Design and Implementation of Educational Games:
Theoretical and Practical Perspectives

Pavel Zemliansky
James Madison University, USA

Diane Wilcox
James Madison University, USA

Information Science REFERENCE

INFORMATION SCIENCE REFERENCE

Hershey · New York

Director of Editorial Content:	Kristin Klinger
Director of Book Publications:	Julia Mosemann
Acquisitions Editor:	Lindsay Johnston
Development Editor:	Joel Gamon
Publishing Assistant:	Deanna Jo Zombro
Typesetter:	Greg Snader, Keith Glazewski, Myla Harty
Production Editor:	Jamie Snavely
Cover Design:	Lisa Tosheff
Printed at:	Yurchak Printing Inc.

Published in the United States of America by
Information Science Reference (an imprint of IGI Global)
701 E. Chocolate Avenue
Hershey PA 17033
Tel: 717-533-8845
Fax: 717-533-8661
E-mail: cust@igi-global.com
Web site: http://www.igi-global.com/reference

Library of Congress Cataloging-in-Publication Data

Design and implementation of educational games : theoretical and practical perspectives / Pavel Zemliansky and Diane Wilcox, editors.
     p. cm.
  Includes bibliographical references and index.
  Summary: "This book will give readers a solid understanding of issues in educational game design and deployment in the classroom"--Provided by publisher.
  ISBN 978-1-61520-781-7 (hardcover) -- ISBN 978-1-61520-782-4 (ebook) 1. Educational games--Design and construction. 2. Simulation games in education--Design and construction. I. Zemliansky, Pavel. II. Wilcox, Diane M.
  LB1029.G3D48 2010
  371.39'7--dc22
                              2009037768

British Cataloguing in Publication Data
A Cataloguing in Publication record for this book is available from the British Library.

All work contributed to this book is new, previously-unpublished material. The views expressed in this book are those of the authors, but not necessarily of the publisher.

Editorial Advisory Board

Table of Contents

Section 1
Theoretical Considerations

Section 2
Applying Theory to Game Design

Section 3
Using Games in Education

Detailed Table of Contents

Section 1
Theoretical Considerations

Chapter 1
Games and Simulations in Training: Factors to Consider When Designing for
> *Courtney Uram, James Madison University, USA*
> *Diane Wilcox, James Madison University, USA*
> *Jane Thall, James Madison University, USA*

The purpose of this chapter is to provide a review of the research literature on the use of gaming and simulation in adult and professional education. The chapter will describe the difference between games and simulation; provide a review of the history of games in adult education; investigate important audience characteristics, including generational differences; examine how games affect motivation; and discuss the application of learning theories and instructional models to game design. The impact of games on learning, especially for those born after 1980, is profound. Games and simulations delivered using a variety of technologies may be an integral part of the educational mix offered by corporate trainers in the near future.

Chapter 2
> *Timo Lainema, Turku School of Economics, Finland*
> *Eeli Saarinen, Turku School of Economics, Finland*

This chapter introduces two views of learning relevant for game-based learning: experiential learning theory and the constructivist view on learning. We will first discuss, how these views explain learning from a perspective that is relevant for game-based learning. We will also evaluate, how these views on learning relate to assessment of learning through gaming. Last, we will concretize the diversity of the potential learning outcomes of gaming: how, for example, the learner's previous knowledge, personality, the team members affect the learning experience and outcome. According to constructivism, learning is a constructive process in which the learner is building an internal representation of knowledge. This is something to which game-based education clearly adds value to.

Chapter 3

David A. Guralnick, Kaleidoscope Learning, USA
Christine Levy, Kaleidoscope Learning, USA

Learn-by-doing simulations can provide tremendously effective learning. This chapter examines previous and current work in the area of educational simulations and looks ahead toward several potential futures in the field. The chapter includes a number of simulation-based success stories and case studies from past years, along with a discussion of why they worked as well as what could have been done better. It also describes approaches to ensure that a simulation is educationally effective while still being engaging and even entertaining. In addition, the chapter includes a design and development process that can be followed in order to maximize the educational value and usability of a simulation

Chapter 4

Tobias Bevc, Goethe-Universität Frankfurt am Main, Germany

This essay will deal with the question of which models of social policy and social structures can be found in video games. This chapter will examine the relationship between these models, the stories (narrations) provided by the games, and the stories and models created by the players themselves. This examination will be followed by a discussion of two types of virtual models of social politics and social structures. In this discussion, light will be shed on the different models of social policy and social structures that appear in the context of video games. In analyzing these models within games, the question is not whether video games have an influence. Rather, the question is what may children and adolescents learn from "off-the-shelf" video games with respect to political education, political socialization and the forming of political identity?

Chapter 5

Ricardo Javier Rademacher Mena, Futur-E-Scape, LLC, USA

There are several theories about entertainment and education. Some, like Caillois' Play Domains, categorize broad domains of play. Others, like Gardner's Multiple Intelligences, categorize narrowly defined types of intelligences. To the author's knowledge however, there has never been a mix of entertainment and education theories in a single conceptual framework. In this chapter, a framework will be systematically built called *The Education and Entertainment (EE) Grid*. This grid will showcase how entertainment theories from Robert Caillois and Richard Bartle can be applied to educational contexts and how educational theories from Benjamin Bloom and Howard Gardner can be applied to entertainment contexts. A wide spectrum of education and entertainment theories will first be reviewed and special attention will be given to the four theories comprising the EE Grid. Two individual grids, the *ENT* and *EDU Grids*, will then be built as a preliminary step to constructing the first version of the EE Grid. Once built, a comparison with other similar frameworks in the field of game design will be discussed. Finally, a few hypothetical examples of how the EE Grid could be used will be presented.

Chapter 6

The idea of bridging literacies has been a topic of much research and theory, and educators continue to struggle to help students understand how their learning transcends the classroom walls. Contributing to the discussion, this chapter focuses on factors influencing video game learning, examining the decisions and game play of eight academically struggling eleventh grade males. Data from two related qualitative studies reveal that direct and peripheral factors influenced students' game play. Findings from these two studies are important to the discussion of educational gaming because they can inform educators of students' struggles and successes in learning outside the classroom. Overall, the evaluation of students' video gaming can provide educators insight into the affordances of this digital literacy and issues affecting student learning outside the classroom.

Section 2
Applying Theory to Game Design

Based on Cognitive Flexibility Theory, this chapter presents a framework for the conception, design, and development of a knowledge network that can be used in exploratory instructional digital games. The instructional structure consists of a set of nodes, each associated with a specific level of conceptual restructuring and a set of resources, both perceptual and physical, that can help the learner/player achieve resolution. The resulting conflict field is used to determine the game structure. Distributed and embodied cognition research is used to link instructional objectives with available game resources at the task level. As a result a better alignment is obtained between the instructional objectives and the game core mechanics. The application of the framework is then illustrated by using it to outline the design process of a game to learn computer programming.

Chapter 8

Play has been an informal approach to teach young ones the skills of survival for centuries. With advancements in computing technology, many researchers believe that computer games[1] can be used as a viable teaching and learning tool to enhance a student's learning. It is important that the educational content of these games is well designed with meaningful game-play based on pedagogically sound theories to ensure constructive learning. This chapter features theoretical aspects of game design from a pedagogical perspective. It serves as a useful guide for educational game designers to design better educational games for use in game-based learning. The chapter provides a brief overview of educational games and game-based learning before highlighting theories of learning that are relevant to educational games. Selected theories of learning are then integrated into conventional game design practices to produce a set of guidelines for educational games design.

Jody S. Underwood, Pragmatic Solutions, Inc., USA
Stacy Kruse, Pragmatic Solutions, Inc., USA
Peter Jakl, Pragmatic Solutions, Inc., USA

The educational research community has been experimenting with educational games with a focus on pedagogy and curriculum, but little effort has been made to assess what students are actually learning in these environments. Designing embedded assessments into games is one of the critical gateways to creating learning tools that are maximally engaging for the learner, using sound pedagogical methodology as a foundation. We review the research in this area and describe technology that facilitates near real-time data collection through embedded assessments, visual data mining, inference mechanisms, and dynamic individualization. We then describe a methodology for creating valid embedded assessments and identify types of data that can be collected from gaming environments along with approaches for analysis, all toward the goal of individualized adaptation.

Jennifer McCabe, James Madison University, USA

This chapter describes the design and development of a game that was created to teach undergraduate students concepts related to health literacy. A brief discussion of the nature of games and how and why they appeal to college students is followed by a synopsis of some of the literature that influenced the design of the game in 2005. The chapter goes on to describe the game in detail, including the learning objectives, gameplay elements, design challenges, and skills included. The chapter will conclude with a discussion of some evaluations that were done on the game and direction for future development.

Paul Peachey, University of Glamorgan, UK

As you read this text you perform an activity. Activity is literally everything we do and yet we are unaware of most of our operations. In this chapter, I will describe activity through a psychological lens and explain how this relates to the process of learning. The conceptual instrument used for analysis is 'activity theory'; a cultural-historical concept that was formulated in Russia during the 1920s. I will offer suggestions as to how activity theory may be used in the design of computer simulation games directed at education and highlight its conceptual underpinnings. In the latter part of the chapter, I offer possible directions for further research in this field.

Philip C. Abrami, Concordia University, Canada
Robert S. Savage, McGill University, Canada
Gia Deleveaux, Concordia University, Canada
Anne Wade, Concordia University, Canada
Elizabeth Meyer, Concordia University, Canada
Catherine LeBel, Concordia University, Canada

In this chapter we summarize the design, development, testing, and dissemination of the Learning Toolkit—currently a suite of three highly interactive, multimedia tools for learning. ABRACADABRA is early literacy software designed to encourage the development of reading and writing skills of emerging readers, especially students at-risk of school failure. We highlight the important modular design considerations underlying ABRACADABRA; how it scaffolds and supports both teachers and students; the evidence on which it based; the results of field experiments done to date; and directions for future research, development, and applications. We also present ePEARL and explain how it can be used with ABRACADABRA to promote self-regulation, comprehension and writing. We briefly discuss ISIS-21 the prototype of a tool designed to enhance student inquiry skills and promote information literacy. As an evidence-based toolkit available without charge to educators, we believe the suite of tools comprising the Learning Toolkit break new ground in bringing research evidence to practice in ways that promote wide scale and sustainable changes in teaching and learning using technology.

Section 3
Using Games in Education

Janice L. Anderson, University of North Carolina – Chapel Hill, USA

In recent years, researchers and classroom teachers have started to explore purposefully designed computer/video games in supporting student learning. This interest in video and computer games has arisen in part, because preliminary research on educational video and computer games indicates that leveraging this technology has the potential to improve student motivation, interest, and engagement in learning through the use of a familiar medium (Gee, 2005; Mayo, 2009; Squire, 2005; Shaffer, 2006). While most of this early research has focused on the impact of games on academic and social outcomes, relatively few studies have been conducted exploring the influence of games on civic engagement (Lenhart et al, 2008). This chapter will specifically look at how Quest Atlantis, a game designed for learning, can potentially be utilized to facilitate the development of ecological stewardship among its players/students, thereby contributing to a more informed democratic citizenry.

This chapter discusses how the quest structure and achievement systems so prevalent in popular videogames can help teachers and directors reform their pedagogy. The idea is to give teachers new ways to guide and motivate students, investing them more fully in the course and encouraging them to deeply explore the subject matter. The chapter provides theoretical support for this model as well as practical advice on its implementation.

Simulations can be powerful tools in helping students learn about strategic management. This paper discusses the value of simulations in helping to illustrate the importance of contingency, the impossibility of a perfect strategy, planning ahead, and aligning internal resources to external environments in strategic management classes. We also discuss the benefits that simulations can offer in going beyond the book and class, being interesting, and the importance of instrumentality in facilitating student learning. This paper then compares self-reported student learning results for each of these variables for two simulations, a professionally packaged simulation and a "home-brewed" one based on a popular board game. We expected the professional simulation to do better on every variable except instrumentality. Surprisingly, the "home-brewed" simulation scored better on most of the dimensions. Therefore, we conclude by encouraging management educators to aggressively explore their instincts for simulation learning opportunities

Children and adolescents with Attention Deficit Hyperactivity Disorder (ADHD) have difficulty maintaining attention, controlling their activity level, and they typically demonstrate poor interpersonal relationships skills. Because of their challenges, educational performance tends to suffer. Paradoxically, when seated in front of a videogame or computer program they enjoy, the performance of individuals with ADHD becomes similar to non-ADHD peers. The purpose of this chapter is to present a conceptual framework for understanding the factors that affect the outcome of individuals with ADHD, and to demonstrate how instructional design models can be used to guide the design and implementation of animated computer education games as instructional tools for this population. Specifically, the FIDGE model and Gagné's Nine Events of Instruction are evaluated for their contributions to understanding the unique technological needs of the ADHD learner.

Chapter 17

This chapter will explore conditions for meaningful adult learning and explain how virtual environments and in-world simulations enable or discourage the development of intellectual skills in adults. Adult learners possess particular characteristics that should influence instructional designs. Issues that affect learning in the real world are also found in the virtual world. Particular problems of cognitive and cultural dissonance in the virtual environment, finding and creating meaningful simulations, and protecting the fidelity of authentic simulations in a public space are discussed. Recommendations and future research directions are provided.

Chapter 18

The purpose of this chapter is to provide a theoretically based argument for using commercial-off-the-shelf (COTS) video games to teach life science topics in the seventh grade science classroom. Specifically, the game Spore™, a turn-based strategy game, will be examined as a potential tool and environment for cultivating knowledge building and model-based reasoning. Though the diversity in methods of the reasoning processes are great and varied, researchers believe that "scientists' work involves building and refining models of the world" (Lehrer & Schauble, 2006, p. 371). The argument forwarded is that Spore™, contextualized by purposeful efforts of instructors and researchers, may facilitate the development and refinement of scientific habits of mind and computational thinking. An exploratory case study derived from an overview of five sections of a seventh grade life science course (n=85), where a two-week lesson on evolutionary biology was significantly revised, illustrates opportunities for and challenges to incorporating COTS games into formal middle school science classroom.

Chapter 19

Video games are serious work for today's students. 93% of the K-12 population plays video games on a regular basis. Educators are now pressed to determine the appropriate integration of this technology into the pedagogy of K-12 classrooms. Research indicates that there are positive effects from playing serious video games, those that aim to teach something. Students are motivated and engaged during such game play. Some speculate that players are using and developing cognitive brain capabilities that have been dormant. The question is whether or not these games, if adequately designed, will teach more than just the skill of playing the game. This chapter takes a look at the evolution of play and games in K-12 education and then seeks to define serious computer games in terms of positive design elements and integration techniques for K-12 classrooms. In conclusion, a research agenda that moves educational gaming forward is explored.

    P.G. Schrader, University of Nevada, USA
    Kimberly A. Lawless, University of Illinois, USA
    Hasan Deniz, University of Nevada, USA

There has been an abundance of writing about video games[1] in education. Characteristic of a young field, much of this work is theoretical and not necessarily based on data (de Freitas, 2006). Classroom integration strategies rely on researchers' arguments, anecdotal evidence, and teachers' pragmatism. Unfortunately, video games are often created for profit and to entertain, leaving many additional issues to consider (i.e., marketing, effectiveness, etc.). Researchers' arguments combined with video games' widespread popularity and potentially spurious advertising may leave teachers confused or misinformed. To exemplify this issue, this chapter contrasts the salient properties of a commercial game (*Spore*), an immersive context with game-like features (*Quest Atlantis*), and a pedagogically based immersive context (*GlobalEd 2*). Specifically, we describe the educational and technological affordances of three contexts, the limitations associated with each, and the necessary yet pragmatic steps involved in their classroom use

    Nava Silton, Fordham University, USA
    Ann Higgins D'Alessandro, Fordham University, USA

The purpose of this chapter is to illustrate that video and eye toy gaming can be used to enhance the social learning of children with autism directly through video modeling and multimedia social story interventions and indirectly through engaging typically developing students with educational videos that increase their sensitivity, knowledge, and behavioral intentions when interacting socially with children with autism, and perhaps other disorders as well. We suggest that it is important to develop typical children's positive attitudes and intentions toward peers with disabilities. Research has shown that this can be accomplished through video which has the power to influence a person's perception and subse-quent behavior in other situations, for instance, in moderating the development and use of stereotypes regarding race (Givens & Monahan, 2005; Ward, Hansbrough, & Walker, 2005). Thinking creatively about the power of gaming to enhance development and social interactions among typical and atypical children, as specifically illustrated here for children with autism, will help bring interventions for atypical children into the 21st century as well as allow the development of much richer research methodologies for tracking and understanding important micro-developmental changes in daily and weekly interpersonal skills development.

Chapter 22

The purpose of this chapter is to provide a brief summary of the military's use of gaming and simulation to accomplish training. Historically, the military has been a forerunner in the exploration of training techniques that incorporate aspects of games and simulations. Training tools emerge in various gaming formats such as simulations, edutainment, commercial-off-the-shelf games (COTS), and serious games. To develop training in the form of games or simulations, elements of instructional design must be considered to include learning objectives, game play, and feedback. Emerging technologies provide possible solutions to training challenges such as achieving affective learning domain objectives and the portability of training. The military, as an early adapter of games and simulation, continues to forge the way by integrating gaming and simulation, instructional design, and emerging technologies to achieve the ever growing demands of training.

Chapter 23

This paper presents the results of a three-year design research study of Gamestar Mechanic, a multiplayer online role-playing game designed to teach middle school children to think like designers by exposing them to key practices behind good computer game production. Using discourse-based ethnographic methods, it examines the ways in which the multimodal meaning representations of the language of games (Gee, 2003) provided within Gamestar Mechanic, have helped learners think and communicate in increasingly sophisticated ways with and about game design. It also examines the implications of these language and literacy skills for other areas of players' lives, as well as for the improvement of the game as a learning environment over time.

Chapter 24

Second Life (SL) is a virtual world that possesses great potential as an innovative teaching tool. SL not only allows users to meet, interact, and collaborate in a virtual space, but also to create their own learning environments. This chapter explores how virtual worlds such as Second Life can be used to enhance the overall educational experience of both traditional and distance education students. We describe applications of SL to teaching diverse classes in art history and museum studies, business, and psychology, and to community building across the university. In general, our experiences with using SL have been positive, and our students report enjoying the creativity and flexibility of SL as well as the opportunity for social interaction in the virtual world. We provide recommendations to those considering the use of SL.

Chapter 25
Paul Pivec, Deakin University, Australia
Maja Pivec, University of Applied Sciences, Austria

Game-based learning has gained popularity in schools and has been proposed for adult education, both at Universities and in the corporate training sector. Games are becoming a new form of interactive content and game playing provides an interactive and collaborative platform for learning purposes. Collaborative learning allows participants to produce new ideas as well as to exchange information, simplify problems, and resolve the tasks. Context based collaborative learning method is based on constructivist learning theory and guides the design of the effective learning environments. In this environment the teacher or trainer becomes the active partner, moderator and advisor of the educational process, not just a repository of the information importing his or her own knowledge to a passive learner as in traditional education. Learners bring their prior skills and knowledge to the classroom community. The trainer structures learning situations in which each learner can interact with other learners to develop new knowledge and fashion their own needs and capacities. Knowledge is generated from experience with complex tasks rather than from isolated activities like learning and practicing separately. Skills and knowledge are best acquired within the context. This helps the learners easily to transfer learning from classroom to "real life" and back, or information from one subject to another. Therefore this method requires that the trainer and learners play nontraditional roles such as interaction and collaboration with each other within the educational process. The classroom drops the physical boundaries and becomes a goal-oriented platform dedicated to learning. Online role-play scenario platforms offers an environment where trainers can define their own role-playing scenarios and provide the opportunity for learners to apply factual knowledge and to gain experience through the digital world. Trainers can define new games or adopt and modify sample games without any programming skills. Some platforms provide a variety of communication means within the scenarios; players can communicate with the use of multimedia discussion forums, text and voice chat modules, as well as through multi-user video conferencing. These platforms foster participation in problem-solving, effective communication, teamwork, project management, as well as other soft skills such as responsibility, creativity, micro-entrepreneurship, corporate culture, and cultural awareness. They are designed for use as a supplement to normal in-class teaching and corporate training, but it is also possible to be used independently from a class course. The constructivist design required for successful Game-Based Learning will be discussed and a model is provided to display how Game-Based Learning occurs in a collaborative online environment. This chapter will present example scenarios and highlight resources available to interested teachers and trainers.

ExerLearning provides parents, educators and others with a solid background of the direct connection between regular, rhythmic aerobic activity, balance, eye-foot coordination and academic success. We can increase students' fitness while simultaneously increasing their academic success. Activity breaks have been shown to improve cognitive performance and promote on-task classroom behavior. Today's exergame and related computer technology can seamlessly deliver activity without over-burdening busy teachers in grades K-12. Activity isn't optional for humans, and our brain, along with its ability to learn and function at its best, isn't a separate "thing" perched in our heads. The wiring, the circulation, the connection between mind and body is very real. The brain is made up of one hundred billion neurons that chat with one another by way of hundreds of different chemicals. Physical activity can enhance the availability and delivery of those chemicals. Harnessing technology to that activity is the ExerLearning solution.

Chapter 27

This chapter is concerned with the potential of serious games as effective and engaging learning resources for people with learning and sensory disabilities. This is considered, followed by detailing of a suitable design methodology and its application, description of a range of types of games that have been successfully developed for this target group, and an explication of accessibility guidelines. Future development in this area is discussed, and it is concluded that there is great potential in the wide range of possible areas of research into, and development of, serious games for supporting people with learning and sensory disabilities, which would contribute greatly to their inclusion in society.

Foreword

25 years ago when my son was nine he and his friends would routinely go to the videogames room in the local mall and play games until their allowance ran out. I saw this as simply entertainment, nothing more, and considered it a waste of time and money, but it was how they wanted to spend what funds they had. Despite my son's frequent urging, I would not go into the noisy and somewhat haphazard videogame room but rather wait for them outside while fretting about his waste of his allowance. Often I suggested other more productive things he could do with his allowance, and he would counter by talking about the value of playing video games -- a point I never grasp. One day when I took him to the mall to play video games I went inside and watched. I had expected to find one boy playing one game mindlessly while exhausting his supply of quarters. What I found, however, was quite different. While one boy was manipulating the controls of the game there were several other boys hovered over it, all engaged in a constant conversation about the game. I was surprised with the sophistication and focus of what they were saying. They were sharing their thoughts on different strategies for playing the particular game and, when asked by the person playing the game, those hovering around would offer guidance about how to be more successful and advance to higher levels in the game. Vygotsky would be pleased!

As a person playing one of these games worked on a task that was very challenging to him those that were more capable provided the necessary scaffolding to help the player learn how to meet the challenge and advance. There was real depth and richness in their conversations as they talk about different strategies for game play. Often several of those who were watching would enter into a rather high level discussion with the player identifying and analyzing potential options for meeting the challenge posed by the game at that moment. They drew from their collective prior experiences to formulate and test hypotheses about the most effective approach to follow. When stumped it was not unusual for one of the boys to run over and grab somebody else who had more experience playing that game and get his suggestions for what to do next. This was rarely a specific suggestion of steps to follow in a 1-2-3-4 fashion. Rather it was usually a discussion of what the player should consider and how he should approach the game situation he confronted at that moment. When I left the videogame room that afternoon I had a very different appreciation of the influence of games on the young people who were playing them. I knew videogames were highly motivating, especially to young boys. I had assumed they may be improving some hand-eye coordination when playing video games but not much more. I had not realized the extent to which sophisticated, high-level thinking was going on while playing these videogames. Nor did I imagine the richness in the conversations among those watching and playing. It had not occurred to me that some of the lessons they were learning while playing video games had any value or relevance to anything other than a videogame. My view on children and games changed that afternoon when I got a better glimpse into what was going on cognitively as they played.

In the years since this experience I have spent more time watching children and adults play video and computer games. I have developed games and worked collaboratively with others in developing games. I have used games in teaching my graduate courses and have taught courses on game development. Like so many, I've seen the explosion in both the hardware and software technologies to support games and in the research that documents the effectiveness of games on learning. In short, during the past 25 years the research, development and applications of gaming in education and training have grown at an astounding rate. Despite what I initially thought, there seems little doubt that games can be very effective in developing learning and motivation. Computer and video games are now routinely used in graduate and professional education as well as corporate and military training to teach sophisticated knowledge and skills. The issue with the use of games in education and training today is not do people learn from games, for that has been long-established. Rather the issue is what can be best taught through the use of games and how can we design games to ensure effective learning.

Professors Zemliansky and Wilcox have edited a comprehensive book that touches on three important themes for the use of games in education. The first section contains chapters that discuss theoretical considerations that underlie the design and use of games for educational purposes. These chapters explain the educational value of games, discuss a framework for studying virtual worlds, describe videogames as adaptive educational systems, discuss political and social factors, identify factors to consider when designing games for adults, and examine online collaboration in role-playing games. The second section contains several chapters that focus on designing computer games for education. These chapters include a discussion of the pedagogical approach for games, the use of activity theory in game design, using evidence-based principles in game design, how to include embedded assessments in games, and factors to consider in designing video games to support learning outcomes. The third section contains chapters describing the use of videogames in education. The chapters in this section document the application of games in a variety of educational settings from K-12 to military education and training. These chapters examine the use of commercial off-the-shelf videogames in education as well as games that were specifically designed for education.

This is a timely book given the emphasis on serious games at all levels in education. People interested in educational uses of games will find much of value to them in this book whether it's a discussion of pedagogical principles that underlie games, techniques for game development, factors to consider when using games, or a rich variety of examples demonstrating how games can be used in various subject matters and at different educational levels. The chapters are written by people on the frontlines describing their experiences with creating and using games for education and training. The book includes a rich blend of both theoretical and practical points of view with regards to educational games.

The doubts I had 25 years ago about the value of games and my difficulty in comprehending any educational benefits from playing games have long since dissipated. In light of following the long line of research studies and many years of practical experience, even a harsh critic of video and computer games as I was would have to acknowledge the substantial educational value that can come from the use of games. The question should not be whether to use educational games, for surely that has to be answered in the affirmative. Rather the question should be how can we design and use educational games to ensure outstanding benefits for our learners. This book by Professors Zemliansky and Wilcox focuses squarely on that question.

Wallace Hannum
University of North Carolina, USA

Wallace Hannum is a faculty member in the educational psychology program at the University of North Carolina and Associate Director for Technology of the National Research Center on Rural Education Support. Dr. Hannum teaches graduate level courses on learning theories, instructional design, and the use of technology in education. Dr. Hannum's research focuses on instructional uses of technology, especially distance education. Dr. Hannum has consulted on instructional uses of technology with many organizations, both public and private. He has participated in the design and implementation of numerous technology-based programs and projects. He has worked extensively on education projects in Africa, Asia and Latin America. Dr. Hannum is author of five books and numerous articles on topics related to technology and instructional design.

Preface

Video games and edutainment began making an appearance in classrooms in the mid to late 1980s. Since 1980, a variety of technologies have been introduced into the classroom and used by preschool, elementary, secondary, and higher education students to augment their learning. These technologies included personal computers, edutainment, VCRs, video games, DVDs, CD-ROMs, the World Wide Web, digital cameras, mp3 players, PDAs, social networking sites, and cell phones. With the introduction of every new technology, instructional designers wonder how the technology in question may optimize learning. Most recently, instructional designers have been examining how best to use games for learning.

The issue of game use for learning is an important one. The field of educational gaming is currently undergoing a transformation. Factors such as economic recession, globalization, and the widespread adoption of a variety of technologies have changed the way we think, learn, and live. Our fast-paced, connected world has demanded that we consider new educational methods and media in order to meet the changing needs of our global society. In addition, an entire generation has been raised with games as a primary vehicle for learning. The purposes of this book is to examine the theories that underly effective educational games, how to apply these theories to game design, and how to use games in learning environments.

As editors, we come to this project with two different but connected perspectives on educational gaming. Being a rhetorician, one us takes a primarily rhetorical approach to game design and implementation for learning, while the other comes to this topic mainly from the point of view of an instructional and multimedia designer. In the next few paragraphs, we'd like to explain why these two perspectives are important for the topic of educational gaming and how each of them adds to the meaning of this collection.

Educational Games as Persuasive Artifacts

Ask anyone what makes educational games different from, say, instructional DVDs, and, more likely than not, people will mention the word «interactivity.» As the readers of this collection will, no doubt, know, the term «interactivity» has been notoriously dificult to define despite its popularity. One way to approach the task of defining interactivity in educational games is to look at ways in which they can be seen as persuasive artifacts.

In recent years, several notable works exploring the persuasive or rhetorical nature of games have been published. One such notable work is the book *Persuasive Games*, by Ian Bogost. In the book, Bogost, himself both a rhetorician and a game designer, argues that carefully crafted video games can persuade and move people to action in ways that traditional texts cannot.

In the book, Bogost proposes the term «procedural rhetoric» which can be explained as the kind of persuasion which relies upon and works when users (players) not only read, hear, or watch persuasive messages, but complete series of steps which result in a new understanding of a problem or, at the very least, the raising of new and important questions.

To illustrate, how this kind of persuasion works, Bogost describes his five-year-old son playing the game *Animal Crossing*, which requires players to «move into a new village and settle into a new life» (Bogost 117). Players are required to interact with a «local real estate tycoon» who can provide them with material possessions, but also get them deeper and deeper into debt. (Bogost 117). Here is how Bogost explains the persuasive consequences of playing *Animal Crossing*:

Animal Crossing is a game about everyday life in a small town. It is a game about customizing and caring for an environment. It is a game about making friends and about collecting insects. But Animal Crossing is also a game about long-term debt. It is a game about the repetition of mundane work necessary to support contemporary material property ideals. It is a game about the bittersweet consequences of acquiring goods and keeping up with the Joneses. Animal Crossing accomplishes this feat not through moralistic regulation, but by creating a model of commerce and debt in which the player can experience and discover such consequences. In its model, the game simplifies the real world in order to draw attention to relevant aspects of that world. (Bogost 119).

According to Bogost, this and other games which he critiques in his book, are examples of procedural rhetorical because they make claims about «how things work» and «make claims about the world» (Bogost 125). And what is important about procedural rhetoric and what differentiates it from other kinds of rhetoric, according to Bogost, is procedural rhetoric's ability to make such claims through processes rather that through one-way messages from the writer or orator to a reader or listener (125).

Elsewhere in his book, Bogost argues not only in favor of the educational potential of procedural rhetoric implemented in carefully designed games, but also for the necessity for educators and parents to become «better critics» of such games, as the world increasingly moves away from replying primarily on lenear media, such as books and movies to the use of «random access» media, such as computer software and games (Bogost 136). According to Bogost's argument, teachers and parents should play games with young learners, but do so critically, unlearning first their own decades old habit of seeing all video games as only mindless distraction (136).

Procedural rhetoric is an important concept for the design and implementation of educational games because it adds yet another dimension to our understanding of the elusive concept of interactivity. Procedural rhetoric may allow us to understand more precisely how «learning by doing» takes place. However, in order to do so, video games must be designed and implemeted very carefully. As Ian Bogost says in the conclusion to one of the chapters of his book, «[games] are not *automatically* (emphasis in the original) rich, sophisticated statements about the world around us.» According to Bogost, both designers and players need to approach games carefully and critically, if those games are to fulfill their potential for persuasion and active learning.

Balancing Instructional Objectives, Learning Principles, and Game Context

While procedural rhetoric may inform how learning by doing takes place in educational games, instructional design provides a framework for addressing audience considerations, the content or skills to be taught, instructional strategies and methods, and ways to evaluate the game player's learning. When designing games, the major challenge for instructional designers is how to balance the standard instructional design framework, which can be linear and regimented, with the creative process required to conceptualize, design, and produce a game that is useful, engaging, and fun. In the corporate sector, most instructional designers follow a 5-step instructional systems design process where each step validates and extends the prior step. As part of a design team, they are usually charged with the creation of instructional objectives and the writing of the curriculum materials, and work with other members of the design team on the development of game play and media elements.

Within the instructional design methodology, it is possible to be creative, but all too often the instructional designer may subordinate his or her creativity to the instructional requirements of the project because of time or resource constraints. When this happens, the end result may be a dull, lifeless game, which fails to achieve its educational goals because the learners are not engaged. For this reason, instructional designers must equally balance their instructional objectives with a consideration for the techniques they will use to capture the imagination of the learners and keep them engaged in the game. This can be accomplished by employing a good, compelling narrative that draws in game players; exciting, interactive game play that provides both context and immediate feedback; and a clear, unified, organized, aesthetically pleasing interface that features carefully designed and judiciously used media elements. When these factors are considered equally, the instructional focus of the game is less apparent as the game context provides a suspension of disbelief, enabling the player become immersed in the imaginary game world. Thomas Malone's (1981) study of what makes computer games intrinsically motivating describes the fantasy, challenge, and curiosity typically associated with the suspension of disbelief required to immerse and engage the learner in the game world.

In addition to creating a motivating game game context, instructional designers also need to consider how the game play, interactivity, and media elements support the learning process, as some uses of multimedia in games may inhibit rather than promote learning. For example, designers may assume that more is better when it comes to multimedia, so complex animations may be used with narration and on-screen stationary or scrolling text without regard to the effect on learning. In this case, the simultaneous display of on-screen text, narration, and animation has the potential to overload working memory and make information more difficult to understand, thus slowing the learning process. Educational games designed without attention to learning principles, specifically how the different media assets affect working memory, may miss the mark entirely when learning is the goal.

Those of us who value, design, and use educational games think they can make a difference in student learning, but the evidence from research studies examining the learning effectiveness of games is not so clear cut. In the second edition of E-learning and the Science of Instruction, Ruth Colvin Clark and Richard E. Mayer (2008) describe several reviews of research on gaming that failed to show an advantage for games when compared to traditional instruction. In other words, some studies indicated that games were more effective than traditional instruction, while other studies showed just the opposite. These mixed research findings are not surprising given the fact that games are frequently designed by teams of people with competing objectives who may or may not understand the importance of carefully designed instruction or the effect of media on learning. For instructional designers, the question is not whether games are more effective than traditional instruction, but how do we apply learning principles to game design to maximize learning?

One way to answer this question is to follow a typical instructional systems design procedure: conduct a content analysis, and then choose a game format, game play, and multimedia elements that facilitate the target audience's learning of the content. The challenge to this type of approach is that games are typically designed by project teams consisting of individuals from a variety of backgrounds, perspectives, and design approaches. The programmer may be concerned with writing elegant and efficient code, but may not be knowledgeable about how a particular interface inhibits or promotes learning. The graphic designer may skilled in creating graphics and animation, but may not understand how a particular combination of graphics with text or narration may impede learning. The audio engineer may be an expert in creating high fidelity audio that creates a mood for the game, but may not understand how some sound effects can be distracting when paired with certain animations or learning challenges that involve problem solving. The necessity for a balance between the art and science of game design cannot be overstated, and it is the instructional designer's job to ensure that all components of the game work in concert to facilitate learning. If not, the team may opt to use multimedia features that are «sexy» rather than instructional, thus minimizing the educational utility of the game.

Another way to answer then question of how to design games that maximize learning, is to follow the five principles for designing games and simulations outlined by Clark and Mayer in Chapter 15 of E-learning and the Science of Instruction. These principles include matching the game type to the learning goal, making learning integral to progress in the game, using features that support the learning process, building in guidance that provides explanations and feedback, providing opportunities for learner reflection and explanation, and finally, and finally minimizing complexity, especially for the game interface. If designers incorporate these five principles when designing educational games, the end result should be a game that promotes learning. Regardless of the design approach used, designers may create a *fun and motivating* educational game if they incorporate fantasy, challenge, curiosity, good narrative, interactivity, context, structure, feedback, the appropriate use of media. Balancing the application of learning principles with context and appropriately used media elements may lead to game design that is both effective and engaging.

Brief Overview of the Book's Sections

In the following paragraphs, we briefly review the three sections of the book. The purpose of this brief review is to provide readers with an overall impression about the structure of this volume and guide them towards those chapters which may be of particular interest to them.

Theoretical Considerations

The first section of the book, entitled Theoretical Considerations, tackles conceptual and theoretical issues in educational game design and deployment theory. With titles like «Educational Simulations: Learning from the Past and Ensuring Success in the Future,» and «Explaining the Educational Power of Games,» the chapters included in this section take a broad view of the subjects they cover. Reading the selections in the first section of the book will prepare the collection's audience for more practical and hands-on discussions of educational game design and deployment which they will encounter in the following two sections.

Applying Theory to Game Design

As its title suggests, the second section of this collection deals with applying game design theory to practical deign situations. While all the selections in this section will be of interest to most readers, notable chapters here include «Moving to the Next Level: Designing Embedded Assessment into Educational Games,» The Design of a Health Literacy Game: Face the Case,» and others. Considering the chapters included in the section will help readers to transition from the consideration of broad theoretical concepts in educational game design to the topics in the third and final section of the book.

Using Games in Education

The third and final section of this collection considers instances of educational game use in real-life learning and teaching settings and for teaching specific subjects. It is the largest section, containing ten chapters. Notable essays include «Animated Computer Education Games for Students with ADHD,» «Quests and Achievements in the Classroom,» and many others. Our hope is that the chapters in this section of the collection, as well as the book as a whole, will give readers a solid understanding of issues in educational game design and deployment in the classroom.

Pavel Zemliansky
James Madison University, USA

Diane Wilcox
James Madison University, USA

REFERENCES

Bogost, I. (2007). *Persuasive Games: The Expressive Power of Videogames*. Boston, MA: The MIT Press.

Clark, R. C., & Mayer, R. E. (2008). *E-Learning and the Science of Instruction: Proven Guidelines for Consumers and Designers of Multimedia Learning*, (2nd Ed.). San Francisco, CA: Pfeiffer.

Malone, T. W. (1981). Toward a Theory of Intrinsically Motivating Instruction. *Cognitive Science, 4*, 333-369.

Acknowledgment

We thank a lot of people who helped us create this book: the authors of the chapters, the development, editorial, and production staff at IGI Global, our colleagues, families, and friends. We thank them all for their ideas, guidance, and for helping us stay on schedule.

Pavel Zemliansky
James Madison University, USA

Diane Wilcox
James Madison University, USA

Section 1
Theoretical Considerations

Chapter 1
Games and Simulations in Training:
Factors to Consider When Designing for Adult Learners

Courtney Uram
James Madison University, USA

Diane Wilcox
James Madison University, USA

Jane Thall
James Madison University, USA

ABSTRACT

The purpose of this chapter is to provide a review of the research literature on the use of gaming and simulation in adult and professional education. The chapter will describe the difference between games and simulation; provide a review of the history of games in adult education; investigate important audience characteristics, including generational differences; examine how games affect motivation; and discuss the application of learning theories and instructional models to game design. The impact of games on learning, especially for those born after 1980, is profound. Games and simulations delivered using a variety of technologies may be an integral part of the educational mix offered by corporate trainers in the near future.

INTRODUCTION

The popularity of video games has led teachers and trainers to investigate the potential uses of games and simulations for continuing, adult, professional, and corporate education. Too often though, designers of adult education materials are unfamiliar with the theoretical and practical design considerations faced when creating games for adult learners. These considerations include an understanding of audience characteristics, generational differences, learning theories, learning motivation, and the use of media elements to promote learning. Games and simulations are learning tools, which have transitioned from "just for fun" entertainment to influential, immersive learning environments for

DOI: 10.4018/978-1-61520-781-7.ch001

knowledge and skill development. Despite the popularity and prevalence of games, the education and corporate sectors have yet to fully realize that computer games are powerful learning devices. This chapter will address the unique design considerations instructional designers and game developers face when designing educational games for the workplace.

WHY GAMES?

Today more than ever, new entrants to the workforce are demanding the smooth, seamless integration of technology and education; the intersection where both meet can be found in interactive computer games. Why games as the new educational impetus for learning? The newest generation of workers has grown up with computer games since early childhood. Games such as *Where in the World is Carmen Sandiego?*, *Reader Rabbit*, *Math and Science Blaster*, *Super Mario Brothers*, and *Pac Man* represent a historical iconography in the lives of these new workers. Moreover, these games embody a new social phenomenon, one in which the language of behavior in the forms of goals, learning, emotion and intention is mediated by the interchange of actors, rules and resources (Klabber, 2003; Mateas, 2003). Taking control and having an effect on the outcome of the game or simulation is a critical motivational element that makes the game a powerful education medium (Bonk & Dennan, 2005).

Today's technology literate, actively engaged students insist that education must be more than the conventional PowerPoint classroom lecture where information is poured into their heads and regurgitated onto worksheets (Oblinger, 2003). Their facility with technology and ability to multitask have led this new generation of learners – Millennials – to want to be actively engaged and in charge of their learning. Consequently, today's students and tomorrow's work force expect teachers and trainers to deliver curricula

in an innovative and creative way; one that will hold the attention of their technology oriented minds (Oblinger, 2003; Bonk & Dennen, 2005). Gaming and simulations provide the extra "spice" that traditional paper-based instructional materials lack. As a generation raised with computers and technology, Millennials expect their training to contain this convergence of technology and curriculum. Gaming and simulation provide these learners with the motivation to "remediate skills and knowledge" (Ricci, Salas, & Bowers, 1996) for generations to come.

As Baby Boomers (those born between 1946 and 1964) retire, the workforce will be replaced with Millennials and subsequent generations raised with games and technology. The early immersion of these individuals in technology rich environments is changing the way they think and learn. Paper-based training in the 21st century is quickly becoming extinct, so why not embrace the coming change? Shifting our learning paradigm from a linear instructional format to a technologically oriented, adaptable instructional platform is critical for human resource development in the 21st century. Using educational games to accommodate the fluid, multitasking, learning orientation of this newest generation is the key to creating motivating continuing adult, professional, and corporate education (Gee, 2003).

GAMES, SIMULATIONS AND SERIOUS GAMES

Games and simulations are not synonymous; rather each has unique characteristics that differentiate it from the other (Prensky, 2006; 2001; Gredler, 2004; Kirkley & Kirkley, 2004; Klabber, 2003; Hogle, 1996; Ricci, Salas, & Cannon-Bowers, 1996). Games are defined by Gredler (2004) as "competitive exercises in which the objective is to win and players must apply subject matter or other relevant knowledge" (p. 571). Simulations conversely are "open-ended evolving situations with many interacting variables" (p. 571). Games are designed to be fun while simulations are designed to emulate reality, which is not necessarily fun. When simulations lack the exciting and fun elements customarily designed into games, they become boring and learners become disengaged (Prensky, 2006; 2001). For this reason, it is important to understand what constitutes fun, especially for the Millennial generation, and take adequate measures to build the fun into training simulations.

Educational games and simulations may be used to facilitate context-based on-the-job learning in a safe environment using simulated patients, processes, systems, cases, and scenarios. They afford learners the opportunity to "apply subject matter knowledge in a new context" (Gredler, 2004, p. 576). Educational games and simulations offer an extensive range of benefits not only for grades K-12, but for adult learners as well (Prensky, 2006; 2001). Research on knowledge acquisition and retention supports the premise that computer games enhance the learning experience and aid in knowledge retention (Ricci, Salas, & Cannon-Bowers, 1996). Attributes of computer-based gaming that contribute to this knowledge acquisition include: active participation, immediate feedback, dynamic interaction, cultural context, competition, the exchange of tacit and explicit knowledge, anthropomorphism, novelty, and goal direction (Klabber, 2003; Mateas, 2003; Prensky, 2001; Ricci, Salas, & Cannon-Bowers, 1996). Additionally, an engaging user interface design and appropriate choice of media elements may foster learner motivation by providing the challenge, fantasy, and curiosity identified by Malone (1980) in his research on what makes computer games fun.

There are three key differences between games and simulations (Gredler, 1996). First, the main objective of the game is to compete against other players and to win. In contrast, the main objective of the simulation is not to compete and win, but to provide learners with an experience that emulates an environment, task, process, role, or scenario in the real world. Second, while games are linear, simulations present players with complex, dynamic, nonlinear environments. Games have a clear structure and linear flow where players make choices, receive feedback, and move forward in the game play. In simulations, on the other hand, the structure is less clear as the focus of the simulation is to emulate a reality. The simulation's complex environment is dynamic and changes based on the input of the player. There is no linear path, but a complex web of possibilities that involve branching. Finally, games have prescribed rules, constraints, rewards, and penalties that enable the player to easily gauge his or her success toward the attainment of the game's goal. Simulations, however, have game constraints that are more amorphous as they reflect relationships between variables that change over time. The simulations structure and outcome are highly dependent on the choices of the player.

Games can encompass a single player or multiple players. In single player games, such as Solitaire, an individual's opponent is the computer. In multiple player games, in contrast, players use their strategy, skill, and knowledge to compete against other players. To parents, guardians, and teachers, a single player game may be viewed as a sheltering or isolating activity where the player is socially removed from his or her peers. However, current research on the use of games by college students (Jones, 2003) indicates that students view online games as a social enterprise, often involving a variety of friends, much like the traditional face-to-face games played by Baby Boomers during their youth. In fact, 20% of the students in the study felt that online games helped them make friends and improved the quality of their relationships. This picture stands in sharp contrast to the image of the solitary child sequestered in a room in front of a computer monitor, devoid of human interaction. Contrary to previous generations, the Millennial generation views online gaming as a very positive and highly social aspect of their life.

Massive multiplayer online games (MMOGs) offer collaboration, and the sharing of knowledge, skills, and values with other players inside and outside of the game (Gee, 2003). Well-designed computer and video games permit people to remake themselves in alternate new worlds, which result in both recreation and profound learning. While little research has been conducted on MMOGs, Dede (2005) claims that these interactive learning environments not only facilitate learning, but also foster identify formation and unique "neomillennial" learning styles related to the immersive experience afforded by MMOGs.

When applied in a non-entertainment realm, digital game-based learning technology results in serious games (Zyda, 2005). Although there are many different definitions for the term serious games, they are simply digital games designed specifically for learning purposes. Serious games cover roughly the same goals as edutainment, but place special emphasis on teaching, training, and informing across all ages (Michael & Chen, 2006). The primary difference between edutainment and serious games is the purpose. Edutainment games are designed primarily to entertain, whereas serious games are designed specifically to teach. Serious games go beyond the rote drill and practice orientation of edutainment to address a wider and deeper range of learning outcomes such as skill acquisition, attitudinal change, specific training on procedures, and complex problem solving. Serious games combine the principles of human performance engineering with entertainment principles, creativity, and technology to offer the possibility of an immersive and motivating teaching environment.

Simulations, which are largely used in professional and organizational training and development (Kriz, 2003; Prensky, 2006; 2001), enable learners to immediately transfer newly acquired knowledge and skills, thus personalizing the learning and making it memorable (Kriz, 2003).

Businesses and professional organizations are using simulations as risk-free employee development tools to improve the knowledge and skills in talent managers, current employees, and specialists (Watters, 2009). When simulations are used to train talent managers, these employees are able to increase their business acumen, practice making decisions, and evaluate the outcomes of their hiring, promotion, and retention decisions. Thus, it is equally beneficial for both the organization providing the simulation as a teaching tool, and the learner who is developing competence.

The notions of free play and free will are critical for a successful simulation. Learners must have the freedom to take control of their learning experiences and make their own decisions. They must be able to see that their actions have an impact. Otherwise, the simulation loses its effectiveness by becoming less engaging, less plausible, less motivating, and certainly less appealing (Luppa & Borst, 2007). If the environment is closed and prevents learners from making decisions or exercising control, skill acquisition and application will be thwarted. This effectively kills learner motivation. Therefore, storylines must web or branch out, provide the opportunity for learners to make decisions, pose questions that facilitate critical thinking, and offer tutoring on difficult-to-learn concepts. When stories are rich and interactive, the narratives and embedded anecdotes act as memory aids, as well as teaching tools.

It is important to remember that although games and simulations differ in many respects, they both foster experiential learning (Gredler, 1996). With both games and simulations, learning is facilitated through reflection and debriefing (Thatcher, 1990; Kriz, 2003), which enable learners to link the game space experience to other similar knowledge residing in their memories, thus personalizing the experience and making it more memorable. Debriefing can be integrated along with reflection; however, it can also be a separate entity.

A BRIEF HISTORY OF GAMES

Games and simulations in education can be traced back to the 1600s (Gredler, 2004). The use of games in military training first occurred in the Roman Empire when military leaders used sand tables to represent battlefields and abstract icons to represent soldiers (Smith, 2009). Games were used extensively in training military officers to help them develop strategies, lead troops, and take command (Roberts, 1976). Chessboards served as terrain maps and chessmen represented the soldiers. Eventually, as civilization became more advanced, terrain maps and wooden blocks replaced the chessboards and chessmen.

Throughout the late 19th and early 20th centuries, war games were used increasingly by many nations to plan both invasions and defenses against invasions (Smith, 2009). World War II represented a turning point in the field of training and development as war games were used by all super powers to develop and train military personnel (Roberts, 1976). As the United States looked for support on the home front, leadership and job training were needed in organizations and manufacturing concerns across the country. Games and simulations provided additional opportunities for training and education in the workplace.

In the 1950s, gaming and simulations were used in business and education primarily to build skills and apply subject matter knowledge (Gredler, 2004; Kirkley & Kirkley, 2004; Hogle, 1996). Often the focus of the simulation was the development of procedural knowledge or the mastery of specific job skills, such as how to operate a particular machine. In the 1960s, Science Research Associates' Educational Laboratory Kit reading programs were designed with three key elements synonymous with computer games: participant self-pacing, competition, and relative autonomy of participant progress (Foorman, Fletcher, Francis, Schatschneider, & Mehta, 1998). Gaming and simulations were also used to enable employees to gain a greater understanding of the organization's culture, processes, and structure (Kriz, 2003) by trying out new roles and scenarios, practicing behaviors, solving problems, and playfully taking chances. For example, the journeyman level employee is free from impunity to try on the new role of first line supervisor—replete with all of the challenges and opportunities inherent in managerial roles.

In the 1980s, educational games were used in K-12 education to foster fact acquisition and content mastery. These games were primarily single player edutainment games based on a drill-and-practice behaviorist paradigm where the game player competed with the computer. Although multi-player games were available in the 1980s, they really did not become popular until the Internet became widespread in the late-1990s. At that time, games became more socially oriented and were used for a broader range of educational purposes. It was also during this time that games and simulations became much more prevalent in the corporate sector. The spread of the Internet, the advent of robust, rich-media technologies, and the dot.com boom converged to create a need in organizations for on demand technology-delivered training. The requirement for ubiquitous, highly inter-active training led to the introduction of games and simulations as more motivating, organizational training tools. Figure 1 provides a brief overview of the history of games.

Games presently serve many purposes in the training industry: as military recruiting tools (Zyda, 2005; Chandler, 2008), educational learning tools (Gredler, 2004; Gee 2003; Chandler 2008), and corporate training tools to foster learning in professional, corporate, or adult education. According to Prensky (2001) there are 53 million children in the K-12 age group, all potential players of educational games. In 2000, the gaming software industry peaked at 1.6 billion dollars.

Educational game use has increased dramatically over the last fifteen years. In the late 1980s and early 1990s, games such as, *Math Blaster, Reader Rabbit, Where in the World is Carmen*

Figure 1. Timeline of games

Sandiego, and *The Oregon Trail*, exposed an entire generation of students to educational games. These former edutainment players are now working adults, many of them playing online games. Edutainment games were followed by another wave of games focused on scientific learning (Prensky, 2001), and included self-help and prevention games such as *Bronkie the Bronchiasaurus*, *Packy & Marlon*, and *Rex Ronan*.

In higher education, games can be used to elaborate on a lecture, as a demonstration, or as a central learning activity (Oblinger, 2004). Games foster a learning environment in which students develop a firmer "sense of how specific social processes and practices are interwoven and how different bodies of knowledge relate to each other" (Squire & Jenkins, 2003, p. 15). Educational games such as *Civilization III*, *Revolution*, and *Thinking Strategically*, enable higher education learners to gain the optimum learning experiences by promoting the transfer of their knowledge and skills into more practical, real world, experiences.

Seventy percent of adult learners over the age of 18 play computer and video games (Prensky, 2001). A recent study by the Pew Internet and American Life Project found that 53% of all Americans over the age of 18 play games on or offline by computer, cell phone, or other device (Lenhart, Jones & MacGill, 2008). Computer games from the 1980's such as *Minesweeper*, *Solitaire*, and *Myst* focused on detail, logic, and thinking, and presented an engaging environment for adults (Prensky, 2001). *Jeopardy*, a competitive television game involving questions and answers, spawned the Jeopardy training game, a Power-Point template widely used in corporate America today to teach a variety of content. Moreover, the popular television game show, *Who Wants to be a Millionaire*, may very well be the next best Digital Game-Based learning tool for adults (Prensky, 2001).

WHO ARE YOUR LEARNERS?

One of the most important considerations in game design is the makeup and complexion of the game's target audience. Absent an in depth understanding of the audience, game design becomes an insurmountable task. When designing games or simulations for the workplace, audience analysis is difficult due to the complexity of the workforce. Currently, there are at least four different generations in the workplace and because of the recent economic down turn, this may broaden to include five generations. With increased globalization, the many nuances of cultural difference must also be considered. The diversity found in today's workforce creates tremendous challenges in communication, and misunderstandings often arise (Zemke, Raines & Filipczak, 2000).

Current generational and age/stage development research have commandeered a wide variety of names and definitions for each specific generation (Gartner, 2000; Glass, 2007; Feiertag & Berge 2008; Rettie, 2002). A recent study by Jones and Fox (2009) of the Pew Internet and American Life Project has further segmented the generations currently using technology and playing games. In their research report, the generations are defined as follows:

- Generation Y (Millennials) born between 1977 and 1990
- Generation X born between 1965 and 1976
- Younger Boomers born between 1955 and 1964
- Older Boomers born between 1946 and 1954
- Silent Generation born between 1937 and 1945
- G.I. Generation born in 1936 or before

Individuals within a generation are a reflection of the times in which they live, making them a product of the cultural, social, political, and technological events that took place during their development (Zemke, Raines & Filipczak, 2000). When one considers a chronology of the social and technological events that unfolded during the youth of each generation, it is easy to see why there would be differences in willingness to use gaming and simulations in learning.

Millennials (Generation Y) are a diverse group who are eager to embrace technology, enjoy playing games, are accustomed to collaboration, and maintain a close relationship with their parents (Oblinger, 2003). This generation was raised on video games, public television, organized sports, standardized tests, and play-based learning. They prefer teamwork, experiential activities, structure, and the use of technology (Oblinger, 2004). Their entry into the workplace has created the need for employers to transfer paper-based training to more interactive, gaming-simulations. Conversely, members of Generation X are independent, adaptable, flexible, require accountability and

autonomy, dislike rigid work requirements and hierarchy, need immediate and ongoing feedback, and are loyal to their work (Dede, 2005; Oblinger, 2004; Tapscott, 1998; Kirkley & Kirkley, 2004; Macedonia, 2002). Generation Xers value family happiness, work-life balance, variety in work, flexibility, and opportunities to grow, develop and prosper (Coates, 2003).

Baby Boomers tend to be optimistic, collaborative, cooperative, introspective, self-absorbed, idealistic, spiritual, and trend setting (Zemke, Raines & Philipczak, 2000). They were raised with traditional training and classroom delivery methods making them comfortable with linear lectures in a face-to-face learning environment. Members of this generation (along with older Generation Xers) are the parents of the Millennials. In many cases, the Boomer parents have made an attempt to keep up with the changing technology in order to maintain currency in their children's lives. In fact, many Younger Boomers and Generation Xers are using instant messaging, playing online games, watching online videos, using social networking sites, downloading music, reading and creating blogs, and playing games on their computers (Jones & Fox, 2009; Lenhart, Jones & MacGill, 2008). For this reason, they will be more open to using games and technology in workplace training.

Despite the distinct generational profiles described by many authors, Kapp (2007) claims that gamers transcend generations. According to Kapp (2007), the gaming generation encompasses those born from the 1960s to 2000. This would include Younger Boomers, Generation Xers and Millennials. The effect that gaming has had on these generations is analogous to many attention deficit disorder characteristics (Hai-Jew, 2007), which may explain why so gamers are self-directed, have short attention spans, and multitask.

The Pew Internet and American Life Project (Lenhart, Jones, and MacGill, 2008) found that American adults over the age of eighteen represent 53% of video game players, with 20% playing daily. Men (55%) are slightly more likely than women (50%) to play video games, and those who have some college education (57%) are more likely to play than those who have not completed high school (40%). The number of gamers varies by generation with the Millennials comprising the largest segment of gamers (81%), followed by Generation X (60%), Boomers (40%), and the Silent Generation (23%). Of note was the fact that although Millennials have the largest number of game players, members of the Silent Generation play games the most frequently. Thirty-six percent of those over age 65 played games daily compared to the Boomers at 19%, Generation X at 20% and Millennials at 20%. The research attributed this finding to the fact that the senior gamers were retired and had more time to play games. Clearly though, the study indicates that both young and older adults find computer and video games an enjoyable and entertaining way to pass time. For this reason alone, it is no wonder educators and human resource professionals are considering the advantages of using games and simulations for teaching and learning.

Jones and Fox (2009) found distinct differences among the generations in how quickly members of each generation adopt new technologies and in how they use the Internet. Although Millennials more readily embrace new technologies, the older age groups are making the transition, too, just more slowly. For example, currently 45% of 70 to 75 year-olds use the Internet, compared to 2005 when only 26% of this age group was online. The researchers found that teens (78%) and Millennials (50%) were far more likely to play online games, but that online game playing was popular with Generation X (38%), Boomers (54%), and the Silent/G.I. Generation (43%), as well.

Despite the aforementioned generational differences in computer game usage, there is an interactive bi-directional learning relationship among generations in the workplace where members of one generation learn from another. Since much can be learned from each generation,

game developers need to design games to foster collaboration among gamers and capitalize on the strengths and preferences of each generation. This will serve to optimize the learning experience for all learners. Older and younger workers "do not respond the same way to training" (Grossman, 2008, p. 43) and, as a result, instructional designers must design training to improve and ensure results (see Figure 2).

Many of the learning differences between the generations may be linked to technology and the ways in which it affects learning (Prensky, 2006; 2001). Learners have changed because of the influence of technology. Research by psychologists has supported this notion. According to the American Psychological Association (2006), multitasking has many hidden costs to children and adults. It divides our attention, which can be dangerous when performing complex tasks, and lowers productivity when we switch from one task to another (Clay, 2009; APA, 2006). Of alarming note is the increase in pedestrian traffic accidents at major Universities resulting from students attempting to multitask around the simple functions of text messaging while, at the same time, observing crossing light signals in heavily congested areas. In the extreme, multitasking may lead to simple distraction or may result in cognitive dysfunction. In either case, issues surrounding multitasking have direct implications for instructional design-

Figure 2. Intergenerational differences model

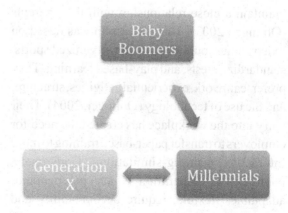

ers. The learner's propensity to multitask and get distracted must be an important consideration in game design. In the end, game design must strike a balance between the need to provide structured guidance to learners and the need for adequate learner control. There must be enough structure in the game to provide clarity but enough choice to engage and motivate the learner.

MOTIVATION AND LEARNING

Seminal research on educational games identified the components of games that made them fun and motivating (Malone, 1980). Game theorists have examined the features, structure, and media elements that make games motivating and enjoyable from the multiple perspectives of fantasy, curiosity, challenge, control (Malone, 1980), visualization, experimentation, creativity of play (Betz, 1995), rules, strategy, goals, competition, cooperation, and chance (Crookall, Oxford, & Saunders, 1987). From each perspective, the designer's desired overall end state is a motivated learner (Garris, Ahlers, & Driskell, 2002).

Motivation "is the most important factor that drives learning" (Gee, 2003, p. 3) and when it dies, so does the learning. Understanding how video games create and sustain motivation in adult learners is the key to fostering meaningful context-based learning that transfers to the learners' jobs and work lives. Further, acknowledging what motivates each generation to learn can create more effective gaming-simulation training. There have been many attempts to explain whether intrinsic or extrinsic motivational factors are the most significant in influencing an individual to learn. (Garris, Ahlers, & Driskell, 2002). While both intrinsic (participation and task accomplishment) and extrinsic (means to an end) factors are important to learner behavior, current research suggests that intrinsic motivation provides the best framework for understanding learner behavior in computer game and simulation design (Squire &

Jenkins, 2003; Garris, Ahlers, &Driskell, 2002; Malone, 1981). Within this intrinsic motivation framework, challenge, fantasy, and curiosity are used to create instruction that maximizes learner engagement (Malone, 1981). Moreover, a broader range of intrinsically motivating factors such as challenge, conflict, curiosity, control, and fantasy help foster both tangible skills and leadership skills (Bonk & Dennen, 2005).

Current research suggests that significant differences of opinion exist on the issues related to motivational appeal in computer-based gaming (Ricci, Salas, &Cannon-Bowers, 1996). Effectively utilizing the attributes of dynamic interaction, competition, and novelty yields "significant differences in learner attitudes" (p. 299). Moreover, learner motivation is governed best by context vice content. In opposition to context as the most influential motivator in learning, Clark (1983) argues that media does not and cannot affect learning outcomes. A consensus in the current research (Joy & Garcia, 2000; Gredler, 2004) supports Clark's (1983, 1994a, 1994b) underlying argument that "methods, not media, are the causal factors in learning" (2004, p. 579).

Taking a more centrist view, Kozma (1994) reframes Clark's argument (1983) and posits that media will influence learning. Kozma (1994) asserts, "both media and methods are part of the instructional design" (p. 8). He further postulates that a similar outcome in different studies does not necessarily mean that they result from the same cause. Current research indicates that both excellent instructional design principles and instructional methods are equally important influences on learner motivation (Joy & Garcia, 2000; Clark,1983).

At the cutting edge of research in motivational learning for computer games, the merging of gaming and simulation together appears to be the next logical step for practitioners (Luppa & Borst, 2007). "Gameplay will breathe life into any simulation" (p. 132) and integrating gameplay elements into simulation potentially yields increased user emotion and user investment. It appears plausible that once designers understand how to effectively break down strong elements of gameplay, then simulation will produce the "desired training and pedagogy to the user" (p. 132).

LEARNING THEORY AND GAME DESIGN

Current trends in gaming point to the increased use of simulations and virtual worlds (i.e.: Second Life, MediaMoos, and MUDs), which are structured around the theory of constructivism and constructionism. Promoting learning through the lens of constructivism enables students to take ownership of their own learning primarily because they create knowledge and make meaning from their own experiences. This experientially based meaning making shifts the instructor's role from that of teacher to facilitator (Driscoll, 2005; Thatcher, 1990; Tapscott, 1998), and switches the student's role from passive to active. Constructivism espouses that knowledge is derived from the assimilation of new experiences into the learner's already existing framework of knowledge. Constructivist learning environments are predicated on the notion that the learner shapes his or her own learning through shared experience with others. In social constructivist learning environments, meaningful learning occurs through the co-construction of knowledge with others. In gaming worlds, this occurs through role-playing, role taking, and feedback. These roles, although difficult to assume, can be "very effective and fulfilling" (Thatcher, 1990, p. 271).

Constructivist learning theory also includes social negotiation as an important element in learning (Vygotsky, 1978; Driscoll, 2005). "Collaboration [is] a critical feature in the learning environment… [which] enables insights and solutions to arise" (Driscoll, 2005, p. 396). Processes that foster collaboration are vital in a learning environment. In social constructivist environments, knowledge

results from shared meaning making between the learner and other knowledgeable members of his or her environment (Berger & Luckmann, 1966). It is only through this negotiated social integration that the learner can learn to interpret the complex systems of signs, symbols and language that constitute new knowledge. In the end, negotiated shared meaning making allows learners to construct knowledge, insights, and solutions to issues, that ordinarily, they may not have considered on their own (Tapscott, 1998).

Second Life, MediaMoos and MUDs have commonalities despite their differences in purpose, intended audiences, and the disciplines addressed. Whether the purpose of learning is intentional or unintentional, users of these worlds can actively construct their own learning and create their own virtual environments through the lens of constructionism. Constructionism combines the social constructivist concept of building on the learner's experience to create meaning with the process of actively building something through experimentation (Papert, 1993). Current examples of constructionist learning projects include SIMcity language acquisition, LEGO animal creation and robotics, and the MOODLE website. Each of these examples requires the learner to experiment through trial and error, to design and redesign, and to learn through the process of doing.

There are two constructionist practices that promote learning in gaming and simulation environments. The first type of construction concerns actively building knowledge from personal experiences in the world. The second type of construction involves the learner actively engaging in creating something meaningful. Knowledge building and meaning making facilitate learning by providing the "opportunity for self-expression…and enhanced sense of community" (Bruckman & Resnick, 1995, p. 94). This approach argues that people learn best by doing, designing and experimenting, as opposed to being told what they need to know (Tapscott, 1998). Constructionism stands in direct opposition to instructionalism.

Discovery learning results in a more meaningful and retention-filled experience than traditional instructional curricula (Tapscott, 1998). From the perspective of constructionism, the instructional designer creates an environment where the learner actively designs, experiments and creates as part of the learning process. However, in today's world, instructional designers are faced with unique challenges when trying to create learning environments for multi-generational learners. Balancing the needs of older, less technology literate learners with those of the Millennial Generation becomes paramount. Millennials are more digitally literate and have been heavily influenced by the information technology world (Oblinger, 2004; Dede, 2005). For this reason alone, it is prudent to consider the advantages afforded by employing interactive gaming simulations to keep and engage the Millennials.

Currently, there are many instructional design challenges in the field of computer gaming and simulation when creating learning environments for training applications. "Existing instructional methodologies do not adequately address how to design and deliver learning in the context of mixed reality and virtual technologies" (Kirkley & Kirkley, 2004, p. 49). Technology friendly and flexible instructional design models must overcome the rigidity and precision of past models. Using a balanced step-by-step model produces "cookie-cutter outcomes" (Prensky, 2001, p. 83) much like the template based training products created when using an Instructional Systems Design (ISD) model. Cookie-cutter outcomes in games and simulations create boring and predictable scenarios. Learners quickly lose motivation to complete the task at hand. The challenge is to incorporate game design elements when creating games and simulations for education and training (edu-training). Though tricky and often difficult to create, blended learning environments should be considered the next step in catering to Millennial learning styles (Kirkley & Kirkley, 2004). Blended learning environments incorporate virtual technologies with traditional technologies and approaches.

Effective game principles should be present in successful game design in order to optimize learning (Prensky,2001). The most successful design configuration counter balances twin principles—easy to learn, yet hard to master. Several important and strategic elements must be considered in every successful game design. These elements include: "balance of challenge, original yet creative, focused and fun, memorable characters, healthy tension that draws the player back for more, and energy" (pp. 133-134). Creating environments that can accommodate all of these elements and principles maximizes the potential for successful instructional game design. Figure 3 illustrates specific elements that should be included for an effective gaming and simulation design.

DESIGN IMPLICATIONS

A pre-assessment is the most important way to address generational and individual learning differences. Theoretically, a pre-game assessment could ask gamers a serious of questions to determine the kind of media elements, colors, kind of narration, or type of language to use to address learner preferences. This type of assessment would serve to make the game environment more personal, and hopefully, optimize the game experience for the learner.

Design implications in Hede and Hede's (2002) integrated model of multimedia effects on learning suggest that multiple factors must be accounted for to properly explain multimedia effects on learning. Awareness of the relationships between and among variables is critical to understand how to promote effective digital-based learning tools. According to Hede and Hede (2002), an understanding of the target audience's abilities and characteristics is critical for successful game design. For this reason, it is imperative to have a clear understanding of the learners and how they will react to the elements and structure of the game.

Figure 3. Effective design model for gaming and simulations

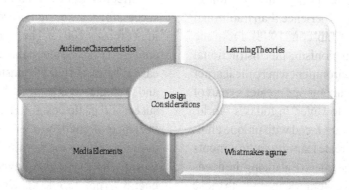

CONCLUSION

Over the next 20 years, the work force will be composed largely of those born after 1980. This generation grew up with the microcomputer, video games, the Internet, digital cameras, cell phones, mp3 players, social networking sites, and the immediate gratification afforded by a variety of technologies. As a collaborative generation used to playing games and dividing their attention among many activities, they will not respond to traditional, linear training techniques.

Gaming and simulation can be seen as the new frontier for adult, professional, and corporate education. Many factors need to be considered when designing training games and simulations. By addressing the topics outlined in this chapter, game designers will be able to foster meaningful learning that transfers to the workplace and other environments.

Design considerations, such as motivation and generational differences are important factors in creating effective simulation scenarios and games. These design considerations combined with an understanding of the learners and the learning process are key to building powerful learning environments. We now know that there is no one-size-fits-all instructional design model for gaming and simulation learning environments. Malone's

(1981) work on intrinsically motivating instruction provides a usable framework for developing the relationships between challenge, fantasy, and curiosity in game and simulation design (Tapscott 1998; Grossman 2008). Additionally, learning is influenced by instructional methods, rather than by media alone (Clark, 1983).

Taken as a whole, effective instructional game designers must have clear goals, an understanding of learning theories and how to apply them to game design, a mastery of the judicious and targeted use of appropriate media elements, and an understanding of how to embed sound learning principles in their learning environments. An application of Constructivist and Constructionist learning perspectives to game design enables game players to more fully engage in learning while providing opportunities for questioning, problem solving, self-expression, and experiential learning. Prensky (2001) gives insight to game design considerations when he states that games must draw in the player by creating a sense of tension between the initial ease of learning and the difficulty in mastering the task. It is the balance of challenging content, appropriate media elements, sound instructional methods, challenge, fantasy, and curiosity that make gaming and simulation both engaging and useful as instructional tools.

REFERENCES

American Psychological Association. (2006, March). Multitasking- switching costs. *American Psychological Association Online.* Retrieved February 24, 2009 from ttp://www.psychology-matters.org/multitask0306.html

Berger, P. L., & Luckman, T. (1966). *The Social Construction of Reality.* New York: Doubleday.

Betz, J. A. (1995). Computer games: Increases learning in an interactive multidisciplinary environment. *Journal of Educational Technology Systems, 24,* 195–205. doi:10.2190/119M-BRMU-J8HC-XM6F

Bonk, C. J., & Dennen, V. P. (2005). *Massive Multiplayer Online Gaming: A Research Framework for Military Training and Education.* Technical Report 2005-1, Department of Defense of the U.S.A.

Bruckman, A., & Resnick, M. (1995). The mediamoo project constructionism and professional community. *Convergence, 1*(1), 94–109.

Chandler, M. A. (2009, January 4). More and more, schools got game. *The Washington Post,* (pp. C1-C4).

Clark, R. E. (1983). Reconsidering research on learning from media. *Review of Educational Research, 53*(4), 445–459.

Clark, R. E. (1994a). Media will never influence learning. *Educational Technology Research and Development, 42*(2), 21–29. doi:10.1007/BF02299088

Clark, R. E. (1994b). Media and method. *Educational Technology Research and Development, 42*(3), 7–10. doi:10.1007/BF02298090

Clay, R. A. (2009, February). Mini-mulitaskers. *Monitor on Psychology.* February 24, 2009, from http://www.apa.org/monitor/2009/02/multitaskers.html

Coates, J. (2003). *Generational learning styles.* River Falls, WI: Lern Books.

Crookall, D., Oxford, R. L., & Saunders, D. (1987). Towards a reconceptualization of simulation: From representation to reality. *Simulation/Games for Learning, 17,* 147-171.

Curtis, C. K., Thomas, K. M., & Ritter, J. (2008). Interactive gaming technologies and air force technical training. *Journal of Interactive Instruction Development, 20*(3), 17–23.

Dede, C. (2005). Planning for neomillennial learning styles. *EDUCAUSE Quarterly, 28*(1), 7–12.

Denis, G., & Jouvelot, P. (2005). Motivation-driven educational game design: Applying best practices to music education. In *Proceedings of the 2005 ACM SIGCHI international Conference on Advances in Computer Entertainment Technology* (Valencia, Spain, June 15 - 17, vol. 265, pp. 462-465). New York: ACM. DOI=http://doi.acm.org/10.1145/1178477.1178581

Driscoll. (2005). *Psychology of learning for instruction* (3rd ed.). New York: Pearson Education, Inc.

Duffy, T. M., & Jonassen, D. (Eds.). (1992). *Constructivism and the technology of instruction: A conversation.* Hillsdale, NJ: Lawrence Erlbaum Associates.

Fiertag & Berge. (2008). Training generation N: How educator should approach the Net Generation. *Education & Training, 50*(6), 457-464.

Foorman, B. R., Fletcher, J. M., Francis, D. J., Schatschneider, C., & Mehta, P. (1998). The Role of Instruction in Learning to Read: Preventing Reading Failure in At-Risk Children. *Journal of Educational Psychology, 90*(1), 37–55. doi:10.1037/0022-0663.90.1.37

Garris, R., Ahlers, R., & Driskell, J. E. (2002). Games, motivation, and learning: A research and practice model. *Simulation & Gaming, 33*, 441–467. doi:10.1177/1046878102238607

Gartner. (2000, May 9). Generation Y Web Shoppers Emerge as Mini-Boomers According to Gartner. *Gartner.*

Gee, J. P. (2003). *What video games have to teach us about learning and literacy.* New York: Palgrave/Macmillian.

Glass, A. (2007). Understanding generational differences for competitive success. *Industrial and Commercial Training, 39*(2), 98–103. doi:10.1108/00197850710732424

Gredler, M. E. (1994). *Designing and evaluating games and simulations: A process approach.* Houston, TX: Gulf Publication Company.

Gredler, M. E. (1996). Educational games and simulations: A technology in search of a (research) paradigm. In Jonassen, D. H. (Ed.), *Handbook of research for educational communications and technology* (pp. 521–539). New York: Macmillan.

Gredler, M. E. (2004). Games and simulations and their relationships to learning. In Jonassen, D. H. (Ed.), *Handbook of research on educational communications and technology* (2nd ed., pp. 571–581). Mahwah, NJ: Lawrence Erlbaum Associates.

Grossman, R. J. (2008, May). Keep pace with older workers. *HRMagazine, 53*, 39–46.

Hai-Jew, S. (2007). Gadgets, games, and gizmos for learning: Knowledge transfer from boomers to gamers?/ Gadgets, games and gizmos for learning. *Journal of Interactive Instruction Development, 20*(1), 42–45.

Hede, T., & Hede, A. (2002). *Multimedia effects on learning: Design implications of an integrated model.* Paper presented at the ASET.

Hogle, J..G. (1996). *Considering games as cognitive tools: In search of effective "edutainment".*

Jones, S. (2003). *Let the Games Begin: Gaming Technology and Entertainment Among College Students.* Pew Internet and American Life Project. Retrieved July 17, 2009. Retrieved from http://www.pewinternet.org/Reports/2003/Let-the-games-begin-Gaming-technology-and-college-students.aspx

Joy, E., & Garcia, F. (2000). Measuring learning effectiveness: A new look at no-significant-difference findings. *Journal of Asynchronous Learning Network, 4*(1). 15. Available online at http://www.aln.org/alnweb/journal/vol14_issue1/joygarcia.htm

Kapp, K. M. (2007). *Gadgets, Games, and Gizmos for Learning.* San Francisco: John Wiley and Sons.

Kirkley, S. E., & Kirkley, J. R. (2004). Creating next generation blended learning environments using mixed reality, video games and simulations. *TechTrends, 49*(3), 42–53. doi:10.1007/BF02763646

Klabbers, J. H. G. (2003). The gaming landscape: A taxonomy for classifying games and simulations. In M. Copier & J. Raessens, (Eds.), *Proceedings of Level Up: Digital Games Research Conference,* (pp. 54-68, 4-6). Utrecht, The Netherlands: University of Utrecht.

Kozma, R. B. (1994). Will media influence learning? Reframing the debate. *Educational Technology Research and Development, 42*(2), 7–19. doi:10.1007/BF02299087

Kriz, W. C. (2003). Creating effective learning environments and learning organizations through gaming simulation design. *Simulation & Gaming, 34*, 495–511. doi:10.1177/1046878103258201

Leemkuil, H., de Jong, T., & Ootes, S. (2000). *Review of educational use of games and simulations.* EC project KITS (Knowledge management Interactive Training System). EC project KITS (IST-1999-3078), KITS Deliverable D1, Enschede: KITS consortium. University of Twente, The Netherlands. Retrieved January 25, 2009, from http://kits.edte.utwente.nl/documents/D1.pdf

Lenhart, A., Jones, S., & MacGill, A. (2008, December 7). *Adults and video games.* Retrieved July 17, 2009 from Pew Internet Website: http://www.pewinternet.org/Reports/2008/Adults-and-Video-Games.aspx?r=1

Luppa, N., & Borst, T. (2007). *Story and simulations for serious games: Tales from the trenches.* Boston, MA: Focal Press.

Macedonia, M. (2002). Games, simulation, and the military education dilemma. In M. Devlin, R. Larson & J. Meyerson, (Eds), Internet and the University: 2001 Forum (pp. 157-167). Cambridge, MA: EDUCAUSE, MIT.

Malone, T. (1981). Toward a theory of intrinsically motivating instruction. *Cognitive Science, 4,* 333–369.

Malone, T. W. (1980). *What makes things fun to learn? Heuristics for designing instructional computer games.* Paper presented at the Joint Symposium: Association for Computing Machinery Special Interest Group on Small Computers and Special Interest Group on Personal Computers, Palo Alto, CA.

Mateas, M. (2003). Expressive AI: Games and Artificial Intelligence. In *Proceedings of Level Up: Digital Games Research Conference,* Utrecht, Netherlands, Nov. 2003.

Oblinger, D. G. (2003). Boomers, gen-xers, and millennials: Understanding the new students. *Educase, 38*(4), 37-47. Retrieved January 26, 2009, from http://www.educause.edu/ir/library/pdf/erm0342.pdf

Oblinger, D. G. (2004). The next generation of education engagement. *Journal of Interactive Media in Education, 8,* 1–18.

Papert, S. (1993). *The Children's machine: rethinking school in the age of the computer.* New York: Basic Books.

Prensky, M. (2001). *Digital game-based learning.* New York: McGraw-Hill.

Prensky, M. (2006). *Don't bother me mom – I'm learning: How computer and video games are preparing your kids for 21st century success – and how you can help.* St. Paul, MN: Paragon House.

Raines, C. (2002). *Managing Millennials.* Retrieved February 28, 2009, from, http://www.generationsatwork.com/articles/millenials.htm

Rettie, R. (2002). Net Generation Culture. *Journal of Electronic Commerce Research, 3*(4), 254–264.

Ricci, K. E., Salas, E., & Cannon-Bowers, J. A. (1996). Do computer-based games facilitate knowledge acquisition and retention? *Military Psychology, 8*(4), 295–307. doi:10.1207/s15327876mp0804_3

Rieber, L. P. (1996). Seriously considering play: Designing interactive learning environments based on the blending of microworlds, simulations, and games.

Rieber, L. P., & Noah, D. (2008). Games, simulations, and visual metaphors in education: Antagonism between enjoyment and learning. *Educational Media International, 45*(2), 77–92. doi:10.1080/09523980802107096

Roberts, N. (1976). Simulation gaming: A critical review. Cambridge, MA: Lesley College and Massachusetts Institute of Technology. (ERIC Document Reproduction Service No.ED 137165).

Smith, R. (2009). *The Long History of Gaming in Military Training.*

Squire, K., & Jenkins, H. (2003). Harnessing the power of games in education. *Insight (American Society of Ophthalmic Registered Nurses), 3,* 6–33.

Susi, T., Johannesson, M., & Backlund, P. (2007). *Serious games: An overview. Technical Report HS-IKI-TR-07-001, University of Skövde. Tapscott, D. (1998). Growing Up Digital: The Rise of the Net Generation.* New York: McGraw-Hill.

Thatcher, D. C. (1990). Promoting learning through games and simulations. *Simulation & Gaming, 21,* 262–273. doi:10.1177/1046878190213005

Vygotsky, L. S. (1978). *Mind in society: The development of higher mental processes.* Cambridge, MA: Harvard University Press.

Watters, C. B. (2009, March). Effective use of simulations in business training. *Talent Management, 5,* 32–35.

Zemke, R., Raines, C., & Filipczak, B. (2000). *Generations at Work: Managing the Clash of Veterans, Boomers, Xers, and Nexters in Your Workplace.* New York: Amacom.

Zyda, M. (2005). From visual simulation to virtual reality to games. *Computer, 38*(9), 25–32. doi:10.1109/MC.2005.297

Chapter 2
Explaining the Educational Power of Games

Timo Lainema
Turku School of Economics, Finland

Eeli Saarinen
Turku School of Economics, Finland

ABSTRACT

This chapter introduces two views of learning relevant for game-based learning: experiential learning theory and the constructivist view on learning. The authors will first discuss, how these views explain learning from a perspective that is relevant for game-based learning. They will also evaluate, how these views on learning relate to assessment of learning through gaming. Last, they will concretize the diversity of the potential learning outcomes of gaming: how, for example, the learner's previous knowledge, personality, the team members affect the learning experience and outcome. According to constructivism, learning is a constructive process in which the learner is building an internal representation of knowledge. This is something to which game-based education clearly adds value to.

INTRODUCTION

Games as an experience-based instructional method have the potential to address many of the limitations of the traditional class-room education. They accommodate more complex and diverse approaches to learning processes and outcomes; allow for interactivity; promote collaboration and peer learning; and, perhaps most important, foster active learning (Ruben, 1999).

We believe that the practice of any instructional design – like educational games – should be based on some conception of how people learn and what it means to learn (Duffy & Jonassen, 1992a). Bednar et al. (1992) argue that effective instructional design emerges from the deliberate application of some particular theory of learning. This is our motivation for introducing the main beliefs in two learning paradigms relevant for game-based education. As researchers we are interested in whether the experiential learning theory (ELT) or the constructivist learning paradigm are able to increase our understanding about the learning processes that take place in game-based learning activities. ELT has been the background for arguing (computerized) game-based learning at least since the early 1980s,

DOI: 10.4018/978-1-61520-781-7.ch002

but it seems that the game community has not fully noticed the constructivist message emerging from the discipline of Education (Lainema, 2009).

Besides of introducing the two learning paradigms, we will also reflect on a recent game-based learning case and describe the diverse nature that may take place through gaming. Finally, we will conclude that learning is a constructive process in which the learner is building an internal representation of knowledge.

In this chapter we use the phrases *game* and *simulation game* interchangeable. The word simulation emphasizes that *the purpose of the game is to describe the behavior of a complex real-world system (like the functioning of a business organization) on a computer model over an extended period of time*. Although not always explicit, our discussion concerns educational (simulation) games and educational gaming. With all of these terms we mean a computerized game, *the goal of which is to help the gamers to learn something relevant that can be transferred into real-world environments*. Business (simulation) game is defined as a sequential decision-making exercise structure around a model of a business operation, in which participants assume the role of managing the simulated operation (Greenlaw et al., 1962).

EXPERIENTIAL LEARNING

According to Experiential learning theory (ELT), the most powerful learning comes from direct experience – through action taking and seeing the consequences of that action. Learning is said to occur through the resolution of conflicts over different ways of dealing with the world. ELT suggests a holistic integrative perspective on learning that combines experience, perception, cognition, and behavior (Kolb, 1984).

Kolb (1984) describes the experiential learning model as: (p. 21): "an integrated process that begins with here-and-now experience followed by collection of data and observations about that experience. The data are then analyzed and conclusions of this analysis fed back to the actors in the experience for their use in the modification of their behavior and choice of new experiences". Learning is conceived as a four-stage cycle shown in Figure 1. Immediate concrete experience is the basis for observation and reflection. Observations are assimilated into a theory from which new implications for action can be deduced. Implications or hypotheses then serve as guides in acting to create new experiences.

Kolb especially notes two aspects of this learning model. The first is the emphasis on

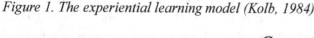
Figure 1. The experiential learning model (Kolb, 1984)

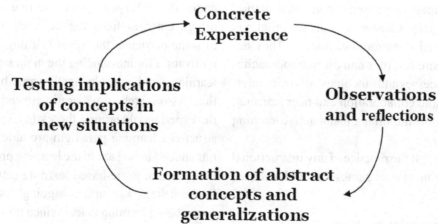

here-and-now concrete experience to validate and test abstract concepts. This experience gives life, texture, and subjective personal meaning to abstract concepts and at the same time provides a concrete, publicly shared reference point for testing the implications and validity of ideas created during the learning process.

The second emphasized aspect of this the information feedback provides the basis for a continuous process of goal-directed action and evaluation of the consequences of that action (Kolb, 1984). The laboratory method (to which also games as learning environments belong to) integrates observation and action into an effective, goal-directed learning process.

Kolb & Kolb (2008) note that the experiential learning cycle is actually a learning spiral. When a concrete experience is enriched by reflection, the new experience created becomes richer, broader, and deeper. As the learner advances in the learning process, her questions become more sophisticated, and her understanding deepens.

There are several different models of experiential learning which all have in common the belief in experience and reflection on it (Cheetham and Chivers, 2001). For example, Argyris and Schön (1978) have described the process of experiential learning in slightly different terms. Ekpenyong (1999) examined several experiential learning strategies and defines experiential learning as (p. 462) "...meaningful learning or problem-solving, which involves purposeful behavior with an anticipation of the probable consequence of such behavior".

At this point, we want to note that in professional education literature, very little has been said about ELT. Ekpenyong (1999) finds two reasons for this: (1) The lack of a formal theory of experiential learning; and (2) The dominance of experiential learning in industrial and non-school settings. Critiques of experiential learning fail to preserve its two fundamental assumptions (Kayes, 2002): (a) the inherent potential of human beings to learn, and (b) the belief that learning

lies in problem solving. Kayes suggests that an alternative approach should preserve the dialectic nature of experience and account for its social aspect more fully.

Despite the criticism, ELT seems to be a widely applied learning theory in game-based learning exercises. The four-stage cycle of experiential learning is very similar to the organizational structure of typical games (Herz and Merz, 1998). We can state that educational games are experiential exercises (Gredler, 1996). Games offer here-and-now concrete experiences to validate and test abstract concepts presented in the gaming environment. Games can be thought as laboratory training including feedback processes and continuous, iterative and goal-directed. While the formulaic way in which Kolb has been interpreted may not represent reality accurately, his theory provides those who wish to be more learner-centered with a starting point for thinking about their practice (Marsick and Watkins, 1990).

CONSTRUCTIVISM

In the simulation gaming community ELT has long been the dominant learning theory and the development and use of games has been argued with ELT. Still, during the 1990's there has been a convergence of learning theories never before encountered (Jonassen and Land, 2000), a phenomenon that should have better been taken into account also within the gaming community. These contemporary learning theories are based on substantially different ontologies and epistemologies than were traditional objectivist foundations for instructional design. According to the objectivist view, knowledge is believed to exist independently of instruction, and there is no need to look at the instructional activities to see what is learned. Rather, a test that stands separate from the instruction is produced, and it is designed to probe the knowledge acquired in an objective way. The objectivist epistemology underlies behaviorism and much of cognitive psychology (Jonassen, 1992).

Constructivism as one of the new theories seems to provide a strong rationale for using games to support learning (Kriz, 2008). Constructivism is not a completely new learning paradigm. For example, the ideas of experiential learning have had influence on constructivism. Duffy and Cunningham (1996) find two similarities among them: (1) Learning is an active process of constructing rather than acquiring knowledge. (2) Instruction is a process of supporting that construction rather than communicating knowledge. Jonassen and Land (2000) list several contemporary conceptions of learning that share many beliefs and assumptions. These views are based on belief that learning is neither a transmissive nor a submissive process, but rather a willful, intentional, active, conscious, constructive practice that includes reciprocal intention-action-reflection activities (similar to the learning cycle in ELT). The views mentioned are, for example, socially shared cognition, situated learning, activity theory, distributed cognitions, and case-based reasoning.

Lave and Wenger (1991) emphasize that learning as internalization – as it is seen in the objectivist view of learning – is too easily construed as an unproblematic process of absorbing the given, as a matter of transmission and assimilation. The focus should be on the skills of reflectivity of the learner, not on remembering. Constructivism focuses on the process of knowledge construction and the development of reflexive awareness of that process (Bednar et al., 1992). Learning is a process of enculturation that is supported through social interaction and the circulation of narrative (Brown et al., 1989).

Instruction should not focus on transmitting plans to the learner but rather on developing the skills of the learner to construct plans in response to situational demands and opportunities. Instruction should provide contexts and assistance that will aid the individual in making sense of the environment as it is encountered (Duffy and

Jonassen, 1992b). The learner is building an internal representation of knowledge, a personal interpretation of experience (Bednar et al., 1992). Learning is an active process in which meaning is developed on the basis of experience. Learning must be situated in a rich context, reflective of real-world contexts for this constructive process to occur. The goal is to portray tasks, not to define the structure of learning required to achieve that task. Thus, we must leave the identification of relevant information and correct solutions open in the instructional situation.

Bednar et al. (1992) have a quite extreme view of how constructivism differs from the old design principles of traditional behavior theory (where the sequence of instruction is specified based on logical dependencies in the knowledge domain). They argue that the learning environments should encourage construction of understanding from multiple perspectives. Effective sequencing or rigorous external control of instructional events simply precludes constructive activity and the possibility of developing alternative perspectives. In traditional instructional design there is a tendency to separate the content from the use of the content. In constructivism the learning of the content must be embedded in the use of that content (Bednar et al., 1992). Knowledge is context dependent, so learning should occur in contexts to which it is relevant (Duffy and Cunningham, 1996).

Spiro et al. (1991) argue that revisiting the same material, at different times, in rearranged contexts, for different purposes and from different conceptual perspectives is essential for attaining the goals of advanced knowledge acquisition. Content must be covered more than once for full understanding because of psychological demands resulting from the complexity of case and concept entities in ill-structured domains. Re-examining a case in the context of comparison with a case different from the comparison context will lead to new insights. Spiro et al. argue that the common denominator in the majority of advanced learning failures is oversimplification, and one serious kind of oversimplification is looking at a concept or phenomenon from just one perspective.

Duffy and Cunningham refer Lave and Wenger (1991) and state that learning is not the lonely act of an individual, but a matter of being initiated into the practices of a community, moving from legitimate peripheral participation to centripetal participation in the actions of a learning community. Meaning making results from conversation (Jonassen et al., 1999). Meaning making is a process of negotiation among the parties through dialogues. This dialogue occurs most effectively within communities where people share their interests and experiences. Also knowledge building requires articulation of what is learned. For usable knowledge to be constructed, learners need to think about what they did and articulate what it meant (verbal, visual, auditory).

Duffy and Cunningham (1996) exemplify constructivism in the form of problem-based learning (PBL). The focus should be on developing the skills related to solving the problem as well as other problems like it. Skills are developed through working on the problem, i.e., through authentic activity. It is impossible to describe what is learned in terms of the activity alone or in terms of the content alone (p. 190): "Rather, it is the activity in relation to the content that defines learning: the ability to think critically in that content domain, to collaborate with peers and use them to test ideas about issues, and the ability to locate information related to the issues and bring it to bear on the diagnosis". The teacher does not teach students what they should do/know and when they should do/know it. Rather, the teacher supports the students in developing their critical thinking skills, self-directed learning skills, and content knowledge in relation to the problem.

The basic message above is that technologies are more effectively used as tools to construct knowledge with - not from, like in programmed instruction or computer-assisted instruction frames. Sophisticated computer applications can also offer genuinely new representations or views of phenomena that would not otherwise be possible, and hence provide new understandings. Duffy and Cunningham (1996) suggest that the technology should be seen as an integral component of the cognitive activity. The focus is not on the individual but on the activity in the environment. The computer opens new opportunities and makes available new learning activities (p. 188): "Success [of learning] will increasingly depend on exploring interrelationships in an information-rich environment rather than on accepting the point of view of one author who pursued one set of relationships and presents conclusions reflecting his or her implicit biases".

Today, the basic principles of constructivism seem to be more or less established: Technologies can support learning if they are used as tools that help learners to think. Jonassen et al. (1999) state that constructivist learning environments are technology-based in which students explore, experiment, construct, converse, and reflect on what they are doing, so that they learn from their experiences. Learners are presented with a complex and relevant problem, project, or experience that they accept or reject as a challenge. Then the learning environment provides them with the tools and resources that they need to understand the problem and to solve it. All these characteristics can be implemented in game-based learning environments. Lainema (2009) has noted that constructivism is very relevant for simulation gaming research, design, and understanding about game participants as knowledge constructors. We see that constructivism supports the basic message of ELT and together these two approaches offer a philosophical perspective on understanding how learning takes place in game-based learning activities.

ASSESSING GAME-BASED LEARNING

Our learning case is from the field of business simulation gaming. Anderson & Lawton (2009) summarize that still today the efficacy of business games in achieving cognitive learning outcomes is unclear. Gosen and Washbush (2004) have come to the same conclusion, stating that there have not been enough high-quality studies to allow us to conclude players learn by participating in simulation games. Objective measures of learning are still limited to the basic knowledge, comprehension, and application stages of cognitive learning. Anderson & Lawton (2009) note that attempts to measure analysis, synthesis, and evaluation stages of the gamers have continued to be limited to participant perceptions of their improved abilities. To this Gentry et al. (1998) have pointed out that learner perceptions of what they state they have learned are inadequate and invalid (authors' note: we do not quite agree on this – see the discussion below). Gentry et al. (1998) note that if the students enjoyed the experience, it is likely that they also perceived the experience useful.

Gentry et al. (1998) also asserted that perceived learning and objective learning indicators measure separate constructs. The findings by Gosen and Washbush (1999) support this assertion: they found a zero correlation between objective learning scores and the perceived learning scores on 10 types of learning measured. Gosen and Washburn further argue that learning measures should be tied to explicit learning goals. They refer to Anderson and Lawton (1997) and claim that it is not possible to construct an assessment activity without knowing what it is we expect to measure.

From epistemological point of view we have a slightly different starting point in our research than the authors above. **First**, we do not believe that it is relevant or even conceivable to state anything else but very general findings about the possible learning that takes place in game-based learning activities. This is because of the huge variety of different (business) games (computerized/ non-computerized, group/individual learning activities, clock-driven/batch-decision games, competitive/non-competitive, functional/ general management, and so on) their differences in object content, method of implementation, user-interfaces, and functional structure. We believe that more or less *every game forms its unique case of learning potential, which might not be relevant compared to other games*.

Second, we believe what Gosenpud (1990) has stated: in games the learner often learns things not intended by the designer, and often this unintended learning is more valuable because it is relevant to the learner. This is challenge for learning research. Quantitative research methods require that the researcher states her research topic (in this case the kind of learning she is studying) before the actual learning incidence. Thus, the research instruments are tuned to catch information only about a certain learning occurrence. This means that it is not possible to cover the whole spectrum of potential learning taking place in and from the experiment, not even the most important learning for the learner. The discussion by Anderson & Lawton (2009), Gentry et al. (1998), Gosen and Washbush (1999), and Anderson and Lawton (1997) we have referred to above seems to be based on the quantitative methodology. Gosenpud (1990) notes also that most researchers stress the importance of keeping dependent measures concrete and specific and measuring dependent variables as precisely consistent with designer goals as possible. We would like to question the idea of quantifying the learning that takes place in gaming. The majority of the simulation gaming learning research seems to follow the objectivist tradition of knowledge where the goal is to strive for the complete and correct understanding. Knowledge is believed to exist independently of instruction and there is no need to look at the instructional activities to see what is learned. Rather, a test that stands separate from the instruction is produced, and it is designed to probe the knowledge acquired in an objective way (Duffy & Jonassen, 1992b).

This discussion about learning assessment should always be connected to the learning theories, as how we believe learning takes place should always affect how we assess learning. For us the starting point is that the ideas of constructivism are relevant and valid for game-based learning. Constructivism holds that there are many ways to structure the world, and there are many meanings or perspectives for any event or concept. Thus, there is necessarily not a correct meaning that we are striving for. It seems that as long as we do not have a tool with which to see inside the minds of the learners, the best way to study the learning is to study participant perceptions. Studying perceptions is utterly difficult, if we select and anchor the learning phenomena under investigation and are not open to any other type of learning outside this selection. Gosenpud (1990) has further stated that game evaluation, defined by the designer (researcher), may miss the real worth of the experiential experience because what is valuable for the learner is defined by the learner and may have nothing to do with the designer's (researcher's) intention. Also this comment seems to favor *qualitative research, in which the possible area of research results is more open than in quantitative research.*

Gosen and Washbush (2004), by stating that objective measures of learning are still limited to the basic knowledge, have also revealed the basic debatable question concerning human beings as learners. This objectivist view of the learning process and the learner underlies behaviorism and much of cognitive psychology (Duffy & Jonassen, 1992b). If we believe that learning is a constructive process in which the learner is building an internal representation of knowledge, then this representation is constantly open to change and has varied forms and stages (Bednar et al., 1992). As noted earlier, the identification of relevant information and correct solutions is left open in the learning situation. Learning is a construc-

tive process in which the learner is building an internal representation of knowledge, a personal interpretation of experience (Bednar et al., 1992). If the outcome of the learning is personal, then this further adds complexity and challenge for the researcher. Personality of the learning outcome further emphasizes research instruments which are open to unexpected learning findings.

As a conclusion on the discussion above, we note that there is a paradoxical and contradictory relation in the educational business gaming field between the games and how they are assessed as learning environments. The games themselves offer an experiential and most of all constructivist learning experience (Lainema, 2009), but the learning research of these environments mainly follow the objectivist view of learning. This contradictory relation clearly requires further research.

A GAME-BASED LEARNING CASE

Next we will concretize the diversity of the potential learning outcomes from gaming. Our case and its analysis do not form a full-blown research case. The purpose of this study is not to assess the learning from the exercises, but to illustrate the complex and multifaceted nature of game-based learning outcomes. Thus, our aim in the remaining of the paper is to illustrate the diversity of the potential learning and how challenging game-based learning assessment is.

Our case is a game-based learning course on virtual team communication and collaboration. The course consisted of experiential learning exercises (business simulation gaming) during which the students made different decisions and analyzed the results from these decisions. The main learning potential from the course was in the areas of (a) the importance of communication in successful collaboration; and (b) cultural differences and their importance in a decision-making environment. During the gaming sessions students collaborated with their team members and other teams. The participants were from several different cultures and faced decision-making situations demanding communication, leadership, and understanding power structures. The course has been arranged four times in 2006-2008. The data we are referring to in this paper is from 2007 and 2008 (including four independent gaming and training groups).

The simulation in use was a clock-driven game called RealGame (Figure 2), in which the task of the participants is to manage their manufacturing company and its different functions, and aim at effective supply chain management and profitable financial result in competition between the other companies. RealGame has earlier been studied, for example, in Kiili & Lainema (2008), Lainema & Lainema (2007), Lainema (2007), and Lainema & Nurmi (2006). These articles describe the content and functioning of the game in question. In this paper we will concentrate on exemplifying the potential learning outcomes of the application of the simulation game.

The course was arranged as a joint collaboration between Turku School of Economics in Finland and Johannes Kepler University in Linz, Austria. The students participated in the simulation game simultaneously in both locations and communicated on-line during the exercise. The simulation game used on the course was real-time processed: it is clock-driven and events and actions are triggered and carried out by the students constantly. The simulation game requires uninterrupted observation and reacting from the participants. This kind of decision-making environment is immersive, meaningful and motivating (Kiili & Lainema, 2008; Lainema & Nurmi, 2006).

In all of the simulation game exercises the students formed teams of 3 or 4 students which were responsible of running their own company. The students in these companies were geographically dispersed: part of each team was located in Linz, Austria, and part in Turku, Finland. The two parties of each company could see the same business decision-making computer interface and both of them could steer the same computer

Figure 2. RealGame participant user interface

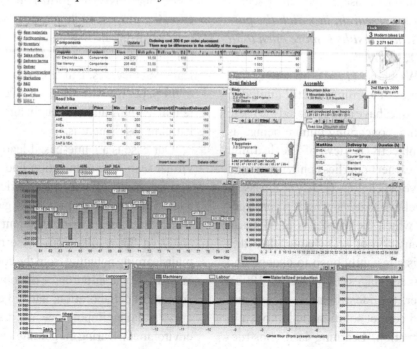

application at the same time. Besides of the web-based simulation gaming platform, these two parties also had an online Skype phone connection so that discussion was taking place constantly between the two locations. Figure 3 below shows a decision-making party in Turku, steering their company and discussing online with their partners in Linz.

In Figure 3 the two students are steering their company in the computer in between them. Both of the students also have a computer of their own on, running Skype and having online connection to their partners in Linz. In addition, the student on the left has an Excel spreadsheet opened, where she maintained production capacity and customer demand calculations in real-time.

During the **first simulation game session** (4 hours) the basic decision-making in the simulation game was introduced. After the first gaming session, the students wrote the **first reflective essay** about their experiences, about predetermined issues, including e.g. decision-making, cultural diversity, power structures and leadership. The results from the first simulation session were discussed in class. After two to three weeks from the first simulation session, the students played the simulation game again **(second/final simulation session**, 4 hours.). After the final simulation game session, the students were again asked to write a **reflective essay**. This time the focus in the reflection was on the learning. They were again guided to discuss predetermined issues. An important part of learning in this setting is the **feedback** given to the teams after the final analysis. The feedback enables the team members to extend their view of the virtual team experience and enables them to compare their subjective conception to this objective evaluation.

We acknowledge that the exercises included many learning topics, which we have not included in our theoretical discussion (like supply chain management, virtual teams, team roles, and cross-cultural communication). Also, we will not argue, why we feel that the case game fulfills the characteristics of an experiential and constructivist learning environment, but content to state that business simulation games in general create environments in which skills are developed

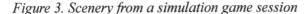

Figure 3. Scenery from a simulation game session

through working on the problem through authentic activity, and the students develop their critical thinking skills, self-directed learning skills, and content knowledge in relation to the problem. It is quite clear that in a typical business game the focus is on exploring interrelationships in an information-rich environment.

FINDINGS

Earlier in this chapter we have claimed that every game forms its unique case of learning potential, which might not be relevant compared to other games. Based on the two views on learning, we argued also that the learning from gaming is such a diverse phenomenon, that to better cover the potential learning, we need qualitative research, which is more open to different kinds of learning results than quantitative research. In the following we will give examples supporting these statements.

Jonassen, Peck & Wilson (1999) note: knowledge building requires articulation of what is learned. For usable knowledge to be constructed, learners need to think about what they did and articulate what it meant (verbal, visual, auditory). Constructivism suggests that we need to assess the meaning that learners have co-constructed from their interactions with the world. Leaning on these principles we use reflective essays in our case.

The reflective essays have had two separate functions. First, they serve as a tool to enhance learning. They support learning by directing the writer to reflect on the experiences. Reflecting itself is an essential part of constructivist understanding of learning as a practice including reciprocal intention-action-reflection activities (see Jonassen & Land 2002). We disregard reflective essays as tools for reflecting separate learning incidents (after each action) but emphasize their meaning as tools for creating a comprehensive picture of all the combined activities. Thus, we see them as facilitators in creating understanding

of greater entities and phenomena. This is in line with Bednar's (1992) real-world contexts meaning that we should build learning environment that captures larger context in which the problems are relevant, like in our experiment, commented by a student:

For me this was the first time actually working in a virtual team and I found it very interesting. Things are quite different when one isn't face to face with the person one is working with. Factors come into account which didn't before, like the functionality of the technical communication channel, i.e. Skype. Others lose their importance, for example how people look or the way they dress.

The experiential learning model is inherent in this learning case as similar tasks are re-assigned and re-reflected in subsequent actions in the simulation game working. Both ELT and constructivism emphasize learning as a cyclical, gradual process. The cyclical nature was also noticed by the students:

Even though we had a few problems concerning our companies success, I profited greatly from the first session, probably exactly for this reason. We made some mistakes but we realized them, reflected on them and will try new methods the next time.

The second function of the essays is that they offer an insight to the different learning processes and different learning levels existing in the learning situation. In the following, we will introduce some descriptive phenomena from the learning case. We will concentrate on presenting some examples of the diversity of learning through gaming – how the very same game experience can produce very different participant experiences:

- Personal negotiation styles: "*The sessions also helped me to realize my negotiation style. While I always thought I was more of a tough negotiator I found that, at least in the second RG session, I was more appeasing and focused on relationship building rather than profits and high prices."*

- Planning: "*I learned the importance to have a plan. It is compulsory when the work is not only influent in your own person.*"
- Dealing with communication problems: "*…when working within a virtual team, it is also important to address arising difficulties and problems… And I consider this as one of the most critical tasks, as talking about problems is already hard when doing it face-to-face, but the virtual context makes it much more complicated.*"
- Trust building: "*Now I know how hard it is to build up trust within a team and to focus on the same goals.*"
- Working in a virtual environment: "*I think this course was very helpful in showing the people how to operate in virtual teams and showing what kind the reality in virtual teams there is.*"
- Learning about oneself: "*I also learnt about myself and my possibilities and how I can manage certain kinds of situations and especially what is most important in team work and specifically in team virtual work.*"
- Learning about cultures: "*I had the chance to negotiate and talk with several different personalities from different countries, which I think of a great chance for future… I definitely will have a better feeling now, when negotiating in a virtual context in the future.*"
- Working in a foreign environment: "*… how it feels to be the only representative of my culture, and in future I will show much more sensibility for exchange students than I have before, because it [loneliness] is sometimes not a very good feeling.*"
- The importance of speaking foreign languages: "*The last point which was very*

valuable for my personal development was to realize that speaking different languages is a quite essential part in today's business. It can bridge gaps of all forms and makes life much effortless for oneself."
- Team work: "*I personally learned that it is important to have members on a team that can contribute equally to the challenge, but also it is important that each member can bring something different to the team. Not every person will have experience with every aspect of a challenge, so it is important that we can bring different experiences to the table.*"

The above quotes are all student reflections on what they considered to be valuable lessons for them in the exercise from the point of view of multiculturalism and virtuality. In addition, there were a countless number of comments on learning about other issues, like business processes, profitability, and how different business functions create a whole of an organization.

All in all, the quotes above simply clarify that learning from the experience depends highly on the learner's previous knowledge, personality, the team members present in the exercise, and the other teaching activities on the course besides the very game. One student reflected: "*I would say what I learned from the session(s) is the experience that both the task to work in a virtual context as well as being a member of a multi-cultural team is nothing to be afraid of*". The other one in the very same team had a different opinion on what has been useful: "*I learned a great deal of this exercise, I basically had the chance of experimenting with learned leadership theories (as I stated in the previous essay, I took "Leadership and organizational psychology" last semester) and I really saw how they worked*". It is natural to assume that these students had different expectations, knowledge, experiences and ambitions prior to the simulation game exercise, which in turn altered the outcome of their experience.

Narrowing the simulation game experiences down to a single team level, another example clarifies this diversity of learning. The following two extracts are from two students working in the same team. Team member A:

There were **virtually no cultural differences** *aside from everyone forced to speak other language than their native one;* **leadership issues** *which I already explained,* **were in a minor role...**

Team member B:

...there are many things to learn before you can make your **virtual teambuilding** *truly effective. ...if you delve deeper into the process* **many obstacles can arise** *such as* **lack of cultural awareness, language barrier, ability to communicate, negotiate, control your emotions, and ability to take responsibility**, *etc. And to be efficient as a group you have to* **learn to listen** *to others speaking due to the absence of eye-contact,* **learn to be tolerant and understanding, to be able to cooperate**, *act not as an individual but as a part of a virtual team, learn to trust your virtual team.*

The two quotes above describe very illustratively how different the personal perceptions from the experience can be. Separate incidents during the simulation game exercises, e.g. unconventional behavior of a single individual, can cause major changes to the learning experience. It means that part of the learning, aside from the original aims, evolves and develops as the situation proceeds. This only highlights our statement that learning in the described simulation game sessions is such a manifold phenomenon and occurs in so many levels, that understanding the whole spectrum of learning, yet alone controlling it, is far beyond the instructors' reach. We can set the themes and guide the situation towards desired directions, but the personal experiences of learning still remain unique and context-bound.

We fully acknowledge that our discussion is more or less hypothetical and the case description and extracts from student essays do not form rigorous research. However, we hope we have been able to make the reader to ponder about the difficulty of assessing the diverse participant comments from the game exercise.

DISCUSSION

Drawing together the theoretical discussion and the findings from our experiment above, we can make a few conclusions. First, every game forms its unique case of learning potential, which might not be relevant compared to other games. Earlier we referred to Gosenpud (1990) who stated that what is valuable for the learner is defined by the learner and may have nothing to do with the game designer's intention. This implies that individuals are different as learners and what an individual learns may differ from what the other individuals learn. We think that our data also supports this assumption. If this is the case within a single game, then it should be quite clear that comparing the learning potential of two or more different games should be even more difficult.

Second, we believe that qualitative research, which better corresponds to the potential diverse learning from gaming, is more suitable to studying learning as phenomenon than quantitative research.

Third, we see that learning is a constructive process in which the learner is building an internal representation of knowledge, a personal interpretation of experience. This is something to which experiential game-based education clearly adds value to, compared to traditional class-room education. Constructivism suggests that we need to assess the meaning that learners have co-constructed from their interactions within the learning environment. If we want to know what gamers have learned, we need to assess their perceptions of them. As learning from gaming clearly is a gradual, iterative process, we need to be able to assess the gamers' assessment of this personal process. This is an utterly interesting research topic, mostly uncover today. At the same time we have to note that participant perceptions are not always necessarily valid, which further makes learning research more difficult.

ELT and constructivism offer also advice on how to design better (game-based) learning environments. Effective design is possible only if the developer has developed reflexive awareness of the theoretical basis underlying the design (Bednar et al., 1992). In other words, effective instructional design emerges from the deliberate application of some particular theory of learning. In our game designs we should make sure that our games encourage construction of understanding from multiple perspectives. The aim should be to facilitate situating cognition in real-world contexts, and construction of multiple perspectives. Furthermore, the learning of the content must be embedded in the use of that content (Bednar et al., 1992). Spiro et al. (1991) argue that revisiting the same material, at different times, in rearranged contexts, for different purposes, and from different conceptual perspectives, is essential for attaining the goals of advanced knowledge acquisition. The case we have described shows all of these characters. However, the case study and the data from it is still work in progress and we will report the case more rigorously in future.

We conclude this chapter by stating that learning is a constructive process in which the learner is building an internal representation of knowledge. This is something to which game-based education clearly adds value to – as researchers we should aim at understanding this process more thoroughly.

REFERENCES

Anderson, P., H. & Lawton, L. (2009). Business Simulations and Cognitive Learning. *Simulation & Gaming, 40*(2), 193–216. doi:10.1177/1046878108321624

Anderson, P. H., & Lawton, L. (1997). Demonstrating the learning effectiveness of simulations: Where we are and where we need to go. *Developments in Business Simulation & Experiential Exercises, 24,* 68–73.

Argyris, C., & Schön, D. (1978). Organizational Learning: A Theory of Action Perspective. Reading, MA: Addison-Wesley.

Bednar, A. K., Cunningham, D., Duffy, T. M., & Perry, J. D. (1992). Theory into practice: How do we link? In Duffy, T. M., & Jonassen, D. H. (Eds.), Constructivism and the technology of instruction: A conversation, (pp. 17-34). Hillsdale, NJ: Lawrence Erlbaum.

Brown, J. S., Collins, A., & Duguid, P. (1989). Situated Cognition and the Culture of Learning. *Educational Researcher, 18,* 32–42.

Cheetham, G., & Chivers, G. (2001). How Professionals Learn in Practice: An Investigation of Informal Learning Amongst People Working in Professions. *Journal of European Industrial Training, 25*(5), 247–292. doi:10.1108/03090590110395870

Duffy, T. M., & Cunningham, D. J. (1996). Constructivism: Implications for the Design and Delivery of Instruction. In D. H. Jonassen, (ed.), Handbook of Research for Educational Communications and Technology (pp. 170-198). New York: Macmillan Library Reference.

Duffy, T. M., & Jonassen, D. H. (1992b). Preface. In T. M. Duffy & D. H. Jonassen, (Eds.), Constructivism and the technology of instruction: A conversation. Hillsdale, NJ: Lawrence Erlbaum.

Ekpenyong, L. E. (1999). A Reformulation of the Theory of Experiential Learning Appropriate for Instruction in Formal Business Education. *Journal of Vocational Education and Training*, *51*(3), 449–471. doi:10.1080/13636829900200092

Gentry, J. W., Commuri, S. F., Burns, A. C., & Dickenson, J. R. (1998). The second component to experiential learning: A look back at how ABSEL has handled the conceptual and operational definitions of learning. *Developments in Business Simulation & Experiential Exercises*, *25*, 62–68.

Gosen, J., & Washbush, J. (1999). Perceptions of learning in TE simulations. *Developments in Business Simulation & Experiential Exercises*, *26*, 170–175.

Gosen, J., & Washbush, J. (2004). A review of scholarship on assessing experiential learning effectiveness. *Simulation & Gaming*, *35*(2), 270–293. doi:10.1177/1046878104263544

Gosenpud, J. (1990). Evaluation of Experiential Learning. In J. W. Gentry (ed.), Guide to Business Gaming and Experiential Learning, (pp. 301-329). London: Nichols/GP.

Gredler, M. E. (1996). Educational Games and Simulations: A Technology in Search of a (Research) Paradigm. In D. H. Jonassen, (ed.), Handbook of Research for Educational Communications and Technology. New York: Simon & Schuster Macmillan.

Greenlaw, P. S., Herron, L. W., & Rawdon, R. H. (1962). Business Simulation in Industrial and University Education. Englewood Cliffs, NJ: Prentice-Hall, Inc.

Herz, B., & Merz, W. (1998). Experiential Learning and the Effectiveness of Economic Simulation Games. *Simulation & Gaming*, *29*(2), 238–250. doi:10.1177/1046878198292007

Jonassen, D. H. (1992). Evaluating Constructivistic Learning. In T. M. Duffy & D. H. Jonassen, (eds.), Constructivism and the Technology of Instruction: A Conversation (pp. 137-148). Mahwah, NJ: Lawrence Erlbaum Associates, Publishers.

Jonassen, D. H., Peck, K. L., & Wilson, B. G. (1999). Learning with Technology; A Constructivist Perspective. New York: Prentice Hall.

Kayes, D. C. (2002). Experiential Learning and Its Critics: Preserving the Role of Experience in Management Learning and Education. *Academy of Management Learning & Education*, *1*(2), 137–149.

Kiili, K., & Lainema, T. (2008). Foundation for Measuring Engagement in Educational Games. *Journal of Interactive Learning Research*, *19*(3), 469–488.

Klabbers, J. H. G. (2003). Interactive learning of what? In Percival, F., Godfrey, H., Laybourn, P., & Murray, S. (Eds.), The international simulation & gaming yearbook, Vol. 11 (257-266). Edinburgh, UK: Napier University.

Kolb, A., & Kolb, D. (2008, October 10). The Learning Way. Meta-cognitive Aspects of Experiential Learning. *Simulation & Gaming*. doi:. doi:10.1177/1046878108325713

Kolb, A., & Kolb, D. A. (2008). *Experiential learning theory bibliography: Volume 2 2006-2008*. Cleveland, OH: Experience Based Learning Systems. Available from the Experience Based Learning Systems Web site, www.learningfromexperience.com

Kolb, A. Y., & Kolb, D. A. (2005). Learning styles and learning spaces: Enhancing experiential learning in higher education. *Academy of Management Learning & Education*, *4*(2), 193–212.

Kolb, D. (1984). Experiential Learning: Experience the Source of Learning and Development. Prentice-Hall, Inc, Englewood Cliffs.

Kolb, D. A., Boyatzis, R., & Mainemelis, C. (2001). Experiential learning theory: Previous research and new directions. In R. Sternberg, & L. Zhang, (Eds.), Perspectives on thinking, learning, and cognitive styles, (pp. 227-247). Mahwah, NJ: Lawrence Erlbaum.

Kriz, W. C. (2008, June 20). A Systemic-Constructivist Approach to the Facilitation and Debriefing of Simulations and Games. *Simulation & Gaming.* doi:.doi:10.1177/1046878108319867

Lainema, T. (2007). Open System View Applied in Business Simulation Gaming. *International Journal of Advanced Technology for Learning on Game-based Learning, 4*(4), 200–205.

Lainema, T. (2009). Perspective Making. Constructivism as a Meaning-Making Structure for Simulation Gaming. *Simulation & Gaming, 40*(1), 48–67. doi:10.1177/1046878107308074

Lainema, T., & Lainema, K. (2007). Advancing Acquisition of Business Know-How: Critical Learning Elements. *Journal of Research on Technology in Education, 40*(2), 183–198.

Lainema, T., & Nurmi, S. (2006). Applying an Authentic, Dynamic Learning Environment in Real World Business. *Computers & Education, 47*(1), 94–115. doi:10.1016/j.compedu.2004.10.002

Marsick, V. J., & Watkins, K. E. (1990). Informal and Incidental Learning in the Workplace. London: Routledge.

Mirvis, P. H. (1996). Historical foundations of organizational learning. *Journal of Organizational Change Management, 9*(1), 13–31. doi:10.1108/09534819610107295

Morecroft, J. D. W. (1992). Executive Knowledge, Models and Learning. *European Journal of Operational Research, 59*(1), 9–27. doi:10.1016/0377-2217(92)90004-S

Ruben, B. R. (1999). Simulations, Games, and Experience-Based Learning: The Quest for a New Paradigm for Teaching and Learning. *Simulation & Gaming, 30*(4), 498–505. doi:10.1177/104687819903000409

Spiro, R. J., Feltovich, P. J., Jacobson, M. J., & Coulson, R. L. (1991). Cognitive flexibility, constructivism, and hypertext: Random access instruction for advanced knowledge acquisition in ill-structured domains. *Educational Technology, 31*, 24–33.

Chapter 3
Educational Simulations:
Learning from the Past and Ensuring Success in the Future

David A. Guralnick
Kaleidoscope Learning, USA

Christine Levy
Kaleidoscope Learning, USA

ABSTRACT

Learn-by-doing simulations can provide tremendously effective learning. This chapter examines previous and current work in the area of educational simulations and looks ahead toward several potential futures in the field. The chapter includes a number of simulation-based success stories and case studies from past years, along with a discussion of why they worked as well as what could have been done better. It also describes approaches to ensure that a simulation is educationally effective while still being engaging and even entertaining. In addition, the chapter includes a design and development process that can be followed in order to maximize the educational value and usability of a simulation.

INTRODUCTION

Learn-by-doing simulations can provide tremendously effective learning: they allow learners to practice skills in a realistic environment in a safe way, free of real-life consequences after mistakes. They also can be incredibly engaging for learners, providing an immersive environment that can feel like a game in many ways. This method is particularly well-suited for corporate training situations in which the end goal for learners is based on the development of skills rather than simply the

acquisition of knowledge, and also has numerous potential applications in university courses. Additionally, well-designed educational simulations allow learners to experiment in a simulated world in ways that real life would not allow.

In this chapter, we will examine previous and current work in the learn-by-doing simulations area and look ahead toward several potential futures in the field. The chapter will include a number of simulation-based success stories and case studies from past years, along with a discussion of why they worked as well as what could have been done better. We will also describe approaches to ensure that a simulation is educationally effective, particularly

DOI: 10.4018/978-1-61520-781-7.ch003

by providing coaching and feedback mechanisms, while still being engaging and even entertaining. In addition, the chapter will include a design and development process that can be followed in order to maximize the educational value and usability of a simulation.

SIMULATIONS VS. GAMES

Over the past several years, there has been significant interest in the use of games and gaming technologies for learning purposes. Not only could games provide new and exciting ways to learn, but they would suit the younger generation of "Digital Natives" (coined by Prensky, 2001), who are comfortable with technology and tend to enjoy and expect a fast-paced, interactive experience.

One question that has arisen is what constitutes a game rather than a simulation. Prensky (2001) notes that "simulations are not, in and of themselves, games—they need…fun, play, rules, a goal, winning, competition, etc.", and that simulations may be boring and non-gamelike. There has been strong interest through the decade from corporations, looking to provide interesting training that resonates with their learners—and turning to game-based models.

Many of the attempts at game-based learning in the corporate world, however, have focused on the "game" elements rather than the learning. For example, some companies have implemented training in the form of "Jeopardy!"-style games, where learners must answer questions (or, more technically, provide questions in "Jeopardy!" format). This type of learning is indeed a game, and can often be fun for the learner. But what is often lost in this style of training is their effectiveness when it comes to improving learners' performance on the job, which, after all, is the goal of the training. Many "educational games" are fun and lend themselves well to the memorization of facts—but fact memorization does not necessarily transfer well to improved job performance. Learn-by-doing

simulations, which will be the focus of the remainder of this chapter, have the ability to incorporate elements that make games fun (including those mentioned by Prensky above), but in a realistic environment in which the learners' experiences will transfer to their real-life jobs.

EARLY HISTORY OF LEARNING SIMULATIONS

Research on the idea of learning by doing, rather than by memorizing, is certainly not new; it dates back at least to the work of John Dewey (1899), and more recent work on situated learning by Brown, Collins, and Duguid (1989) and Lave and Wenger (1991) has further demonstrated the effectiveness of learning-by-doing methods. Computer-based simulations of various types have been developed for many years. Yet the idea of educational learn-by-doing simulations—simulations designed based on learning theory—became popular much later, in the late 1980s, when Roger Schank formed the Institute for the Learning Sciences (ILS) at Northwestern University in Evanston, Illinois. ILS was formed with funding from Ameritech, IBM, and Andersen Consulting (now Accenture), among others, and brought together researchers from the areas of education, computer science (particularly artificial intelligence), and cognitive psychology, with the goal of designing innovative software for educational purposes.

One of the core design philosophies from Dr. Schank's lab was that of goal-based scenarios, defined as follows (Schank et al, 1992):

"Goal-based scenarios allow students to pursue well-defined goals and encourage the learning of both skills and cases in service of achieving those goals. Goal-based scenarios may be quite artificial in the sense that they may ask students to do something that they never would do in real life as a way of getting them to understand something. It helps if the scenario is something that

someone actually does, however. For example, one could teach history by asking a student to play the role of the President of the United States at a particular period and present him with decisions that need to be made. Accomplishing this goal would cause the student to need to know certain cases, learn certain skills, and understand certain processes."

While the concept of goal-based scenarios was originally conceived with a traditional education audience—students from K-12, college, and perhaps even graduate school—it turned out that putting such a novel educational model into practice, including placing computers in the schools, was quite a challenge and that schools were not completely ready for this yet. However, the world of professional education, through ILS sponsor Andersen Consulting and others, had the technical infrastructure and (with the right business case) the funding to explore and implement these novel methods. David Guralnick, one of the authors of this chapter, was asked to design a

methodology that could quickly move beyond the demonstration and prototype stages and feasibly be put into practice—and soon—in a real corporate training environment.

The plan was to begin with simpler, "procedural" tasks and create pedagogically-sound, engaging, effective simulations that could be completed, tested, and deployed in actual client environments. This was no easy task in the pre-World Wide Web days of 1991; in addition, these computer-based training methods were brand new, fresh out of the research lab, and it required somewhat of a leap of faith on the part of a training department to decide to use simulations for training. No matter how compelling the research arguments were for the method's effectiveness, practical considerations needed to be weighed, and this revolutionary approach to training was as intimidating to some people as it was inspiring and exciting to others.

The first learn-by-doing simulation for corporate training use was 1991's Boston Chicken Cashier Trainer (see Figure 1 for a screen shot from this program).

Figure 1. The Boston Chicken Cashier Trainer

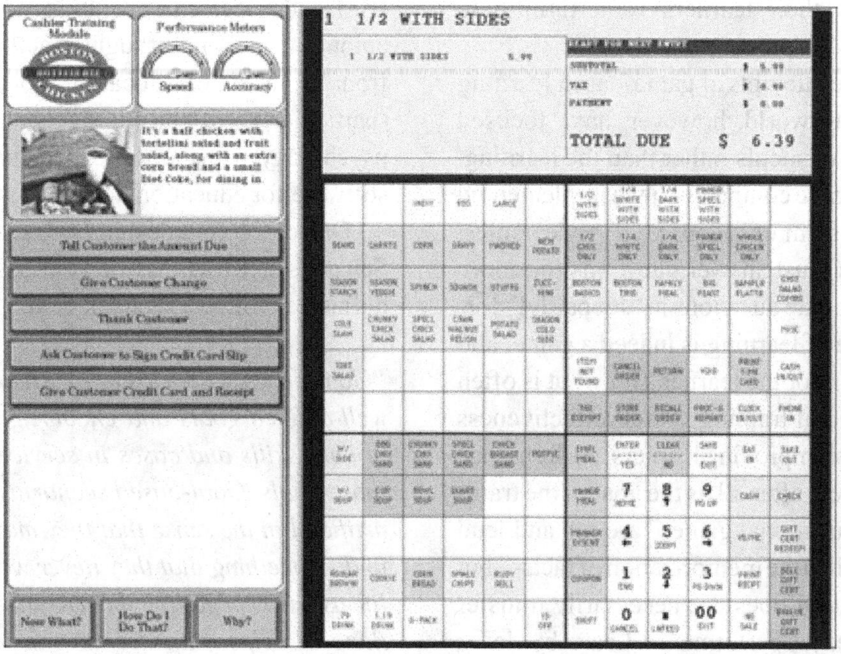

The Cashier Trainer instituted a learn-by-doing simulation model with a gamelike element—the learner's speed and accuracy were constantly measured and displayed on-screen. The model also included substantial coaching guidance and feedback, with the feedback in the form of both realistic results (e.g., an incorrect total on the cash register) and intervention from the tutoring component.

This model proved successful and was later expanded to other procedural tasks, most notably the Directory Operator Assistance Training program for Ameritech (Guralnick, 1996) and script-based customer service, in the Target Guest Service Training System (described in Schank, 1997). The underlying model and authoring tool (Guralnick, 1996) was then commercialized and reused at Dr. Schank's startup, Learning Sciences Corporation, and related, expanded approaches to these problems were later used—and continue to be used—in Dr. Guralnick's own company, Kaleidoscope Learning.

FROM PAST TO PRESENT

As corporate internets developed in the late 1990s, corporate trainers' focus shifted to "putting content online," and learning by doing (along with other effective online learning methods) was generally ignored for some time, with a handful of exceptions, in the corporate training world. Kaleidoscope Learning continued to create simulations; Accenture (formerly Andersen Consulting) and its spinoff Indeliq took the ILS methods and looked to create "business simulations"; and a handful of other companies, such as Texas-based Enspire Learning, worked in the simulation field. Clark Aldrich's Virtual Leader simulation (Aldrich, 2004) took a slightly different approach than the work from ILS and Kaleidoscope, putting learners in a virtual world in which they interacted with avatars, and focusing more on computer-game aspects than on pedagogical constructs such as coaching and feedback.

By 2005 or so, simulations regained some publicity in the corporate training world, if not in university e-learning, and companies looked to create more simulations, though large-scale simulations still suffered from a reputation as being expensive to implement. Mini-simulations for teaching software skills, based on screen captures and simple interactions, became a popular method, with an off-the-shelf tool called RoboDemo and its later versions, after acquisition by Adobe Corporation, called Captivate. These simulations tended to be simplistic and often taught operations out of context, thus missing a key factor that had made earlier learn-by-doing simulations successful. Further, the feedback to learners who took the wrong action was often of the simple, generic "That's not correct" form, failing to provide learners with the pedagogical constructs needed for them to truly learn effectively and form correct abstractions. With the increased commonality by 2009 of Captivate mini-simulations, and the consideration of virtual worlds such as Second Life for use in simulation-based learning, it is crucial to consider what defines a successful *learning* simulation—that is, not solely a simulated world, or even a gamelike, engaging environment, but a true learning environment in which learners acquire skills. We explore this question in detail in the following section.

WHAT MAKES FOR A SUCCESSFUL LEARNING SIMULATION?

The primary appeal of learn-by-doing simulations is that they can provide tremendously effective and engaging learning, allowing learners to practice skills in a realistic environment in a safe way, free of real-life consequences after mistakes. As we have discussed earlier in this chapter, this method is particularly well-suited for corporate training situations in which the goal is for learners to perform their jobs as well as possible. The success—in terms of improved skill development and job performance—of an educational simulation requires an emphasis on the educational components rather than just the simulation aspect. All too often, corporate simulation-based training programs focus solely on the simulated environment and do not give enough thought to the educational aspects of the training, and thus do not have an optimal effect on job performance. In order to provide an effective, efficient learning experience, a simulation should not only provide a practice environment, but provide a specific learning environment (with some type of guidance and feedback for the learner) and carefully-created situations in order for the learner to become proficient in the required skills. In this section, we will explore what makes for a successful simulation from an educational—and job performance improvement—perspective.

SIMULATIONS VS. REAL-LIFE EXPERIENCE

Online simulation is such an appealing method because it allows people to learn from experience in a safe, simulated environment—"safe" in that learners can experiment in ways that they cannot in real life, and in that mistakes made in the simulation will not have real-life consequences, such as a crashed plane or an angry customer, as they would in real life. While in some ways there is no substitute for actual experience, a well-constructed simulation can provide two key factors that real-life experience cannot match:

- A simulation can be built around scenarios and situations that have been carefully designed to bring out key learning points. This approach can accelerate the learning process by ensuring that learners face certain situations.
- A simulation can provide appropriate coaching guidance, feedback, and relevant expert stories to the learner, while real-life experiences often can pass by without

the learner taking away the key points. Different, successful learn-by-doing simulations (Guralnick, 1996; Guralnick, 2005) to teach a variety of skills – customer service, sales, and technical skills, to name a few – have employed various methods of guidance and feedback. Each of these successful simulations did include the following:

° A *"coaching guidance" component* to help the learner through the tasks and to provide advice at various levels of detail along the way. This component can include specific suggestions about how the learner should proceed at a particular moment, as well as higher-level suggestions and answers to more general questions. It may include the use of relevant real-life stories when appropriate. More sophisticated coaching components can include asking the learner to engage in a Socratic dialog with the online system.

° A *feedback component* that provides the learner with information on how well he or she performed the task. This can include both immediate and delayed feedback, and is designed to help learners foster the correct abstractions. This component generally includes both feedback from the simulated world itself (such as a video-based customer getting angry at the learner for providing poor service) and feedback from a tutoring component (to explain what went wrong and help learners abstract from their mistakes). In addition, real-life stories are often useful at moments in which the learner has made a mistake (Schank, 1997; Guralnick, 2005).

We will examine some specific learn-by-doing simulations in more detail in the next section. The specific situations, the overall design concept of the simulation, and the use of coaching guidance and feedback, in each of these simulations, was carefully designed to suit the audience and the skills being taught.

EXAMPLES AND SUCCESS STORIES

Over the years, we have developed a variety of successful educational simulations, each simulating very different environments, and each using a variety of related guidance and feedback methods. In this section, we examine some of these educational simulations to identify what made them successful and to explore some ways in which simulation-based learning has evolved over the years.

411: Directory Assistance Operator Training

- *Description*: This course was a significant part of the training for directory assistance operators, teaching them how to find telephone listings in a fast and accurate way. Learners using this program took calls from simulated customers, via audio, and needed to answer their information requests as quickly and accurately by looking up listings using a specialized keyboard and by following "keying strategies" for each type of request.
- *Guidance*: At any point in the simulation, the learner can ask the questions "Now What?, and the follow-up questions "How?" and "Why?". "Now What" provides some assistance regarding what the learner should do next, at a conceptual level. "How?" explains specifically how to perform the action, and "Why?" provides an explanation about what just happened or what the learner is asking about. There is also a small amount of general, non-context-dependent guidance, mainly in the

form of the "Tour of the Operator Screen," which shows the learner what each symbol on the screen means.

- *Feedback*: When a learner makes a mistake, the tutoring component intervenes immediately and explains what the learner did wrong. If the error would not be trivial to recover from in real life—for example, if the learner moves the cursor to the wrong field—then the learner must "recover" from this error in the simulation. For other errors, the tutoring component jumps in but the learner then simply can continue. Additionally, on-screen meters show the real-life metrics on which directory assistance operators are evaluated: speed and error rate.

See Figure 2 for a screenshot.

Guest Service Training for Retail Employees

- *Description*: This project taught customer service skills to "service desk" staff members at a large U.S. retailer. Service desk staff members need to learn how to handle customers' returns—the customers are returning merchandise that they had purchased—and understand how to appropriately treat a customer, particularly one who may be angry. Learners using this simulation played the role of a "service desk" staff member and had to handle customers who "approached" them in video.
- *Guidance:* As in 411, guidance is available via "Now What?," "How?," and "Why?". "Now What?" advice is intended to be at the conceptual level, while "How?" gets down to the level of what specific things the learner might say to the customer. It is more difficult than in 411 to keep the "How?" tutoring from giving away the

Figure 2. A screen from 411, Directory Assistance Operator Training, showing tutoring guidance.

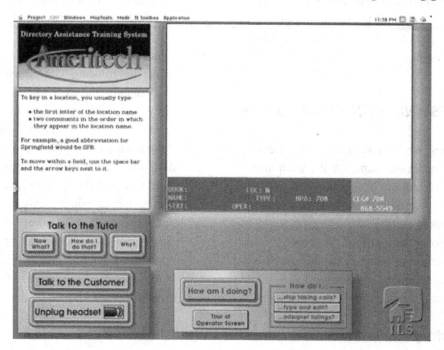

answer though; in 411, "How?" could take the form of a rule or a visual, while in Guest Service, "How?" tends to be a bit more direct.

- *Feedback:* When the learner takes a wrong action, three things may happen:
  - The customer reacts badly, providing the learner with realistic feedback.
  - The tutoring component provides feedback in the form of structured text, in order to help the learner make the appropriate generalizations.
  - An advice or story video clip is provided, with either an expert explaining a concept in more detail, or a peer telling a story of a similar experience.

Text feedback is always provided, whether or not there is a story or advice clip, or a customer reaction.

See Figure 3 for a screenshot.

Radio Frequency Unit Technical Training

- *Description*: Our client for this project was a U.S. retailer with over 1200 stores, who use the handheld devices shown above for a myriad of purposes. The applications on the device, and the tasks the device were used for, were many and varied. Under the simulation method used here, learners are given realistic tasks and a simulated version of the "RF unit" online. They must quickly and accurately perform the requested tasks using the simulated RF unit.
- *Guidance:* The guidance for the learner in this simulation is very simple: there's a "Hint" button that is always available for the learner to click. Text guidance then appears in the box in the lower left-hand corner of the screen.
- *Feedback:* When the learner makes a mistake, text appears in the box in the lower left-hand corner. This text will explain any

Figure 3. A screen from the Guest Service Training System, showing the tutor intervening

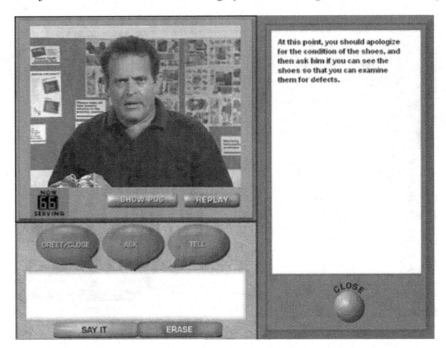

likely misconception that the learner may have, if any, and may also help the learner decide how to correctly perform the action.

See Figure 4 for a screenshot.

Anti-Bias Training for High School Teachers

*   *Description:* This course, designed primarily for high school teachers, raises teachers' awareness of their own biases and provides them with the knowledge and skills to improve their own classrooms and schools. The course is delivered entirely online, making substantial use of video and with a variety of interactive exercises. The course includes twelve modules and takes approximately twenty hours to complete. The centerpiece module uses a method called character-based simulation, in which learners control the main character, a high-school teacher who is forced to deal with difficult situations of bias involving students, faculty, parents, and administrators. At each "turn" in this simulation, the learner must decide what the "teacher" character in the simulation should do. Along the way, learners can get advice from experts via context-sensitive questions, learn what the simulation's characters are thinking at any given time via "character insights" (a feature that is not available in a learn-by-doing simulation, or in real life!), and explore a print-based guide for handling situations of bias. At the end of the scenario, the learner receives a summary of his or her performance.

*   *Guidance:* Learners have three sections that can provide in-context guidance of some sort: "character insights," which let the learner get inside the head of a character to help them decide what to do; questions which are answered in text; and stories from peers who have encountered similar

Figure 4. A screen showing a hint in RF Unit Training

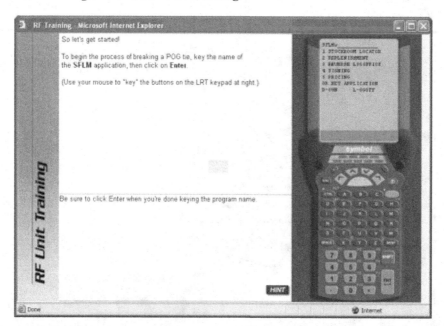

situations. In addition, learners can refer to the context-independent "zero-indifference guide" for general rules of behavior.

- *Feedback:* When a learner takes an action, he or she sees the playout of that action—the story continues. Since these situations are complex, the notion of "failure" or "success" is not quite as defined as in the other examples discussed above; however, the learner can see if the situation is improving (sometimes time elapses), and if not, the learner is faced with a new set of choices and must again make a decision. In addition to the immediate feedback of seeing how a decision worked, the learner receives a summary at the end of a scenario, recapping the good and bad decisions.

ANALYSIS

The above projects, and their guidance and feedback methods, have been considered to be "successful" in that they performed well on usability tests and received very positive responses from the end-users once the product was in use. The 411 product also involved a study which demonstrated improved performance for those learners who took the online course as opposed to the classroom-only course it replaced; it was not feasible for budget reasons for the other products to be studied in such detail. Learners did find the situations to be realistic, engaging, and relevant, and the coaching guidance and feedback relevant and helpful on all projects. Based on our experience, the design decisions made, particularly choices about the simulated environment and on the guidance and feedback, were critical contributions to making these projects successful. There is not a single correct method, but rather a set of potentially-effective components that are appropriate for different situations.

For example, as seen in the examples above, we have used several different coaching guidance and feedback components. Those include:

- *Text-based guidance*: This comes at a conceptual level (e.g., answering a "Now What?" question, specific level (such as in the answer to a "How?" question or in some of the RF hints), or as an explanation (as in "Why?" answers). Whenever possible, this is presented in a very structured form, clearly written and with examples, to aid learners in making appropriate generalizations.

- *Visual guidance*: This was shown in the second "How?" example in 411, in which the guidance system demonstrates the location of a hard-to-find key.

- *Ratings:* When appropriate, simulations provide real-life metrics showing user performance. These ratings may include speed and error rate.

- *Character insights:* These are not strictly a form of guidance, but do provide additional information that helps a learner think through the situation and decide what to do next.

- *Text-based immediate feedback*: When a learner makes a mistake, sometimes a feedback component intervenes immediately with structured text feedback, again intended to aid generalization.

- *Video stories:* These have been used both as guidance (in the anti-bias model), and as part of immediate feedback (in the Guest Service model). Relevant stories are particularly effective when delivered in-context at a "failure" point (Schank, 1982).

- *Video advice clips:* These clips work best when the person giving the advice is either well-known to the learners (e.g., someone famous, or someone known and respected within the learner's company), or is particularly charismatic on-camera.

- *Realistic simulation consequences:* One of the most effective types of feedback in a simulation, learners get to see the real consequences of their actions. But such feedback is most effective when paired with a feedback component (whether immediate or at a later point) that helps the learner understand his or her actions, reflect on them, and make appropriate generalizations.

- *Scenario summary*: Summaries of the learners' actions and failures are especially useful if they are *diagnostic*—they provide some categorization of the learner's strengths and weaknesses—and *prescriptive*—they suggest what the learner can do to shore up his or her weaknesses, such as redoing a particular part of the training.

USING PAST SUCCESSES TO INFORM FUTURE DESIGN DECISIONS

After examining past instances of successfully-implemented simulations, a key question, then, is when designing a learn-by-doing simulation, and assuming that we want to include coaching guidance and feedback in some form, how do we determine which specific methods to use? Some of the key factors are:

- *Teaching "soft skills," such as customer service or sales, vs. teaching technical skills:* Technical skills may lend themselves better to a Now What/How/Why style, while providing specific questions seems to work better for soft skills.

- *The complexity of the decisions the learner must make on the job:* If the job, and therefore the simulation, involves simple decisions, immediate intervention by a tutoring component often works well (as seen in 411 and most of the customer service examples). More-complex decisions such as those in the anti-bias training example generally benefit from deferred feedback, in which the learner has time to explore and reflect deeper into a storyline before the coach or tutor steps in.

The series of design decisions in any learn-by-doing simulation project involves these factors and others.

A DESIGN AND DEVELOPMENT APPROACH

Another key question is how to design and develop an effective learning simulation—how can a training designer get from high-level skills to be taught all the way to producing an effective simulation? A skeleton design process that we have used for years is described below. Several content-development stages from an overall process have been omitted, in the interests of focus.

Step 1: Specify the Audience and its Characteristics

At this step, the design architect should be as specific as possible about who the audience for the program is, including primary and secondary audiences.

Step 2: Articulate the Goals

Define the goals of the program clearly and concisely; this step covers what learners should be able to do at the completion of the course.

Step 3: Develop Concept and Learning Methodology

In this step, the overall concept is established for the program, meaning what methods will be used and what the learner will do in the program.

Step 4: Develop Specific Teaching Points, Scenario Overviews

In this composite step, the specific things the learner will be able to do after the training are articulated, along with (in the case of a learn-by-doing simulation) the scenarios the learner will be asked to encounter in order to sufficiently cover all teaching points. This step is dependent on the concept determined in step 3; for example, if we were evaluating a performance-support program, this step would not be the same.

Step 5: Design Sketch: Wireframes

The process here involves sketching out wireframes—black and white sketches showing the layout and positioning of items on the screen. The reason for wireframes rather than graphics at this step is to keep the focus on the learner's conceptual actions. The designer should focus on actions and layout, rather than graphics, at this stage, and design the primary (most heavily-used screens) first if possible.

Step 6: Sample Screens/ Storyboard (Full Graphics)

A set of sample graphical screens are produced, showing the intended look of the screens the user will see. These are often best produced in a sequence that shows a part of a realistic interaction that a user might have. The design architect should look for several things at this stage (and this stage is often iterative), including the following:

- The graphical look should support the tasks and layout from the wireframes, and in an ideal world improve upon them. This means that, for example, the relative sizing of things is as defined in the wireframes.
- The colors should be appropriate for the audience (and, in a client project, the client's needs), and color should further allow, for example, the learner's eye to be drawn to the parts of the screen the designer needed it to be drawn to.

This generally should be the first interface design stage that outside groups—the target audience and client—should be able to see and react to. Their feedback should then be incorporated;

specific methods for doing so are beyond the scope of this paper, but the philosophy is that the feedback should be taken seriously, but not literally, and many questions should be asked. For example, if a reviewer said they thought a particular button should be blue, one would want to uncover why they thought so, and work the feedback into a holistic set of design changes to address the goals and concerns raised by the reviewers, rather than specific solutions raised. While not listed here as a separate step, changes will generally be made after the review, and either the screens will be reissued or the changes can be incorporated into Step 7, depending on the degree of change required.

Step 7: Single-Path Demonstration

At this stage, an online demonstration is produced, showing a carefully-constructed path as the learner would interact with the program. The path should be designed to tell a realistic, compelling story of the learner's interaction, and should very specifically explain what the learner does at each stage of the demo and what happens on-screen, so that the graphics and programming, however they are done, are exactly what the designer had in mind.

- The demonstration should be shown from the point of view of the learner, so the audience viewing the demo can get a feel for what it is like for a learner to use it.
- The designer, when reviewing the demonstration, should look to be sure all screens are correct and that the interactions seem smooth to a learner; for example, the screen does not "jump" (no graphics move slightly, accidentally, on-screen), and unnecessary portions of the screen are not "redrawn."
- It is not necessary for all features to work correctly technically at this stage—it is only necessary for things to appear as if they are working to the viewer. For example, a

PowerPoint slide show often can make a good demo, though this demo would only function by following a single path no matter what action a learner tried. For demo purposes, this is sufficient and this method is often a good use of resources.

The demonstration is another major deliverable that the target audience should be able to see and react to. Feedback should be treated as in Step 6—seriously but not literally, with an emphasis on goals.

Step 8: Design Document

This document should describe the program's behavior completely, including all screens and actions (building on the work done in previous steps). All graphics should be approved and referenced in this document as well (so a smaller step, omitted from our major steps but a prerequisite to this one, is to sketch and then receive and approve all artwork from the graphic artist). The design document is used by the programmer to implement the program.

Step 9: Prototype Version and Primary Usability Testing

The prototype is a working program, generally with most of the features implemented and most of the content included. The prototype is particularly crucial for everyone, beginning with the design architect, to first get to interact with the real program. This version, after changes from the architect's review, generally should go to the target audience for the most significant usability test, to determine how clear it is to use.

Step 10: Implementation Completion and Pilot Testing

The program is completed and ready for final testing. Interface issues may still arise, though, because there is new content, which may not be clear. Sometimes it is arguable whether to categorize such points of learner confusion under "interface," but under our holistic process, any concerns certainly need to be addressed.

The above process helps ensure that the designer thinks carefully at all stages of design and development about the educational impact and clarity of the writing in the simulation. The inclusion of several checkpoints—both external testing and internal documents such as the scenario matrix—helps tremendously in this regard. The process has generalized well to work for a large number of learning simulation projects.

SIMULATION AUTHORING: THE RIGHT TOOLS FOR THE JOB

E-learning design and development today relies more on technological tools than ever before. In today's world, for budget and efficiency reasons, a large percentage of e-learning is created by people without a technical background, using the platforms and authoring tools that are available to them. While this process is natural and in some ways unavoidable, the result is that e-learning design is often dictated as much by the capabilities of existing authoring tools as by educational goals and sound design principles. For example, in a 2008 survey by the E-Learning Guild (Wexler et al., 2008), corporate trainers were asked what they look for in an authoring tool. The most common responses focused on the following areas:

- Simplicity of updating of existing content
- Short learning curve to learn how to use the tool
- Support for particular output formats

Not mentioned in these results is the ability of the tool to aid in the creation of effective e-learning. This is a particularly problematic issue with learning simulations, where a simulation that is not well-designed and well-written can

easily end up being very ineffective—and ineffective simulations could dissuade people from using the simulation method in the future. The prevailing theory, according to the E-Learning Guild survey and report, is that the quality of the product depends solely on the people creating it, not on the tool.

Most popular authoring tools today are simpler tools, such as Lectora or even the general HTML tool Dreamweaver, that make it easy to build simple, page-turning e-learning, or course management systems such as Blackboard which are intended mainly to support classroom-based courses. These tools have their roles, but for the purposes of designing rich, effective, standalone e-learning, they suffer from the following problems:

- They typically don't encourage good design (do not contain a philosophy), or do encourage the design of simple, ineffective, page-turning courses
- They can make it difficult for trainers to produce well-designed, effective e-learning—it's often lots of extra implementation effort to create something that's pedagogically effective, even if it's possible in the tool.

Our perspective on authoring tools is that such general-purpose tools need to be supplemented—and in many cases surpassed—by new, specialized authoring tools, which are designed specifically for particular pedagogical models. Specialized authoring tools under our definition have the following characteristics:

- Incorporate a philosophy—they don't build everything, they build particular types of products easily
- Can be very fast and easy to use, when designed well, and also inexpensive
- Can work in place of or in addition to the general-purpose tools of today.

Kaleidoscope Learning's EncompassLite is a specialized authoring tool that contains templates based on e-learning methodologies that have been shown to be successful. The first EncompassLite release contains a customer service learning-by-doing simulation template with built-in structures for coaching guidance and feedback, thus making it fast and easy for trainers to follow this successful model and also encouraging them to do so. Additional templates for EncompassLite will be suited for different content areas and, in some cases, will provide more general structures. We believe that this special-purpose approach to tools has the potential to greatly increase e-learning effectiveness at a reasonable cost.

WHERE DO WE GO FROM HERE?

As we have seen, skill transfer from a well-designed simulation to a real-life job position can be very high; this stands in stark contrast to the transfer ability of traditional educational methods that are not performance-based in the way that simulation is. However, not all simulations are necessarily good tools for learning; people do not always learn—or do not learn quickly—simply by experiencing something, or from playing a game, but instead need assistance and feedback to help them understand the situations they have faced and what has gone well or badly, and why.

Educational simulations have the potential to vastly change not only the e-learning landscape, but learning and education in an even larger sense. To this point, simulation-based learning has had its success stories, but we seem now to be at a crucial stage in the design, development, and scalability, and acceptance of educational simulations in corporate training and universities. There's still a huge gap between the level of success of learning simulations and their potential; simulation-based learning is, in many ways, still in its infancy even though it has been around for many years.

Yet the potential of e-learning is becoming even greater than ever before: technological advances such as faster networks, better video compression, and Ajax programming techniques make it possible to create simulations that run better technically than in years past, and virtual worlds such as Second Life allow programming and also show tremendous potential (such as a learning simulation called Second China (PhysOrg.com, 2008), developed at the University of Florida, in which learners get to experience simulated experiences in a simulated China). The development of new, special-purpose authoring tools such as EncompassLite should improve the quality of learning simulations and bring the ability to create true learn-by-doing simulations to a larger audience. At a more detailed level, research continues into more sophisticated forms of guidance and feedback, such as realistic Socratic dialogues to assist learners as they work in a simulated environment. In all ways, the future of simulation learning has the potential to be very bright, as this method may begin to reach the potential it has shown for so many years.

REFERENCES

Aldrich, C. (2004). Simulations and the Future of Learning: An Innovative (and Perhaps Revolutionary) Approach to e-Learning. San Francisco: John Wiley & Sons, Inc.

Brown, J. S., Collins, A., & Duguid, P. (1989). Situated cognition and the culture of learning. *Educational Researcher*, *18*, 32–42.

Dewey, J. (1899). The School and Society. Chicago, IL: University of Chicago Press.

Freedman, D. H. (1994). The Schank Tank. *Wired magazine, 2*.08, August 1994.

Guralnick, D. (1996). An Authoring Tool for Procedural-Task Training. Evanston, IL: Northwestern University Press.

Guralnick, D. (2000). A Step Beyond Authoring: Process-Support Tools. WebNet 2000. San Antonio, TX: Association for the Advancement of Computing in Education.

Guralnick, D. (2005). Creating Online Simulations to Teach Social Skills. In *European Conference on E-Learning*, Amsterdam.

Guralnick, D. (2006). How to Design Effective, Motivating User Interfaces. In *American Society for Training & Development TechKnowledge Conference*, Denver, CO.

Lave & Wenger. (1991). *Situated Learning: Legitimate Peripheral Participation.*

Nielsen, J. (1993). Usability Engineering. San Diego, CA: Academic Press.

Nielsen, J., & Molich, R. (1990). Heuristic Evaluation of User Interfaces. In *Proceedings of the. ACM CHI '90 Conference* (Seattle, WA, 1-5 April), (pp. 249-256).

PhysOrg.com. (2008 October 29). Issue retrieved from http://www.physorg.com/news144510236.html

Prensky, M. (2001). Digital Natives, Digital Immigrants. *Horizon, 9*(5).

Prensky, M. (2001). Digital Game-Based Learning. New York: McGraw-Hill Companies.

Schank, R. C. (1982). Dynamic Memory. Cambridge, UK: Cambridge University Press.

Schank, R. C. (1997). Virtual Learning: A Revolutionary Approach to Building a Highly Skilled Workforce. New York: McGraw-Hill Companies.

Wexler, S., Schlenker, B., Bruce, B., Clothier, P., Miller, D. A., & Nguyen, F. (2008). Authoring & Development Tools. Santa Rosa, CA: The eLearning Guild.

Chapter 4
Models of Politics and Society in Video Games

Tobias Bevc
Goethe-Universität Frankfurt am Main, Germany

ABSTRACT

This essay will deal with the question of which models of social policy and social structures can be found in video games. It will examine the relationship between these models, the stories (narrations) provided by the games, and the stories and models created by the players themselves. This examination will be followed by a discussion of two types of virtual models of social politics and social structures. In this discussion, light will be shed on the different models of social policy and social structures that appear in the context of video games. In analyzing these models within games, the question is not whether video games have an influence. Rather, the question is what may children and adolescents learn from "off-the-shelf" video games with respect to political education, political socialization and the forming of political identity?

WHY ARE VIDEO GAMES SO ATTRACTIVE: MOTIVATION OF PLAY AND POLITICAL SOCIALIZATION

The models and structures of politics in video games are of great importance as they contribute to the forming of a political identity by their recipients. The main issues in popular video games are power, supremacy and control.[1] These are the components that render video games attractive for the players and make them play these games (Fritz, 2005; cf. for games in general Oerter, 1999, pp. 210-218).

DOI: 10.4018/978-1-61520-781-7.ch004

Further factors, which Klimmt has shown as pivotal for the entertainment experience in video games, are self-efficacy, the principle of suspense and resolution, and the simulated experience of life (Klimmt, 2006a, pp. 75-115; cf. for self-efficacy: Bandura, 1997).[2] With the first factor, self-efficacy, the player learns while playing that his actions make the determining difference, i.e. that his actions and decisions are the deciding factor of the further development of the game the player is playing, that he is the decisive factor in failing or succeeding. The second factor signifies that the game itself is a continuing process of building up suspense through the events in the game itself. The player is forced to develop a strategy to resolve the problems and to achieve a solution of the problem by employing it. This then results in the resolution of the suspense through the successful utilization of his strategy. The third factor, the simulated experience of life, offers the player the possibility to take an interactive role in the game. This model, derived from developmental psychology, provides the players with the opportunity to assume different identities and to act accordingly. Thus, roles can be assumed that may not be attainable in reality, such as the roles of Cowboy, Alien or Star; or may only be attainable in adulthood, e.g. the role of a parent (cf. Klimmt, 2006a, pp. 95-102; cf. Oerter, 2000, pp. 50-52).

A further factor of playing video games, which is often mentioned with reference to Massively Multiplayer Online Role-Playing Games (MMORPG), is the communal life aspect of the social contacts that can be won and cultivated. This aspect will be discussed in more detail later in this chapter.

Political Socialization by Entertainment in Media

Media-literacy, or the lack thereof, is the deciding factor in the classification and the understanding of the content brought to bear by the entertainment media and submitted to the recipients (Theunert, 1999, 2005). To aggravate the situation it must be noted that entertainment media – be it in video games or telecasts – are perceived differently than serious news telecasts or other serious television programs (cf. Baum, 2006; Dörner, 1999; 2001; Holbert, 2005). This perception mode is based on a different and less critical attitude that accepts the content much more readily. Dörner calls this perception-mode the "Feel-Good-Mode," which presents itself automatically in all entertaining "As-If-Worlds". In transmissions dealing with serious Information, however, the recipients know that they are to receive information on the world which may be wrong or even guided by

particular interests and are therefore suspicious (Dörner, 1999; 2001, pp. 11-111). Moreover, it must be stated that many people admit that they use entertainment programs explicitly to inform themselves on politics. They say that they get information of and their opinion about politics and social structures as well as this makes them start to think about their own living conditions based on these transmissions (Mikos, 1994; Bente & Fromm, 1997). The fictional content of these kinds of entertainment programs does not necessarily influence the reflection of the recipient on politics and society and the person's own conditions of living in a negative way. However, it should always be taken into consideration that the content of the entertainment is always fictional.

For this reason it is important to realize that most video games are based on more or less fictional assumptions of politics and social order and assume certain social structures and operation modes (Bevc, 2006; 2007; 2008a; Höglund, 2008; Sample, 2008). These assumptions which are offered by video games may exercise an influence on recipients' political socialization and on children's, the adolescents' and the (young) adults' development – evidently, to different degrees depending on age, media-literacy and education of the respective person (Eyal et al., 2006; Kuhn, 2000, Schorb, 2005; 2008). For this reason video games have a similar importance for the individual understanding of politics and political socialization as conventional mass media (Fromme, 2006), especially in consideration of the fact that the peak of the political socialization and the development of identity falls into the same time when the utilization of video games is the most intensive and the political socialization and the development of identity is genuinely to be understood as conflict of the individual with his/her environment – including the medial environment. This aspect looks plausible even though empirical validation particularly for video games has still to be undertaken. A pilot study among adolescents has definitely shown that video games' political content and moral concepts exert an influence on the recipients of these games (cf. Klimmt, 2006b).

Dörner has emphasized the relevance of modern mass media for the development of political identity in his study "Politainment" and also highlighted that mass media have caught up with the various traditional instances of socialization such as family and school (Dörner, 2001, pp. 105-108). Communications scientists as well consider the influence of mass media on the individual and society as important (Saxer, 2007; Schulz, 1989, p. 140). This originates not least from the fact that media through their choice and their emphasis on certain themes determine to a high degree what the recipients learn and understand of politics and society – and to a large degree everything that is beyond the life-world of the recipient.[3]

Issues and Approaches to Research With Regard to the Recipient

One must consider as well that the recipients utilize the media in very personal ways and are also very creative in dealing with the media content as shown in the "Cultural Studies" as well as in the "Uses-and-Gratifications" approaches. These two approaches of media-research have a common base, i.e. the assumption that recipients absorb the media content to meet their own information and entertainment demands, and are able to use the content creatively for their own interest and intention (Hall, 1980a; 1980b; Jäckel, 2005, pp. 70-75). This means that the recipient and his motives for reception will have to be taken seriously in any analysis of video games.[4]

When making these general statements about socialization and reception, it must be borne in mind that the age, education and media-literacy affect the recipient's interaction with the media content. From that point of view, it is impossible to issue generally applicable judgments with regard to well-defined effects of games as far as their content is concerned. However, there are differ-

ent empirical theories that explain the impact of media on the recipient which suggest that video games can indeed have an influence on political socialization:

- The research into the *cultivation of beliefs* explains the formation of ideas about the world on the basis of media information, which stems also from the content of the entertainment media (e.g. Holbert et. al., 2003; Roskos-Ewoldsen et al., 2004; Williams, 2006). Thus, the key factor to problem solving in very many video games, i.e. violence, would be an example for the cultivation of problem solving mechanisms. These would be transferred from the media to the recipient through the individual's perception and interpretation. That way, medial modes of problem solving are transferred from the virtual world as conceptions into the real world. This affects mainly the knowledge element of political socialization. [5]

- The *narrative persuasion theory* assumes a potential to affect (politically based) views (Slater et al., 2006; Green & Brock, 2000; Green et al., 2002), especially in cases of strong entertainment experiences. In this case, it is the effect identified by the authors that counts, i.e. that controversial public-policy content causes priming. Such content can change the recipient's underlying values that are linked to the story, as well as to public policy. Priming then denotes a possible change in the recipient's value-system by providing content that links the entertainment program to reality (Slater et al, 2006, pp. 237-238).[6]

- Finally, also relevant are reflections of entertainment research, which are based on *identity theory* (cf. Vorderer, 1996; Vorderer, 2001) for the establishment of models on political socialization, as these approaches more precisely characterize the way entertainment offers orientation and thus help to explain the identity forming effect of Politainment. This approach is particularly useful to explain who uses which media-based content. "Recipients will choose the (fictitious) stories that will appear useful to master their individual development challenges. Useful or functional in turn are such stories whose content leads to a sensation of being in the middle of the story and thus help to master the problems of life" (Vorderer, 1996, p. 322). These considerations point out that the identity formation process of the recipient determines the choice of media-based content.

The approaches presented so far seek to explain the perception and impact of media, and assume at the same time conscious and unconscious causes for media utilization. The unconscious processes, that take place while using media, however, have to be understood as the knowledge used for problem-solving that is consciously not available (Oerter, 1999, p. 265; Lewicki et. al., 1992; Greenwald 1992).[7]

The existence of "non-conscious cognitive information- and storage processes" is explicitly pointed out in these studies (Oerter, 1999, p. 265) and make clear that the recipients of media absorb and process content unknowingly. This needs to be emphasized in particular since this aspect of the impact of media is often neglected.

VIRTUAL MODELS OF POLITICS AND SOCIETY: AN OVERVIEW[8]

In the different genres of video games, one finds an infinite number of societies, societal fabric, their structure and control (i.e. politics). This essay will develop a system of the most important models of politics and social structures to facilitate their classification so that one can sort them out and consider their implications. Firstly,

we will use Weber's classification of the three legitimate forms of governance to categorize the various conceptions of authority that make their appearance in video games (Weber 1972: 124). At the same time, the construction of the society itself as society or community is of major interest for the practical (useful) categorization of virtual models of politics and social structures (Tönnies 2005: 8-83).

Forms and Models of Government and Society

The term society is the one that is valid for today's mass society. It is based on the assumption that the various individual interests will approach each other by means of categories of exchange in the respectively relevant items and thus enable a cooperation. Hence, the result is an open society – at least for all those who have something to exchange – i. e. pluralistic and tolerant. The community on the other hand is to be looked at as a parochial community, and thus to be localized in the pre-modern forms of civilization and social structure. In the latter, the life world is distinctly larger, and so are the regimentation and the closeness. From today's perspective, one can hold onto Tönnies' opinion that the organic community based on tradition and religion provides people with a limited and closed perception of the world. It distinguishes itself by a collective volition, common mores and common customs and practices. Society, however, is based on contracts, laws and justice. Power is delegated and not organized in a patriarchal way. Society is kept together by rules, norms and sanctions that – at least to a certain extent – depend on consensus. This is not so, however, for the rules, norms and sanctions of the community. These differences, only tersely elaborated in this context, make it clear that the concept of society is an open concept where differences and foreign ideas are up to a certain degree considered normal and are tolerated, if not even accepted. Heterogeneity is its deciding characteristic. Society is therefore marked by uncertainty, complexity and the absence of unambiguousness. Nothing is evident, but everything is ambivalent. The individual has to find his or her place autonomously in this society and has to carry all the risks (Beck, 1986). Failure and success can only be attributed to oneself which is, particularly in the first case, rather unpleasant.

The community, however, disapproves of differences and foreign ideas; it rests on homogeneity and closeness of its world of thought.[9] The community presents itself as a world which has clearly defined and controlled borders. In it, each member has a place, which provides security and an unambiguous localization to the particular individual in the communal hierarchy. Right and wrong, good and bad are clearly defined and are easily recognizable. With regard to the individual subjects, a similar antagonism exists: In the society, individuals are autonomous (at least to a large extent). In the community, however, they are heteronomous.[10]

This classification of Tönnies matches nicely two of Weber's legitimate forms of governance. To a large extent, the community meets the traditional governance, which is marked by values handed down through history and by a conservative self-conception.[11] The modern society and with it the organizational form of the modern state, however, corresponds with Weber's concept of rational governance. It corresponds as well with the form of the modern parliamentary democracy with its written constitution and laws and its administration which is supposed to dispense equal treatment. The charismatic governance finally is a bit more difficult to localize in Tönnies differentiation. It could, beyond modernity, create a new political community or bring a charismatic leader to the top of a state, who then can quite possibly establish a system of non-legitimate governance: a totalitarian state. Weber's kinds of legitimate governances are obviously only ideal types which in reality will appear as a combination of the various types, and rarely in their pure form.

In video games accordingly, one will not find pure forms of social cohabitation or political order. However, for the orientation and classification the scheme "traditional governance – rational governance" and the scheme "community – society" will still be used.

The quadrant 2 which shows the political and societal configuration of western capitalist democracies (Figure 1) is rarely found in video games, with the exception of the game *Genius – Im Zentrum der Macht* (2007). Particularly popular MMORPGs usually take place in pre-modern societies with corresponding structures.[13] Too, many of the guilds that can be developed by the players themselves in these games cannot be localized in quadrant 2 but in the three remaining quadrants, depending on their own definition and preference. This illustrates nicely that the factor "community" in MMORPGs is one of the main motivators for many players. This has already been frequently stressed (Jakobson & Taylor, 2003; Yee, 2006; Bartle, 1997), but it means as well that these communities do not have to be inevitably authoritative. Yee (2006; n.d.), however, points out that one cannot, as Bartle (1996) has done, really separate the players by types. As Yee pointed out, it is rather a question of categorizing the player types in respect to their motivation of play (Figure 2).

Yee emphasizes that almost all players belong only primarily to one of these categories, but also will draw their motivation from the categories. According to Yee, the distribution of gender in the three main categories shows that women have obviously different motivations than men. These are mainly from the category "social" (25.1%) and "immersion" (30.9%) (Yee, n.d., p. 11). (See Figure 3)

While men have a wider range of game motivations, women's interest focuses primarily on "relationship", "role play" and "customization". In Yee's statistics, one can see that the thesis of developing community in role-play (in the afore mentioned sense) cannot be dismissed and

Figure 1. Ideal types of governance between society and community [12]

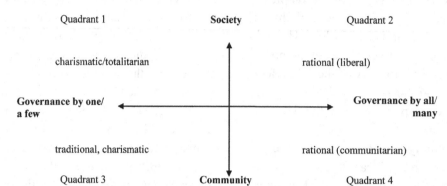

Figure 2. Categorization of the motivation of play after Yee (2007; n. d., p. 6)

Categories of Motivation	Achievement	Social	Immersion
Forms of appearances	Advancement	Socializing	Discovery
	Mechanics	Relationship	Role-Playing
	Competition	Teamwork	Customization
			Escapism

Figure 3. Gender Differences in Subcomponents after Yee (Yee, n.d., p. 11)

Categories	Female	Male
Advancement	2,6 %	10,1 %
Mechanics	1,9 %	11,6 %
Competition	3,5 %	11,4 %
Socializing	9,5 %	8,7 %
Relationship	27,0 %	8,5 %
Teamwork	8,4 %	11,6 %
Discovery	11,2 %	9,4 %
Role-Play	14,0 %	10,7 %
Customization	12,1 %	7,7 %
Escapism	10,0 %	10,3 %

deserves a specific study. For the male players, this motivation is absolutely present, but it is not stronger than other motivations. One can see by means of the numbers that men approach a game in a performance-oriented utilitarian way to achieve a large advance in the game as quickly as possible, and that these advances manifest themselves in material matters (such as arms, armament, gold) and matters that may decide the game (i.e. game levels). However, the effect is the same in a world of people with the same objective: the appreciation and acceptance by the others. The immersion into the community for the male players happens through the restitution of the traditional roles: they are useful and work goal-oriented, while the female players look after the social component and the warmth and "security of the home". Both these tasks are considerably more difficult to achieve in the real life of the 21ˢᵗ century than in the games of this century, which are obviously tailored to meet these needs of their recipients. This bias for the community reflects itself in the organization und the structure of the guilds and clans.

While the community aspect in the MMORPGs is understandable, one can ask why quadrant 2 is practically absent in the other games and why in most cases only the forms of human cohabitation are shown that stress the community factor. So even the societies in video games appear as communities. This is all the more surprising since in reality the western capitalist societies represented in these games do not show anymore any communal life traits particularly not if viewed at the meta-level. From that point of view it has to be stated that the reduction of complexity in video games will lead to misinterpretation. The generally positive representation of the community in the video games will generate further problems with regard to the political socialization and development of identity in the social reality of the 21ˢᵗ century. Questions of exclusion, heteronomy, and priority of the collective are issues that are not broached at all in these games. Thus, the community is without reservation being presented as a positive, problem-free form of human cohabitation. In these games the longing of the people for identity, unambiguousness, clearness of the situation is being satisfied. Hence, it seems obvious that video games satisfy a need to replace the increasingly confusing world of few constants and causalities with a world that is cozy, comfortable, explainable, and transparent. The individual is unburdened by the community which keeps a place for the individual in its midst providing he sticks to the rules and does not have too many independent views.

Political Structures and Protagonists

The terms political structures and protagonists signify by whom and how the state and its representatives are symbolized in a game. This is different from game to game. For example, in *SimCity* (1989ff), the role of the mayor will have to be assumed by the player who has to incorporate the role of the legislature. In this function he has also the possibility to run the executive authority dry. The mayor may be considered the absolute ruler since he/she is the only one responsible for cultivating and entertaining relations with neighboring municipalities, promoting the development of the town, and organizing the formation of continuing education. The mayor is practically omnipotent and mainly guided by the results of opinion, which might force resignation if and when the subjects are unhappy with his or her actions. In SimCity, much as in many other games, the player assumes the role of an omnipotent ruler who has to make and to implement all the decisions that will decide the fate of the game. This is not without consequences for the representation of the structures and protagonists in the games, and gives a nice insight into the image of politics promoted by these games.[14] To stay with the example of SimCity: a town council to which the mayor will have to answer does not exist and – quite evidently – neither a political opposition.

As Strohmeier (2005) already shows in his investigation into child radio play, the attribution of roles and the stereotyping of these in entertainment media are appallingly short-witted and low in complexity. With regard to video games, though, one cannot maintain that they would always be pejorative. But even the positive stereotyping of political protagonists and structures is not helpful to the question of political socialization. For example, the media are very often presented as the ones owning the treasure of truth, as the authentic representative of people's voice, or as a trustworthy chronicler of events, respectively.[15] Ambivalence, perspective-taking, plurality of opinions and views, and the existence of different media offers with divergent notions, however, do not seem to exist.

What does this mean with regard to the issue of virtual models of politics and social structures? The representation of political structures and protagonists in video games is not a suitable means to create understanding for real world political structures due to the stereotyping and the reduced complexity applied in video games. This does not necessarily mean that political structures and stereotypes look alike in all video games; however, each reduces complexity and applies stereotyping. Thus, the impact is the same. In video games, matters are unambiguous and clear. The players – having been molded by these games – then turn to the real world and are surprised that nothing is unambiguous and clear. But particularly for the political socialization and development of identity in a democratic society it is indispensable to know about plurality, conflicts of interest even within a society with justified demands from everybody and the complexity to execute decisions once taken.

Further protagonists, who would come under Strohmeier's category of latent political socialization, are e.g. policemen acting on their own account and beyond law and order as for example *Max Payne* (2001, 2003). In this case the police, on the one hand, is corrupt and therefore not in a position to fight the drug mafia. On the other hand, the protagonist Max Payne, who is represented by the player, takes law and order into his own hands and alone destroys the mafia-like organization from New York. In this case vigilantism, excessive police power and torture are presented as quite legitimate forms of police procedures (Max Payne 2001, 2003). Especially such questions as the application of torture seem to be coming back into fashion and are in some cases unambiguously replied to as for example in the television series *24* (2001ff.). Here torture is an integral and legitimate part of police procedures. With regards to political socialization all this is – with a timid regard to the constitution – questionable.

Political Processes

The term political process shall here be defined as the procedures used to arrive at decisions and the passing of resolutions. In democracies, the political process unfolds using well-defined routines that will eventually lead to either the passing of a law or its rejection. As these processes are public, they can be comprehended by everybody who is interested. In most video games, processes or their representation do not exist.[16] Here again the reduced complexity of the game structures becomes obvious. However, this is understandable from the point of view of the game producers, designers, and publishers, as well as of that of most of the players. Most of the fun of the games would be lost, if the complex structures were made visible (cf. Wechselberger, 2009). But this can only partially explain and exonerate the frequently awful political and social structure in these games. Thus in *Civilization,* one converts the form of governance from democracy to fascism by pushing a button. The idea alone of such an all-encompassing structural change of society, which affects all sections of public and private life, makes one suffer from vertigo.

In *games* like *Civilization,* such a process is presented as being not much more difficult to accomplish then the daily brushing of teeth. The consequences that such a radical change of social systems might engender, however, are rather restricted in *Civilization*: If you choose democracy for example, the mood of the population might augment to a somewhat higher level, but the state and the government in turn will have some more difficulties to set up new military units. It seems that one is dealing with a zero - sum game.[17] The transition phase is marked by a revolution followed by anarchy and by the fact that nothing is being produced anymore (cf. Biermann &Fromme, 2009).[18] With such representation, the differences between the various forms of government are not only blurred, but at the same time authoritative forms are massively played-down. These games can be played with fascism as the form of government (disguised as police state) and in a sense there is nothing to criticize on fascism. It seems to be just one of many forms of government that are possible. And what leads to success has necessarily to be the right thing.[19] Here we do not talk of missing complexity or a wrong historical representation of forms of government, but we talk about the nonchalance used in putting authoritative-repressive forms of government at the same level as other forms of government that at least try to respect the dignity of man.[20]

History as the Basis of the Development of Political Identity

History is used in many ways in video games as the background for the plot, or plays even an explicit role (cf. Bevc, 2008; Wesener, 2007). For this chapter, an accurate representation of history is not important. It is rather interesting to examine how particular ideas of the philosophy of history are implemented and prevail in these games, and which idea there is in the background. Important components to look at in this context are the progress and development of humanity, the means of production and the way they produce, the economic base and the cultural superstructure. Thanks to the generally accepted archetypes and ideas of games it is almost always the same type of history (and its philosophy) that is "hidden" in the video games. That is the form that once helped the European countries to their unprecedented rise: conquer, colonize, destroy and suppress where the means of the European countries' rise to become the masters of the world (Stephenson, 1999; cf. Wallerstein, 2004). In similar games like Age of Empires (1997ff.), Civilization, Galactic Civilizations (2003ff) it is the same. Games of this kind design man as man's wolf and project subjugation of the opponent as the only possible alternative of action – with all the adequate means that are permissible in the respective game. The different approaches of the philosophy of history with their eschatology, like messianism, history as life cycle, history as apocalypse etc. do not exist. Only the history of progress in its most naïve social democratic excrescence is offered as always the same model (Benjamin 1991a: Thesis XI, XV; 1991b). The problem there is that all the different

images of history result simultaneously from past experience and future expectations. "People assure themselves of their present situation by focusing on the past to deduce from this the future or, vice versa, project their expectations of the future into the past. The mutual and suspenseful relation of interpretation of the past, understanding of the present time and future perspectives creates historical consciousness." (Rohbeck, 2004, p. 13f, my translation).

But if a video game allows only one possibility of interpretation in order to win the game, then all the other historical realms of experience are closed to the player. Insofar the development of identity through historical consciousness for the individual is possible only in the way, which the producer or the author of the game has provided. As a result necessary realms of experience are made inaccessible to the player and, therefore, the possibility to build up his own interpretation of history and, following this, the development of his identity will be limited (Cassirer, 1996; Bevc, 2005, pp. 113-124, pp. 175-193, pp. 202ff)[21].

Religion as the Basis of the Development of Political Identity

Since the Muslim terrorist attack on the towers of the World Trade Center in New York, religion has become a delicate subject. One can see this in the instructions of *Civilization IV* where the developers feel compelled to formulate a special disclaimer that the representation of religion is not meant to hurt anyone's feelings and is in absolutely not meant disparagingly (Civilization IV, 2004, 69). It can be established that religion in games – regardless of which religion – has a positive influence. Subtly one could of course criticize this as a discrimination of atheists. Unfortunately such a sensibility is not widespread. In most games that prominently feature religion, it is used as a symbol to raise specific connotations and come up to certain expectations respectively. An example for this would be the war games *First to Fight* and

Full Spectrum Warrior. In these games, Islam is definitely represented negatively. It represents brutal force, intolerance and backwardness.

In other games, as well, that take place in a fictitious scenario such as *Siedler* (1993ff.) or *Anno 1701* (2006), there is only the possibility to construct a Christian church One wonders why it is not possible to build e.g. a mosque or a synagogue.[22] For his salvation the player has to use a Christian religion. The possibility of atheism or agnosticism is not even taken into consideration. Here, as well as in the issue of historical awareness, interpretative authority is exercised by the producers of the games – namely on central aspects of human existence which are closely entangled with the development of the personal, social and political identity.

With the utilitarian functions of religion, as in *Civilization IV* and in *Siedler,* one notices immediately the purpose that religion is to supposed to meet: It is in the true sense Opium to the People (Marx, 1956, pp. 378-385)! If it is introduced one has fewer problems with one's subjects, they are easier to be satisfied in their needs. This again is an example that certain components of games – regardless how innocently meant – can easily assume a political nature – however not in an educational-emancipating sense but in a way which shows that all areas of life will only be considered using the criterion of utility.

DISCUSSION

Social and political structures as well as issues evident in video games may contribute to the political socialization and development of the game players.

It can be stated that the representation of political processes, ideologies and of ways to explain the world as well as political protagonists and structures with reduced complexity leads to unambiguous statements which do not necessarily need to be deliberate and can rather be related to latent forms of political socialization. The normative equal treatment of e.g. police state/fascism and representation/constitution as legitimate form of government and the treatment of people is a profoundly political statement which can lead to confusion at least for children and adolescents. The same is true for the statement that all religions will have positive impacts on the satisfaction of people and the productivity of cities. Form and function of religion as a simply utilitarian tool on the way to world domination is devalued to a function that purely helps to improve domination and has not anymore anything to do with salvation and faith that the individual subject may have. Functionalized this way it does not matter anymore in which god or gods one believes as long as it is believed and economy and domination are functioning more effective. This representation of religion does not really contribute to a positive examination of questions of the transcendental mental state of the recipients. Even more questionable is, however, the unambiguous stereotyping of religion in war games, i.e. – as in this moment – the Islam. Here a religion is systematically shown negative so that an examination without prejudice is impossible. With this goes along a stigmatization of Arabs which has already a long tradition in Hollywood cinema.[23]

Virtual models of politics and social structures are consequently functional structures reduced to serve the objective of the game although it "quotes" constantly the reality but once closely analyzed has nothing in common with it. In these games an image of cohabitation of humanity is being drawn up that has absolutely nothing or almost nothing in common with the modern society of the 21st century. In most cases an image of a society is drawn up that has common interests, objectives of life and – most important – mutual clearly identified enemies.

Looked at it from this perspective and recalling that many of the recipients of these games find themselves at this very moment in the process of political socialization and development of identity the virtual images of politics and society in video games are not exactly furthering the democratic consciousness of an open society. From the point of view of political education whose primary objective is to develop the ability to make one's own judgments these games are rather inapt due to the causality, the homogeneity and the unambiguousness of social structures and the getting along together.

In summary, one can state that the aspect of community mainly prevails in video games. This is the case for the games themselves, their narration, and for MMORPGs. The narrations of the MMORPGs are community oriented and the play itself is structured in a way that requires concerted action to be successful. With regard to the basic question as to the virtual models of politics and social structures in video games, democracies as seen in western industrialized countries are very rarely found in video games, and when they are present, they show a strong community focus.

Generally speaking the matter represents itself in a way that the virtual models of politics and social structures in video games often do not go far enough and destroy the surface plurality of the statements they contain. By this they lose their existing potential to be meaningful plane for politics and society by means of which the recipients could playfully penetrate into the plural society in which they live and could learn to appreciate this plurality since only the real plurality actually offers different ways to live one's life and to shape the world.

Video games teach in their community oriented, pre-modern conceptions of politics and social structures the opposite of what should be taught by political education: that each individual is free and equal and may think and do whatever he likes to in whatever way he thinks to. Political education should enable its subjects to build their own opinion. But therefore, the subjects have to have the possibility to choose from a plurality of sources, opinions and possible (future) paths (Bevc 2007b).

REFERENCES

Bandura, A. (1997). Self-Efficacy: The Exercise of Control. New York.

Bartle, R. (1997). Hearts, Clubs, Diamonds, Spades: Players Who Suit MUDs. *The Journal of Virtual Environments, 1.* Retrieved February 25, 2009, from http://www.brandeis.edu/pubs/jove/HTML/v1/bartle.html

Baum, M. (2006). Soft News goes to war: public opinion and American foreign policy in the new media age. Princeton, NJ: Princeton.

Beck, U. (1986). Risikogesellschaft. Auf dem Weg in eine andere Moderne. Frankfurt/M, Germany: Suhrkamp.

Benjamin, W. (1991a). Über den Begriff der Geschichte. In R. Tiedemann & H. Schweppenhäuser (Eds.), Walter Benjamin. Gesammelte Schriften in 7 Bänden, (Vol. 2, pp. 691-704). Frankfurt/M, Germany: Suhrkamp-Verlag.

Benjamin, W. (1991b). Eduard Fuchs, der Sammler und Historiker. In R. Tiedemann & H. Schweppenhäuser (Eds.), Walter Benjamin. Gesammelte Schriften in 7 Bänden, Vol. II.2, 465-505, Frankfurt/M, Germany: Suhrkamp-Verlag.

Bente, G., & Fromm, B. (1997). Affektfernsehen: Motive, Angebotsweisen und Wirkungen. Opladen, Germany: Leske und Budrich.

Bevc, T. (2005). Kulturgenese als Dialektik von Mythos und Vernunft. Ernst Cassirer und die Kritische Theorie. Würzburg, Germany: Verlag Königshausen & Neumann.

Bevc, T. (2006). Affirmation des Bestehenden. Konstruktion von Politik und Gesellschaft in Computerspielen. *Telepolis*, 07.12.2006. Retrieved March 1, 2009, from http://www.heise.de/tp/r4/artikel/24/24129/1.html

Bevc, T. (2007a). Konstruktion von Politik und Gesellschaft in Computerspielen? In T. Bevc (Ed.), Computerspiele und Politik. Zur Konstruktion von Politik und Gesellschaft in Computerspielen (pp. 25-54). Münster, Germany: Lit Verlag.

Bevc, T. (2007b). Political Education via Video Games? In D. Remeny (Ed.), *Proceedings of the European Conference on Game Based Learning. 25-26. 10. 2007 in Paisley, Scotland* (pp. 27-34). Reading.

Bevc, T. (2008). Gesellschaft und Geschichte in Computerspielen. *Einsichten und Perspektiven*, 1/2008, 50-59. Retrieved March 10, 2009 from http://www.km.bayern.de/blz/eup/01_08/4.asp

Bevc, T. (2009). Visuelle Kommunikation und Politik in Videospielen: Perspektiven für die politische Bildung? In K. Thimm (Ed.), Das Spiel - Muster und Metapher der Mediengesellschaft? (pp. 169-190). Wiesbaden, Germany: VS Verlag.

Bevc, T., & Zapf, H. (Eds.). (2009). Wie wir spielen, was wir werden. Computerspiele in unserer Gesellschaft. Konstanz, Germany: Universitätsverlag Konstanz.

Biermann, R., & Fromme, J. (2009). Identitätsbildung und politische Sozailisation. In: T. Bevc & H. Zapf (Eds.), Wie wir spielen, was wir werden. Konstanz, 113-138.

Cassirer, E. (1996). Versuch über den Menschen. Eine Philosophie der Kultur. Hamburg, Germany: Felix Meiner Verlag.

Eyal, K., Metzger, M. J., Lingsweiler, R. W., Mahood, C., & Yao, M. Z. (2006). Aggressive political opinions and exposure to violent media. *Mass Communication & Society*, 9(4), 399–428. doi:10.1207/s15327825mcs0904_2

Fritz, J. (2005). Warum eigentlich spielt jemand Computerspiele? Macht, Herrschaft und Kontrolle faszinieren und motivieren. In *Bundeszentrale für politische Bildung, Thema Computerspiele*. Retrieved March 10, 2009 from http://www.bpb.de/themen/RSE41Q,0,Warum_eigentlich_spielt_jemand_Computerspiele.html.

Fromme, J. (2006). Socialisation in the Age of New Media. *MedienPädagogik. Zeitschrift für Theorie und Praxis der Medienbildung*. Retrieved January 17, 2009 from http://www.medienpaed.com/05-1/fromme05-1.pdf

Green, M. C., & Brock, T. C. (2000). The role of transportation in the persuasiveness of public narratives. *Journal of Personality and Social Psychology*, 79, 701–721. doi:10.1037/0022-3514.79.5.701

Green, M. C., Strange, J. J., & Brock, T. C. (2002). Narrative impact: Social and cognitive foundations. Mahwah, NJ: Lawrence Erlbaum.

Hall, S. (1980a). Encoding/Decoding. In S. Hall, et al. (Eds.), Culture, Media, Language, (pp. 128-138). London: Hutchinson.

Hall, S. (1980b). Cultural Studies: Two Paradigms. *Media Culture & Society*, 2(1), 57–72. doi:10.1177/016344378000200106

Heidenreich, B. (1999). Vorwort. In B. Heidenreich (Ed.), Politische Theorien des 19. Jahrhunderts. I. Konservatismus (pp. 7-10). Wiesbaden.

Höglund, J. (2008). Electronic Empire: Orientalism Revisited in the Military Shooter. *GameStudies. The international journal of computer game research*, 8(1). Retrieved January 28, 2009 from http://gamestudies.org/0801/articles/hoeglund

Holbert, R. L. (2005). A typology for the study of entertainment television and politics. *The American Behavioral Scientist*, 49, 436–453. doi:10.1177/0002764205279419

Holbert, R. L., Shah, D. V., & Kwak, N. (2003). Political Implications of Prime Time Drama and Sitcom use: Genres of Representation and Opinions Concerning Women's Rights. *The Journal of Communication, 53*(1), 45–60. doi:10.1111/j.1460-2466.2003.tb03004.x

Holbert, R. L., Shah, D. V., & Kwak, N. (2004). Fear, authority, and justice: Crime-related TV viewing and endorsement of capital punishment and gun ownership. *Journalism & Mass Communication Quarterly, 81*(2), 343–363.

Holtz-Bacha, C. (1988). Unterhaltung ist nicht nur lustig. Zur politischen Sozialisation durch Medieninhalte. *Publizistik, 33*(2-3), 493–504.

Horkheimer, M., & Adorno, T. W. (2007). Dialektik der Aufklärung. Philosophische Fragmente. In A. Schmidt & G. Schmid Noerr (Eds.). Max Horkheimer. Gesammelte Schriften. Bd. 5, Frankfurt/Main, 11-290.

Jäckel, M. (2005). Medienwirkungen. Ein Studienbuch zur Einführung. Wiesbaden, Germany: VS Verlag für Sozialwissenschaften.

Klimmt, C. (2006a). Computerspielen als Handlung. Dimensionen und Determinanten des Erlebens interaktiver Unterhaltungsangebote. Köln, Germany: von Halem.

Klimmt, C. (2006b). *Computerspielkonsum und Politischer Konservatismus unter Jugendlichen.* Paper presented at the Workshop „Konstruktion von Politik und Gesellschaft in Computerspielen?" of the Arbeitskreis Visuelle Politik/Film und Politik der DVPW. München.

Kuhn, H.-P. (2000). Mediennutzung und politische Sozialisation. Eine empirische Studie zum Zusammenhang zwischen Mediennutzung und politischer Identitätsbildung im Jugendalter. Opladen.

Marx, K. (1956). Zur Kritik der Hegelschen Rechtsphilosophie. Einleitung. In Institut für Marxismus-Leninismus beim ZK der SED (Ed.), Marx/Engels Werke, Bd. 1 (pp. 378-391). Berlin: Dietz Verlag.

Mikos, L. (1994). Fernsehen im Erleben der Zuschauer: vom lustvollen Umgang mit einem popularen Medium. Berlin: Quintessenz-Verlagsgesellschaft.

Oerter, R. (1999). Psychologie des Spiels. Ein handlungstheoretischer Ansatz, Weinheim, Germany: Beltz.

Oerter, R. (2000). Spiel als Lebensbewältigung. In S. von Hoppe-Graff & R. Oerter (Eds.). Spielen und Fernsehen. Über die Zusammenhänge von Spiel und Medien in der Welt des Kindes, (pp. 439-454). Weinheim, Germany: Juventa.

Peter, J. (2002). Medien-Priming - Grundlagen, Befunde und Forschungstendenzen. *Publizistik, 47*, 21–44. doi:10.1007/s11616-002-0002-4

Rohbeck, J. (2004). Geschichtsphilosophie zur Einführung. Hamburg, Germany: Junius.

Roskos-Ewoldsen, B., Davies, J., & Roskos-Ewoldsen, D. R. (2004). Implications of the mental models approach for cultivation theory. *Communications: The European Journal of Communication Research, 29*(3), 345–364.

Sample, M. L. (2008). Virtual Torture: Videogames and the War on Terror. *GameStudies. The international journal of computer game research, 8*(2). Retrieved January 28, 2009 from http://gamestudies.org/0802/articles/sample

Saxer, U. (2007). Politik als Unterhaltung. Zum Wandel politischer Öffentlichkeit in der Mediengesellschaft, Konstanz, Germany: UVK.

Schulz, W. (1989). Massenmedien und Realität. Die „ptomeläische" und die „kopernikanische" Auffassung. In M. Kaase & W. Schulz (Eds.), Massenkommunikation. Theorien, Methoden, Befunde (pp. 135-149). Opladen, Germany: Westdeutscher Verlag.

Shaheen, J. G. (2001). Reel Bad Arabs. How Hollywood Vilifies a People. New York: Olive Branch Press.

Slater, M. D., Rouner, D., & Long, M. (2006). Television dramas and support for controversial public policies: Effects and mechanisms. *The Journal of Communication, 56*(2), 235–254. doi:10.1111/j.1460-2466.2006.00017.x

Stephenson, W. (1999). The Microserfs are Revolting Sid Meier's Civilization II. *Bad Subjects, 45*. Retrieved March 9, 2009 from http://bad.eserver.org/issues/1999/45/stephenson.html

Strohmeier, G. (2005). Politik bei Benjamin Blümchen und Bibi Blocksberg. *Aus Politik und Zeitgeschichte, 41*, 7–15.

Theunert, H. (1999). Medienkompetenz. Eine pädagogische und alterspezifisch zu fassende Handlungsdimension. In F. Schell, E. Stolzenburg & H. Theunert, (Eds.), Medienkompetenz. Grundlagen und pädagogisches Handeln, (pp. 50-59). München, Germany: KoPäd-Verlag.

Theunert, H. (2005). Medien als Orte informellen Lernens im Prozess des Heranwachsens. In Sachverständigenkommission Zwölfter Kinder- und Jugendbericht (Ed.), Kompetenzerwerb von Kindern und Jugendlichen im Schulalter, Bb. 3, München (pp. 175-300).

Tönnies, F. (2005). Gemeinschaft und Gesellschaft: Grundbegriffe der reinen Soziologie. Darmstadt, Germany: Wissenschaftliche Buchgesellschaft.

Trend, D. (2007). The Myth of Media Violence: A Critical Introduction. Oxford, UK: Blackwell.

Vorderer, P. (1996). Rezeptionsmotivation: Warum nutzen Rezipienten mediale Unterhaltungsangebote? *Publizistik, 41*, 310–326.

Wagner, U. (Ed.). (2008). Medienhandeln in Hauptschulmilieus. Mediale Interaktion und Produktion als Bildungsressource. München, Germany: KoPäd-Verlag.

Wallerstein, I. (2004). Das moderne Weltsystem, 3 Bde. Wien, Germany: Promedia Verlagsgesellschaft.

Weber, M. (1972). Wirtschaft und Gesellschaft, Tübingen, Germany.

Wechselberger, U. (2009). Einige theoretische Überlegungen über das pädagogische Potential digitaler Lernspiele. In T. Bevc & H. Zapf (Eds.), Wie wir spielen, was wir werden (pp. 95-111). Konstanz, Germany: UVK.

Williams, D. (2006). Virtual Cultivation: Online Worlds, Offline Perceptions. *The Journal of Communication, 56*, 69–87. doi:10.1111/j.1460-2466.2006.00004.x

Yee, N. (2006). Motivations of Play in Online Games. *Journal of Cyber Psychology and Behavior, 9*, 772–775. doi:10.1089/cpb.2006.9.772

Yee, N. (n.d.). *Motivations of Play in MMORPGs. Results from a Factor Analytic Approach.* Retrieved February 26, 2009 from http://www.nickyee.com/daedalus/motivations.pdf

ENDNOTES

[1] Power, supremacy and control in this case are not to be understood in the sense of political or sociological science but in a psychological sense

[2] Cf. the essays in "Communication Theory" (14), 2004, 4, 285-408, which address the topic of 'media enjoyment'.

3   Also compare David Trend who makes very enlightening statement with regards to media violence: »Media violence may not provoke people to become aggressive or commit crimes, but it does something more damaging. Media violence convinces people that they live in a violent world and that violence is required to make the world safer. The anxieties and attitudes that result from these beliefs about the world have profound consequences in the way people live their lives and the way society is organized. People's behaviour at home and in public, at work, at school, and in leisure activities becomes affected. Anxieties about violence influence the television people watch, what they read, and what they discuss with friends. They cast a shadow on the ways they plan their time, where they decide to go, and what they buy. Ultimately media violence takes a toll on the way people imagine their lives and how they think about the future. This anxious worldview is the result of a culture of violence that forges our core identities in fear.« (Trend 2007: 58).

4   This has been done in a recent study in Germany. The results are devastating and surprising at the same time. The target group of the study were pupils of the "Hauptschule". There is no proper translation for this type of school in English. Therefore I use the German term. The definition, of the Bavarian Ministry of Education and Culture is: "General education secondary school (level I, yrs 5-9), oriented to the world of work, compulsory for all pupils who do not transfer to other secondary schools." The results of the study show, that a lot of the pupils do not at all understand what the games are about and what they have to do. But if they have problems with the complexity of the game they find creative solutions which aren't intended by the game designers. (Wagner, 2008, pp. 119-185).

5   Cf. Endnote 3.

6   Peter defines media-priming as the "process with which (1) information communicated by mass-media (as "primes") will make knowledge items in the memory of the recipient (2) more easily accessible. Thereby the probability increases, (3) that these knowledge items which are now more easily accessible will be activated and used in the reception, interpretation and appraisal of subsequently found information on the environment […] rather knowledge that is not as easily accessible (and as a consequence the former can also influence attitudes). The activation and utilization of information that is accessible more easily is as a matter of fact the more likely (4) the shorter the time the media-prime has been published or (5) the more often it arises. A further fundamental condition of the activation und utilization of such easily accessible knowledge items is (6) that they are applicable to the following environmental information. (Peter, 2002, p. 22)

7   Cf. the discussion in the "American Psychologist" 1992, vol 47, nr. 6, 761-809

8   In German there is only one concept for the English trias polity, politics and policy. All three are meant here.

9   Particularly conspicuous in a negative sense is this community concept in the game *City Life* (2006) in which 6 different groups of people live in a city. daytaler, hippies, workers, trend-setters, white collar workers and rich people. Of these groups always only two get well along with each other, i.e. even here we find already micro-communities. The social segmentation is being brought to the point and established in this game (apart from the fact that the different groups of population are nonsense. On poses oneself the question what can be learned? That a society is not homogeneous but should be?)

[10] Barring the critical ideological theories of Marxist origin of the 20th century where, naturally, in the here outlined societies the individuals were not considered to be autonomous.

[11] Conservative thinking is marked by the following points: 1. God's intention guides society and the human conscience, the individual as well as politics have to answer to Him; 2. respect for the human dignity, whether for an unborn, a living or a dying person; 3. respect for nature as God's creation; hence the obligation to preserve and to protect it – and not to exploit it; 4. the firm conviction that property and liberty are inseparable and economic equalization is nonsense; 5. the role of the family as the nucleus of society; 6. trust in the traditional values and opinions, high regard and respect for the ancestors; 7. scepticism versus the zeitgeist and the conviction that reforms may be necessary, however, have to be performed slowly and with a sense of proportion (cf. Heidenreich, 1999, p. 8f.)

[12] Rational governance is attributed to society and community. Decisive is here the add-on of "liberal" and "communitarian" to it. The communitarian form of democracy has up to now only made a theoretical appearance (in reality) – it is, however, in MMORPGs by all means a reality (i.e. in virtual reality).

[13] Or they are located in a not further defined future. The models of politics and society localized there are, however, in their majority taken from "premodern Times".

[14] Many a juvenile *SimCity* player was wondering about the incapability of real world mayors of many an indebted city with high unemployment and a high criminal record. After all he, with no adequate education, as simple pupil, has lead many a city in *SimCity* which was reduced to rubble back into a glorious future.

[15] Whereas there are naturally positive examples as well which show the ambivalence of the activity of the media: The *Global Conflicts* series which requires that the player assumes the role of a journalist. This makes it nicely evident that for each event there exist always different "truths" (Global Conflicts: Palestine, 2007; Global Conflicts: Latin America, 2008).

[16] There are exceptions like *Genius Politik* which deals explicitly with politics and political processes (2007).

[17] What it isn't. The point is that the respective forms of government in *Civilization* go along with certain development levels of the organisation of production. It is for a game of western origin evident, that capitalism is the equivalent of the highest level of production organisation and comes along with a parliamentary democracy.

[18] One could think, that a revolution and anarchy are quite some consequences. But: what a revolution and phase of anarchy is this, where the outcome is clear before they even started? Hence, the revolution and anarchy seem to be the troublesome concomitants of a change of the political system and are only to be understood as some disturbances before the new regime may take hold of society. Which is – again – a distorted and reified comprehension of political processes.

[19] This is no new finding, it is simply easier to digest the way it is presented here compared to remarks of Horkheimer and Adorno (1997). 'Success' obviously is an ambivalent matter. But in *Civilization* as in many other games it is not. There, success is naturally measured by technical progress, the ability to become as powerful as possible to be able to shape the world according to one's own visions. Which is, if one was fascist, very unfortunate for all the antifascists as well as for all those who do not meet the fascist image of the world. As far as the topic "police state"

is concerned the rule book of *Civilization IV* succinctly says: "Pre-condition: Fascism, running costs: High, effects: +25% production of military units, - 50% war fatigue. In a police state the government exercises (and the secret service) a rigorous control and surveillance" *(Civilization IV*, 2004, p. 76).

[20] It should be clear even in video games that fascism is a crime and not possible alternative of political action. If one has to borrow from real history then these borrowings have to be put into their correct relation and the consequences have to be shown. Thus pacifism has absolutely nothing to do with the assumption that God does not want war as wants us to believe the handbook of *Civilization* (2004, p. 81).

[21] Cassirer interprets History as one possibility of perception in which the past is actualized and thereby the presence and future can be shaped. Hence, if I am determined in my perception of history, I am also determined in shaping my presence as well as my future.

[22] In the preview of *Anno 1404* which is supposed to be published 2009 one can see a mosque on the screenshots… however under "monuments". Whether this is an implementation of different religions that will have implications on the gaming of the game or whether it is only a design element will be an interesting question. If one reads the story, however, everything seems to point again into the direction of colonialization: *"Anno 1404"* captivates the players by pulling them into the spell of the Orient in the 15th century. An abundance of new features put the proven principles of the game on a new level. For the first time in the history of this series players can interact with a new culture and settle in a new land. When travelling into the Orient players find new exotic commodities, technological accomplishments and a foreign architecture which needs to be capitalized on through diplomatic aptitude and economic relations. The newly acquired knowledge of an advanced civilization and the intense trade with the oriental culture will lead to a situation where the player will be held in high esteem. In this way he can populate the fascinating world of the Orient and lead the Occident to a new bloom" http://anno.de.ubi.com/history1404.php

[23] Cf. Shaheen's book "Reel Bad Arabs. How Hollywood Vilifies a People" shows in an impressive overview of more than 900 movies that Hollywood uses since 1896 always the same stereotypes to characterize Arabs:: »Seen through Hollywood's distorted lenses, Arabs look different and threatening. Projected along racial and religious lines, the stereotypes are deeply ingrained in American cinema. From 1896 until today, filmmakers have collectively indicted all Arabs as Public Enemy #1 – brutal, heartless, uncivilized religious fanatics and money-mad cultural »others« bent on terrorizing civilized Westerners, especially Christians and Jews.« (Shaheen, 2001, p. 2).

APPENDIX

Games

Global Conflicts: Palestine
Global Conflicts: Latin America
Im Zentrum der Macht. Genius Politik
Civilization
SimCity (Maxis Games 1994ff.)
Anno 1404 (2009): Related Designs, Ubisoft: Deutschland.
Anno 1503 (2002): Max Design, Sunflowers: Deutschland.
Anno 1602 (1998): Max Design, Sunflowers: Deutschland.
Anno 1701 (2006): Related Designs, Sunflowers: Deutschland.
Civilization IV (2005): Firaxis, Infogrames: Frankreich.
Close Combat: First to Fight (2005): Destineer, 2K Games: USA.
Die Siedler II – Die nächste Generation (2006): Thomas Häuser & Peter Ohlmann (Programmierung),
    Christoph Werner & Adam Sprys (Grafik), Blue Byte: Deutschland.
Full Spectrum Warrior (2004): Pandemic Studios, THQ: USA.
Genius – Im Zentrum der Macht (2007): SpielArt Entertainment OhG, Cornelsen/BpB: Deutschland.
Global Conflicts: Latin America (2008): Serious Games Interactive: Dänemark.
Global Conflicts: Palestine (2007): Serious Games Interactive: Dänemark.
Max Payne (2001): Remedy, Gathering of Developers: USA.
Max Payne 2 (2003) Remedy, Rockstar Games: USA.
SimCity (1989): Maxis, Maxis: USA.
SimCity 2000 (1994): Maxis, Electronic Arts: USA.
SimCity 4 Deluxe Most Wanted (2006): Maxis, Electronic Arts: USA.
World of Warcraft (2004): Blizzard Entertainment, Vivendi: Frankreich.

Chapter 5
A Proposed Framework for Studying Educational Virtual Worlds

Ricardo Javier Rademacher Mena
Futur-E-Scape, LLC, USA

ABSTRACT

There are several theories about entertainment and education. Some, like Caillois' Play Domains, categorize broad domains of play. Others, like Gardner's Multiple Intelligences, categorize narrowly defined types of intelligences. To the author's knowledge however, there has never been a mix of entertainment and education theories in a single conceptual framework. In this chapter, a framework will be systematically built called The Education and Entertainment (EE) Grid. This grid will showcase how entertainment theories from Robert Caillois and Richard Bartle can be applied to educational contexts and how educational theories from Benjamin Bloom and Howard Gardner can be applied to entertainment contexts. A wide spectrum of education and entertainment theories will first be reviewed and special attention will be given to the four theories comprising the EE Grid. Two individual grids, the ENT and EDU Grids, will then be built as a preliminary step to constructing the first version of the EE Grid. Once built, a comparison with other similar frameworks in the field of game design will be discussed. Finally, a few hypothetical examples of how the EE Grid could be used will be presented.

INTRODUCTION

Over the centuries and across species, play has always been used as a means of education. The vigorous romping of young puppies is teaching them how to socialize and hunt. A chess game between two nobles was a means of teaching strategy and warfare in ancient times. However as the notion of a frivolous childhood took root in modern society, that age and its play were likewise considered frivolous. As such, play lost its educational context and was relegated purely to entertainment within the nursery or playground. However in the past 20 years, with the rise of the cultural acceptance of video games, there has been much work done in restoring play to the classroom such as the Serious Games movement (Michael & Chen, 2006) and the New Literacy Studies (Gee, 2007).

DOI: 10.4018/978-1-61520-781-7.ch005

The classroom is itself not devoid of radical change. In the last five years, we have seen the rise of the pure online university and thus the pure online class (Rademacher, 2009a). These online classes set up virtual communities of learning, every bit as relevant as a real community of learning. Countless students are now engaging in purely virtual education in fields such as education, nursing, and law. This new style of teaching is revolutionizing how students are reached as well as the very concept of what a classroom is. These revolutions are also playing out in the area of virtual worlds. In a purely entertainment context, the virtual world is known as a Massively Multiplayer Online Game (MMOG). Hundreds of these games are played by millions of people worldwide all of whom can interact with each other simultaneously within their game world. Several books have already commented on the educational value of these worlds and the people that inhabit them (Aldrich, 2005; Castronova, 2006; Guest, 2008). As will be shown, aside from studies within current commercial worlds, there are also many worlds specifically built for education and research.

It is the philosophy of this chapter to treat education and entertainment as complementary principles and not decree one to be superior to the other; the play mentality is assumed to be related to the learning mentality and vice versa. To examine these ideas, research and theory from the educational and entertainment sectors will be reviewed. For each sector, two theories will be chosen and then presented in the form of a grid, an *ENT Grid* and an *EDU Grid*. Once each grid's independent message has been elucidated, they will be put together into one large grid. This large grid is the centrepiece of the chapter. Known as the *Entertainment and Education (EE) Grid,* this unique presentation of entertainment and education theories will help us better understand and use these theories by organizing them within and without their native sectors. Finally, how this grid compares to other game frameworks, how it might

be used, and how it will be tested in an upcoming survey will be discussed.

While this research is grounded in the realm of virtual worlds, it may be possible to extrapolate these results to single player or off-line games. As well, while the educational focus is on the subject of physics due to the author's familiarity with the subject, it should be possible to extrapolate these results to other subjects. While these are important topics for discussion, given the space limitations of the chapter these ideas will not be openly explored here.

VIRTUAL WORLD REVIEW

Viewing a timeline of online entertainment (Koster, 2002) shows its start with Tolkien in 1937 up to Disney's Toontown™ in 2002. And the history of distance education (*Distance Education Timeline*, 2000; *Online Learning History*, 2008) shows its beginnings with teaching by mail in 19th century England leading to its modern incarnation with e-Learning in the 21st. With such a rich history, it will be important to explicitly define the space that will be studied. Richard Bartle (2003) defines a Virtual World (VW) by three criteria: an environment simulated by a computer, that is shared by several players (a.k.a. avatars), and that continues to exist and develop internally even when there are no players in the world (persistent). *Based on his definition, for this chapter a Virtual World is defined as 1) an environment and 2) a community 3) inhabited by avatars and 3) implemented through the Internet.* Note that persistence is not part of this definition. This means that there are persistent VWs (e.g., online role playing games) and non-persistent VWs (e.g., online first person shooters). With this in mind, we will focus on the MMOG as an example of a persistent VW and the Online Classroom as an example of a non-persistent VW.

The MMOG is responsible for bringing VWs to the cultural foreground. With games like World of Warcraft™ drawing millions of users and billions of dollars, the popularity of these games is unmatched. Because of this rise in popularity and thus a general awareness of the possibilities within a VW, there has been much work done in researching virtual worlds over the last 20 years. Here are three recent examples of this type of research. The first is by Kafai (2008) and is based on the longest running educational VW, Whyville™ (http://www.whyville.com). Launched in 1999, Whyville™ is a browser-based VW aimed primarily at children and preteens. It has a vast curriculum covering science, history, and more. Kafai's study followed 35 players as the Whypox, an in-game virus, spread through Whyville™. They report on the assumptions the players make about viruses and ecology before and after the epidemic. The second example is a VW specifically built for research, Celia Pearce's Mermaids™. As part of Georgia Tech Experimental Game Lab, Mermaids™ runs on the MultiVerse™ MMOG platform and aims to research emergent social behavior in VWs through non-violent gameplay (Pearce & Ashmore, 2007). This was a private study and thus the world is not open to the public but information can be found at http://www.mermaidsgame.net. The final example comes from the Minnesota Zoo and is called WolfQuest™ (http://www.wolfquest.org). This is a fascinating exploration of wolf dynamics and teaches about wildlife preservation by making players part of a wolf pack (Shaller & Allison-Bunnell, 2008).

The field of distance education also has a rich and active research history. This is evidenced by the number of journals specifically devoted to this subject such as *Open Learning* (ISSN 0268-0513), the *American Journal of Distance Education* (ISSN 0892-3647), and *Educational Technology and Society* (ISSN 1436-4522). And while papers on VWs do occasionally appear in these publications, the idea of an Online Classroom as a VW has not been explored to the author's knowledge. The idea is thus put forth that the Online Classroom does in fact fulfil this chapter's definition of a VW. It has an online environment which is implemented via standardized Learning Management Systems such as Moodle™ (http://moodle.org) or eCollege™ (http://www.ecollege.com). It has a community held together by the textual chat and discussion-based forums that are the exclusive means of communication within these classrooms. This is reminiscent of the early days of VWs with Multi User Dungeons (MUDs) and Bulletin Board Systems (BBSs) which were also entirely textural. And like these early VWs, it has an avatar that is not seen but defined by the actions of the student within the class. (Rademacher, in press).

ENTERTAINMENT AND EDUCATIONAL THEORIES

In the process leading up to the EE Grid, two theories will be chosen from the educational domain and two from the entertainment domain. The choice of theories in the educational domain is not motivated by an extensive review of the fields of instructional design, e-learning, or educational technology; there may in fact be better theories for this framework. However, the entertainment field has been extensively covered. In both domains, the theories were chosen because of the author's familiarity, having used these theories in both offline and online classes. As well, these theories have discrete elements and thus lend themselves to easy quantification.

The first theory comes from Robert Caillois (1958), a renowned French anthropologist, who wrote *Le Jeux et le Homme*. He set out to observe how children play and then categorized the different styles. He also looked to nature and animal play for insight into our own play. In his book he proposes a taxonomy of play based around two axes: "Play Domain" and "Play Structure". The Play Domains are: **Competition, Vertigo, Chance, and Mimicry**. Thus examples of Competition play would be a game of tennis; of Vertigo play, jump rope; of Chance play, roulette; and of

Mimicry play, theatre. He broke up Play Structure into Freeform and Structure, with freeform play having fewer rules and being more chaotic than structured play. By intersecting these two axes a grid is formed and six distinct categories emerge such as Free-form Competition, Structured Competition, Free-form Chance, etc. An example of Free-form Competition would be boxing while an example of a Structured Competition would be Judo. While not comprehensive and serving as a classification of play and not games, Caillois' taxonomy is by far the most useful way of organizing games that the author has found. And even though it was posited before the advent of the computer age, these Play Domains still hold up in today's digital market. Since Play Structure is a linear commentary on the complexity of a game and does not lend itself to easy quantification, the Play Domains will be the initial focus for the grids construction.

We advance several decades for the second entertainment theory. Richard Bartle (1996) is a professor at Essex University and author of a seminal paper on VWs entitled *Hearts, clubs, diamonds, and spades: players who suit MUDs.* In it, Dr. Bartle synthesizes his experiences with the textual VWs of the 80's and early 90's known as MUDs. He organized his observations along two axes: "Interaction Type" (interact or act) and "Interaction Target" (world or player). As with Caillois, a grid is formed from the intersection of these axes and Player Types emerges at each quadrant: **Socializer, Explorer, Achiever, and Killer**. The Socializer (interact+player) is mainly concerning with establishing relationships with other players. The Explorer (interact+world) is primarily focused on discovering the boundaries of the game, both rules and environment. The Achiever (act+world) is primarily interested in receiving the rewards the world has to offer. And finally the Killer (act+player) is focused on disrupting the play experience of others. The model was later expanded (Bartle, 2003) by adding a third axes of "Interaction Style" (implicit or

explicit) which bifurcated his initial four Player Types into eight. For example the Socializer becomes a Networker interacting implicitly with players (transitory associations and friendships) and a Friend interacting explicitly with players (long-lasting bonds and friendships). This model of Player Types, though initially based on textual VWs, has held up when applied to modern VWs. Due to its simplicity and wide acceptance in the VW community, Bartle's initial four player types will be used for the first version of the grids.

Switching to education, Benjamin Bloom (1956) and several of his colleagues identified three areas of educational activity: the cognitive, effective, and psychomotor. The most popular outcome of this classification is in the realm of the cognitive in what is normally known as Bloom's Taxonomy. In this work, he outlined an eight element hierarchy of cognitive processes involved in learning. Starting from the lowest level of "Knowledge" and reaching to the highest level of thinking through "Evaluation", this taxonomy has been a standard part of many curriculums for the last 50 years. Recently, Lorin Anderson (2001), a former student of Dr. Bloom, and colleague David Krathwohl revised Bloom's Taxonomy and relabelled its terms. For example "Knowledge" was relabelled "Knowing" and "Evaluation" was relabelled "Creating". This renaming emphasized the procedural nature of this taxonomy. In this work they also identified four Knowledge Domains: **Factual, Procedural, Conceptual, and Metacognitive**. For example, in physics the Factual domain would consist of the name of an equation, the Procedural domain would address how this equation can be manipulated, the Conceptual domain would address what the equation means, and the Metacognitive domain would address how the equation is part of a bigger system. The focus for this chapter will be exclusively on the Knowledge Domains so as to quantify the types of knowledge and not delve into the procedures to develop them. Integration of the revised taxonomy will be left for a later publication.

The final theory to be used was proposed over 20 years after Bloom. Howard Gardner (1983) of Harvard University is the author of the theory of Multiple Intelligences (MI). This theory rejects the notion of a single intelligence "g" factor, the ubiquitous IQ, and instead proposes several different yet interconnected forms of intelligence. His initial seven intelligences are: **Physical (renamed from Bodily), Spatial, Logical, Lingual (renamed from Linguistic), Interpersonal, Intrapersonal, and Musical**. The criteria Gardner chose for his intelligences were that each intelligence be rooted in the biological origins of problem solving, that they represent a majority of the healthy population, that they are valued by one or more cultural settings, and that they have an identifiable core set of operations. He asserts that every individual has a certain combination of these intelligences and that these intelligences have their roots in evolutionary as well as neural development theory. He also maintains that each intelligence can be demonstrated by a particular job that relies on it. Thus a pianist has a strong Musical intelligence, a physicist has a strong Logical intelligence, and a politician has a strong Interpersonal intelligence. He later extended his model (Gardner, 1999) by adding the Natural Intelligence which is related to a holistic view of flora and fauna and also allowed for the pos-sibility of a Spiritual and Existential intelligence. Nature and spirituality will be excluded for now and the focus will be on Gardner's original seven intelligences for now.

CONSTRUCTING THE ENT GRID

Having defined the theories, the entertainment theories are now put together into the first grid. As shown in Figure 2, Caillois' Play Domains has been placed on the x-axis and Bartle's Player Types on the y-axis. This creates a 4x4 grid of entertainment Domains versus Types known as the *ENT Grid*. Notice the "virtual" tag in the Play Domain. Caillois' Vertigo play is related to the movement of the body and our enjoyment therein. But given that our bodies are in a chair while accessing a VW, the real Play Domain needs to be reinterpreted to apply to a virtual Play Domain. The assumption is therefore put forth that Vertigo gameplay in a VW applies to the player's avatar and not the player themselves. Thus where Caillois' would use spinning around in circles as an example of Free-Form Vertigo play, in a VW an avatar spinning around in circles would be an example of Free-Form Virtual Vertigo play.

With this assumption in place, each intersection of Player Types and Play Domains gives a unique

Figure 1. The ENT Grid and hypothetical values for a MMORPG

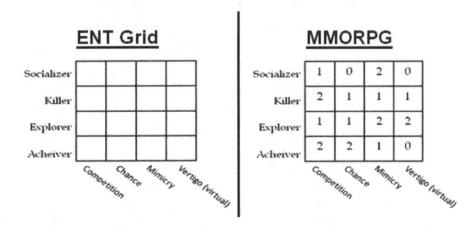

perspective on VWs which can be put in the form of a question. For example at the intersection of the Socializer with Competition the question is asked "Does the socializer player type, a player prone to communicate with other players, engage in any games from the competitive domain, such as tennis or poker?" In the grid box to its right the same question would be asked about Chance: "Does a socializer play games of chance?" Or in the box below: "Does the killer play competition style games?" The way to quantify these questions on the grid is to assign each of the 16 boxes a number based on the strength of the response to the question: "0" if that Player Type and Play Domain are not present in a VW, "1" if it there is weak evidence of the Player Type engaging in the Play Domain, and "2" if there is strong evidence of the same. As an example of how to use the ENT Grid, on the right in Figure 1 is a filled-in grid representing the author's ad hoc analysis of a Massively Multiplayer Online RolePlaying Game (MMORPG), such as World of Warcraft™ or Lord Of The Rings Online™.

The analysis starts by looking at the players. As seen in the figure, it is believed that a Socializer is not engaging in games of Chance or Vertigo. Neither of these Domains require interaction with another person. However games of Competition or Mimicry would be of interest to a Socializer as they necessitate two or more people. The Killer would see games of Competition, like the combat system, to be the primary way to disrupt a player's experience. However, they can still find ways to disrupt in other Play Domains including Vertigo, with the famous example of Killer behavior in MMORPGs with large ogres, small doors, and collision detection. The Explorer is not surprisingly strongest in the Vertigo Domain. As they set out to explore the world, they will need to understand their avatar's bodies and limits. Finally, the Achiever is interested in that which will give them the most tangible rewards. As such, games of Competition and Chance are of primary interest as players are rewarded for engaging in these games with in-game gold or experience points. In contrast, engaging in Mimicry or Vertigo play is seldom tangibly rewarded and thus not of interest to the Achiever. It is interesting to note that based on this hypothetical analysis, the Socializer is the Player Type that is least engaging in Caillois style play. This is interpreted to mean that while Socializers are given a lot of attention in MMORPGs, there is actually surprisingly little gameplay directly made for them.

Figure 2. The EDU Grid and a hypothetical example for an online physics classroom

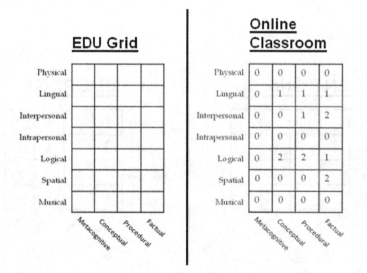

A MMORPG can also be analyzed by looking at the type of play present. As this is a Role Playing Game, it is no surprise that Mimicry is strongly represented in this analysis. Likewise, since most of these games employ some type of combat system, games of Competition are also well represented on the grid. Games of Chance may also be present depending on whether the MMORPG has other gameplay aside from combat. However, most MMORPGS have very little in the way of games like roulette or craps and thus this Play Domain is only weakly represented. And even with the assumption of Vertigo play applying to a player's avatar and not the players themselves, it is still the weakest Domain in these games; MMORPGs simply do not give much attention to gameplay using the body. A notable exception to this is dancing in Star Wars Galaxy™ wherein the game's mechanic was directly tied into an avatar's sense of Vertigo (Squire & Steinkuehler, 2006).

CONSTRUCTING THE EDU GRID

With the creation of the ENT Grid, we are half way to our final goal. In this section, its educational counterpart is built. As shown in Figure 2, the Revised Bloom (aka: Anderson & Krathwohl's) Knowledge Domains have been placed on the x-axis and Gardner's Multiple Intelligence Types on the y-axis. This sets up a 4 x 7 grid called the *EDU Grid*. Like the previous grid, these boxes will be filled-in by asking key questions about the VW to be studied. For example, at the intersection of the Lingual Intelligence Type with the Factual Knowldege Domain the question is: "What types of language based facts are present or represented in the VW?" or "How are the facts of language, like the vocabulary, presented in the VW?" In the box to the left the question becomes: "What procedures are present or presented in the VW related our language?" or "How is the grammar

of the VW presented?" Thus like the ENT Grid, each of the 28 boxes in the EDU Grid represents a unique question probing the Types and Domains of the VW to be examined.

As an example of how to use this grid, shown on the right in Figure 2 is the author's analysis of a purely online physics classroom. The entire curriculum is conveyed online through Learning Management Systems and this is why there is a complete lack of Physical intelligence. Also lacking are any elements of an Intrapersonal intelligence since introspection about oneself is not part of an online physics class. Unfortunately introspection about physics itself is not present in these classes and thus the Metacognitive domain is excluded. From what remains Logical is the most strongly represented since these classes rely on logic and math. In these classes there is also a lot of work defining space and thus Factual-Spatial intelligence is strongly represented. However as these ideas are merely presented but not used, the Procedural and Conceptual boxes have been left empty. Finally, given that most of the work in the online environment relies on text and written discussions, there are contributions to the Lingual intelligence from all but the Metacognitive domain.

While the EDU Grid is sparse in the realm of the online physics class, it can be shown that is it much richer in other educational domains. While due to space constraints such analyses are not presented here, the EDU Grid does in fact give interesting insights into other class formats (Rademacher, 2009b). For example, when applying the ideas of Physics Education Research (Hake, 2000; McDermott, 2001) to the classroom, there are contributions from the Metacognitive domain since this research is focused on how physics relates to teachers and students. This research also places an emphasis on how physics relates to the individual which means that the Interpersonal and Intrapersonal intelligences are also present.

CREATING THE EE GRID

While the EDU and ENT grids are interesting in their own way, the subject for the remainder of the chapter is shown in Figure 3. The construction of the EE Grid is motivated by similar axes in both the education and entertainment sector. In each case there are labels that identify distinct objects within that sector, the Types. As well, each sector contains a set of Domains of which each type may or not be a member. Formally, the Grid is created by placing the previously created ENT Grid in the first quadrant and EDU Grid in the third quadrant. This is done to explicitly show each theory in its uncoupled state. The coupling of the ENT and EDU theories as represented by the second and fourth quadrants will not be discussed here and is reserved for a future publication.

Borrowing the idea of Virtual Vertigo play in the entertainment sector, the assumption is put forth that in a virtual environment, virtual analogues of intelligence must be considered. So for example knowing how to throw a fastball or dance in a ballet (both examples of a real Physical intelligence)

is of no use in a VW but knowing how fast an avatar can move or where they may go based on body size (both examples of a Virtual Physical intelligence) can be critical for game enjoyment. As well, the Interpersonal intelligence, formerly related to a real person-to-person interaction, is reinterpreted to now apply to an avatar-to-avatar interaction in deference to the online mode of communication. Intrapersonal intelligence, formally meaning a self-to-self interaction, is now similarly reinterpreted as a self-to-avatar interaction reflecting a player's knowledge of themselves gained by interacting with their avatar. These virtual Personal intelligences have been the subject of much discussion in VWs as related to issues of identity, anonymity, behavior, and more (Dibbell, 93; Meadows, 2008). Unlike the redefinitions of what our body is (Physical intelligence) and who our body is communicating with (the Personal intelligences), the Lingual, Spatial, Logical, and Musical intelligences have no such redefinitions. This is due to the belief that these intelligences are the same in a real or virtual context. Thus these intelligences would have the same facts,

Figure 3. The EE Grid

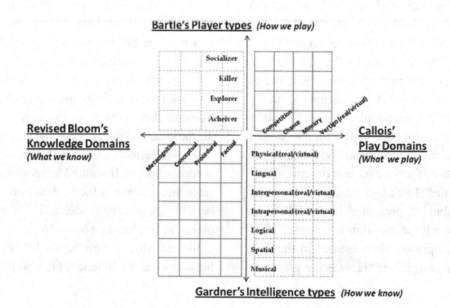

procedures, concepts, and metacognition whether online or off. For the purposes of analysis, this assumption will mean that if an offline environment is to be analyzed, like a traditional physics classroom, the real interpretations of Vertigo and the MI's must be used. If on the other hand a VW is the subject of analysis, then their virtual analogues would be used.

While there are no frameworks that address education and entertainment in the manner presented in this chapter, there are several works that we can compare to the framework presented here. In his book, Gee (2007) identifies three identities that a person takes in a video game: the virtual (representing their game persona), the real (representing the real person), and the projective (representing how the real identity projects into the virtual one). While the Virtual Intelligence is not to be confused with Gee's idea of a virtual identity, it is in correspondence with his projective identity in that this intelligence is being projected into the virtual space. This classification lends insight into his ideas by showing which types of intelligences change when projected into the virtual world and which remain the same. Another popular set of game schema is put forth by Katie Salen and Eric Zimmerman (2004). In their seminal book *Rules of Play,* they lay out three schemas by which to view games: rules, play, and culture. In terms of this chapter's framework, the rules schema is completely dominated by the Logical intelligence while the play schema is dominated by Caillois Play Types. The culture schema derives strongly from the type of view presented by Bartle and his Player Types. As well, the Personal intelligences are used in this schema since culture requires interaction among people. These results are not too surprising considering that they used several of the same theories used in the construction of the EE Grid. Yet another classification is presented by Friedl (2003). In his book, he identifies three realms of online interactivity: player-to-computer (interaction with hardware), player-to-player (interaction with others), and player-to-game (in-

teraction with gameplay). Using the educational theories, the player-to-computer would require Spatial and Physical intelligences as they relate to how a player physically interacts with the hardware. The player-to-player interaction is clearly dependent on the Interpersonal intelligence while the player-to-game would rely on the Logical, Lingual, and Musical intelligences to play the game. Based on the framework presented in this chapter, a player-to-avatar interaction is suggested as a necessary extension to Friedl's framework. This would represent a type of interaction in which the player is not relating to the game, hardware, or others but rather to themselves as projected in the game. This new proposed interaction would be dominated by the Intrapersonal intelligence. The final framework presented is Barab et al's (2006) Conceptual Play Space. Through their work on Quest Atlantis (Barab et al, 2005) they came up with four participations: conceptual (related to the potential to engage in meaningful tasks), immersive (related to losing oneself in the game and story), impactive (related to the understanding of cause and effect), and reflexive (related to the understanding of actions as they relate to self). Analyzed within the context of the educational sector, Barab is not surprisingly well represented across the educational spectrum. Conceptual participation is directly related to the Conceptual and Procedural domains. This is because this participation is more about what can be done and what will be done, the concepts and procedures that will carry a player forward on their tasks. Immersive participation clearly has a strong environmental aspect and thus the Spatial intelligence comes to the fore. As well, since Quest Atlantis is a multiplayer game, a large part of immersion has to do with the community of people and this bring Interpersonal intelligence to bear. Impactive participation is clearly Logical as it deals with a rational understanding on your effect on the game. Finally, reflexive participation, with its focus on understanding the player's role in the world, is a clear combination of the Intrapersonal intelligence and Metacognitive domain since they both deal with the type of introspection that impactive participation requires. This analysis thus shows that several other frameworks can be expanded or analyzed using the framework presented in this chapter.

SAMPLE USE OF THE EE GRID

The initial procedure for using the EE Grid will be the same in both educational and entertainment applications. In each case, a previously constructed grid is pasted onto the EE Grid and then the other empty grid is filled-in. So for example to analyze a game, the EE Grid is seeded with a previously filled out ENT Grid and then the empty EDU Grid components of the EE Grid are filled by asking which intelligences and domains are present or represented in that particular game. If on the other hand a classroom is analyzed, the EE Grid is seeded with a previously filled out EDU Grid and the missing ENT Grid is filled by asking what type of play or activities are present in the classroom and how do they relate to the roles that students take in virtual worlds.

The first example will be from the realm of entertainment and thus the EE Grid is seeded with the analysis of a MMORPG as was previously shown in Figure 1. Since this is the domain of VWs, the previously established virtual reinterpretations are used. With this in mind, on the left of Figure 4 it can be seen that this type of game is filled with facts and procedures. For example in terms of Physical intelligence, the facts of an avatar are best represented by a "character sheet" and the procedures the avatar can take by an "action bar"; or in terms of Lingual intelligence, the facts are the unique vocabulary of the world (such as AFK, BRB, or LFG) and the procedures are how to use these within the game. Personal intelligences are also well represented in this analysis. This is indicative of the strong social aspect that is part of every MMORPG. The lack of the Socializer presence in the entertainment sector that was mentioned in Section 3 can be explained by noting that the Socializer is not engaging in play, but rather doing what is Socializer like to do best and that is using their Personal intelligences. The Lingual intelligence is also well used in these VWs befitting the role that text still plays as the primary form of communication amongst players.

Figure 4. Hypothetical filled EE Grid examples

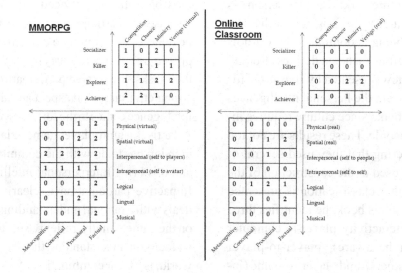

However, if Voice over IP (VoIP) becomes more common in these types of games, there may be a shift from the Lingual to the Musical intelligence as information is also communicated by the tone and pitch of a person's voice.

In the second example, the seed is the online physics classroom EDU Grid as was seen in Figure 2. With this seed in place, the entertainment sector is now filled; this is shown on the right in Figure 4. This is a test of the assumption that Bartle's Player Types can be applied outside the domain of VWs. The Killer Player Type is automatically excluded as well as games of Chance. This represents the idea that in the classroom environment, disruptive behavior as personified by the Killer is not tolerated and soon excised from the class. As well, by its very nature there is no Chance in a Newtonian presentation of physics; a quantum mechanics classroom on the other hand might have this element present. In this severely excluded space, the Explorer is strongly represented followed by the Achiever. This reflects the idea that in a physics class the Explorer, a person who fundamentally wants to understand how things works, is exactly the type of person for whom a traditional physics class is designed for and thus will stand to get the most out of this environment. The Achiever is after any tangible rewards in the VW and in the case of the classroom, this reward is clearly the alphanumerical grades given during the class. When this analysis is correlated with the educational sector, the Socializer's low representation in the entertainment sector is mimicked by a low Intrapersonal representation and outright lack of Intrapersonal intelligence. The Socializer is therefore all but absent in these environments. Finally, the Explorer and Achiever would naturally have to engage their Spatial and Logical intelligences in order to meet their goals within this environment. Using the ENT sector to analyze this classroom quantifies the author's experiences and these classrooms lack of social elements and single minded emphasis on math and logic.

CONCLUSION

In this chapter, the EE Grid has been systematically built. It is formally a two-dimensional matrix with educational and entertainment Types as one axis and Domains as another. This forms three sectors: pure entertainment, pure education, and mixed entertainment/education. In this work, the pure sectors were examined by independently analyzing an ENT and EDU Grid. In the course of building the EE Grid, examples of a MMORPG and an online physics classroom were used. And as was shown, a classroom can be analyzed in terms of an EDU Grid, this EDU Grid is then used as a seed for the larger EE Grid, and then the entertainment portion of the EE Grid is filled. This procedure is replicated in analyzing a game and while not presented in this chapter, it can be taken a step further by exploring the intersections of education and entertainment on the EE Grid to gain deeper insight into how people play and learn.

There is already work on a second version of this grid. This new version will incorporate insights gained from the first version (Rademacher, 2009b). For example, there is a strong correlation between Bartle and Caillois model. What Bartle considers an "Implicit" action, Caillois speaks of "Free-Form". Also, when Bartle mentions an "Explicit" action, it is very much in line with how Caillois speaks of "Structured" play. As well, the idea of a Virtual Intelligence as an extension to Gardner's Multiple Intelligence is very promising. By analyzing each intelligence and seeing if and how it changes in a virtual setting, preliminary results show that virtual worlds might be organized on a deeper, holistic level.

Aside from working on a second theoretical model, the author is also in the process of giving the EE Grid some experimental backing by conducting a survey. This survey will ask a series of questions, each inspired by one of the grid boxes, to a wide range of academics, students, and the public. This is exactly the process used in the examples of the previous sections to fill in the grids. By evaluating their responses, the effectiveness of the EE Grid can be fine-tuned to better quantify an environment's educational and entertainment value. As well, this will also build a catalogue of responses which may be a useful dataset as it would show how people view games through this framework.

REFERENCES

Anderson, L. W., & Krathwohl, D. R. (Eds.). (2001). A taxonomy for learning, teaching and assessing: A revision of Bloom's Taxonomy of educational objectives: Complete edition. New York: Longman.

Barab, S. A., Dodge, T., & Ingram-Goble, A. (2006). *Conceptual play spaces: A 21st Century pedagogy.* Paper presented at the Annual Meeting of the American Educational Research Association, Chicago, IL.

Barab, S. A., Thomas, M., Dodge, T., Carteaux, R., & Tuzun, H. (2005). Making learning fun: Quest Atlantis, a game without guns. *Educational Technology Research and Development, 53*(1). doi:10.1007/BF02504859

Bartle, R. A. (1996). *Hearts, Clubs, Diamonds, Spades: Players who suit muds.* Retrieved April 14, 2009, from Richard Bartle's webpage: http://www.mud.co.uk/richard/hcds.htm

Bartle, R. A. (2003). Designing Virtual Worlds. Indiana: New Riders Publishing.

Bloom, B. S. (1956). Taxonomy of Educational Objectives, Handbook I: The Cognitive Domain. New York: David McKay Co Inc.

Caillois, R. (1958). Les jeux et les hommes. Paris: Gallimard.

Castronova, E. (2006). Synthetic worlds: the business and culture of online games. Chicago: The University of Chicago Press.

Crawford, C. (1984). The art of computer game design. Berkeley, CA: Osborne/McGraw-Hill.

Dibbel, J. (1993). *A rape in cyberspace.* Retrieved April 14, 2009, from Julian Dibbell's webpage http://www.juliandibbell.com/texts/bungle.html

Distance education timeline. (n.d.). Retrieved April 14, 2009, from Baker's Guide http://www.bakersguide.com/Distance_Education_Timeline.

Friedl, M. (2003). Online game interactivity theory. London: Charles River Media.

Gardner, H. (1983). Frames of mind: The theory of multiple intelligences. New York: Basic Books.

Gardner, H. (1999). Intelligence reframed: Multiple Intelligences for the 21st century. New York: Basic Books.

Gee, J. (2007). What Video Games Have to Teach Us about Learning and Literacy, (2nd Ed.). Basingstoke, UK: Palgrave Macmillan.

Guest, T. (2008). Second Lives: a journey through virtual worlds. New York: Random House.

Hake, R. R. (2000). What *Can We Learn from the Physics Education Reform Effort?* Presented at the ASME Mechanical Engineering Education Conference, Fort Lauderdale, Florida.

Kafai, Y. B. (2008). Understanding Virtual Epidemics: Children's Folk Conceptions of a Computer Virus. *Journal of Science Education and Technology, 17*(6). doi:10.1007/s10956-008-9102-x

Koster, R. (2002). *Online world timeline.* Retrieved April 14, 2009, from Raph Koster's website: http://www.raphkoster.com/gaming/mudtimeline.shtml

McDermott, L. (2001). Oersted Medal Lecture2001: Physics education research – The Key to Student Learning. *American Journal of Physics, 69*(11). doi:10.1119/1.1389280

Meadows, M. (2008). I, Avatar: The culture and consequences of having a second life. Indianapolis: New Riders.

Michael, D., & Chen, S. (2006). Serious Games. Boston: Course Technology Ptr.

Online Learning History. (2008). Retrieved April 14, 2009, from Moodle Website: http://docs.moodle.org/en/Online_Learning_History

Pearce, C., & Ashmore, C. (2007). *Principles of emergent Design in Online Games: Mermaids Phase 1 Prototype*. Presented at the SIGGRAGH Sandbox, Sand Diego, California.

Rademacher, R. J. (2009a). *An assessment of current pure online physics courses*. Presented at the American Association of Physics Teachers Winter meeting, Chicago.

Rademacher, R. J. (2009b). *A proposed framework for studying educational virtual worlds*. Presented at the Indipendent Massively multiplayer Game Developers conference, Las Vegas, Nevada.

Rademacher, R. J. (in press). Best practices in teaching and designing a pure online science classroom. In Y. Katz, (Ed.), Learning Management Systems Technologies and Software Solutions for Online Teaching: Tools and Applications. Hershey, PA: IGI Global.

Salen, K., & Zimmerman, E. (2004). Rules of Play. Cambridge, MA: MIT Press.

Schaller, D. & Allison-Bunnell. (2008). *Wolfquest: How do we know if a learning game really works?* Presented at the Games+Learning+Society Conference, Madison, WI.

Squire, K. D., & Steinkuehler, C. A. (2006). Generating CyberCulture/s: The case of Star Wars Galaxies. In D. Gibbs & K. L. Krause (Eds.), Cyberlines: Languages and cultures of the Internet (2nd ed.). Albert Park, Australia: James Nicholas Publishers.

Chapter 6
The Dynamics of Video Gaming:
Influences Affecting Game Play and Learning

Sandra Schamroth Abrams
St. John's University, USA

ABSTRACT

The idea of bridging literacies has been a topic of much research and theory, and educators continue to struggle to help students understand how their learning transcends the classroom walls. Contributing to the discussion, this chapter focuses on factors influencing video game learning, examining the decisions and game play of eight academically struggling eleventh-grade males. Data from two related qualitative studies suggest that direct and peripheral factors influenced students' game play. Findings from these two studies are important to the discussion of educational gaming because they can inform educators of students' struggles and successes in learning outside the classroom. Overall, the evaluation of students' video gaming can provide educators insight into the affordances of this digital literacy and issues affecting student learning outside the classroom.

INTRODUCTION

It comes as no surprise that students choose activities they find pleasurable (Csikszentmihalyi, 1990; Smith & Wilhelm, 2002) and that their personally relevant experiences beget meaningful learning (Dewey, 1916; Rousseau, 1911/2003). Part of the call to bridge students' literacies (Alvermann, 2002; Goodson & Norton-Meier, 2003; Hull, 2003; Norton-Meier, 2005; Smith & Wilhelm, 2002) is to sanction these personally relevant experiences and help students connect what they learn outside

school to what they learn inside school. Doing so inherently involves recognizing the value of students' outside-of-school knowledge and the forces shaping text choice and perception. In other words, bridging the gap requires an understanding and an espousal of students' traditional and multimodal literacies and how such multi-textual, multimodal learning can transcend the classroom walls.

This chapter provides a closer examination of video gaming, revealing some influences affecting students' game play and offering insight into some of the forces shaping student learning outside the classroom. Data emerging from my investigation of the literacies of eight adolescent male video gamers

DOI: 10.4018/978-1-61520-781-7.ch006

suggest that real and virtual factors influenced the participants' game choice and knowledge acquisition; membership (Moje, 2000), competence (Smith & Wilhelm, 2002) and *identity performance* (Goffman, 1959) motivated gamers to engage in specific video gaming activities. Understanding how these forces may affect game play is central to the discussion of educational gaming, as educators can become cognizant of students' struggles and successes in learning outside the classroom, gain awareness of undercurrents that may exist inside the classroom, and help students connect to their academic material with greater ease.

BACKGROUND

Video game playing is a complex activity. It is a digital literacy that involves the use of and interaction with real and virtual tools and images in accordance with the design of a video game program. Such interaction includes, but is not limited to, the use of semiotic tools, the understanding of changing images and their functions, the recognition and response to audio and visual cues, and the assumption of virtual identities.

Multimodality (Jewitt, 2003; Kress, 2003; Kress & Van Leeuwen, 2001), provides a context for the discussion of video gaming, literacy, and meaning making. Unlike traditional ways of defining literacy as reading or writing letters on a page, multimodality accounts for all the elements that are part of the meaning making process, extending the concept of "text" to include any mode—be it music, video, movement, image—and valuing a wide variety of literacy experiences, including video game playing (Kress & Jewitt, 2003). Acknowledging multimodalities inherently validates students' digital literacies, such as video gaming, and reinforces how critical thinking is equally important in traditional and virtual learning environments (Leu, Castek, Henry, Coiro, & McMullan, 2004, p. 500).

The Great Video Game Debate

Though critics of video gaming may contemplate the negative effects of violent content (Anderson & Dill, 2000; Giumetti & Markey, 2007; Sheese & Graziano, 2005; Shibuya, Ihori, & Yukawa, 2008) and game addiction (Young, 2004), and suggest a relationship between gaming and poor academic performance (Anand, 2007), other research and theory on video gaming suggest that, for children and adolescents, video game playing can be motivating and rewarding (Chute & Miksad, 1997; Rosas et al., 2003; Smith & Wilhelm, 2002) and can have potential academic benefits (Alberti, 2008; Din & Calao, 2001; Gee, 2003; Greenfield, 1984; Lacasa, Méndez, & Martínez, 2008; Rosas et al., 2003). Some have suggested the benefits of frequent playing (Green & McNeese, 2008; Schrader & McCreery, 2008), proposing that video games can improve mental rotation and perceptual skills (Boot, Kramer, Simons, Fabiani, & Gratton, 2008; Cherney, 2008), and some have recommended ways in which games can be implemented in school (Charsky & Mims, 2008; Lacasa, Méndez, & Martínez, 2008). Further, extant research has addressed the relationship between gamers' personal interests and their game choice (Crawford, 2005; Malliet, 2006), and advocates (Gee, 2003; Prensky, 2001) have contended that most video games require players to be active, engaged learners who advance through experimentation, critical thinking, and practice.

This chapter looks outside this great debate and explores the forces affecting game play—from the media, to the social, to the self—revealing some of the influences both on students' game play and their understanding of texts outside of school. Students' situated identities are at the center of this discussion, and Discourse theory (Gee, 1989, 2001), along with the concepts of the *projective identity* (Gee, 2003) and *identity performance* (Goffman, 1959), help to frame the examination and analysis of the participants' situated identities and video game activities.

Discourses and Identity

To be a video gamer means that one must enact a specific identity, utilizing language, knowledge, behavior, and belief systems that are related to video game playing. Gee's (1989, 2001) concept of "Discourses with a capital 'D'" (Gee, 1989, p. 6) is helpful because it highlights how identity, perception, and action (verbal and non-verbal) are socially and culturally constructed. A Discourse involves a way of being, and "integrates ways of talking, listening, writing, reading, acting, interacting, believing, valuing, and feeling (and using various objects, symbols, images, tools, and technologies) in the service of enacting meaningful socially situated identities and activities" (Gee, 2001, p. 719). Video games provide an alternate, virtual space for experimentation with language and identity, and navigation within this space hinges upon one's knowledge and manipulation of game-specific tools and images. "Being" a gamer not only reveals what one does, but also provides insight into the language, knowledge, experiences, and perceptions that are formed in relation to or as a result of video game playing.

Discourse theory calls attention to one's situated identity, perception, and activity and it was a useful frame for evaluating how the participants in my studies viewed themselves as students, learners and video gamers. However, when considering what happens in virtual reality, Gee's (2003) concept of the *projective identity* and Goffman's (1959) notion of *identity performance* provided insight into the ways gamers related to their virtual characters and enacted specific identities.

Video games complicate the discussion of identity because, as Gee (2003) explains, a gamer has three identities: "virtual, real, and projective" (p.54). In addition to distinguishing one's real identity (e.g., a person, student, gamer), and the virtual character on the screen, Gee defines the *projective identity*, or the extension of one's values and feelings upon a virtual character. The projective identity helps to explain one's emotional investment in a character, uncovering the gamer's personal connection to that character and the virtual world. More specifically, one's projective identity can reveal how the gamer capitalizes from a virtual character's accomplishments; gaming skills can lead to social achievement, thereby solidifying one's membership to the gaming community.

Though the projective identity helped to explain the extension of the gamer's feelings onto the virtual character, the concept did not help to clarify the function of the assumed identity. Goffman's (1959) discussion of *identity performance* proved useful for exploring and explaining the identities gamers enacted on *and* off the screen. Identity performance means that people adopt specific Discourses and behave in certain ways in order to present a particular identity to their audience (e.g., an expert, a diligent student, a teacher). As Moje's (2000) study of "gansta" youth reveals, identity performance can be directly related to one's desired membership to a specific social group. Overall, the confluence of Gee's and Goffman's theories has allowed me to examine the gaming practices of the adolescent males in my study, thereby enabling me to address the gamers, their Discourses, and the significance of their situated identities on and off the screen.

RESEARCH DESIGN AND METHOD

This discussion draws upon data from a pilot and subsequent study of a total of eight academically struggling adolescent males and how they understood their traditional and multimodal literacies in relation to their video gaming experiences. Though the pilot study examined students' outside-of-school literacies and activities, it immediately became clear that the students' video gaming experiences were central to the research; during my initial discussions with students in the pilot study, I began to question how the students chose their games, why the students played the games they did, and how they knew about the moves they used. As a result, I developed the following research questions to help guide both the pilot and subsequent inquiry:

1. For video gamers, what influences game choice, game play, and game knowledge?
2. How might these influences impact game play, understanding, and learning?

For a combined total of 12 months, I collected data at a suburban, New Jersey public high school situated in a middle-to-upper-middle-class neighborhood where students had access to the technology, such as personal computers and video games, necessary for this study. Data from the eight case studies provide insight into the students' real and virtual Discourses, revealing the impetus driving much of their video gaming experiences.

The Participants

The eight eleventh-grade males who volunteered for this study all exhibited academic struggles, and they attended English and/or math classes designed for those needing additional support and/or material taught at a modified pace. Not only has research suggested that males play video games more frequently than females (Bonanno & Kommers, 2005; Green & McNeese, 2008; Lucas & Sherry, 2004), but also statistical data has shown seventeen-year-old males trailing 14 points below the average female score for reading (National Center for Educational Statistics [NCES], 2007). By limiting recruitment to eleventh-grade males, this study contributes to the research into adolescent male literacy, responding to the call to "think hard about what we can do to help [boys]" (Smith & Wilhelm, 2002, p. xx). Insight into some factors influencing students' literacy practices may provide educators a better understanding of how students may make their literacy decisions outside of school.

Data Collection and Analysis

The initial study, conducted over four months in 2004, included four observations of eleventh-grade English classes tracked for those struggling in that subject. Solicitation yielded four volunteers who participated in two individual interviews and one focus group interview. Inspired by the data from the pilot study, I conducted additional research four years later, in 2008, modifying classroom observations to include math classes also designed for eleventh graders needing additional support, and increasing the frequency of observations according the teachers' schedules. I observed a total of 37 English and 74 math classes, which provided me greater insight into the participants' experiences in school and enabled me to develop a better rapport with the participants. The second, eight-month-long study included five individual and one focus group interview, participant observation in three other academic subjects, electronic literacy logs, and stimulated recall of game play. These modifications helped me to access students' reflections about their gaming and the factors influencing their video game practices. In both studies, the initial interview included a literacy survey that provided insight into the students' "personal preferences and interests" (Smith & Wilhelm, 2002, p. 20), and the interview questions continuously built upon collected data and emerging themes.

The 2008 study included stimulated recall of game play as a means to engage students in critical, reflective thinking about their decisions; the students and I choose two familiar games that were appropriate to play in school (e.g., no "M" rated games), and, during two separate sessions, I videotaped the students' video game playing and immediately played back the footage, asking students about their moves, intentions, and thoughts. Given that think aloud protocols may not be helpful in measuring the cognitive processes of time-constrained situations that involve complex interaction (Lyle, 2003), this protocol enabled me to question students' knowledge of content and game design, while also learning about factors affecting their choices and perception.

Once I collected the data, I coded and analyzed all the data according to larger categories, such as Discourses, performed identity, projective identity, and shared experiences, which initially helped me organize the data. After reviewing the categories, I returned to code the data using elements of Discourses—believing/knowing, valuing, and doing—to help me identify specific instances of being and doing, identity and action, competence and decisions. Such an approach elicited the connection between what gamers did, be it performing an identity, projecting an identity or sharing information, and what occurred as a result of their gaming, such as making choices, feeling competence, and engaging in social activity. Finally, member checking, researcher reflexivity, triangulation, peer debriefing, and thick, rich description all helped to validate the data.

THE DYNAMICS OF GAME PLAY

Game play involves real and virtual interaction with a video game program, and, given the complex relationship between gaming and identity, it seems logical that there would be multiple factors influencing the participants' video game playing. When learning about the students' video gaming experiences, I found that students' game choice, game play, and game knowledge were informed by factors peripherally and directly related to the students. Television advertisements, Internet sites, social pressure, and collaborative discussions all seemed to teach the students about game moves and/or inspire them to play specific games. The students also were motivated to play specific games because of the latitude and comfort the virtual world afforded them. The following sections reveal the influence of the media, the social, and the self on students' game play.

The Media

Video game advertisements are pervasive, and they informed the students' game play. Three students explained how they learned about game play and remembered game features from commercials or online reviews and discussions. For instance, J.D. (all names are pseudonyms) discovered a specific *Super Mario Cart* maneuver from a television commercial, and he modeled that technique during his game playing session with me; J.D. shook the control because "they did it in the commercials... like pop a wheelie like when the guy's doing a jump...showing people shaking the controller." In other words, the advertisement J.D. unexpectedly encountered served as a multimodal tutorial informing his game play.

Unlike J.D., Robbie and Eric purposely visited gaming websites, sought desired information, and critically thought about and applied their newfound knowledge to their game play. Robbie visited gamefaqs.com to learn about *Super Mario Cart* strategy; during the stimulated recall, Robbie explained that "he's [his computerized opponent] supposed to make me crash, but I know how to block him," a move Robbie knew because "I looked that up," intentionally using gamefaqs.com as a reference. Further, Eric frequented IGN.com, a website that touts itself as the "the web's number one videogame information destination" ("Passionate about entertainment," n.d.), where Eric watched a film trailer for *Saints Row II*, and "the movies were like you can do this and then it would like show you. And I was like you know the game play looks a lot smoother than in *Saint's Row I*... it was such good like advertising like [it] stuck in my head." Inspired by the advertisements, Eric rented *Saints Row II* and experimented with the advertised features. For the three participants, the media informed their game play by modeling behavior and/or providing useful information. Appealing to their game playing audience by promoting gaming techniques and using game-specific language, these media sources seemed to honor gaming Discourses and value and motivate game play.

The Social

Though the media may have informed some students' video gaming, a more powerful influence over game play appeared to be the power of membership (Moje, 2000). Social inclusion and undercurrents of peer pressure seemed to shape students' game choices. Garret revealed how important it was for him to share in his friends' experiences: "Pretty much…all my friends were talking about it [*Madden 08*], so I was like, obviously made me go out and nag my parents into letting me play this game." Perhaps Garret feared exclusion, but it is possible that social collaboration motivated him to play *Madden 08,* because, as Brad explained four years earlier, the *Madden* games were a "popular choice," and Brad enjoyed playing *Madden 04* "with my friends because we can always joke on each other…Maybe screw each other up—play around like that you know." In other words, Garret and Brad felt socially included when they were involved in the shared gaming event, and this sense of community and belonging motivated them to engage in specific game play.

At times, social inclusion appeared in the form of peer pressure. When J.D. realized that his friends were online competing as a team in the shooter game, *Call of Duty*, he began playing *Call of Duty* because "if I have it [the game] and my friends are like, come on, we're all on, I'll play it. I'm not going to *not* play with my friends." Inclusion in the social activity required J.D. to join his friends' established *Call of Duty* clan, a difficult task because the clan already was on the twelfth level. Therefore, J.D. dedicated days to learning the game and completing all twelve levels on his own. He sensed an obligation to play well, explaining how "I'm getting better to play with [my friends] and that way they're not ridiculously better and I'm bringing their team down." Membership (Moje, 2000) to that virtual community required J.D. to demonstrate his knowledge of gaming Discourses and his value to the team. Membership motivated J.D. to learn an unknown text and contribute to a collaborative effort.

As is evident from J.D.'s example, the desire to be part of a popular activity seemed strong enough to modify one's behavior. Further, video game knowledge and experience seemed to be social currency, providing a status transcending social stigmas. For example, Steven felt that others often ridiculed him, but he recognized how he gained social acceptance by performing the identity (Goffman, 1959) of a video game "guru." He explained that his peers would often approach him, asking "'What's a good game' you know. And I'm like, 'What kind of games are you into?' And then they all tell me the kind of games they like. And, I'm like, 'You might want to try this game if you like that type.'" Steven's example illustrates not only the power of gaming knowledge, but also the value gamers placed on sharing information. In this way, communication was a powerful learning tool within the gaming community.

Talking about a game seemed to be part of everyday conversation among gamers, even if they were not friends. In 2004, Brad had implied that talking about video games was standard practice in that Discourse community: "I'm a big *Madden* fan, so everyone's like, 'Did you get the *Madden* game?' And I'm like 'Yeah, you know, it's got new graphics, it's got new features to it.'" Four years later, during the 2008 focus group interview, J.D. mentioned that he wanted "to try the *Left for Dead* demo," and Eric (who was not friends with J.D.) immediately offered his assessment of the game: "That's good. It's a great game. Bought it over Christmas." This brief conversation was informative in content yet natural in turn, suggesting that such communication among gamers was a common, accepted practice. Unlike the commercials intended to lure gamers to try a game, word-of-mouth critiques reached gamers on a social level because gamers seemed to embed their knowledge and opinions into their conversations. Such informal contributions seemed to be part of the learning and gaming experience, with gamers valuing peer teaching in the form of information exchange and feedback.

The Self

As is evident in many of the examples above, students felt a sense of community when they participated in and discussed their game play. However, when the participants spoke of their independent game play, they indicated a sense of competence they otherwise appeared not to feel. The participants played video games that not only represented their personal interests (Crawford, 2006; Malliet, 2006), but also validated their desires and empowered them with the freedom to experiment with identities, decisions, and moves they might have longed for in reality. For instance, *Madden 08* enabled Garret, who referred to himself as "the fat, slow lineman," to assume the role of a "6'2" or 6'3" quarterback...getting the interception, running back for a touchdown. Always wanted to do that...[but can't do that because] I'm not fast enough." Likewise, the online shooter game, *Battlefield 1942*, allowed Robbie, the reticent history enthusiast, to model his gaming decisions after historical events and control the outcome by modifying decisions that had made real leaders face defeat. When Robbie eventually decided to join a *Battlefield 1942* online clan, he used his knowledge of history to perform the identity (Goffman, 1959) of an expert and feel competent "being at the top, like generals." Further, J.D., who taught snowboarding, liked playing the snowboarding game, *Amped*, to "do like back flips in the game and do like 20 of them off of the jump," experimenting with moves he otherwise could not achieve. In other words, the gamers experienced competence through their game play; they sensed achievement not only because they performed an identity in the virtual world, but also because they emotionally connected to their character through their projective identity.

Video games also gave some the opportunity to experiment and learn without having to suffer the physical or emotional consequences of poor performance. Virtual tennis enabled unathletic Michael to play the sport without feeling awkward or ashamed:

In gym, I played tennis. And I was really bad at it. I mean all I kept doing was hitting balls over the fence and go into the road...But with this game... like if you mess up, then I mean you know you're the one that did it but ... I mean you really don't feel embarrassed as much as you do if you were playing an actual sport.

Michael's anonymity gave him comfort in and control of the virtual athletic experience, allowing him to gain competence because he could play and improve without feeling judged by others. Further, video games allowed players to try various activities with relative impunity, as Garret explained, "Like in the game you can mess up. You can always go back. But, in real life, you can't. Like you have to make the play or you're screwed...[but with video games] you can always just press start and like go to restart the game." Likewise, J.D. noted that he wasn't worried about losing a game or making a bad move because "You're not going to mess anything up because you can always restart it and then just try something else." In other words, there always is a chance to begin anew, something difficult for many academically struggling students to achieve in school given the nature of traditional grading.

In general, video games seemed to empower players because, as Brad so aptly explained, "I guess in a video game you're more in charge of what happens." Caleb expanded on this idea in the 2004 focus group interview, noting the autonomy he felt playing *Madden 04*: "In the [video] game, *you're* coaching the team; *you're* picking the plays. When you play on the field, you don't pick the plays." Unlike most traditional learning conditions, the virtual world enabled the students to be designers of their own learning, an important pedagogical concept (New London Group, 1996). In this way, we can see how the video game experience can be personally relevant and meaningful, as gamers were able to project their knowledge and feelings onto the characters, perform a desired identity, and gain competence mastering moves they otherwise could not accomplish in reality.

What's Competence Got to Do With It?

Embedded in the discussion of the media, the social, and the self is the issue of competence. Across the cases, feelings of or desire for competence seemed to be associated with the students' game choice, game play, and game knowledge. J.D., Robbie, and Eric felt competent enough as gamers to experiment with advertised moves and games; desire for social competence prompted J.D., Brad, and Garret to play specific games; Steven's gaming competence and knowledge yielded social acceptance; performing identities in the virtual world enabled Garret, Robbie, and J.D. to feel competent enacting expert moves; and the anonymity of the virtual world made Michael feel competent enough to play a virtual sport. Overall, the students in my studies realized a degree of competence because they gained a sense of autonomy during game play and/or they felt others valued their knowledge and experiences. Though the social aspect of video gaming was powerfully influential, the comfort in playing alone and experimenting with identities and moves also was empowering. Regardless of the independent or collaborative practice, it is apparent that students felt validated through their game play.

In Smith and Wilhelm's (2002) study, the adolescent male participants continually "talk[ed] about how a feeling of competence kept them involved in an activity" (p.32). The boys "championed a sense of control" (p. 109) and preferred activities in which they perceived mastery and security. Similarly, many of the participants in my studies valued the degree of competence and control they experienced from video gaming, and, as Caleb, J.D., Michael, and Brad acknowledged, gamers could be authorities, experimenting with moves, making mistakes, and starting over at their own discretion. Many of the gamers also felt a level of accomplishment through their performed and projective identities, sensing an emotional connection to their virtual character and their virtual abilities. Further, as J.D., Robbie, Garret, Brad

and Steven revealed, belonging to a Discourse community and accessing a shared event was empowering; in many ways, membership became a sign of competence, and competence became a sign of membership.

Overall, the data from the case studies reveal how the students' competence or desire for competence was related to their game choice, game play, and game knowledge. Given the various forces influencing the students' game play, it seems clear that the examination of video gaming should include the discussion of gamers' socially situated identities and literacies. The impetus to play video games may vary, but the data suggest that the forces shaping student learning outside the classroom may have inherent emotional and/or social implications, thereby making gaming a relevant and meaningful activity.

RECOMMENDATIONS

Educators can benefit from understanding some of the forces affecting video game play, as they can gain insight into their students' needs, perceptions, and motivations. The examples from my data suggest that the desire for social inclusion can impact students' behavior and gaming knowledge can be social currency. If students, such as Steven, often feel excluded except when imparting game knowledge, then educators may look to build upon students' Discourses to help students find a common ground within the classroom. Similarly, if students gain competence when adopting an alternate persona, then perhaps educators may provide a similar context for experimentation in school. In addition, the academically struggling students in my studies appeared to develop critical thinking skills that enabled them to search and find information and/or understand the application of game information; these are skills they need to bring into the classroom, and perhaps educators can harness the students' knowledge of and motivation to utilize resources.

When we consider ways to build upon students' outside-of-school literacies, such as video gaming, we need to remain sensitive to the issues that can transcend academic and social realms. We also need to find practical ways to enable students to appreciate autonomy and experimentation in school without "burying youth's pleasures by exposing them to adult critique" (Alvermann & Heron, 2001, p. 121). In order to effectively bridge inside- and outside-of-school literacies, educators need to recognize and value students' Discourses, feeling comfortable welcoming students' voices and experiences in the classroom (Labbo et al., 2003; Marsh, 2004; Millard, 2003).

FUTURE RESEARCH DIRECTIONS

My two studies reveal the gaming practices of eight academically struggling adolescent males and the powerful forces impacting their game choices, feelings of competence, and social activity. Additional research is needed to examine if and how the dynamics of video gaming presented in my studies may influence female gamers in similar and/or different ways. Further, investigations can examine if there exists, for some, a relationship between one's academic standing and game choice.

The data from my two studies also suggest that video gaming should not be evaluated in isolation; the gaming experience may be distinct, but it is related to, and informed by, other socio-cultural experiences. Some studies (Crawford, 2005; Malliet, 2006) suggest a relationship between one's real interests and one's virtual game play, and additional research is needed to examine the knowledge acquired in and transferred to real and virtual settings and vice versa. Such research would help to reveal the affordances and constraints of commercial games as pedagogical tools, providing insight into the ways students' use of commercial games outside school could be a vehicle for learning inside school.

In addition, there are methodological implications for the use of stimulated recall sessions to promote students' critical reflection of game play. The students in my 2008 study seemed to have gained a heightened awareness of their gaming and their moves because of this technique. Research is needed into the effectiveness of this method as a supplementary or complementary technique to reflective journals, and the extent to which it can prompt and promote the degree of student reflection the researcher desires. Overall, examinations of this technique could provide insight into the range of its research and classroom applications.

CONCLUSION

In the discussion of educational gaming, it is important to consider the influences affecting students' game play. As the data from my studies reveal, the students' game choice and knowledge acquisition were shaped by real and virtual factors; when the gamers played alone, they were designers of their own learning, researching moves and game strategies, experimenting with virtual identities and game moves, and feeling empowered by the control and competence they achieved in the virtual world. In light of gaming as a social activity, the data suggest that the gaming community valued the sharing of knowledge and experiences, and membership to this community involved collaborative gaming and discussions of game play.

By valuing and understanding gamers' learning experiences, educators can create practical ways to summon inside school the motivation, the collaboration, and the competence achieved in most video gaming experiences. Overall, with an awareness of students' video game practices and the various influences affecting game play, educators can become more knowledgeable of students' Discourses and perhaps discover new ways to motivate students, validate their interests, and promote meaningful learning.

REFERENCES

Alberti, J. (2008). The game of reading and writing: How video games reframe our understanding of literacy. *Computers and Composition, 25*, 258–269. doi:10.1016/j.compcom.2008.04.004

Alvermann, D. E. (2002). Effective literacy instruction for adolescents. *Journal of Literacy Research, 34*(2), 189–208. doi:10.1207/s15548430jlr3402_4

Alvermann, D. E., & Heron, A. H. (2001). Literacy identity work: Playing to learn with popular media. *Journal of Adolescent & Adult Literacy, 45*(2), 118–122.

Anand, V. (2007). A study of time management: The correlation between video game usage and academic performance markers. *Cyberpsychology & Behavior, 10*(4), 552–559. doi:10.1089/cpb.2007.9991

Anderson, C. A., & Dill, K. E. (2000). Video games and aggressive thoughts, feelings, and behavior in the laboratory and in life. *Journal of Personality and Social Psychology, 78*(4), 772–790. doi:10.1037/0022-3514.78.4.772

Bonanno, P., & Kommers, P. A. M. (2005). Gender differences and styles in the use of digital games. *Educational Psychology, 25*(1), 13–41. doi:10.1080/0144341042000294877

Boot, W. R., Kramer, A. F., Simons, D. J., Fabiani, M., & Gratton, G. (2008). The effects of video game playing on attention, memory, and executive control. *Acta Psychologica, 129*, 387–398.

Charsky, D., & Mims, C. (2008). Integrating commercial off-the-shelf video games into school curriculums. *TechTrends, 52*(5), 38–44. doi:10.1007/s11528-008-0195-0

Cherney, I. D. (2008). Mom, let me play more computer games: They improve my mental rotation skills. *Sex Roles, 59*, 776–786. doi:10.1007/s11199-008-9498-z

Chute, R., & Miksad, J. (1997). Computer assisted instruction and cognitive development in preschoolers. *Child Study Journal, 27*(3), 237–254.

Crawford, G. (2005). Digital gaming, sport and gender. *Leisure Studies, 24*(3), 259–270. doi:10.1080/0261436042000290317

Csikszentmihalyi, M. (1990). Flow: The psychology of optimal experience. New York: Harper and Row.

Dewey, J. (1916). Democracy and Education. New York: The Free Press.

Din, F. S., & Calao, J. (2001). The effects of playing educational video games on kindergarten achievement. *Child Study Journal, 31*(2), 95–102.

Gee, J. (1989). Literacy, discourse, and linguistics: Introduction. *Journal of Education, 171*(1), 5–17.

Gee, J. (2001). Reading as situated language: A sociocognitive perspective. *Journal of Adolescent & Adult Literacy, 44*(8), 714–725. doi:10.1598/JAAL.44.8.3

Gee, J. (2003). What video games have to teach us about learning and literacy. New York: Macmillan.

Giumetti, G., & Markey, P. M. (2007). Violent video games and anger as predictors of aggression. *Journal of Research in Personality, 41*(6), 1234–1243. doi:10.1016/j.jrp.2007.02.005

Goffman, E. (1959). The presentation of self in everyday life. Garden City, NY: Doubleday.

Goodson, F. T., & Norton-Meier, L. (2003). Motor oil, civil disobedience, and media literacy. *Journal of Adolescent & Adult Literacy, 47*(3), 258–262.

Green, M. E., & McNeese, M. N. (2008). Factors that predict digital game play. *The Howard Journal of Communications*, *19*, 258–272. doi:10.1080/10646170802218321

Greenfield, P. A. (1984). Mind and media: The effects of television, video games and computers. Cambridge, MA: Harvard University Press.

Hull, G. A. (2003). Youth culture and digital media: New literacies for new times. *Research in the Teaching of English*, *38*(2), 229–233.

Jewitt, C. (2003). Computer-mediated learning: The multimodal construction of mathematical entities on screen. In C. Lankshear, M. Knobel, C. Bigum, & M. Peters (Series Eds.) & C. Jewitt & G. Kress (Vol. Eds.), New literacies and digital epistemologies: Vol. 4. Multimodal literacy (pp. 34-55). New York: Peter Lang.

Kress, G. (2003). Genre and the multimodal production of 'scientificness.' In C. Lankshear, M. Knobel, C. Bigum, & M. Peters (Series Eds.) & C. Jewitt & G. Kress (Vol. Eds.), New literacies and digital epistemologies: Vol. 4. Multimodal literacy (pp. 173-186). New York: Peter Lang.

Kress, G., & Jewitt, C. (2003). Introduction. In C. Lankshear, M. Knobel, C. Bigum, & M. Peters (Series Eds.) & C. Jewitt & G. Kress (Vol. Eds.), New literacies and digital epistemologies: Vol. 4. Multimodal literacy (pp. 1-18). New York: Peter Lang.

Kress, G., & Van Leeuwen, T. (2001). Multimodal discourse: The modes and media of contemporary communication. London: Arnold.

Labbo, L., Leu, D. Jr, Kinzer, C., Teale, W., Cammack, D., & Kara-Soteriou, J. (2003). Teacher wisdom stories: Cautions and recommendations for using computer-related technologies for literacy instruction. *The Reading Teacher*, *57*(3), 300–304.

Lacasa, P., Méndez, L., & Martínez, R. (2008). Bringing commercial games into the classroom. *Computers and Composition*, *25*, 341–358. doi:10.1016/j.compcom.2008.04.009

Leu, D. J. Jr, Castek, J., Henry, L. A., Coiro, J., & McMullan, M. (2004). The lessons that children teach us: Integrating children's literature and the new literacies of the Internet. *The Reading Teacher*, *57*(5), 496–503.

Lucas, K., & Sherry, J. L. (2004). Sex differences in video game play: A communication-based explanation. *Communication Research*, *31*(5), 499–523. doi:10.1177/0093650204267930

Lyle, J. (2003). Stimulated recall: A report on its use in naturalistic research. *British Educational Research Journal*, *29*(6), 861–878. doi:10.1080/0141192032000137349

Malliet, S. (2006). An exploration of adolescents' perceptions of videogame realism. *Learning, Media and Technology*, *31*(4), 377–394. doi:10.1080/17439880601021983

Marsh, J. (2004). The techno-literacy practices of young children. *Journal of Early Childhood Research*, *2*(1), 51–66. doi:10.1177/1476718X0421003

Millard, E. (2003). Towards a literacy of fusion. New times, new teaching and learning? *Reading*, *37*(1), 3-8.

Moje, E. B. (2000). 'To be part of the story': The literacy practices of gangsta adolescents. *Teachers College Record*, *102*(3), 651–690. doi:10.1111/0161-4681.00071

National Center for Educational Statistics. (2007, February 22). *The Nation's Report Card: Reading 2007*. Retrieved October 25, 2007, from http://nces.ed.gov/pubsearch/pubsinfo.asp? pubid=2007496

New London Group. (1996). A pedagogy of multiliteracies: Designing social futures. *Harvard Educational Review, 66*, 60–92.

Norton-Meier, L. (2005). Joining the video-game literacy club: A reluctant mother tries to join the "flow.". *Journal of Adolescent & Adult Literacy, 48*(5), 428–432. doi:10.1598/JAAL.48.5.6

Passionate about entertainment. (n.d.). Retrieved October 13, 2008, from http://corp.ign.com/

Prensky, M. (2001). Digital game-based learning. New York: McGraw-Hill.

Rosas, R., Nussbaum, M., Cumsille, P., Marianov, V., Correa, M., & Flores, P. (2003). Beyond Nintendo: Design and assessment of educational video games for first and second grade students. *Computers & Education, 40*, 71–94. doi:10.1016/S0360-1315(02)00099-4

Rousseau, J. J. (2003). Émile. London: Orion Publishing Group. (Original work published in 1911).

Schrader, P. G., & McCreery, M. (2008). The acquisition of skill and expertise in massively multiplayer online games. *Educational Technology Research and Development, 56*(5-6), 557–574. doi:10.1007/s11423-007-9055-4

Sheese, B. E., & Graziano, W. G. (2005). Deciding to defect: The effects of video-game violence on cooperative behavior. *Psychological Science, 16*(5), 354–357. doi:10.1111/j.0956-7976.2005.01539.x

Shibuya, A., Ihori, A. S. N., & Yukawa, S. (2008). The effects of the presence and contexts of video game violence on children: A longitudinal study in Japan. *Simulation & Gaming, 39*(4), 528–539. doi:10.1177/1046878107306670

Smith, M. W., & Wilhelm, J. D. (2002). Reading don't fix no chevys. Portsmouth, NH: Heinemann.

Young, K. S. (2004). Internet addiction: A new clinical phenomenon and its consequences. *The American Behavioral Scientist, 48*(4), 402–415. doi:10.1177/0002764204270278

ADDITIONAL READING

Brozo, W. G., & Young, J. P. (2001). Boys will be boys, or will they? Literacy and masculinities. *Reading Research Quarterly, 36*(3), 316–325. doi:10.1598/RRQ.36.3.4

Cavazos-Kottke, S. (2005). Tuned out but turned on: Boys' (dis)engaged reading in and out of school. *Journal of Adolescent & Adult Literacy, 49*(3), 180–184. doi:10.1598/JAAL.49.3.1

Cocking, R. R., & Greenfield, P. M. (1996). Effects of interactive entertainment technologies on children's development. In P.M. Greenfield & R.R. Cocking (Eds.), Interacting with Video (pp. 3-7). Norwood, NJ: Ablex Publishing.

Cope, B., & Kalantzis, M. (2000). Multiliteracies: Literacy, learning, and the design of social futures. London: Routledge.

Delpit, L. (1995). Other people's children: Cultural conflict in the classroom. New York: The New Press.

Gailey, C. W. (1996). Mediated messages: Gender, class, and cosmos in home video games. In P.M.

Gee, J. (1996). Social linguistics and literacies: Ideology in Discourses (2nd ed.). London: Taylor & Francis.

Gee, J. (1999). An introduction to Discourse analysis. New York: Routledge.

Gee, J. (2000). Teenagers in new times: A new literacy studies perspective. *Journal of Adolescent & Adult Literacy, 43*(5), 412–420.

Goodson, I. F., Knoebel, M., Lankshear, C., & Mangan, J. M. (2002). Cyber spaces/Social spaces: Culture clash in computerized classrooms. New York: Palgrave Macmillan.

Greenfield & R.R. Cocking (Ed.). Interacting with Video (pp. 9-23). Norwood, NJ: Ablex Publishing. (Reprinted from Journal of Popular Culture, 27(1), 81-97, 1993)

Hunsberger, P. (2007). 'Where am I?' A call for 'connectedness' in literacy. *Reading Research Quarterly*, *42*(3), 420–424. doi:10.1598/RRQ.42.3.7

Hynds, S. (1997). On the brink: Negotiating literature and life with adolescents. New York: Teachers College Press.

King, J. R., & O'Brien, D. G. (2002). Adolescents' multiliteracies and their teachers' needs to know: Toward a digital détente. In D. E. Alvermann (Ed.), Adolescents and Literacies in a Digital World (pp. 40-50). New York: Peter Lang.

Lim, C. P. (2008). Spirit of the game: Empowering students as designers in schools? *British Journal of Educational Technology*, *39*(6), 996–1003. doi:10.1111/j.1467-8535.2008.00823_1.x

Lotherington, H. (2003). Emergent metaliteracies: What the Xbox has to offer the EQAO. *Linguistics and Education*, *14*, 305–319. doi:10.1016/j.linged.2004.02.007

Luke, A., & Elkins, J. (1998). Reinventing literacy in 'New Times.'. *Journal of Adolescent & Adult Literacy*, *42*(1), 4–7.

Maynard, T. (2002). Boys and literacy: Exploring the issues. New York: Routledge.

McGinnis, T. A. (2007). Khmer rap boys, X-Men, Asia's fruits, and Dragonball z: Creating multilingual and multimodal classroom contexts. *Journal of Adolescent & Adult Literacy*, *50*(7), 570–579. doi:10.1598/JAAL.50.7.6

McMillan, S., & Wilhelm, J. (2007). Students' stories: Adolescents constructing multiple literacies through nature journaling. *Journal of Adolescent & Adult Literacy*, *50*(5), 370–377. doi:10.1598/JAAL.50.5.4

O'Brien, D., & Scharber, C. (2008). Digital literacies go to school: Potholes and possibilities. *Journal of Adolescent & Adult Literacy*, *52*(1), 66–68. doi:10.1598/JAAL.52.1.7

Prensky, M. (2008). Students as designers and creators of educational computer games: Who else? *British Journal of Educational Technology*, *39*(6), 1004–1019. doi:10.1111/j.1467-8535.2008.00823_2.x

Smith, M. W., & Wilhelm, J. D. (2006). Going with the flow. Portsmouth, NH: Heinemann.

Stone, J. C. (2007). Popular websites in adolescents' out-of-school lives: Critical lessons on literacy. In M. Knobel and C. Lankshear (Eds.), A New Literacies Sampler (pp. 49-66). New York: Peter Lang.

Turkle, S. (1997). Life on the screen: Identity in the age of the internet. New York: Touchstone.

Vasudevan, L. M. (2006). Looking for Angels: Knowing adolescents by engaging with their multimodal literacy practices. *Journal of Adolescent & Adult Literacy*, *50*(4), 252–256. doi:10.1598/JAAL.50.4.1

Wolf, M. J. P., & Perron, B. (2003). Introduction. The Video Game Theory Reader. New York: Routledge.

Section 2
Applying Theory to Game Design

Chapter 7
Exploratory Digital Games for Advanced Skills:
Theory and Application

Juan Carlos Sanchez-Lozano
Concordia University, Canada

ABSTRACT

Based on Cognitive Flexibility Theory, this chapter presents a framework for the conception, design, and development of a knowledge network that can be used in exploratory instructional digital games. The instructional structure consists of a set of nodes, each associated with a specific level of conceptual restructuring and a set of resources, both perceptual and physical, that can help the learner/player achieve resolution. The resulting conflict field is used to determine the game structure. Distributed and embodied cognition research is used to link instructional objectives with available game resources at the task level. As a result a better alignment is obtained between the instructional objectives and the game core mechanics. The application of the framework is then illustrated by using it to outline the design process of a game to learn computer programming.

INTRODUCTION

There is a fundamental difference between games and what we usually identify as formal education. Huizinga (1955) notes the capacity of play to absorb and impart meaning to activities that would otherwise be inconsequential. Some consider play a central factor in human learning (Apter, 1991) whereas others point out that learning is the essential motivation behind play (Crawford, 1982). Meaningful play occurs within the 'magic circle' (Salen

& Zimmerman, 2004) which is the game's own space and time where people voluntarily participate (Huizinga, 1955). Within this space it is possible to experience a high level of excitement and take risks within a protective frame (Apter, 1991). Motivation is increased by the presence of fantasy, challenge and curiosity (Malone, 1981).

This chapter takes an ecological stance on games. The digital medium allows the player to actively explore –spatial quality– and act on the virtual world –participatory affordance– (Murray, 1997). Furthermore, since the player can perceive possibilities for action in the game space, and is given tools to act

DOI: 10.4018/978-1-61520-781-7.ch007

upon those possibilities to reach a goal, games fit the description of lived environments (Allen, Otto, & Hoffman, 2003). From this perspective, the purpose of instruction is to motivate the learner to set specific goals and detect relevant information and actions in the environment that can lead to these objectives (Young, 2003). Whether those goals emerge from the interaction with the environment (Young, Barab, & Garrett, 2000) or are personal, an important skill will be identifying which of the affordances are most effective to achieve specific goals (Gee, 2008). Learning is then the result of this perceiving-acting cycle (Young, 2003, 2004; Young et al., 2000).

In line with the previous argument, computer games for instruction can benefit from an instructional strategy consistent with the characteristics of the digital medium. Steinkuehler (2006) states that "games typically consist of overlapping well-defined problems enveloped in ill-defined problems that render their solutions meaningful" (p. 2). Designers of games that have this structure, however, have no clear guidelines on how to create the underlying network of well-defined problems that can be explored rather than completed sequentially as it happens in traditional instruction. Cognitive Flexibility Theory (Spiro, Feltovich, Jacobson, & Coulson, 1992; Spiro & Jehng, 1990; Spiro, Vispoel, Schmitz, Samarapungavan, & Boerger, 1987) is presented here as the basis of an approach that can guide the conceptualization of the knowledge structure, one that will better use the affordances of the digital environment while at the same time providing the learner with the opportunity to gain a deeper understanding of the specific domain. The result is a network that can act as the underlying structure of the game, inducing learning through exploration and conflict resolution. The idea of cognitive conflict is further explored in the context of a critical thinking/problem-solving continuum which can inform learner progression as well as the type of tasks involved.

From the point of view of the learning processes involved, current work tends to focus on either internal processes or context but what is desirable is a theory that integrates mental processes with the perceptual, motor, and embodied dimensions of learning, among others (Gee, 2008). Beyond internal cognitive processes, the perceiving-acting cycle suggests that the resources present on the screen play a very important role. For example, Massively Multiplayer Online Games (MMOGs) can be optimal educational playgrounds (Squire, 2006) where large amounts of information are present through a variety of interface elements. However, it is unclear how players interact with the many resources available or how this interaction can be of use in instruction (Schrader & Lawless, 2008). Commercial game designers are starting to approach this issue from a human-computer interaction perspective (Dyck, Pinelle, Brown, & Gutwin, 2003; Jorgensen, 2004). This chapter argues that the Distributed Information Resources Model (DIRM) (Wright, Fields, & Harrison, 2000) provides a reference that can help in this analysis. Although this model is more relevant when learning how to use a computer application, it can help determine what kinds of resources are desirable in an instructional game.

Furthermore, interaction with a digital environment is not limited to cognitive and perceptual skills. The use of the keyboard, mouse, and game controllers require motor skills that can be central to the gameplay. Studies on embodied cognition (Ballard, Hayhoe, Pook, & Rao, 1997; Gray & Fu, 2004; Gray, Sims, Fu, & Schoelles, 2006) can inform the analysis of how individuals choose between cognitive, perceptual, and motor skills, the way in which this decision impacts learning, and therefore the way we design the physical interaction with an instructional game.

Many authors have proposed frameworks and guidelines for the design and development of instructional games (Boocock and Schild, 1968; Abt, 1968; Duke, 1974; Greenblat and Duke,

1981; Garris and Ahlers, 2002). Nevertheless there is no generally accepted framework, which has led designers to insert instructional modules in existing commercial games or rely on intuition and experience (Boyd, 1983.

Two main features characterize the work presented here:

1. It applies instructional theories that help organize the instructional content, define learning tasks and map learner progression in the game knowledge network, while at the same time better harnessing the affordances of the digital medium.
2. It presents and incorporates recent theories that can help understand how the game assets and controls are linked to the type of skills brought into the learning process. This understanding in turn allows for better alignment between instructional and game objectives.

In spite of the fact that designing and implementing educational games is no simple matter, they have been successfully used in education in areas such as computer programming (Cooper, Dann, & Pausch, 2000), language (Piirainen-Marsh & Tainio, 2009), physics (Squire, Barnett, Grant, & Higginbotham, 2004), science and social studies (Barab, Thomas, Dodge, Carteaux, & Tuzun, 2005), and history and the environment (Squire, 2006). Educators have either applied lessons learned from commercial games (Barab et al., 2005) or modified existing ones (Hayes & Games, 2008). Commercial games rely heavily on the design document for game design and development (Rollings & Morris, 2004). Design documents for serious games have been proposed (Bergeron, 2006). Because of the unique and differentiating quality of serious games, the instructional component should be explicitly present and carefully integrated but, as Bergeron (2006) notes, in some cases instructional game design documents end up looking very similar to

their commercial counterparts. The instructional structure of educational games is the first issue addressed here.

THE INSTRUCTIONAL STRUCTURE OF EDUCATIONAL GAMES

Games can be considered environmental narratives that allow the player to create associations, experience events, absorb information, or collectively construct meaning (Jenkins, 2004). As opposed to creating a cohesive whole that can be explored and appropriated, in formal education knowledge is dissected and structured with the objective of facilitating learning. In the process, we run the risk of stripping knowledge off its meaning, and hence, off its complexity and beauty.

Cognitive Flexibility Theory (CFT) argues that the organization of knowledge in simpler, sequential blocks might be adequate for simple structured domains but not for ill-structured ones (Spiro et al., 1992; Spiro & Jehng, 1990; Spiro et al., 1987). In ill-structured domains cases are not clear-cut and require deep conceptual understanding rather than the use of 'recipes' (case- and concept-complexity). Even similar cases within the same domain require mastering different concepts and/or applying them in different ways (across-case irregularity). CFT maintains that the traditional approach leads to poor conceptual understanding and oversimplification, not only of content, but also of the learning process and the instructional strategies used (Spiro & Jehng, 1990). "Simply explaining concepts or stating facts will not be effective because it does not permit indexing according to the features of the situations in which the concepts or facts are relevant" (Schank, Fano, Bell, & Menachem, 1994, p. 306). This argument is in line with situated cognition which argues that the nature of the task will depend on the context (Brown, Collins, & Duguid, 1989).

In order to convey the real complexity of the domain and foster the adequate application of knowledge under different circumstances and scenarios, CFT proposes a network or landscape where the learner can explore conceptual complexity of the domain in many directions, appreciating relationships and the way in which context can influence the use of models, ideas, and processes (Spiro & Jehng, 1990). The instructional principles derived from this approach include representing knowledge in a variety of ways, showing how concepts and facts are applied in different situations, making interrelations between concepts evident, and encouraging the construction of knowledge over mere fact retrieval (Jacobson & Spiro, 1993).

Computers seem ideally suited for the implementation of environments based on CFT. Digital environments allow people to get involved through participation, can be explored because of their spatial quality, and can store large amounts of information (Murray, 1997). However, non-linearity presents challenges of its own. A certain structure has to be in place to guide the learner in the exploration of the network-landscape. Spiro and Jehng (1990) used a network of mini-cases where each node had an associated vector with specific attributes that allowed the user to visit nodes by connecting them according to topic. The use of mini-cases seems to be supported by successful instructional games like the Monkey Wrench Conspiracy (Prensky, 2004). The creation of a mesh is also proposed by Crawford (2005) to represent knowledge and provide a narrative landscape. CFT has been successfully applied to various areas such as transfusion medicine (Jonassen, Ambruso, & Olesen, 1992), pharmacy (Oliver, 1997), literary interpretation (Spiro, Feltovich, Jacobson, & Coulson, 1992), and art education (Taylor & Carpenter, 2002).

Indeed, a computer game can be seen as the materialization of an underlying model or structure, that of the designer. And, as with any software application, the player's model of the system does not necessarily match the designer's model (Sasse, 1997). An experienced designer will

manage to link the player's actions with all the game elements in order to shape the perceptions, cognitive processes and behaviors of the learner/player (Raybourn, 2007). Through meaningful action learning takes place as the player recognizes elements, relationships, and patterns in the knowledge space (Gee, 2003), which is also what Koster (2004) defines as 'fun' in games. This interaction will inevitably lead to conflict (Crawford, 1982).

CONFLICT MAP

Conflict is a key element in games (Crawford, 1982), stemming primarily from the struggle to achieve an objective (Salen & Zimmerman, 2004). In games, conflicts can be perceived as puzzles rather than as annoying obstacles (Apter, 1991). Each task in the game can be seen as a source of conflict and an opportunity to induce conceptual change (Limon, 2001). Task 'conflict' can involve weak restructuring such as fact acquisition or radical restructuring such as view changes (Vosniadou & Brewer, 1987). Learning from cognitive conflict requires a meaningful context (Limon, 2001), which games are ideally suited to provide.

Thus, the non-linear structure proposed by Cognitive Flexibility Theory can be seen as a network of conflict nodes that can receive different kinds of input, such as prior knowledge and system resources, resulting in a certain output, such as a learning outcome, conflict resolution, or choice. Implicit in this representation is the fact that there is resolution of the conflict through the appropriate use of different resources, which are not necessarily the same all the time. Several paths can lead to resolution of the same issue, an idea based on Edelman's (2004) view of how the brain works. Underlying instructional game models can be seen as fields of conflict that can be resolved in different ways, as shown in figure 1. It is proposed here that this conflict field can be the basis for the game's constitutive rules

(Salen & Zimmerman, 2004) or their underlying mathematical structure. Constituative, operational and implicit rules give structure to the game and define what is and what is not possible inside the magic circle.

CONFLICT SOURCE

Different tasks can be associated with different levels of conflict, depending on the degree of uncertainty in those tasks. At the simplest level we find deterministic step-by-step procedures such as pressing the correct buttons in the right sequence to obtain money from ATM. Complex tasks, such as buying the best stocks for a portfolio in order to maximize profit, have a higher level of uncertainty. Tasks that can be considered transformational (Mezirow, 1978) or emancipatory (Brookfield, 1987) include finding the meaning of one's existence. Life changing conflict will naturally be greater than merely learning new facts.

What skills are necessary to solve these situations? Mezirow (1978) argues that critical thinking is an essential skill in achieving perspective transformation. What about weaker forms of restructuring? Many would think of problem-solving skills in that case. Garrison (1991) suggests that critical thinking involves heuristic metacognitive

processes and is related to ill-structured situations. In contrast, problem solving is associated with algorithmic cognitive processes and structured situations. This differentiation is compatible with the definition of critical thinking provided by the Delphi report (Facione, 1990). Few people would consider the search for meaning in life 'solving a problem', but rather critically reflecting on one's existence. Getting cash from an ATM would likely be associated with problem-solving and not with critical thinking.

Confining problem-solving to well-defined goals and situations (algorithmic) and critical thinking to ill-defined ones (heuristic) may be too drastic. For example, a problem that is ill-defined, such as deciding what stocks to buy in a market shaken by previously inexistent circumstances, may have both algorithmic processes involved based on domain specific knowledge (such as return-on-investment calculations), and also a judgment component, which will rely more on a critical reflective process and insight. It is one single problem and rather than stating that we are solving a problem or critically thinking about it, both seem to coexist in the same scenario. Figure 2 shows how different components and their degree of interaction can be visualized in a continuum.

The continuum would have 'pure' problem-solving at one end, and 'pure' critical thinking at

Figure 1. Conflict node and conflict field

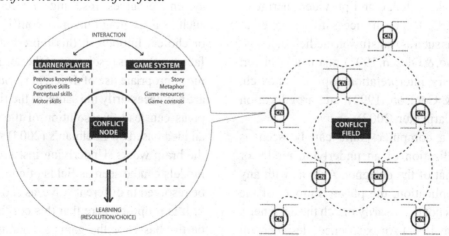

Figure 2. (a) Critical thinking continuum (b) Conflict variability

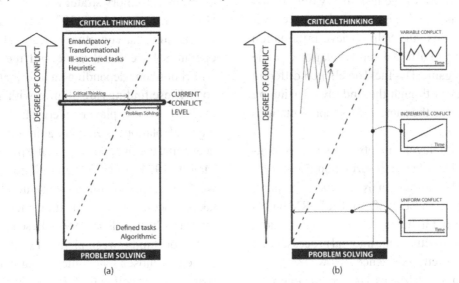

(a)   (b)

the other. What this means is that task complexity would go from structured and algorithmic to ill-structured and heuristic. A specific situation would be a slice in the continuum, where critical thinking would coexist with problem-solving. The degree of 'coexistence', which is not an exact percentage, would largely depend on the context and the specific task at hand. This 'slice' would show observable evidence of the use of each construct. This in turn would help determine the instructional interventions as well as measurable outcomes. It is important to note that higher conflict refers to a higher degree of uncertainty and restructuring, but not necessarily difficulty. For example, in the game Simon Says the player is simply required to repeat the sequence generated by the computer by pressing the buttons in the correct order. Longer sequences will be more difficult because of memory demands, but the player will still be at the same level of restructuring complexity since no new skills are required. A game such as Age of Empires involves different tasks with various levels of complexity, from creating an army to planning a campaign.

A slice in the graph can represent a node or series of nodes, a single task in the game or an entire game level. It is at the node level that conflict will appear and interaction with the game will hopefully lead to resolution and learning. The resources available, as well as how the player is expected to interact with them should support the learning process. How external resources and physical interaction affects learning is an important consideration since these elements are key components of both the game mechanics and gameplay.

INTERACTION WITH GAME RESOURCES

Situated cognition argues that individuals use external artifacts to build solutions to problems (Brown et al., 1989). Such artifacts can be domain specific, social, or cultural (Driscoll, 1994; Henning, 2003). Distributed cognition sees information as distributed among and flowing between different representations (Hutchins, 1995; Hutchins & Klausen, 1996). Representational properties can support or hinder information flow. Zhang and Norman (1994) have shown that external representations have the power to change the nature of the task, the way in which information is perceived, structure internal cognitive mechanisms, and help retrieve information from memory. Different representations of the well-known game Tic-Tac-Toe elicited different strategies, even though the underlying winning mechanism was the same across representations (Zhang, 1997).

In line with developments in distributed cognition, the Distributed Information Resources Model (DIRM) can help analyze human-computer interaction (Wright et al., 2000). The DIRM builds on evidence that in human-computer interaction, abstract data structures cue internal processes that lead to correct action sequences (Howes & Payne, 1990; Larkin, 1989; Mayes, Draper, McGregor, & Oatley, 1988; Payne, 1991). The DIRM presents a non-exhaustive list of possible data structures that can be represented in the system: plans, goals, possibilities, history, action-effect relations, and states. The model also suggests strategies that the individual may use to coordinate those resources and take action: plan following, plan construction, goal matching, and history-based selection and elimination. Games can be seen as distributed systems where cognition is the result of the individual's close coupling with external resources (Kirsh, 2006). These resources can involve visual and aural elements, physical interaction, or other players. The DIRM can be used as a starting point to relate tasks to external resources and determine the type of game elements that will be made available in each conflict node.

Interaction analysis should not be limited to resources on the screen. It has been shown that physical interaction is related to cognitive and perceptual mechanisms. Ballard et al. (1997) have argued that at very small time scales, physical interaction will impact and connect perceptual and cognitive processes. It has been suggested that individuals will prefer to use perceptual/ motor skills rather than retrieval from memory,

a 'minimal memory strategy' (M. Wilson, 2002). However, Gray and Fu (2004) refuted this position, arguing that cognitive, perceptual, and motor operators have equal value and the individual will choose one depending on information access cost. These findings are aligned with an analysis of Tetris where players were shown to favor physical rotation instead of cognitive operations to determine the final position of the piece (Kirsh & Maglio, 1994). Even though Ballard et al. (1997) were criticized for implying that embodiment only takes place at very small time intervals (Feldman, 1997; R. Wilson, 1997) these studies show a relationship between physical systems and the strategies chosen when interacting with a digital space. More specifically, Gray and Fu (2004) have also pointed out that if the objective is to make information readily available, then information cost should be low, but if the objective is to learn something, then information cost should be high so the effort will help retention.

The careful selection of resources and their access cost will influence the strategies used. Although it has been argued that learning resources should be configured to reduce cognitive load (Kirschner, Sweller, & Clark, 2006; van Merrienboer, Kirschner, & Kester, 2003; van Merrienboer & Sweller, 2005), video games work under a different set of values (Barr, Noble, & Biddle, 2007). In gaming environments players not only welcome some forms of cognitive load but also come up with approaches to overcome them (Ang, Zaphiris, & Mahmood, 2007).

Summarizing, distributed and embodied cognition suggest that the elements present in a gaming environment and the way the user interacts with them will influence the choice of strategies that will be applied, and this can in turn impact learning. These considerations should be incorporated in design frameworks. New research will be needed as new forms of interaction emerge.

INSTRUCTIONAL GAME DESIGN FRAMEWORK

The final step is the integration of the instructional structure in the larger game design process. Crawford (1982) has proposed a simplified game design scheme. The designer selects the goal of the game (abstract) which is then expressed through the topic (concrete). Once the goal and the topic have been selected, three related structures have to be developed simultaneously. These are:

- Input/Output structure, which accounts for the interaction between the computer system and the player. The input structure reflects the physical interaction with the game through which the player executes meaningful choices. The output structure incorporates the display and new types of controls, such as the vibration of the Wii command.
- Game structure, which translates the goal into an operational system.
- Program structure, which is the software/hardware system itself.

The instructional elements presented in this chapter can be incorporated into this general scheme. The conflict map previously discussed is intimately related to the game structure, and the content of each node determines the type of resources necessary and the desired forms of interaction with the system (Input/Output structure). The software and hardware structure establishes possibilities and limitations depending on available technology. Figure 3 shows the integrated design framework.

EXAMPLE: PROGRAMMING GAME

This example illustrates how the framework is being applied to build a game to teach ActionScript, a scripting language used in Adobe Flash, a rich internet applications development platform. In this particular case it was decided that the goal of the game would be to access an alien race computer network and disable their weapons. Otherwise, they would annihilate the human race. This topic was selected because it offers a context for the programming tasks involved and also a rich

Figure 3. Instructional game design framework

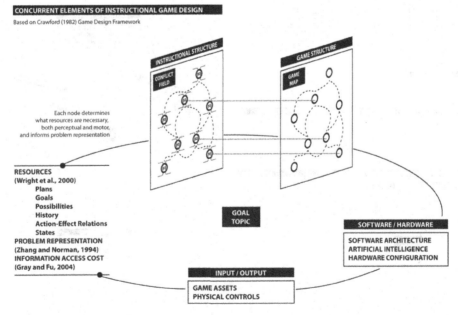

source of visual representations that can provide meaning. Please note that the example has been greatly simplified for clarity.

A quick literature review will reveal that many researchers agree that programming involves three types of knowledge: syntactic, conceptual, and strategic (Bayman & Mayer, 1988; McGill & Volet, 1997). Syntactic knowledge refers to the rules and syntax of the language. It is this level that is normally achieved in introductory courses. Conceptual knowledge refers to semantic understanding of computer structures. Strategic knowledge is the capacity to design, implement, and debug new programs. Notice that these types of knowledge are easily located in the critical thinking continuum as shown in figure 4. The designer can choose to target only one level of conflict (e.g. only language syntax), take the learner from low conflict to high conflict (e.g. incremental from syntactic to strategic), or produce a trajectory that will have variable conflict (all three types of knowledge simultaneously). In fact, McGill and Volet (1997) suggest this last option, the concur-

rent teaching of all three types of knowledge, to teach programming.

The general theoretical outline is presented in figure 4. Three processes take place simultaneously: creation of the network, outline of possible progressions, and determining what kind of resources and interactions can support specific learning at the node level. This is not a guessing process, but once again should be based on existing research. In this case, it has been shown that programming is not a purely intellectual effort (Jonsson, Tholander, & Fernaeus, 2009). Visual cues (distributed cognition), social artifacts present in software development teams (situated cognition), and physical language design (embodied cognition) can inform the selection of resources available to resolve a specific conflict, and open new possibilities for information flow at the perceptual and physical level that will lead to learning.

To begin with, the nodes and their content are in essence a representation of the knowledge that will hopefully be communicated and acquired

Figure 4. Programming game

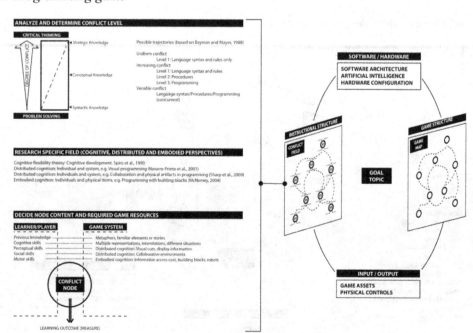

through the game. As Scandura (2003) mentions, knowledge representation is not an easy task, particularly if it has to be represented using a computer system or automated in any manner. Specific tools such as Structural Learning Theory (Scandura, 2006) can help create highly detailed knowledge representations at various levels of granularity and expertise.

Figure 5 shows a simplified representation matrix for this example. As noted earlier, each case or node has a set of requirements and produces a specific output. The simplest exercise found at the bottom left is a loop. It requires previous knowledge about variables, and certain operators. The node requires that the learner produce a simple output: 012345678. Once the code has been successfully mastered, the loop structure can be added as an output to the current level of knowledge of the learner.

The matrix is superimposed over the critical thinking/problem-solving continuum. The previous example is clearly a problem-solving case. Exercises similar in complexity and structure can be found by moving horizontally. In this example, the exercise to the right of the previous one requires the learner to output certain numbers in reverse order: 54321. This introduces the

'greater or equal than' (>=) and the 'decrement' (--) operators, but the loop structure is almost identical. Alternatively, more complex topics such as functions, parameters and events are introduced using a vertical path of nodes not specified in the figure ({...}) until the most complex case in this simple matrix appears at the top: creating the code to enable a button to jam the weapons. Although the code is simple, 'listeners', as they are called, are conceptually more challenging than simple loops. In a real matrix additional syntactic, conceptual and strategic cases would be present. Higher levels would include organizing blocks of code, creating objects, and suggesting efficient patterns. However, the design process would be very similar. By carefully matching input and output between nodes, and their level of complexity, different paths can be constructed resulting in a node network or conflict field, as shown by the dotted lines in figure 5.

The next issue is to visit each of the nodes and decide what kinds of resources are required, what possible actions can be taken, and what kind of visual representations are adequate within the game. Figure 6 shows one possible representation for the simplest exercise in the matrix, the loop. The node has been transformed into a completion

Figure 5. Sample node matrix

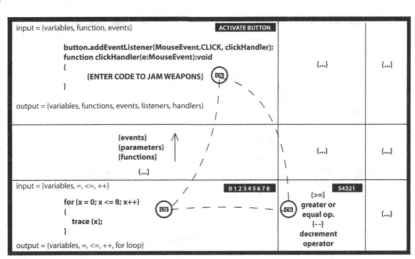

exercise. In order to access the alien system, the learner needs to enter a code.

The visual representation uses an obvious metaphor. However, instead of just clicking the numbers, the learner has to complete the loop structure. Based on Wright et al. (2000) the link between game assets and task requirements can be established. The main resource, the goal, is made explicit. The exercise offers the opportunity to follow a plan as the basic structure is already there and it only requires certain elements to work. If the learner correctly drags and drops one item, then the system will provide a visual cue allowing the item to be inserted in the structure (action-effect). Checked items show what steps have already been completed (history). In this very specific case of programming instruction, two options are offered (possibilities): pseudo-code and code. Pseudo-code is a more conceptual approach whereas pure code is more rule-based. Notice that in this case the pseudo-code instructions and their code equivalent are not side-by-side, adding another level of complexity. By offering and synchronizing both options, the learner can better understand the exercise. In addition, small snippets of text or video can be offered to further explain the topic if necessary. Similar nodes can be represented dif-ferently to exemplify their relevance in a variety of contexts, in agreement with CFT.

Completing the exercises in the matrix in a sequential fashion without any context or unifying concept would be boring at best, but exploring them in different ways under the coherent frame of a game allows for a deeper level of understanding as well as motivation. The representations and type of resources that can be made available to the player are determined both by the instructional content and the game topic. In *Supercharged!* animations make electromagnetism concepts easier to understand, and the interaction is not limited to a simple drag-and-drop operation but involves controlling a virtual ship (Squire et al., 2004). The previous design steps do not take place in a linear fashion but require a back-and-forth approach. A wide variety of representations are possible and determining the best ones requires involving the users. As innovative learning environments, instructional games benefit from extensive testing and a refining iterative process. Players become participants in the design process, enabling researchers to better understand the dynamics involved and modify the game accordingly (Barab & Squire, 2004).

Figure 6. Sample node

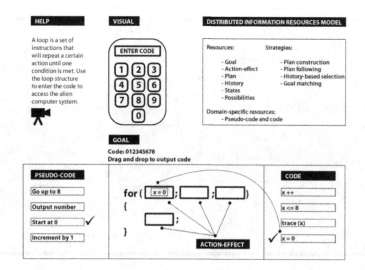

CONCLUSION

This chapter has presented a framework that links the instructional component of the game with other game structures. It has also underlined the importance of incorporating perceptual and physical components in the analysis for better alignment between the instructional objective and the gameplay. Although it is not applicable to every type of game, designers of games that can benefit from an underlying knowledge network may find it useful. More research is necessary to understand the impact of new game features such as graphics, sound, and controls on the learning process. The continued contribution of researchers and practitioners will help us better understand new elements of games and may lead us to design digital environments that will not only educate but will radically transform people's lives and society in general.

REFERENCES

Abt, C. (1968). Games for Learning. In S. Boocock & E. Schild (Eds.), Simulation Games in Learning. Beverly Hills, CA: Sage.

Allen, B., Otto, R., & Hoffman, B. (2003). Media as Lived Environments: The Ecological Psychology of Educational Technology. In D. Jonassen (Ed.), Handbook of Research on Educational Communications and Technology. Mahwah, NJ: Lawrence Erlbaum Associates, Inc.

Ang, C. S., Zaphiris, P., & Mahmood, S. (2007). A Model of Cognitive Loads in Massively Multiplayer Online Role Playing Games. *Interacting with Computers*, *19*(2), 167–179. doi:10.1016/j.intcom.2006.08.006

Apter, M. (1991). A Structural Phenomenology of Play. In J. Kerr & M. Apter (Eds.), Adult Play: A Reversal Theory Approach. Amsterdam: Swets & Zeitlinger.

Ballard, D., Hayhoe, M., Pook, P., & Rao, R. (1997). Deictic Codes for the Embodiment of Cognition. *The Behavioral and Brain Sciences*, *20*, 723–742.

Barab, S., & Squire, K. (2004). Design-Based Research: Putting a Stake in the Ground. *Journal of the Learning Sciences*, *13*(1), 1–14. doi:10.1207/s15327809jls1301_1

Barab, S., Thomas, M., Dodge, T., Carteaux, R., & Tuzun, H. (2005). Making learning fun: Quest Atlantis, a game without guns. *Educational Technology Research and Development*, *53*(1), 86–107. doi:10.1007/BF02504859

Barr, P., Noble, J., & Biddle, R. (2007). Video Game Values: Human-Computer Interaction and Games. *Interacting with Computers*, *19*(2), 180–195. doi:10.1016/j.intcom.2006.08.008

Bayman, P., & Mayer, R. (1988). Using Conceptual Models to Teach BASIC Computer Programming. *Journal of Educational Psychology*, *80*(3), 291–298. doi:10.1037/0022-0663.80.3.291

Bergeron, B. (2006). Developing Serious Games. Hingham, MA: Charles River Media.

Boocock, S., & Schild, E. (Eds.). (1968). Simulation Games in Learning. Beverly Hills, CA: Sage Publications.

Boyd, G. M. (1983). *The Use of Heuristics Based on Frank's Political-Value Triangle for the Analysis and Design of Legitimate Educational Games*. Paper presented at the International Conference on Cybernetics, Namur, Belgium.

Bredemeier, M., & Greenblat, C. (1981). The Educational Effectiveness of Simulation Games: A Synthesis of Findings. *Simulation & Games*, *12*(3), 307–332. doi:10.1177/104687818101200304

Brookfield, S. (1987). Developing Critical Thinkers: Challenging Adults to Explore Alternative Ways of Thinking and Acting. San Francisco: Josey-Bass Inc.

Brown, J., Collins, A., & Duguid, P. (1989). Situated Cognition and the Culture of Learning. *Educational Researcher*, *18*(1), 32–42.

Cooper, S., Dann, W., & Pausch, R. (2000). *Alice: A 3D tool for introductory programming courses.* In Proceedings of the 5th Annual CCSC Northeastern Conference 2000, Ramapo, NJ.

Crawford, C. (1982). *The Art of Computer Game Design*. Retrieved October 7, 2006, from http://www.vancouver.wsu.edu/fac/peabody/game-book/Coverpage.html

Crawford, C. (2005). Chris Crawford on Interactive Storytelling. Berkeley, CA: New Riders.

DeNike, L. (1976). An Exploratory Study of The Relationship of Educational Cognitive Style to Learning from Simulation Games. *Simulation & Games*, *7*(1), 65–74. doi:10.1177/104687817600700105

Driscoll, M. (1994). Psychology of Learning for Instruction. Boston: Allyn and Bacon.

Duke, R. (1974). Toward a General Theory of Gaming. *Simulation & Games*, *5*(2), 131–146. doi:10.1177/003755007452001

Dyck, J., Pinelle, D., Brown, B., & Gutwin, C. (2003). *Learning from Games: HCI Design Innovations in Entertainment Software*. Paper presented at the Graphics Interface Conference, Halifax, Canada.

Edelman, G. (2004). Wider Than the Sky: The Phenomenal Gift of Consciousness. New Haven, CT: Yale University Press.

Facione, P. (1990). Critical Thinking: A Statement of Expert Consensus for Purposes of Educational Assessment and Instruction. Millbrae, CA.

Feldman, J. (1997). Embodiment is the Foundation, Not a Level. *The Behavioral and Brain Sciences*, *20*(4), 746–747. doi:10.1017/S0140525X9727161X

Garris, R., & Ahlers, R. (2002). Games, Motivation, and Learning: A Research and Practice Model. *Simulation & Gaming*, *33*(4), 441–467. doi:10.1177/1046878102238607

Garrison, D. R. (1991). Critical Thinking and Adult Education: A Conceptual Model for Developing Critical Thinking in Adult Learners. *International Journal of Lifelong Education*, *10*(4), 287–303. doi:10.1080/0260137910100403

Gee, J. P. (2003). What Video Games Have to Teach Us About Learning and Literacy. Houndmills, NY: Palgrave Macmillan.

Gee, J. P. (2008). Video Games and Embodiment. *Games and Culture*, *3*(3-4), 253–263. doi:10.1177/1555412008317309

Gray, W., & Fu, W. T. (2004). Soft constrains in interactive behavior: the case of ignoring perfect knowledge in-the-world for imperfect knowledge in-the-head. *Cognitive Science*, *28*(3), 359–382.

Gray, W., Sims, C., Fu, W. T., & Schoelles, M. (2006). The Soft Constraints Hypothesis: A Rational Analysis Approach to Resource Allocation for Interactive Behavior. *Psychological Review*, *113*(3), 461–482. doi:10.1037/0033-295X.113.3.461

Greenblat, C., & Duke, R. (1981). Principles and Practices of Gaming-Simulation. Beverly Hills, CA: Sage.

Hayes, E., & Games, I. (2008). Making computer games and design thinking. *Games and Culture*, *3*(3-4), 309–332. doi:10.1177/1555412008317312

Henning, P. (2003). Everyday Cognition and Situated Learning. In D. Jonassen (Ed.), Handbook of Research on Educational Communications and Technology. Mahwah, NJ: Lawrence Erlbaum Associates, Inc.

Howes, A., & Payne, S. (1990). Display-Based Competence: Towards User Models for Menu-Driven Interfaces. *International Journal of Man-Machine Studies, 33*(6), 637–655. doi:10.1016/S0020-7373(05)80067-7

Huizinga, J. (1955). Homo Ludens: A Study of the Play Element in Culture. Boston: Beacon Press.

Hutchins, E. (1995). How a Cockpit Remembers its Speeds. *Cognitive Science, 19*(3), 265–288.

Hutchins, E., & Klausen, T. (1996). Distributed Cognition in an Airline Cockpit. In L. Resneck, R. Saljo, C. Potecorvo & B. Burge (Eds.), Tools, and Reasoning: Essays in Situated Cognition. Vienna, Austria.

Jacobson, M., & Spiro, R. (1993). Hypertext Learning Environments, Cognitive Flexibility, and the Transfer of Complex Knowledge. [Center for the Study of Reading.]. *Urbana (Caracas, Venezuela)*, IL.

Jenkins, H. (2004). Game Design as Narrative Architecture. In N. Wardrip-Fruin & P. Harrigan (Eds.), First Person: New Media as Story, Performance, Game. Cambridge, MA: MIT Press.

Jonassen, D., Ambruso, D., & Olesen, J. (1992). Designing hypertext on transfusion medicine using cognitive flexibility theory. *Journal of Educational Multimedia and Hypermedia, 1*(3), 309–322.

Jonsson, M., Tholander, J., & Fernaeus, Y. (2009). Setting the Stage - Embodied and Spatial Dimensions in Emerging Programming Practices. *Interacting with Computers, 21*(1-2), 117–124. doi:10.1016/j.intcom.2008.10.004

Jorgensen, A. (2004). *Marrying HCI/Usability and Computer Games: A Preliminary Look*. Paper presented at the Third Nordic conference on Human-Computer Interaction, Tampere, Finland.

Kirschner, P., Sweller, J., & Clark, R. (2006). Why Minimal Guidance During Instruction Does Not Work: An Analysis of the Failure of Constructivist, Discovery, Problem-Based, Experiential, and Inquiry-Based Teaching. *Educational Psychologist, 41*(2), 75–86. doi:10.1207/s15326985ep4102_1

Kirsh, D. (2006). Distributed Cognition: A Methodological Note. *Pragmatics & Cognition, 14*(2), 249–262. doi:10.1075/pc.14.2.06kir

Kirsh, D., & Maglio, P. (1994). On Distinguishing Epistemic from Pragmatic Action. *Cognitive Science, 18*(4), 513–549.

Koster, R. (2004). Theory of Fun for Game Design. Phoenix, AZ: Paraglyph.

Larkin, J. (1989). Display-Based Problem Solving. In D. Klahr & K. Kotovsky (Eds.), Complex Information Processing: The Impact of Herbert A. Simon. Hillsdale, NJ: Lawrence Erlbaum.

Limon, M. (2001). On the Cognitive Conflict as an Instructional Strategy for Conceptual Change: A Critical Appraisal. *Learning and Instruction, 11*(4-5), 357–380. doi:10.1016/S0959-4752(00)00037-2

Malone, T. W. (1981). Toward a theory of intrinsically motivating instruction. *Cognitive Science, 5*(4), 333–369.

Mayes, J., Draper, S., McGregor, A., & Oatley, K. (1988). Information flow in a user interface: the effect of experience and context on the recall of MacWrite screens. In D. M. Jones & R. Winder (Eds.), People and Computers IV. Cambridge, UK: Cambridge University Press.

McGill, T., & Volet, S. (1997). A Conceptual Framework for Analyzing Students' Knowledge of Programming. *Journal of Research on Computing in Education, 29*(3), 276–297.

Mezirow, J. (1978). Perspective Transformation. *Adult Education, 28*(2), 100–110. doi:10.1177/074171367802800202

Murray, J. (1997). Hamlet on the Holodeck: The Future of Narrative in Cyberspace. New York: The Free Press.

Oliver, K. (1997). *A Case-Based Pharmacy Environment: Cognitive Flexibility + Social Constructivism.* Paper presented at the ED-MEDIA/ED-TELECOM, Calgary, Canada.

Payne, S. (1991). Display-Based Action at the User Interface. *International Journal of Man-Machine Studies, 35*(3), 275–289. doi:10.1016/S0020-7373(05)80129-4

Piirainen-Marsh, A., & Tainio, L. (2009). Collaborative game-play as a site for participation and situated learning of a second language. *Scandinavian Journal of Educational Research, 53*(2), 167–183. doi:10.1080/00313830902757584

Prensky, M. (2004). Digital Game-Based Learning. New York: McGraw-Hill.

Raybourn, E. (2007). Applying Simulation Experience Design Methods to Creating Serious Game-Based Adaptive Training Systems. *Interacting with Computers, 19*(2), 206–214. doi:10.1016/j.intcom.2006.08.001

Rollings, A., & Morris, D. (2004). Game Architecture and Design: A New Edition. Berkeley, CA: New Riders Publishing.

Ruben, B. (1999). Simulations, Games and Experience-Based Learning: The Quest for a New Paradigm for Teaching and Learning. *Simulation & Gaming, 30*(4), 498–505. doi:10.1177/104687819903000409

Salen, K., & Zimmerman, E. (2004). Rules of Play: Game Design Fundamentals. Cambridge, MA: The MIT Press.

Sasse, M. A. (1997). *Eliciting and Describing User's Models of Computer Systems.* Unpublished Doctoral Thesis, University of Birmingham, Birmingham.

Scandura, J. M. (2003). Domain Specific Structural Analysis for Intelligent Tutoring Systems: Automatable Representation of Declarative, Procedural and Model-Based Knowledge with Relationships to Software Engineering. *Technology, Instruction. Cognition and Learning, 1,* 7–57.

Scandura, J. M. (2006). Abstract Syntax Tree (AST) infrastructure in problem solving research. *Technology, Instruction. Cognition and Learning, 3,* 1–13.

Schank, R., Fano, A., Bell, B., & Menachem, J. (1994). The Design of Goal-Based Scenarios. *Journal of the Learning Sciences, 3*(4), 305–345. doi:10.1207/s15327809jls0304_2

Schrader, P. G., & Lawless, K. A. (2008). Gamer Discretion Advised: How MMOG Players Determine the Quality and Usefulness of Online Resources. In K. McFerrin et al. (Eds.), Proceedings for the Society for Information Technology and Teacher Education (pp. 710-715). Chesapeake, VA: AACE.

Spiro, R., Feltovich, P., Jacobson, M., & Coulson, R. (1992). Cognitive Flexibility, Constructivism and Hypertext: Random Access Instruction for Advanced Knowledge Acquisition in Ill-Structured Domains. In T. M. Duffy & D. H. Jonassen (Eds.), Constructivism and the technology of instruction: A conversation. Hillsdale, NJ: Erlbaum.

Spiro, R., & Jehng, J. (1990). Cognitive Flexibility and Hypertext: Theory and Technology for the Nonlinear and Multidimensional Traversal of Complex Subject Matter. In D. Nix & R. Spiro (Eds.), Cognition, Education and Multimedia: Exploring Ideas in High Technology, (pp. 163-205). Hillsdale, NJ: Lawrence Erlbaum Associates.

Spiro, R., Vispoel, W., Schmitz, J., Samarapungavan, A., & Boerger, A. (1987). Knowledge Acquisition for Application: Cognitive Flexibility and Transfer in Complex Content Domains. In B. C. Britton, (Ed.), Executive Control Processes, (pp. 177-200). Hillsdale, NJ: Laurence Erlbaum Associates.

Squire, K. (2006). From content to context: Videogames as designed experience. *Educational Researcher*, *35*(8), 19–29. doi:10.3102/0013189X035008019

Squire, K., Barnett, M., Grant, J., & Higginbotham, T. (2004). *Electromagnetism supercharged!: learning physics with digital simulation games.* Paper presented at the Proceedings of the 6th international conference on Learning Sciences, Santa Monica, CA.

Steinkuehler, C. (2006). Why Game (Culture) Studies Now? *Games and Culture*, *1*(1), 97–102. doi:10.1177/1555412005281911

Taylor, P., & Carpenter, S. (2002). Inventively Linking: Teaching and Learning with Computer Hypertext. *Art Education*, *55*(4), 6–12. doi:10.2307/3193962

Van Merrienboer, J., Kirschner, P., & Kester, L. (2003). Taking the Load Off a Learner's Mind: Instructional Design for Complex Learning. *Educational Psychologist*, *38*(1), 5–13. doi:10.1207/S15326985EP3801_2

Van Merrienboer, J., & Sweller, J. (2005). Cognitive Load Theory and Complex Learning: Recent Developments and Future Directions. *Educational Psychology Review*, *17*(2), 147–177. doi:10.1007/s10648-005-3951-0

Vosniadou, S., & Brewer, W. (1987). Theories of Knowledge Restructuring in Development. *Review of Educational Research*, *57*(1), 51–67.

Wilson, M. (2002). Six Views of Embodied Cognition. *Psychonomic Bulletin & Review*, *9*(4), 625–636.

Wilson, R. (1997). Pointers, Codes, and Embodiment. *The Behavioral and Brain Sciences*, *20*(4), 757–758. doi:10.1017/S0140525X97421611

Wright, P., Fields, R., & Harrison, M. (2000). Analyzing Human-Computer Interaction as Distributed Cognition: The Resources Model. *Human-Computer Interaction*, *15*(1), 1–41. doi:10.1207/S15327051HCI1501_01

Young, M. (2003). An Ecological Psychology of Instructional Design. In D. Jonassen (Ed.), Handbook of Research on Educational Communications and Technology. Mahwah, NJ: Lawrence Erlbaum Associates, Inc.

Young, M. (2004). *An ecological description of video games in education.* Retrieved July 14, 2009, from http://web2.uconn.edu/myoung/EISTA04Proceed.pdf

Young, M., Barab, S., & Garrett, S. (2000). Agent as detector: An ecological psychology perspective on learning by perceiving-acting systems. In D. H. J. S. M. Land (Ed.), Theoretical foundations of learning environments (pp. 147-172). Mahwah, NJ: Erlbaum.

Zaphiris, P. & ang, C. S. (2007). HCI Issues in Computer Games. *Interacting with Computers*, *19*(2), 135–139. doi:10.1016/j.intcom.2006.08.007

Zhang, J. (1997). The Nature of External Representations in Problem Solving. *Cognitive Science*, *21*(2), 179–217.

Zhang, J., & Norman, D. (1994). Representations in Distributed Cognitive Tasks. *Cognitive Science*, *18*(1), 87–122.

Chapter 8
Designing Educational Games:
A Pedagogical Approach

Stephen Tang
Liverpool John Moores University, UK

Martin Hanneghan
Liverpool John Moores University, UK

ABSTRACT

Play has been an informal approach to teach young ones the skills of survival for centuries. With advancements in computing technology, many researchers believe that computer games[1] can be used as a viable teaching and learning tool to enhance a student's learning. It is important that the educational content of these games is well designed with meaningful game-play based on pedagogically sound theories to ensure constructive learning. This chapter features theoretical aspects of game design from a pedagogical perspective. It serves as a useful guide for educational game designers to design better educational games for use in game-based learning. The chapter provides a brief overview of educational games and game-based learning before highlighting theories of learning that are relevant to educational games. Selected theories of learning are then integrated into conventional game design practices to produce a set of guidelines for educational games design.

INTRODUCTION

Computer gaming is an extremely popular trend among youth in the 21st century (Pearce, 2006) yet is often seen as a concern by the general public with the potential harm it may introduce based on studies of video gaming effects in the 1980's and 1990's. But should those concerns neglect the educational potential of computer games? Computer games are able to generate enormous levels of motiva-

DOI: 10.4018/978-1-61520-781-7.ch008

tional drive for game players as opposed to formal classes which are perceived as "boring" or rather "dry" (BECTa, 2006; Prensky, 2002). The energy that game players often invest for computer games is phenomenal. Though some may comment that aspects of learning in computer games may not be suitable for academic learning, e.g. (Adams, 2005), nevertheless exploiting such technology to aid learning is still possible when used appropriately.

Educational games, also known as *instructional games*, take advantage of gaming principles and technologies to create educational content. Early versions of educational games were often incarnations of interactive multimedia courseware that incorporated simple mini-games such as puzzles and memory games as rewards attempting to inject fun into learning (albeit often developed by inexperienced educational game designers). Most educational games were developed for children who have lower expectations of interactive content as compared to teenagers and adults. Financial and technological constraints presented major barriers to production of high quality educational games that could meet teenage and adult expectations, and such constraints still exist today. Hence there is a common misconception that educational games are simply for children.

In actual fact, there are a number of educational games for adults aimed mainly in medical (Moreno-Ger, Blesius, Currier, Sierra, & Fernández-Manjón, 2008) and business education (Faria, 1998). *Training simulators* (a term more familiar to the adult population) simulate real-world experience intended for development of skills where the challenges presented accurately replicate real-world scenarios requiring the user to overcome problems using realistic procedural acts defined through hardware interfaces. Training simulators are most popular in the fields of aviation (Telfer, 1993), medicine (Colt, Crawford, & III, 2001) and military applications (Nieborg, 2004). *Serious games* is a more recent term used for representing software applications that employ gaming principles and technologies for non-entertainment purposes including education and training (Sawyer & Smith, 2008; Zyda, 2005).

Designing games with good game-play is not a science or an art, but often quoted as a 'craft' requiring skills to engage and immerse game players in a realistic setting while also encouraging replayability. Game designers are brilliant at creating "hooks" to engage gamers, but in the context of game-based learning it is important to emphasize the aspects of academic value that can develop skills that are useful to the learner. This chapter presents a general model and guidelines for designing educational games by incorporating theories of learning into games design practices. Variables influencing learning and a selection of theories of learning related to educational games design are described before being mapped to elements of game design to form guidelines for designing educational games. Some conclusions from this work are presented at the end of this chapter.

VARIABLES INFLUENCING LEARNING

Learning is generally perceived as the process of acquiring new knowledge which often takes place in a formal classroom setting. However, learning can also take place informally after school hours through interactions with peers and the surrounding environment making learning a constant process. The ability to learn and adapt are crucial in our daily lives and has a direct relationship with human performance when executing tasks. Learning is enriched us with knowledge and skills gained through experience from direct and indirect interaction with the subject matter which proves useful in future similar events and scenarios.

Learning as a cognitive process is affected by a number of psychological factors which can be categorised as internal or external. Internal factors are factors originated by the learner them self and are closely related to the functioning of the human mind and emotions (Bransford, L., & Crocking, 1999). External factors can be those that are sourced from teachers, peers or the environment for example (Hattie, 2005). Some internal factors can be controlled using appropriate pedagogy to ensure learners achieve the learning objectives associated to a lesson, while others require discipline, dedication and effort from learners. Learning requires full commitment from participants as learners themselves account for 50% variance of achievement, whereas the teacher (amongst the external factors) contribute to a learner's achievement with a variance of 30% (Hattie, 2005).

It is important to recognise that teachers and effective teaching strategies can impact learning. Creemers (1994) identified nine variables relating to teaching instruction as *advance organisers*; *evaluation*; *feedback*; *corrective instruction*; *mastery learning*; *ability grouping*; *homework*; *clarity of presentation* and *questioning*. Meta-analysis on teaching and learning can also provide additional pointers on variables that influence learning. Hattie (2003) in his study identified 33 variables. Amongst the additional variables that provide a positive effect on learning are *quality of instruction; class environment; challenge of goals*; *peer tutoring; teaching style; peer effects*; *simulation and games*; *computer-assisted instruction*; *testing*; *instructional media*; *programmed instruction*; *audio-visual aids*; *individualisation* and *behavioural objective*. These influential variables are essential inputs for designing educational games that can maximise the positive effect on learners.

In a recent quantitative meta-analysis on computer games as learning tools, 35 of the 65 studies reported that computer games have significant positive effects on learning, 17 with mixed results, 12 indicated similar effects to conventional instruction and one study reported otherwise (Ke, 2009). It is not surprising that the correlation between computer games and learning has increased the effect size from 0.34 (Hattie, 2003) to 2.87 (Marzano, 2009) as computer games have emerged as popular culture among the multimedia generation. These findings affirm the claims by supporters of game-based learning that computer games have tremendous potential for positive learning. However, the extent of this impact is still very much dependent on the abilities of educational game designers.

THEORIES OF LEARNING

Applications of theories of learning often relate to instructional design concerned with research and theory about instructional strategies and the process of developing and implementing those strategies. In the context of designing game-based learning content, it is important that educational games are developed using pedagogically sound theories that are relevant to instructional design. For brevity we will therefore focus only on theories of learning which are deemed useful in designing educational games.

SHAPING LEARNERS' BEHAVIOUR

A crucial part of learning is to shape the learner's behaviour by encoding knowledge of cause and effect. *Behaviourism* is built upon the belief that learners can be conditioned to make a response in which learning is perceived as the result of association forming between stimuli and responses. Thorndike's 'Law of Effect' (Thorndike, 1933) suggests that stimulus and response can be strengthened through rewards and can, over time, become habitual. Conversely, the connection between stimulus and response is weakened when discomfort is experienced. Skinner's 'Operant Conditioning theory' (Skinner, 1935) states that learners can be conditioned to respond to stimulus through reinforcement, and over time continue to behave as such even when the stimuli is not present.

Hull's 'Drive Reduction theory' (1951) focuses more on human behaviour and argues that motivation is essential in order for responses to occur. It suggests that responses can become habitual when the stimuli and response cycle is reinforced reducing the latency of such responses. His framework can be closely tied with Maslow's 'Hierarchy of Needs theory' (Maslow, 1946) and the work of Thorndike and Skinner.

Weiner's 'Attribution theory' (1979) extends the concepts of motivation and his findings on attributions to achievement; ability, effort, task difficulty and luck (luck is interpreted as being at the right place in right time and the right execution of action) is also worthy of mentioning in this chapter.

ADAPTING TO LEARNERS' COGNITIVE NEEDS

Human cognition is a combination of short-term and long-term memory. Short-term memory provides the working memory for cognitive processing, while long-term memory stores cognitive constructs which are composed of multiple elements of information grouped into one single representation. Miller's 'Information Processing theory' (2003) presents an interesting principle on the limitation of a human's cognitive capacity reporting that an average human can remember between five to nine elements of information in his infamous 'seven ± two' theory. It explains why humans cluster elements of information to address the capacity of short-term memory before encoding it permanently into the long-term memory.

Sweller's 'Cognitive Load theory' (1994) focuses on the interaction between information structure and working memory in relation to learning. It suggests that cognitive load should be kept to a minimum in the learning process for optimal learning through elimination of working memory load for tasks which can be completed physically, usage of worked examples of problem solving methods and usage of audio and visual components to increase working memory capacity.

In designing learner-oriented instructional material for computer-based training, Carroll's 'Minimalism theory' (1998) suggests that all learning tasks should be meaningful, interactive, contain error recognition and be relevant to the real-world scenario.

AN ENVIRONMENT FOR KNOWLEDGE CONSTRUCTION

Constructivists view learning as a process of knowledge construction through active participation. Bruner's 'Constructivist theory' (1960) presents a general framework to many other constructivists' work proposing that a theory of instruction should address four major aspects: predisposition towards learning; approaches to structure knowledge for ease of understanding; methods of presenting learning material; and nature of rewards and punishment. This was the basis for 'Discovery Learning' which instructs learners to solve situational problems based on their experience and knowledge (Bruner, 1961). The approach encourages learners to discover the facts and relationships themselves through interactions with the environment in search for solutions for the given problems.

Gagne's 'Conditions of Learning theory' (1970) advocates that effective learning takes place when learners are exposed to the right conditions. The theory proposes nine instructional events and corresponding cognitive processes: (i) *gaining attention* (reception); (ii) *informing learners of the objective* (expectancy); (iii) *stimulate recall of prior learning* (retrieval); (iv) *presenting the stimulus* (selective perception); (v) *providing learning guidance* (semantic encoding); (vi) *eliciting performance* (responding); (vii) *providing feedback* (reinforcement); (viii) *assessing performance* (retrieval); and (ix) *enhancing retention and transfer* (generalization) to facilitate learning at various levels.

This work has a similar objective to Reigluth's 'Elaboration theory' (1980) which postulates that instructions should be organised with increasing complexity for optimal learning. Sequencing instructions promotes semantic development allowing subsequent ideas to be incorporated. The 'Elaboration theory' proposes seven major strategy components: (i) *an elaborative sequence*; (ii) *learning prerequisite sequences*; (iii) *summary*; (iv) *synthesis*; (v) *analogies*; (vi) *cognitive strategies* and (vii) *learner control*.

Bloom's 'Taxonomy of Educational Objectives' (1956) categorises cognitive development into six major components: (i) *knowledge*; (ii) *comprehension*; (iii) *application*; (iv) *analysis*; (v) *synthesis* and (vi) *evaluation*. Learning can also be clustered into affective and psychomotor domains. Learning in the affective domain focuses on development of emotions and can be categorised into (i) *receiving phenomena*; (ii) *responding to phenomena*; (iii) *valuing*; (iv) *organization* and (v) *internalising values* (Krathwohl, Bloom, & Masia, 1964). The psychomotor domain focuses on development of physical movement and coordination which can be measured in quality of execution. Learning in such a domain can be categorised in increasing behaviour complexity: (i) *perception*; (ii) *readiness*; (iii) *guided response*; (iv) *mechanism*; (v) *complex overt response*; (vi) *adaptation* and (vii) *origination* (Simpson, 1972).

Anderson & Krathwohl et. al. (2000) redefine Bloom's Taxonomy by renaming and reorganizing the cognitive processes as (i) *remember*; (ii) *understand*; (iii) *apply*; (iv) *analyse*; (v) *evaluate* and (vi) *create* which are simpler to understand and apply. In addition, the revision also includes dimensions of knowledge categorised into *factual*, *conceptual*, *procedural* and *meta-cognitive* which are used with cognitive processes to categorise knowledge comprehensively.

Marzano & Kendall's 'New Taxonomy of Educational Objectives' (2006) is a comprehensive and more recent revision of Bloom's work. Based on Bloom's work, the new taxonomy organises the six levels of processing as: (i) *retrieval*; (ii) *comprehension*; (iii) *analysis*; (iv) *knowledge utilization*; (v) *meta-cognitive system*; (vi) *self system*. These are grouped into three systems of thought: the cognitive system (level 1 to level 4), the meta-cognitive system (level 5) and the self system (level 6). Each level correlates with different knowledge domains – *information*, *mental procedures* and *psychomotor procedures*.

LEARNING IN ADULTHOOD

Adult learning is mostly supported by theories on experiential learning. Knowles' 'Andragogy theory' (1996) notes that adults should be informed of the learning objectives and that learning should be problem-centred reflecting current issues. More importantly, he suggested that adults should learn experientially.

Kolb's 'Learning Cycle theory' (1984) presents a useful descriptive model of the adult experiential learning process known to many educators at the tertiary level. The model suggests that the adult learning process is a cycle of four stages better described as (i) *Concrete Experience*; (ii) *Reflective Observation*; (iii) *Abstract Conceptualization*; and (iv) *Active Experimentation*. The model was then adopted by Honey and Mumford (1982) in their proposal of a typology of learners that distinctively describes the learning styles in each stage.

EDUCATIONAL GAMES DESIGN

Designing computer games is a creative and innovative process of imagining and describing the 'game world' in a detailed manner. There are two approaches employed for designing educational games: *instructor* where the designer places education as a high priority; and *entertainer* where the designer places entertainment as a high priority. There have been several proposals on designing educational games from the *instructor* perspective focusing on various aspects of educational games:

- Malone (1980) in his early thoughts of designing educational games presented interesting guidelines through his study of fun by identifying the essential characteristics of a good computer game as *challenge*, *fantasy* and *curiosity*.
- Prensky (2001) in his well-received book "Digital Game-based Learning" shares his research findings on types of learning and possible game styles.
- Pivec, Dziabenko and Schinnerl (2003) proposed six steps of educational game design as: (i) *determine the pedagogical*

approach; (ii) *situate the task in a model world*; (iii) *elaborate the details*; (iv) *incorporate underlying pedagogical support*; (v) *map learning activities to interface actions*; and (vi) *map learning concepts to interface objects*.

- Paras and Bizzocchi's (2005) propose an integrated model for educational games design promoting Csikszentmihalyi's (1991) 'Flow theory' as the bridge for understanding and implementing motivation through play.
- Denis and Jouvelot's (2005) motivation-driven educational game design principles namely (i) *reify values into rules*; (ii) *give power*; (iii) *tune usability*; (iv) *derail the game-play*; and (v) *favour communication* centred on Ryan and Deci's (2000) 'Self Determination Theory'.
- Fisch (2005) emphasises the importance of *making educational content an integral part of game-play*, *relating game challenges to learning*, *providing feedback* and *creating linkages for offline learning* as considerations for making educational games educational.

These proposals are certainly useful in designing educational games. Building upon the existing knowledge in this domain, this section compiles the best practices on educational games design and presents insights on educational game design based on the theories of learning introduced earlier from both entertainer and instructor perspectives.

ELEMENTS OF PEDAGOGY IN EDUCATIONAL GAMES

Before delving into models and guidelines for designing educational games, it is important to identify and understand the elements of pedagogy within educational games. Studies on the various aspects of computer games have provided enough information to identify the pedagogic elements in educational games that could be used as learning subjects. These pedagogic elements exist in educational games in the form of (i) *the properties and behaviour of in-game components*; (ii) *the relationships between in-game components*; and (iii) *the solving of problems in the scenario defined* (Tang, Hanneghan, & El-Rhalibi, 2007). The following subsections describe and map each pedagogy element previously mentioned to the 'Taxonomy of Educational Objectives' in each learning domain. This is offered as an aid to teachers for defining assessable learning objectives and designing suitable learning activities in educational games. In this chapter, Anderson & Krathwohl *et. al.*'s taxonomy for cognitive domain is favoured over Marzano & Kendell's for its simplicity and relation to the widely practiced Bloom's taxonomy (See Figure 1).

Properties and Behaviours of In-Game Components

Actors and objects, as in-game components represented in educational games, are valid subjects for learning. Learners can learn by simply observing the properties of these in-game components that are presented visually and aurally. Learners can also interact with these in-game components to learn about the physical and cognitive behaviour possessed by these in-game components. The amount of knowledge extracted from these in-game components depends on the detail provided within the actors' and objects' identity. Some classes of actors can be programmed with the ability to converse with other actors through dialogue to guide or direct learners. The content of this dialogue can be presented aurally or visually by using user interface components. Learning about the properties and behaviours of actors and objects allows learners to develop an understanding toward these in-game components and relationships between the encoded properties and behaviours. The properties and behaviour of

Figure 1. Pedagogy elements in educational games organised in taxonomy of educational objectives in cognitive, affective and psychomotor domains

Elements of Pedagogy in Educational Games	Cognitive Domain	Affective Domain	Psychomotor Domain	
Tasks and Problems in Scenario	Create Evaluate Analyse Apply	Internalising Values Organization	Origination Adaptation Complex Overt Response Mechanism Guided Response	Difficulty
Relationship of in-game components	Understand	Valuing Responding to Phenomena	Set	
Properties of in-game components	Remember	Receiving Phenomena	Perception	

in-game components are pedagogy elements can be assessed using the *'remember'* cognitive process. It can also be assessed in the affective and psychomotor domains as *'receiving phenomena'* and *'perception'* respectively.

Relationship between In-Game Components

Learning about the properties and behaviours of in-game actors and objects allows learners to classify these into their distinctive classes and subsequently develop knowledge of understanding of the relationships that are defined among actors and objects. These relationships can be learned by observing the cause and effect of an interaction. Every action taken by the learner is associated with a meaningful response that can be represented visually or aurally (or both) to foster construction of knowledge. Interacting with in-game components can help learners to develop knowledge and promote understanding of the usage of the real-world equivalents of these in-game components in solving problems. The relationship between in-game components can also help learners to develop greater understanding toward actors and objects observable via emergent properties that are introduced through interactions. Emergent properties are noticeable once learners have developed an understanding of the relation-

ships and applications of the collection of parts as a combined whole. Problem semantics defined through relationships in educational games are assessable via the *understanding, responding to phenomena* and *valuing* categories in the affective domain, and *set* category in the psychomotor domain.

Tasks and Problems in a Given Scenario

Performing tasks and solving problems interactively in a scenario staged by appropriate domain experts provides learners with the cognitive, affective and psychomotor challenges at a higher level in the taxonomy of educational objectives. Tasks are direct interactions with in-game components that serve a specific purpose. Performing a task in an educational game requires the learner to have knowledge of the properties and behaviour of the in-game components involved and the relationships that exist between these components. Defining and arranging a set of tasks to cognitively challenge learners is the essence of designing problems in educational games. These problems can be designed to reflect educational objectives that require learners to perform *analysis, application, evaluation* or *creation* in order to complete the tasks assigned. Tasks can be combined to form complex problems in a defined scenario.

Tasks are measurable interactions and therefore problems presented to learners are also assessable. Performing tasks and solving problems are learning activities that help in building learners' experience and cognitive skills when approaching similar problems in the real world. An example of a real-world task might be demonstration of knowledge of safe handling of a certain chemical or operating a machine correctly in the virtual environment. Social problems in the scenario can be assessed also through the affective domain requiring learners to organise values in priority when resolving conflicts and demonstration of internalised values when similar social problems arise. In the psychomotor domain learners can be assessed on *mechanism*, *complex overt response*, *adaptation* and *origination* of actions to perform the given tasks or solve a problem. Some of these categories are often best assessed on specific hardware interfaces such as a steering wheel, joystick or other specialised controllers.

EDUCATIONAL GAME DESIGN METHODOLOGY

Designing computer games is a process of (1) imagining the game; (2) defining the way it works; (3) describing the elements that construct the game; and (4) communicating the information to the development team. Computer games often begin life either as a genuinely novel game idea, technology-driven concept or based upon existing intellectual property (IP) from movies, comics and novels. Designing educational games differs greatly from conventional game design process because it principally involves pedagogy. Teachers often begin by defining learning objectives or learning outcomes (depending on the adopted instructional design model) when designing lessons rather than applying mechanisms that promote fun (Kelly, et al., 2007). Topics are then identified and structured, and relevant learning activities are devised to complement.

When designing educational games, there is a need to adopt a hybrid game design methodology that infuses activities from instructional design beginning with the definition of learning objectives. Rules and game-play are then designed to support the learning objectives but yet remain interesting to captivate learner, and hence the need to place education first and entertainment second. These differences in approach require close collaboration between teachers and the game design team during the process of educational game design and often require a number of iterations (involving various stages of design, rapid prototyping, play-testing and revision) before it is released for use (Kelly, et al., 2007). These measures are taken to ensure that actual learning takes place within educational games. Building on Morrison, Ross and Kemp's (2006) model of instructional design plan for designing learning software, an educational game design methodology is presented in Figure 2.

The methodology consists of thirteen activities that are grouped into three phases; *plan*, *prototype* and *finalise*. In the planning phase, teachers are expected to define the learning objectives and design goals, understand the learners, identify the learning activities, sequence it and design a story to set the scene for the educational game and to link the learning activities defined. Planning activities are similar to early phases of instructional planning and are carried out by the teacher with the game designer (although this may in fact be the same person!) and the development team in building working prototypes of the game levels (where each level may form a specific problem for the end-user). During the prototyping phase, the development team will be involved in designing details of the game level, prototyping, evaluating and refining the game level. If required, they may go through the design activities again to make necessary adjustments so as to meet the learning objectives and design goals defined or to further satisfy the learners' needs. It is best to have the prototyped game level play-tested by a focus group as part of the evaluation process. Once all game

Figure 2. Educational game design methodology

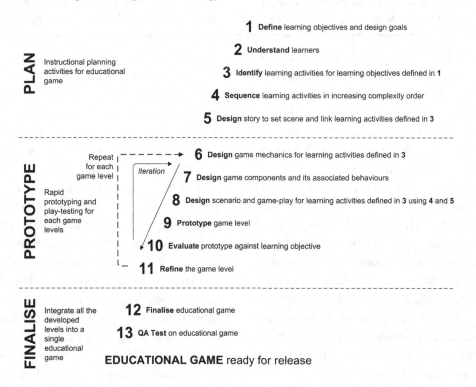

levels are completed, the complete game can then be finalised and tested against quality parameters before its final release.

DESIGN GUIDELINES FOR EDUCATIONAL GAMES

Complementing the educational game design methodology is a set of design guidelines to help design better educational games with pedagogy in mind while still maintaining the element of entertainment. These guidelines focus on four core areas in educational game design namely: *game-play and challenges*; *game structure*; *embedding pedagogic content*; and *motivational design*.

Game-Play with Embedded Pedagogy

Play can be regarded as an activity having its rules constantly under negotiation. In game design, designers often regard game-play as series of goal-directed activities with interesting choices designed for the purpose of enjoyment. Educational game designers however should design game-play as meaningful activities derived from the practice of a particular knowledge domain. The semantics of such activities can be derived from the relationships between the available actions and responses present within the game and should be discernible and integrated into the larger context of a game (Salen & Zimmerman,

2003). Such a proposal is not meant to restrict the designer's creativity, but rather issues a plea to them not to take short-cuts in designing such activities, for example by blending "hack and slash" or "shoot-em up" genres into educational games. Although studies shows that game players are aware of the consequences of violent and irresponsible acts in real-life (Dawson, Cragg, Taylor, & Toombs, 2007), such game-play activities may not be appropriate for educating learners in many domains. Instead designers should think of innovative ways to maximise the "education factor" within educational games. There are various ways to introduce "fun" experiences to game players; it does not necessarily mean that design choices should be irresponsible or mere fantasy. Each interesting choice in the game can also be designed with responsibilities that actions taken within the game world will be able to educate game players about knowledge and also ethical values in the real world (Sicart, 2005).

To create game-play adhering to such a context we propose the following guidelines:

- Activities should be in line with defined learning objectives and assessable.
- Activities should be of increasing difficulty order and achievable.
- Activities should be a form of intellectual exercise (or psychomotor challenge if challenges are meant for assessing the psychomotor domain) with minimal abstraction.
- Activities should be applicable and readily transferable to a real world scenario.
- Activities should be carefully balanced and achievement should be based on Weiner's 'Attribution Theory' rather than predestined winning.
- Learners should be given feedback (either in the form of positive or negative reinforcement or rewards) to assist in success and error recognition.

Challenge in computer games is important as it invites participants to be involved in an action or series of actions that can distinctively justify their superiority in mastering it. As challenges are part of game-playing, challenges should be tied closely with the defined activities. Challenges can be either *pure* or *applied*, each requiring different approaches to solve the problems expressed therein (see Table 1 below). A more detailed description of the challenges presented in Table 1 is described in (Rollings & Adams, 2003).

Challenges designed for educational games should be relevant to the learning objectives to elicit meaningful game-play. More importantly these challenges should be tied closely with the educational content and emphasize that overcoming these challenges requires mastery over the learning content presented. Though most challenges are applicable in defining engaging game-play, not all are necessarily suitable for assessing all categories of the learning domain. It is entirely up to designers to design the most appropriate type of challenge to assess the desired learning objectives and this may require some revision after user-testing before it can be deemed educationally suitable.

One of the simplest forms of cognitive challenge, used to test learners' ability to remember factual information embedded within storytelling or game-play, is the memory-based challenge.

Table 1. Forms of Pure and Applied Challenges (Rollings & Adams, 2003)

Pure Challenges	Applied Challenges
Logic and Inference Challenges	Races
Lateral Thinking Challenges	Puzzles
Memory Challenges	Exploration
Intelligence-Based Challenges	Conflict
Knowledge-Based Challenges	Economies
Pattern Recognition Challenges	Conceptual Challenges
Moral Challenges	
Spatial Awareness Challenges	
Coordination Challenges	
Reflex Challenges	
Physical Challenges	

For example, a challenge can be designed to be a progression barrier (i.e. a roadblock or assessment point) that requires learners to collect a list of items in which the answer is presented in the cut-scene prior to the game-play. A challenge can also incorporate more than one applied or pure challenge to add complexity and depth. For example, the task can be made more complex and interesting by requiring the learner to interact with various non-player characters in order to obtain each item while possibly incorporating trading of existing items to obtain further items.

For challenges that require a higher level of cognition, educational game designers can incorporate tasks that require learners to devise a solution for a given purpose. Mind Rover[2], an intelligent robot simulation, is an example of a computer game that presents lateral-thinking challenges. The learner takes the role of a researcher to program the intelligence of robotic vehicles to race around tracks and battle against other robotic vehicles.

The affective domain can also be tested through moral challenges and conflict. These different levels may not be directly assessable in all games but quite often present themselves in multiplayer modes which invite collaboration between game players and promote development of social values during post-game sessions.

As for the psychomotor domains reflex challenges are the simplest form of challenges available for designers to stimulate a game player's sensory mechanism. Races and coordination challenges are suitable for exercising higher levels of the psychomotor domain that involve programmed responses, responding to different circumstances and creation of a new regime for optimal response. Challenges involving physical movements are now becoming increasingly popular thanks to innovative input technologies such as the Nintendo WiiMote and WiiFit, the Apple iPhone, the Sony Sixaxis controller and PlayStation Eye camera system.

A Structure for Integrated Learning

Game structure represents the main construct of a computer game and is usually organised in the form of levels which further broken down into achievable objectives within the game scenario. Such a structure is relevant, but it should be presented in an environment that can assist knowledge construction. In many commercial computer games, it is noticeable that levels are ordered in increasing difficulty, organised in a hierarchical or linear structure and often driven by storytelling. An ideal structure for educational games should depict the characteristics from well-designed commercial computer games to include spaces for pedagogies such as *active learning*, *experiential learning*, *problem-based learning* and *situated learning*. Based on the theories of learning by Gagne, Reigluth and Kolb, an ideal educational game structure is proposed in Figure 3.

The proposed structure closely resembles that of well-designed computer games but aims at the presentation of learning material in a guided and elaborative manner closely integrated with meaningful activities introduced as a form of play. It organises game events into a series of instructional events for learning to take place within educational games. These events are grouped as segments of a game, similar in concept to chapters in a book. Events are made up of game elements such as the game screen and cut scene (or animated information segment) to attract the learner's attention, inform of learning objectives, link learners to previous lessons and provide summative feedback on the learner's performance. The game scenario, the core element in a computer game, provides a stage for other instructional events such as presentation of stimuli to learners, assessment of a learner's performance and providing learners with guidance and feedback during game-play. Tutorials and levels each represent a different form of learning activity within a game scenario. A tutorial provides the learner with guidance while a level is used for assessment of and transfer of

Figure 3. An integrated learning structure for educational games

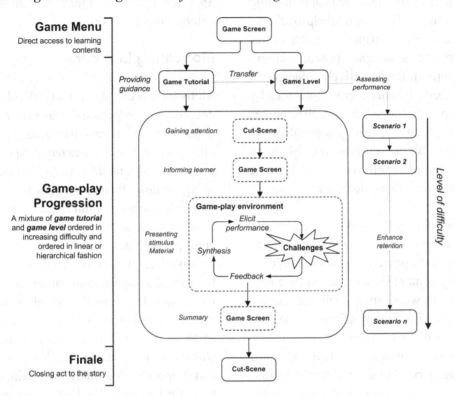

knowledge or skills. Different forms of challenge can be used to assess the different forms of learning outcome associated with the scenario. Similar challenges can be assessed in subsequent levels to enhance retention of knowledge and fine-tune skill acquisition. Scenarios presented during a tutorial or level should be organised in increasing difficulty order as an attempt to introduce 'scaffolding' or a learning growth mechanism. As the design process continues, game-play spaces can be identified and coupled with relevant learning material making learning more integrated within educational games rather than isolated using a so-called 'blended learning' approach.

Embedding Pedagogic Content

One of the goals of exploiting computer games as a learning tool is to present educational materials within the familiar gaming environment.

Factual information, descriptive information and scenarios are common forms of knowledge that need to be conveyed to learners. Learning content in educational games should be congruent with any lesson given in the event that the educational game is used as a support mechanism either in a classroom setting or during private study. In this context, game-play is used as an exercise to revise and practice the knowledge in a simulated environment to enhance understanding or to provide reinforcement. Rather than embed an entire 'textbook' into an educational game, Fisch (2005) proposes that designers should attempt to create linkages for offline learning by means of testing concepts or by requiring game players to search for information which is not provided within the game itself. Although such an approach may reduce the degree of immersion in educational games, it is necessary to have game players apply what they have learnt in the classroom within educational games to enhance their understanding in the subjects taught. This can then help to achieve the primary objective of using computer games as a medium to educate learners with fun and meaningful activities. Alternatively, educational games can embed all the necessary information by linking game players to appropriate web resources where this information is readily accessible.

To reiterate this we propose the following guidelines as part of our efforts to make learning material more accessible to learners:

- Learning content should be embedded within the storytelling and narrative components of the game whenever possible.
- Learning content should use multiple representations where appropriate (i.e. use auditory and visual information) and be concise but avoid oversimplification.
- Learning content should contain challenges allowing learners to apply acquired knowledge in the present (and any future unseen) scenario and thus increase retention of the concepts therein.
- Learning content should not have more than seven key concepts in order to aid information recall.

Extending the discussion on pedagogic content in educational games is the issue pertaining to the quality of graphics both in art and in technology suitable for educational games. The "graphics versus game-play" debate is a long-standing argument. A game with stunning graphics attracts game players but poor game-play is often equated with poor replayability. In addition, poor graphics quality may affect the learner's first impressions of the whole offering thereby discouraging their commitment to invest time in the game. In the context of educational games however, game-play should be given higher priority and graphics should be used merely for visualisation purposes. This is often born out of necessity since the development budgets for educational games

are often a fraction of that spent on commercial entertainment software.

Motivating Learners

Motivation is the 'drive' that individuals experience either for personal reasons or to receive external rewards (or avoid external punishments). Highly motivated learners tend to spend a greater proportion of time devoted to learning a subject area. It follows then that we should aim to better motivate learners within the context of an educational game to promote deeper learning of the concepts within.

Bixler (2006), in his studies of motivation in relation to educational games, compared four motivational frameworks, namely Keller's ARCS Model; Wlodkowski's Time Continuum Model of Motivation and Motivational Framework for Culturally Responsive Teaching; and Malone and Lepper's Taxonomy of Intrinsic Motivations for Learning. His findings reveal common motivational constructs such as: (i) *obtain and sustain the learners' attention*; (ii) *relate learning objectives to learners*; (iii) *develop the learners' competency in subject area*; and (iv) *provide control to learners in achieving the learning objectives*. Further evidence can be found in the motivational frameworks within the theories of learning proposed by Gagne and Reigluth. Malone and Lepper (1987) in their framework state individuals can be motivated by providing the right *challenge*, arousing their *curiosity*, providing the *controls* and creating a *fantasy* to aid learners in experiencing well-deserved satisfaction over achievements within the virtual world. *Competition, cooperation* and *recognition* are parameters affecting motivation on the intrapersonal level defined in the framework.

In practice game designers introduce events that hold the game player's interest through creative storytelling or artwork and attempt to create psychological proximity to immerse game players into the game (Schell, 2005). This can be achieved via the conceptual design of the virtual world, the user interface, the chosen avatar (or player and non-player characters within the game world) and the storyline. Story and narrative provides access to degrees of awareness by manipulating a game player's abilities such as imagination, empathy and focus in the virtual world. Immersion can be divided into three stages; *engagement, engrossment* and *total immersion* (Brown & Cairns, 2004). When game players are totally immersed, they tend to ignore their physical surroundings and focus only on the game-play. Well-designed and balanced game-play often provides game players the optimal experience described by Csíkszentmihályi (1991) as *flow* which is the ultimate goal of motivated game-play. A game player who is experiencing flow is focussed, energised and committed to complete the challenges presented.

Educational game designers should consider the following further guidelines which are relevant in designing motivation in educational games.

- Complex activities designed should be made of smaller, achievable tasks to guide learners in achieving the main objective.
- The story and narrative used should be closely related to common cases in the real world.

The user interface also plays an important role in motivation. In addition to being thematic, the user interface should also be designed to be functional to provide learners the control required in the virtual environment to accomplish the tasks assigned.

- Controls should be made simple and natural to reduce the learning barrier in using computer games as a medium for learning.
- Graphical User Interface (GUI) components should be grouped logically with each group not exceeding seven items to aid learners in remembering.

CONCLUSION

Educational games are commonly used at home as learning aids to encourage children to learn or as a computer-aided learning tool in the case of adult learner. In the past, both these approaches have gained significant support from academia, government and industry bodies. With the current generation of 'digital natives' being exposed to interactive entertainment during childhood years (Rideout, Vandewater, & Wartella, 2003) and being brought up in the digital era, it is widely thought that game-based learning will become a preferred method of learning for many of this generation in the future. Although game-based learning has some of the accepted and desirable learning approaches embedded such as active learning, experiential learning, situated learning and problem-based learning (Tang, Martin Hanneghan, & El-Rhalibi, 2009), it should be pointed out that it is not a panacea. Educational games are a viable alternative to existing computer-aided learning technologies that can assist in persuading and encouraging digital natives to acquire knowledge. This new medium can make learning more effective since the approach is more relevant to this particular target group's lifestyle. There are still substantial barriers for teachers (technical, pedagogical and social) to convince this group to immerse themselves in actual game-based learning. Therefore it is important that educational games are designed with pedagogically sound theories to encourage further learning when disconnected from the virtual learning environment. The effect video gaming has on society should not be ignored; instead such knowledge should be used to help channel appropriate energy and resources to promote learning adaptable to the learning styles of today's entertainment-generation.

REFERENCES

Adams, E. (2005). *Educational Games Don't Have to Stink!* Retrieved 31 January, 2009, from http://www.gamasutra.com/features/20050126/adams_01.shtml

Anderson, L. W., Krathwohl, D. R., Airasian, P. W., Cruikshank, K. A., Mayer, R. E., Pintrich, P. R., et al. (2000). A Taxonomy for Learning, Teaching, and Assessing: A Revision of Bloom's Taxonomy of Educational Objectives (2nd ed.). Boston: Allyn & Bacon.

BECTa. (2006). *Computer Games in Education: Findings Report.* Retrieved 19 February, 2008, from http://partners.becta.org.uk/index.php?section=rh&rid=13595

Bixler, B. (2006). *Games and Motivation: Implications for Instructional Design.* Paper presented at the 2006 NMC Summer Conference.

Bloom, B. S. (1956). Taxonomy of Educational Objectives, Handbook I: The Cognitive Domain. New York: David McKay Co. Inc.

Bransford, J. D. L., B. A., & Crocking, R. R. (1999). How People Learn: Brain, Mind, Experience, and School. Washington, DC: National Academic Press.

Brown, E., & Cairns, P. (2004). *A grounded investigation of game immersion.* Paper presented at the Conference on Human Factors in Computing Systems.

Bruner, J. S. (1960). The Process of Education. Cambridge, MA: Harvard University Press.

Bruner, J. S. (1961). The act of discovery. *Harvard Educational Review, 31*(1), 21–32.

Carroll, J. M. (Ed.). (1998). Minimalism Beyond the Nurnberg Funnel (Technical Communication, Multimedia and Information Systems). Cambridge, MA: MIT Press.

Colt, H. G., & Crawford, S. W., & III, O. G. (2001). Virtual Reality Bronchoscopy Simulation*: A Revolution in Procedural Training. *Chest, 120*(4), 1333–1339. doi:10.1378/chest.120.4.1333

Creemers, B. P. M. (1994). The Effective Classroom. London: Cassell.

Csíkszentmihályi, M. (1991). Flow: The Psychology of Optimal Experience. New York: Harper Perennial.

Dawson, C. R., Cragg, A., Taylor, C., & Toombs, B. (2007). Video Games Research to improve understanding of what players enjoy about video games, and to explain their preferences for particular games. London: British Board of Film Classification (BBFC).

Denis, G., & Jouvelot, P. (2005). *Motivation-Driven Educational Game Design: Applying Best Practice to Music Education.* Paper presented at the Advances in Computer Entertainment (ACE) 2005.

Faria, A. J. (1998). Business Simulation Games: Current Usage Levels - An Update. *Simulation & Gaming, 29*(3), 295–308. doi:10.1177/1046878198293002

Fisch, S. M. (2005). *Making Educational Computer Games "Educational".* Paper presented at the 4th International Conference on Interaction Design and Children (IDC2005).

Gagne, R. M. (1970). The Conditions of Learning and Theory of Instruction, (2nd ed.). New York: Holt, Rinehart & Winston.

Hattie, J. A. (2003). Teachers make a difference: What is the research evidence? *2003 Australian Council for Educational Research Conference.* Melbourne.

Hattie, J. A. (2005). *What is the nature of evidence that makes a difference to learning?* Paper presented at the Research Conference 2005 VIC: Australian Council for Educational Research.

Honey, P., & Mumford, A. (1982). Manual of Learning Styles. London: P. Honey.

Hull, C. L. (1951). Essentials of behavior. New Haven, CT: Yale University Press.

Ke, F. (2009). A Qualitative Meta-Analysis of Computer Games as Learning Tools. In R. E. Ferdig (Ed.), Handbook of Research on Effective Electronic Gaming in Education (Vol. 1-32). Hershey, PA: Information Science Reference.

Kelly, H., Howell, K., Glinert, E., Holding, L., Swain, C., & Burrowbridge, A. (2007). How to build serious games. *Communications of the ACM, 50*(7), 44–49. doi:10.1145/1272516.1272538

Knowles, M. (1996). Androgogy: An emerging techology for adult learning. In R. Edwards, A. Hanson & P. Raggatt (Eds.), Boundaries of Adult Learning (pp. 82-96). London: Routledge.

Kolb, D. A. (1984). Experiential Learning. Englewood Cliffs, NJ: Prentice-Hall.

Krathwohl, D. R., Bloom, B. S., & Masia, B. B. (1964). Taxonomy of Educational Objectives: Classification of Educational Goals, Handbook II: Affective Domain New York: David McKay Co., Inc.

Malone, T. W. (1980). *What makes things fun to learn? heuristics for designing instructional computer games.* Paper presented at the Proceedings of the 3rd ACM SIGSMALL symposium and the first SIGPC symposium on Small systems.

Malone, T. W., & Lepper, M. R. (1987). Making Learning Fun: A Taxonomy of Intrinsic Motivations for Learning. In R. E. Snow & M. J. Farr (Eds.), Aptitude, Learning and Instruction: Conative amd affective process analyses (Vol. 3, pp. 223-254). Hillsdale, NJ: Lawrence Erlbaum Associates.

Marzano, R. J. (2009). *MRL Meta-Analysis Database Summary.* Retrieved 5th July 2009: http://files.solution-tree.com/MRL/documents/strategy_summary_6_10_09.pdf

Marzano, R. J., & Kendall, J. S. (2006). The New Taxonomy of Educational Objectives (2nd ed.). Thousand Oaks, CA: Corwin Press.

Maslow, A. H. (1946). A Theory of Human Motivation. In P. L. Harriman (Ed.), Twentieth Century Psychology: Recent Developments in Psychology (pp. 22-48). New York: The Philosophical Library.

Miller, G. A. (2003). The Magical Number Seven, Plus or Minus Two: Some Limits on Our Capacity for Processing Information. In B. J. Baars, W. P. Banks & J. B. Newman (Eds.), Essential Sources in the Scientific Study of Consciousness (pp. 357-372). Cambridge, MA: MIT Press.

Moreno-Ger, P., Blesius, C., Currier, P., Sierra, J. L., & Fernández-Manjón, B. (2008). Online Learning and Clinical Procedures: Rapid Development and Effective Deployment of Game-Like Interactive Simulations In Z. Pan, A. D. Cheok, W. Müller & A. E. Rhabili (Eds.), Transactions on Edutainment I (Vol. 5080/2008, pp. 288-304). Berlin Heidelberg: Springer Verlag.

Morrison, G. R., Ross, S. M., & Kemp, J. E. (2006). Designing Effective Instruction (5 ed.). London: Wiley.

Nieborg, D. B. (2004). *America's Army: More Than a Game.* Paper presented at the Transforming Knowledge into Action through Gaming and Simulation, Munchen: SAGSAGA.

Paras, B., & Bizzocchi, J. (2005). *Game, Motivation, and Effective Learning: An Integrated Model for Educational Game Design.* Paper presented at the DiGRA 2005 – the Digital Games Research Association's 2nd International Conference, Simon Fraser University, Burnaby, BC, Canada.

Pearce, C. (2006). Productive Play: Game Culture From the Bottom Up. *Games and Culture, 1*(1), 17–24. doi:10.1177/1555412005281418

Pivec, M., Dziabenko, O., & Schinnerl, I. (2003). *Aspects of Game-Based Learning*. Paper presented at the Third International Conference on Knowledge Management (IKNOW 03), Graz, Austria.

Prensky, M. (2001). Digital Game-Based Learning. New York: Paragon House.

Prensky, M. (2002). The Motivation of Gameplay or the REAL 21st century learning revolution. *Horizon, 10*, 1–14.

Reigeluth, C. M., Merrill, M. D., Wilson, B. G., & Spille, R. T. (1980). The elaboration theory of instruction: A model for sequencing and synthesizing instruction. *Instructional Science, 9*(3), 195–219. doi:10.1007/BF00177327

Rideout, V. J., Vandewater, E. A., & Wartella, E. A. (2003). Zero to Six: Electronic Media in the Lives of Infants, Toddlers and Preschoolers. Menlo Park, CA: Kaiser Family Foundation.

Rollings, A., & Adams, E. (2003). Andrew Rollings and Ernest Adams on Game Design. St. Carmel, IN: New Riders Publishing.

Ryan, R. M., & Deci, E. L. (2000). Self-determination theory and the facilitation of intrinsic motivation, social development and well-being. *The American Psychologist, 55*(1), 68–78. doi:10.1037/0003-066X.55.1.68

Salen, K., & Zimmerman, E. (2003). Rules of Play: Game Design Fundamentals. Cambridge, MA: The MIT Press.

Sawyer, B., & Smith, P. (2008). *Serious Games Taxonomy*. Retrieved 26 March, 2008, from http://www.dmill.com/presentations/serious-games-taxonomy-2008.pdf

Schell, J. (2005). Understanding entertainment: story and gameplay are one. [CIE]. *Computers in Entertainment, 3*(1), 6. doi:10.1145/1057270.1057284

Sicart, M. (2005, 16-20 June 2005). *The Ethics of Computer Game Design*. Paper presented at the DiGRA 2005 - the Digital Games Research Association's 2nd International Conference, Simon Fraser University, Burnaby, BC, Canada.

Simpson, E. J. (1972). The classification of educational objectives in the psychomotor domain: The psychomotor domain (Vol. 3). Washington, DC: Gryphin House.

Skinner, B. F. (1935). Two Types Of Conditioned Reflex And A Pseudo Type. *The Journal of General Psychology, 12*, 66–77.

Sweller, J. (1994). Cognitive load theory, learning difficulty, and instructional design. *Learning and Instruction, 4*(4), 295–312. doi:10.1016/0959-4752(94)90003-5

Tang, S. Martin Hanneghan, & El-Rhalibi, A. (2009). Introduction to Games-Based Learning. In T. M. Connolly, M. H. Stansfield & L. Boyle (Eds.), Games-Based Learning Advancements for Multi-Sensory Human Computer Interfaces: Techniques and Effective Practices (pp. 1-17). Hershey, PA: Idea-Group Publishing.

Tang, S., Hanneghan, M., & El-Rhalibi, A. (2007). *Pedagogy Elements, Components and Structures for Serious Games Authoring Environment*. Paper presented at the 5th International Game Design and Technology Workshop (GDTW 2007), Liverpool, UK.

Telfer, R. (1993). Aviation Instruction and Training. Aldershot, UK: Ashgate.

Thorndike, E. L. (1933). A proof of the law of effect. *Science, 77*, 173–175. doi:10.1126/science.77.1989.173-a

Weiner, B. (1979). A Theory of Motivation for Some Classroom Experiences. *Journal of Educational Psychology, 71*(1), 3–25. doi:10.1037/0022-0663.71.1.3

Zyda, M. (2005). From Visual Simulation to Virtual Reality to Games. *Computer*, *38*, 25–32. doi:10.1109/MC.2005.297

ENDNOTES

[1]   The terms 'computer games' and 'video games' refer to digital games on a home computer and console platform respectively and are often used interchangeably. For clarity, this article uses the term 'computer games' to represent digital games on all platforms.

[2]   More details of Mind Rover can be found at http://www.lokigames.com/products/mindrover/.

Chapter 9
Moving to the Next Level:
Designing Embedded Assessments into Educational Games

Jody S. Underwood
Pragmatic Solutions, Inc., USA

Stacy Kruse
Pragmatic Solutions, Inc., USA

Peter Jakl
Pragmatic Solutions, Inc., USA

ABSTRACT

The educational research community has been experimenting with educational games with a focus on pedagogy and curriculum, but little effort has been made to assess what students are actually learning in these environments. Designing embedded assessments into games is one of the critical gateways to creating learning tools that are maximally engaging for the learner, using sound pedagogical methodology as a foundation. The authors review the research in this area and describe technology that facilitates near real-time data collection through embedded assessments, visual data mining, inference mechanisms, and dynamic individualization. They then describe a methodology for creating valid embedded assessments and identify types of data that can be collected from gaming environments along with approaches for analysis, all toward the goal of individualized adaptation.

INTRODUCTION

Educational games are being used by many different people (Rieber, 1996): parents buy games for their children, teachers find games online that address the content they are focusing on, and many students find these environments engaging and worthwhile. Most research on using games for learning look at the outcome as a single unit, for example, students learned to add fractions. To make the most of digital learning environments, it would be useful to know what happened inside the game, when it happened, and how it happened. How can the learner get more of what they want or need, and less of what they do not want or need? To answer these questions, more in-game data needs to be collected, and sense made of the data. No small task, to be sure.

DOI: 10.4018/978-1-61520-781-7.ch009

In some sense, there is nothing new here. Human tutors have always answered these questions about individuals. However, while digital games provide environments for one-on-one learner interaction, they do not yet collect data about learner behavior and needs to determine the best course of action for the individual.

The focus of this chapter is on how to use game environments to provide one-on-one learning experiences. Even with advances in technology, there is still a need for humans to oversee individual learning, but digital games can scale, in ways that teachers cannot, to provide one-on-one experiences in the form of adaptive environments from the results of embedded assessments. This approach is key to fostering both engagement and learning, where the challenge must be neither too easy (promoting boredom) nor too hard (discouraging continued play).

BACKGROUND

What is Embedded Assessment

Embedded assessment is the process of measuring knowledge and ability as *part* of a learning activity rather than after the fact, when it is only an approximation of learner behavior. Student actions can be evaluated within context while carrying out tasks, or otherwise interacting in a gaming environment. (Note that we will use the terms "gaming environment" and "game" to refer to any online game that is intended for learning, including computer games, puzzles, drills, simulations, and 2D and 3D immersive spaces. By "online," we mean any environment that communicates with the Internet, either in real-time or at some point.) These actions can be collected, viewed, and analyzed either immediately or after the session. Sometimes "so-called" embedded assessments are implemented as pop-up quizzes that a learner cannot bypass. We identify these as possible "tools" an educator might employ within

a larger framework, but not as fully-realized embedded assessment.

Embedded assessments in games can focus on such things as content knowledge, process and procedures, and higher-order 21st century skills such as collaboration and strategic thinking (hereafter called "higher-order skills"; Partnership for 21st Century Skills, 2009). Stakeholders may obtain reports detailing student proficiencies and challenges – who needs help in teamwork, who is accelerating in math skills, and how well individuals compare with the larger population taking the course. Parents, teachers, administrators and others may gain valuable information that can be elusive during the course of traditional instruction.

Why Focus on Embedded Assessment

Assessment is not new. Tests are used successfully as gauges and gateways--for example, college entrance exams such as SAT or ACT, driving tests, and for fields such as medicine, cosmetology, and interior design. Assessment is also done successfully in the classroom, both formally and informally – teachers give quizzes and tests, they look into faces to gauge students' grasp of the material, and they ask questions. If traditional assessments have been so successful, why turn to alternative types of assessments? Research and development of traditional high-stakes assessments have been going on for decades to maintain their validity and reliability. Alternative assessments fill a gap created by traditional assessments, which often label individuals unfairly and constrain them with limited goals (Reeves & Okey, 1996).

Why assess learning in games? While they are recommended as engaging approaches to learning, the adoption in education of games is slow because they have not yet been shown to be effective (Federation of American Scientists, 2006). One way to show they are effective is to measure the learning that occurs during play.

Without knowing *how* students interact with these games, *where* they encounter moments of challenge and success, *what* they have done in the past with all relevant games, and *how* they compare against their peer groups, useful information that can support learning for individuals is lost. In addition to giving learners the type of one-on-one experience they might otherwise find with human tutors, the answers to these questions will help parents and educators determine how to intelligently use games for instruction and intervention.

Finally, embedded assessments provide information to adapt the game environment to the learner. Games can be, by their very nature and design, outstanding forums for providing formative feedback to the learner in a familiar, low-stress fashion, creating a space in which learners are free to explore and are receptive to help.

How can games, including puzzles, simulations, and other immersive spaces, be designed so that embedded assessments are seamless, expedient, and valid? How can higher-order skills be assessed? How can we assess process and infer behavior, in addition to content knowledge? How can embedded assessments be technologically implemented? How can games be adapted to individuals? These are the questions this chapter addresses. We start with background on the state of the art of embedded assessment in educational research.

Research on Embedded Assessment in Educational Games

Video games that were designed for entertainment actually provide an environment in which players learn (Gee, 2003). Tutorials are meant to help players learn to play the game, typically presenting a few new things at a time so the player can steadily assimilate them. Games also assess the player through levels, scoring, and other in-game resources. The challenge of educational games is to use these methods to help people learn particu-

lar content, skills, and behaviors. Many existing efforts use mechanisms such as engaging online quizzes to assess student learning, and that is the extent of the "game." Following is a review of the research and development efforts of both the educational research and serious games communities, who are both addressing very similar issues related to the use of games and of embedded assessment for learning.

Intelligent Tutoring Systems

Many educators and researchers have long sought to use assessment in tutoring environments (e.g., Snow & Mandinach, 1991), leading to the development of several systems, including: *Cognitive Tutors* (Anderson, et al., 1995; Koedinger et al., 1997), which keep track of students' knowledge through the use of a cognitive model to offer immediate feedback and guidance; *ASSISTments* (Razzaq et al., 2005), which represent a derivation of the cognitive tutoring approach by merging instructional assistance with robust assessment; and *Assessment and Learning in Knowledge Spaces* (*ALEKS;*Falmagne, et al., 2004), which dynamically generates interactive courses adapted to a student's goals, preferences, capabilities, and knowledge. While these tutoring systems have shown significant positive learning effects, they focus on procedures, constrain students to particular problem-solving paths, and eventually provide answers to problems instead of letting students attempt solutions and learn from their mistakes. Many lessons can be learned from these efforts to provide more open-ended environments for students to explore subject matter knowledge, procedures, and 21st century skills.

Virtual Environments for Learning

Research into educational uses of virtual environments has been a steadily developing field, where participants guide avatars through complex worlds, interacting with objects they encounter in authentic ways while collaborating with peers. Researchers have looked at feasibility issues for learning, such as design questions for creating multi-user virtual environment-based curricula (e.g., Nelson, Ketelhut, Clarke, Bowman, & Dede, 2005; Slator, Hill, & Del Val, 2004), and student engagement and identity development (e.g., Barab, Arici, & Jackson, 2005). In many of these environments, there has been a focus on providing a pedagogically sound environment, but little effort on how to assess what content students are actually absorbing in-game or how the games contributed to student learning (Kafai, 2006).

External Assessment of What is Learned in Games

There has been a fair amount of research on external assessment of learning in games. Some efforts require students to submit solutions, responses, or summaries of game interactions to an instructor or other real person, who then grades them (e.g., Barab, Arici, & Jackson, 2005; Chen & Michael, 2005). Other efforts do conversation analysis of discussions that take place in-game (e.g., Shaffer, 2007) and out-of-game (e.g., Steinkuehler, 2008), but neither looks at game activity directly. Another approach is to carry out a pre- and posttest experimental design to determine what the student has learned (e.g., Zapata-Rivera, VanWinkle, Shute, Underwood, & Bauer, 2007). By administering external tests, teachers may lose much of the value of the games since learners are already inherently demonstrating their knowledge and skills by interactions *during* gameplay. Assessments embedded into games will, in addition, reduce the often artificial separation between performance and assessment in school (Reeves & Okey, 1996).

Each of these approaches has shown that students are learning in the gaming environment. However, there has been little effort to study in-game activity to see what is being learned, or what facilitates or creates bottlenecks to achieving the desired learning goals. As Jim Gee indicated at the American Educational Research Conference (Gee, 2009), "If you are testing outside the game, you had better have good reason for doing it. The very act of completing a game should serve as an assessment of whatever the intervention was designed to teach or measure."

Using Gaming Environments *as* Assessment

Research efforts are beginning to address how to embed assessment validly, reliably, and without interrupting play. These efforts mostly use games *as* assessment, and may provide engaging virtual environments and feedback (e.g., Clarke & Dukas, 2009; Hickey, 2009). These are generally performance assessments that take place after a course of learning, another example of "external" measures. These efforts, while successfully assessing such competencies as critical thinking, are addressing many good questions for how to have engaging assessments in a *virtual* environment, but they are not addressing the issue of how to integrate them into a *learning* environment.

Embedded Assessment in Gaming Environments

People are starting to realize that integrating assessments into gaming environments is important and that external multiple-choice questionnaires and human-scored artifacts are not sufficient to assess all that people may be learning in games, since the latter are time-wise inefficient and do not scale easily. Both the Digital Media Collaboratory (out of U. Texas at Austin) and the EduMetrics Institute advocate addressing assessment issues as an initial part of serious game design (Chen & Michael, 2005). Shute et al. (2008) propose an approach for embedding assessments into games to reveal what is being learned during the gaming experience, where the focus is not only on content knowledge, but also higher-order skills. Some efforts are interested in analyzing a sequence of events to infer abilities such as problem-solving strategies (e.g., Ketelhut, Nelson, & Schifter, 2009). Others have begun to implement embedded assessments to gauge content learning (e.g., Zapata-Rivera, 2009). PIXELearning creates sophisticated training simulations that give the player appropriate feedback so that players come to understand the connection between their in-game actions and the outcomes (Chen & Michael, 2005). Shute et al. (2008) and Shute (2009) propose an approach for embedding assessments into immersive games to reveal what is being learned during the gaming experience, with a focus on creative problem-solving and systems thinking. Their work takes a similar approach to that described here, such as using evidence-based assessment design and doing statistical analysis to make inferences based on in-game behavior. However, our paths quickly diverge. In this theoretical work (i.e., not yet tested), they overlay an expert student model onto the learner's experience to determine whether the student is doing the right thing at the right time (in the same way intelligent tutoring systems work), and to identify misconceptions. Where they need to build a new expert student model for each problem to be solved, we are interested in building a general model of mathematical knowledge that will apply to many learning situations. And where they focus on correcting misconceptions, we are interested in determining learners' prior knowledge so the system can help them build on that directly. Our efforts, described in later sections, build on these experiences by providing data analysis and mining capabilities, and adapting the environment to the individual learner.

HOW TO APPROACH EMBEDDED ASSESSMENT

Educational games, in order to be effective, should be designed as constructivist learning environments where learners can explore, experiment, and actively solve problems (Reeves & Okey, 1996), with a focus on both learning outcomes and the actions and processes taken toward a goal. In this section we will briefly list the types of things that can be measured, then describe an approach to designing assessments and embedded assessments, including challenges, technology to address these challenges, measurement, and validation.

What can be Measured

For games that lend themselves to learning by drill, content knowledge (e.g., math facts, following foreign language directions, other right/wrong content) can be readily assessed. It is simple only in the sense that assessment design research has a long history of focusing on content knowledge. There are still design principles to follow to make sure the assessments are valid, that is, that they measure what is intended to assess. We will talk about measurement and validity in later sections.

Process is a bit more difficult to measure. Process includes such things as procedures for solving algebraic equations, and paths taken toward a goal like racing a car or constructing a bridge. It is generally easy to discern whether the outcome is correct, but it is more difficult to discern whether the path taken was good or efficient, as in the case where mistakes in process lead to correct answers. In an interactive environment, fine-grained actions can be collected to help measure process.

Even more challenging to measure are skills, including higher-order skills (e.g., critical thinking, decision-making, and problem solving) and behavioral skills (e.g., teamwork, leadership). It is possible to directly test these skills in an interactive environment, but a theory of how these skills can be demonstrated is still needed.

Assessment Design Methodology

In this section, we describe an approach to assessment design based on Educational Testing Service's evidence-centered design (ECD; Mislevy, Steinberg, & Almond, 2003), which provides an evidentiary argument for a test's validity.

The questions to be answered, in order, are:

1. What do we want to do with the results of the assessment?
2. What claims do we want to make about the learner based on performance in the game?
3. What observations of learner actions would provide evidence for the claims?

What do We want to do With the Assessment Results?

How can assessments be designed to be embedded into games? Valid assessments are best designed in a top-down fashion, starting with the goal of determining what to do with the assessment results. Experience shows that if this part is postponed until the end, the data to be collected would likely need to be redefined. It is simply more efficient to define these, for example, as pedagogical goals such as feedback or adaptivity, at the beginning, and to periodically revisit them to ensure that they use the types of data that *can* be collected. It is an iterative process.

Much can be learned from modern entertainment games which already employ embedded assessment and feedback, though for different purposes. Their goal is to foster high engagement in order to extend the playability of a title. For example, they have tutorials that slowly introduce features of the game to the player and offer players a chance to practice certain skills. They provide scores as feedback to demonstrate what is important in game play, leaderboards for comparison to other players, and persistent scoring that allows players to monitor their own progress. These features essentially show the results of embedded assessments and if used appropriately in educational games may, in fact, greatly enhance levels of learner interest and engagement.

As an example, our group supports *America's Army* (AA), a serious game produced by the U.S. Army to inform the public about Army life, Army career opportunities, and the Army's core values. Players get feedback in the form of medals and ribbons for completing various training exercises as well as for teams completing missions. The AA environment also adapts to players according to training and performance.

We have identified four general pedagogical goals that can leverage the results of embedded assessments in games:

*   Provide custom feedback to learners during games
*   Provide custom feedback to learners after games
*   Tailor which games learners experience
*   Tailor how learners experience the games

Custom feedback *during games* includes suggestions to help learners overcome weaknesses – perhaps via non-player agents, providing practice areas, or other creative mechanisms; similarly, persistent scores can be displayed as an ongoing gauge of proficiency of necessary knowledge, process, and skills. Underwood (2008) presents some guidelines for pedagogically sound feedback.

For learners who have a competitive streak, it is helpful to provide leaderboards or other mechanisms *after the game* by which learners can compare their performance with others. High scores may not be the only thing learners are interested in, however, so it would also be useful to provide such measures as accuracy (e.g., knowledge displayed), efficiency (e.g., in procedures), behavior, creativity, or other things different types of learners will value.

To help learners *across games*, suggestions can be made for games learners seem to be ready for, either for remediation or challenge (see Figure 1). Guiding these selections, learning is optimized when the difficulty of the activity lies in the learner's zone of proximal development

Figure 1.

(Vygotsky, 1978), where it is a challenge for the learner, but can still be accomplished with scaffolding via hints or peer discussions.

Finally, in-game performance can be used to *adapt the game environment* to suit the learner. Adaptations can take the form of dynamically swapping media (e.g., auditory learner gets audio cues, visual learner gets visual cues), making content simpler or harder (e.g., using an aggressive boss in a simulation of "learning to be agreeable" if the player is successful with an approachable boss), or otherwise "re-skinning" graphical elements in a game (e.g., changing genders of non-player characters, altering billboards and street scenes). Figure 2 shows an example of adaptivity in AA, where the number of weapons available to a player is reduced based on his displaying low responsibility.

What Claims can be Made Based on Performance in the Game?

Claims are statements we want to be able to make about a learner's knowledge, higher-order skills, or other attributes based on their performances.

Claims are a way to communicate performance and may be very general (e.g., learner can read at the second grade level) or specific (e.g., learner can decode initial consonants). Some examples include:

- Tom mastered the addition of fractions with common denominators (92%). He needs help with fractions without common denominators.
- Pat is not always efficient in the paths taken, though the solutions are 95% correct.
- Jane's leadership skills need help, as is evidenced by her team not successfully completing all their tasks.

The last claim shows a certain level ("needs help") of achievement in *leadership*. It is useful to break that down into strengths and weaknesses of sub-skills, including communication, delegation, and team-support, in order to reach measurable actions.

In enumerating these claims, we are both identifying the skills we want to measure and how we want to report them, for example, as numeric

Figure 2.

or percentage scores, categorical (e.g., "needs help"), or some other way. This information can be used to help learners improve, as well as to improve the gaming environment. These claims are defined *before* determining which actions will provide evidence for them. This is because we want to focus on the best way to help the learners, remaining open to the myriad types of data available to collect and measure.

What Observations of Learner Actions Would Provide Evidence for the Claims?

In this step, we identify ideal types of evidence that would support the claims about learner performance. This is immediately balanced with the practicality of measuring the skill in the game, since there are certainly limitations.

For example, to satisfy the claim that a learner has mastered the skill of adding fractions, we might decide that the learner must display correct solutions for 94% of the fraction addition problems that appear in the game. Embedded *into* the game, the tests can appear as problems to be solved in order to do such things as build or to break a code. Also needed to be identified is what behavior shows lack of the skill. For example, if learners only correctly solve easier problems, they

may still need help with more complex ones. This list needs to be enumerated with as much detail as will be required by the pedagogical goals of the gaming environment.

To meet the claim of a player performing well in leadership, these actions might display evidence of some appropriate sub-skills:

- Communication: how often the leader initiates on-task communication
- Delegation: how often the leader delegates responsibilities that get completed
- Team-support: how often the leader leads team members to action, gives advice

Given a list of observables and actions that will provide data to support claims, we must also determine what is feasible to measure in a gaming environment and how to design it unobtrusively using normal game mechanics .

The Challenges of Embedded Assessment

We just described an evidence-centered methodology for assessment design. The points that focus on creating an immersive and motivating educational game are:

- *Adapt the environment to the learner.* We identified four ways to adapt the environment to support learning.
- *Assess process and skills, not just content.* Some of these are easy to measure, and some more challenging.
- *Embed assessments into the fabric of the game.* If a test feels like school, learner motivation can be lessened. Embedding assessments can help overcome this problem.

These are the challenges in creating embedded assessments in gaming environments. They include how to:

- *Maintain flow while collecting in-game data.* This is both a design and technological problem. The game has to be designed so that actions in the game provide evidence of a pedagogical goal to be measured. The technology has to collect data in real-time so as not to interrupt gameplay.
- *Analyze the data.* Appropriate techniques should be used to measure performance, including statistical, visual, and other data mining approaches. Analyzing content knowledge is relatively simple; process and skills are harder, as described earlier.

A Technological and Analytical Solution

Constructivist educators stress that learning is personal, unique, and contextualized for each learner (Reeves & Okey, 1996). Toward that end, we argue that games, along with technology that is finally available today, provide environments that can be adapted to the individual learner according to constructivist maxims.

Pragmatic Solutions (aka Pragmatic; www.pr-sol.com) has developed a suite of tools (Leverage™) that facilitate the implementation of embedded assessment, analysis and reporting, and adaptive gaming environments (Underwood,

Kruse, & Jakl, 2009). This section describes the technological capabilities of Leverage and how it supports our assessment methodology and addresses the challenges of embedded assessment.

Done in real-time through Pragmatic's infrastructure, in-game data is collected to update learner profiles without impeding the flow of the environment (Csikszentmihalyi, 1990), a requirement that is critical to fostering both engagement and the potential for learning (Shute, et al., 2008). Leverage supports the dynamic delivery and modification of any and all elements in the game, with the capability of providing individualized content to a large user base in near real-time. Elements dynamically delivered into the environment may include static or scrolling textual content, images, audio, video, or other in-game objects, as defined by the pedagogical framework of the game.

Leverage (see Figure 3) includes an attribute tracking system (ATS) to collect and organize data dynamically, a rule-based statistical tracking system (STS) to summarize acquired data, a dynamic content delivery system (DCDS), a behavioral inference engine (*Inflection*), and an interactive data visualization application (*Visual IQ*™). ATS, the heart of this database-driven application, collects data of any grain-size in real time from embedded assessments and manages the results to adapt the game to an individual learner's needs. STS tracks in-game events and is highly scalable using massive parallel processing methodology. STS summaries, which include such things as correlation, regression, and factor analysis, are automatically fed into Visual IQ. Subject matter experts construct the processing rules for ATS and STS. DCDS delivers individualized content to any game. *Inflection* uses genetic algorithms and other data mining techniques to construct inferences and make predictions about learner behavior and performance. In short, Leverage collects information about what learners do in the game, processes that information, and returns a best course of action back to the learner. As more data is collected, the system continues to

Figure 3.

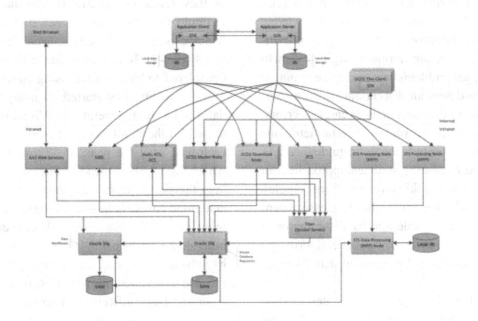

be refined to improve inference and adaptivity. Finally, Leverage is modular and platform-agnostic, allowing it to be used with any database, operating system, or gaming platform.

Visual IQ provides data visualization and real-time analytic support tools, allowing stakeholders to analyze data of a learner population, drill-down into individual learner profiles, and define custom groups. Visual IQ provides various interactive charting and graphing tools, custom reporting options, and input of external "events" (e.g., completion of a course unit, a holiday) against which to track data. Since the Leverage platform uses attribute-value architecture, there is no limit to the number of variables that may be tracked about learner activity. Leverage collects the data; Visual IQ helps stakeholders create layers of context for the data.

Leverage has been developed to support *America's Army*. With each new release, Leverage scaled to support more and more in-game actions and more players. With the release of *America's Army 3* (AA3), Leverage now fosters learning by filtering a player's in-game actions through a complex set of rules related to the Army's "core

values" (loyalty, duty, respect, selfless service, honor, integrity, personal courage), with specific actions serving as a measure of a player's understanding and demonstration of core values, which in turn impacts future actions in the game, providing implicit feedback as authentically as possible. For example, if you do not display traits such as integrity, you will be negatively impacted in battle; excel in these areas and you will reap the rewards by being nimble, accurate, and effective.

Pragmatic is partnering with educational institutions (e.g., NYU) to integrate Leverage into educational games, continuing to discover new insights into collaborative learning and how people make decisions and acquire knowledge.

Measurement in a Gaming Environment

We have just described technology that can implement embedded assessments, analyze them, incorporate their results, and facilitate individualized adaptivity into educational games. Here we will describe some mechanisms to measure content knowledge, process, and higher-order skills.

As noted earlier, content knowledge is relatively easy to measure. Right/wrong knowledge can be compared to correct answers, just as in traditional tests; a structured formula can give weight to more complex problems than easier ones; content analysis can determine that certain incorrect solutions showed misconceptions or careless errors, and weight them accordingly. Psychometricians often use item response theory to guide them. As complicated as these measurement approaches can get, procedures and skills are even more complex to assess, and other approaches to measurement are required, for example, a probabilistic approach (e.g., Bayesian networks or genetic algorithms) can score actions and patterns of actions more subjectively.

Through ECD, a game can be designed to facilitate the measurement of process for students taking known paths. However, in a well-designed game, learners will often come up with approaches not considered by the game designer. Visual IQ and Inflection can help address the "long tail" of learners, that is, the many individual learners who do not fall into statistical groups. Research in this area is just beginning.

We are investigating ways to find patterns in solution paths as they are related to correct answers. In River City, Harvard University's immersive inquiry-based science environment, we are mining the paths of actions students take

as they relate to hypothesis formulation. For example, the time at which each student made a hypothesis can be aligned for visual data-mining (see Figure 4). To align the data, all students are considered to have started using River City on 1/01 (in reality they started on many different dates). The chart, generated by Visual IQ, shows growth in the number of hypotheses generated each day, until the peak of 871 on 1/08, after which the numbers steadily decrease. This can help the designers of the gaming environment determine how to help students be more efficient in their paths, for example, by drilling down into individual student paths for those who generate hypotheses early and late in the process. We are also experimenting with Leverage's genetic algorithm-based Inflection to find patterns in those sequences of actions that correspond to early and late hypothesis generation.

Even more challenging than assessing process are higher-order skills (e.g., leadership, strategic thinking). A mix of structured and probabilistic formulae may be the best way to measure these skills. Traditional strategic thinking tests are usually in the form of asking what someone would do in a particular situation, sometimes called "situational judgment" tests. These tests can provide some information about how people *think* they would act in a situation, but they can have validity issues (Ployhart & Ehrhart, 2003), that is, people

Figure 4.

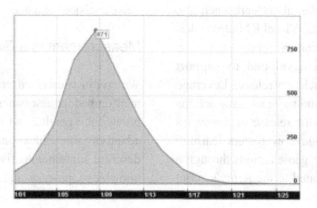

do not always act the way they think they would act. Game environments create the opportunity to more directly test these skills. Similar to measuring process, measurement can begin by defining rules for known or expected skill performance as defined in the assessment design, supplemented by visual data mining tools and more open-ended pattern matchers. In one analysis study, Inflection predicted gender based on gameplay in River City with 75% accuracy. An example of rule-based analysis was done in AA3, where in-game actions inform a player's demonstration of the Army core values (see Figure 5), which then affect the environment later in the game. Players can also be provided information about their expected and actual performance.

Validation

The main challenges in designing valid assessments are captured by the following questions:

- How do you know that students are learning what you claim they are learning?
- How do you know you are measuring what you claim you are measuring?

Assessment validity is an area that psychometricians have been researching for many years. The main purpose of assessment design is to have a

test (e.g., college entrance exam) where student performance can confidently predict the relationship to a goal (e.g., performance in the first year of college). For these high-stakes cases, specialized statistical analysis is used and continual adjustments of the test are made so that it maintains correlation with the ultimate goal. Traditional psychometricians seem to over-emphasize measurement of decontextualized knowledge, assuming that the less contextualized their instruments, the more likely they are to assess generalizable knowledge and skills.

Proponents of authentic assessment seek to estimate learning within specific contexts that approximate the ill-defined, uncontrollable aspects of the real world, a world in which the generalizability of standardized tests may have little relevance (Reeves & Okey, 1996). The goals of educational games are not as critical (i.e., high-stakes) as college entrance exams, but the assessments still need to be valid.

Evidence-centered design helps ensure validity, leaving an evidentiary trail of design decisions. However, it is advisable to do explicit validation. For such things as math knowledge, running pilot studies with pre- and post-tests can provide the proper level of validation. For higher-order skills, expert opinions on what constitutes the skill will be sufficient; these experts can also assign ratings to game behavior. Learners and teammates can

Figure 5.

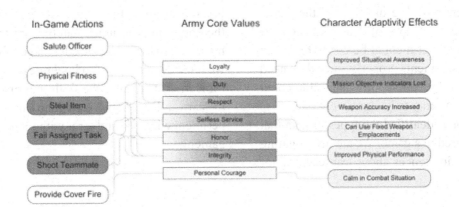

rate themselves and each other, and these can be compared to computed scores. Learners can also be asked to react to the scores. As always, the game and embedded assessments should continually be adjusted to get closer to more accurate measurement.

DISCUSSION

Why have adaptive gaming environments like these never been created before? The reality is that advances in technology are finally at the point to make it possible, addressing such things as fast connection speeds, storage of large amounts of data, and the like. But there are still areas that need to be explored. For example, digital gaming environments make it easy to collect every keystroke learners make, but it is not clear that this is the best approach. Focusing on the wrong data could lead to incorrect conclusions about learner needs. Theories for what to look at still need to be developed. Another limitation is that, even with all the data now available, we still do not know other things about the learners, like their feelings at the moment, what else is on their screen, as well as other distractions and pressures, opening up other areas of research.

What are the disadvantages of embedded assessment? If embedded assessments are not truly part of the game environment, they start to seem like "school" by popping out or otherwise taking away the learners' focus from the game, where learners will lose the flow of the game, and therefore, the flow of learning. Another disadvantage is that it could be costly to design embedded assessments properly since they need to be designed by people knowledgeable about game design in order to be done well.

This chapter identified the types of data that can be measured in a game. We are investigating how to make inferences about learner behavior using such techniques as genetic algorithms and visual data-mining. Additional directions should include natural language and speech understanding, in order to automatically and in real-time analyze communication for the purpose of assessing higher-order skills such as leadership.

Finally, we must ask how reliable are embedded assessments? This is an open question, since each is as reliable as the assessment itself. There have been many studies on how effective educational games are for learning, but they generally lump all games into one category (e.g., Virvou, Katsionis, & Manos, 2005). Furthermore, they do not evaluate the learning that occurs during gameplay. In a game that is well-designed, immersive, and engaging, embedded assessments should be valid and reliable and not distract the learner, but these are also areas ripe for research.

CONCLUSION

The time is ripe to create educational gaming environments since technology is now available to integrate assessments and implement data collection and adaptivity in near real-time. We have developed a set of capabilities to design and integrate assessments into games, visualize and analyze data, and individually adapt games. Additionally, we are continuing to research and develop methods for making inferences about behavior and learning in gaming environments. Embedded assessments that are truly integrated into the design of the game provide learners with the opportunity to immediately learn from their mistakes. In order to take advantage of this idea, we must design games to integrate opportunities for learners to display the skills they are intended to learn, allowing the learner to enjoy and experiment with trial and error without interrupting gameplay.

ACKNOWLEDGMENT

The authors would like to thank Brian Nelson, Steve Zuiker, and two anonymous reviewers for reviewing earlier versions of this chapter.

REFERENCES

Anderson, J. R., Corbett, A. T., Koedinger, K. R., & Pelletier, R. (1995). Cognitive tutors: Lessons learned. *Journal of the Learning Sciences*, *4*, 167–207. doi:10.1207/s15327809jls0402_2

Barab, S. A., Arici, A., & Jackson, C. (2005). Eat your vegetables and do your homework: A design-based investigation of enjoyment and meaning in learning. *Educational Technology*, *65*(1), 15–21.

Chen, S., & Michael, D. (2005). *Proof of learning: Assessment in serious games*. Retrieved on December 10, 2008 from http://www.gamasutra.com/features/20051019/chen_01.shtml

Clarke, J., & Dukas, G. (2009). Studying the potential of virtual performance assessments for measuring student achievement in science. Presentation at AERA 2009, San Diego, CA.

Csikszentmihalyi, M. (1990). Flow: The psychology of optimal experience. New York: Harper Perennial.

Falmagne, J.-C., Cosyn, E., Doignon, J.-P., & Thiery, N. (2004). *The assessment of knowledge, in theory and in practice*. Retrieved February 20, 2006 from http://www.business.aleks.com/about/Science_Behind_ALEKS.pdf

Federation of American Scientists. (2006). *Harnessing the power of video games for learning*. Report from the Summit on Educational Games. Retrieved March 12, 2009 from http://www.fas.org/gamesummit/Resources/Summit%20on%20Educational%20Games.pdf

Gee, J. P. (2003). What video games have to teach us about learning and literacy. New York: Palgrave Macmillan.

Gee, J. P. (2009). Discussant for the session Peering behind the digital curtain: Using situated data for assessment in collaborative virtual environments and games. AERA, San Diego, CA.

Hickey, D. T. (2009). Designing assessments and assessing designs in educational videogames. Presentation at AERA 2009, San Diego, CA.

Kafai, Y. B. (2006). Playing and making games for learning: Instructionist and constructionist perspectives for game studies. *Games and Culture*, *1*(1), 36–40. doi:10.1177/1555412005281767

Ketelhut, D. J., Nelson, B., & Schifter, C. (2009). Situated assessment using virtual environments of science content and inquiry. Presentation at AERA, San Diego, CA.

Koedinger, K. R., Anderson, J. R., Hadley, W. H., & Mark, M. A. (1997). Intelligent tutoring goes to school in the big city. *International Journal of Artificial Intelligence in Education*, *8*, 30–43.

Mislevy, R. J., Steinberg, L. S., & Almond, R. G. (2003). On the structure of educational assessment (with discussion). *Measurement: Interdisciplinary Research and Perspectives*, *1*(1), 3–62. doi:10.1207/S15366359MEA0101_02

Nelson, B., Ketelhut, D. J., Clarke, J., Bowman, C., & Dede, C. (2005). Design-based research strategies for developing a scientific inquiry curriculum in a multi-user virtual environment. *Educational Technology*, *45*(1), 21–27.

Partnership for 21st Century Skills. (2009). *Skills framework*. Retrieved April 3, 2009, from http://www.21stcenturyskills.org/index.php?option=com_content&task=view&id=254&Itemid=120

Ployhart, R. E., & Ehrhart, M. G. (2003). Be careful what you ask for: Effects of response instructions on the construct validity and reliability of situational judgment tests. *International Journal of Selection and Assessment, 11*, 1–16. doi:10.1111/1468-2389.00222

Razzaq, L., Feng, M., Nuzzo-Jones, G., Heffernan, N. T., Koedinger, K. R., & Junker, B. (2005). The assistment project: Blending assessment and assisting. In *Proceedings of the 12th artificial conference on intelligence in education*, (pp. 555–562). Amsterdam: ISO Press.

Reeves, T. C., & Okey, J. R. (1996). Alternative assessments in constructivist learning environments. In B. G. Wilson (Ed.), Constructivist Learning Environments: Case Studies in Instructional Design, (pp. 191-202). Englewood Cliffs, NJ: Educational Technology Publications.

Rieber, L. P. (1996). Seriously considering play: Designing interactive learning environments based on the blending of microworlds, simulations, and games. *ETR&D, 44*(2), 43–58. doi:10.1007/BF02300540

Shaffer, D. W. (2007). How computer games help children learn. New York: Palgrave Macmillan.

Shute, V. J. (2009). Simply assessment. *International Journal of Learning and Media, 1*(2), 1–11. doi:10.1162/ijlm.2009.0014

Shute, V. J., Ventura, M., Bauer, M. I., & Zapata-Rivera, D. (2008). Melding the power of serious games and embedded assessment to monitor and foster learning: Flow and grow. In U. Ritterfeld, M.J. Cody, & P. Vorderer, (Eds.), The Social Science of Serious Games: Theories and Applications. Philadelphia, PA: Routledge/LEA.

Slator, B. M., Hill, C., & Del Val, D. (2004). Teaching computer science with virtual worlds. *IEEE Transactions on Education, 47*(2), 269–275. doi:10.1109/TE.2004.825513

Snow, R. E., & Mandinach, E. B. (1991). *Integrating assessment and instruction: A research and development agenda* (ETS Research Report No. 91-08). Princeton, NJ: ETS.

Steinkuehler, C. (2008). Pop cosmopolitanism, cognition, and learning on the virtual frontier. Keynote presentation at the International Society for the Learning Sciences (ICLS), Utrecht, Netherlands.

Underwood, J. S. (2008). Effective feedback: Guidelines for improving performance. In *Proceedings of the International Conference of the Learning Sciences*, Utrecht, The Netherlands.

Underwood, J. S., Kruse, S., & Jakl, P. (2009). *Embedded assessment: Evaluating in-game data to adapt the learning environment*. Presentation at Games, Learning + Society Conference, Madison, WI.

Virvou, M., Katsionis, G., & Manos, K. (2005). Combining software games with education: Evaluation of its educational effectiveness. *Educational Technology & Society, 8*(2), 54–65.

Vygotsky, L. (1978), Mind in society: The development of higher mental processes. Cambridge, MA: Harvard University Press.

Zapata-Rivera, D. (2009). Assessment-based gaming environments. Presentation at AERA, San Diego, CA.

Zapata-Rivera, D., VanWinkle, W., Shute, V. J., Underwood, J. S., & Bauer, M. (2007). English ABLE. In R. Luckin, K. Koedinger, & J. Greer (Eds.), Artificial intelligence in education - Building technology rich learning contexts that work (pp. 323-330). Amsterdam, The Netherlands: IOS Press.

Zuiker, S. (2009). Assessment for "Learning to Be" in educational videogames. Presentation at AERA, San Diego, CA.

Chapter 10
The Design of a Health Literacy Game:
Face the Case

Jennifer McCabe
James Madison University, USA

ABSTRACT

This chapter describes the design and development of a game that was created to teach undergraduate students concepts related to health literacy. A brief discussion of the nature of games and how and why they appeal to college students is followed by a synopsis of some of the literature that influenced the design of the game in 2005. The chapter goes on to describe the game in detail, including the learning objectives, gameplay elements, design challenges, and skills included. The chapter will conclude with a discussion of some evaluations that were done on the game and direction for future development.

BACKGROUND

This chapter describes the design and development of a game created to teach pre-professional health and nursing students about the health literacy challenges facing their future patients and clients. The purpose of the game is not to improve the health literacy of the player; rather the goal of the game is to educate players about the ways in which compromised health literacy affects people and to expose the players to strategies for working through the barriers that compromised health literacy places between patients and effective health care.

DOI: 10.4018/978-1-61520-781-7.ch010

For the purposes of the game and this chapter, the definition of health literacy is "the degree to which individuals have the capacity to obtain, process, and understand basic health information and services and make appropriate health decisions." (National Library of Medicine, 2000).

While the amount of information available on the Internet has in some ways leveled the playing field for consumers of information, it has been a mixed blessing. Consumers using the Internet to research health conditions are deluged with information that varies wildly in credibility, objectivity, reading level, and usability. When seeking health care these same consumers are expected by health care practitioners to play a specific part in the treatment. They are expected to be literate, to have math skills, to have reasoning abilities, and to have cultural beliefs that make them compliant with instructions delivered by practitioners. However, the diversity in literacy, socio-economic status, religious and cultural beliefs and cultural practices makes it impossible for all consumers to experience the same level of care. Health care practitioners and social service providers have an obligation to assess their clients' health literacy and address barriers they face to receiving health care that is often designed as "one size fits all". It is this assessment and identification of barriers that the game was designed to address.

The concept of health literacy is one that has received a good deal of attention from both public and private funding agencies. The game that this chapter describes was funded by a National Leadership Grant from the Institute for Museum and Library Services. The impetus for creating the game was a request from the then-director of the JMU based Institute for Innovation in Health & Human Services. Initially a tutorial was requested that would help pre-professional health students understand health literacy. However, because the students who made up the potential players and their backgrounds were so diverse, a decision was made to create a game rather than a tutorial. This decision required a major shift in how "instruction" was approached as well as the kinds of resources required to create the game. The then-current work of Diana Oblinger and Marc Prensky influenced this decision.

INFLUENTIAL LITERATURE

The design of Face the Case (FTC) was more a creative endeavor than a work of research; therefore design choices were influenced more by playing games than by a formal review of the literature. There are several writers and scholars, however, whose work influences contemporary thinking about the creation of educational games.

Marc Prensky, author of Digital Game Based Learning, initially suggested that games needed six structural elements in order to be considered a game. Prensky's elements are rules, goals and objectives, outcomes and feedback, conflict/competition/challenge/opposition, interaction, and representation or story (Prensky, 2001). These elements were used, in unequal measure, to guide design decisions related to Face the Case. While Prensky's ideas provided insight into the design of games that can be used in educational settings, it should be noted that he has been heard to say that trying to design learning into a game "sucks the fun out of it." His central dogma relates to the idea that we can learn from games and the way that they engage students, but that as soon as educators try to design games that intentionally teach anything, they cease to be games and become dressed up tutorials. Prensky's devil's advocate style, while decidedly unscholarly, served as an important warning throughout the design of Face the Case.

The work of James Paul Gee was also influential in many design decisions related to Face The Case. Gee heads the Games and Professional Practice Simulations program at the University of Wisconsin, and is the author of the influential work *What Video Games Have to Teach us About Learning and Literacy*. In his various writings Gee argued that well designed video games illuminate the fact that humans enjoy learning. Games excel at encouraging players to engage in the process of knowledge creation in ways that traditional educational methods do not. For example, Gee argues that games can encourage risk taking, interaction, and relationship building in a safe way that appeals to players' senses of fun (Gee, 2005). The challenge Gee considers paramount to educators today is how to make learning more game-like.

Several of the design decisions in Face The Case were directly influenced by Gee's learning principles. The self knowledge principle was used in making decisions about the game world and the cultural competence questions. In the cultural competence questions players are asked to reflect on their own heritage and values. The regime of competence principle was another driving force in the game mechanics. The player received cases and questions that became increasingly difficult as they were solved. In this way the game was designed to keep the player at the edge of their abilities. The multimodal principle was used in creating the virtual world that included familiar and imaginary buildings, varying ambient sounds, and non-player characters who delivered essential information.

Many other scholars have built on the arguments that Gee makes in favor of integrating games into education. Henry Jenkins, director of the Comparative Media Studies program at MIT, makes a compelling case when he states "The worst thing a kid can say about homework is that it is too hard; the worst thing a kid can say about a game is that it is too easy."(Jenkins, 2005). He refers to the concept of "hard fun" noting that it exploits Gee's regime of competence learning principle and is present in the most successful commercial video games. Because Face The Case was designed to address a complicated, multidimensional topic, the concept of hard fun played an important role in decisions regarding when to challenge players and how to reward them. We wanted to push players to make hard choices and reward them immediately.

The writing of Diana Oblinger provided valuable insight into the characteristics of the population for whom the game was being designed. Oblinger is the president and CEO of EDUCAUSE and has extensive experience in higher education coupled with unique insight into the nature and expectations of undergraduate students. Oblinger argues that students were heavily influenced by growing up with Nintendo, a game system that emphasized trial-and-error problem solving and allowed players to learn from losing (the game). This experience coupled with students' proclivity for group work and their belief in the value of

performance influenced the decision to include collaborators and to design a game that emphasizes practice as preparation (Oblinger, 2003).

Joe Landsberger's interview with Kurt Squire, professor at the University of Wisconsin and visiting research fellow at MIT also provided some important insight into how to design engaging games. Squire suggests that the most important preparation for designing a game is playing games. Educational games span the gamut of game types, but in order for a game to be a useful, well designed educational tool, it must first be a well designed game. Game players, Squire points out, are quickly irritated by poorly designed games. Squire also suggests that the instructional theories of problem-based or case-based studies lend themselves well to gaming, an idea that spawned the basic design structure of Face The Case (Landsberger, 2004).

In a 2005 Library Journal article Constance Steinkuehler and Kurt Squire argued that game playing promotes various kinds of information literacy and require research skills and compels lots of writing (Squire & Steinkuehler, 2005). Librarians, they state, cannot afford to ignore games as legitimate instructional instruments. One unique appeal of games that Squire and Steinkuehler discuss is their equalizing power. In games the player is equal parts creator and consumer of information. This position may explain the popularity of games as well as one challenge that librarians and many educators face; namely the struggle to get students to accept the core concepts and values on which the content they must master is based. Perhaps if the students were able to participate in the content creation itself earlier in their studies they would engage as deeply with it as they do with the games they play.

Constance Steinkuehler has gone on to conduct substantial research that, while conducted subsequent to the design of Face The Case, bears some conceptual relationship to it. Perhaps the most interesting study was a collaboration between Steinkuehler and Sean Duncan in which they analyzed the transcripts of World of Warcraft discussion posts for evidence of scientific reasoning (Steinkuehler & Duncan, 2008). The extra-game discussions, they found, contained evidence of the spontaneous development of "scientific habits of mind". In other words, players of the game were seen to communicate and reason in ways that the academy accepts as soundly scientific. Certainly the creators of World of Warcraft never intended for it to be a scientific reasoning tool, however it succeeded where many more traditional attempts have failed.

WHAT IS FUN?

This chapter is not the place for a discourse on the epistemology of fun. Fun is manifest in many diverse and often contradictory ways. Formal definitions of fun tend toward the mundane; the Oxford English Dictionary defines it as a "Diversion, amusement, sport; also, boisterous jocularity or gaiety, drollery. Also, a source or cause of amusement or pleasure" (*Oxford english dictionary*). Even the ever-popular common law encyclopedia Wikipedia offers the generic definition "Recreation or fun is the expenditure of time in a manner designed for therapeutic refreshment of one's body or mind" (*Recreation*.n.d.). There is a dearth of formal scholarship of the nature of fun which presents a unique challenge to anyone intent on designing an experience that equally emphasizes fun and learning equally.

Another way to approach thinking about fun is to consider the activity of play. Play is recognized by educators, psychologists, and other professionals as an essential element of learning. It is, after all, the way humans choose to learn before they are forced into formal academies. In his writing on the integration of digital games into education, Marc Prensky's uses Fabricatore's definition of play "... an intellectual activity engaged in for its own sake, with neither clearly recognizable functionalities nor immediate biological effects...and related to

exploratory processes that follow the exposure of the player to novel stimuli" (Fabricatore, 2000) The key to this definition is the phrase *engaged in for its own sake;* in other words, fun.

Our solution to understanding fun was to approach the definition of fun backwards. Rather than asking people to define what fun meant to them, we asked them what they activities and experiences they considered to be fun. After a lengthy and decidedly *un*scientific survey, a pattern began to emerge. While individuals' experiences of fun varied wildly from high adventure (e.g. whitewater rafting) to contemplative (e.g. hiking the Appalachian Trail) to performance (e.g. competitive sports) to creative (e.g. crafts, music performance) and beyond; all of the activities reported tended to fall into one or more of the following three categories: sensual, surprising, challenging. Sensual activities were those that appealed directly to any of the five senses, sight, smell, hearing, touch, and taste. The element of surprise presented itself as integral to fun insomuch as it removed the person experiencing it from the mundane experience of daily life. This is the category into which most of what is normally considered funny falls. Much humor is based largely on surprise. Finally, the challenge that made many activities fun was seen as the result of a sense of competitiveness that is present in most people, though expressed in very different ways. The challenge of learning a new knitting stitch represented conquering the pattern and developing a new skill. Likewise the challenge associated with a competitive sport represented conquering the opposing player or team while further developing one's own athletic skills.

Many activities described as fun contained elements of all three categories. The activities offered were either appealing to the senses - visually rewarding, delicious, tactile - or surprising, a category that most closely overlapped with *funny*, or challenging. The challenging experiences were the ones that intrigued the designers most, as this was where learning could be connected to the overall experience of the game. Andrea diSessa stated that people learn best when they are performing within the *regime of competence* (DiSessa, 2000). The regime of competence is the experience of being good enough to perform a task, to enjoy it for its own sake. James Paul Gee elaborated on this theory by suggesting that games are valuable learning tools because they encourage players to expand their regime of competence, to perform a mastered task better or faster, or in a new way (Gee, 2005) p. 36). This is where learning takes place. In other words, they must stretch themselves and their abilities in order to expand their skill base and efficacy.

This general taxonomy of fun guided the design decisions that allowed us to take a decidedly complex and almost pedantic topic like health literacy and wrap it around an interactive experience that was fun.

WHAT MAKES A GAME A GAME/ WHAT MAKES THIS A GAME

Many writers have written at length about what constitutes a game and how games can and must differ from simulations, tutorials, and other forms of interactive instruction. An in-depth discussion of what constitutes a game can be found elsewhere in this collection. Like many new concepts, there is still a variety of definitions of games and the essential elements of them. The literature revealed a laundry list of essential elements for a game and principles that must be incorporated into games. Games must have rules, goals and objectives, outcomes and feedback, conflict/competition/challenge/opposition, interaction, and representation (Prensky 2001 p. 118-119). Games must encourage players to identify with them, must provide feedback, must reward risk taking, must situate the meaning of words within actions and images, must encourage players to think about relationships, etc (Gee, 2005). Kurt Squire asserts simply that a game is "a goal-based activity governed by rules for the purpose of entertainment."(Landsberger,

2004) This section will only address the elements of Face the Case that were designed specifically to make it a game. The design of FTC was guided by the principles that a game must have the following three elements: it must have levels of difficulty; it must grant the player new powers and it must reward performance.

The main challenges of designing Face the Case were to create a game that met all three criteria above, was fun, and fulfilled the learning objectives stated in the funding proposal. The learning objective for the game was stated in the grant application as "(To) develop interactive games that will prepare students to identify compromised health literacy, and to help patients access and use appropriate information." In the context of an online game, how could levels, powers, and rewards be established?

We decided to create a game based on case studies. These cases would increase in complexity as the player solved them. The cases would be presented as narratives, describing patients and their families, their health care needs as well as their beliefs and deficits in knowledge. Players would participate in a series of mini-challenges (games within the game) in order to acquire skills, which would ultimately be matched to the needs expressed in the cases. Players would also "collaborate" with other characters in the game. These collaborators had discrete skills which would be required by some cases. Correctly matching the skills and collaborators with the case would result in resolution of the case, and the player would be awarded points with which their game avatar could purchase rewards. As the player successfully solved the case, subsequent cases would become increasingly complex, requiring more skills and collaborators. This principle represented levels of difficulty.

The mini-challenges were essentially quizzes that reinforced the individual learning objectives. Presented in Flash, players would answer short questions, fill in the blanks, change the order of words, isolate keywords, and even do simple mathematical calculations. Mini-challenge content was always paired with the kind of skill the player needed. For each question they answered correctly, they would get points, and these points earned would be used to "purchase" the skills needed to solve the cases. Skills acquired represented new powers.

FACE THE CASE GAME OBJECTIVES

Many of the design considerations as well as the learning objectives of the game were set out in the funding application. Face The Case was designed for a well-understood population of players: undergraduate nursing, allied health, and social work students at James Madison University. We knew these students to be mostly female, aged 18-22, with moderate information seeking skills. Because of the assessment activities that take place at the University, there is a well developed information literacy program in place, with assessment data to indicate which information seeking skills the student body possesses.

The first step in fulfilling the promise of the funding application was to define the main concept of health literacy and to identify the corollary skills to be developed. Health literacy was therefore broken down into three essential skills sets; information seeking, communication, and cultural competence. These skills sets, used together, formed the basis for understanding and measuring the health literacy of a health care consumer. Each skill set could be further broken down into core skills that were relevant to healthcare. Once identified these core skills would become the basis for the mini-challenges and would be mapped to the series of cases that would form the basis for the game.

Compiling the list of information seeking skills began with an examination of the Association of College and Research Libraries Information Literacy Competency Standards for Higher Educa-

tion. These also formed the basis for the assessment that all JMU freshman take. The competency standards approach information seeking and use in five phases; identifying information needs, accessing needed information, evaluating information critically, applying information, and understanding information use ethics. The standards were written for an academic context, therefore only some of them are relevant to the healthcare setting. Core information seeking skills that were chosen for Face the Case were: the ability to find reliable information, the ability to find information online, the ability to organize information, the ability to understand new information, the ability to critically evaluate new information, the ability to summarize and combine new information with pre-existing beliefs, the ability to apply new information to a novel situation, and the ability to explain information to another.

The next category of skills to be developed was the communication skills. Communication is essential to the provision of healthcare, and it can be compromised in a variety of ways. Literacy in one's native language, literacy in the language common to the patient and provider, one's education level, and one's socio-economic status all affect self expression. But this is only half of the communication process; active listening, the ability to communicate in the face of anger, fear, and confusion, and the ability to communicate in a variety of media are also essential skills. The skills identified as essential communication skills for the purpose of the game were: active listening, the ability to elicit information, the ability to help another person understand, the ability to provide comfort, the ability to provide clear instructions, the ability to communicate with an angry person, the ability to communicate with a confused person, the ability to communicate with an anxious person, and the ability to provide written and graphical instructions.

The final set of skills to be developed was the cultural competency skills. These skills represent the rich variations in beliefs, practices, and behaviors that people from different cultures have that intersect with their ability to receive healthcare and comply with healthcare plans. Cultural competence was the most difficult skill set to define because it is commonly seen as a "journey" rather than a "destination". Unlike the information seeking and communication skill sets, the most important component of cultural competence is a mindset rather than a skill. Humility and the desire to expand one's world view are the hallmarks of cultural competence. With this in mind, the following cultural competence skills were identified: understanding one's own personal beliefs, the ability to identify biases, the ability to understand others' beliefs, and an awareness of relevant community support services.

In resolving the issue of matching core skills to cases, there was one final challenge. Health and human services, like most services, occur as the result of collaboration between professionals. No single professional can have all of the skills needed to resolve any but the simplest cases. Therefore we had to decide how to make unique skills, like fluency in another language, available to our players without adding to the already long list of skills they would be building through the mini challenges described previously. We decided to create collaborators, where the player could essentially borrow the skills of another professional.

In order to establish collaborators, a group of non-player characters was created, each with a unique persona and skill or skills. These characters were placed in a space in the game called the "Collaboration Café". Players could enter the café and select a potential collaborator. The collaborator would then display a brief dialogue box describing what their specific skills were. If the player decided that the skills described might help resolve the case at hand, s/he could accept a virtual business card for the collaborator, which would go into a collaborator slot in the PDA. When the time came to resolve the case by matching skills to it, the option of applying a collaborator's skills

would be available. Collaborators present in the café would change on each visit, so that the player would have to choose between collaborators with relevant skills and irrelevant skills.

FTC GAME DESIGN

The design team for the game consisted of a librarian as the principal investigator on the grant, a computer programmer, several JMU staff who provided part-time support, and an external contractor who provided the game graphics, music, and Flash programming. Usability testing of the game interface in various stages was conducted and coordinated by other library employees.

The librarian, principal investigator on the grant, was also the project manager for the creation of the game. She was charged with providing the bulk of the intellectual content; isolating the essential skills, creating the "mini-challenges" to teach the skills, writing the case narratives, describing each non-player character and collaborator, describing collaborators' skills, mapping the skills to the cases, and providing the in-game content on health literacy.

The computer programmer in the Center for Instructional Technology at JMU created a database that ran behind the scenes of the game and kept track of the scores, players, and their status in the game. The database also manages the question content for the mini-challenges. The database was designed so that content could be easily added to the game in the form of new case narratives, new skills, new collaborators, and new mini-challenges.

An external contractor was secured to do the graphic design work and Flash programming for the game. This consisted of designing the game world itself, including six interiors and an exterior that was designed as a loop so that players would never reach a dead end. The game world was designed to be expandable, with many store-fronts inactive but ready for use. The graphic designers also had to design the player avatar system, the entire collection of rewards, the interface for the mini-challenges, the score keeping, and a common area where players and their scores could be viewed. Because there was so much graphic design work, complexity of the visual experience was sometimes compromised in favor of variety.

TESTING

Formal usability testing was done at a mid-point in the game design, after the game play mechanics were in place but prior to the final launch. This was done using Morae software and was facilitated by library staff members not associated with the game's creation. Video recordings of novice players working through the game provided valuable insights into player behavior and expectations. Several changes to the game world graphics were implemented as the result of the usability testing. A series of introductory slides were also designed with the rules of the game presented graphically.

After its completion the game was evaluated by several classes of nursing students and one health communication class. Each group of students was given a formal evaluation to complete and received some form of class credit. The nursing students discussed their experiences with the game in an online forum, the transcript of which was later shared with the game designer. As expected, the nursing students gave the game high marks for interactivity, as well as the graphics, and the shopping elements. One student specifically mentioned liking the familiar buildings that were used to create the game world. Other elements that were mentioned as positive included the skill acquisition activities (mini-challenges), the reward of earning points for correct answers, and the variety of sounds programmed in the various environments. One student mentioned that she liked the fill-in-the-blank questions that required the player to contribute and analyze their own

world view. This style of question was used in the area of the game where cultural competence skills could be acquired.

The health communication students filled in a detailed worksheet with questions about which cases they received, skills acquired, and their definition of health literacy. It was clear upon reviewing the worksheets that students concluded with an acceptable working knowledge of health literacy and how it relates to individuals and communities. The most frequently repeated complaint had to do with the lack of instructions and feedback when the cases were not solved successfully. That students requested instructions or a tutorial surprised the game developers, since they believed that the game itself would provide sufficient instruction. This may be a reflection of the ultimate finding that the game was too hard. No students were able to solve more than a few cases. The majority of the health communication students reported that they were not regular game players.

PEDAGOGICAL ELEMENTS

At the time that the development and design of the game were taking place, the study of health literacy was in its youth. The game team decided to use the definition of health literacy that had been coined in 2000 "the degree to which individuals have the capacity to obtain, process, and understand basic health information and services and make appropriate health decisions" (National Library of Medicine, 2000). Since the audience for the game was not healthcare consumers, but future healthcare practitioners, the definition had to be deconstructed into the essential skills that healthcare providers would need in order to provide services to a population that had compromised health literacy. For the purposes of the game, health literacy was considered to be composed of information seeking, communication, and cultural competence skills. These discrete skills would be developed by means of "mini-challenges": essentially drills and quizzes that rewarded players with points for correct answers. The mini-challenge questions were entered into a database with randomization such that players would not see questions they had answered correctly, but would get multiple chances to answer questions they answered incorrectly.

The skills acquired would be applied to cases which the player (via her avatar) would have received as an email assignment. The cases varied in complexity through the number of skills required to solve them. An example of a case is provided in illustration 1.

To solve this case, the player needs to have acquired three skills; the ability to seek another's beliefs (cultural competence), the ability to summarize the main concept from a variety of sources (information seeking), and the ability to evaluate sources of information (information seeking). The player must explore the game world, earn points, and acquire these skills to solve the case.

GAMEPLAY ELEMENTS

The essential steps of the game are as follows:

1. A new player configures her avatar (an in-game virtual representation of the player).

2. The avatar receives an email message from a non-player character via a personal digital assistant (PDA). The message contains the narrative of a case describing another non-player character and a healthcare challenge they are facing.

3. The avatar travels through the game world.

4. The avatar enters various retail settings in which s/he receives a series of questions related to the essential skills that comprise health literacy.

5. Upon correctly answering the questions, the avatar then acquires skills s/he deems necessary to the solving the case at hand.

6. The avatar enters the collaboration space and receives proxy skills via a collaborator character.

7. Once the avatar decides s/he has the appropriate skills and collaborator, s/he matches them to the case using a drag and drop application in an office space in the game.

8. If the correct choices are made, the player receives additional points for solving the case.

Figure 1.

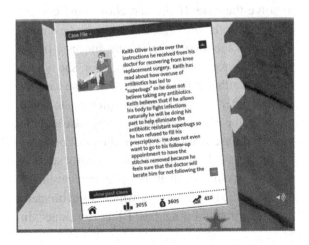

Figure 2.

Keith Oliver is irate over the instructions he received from his doctor for recovering from knee replacement surgery. Keith has read about how overuse of antibiotics has led to "superbugs" so he does not believe taking any antibiotics. Keith believes that if he allows his body to fight infections naturally he will be doing his part to help eliminate the antibiotic resistant superbugs so he has refused to fill his prescriptions. He does not even want to go to his follow-up appointment to have the stitches removed because he feels sure that the doctor will berate him for not following the drug regimen. You need to figure out why Keith has such a low opinion of his care, and help him understand some of the information he is finding.

9. The player can use the new points to acquire new clothing or accessories or make changes to her appearance in a retail space designed for this purpose.
10. The player receives a new case via email on her PDA.

The first time a player plays Face the Case he or she must configure an avatar. They do this through a process of choosing their gender and physical attributes. This element of the game was an intentional decision to give the player a sense of control over their own in-game identity. The literature of game design indicates that choice is an element of gameplay that makes a game fun. It appeals to the visual sense and helps the player identify with the game world. The budget for development limited the amount of game-world customization that could be programmed and designed in. Allowing the player to design their avatar was an affordable option that proved to be highly enjoyable to the players. The avatar is customized further later in the game when the player has amassed points and can purchase additional clothing, jewelry, and other personal characteristics in the "Bling Boutique".

Once the avatar is set up, they receive an email message on a virtual personal digital assistant (PDA) presenting them with their first case. The message is sent from a non-player character, Lois the Mentor. The first case assigned was the same for all players, and was written specifically to encourage exploration of the game world. The PDA becomes an essential record keeping tool for the player, as it tracks their scores, the cases they have been assigned, the collaborators they have contacted, and the skills they have acquired.

The essential skills that make up health literacy were divided into three categories and short answer quizzes and drills were designed to allow players to amass points. Once they had sufficient points they would choose which skill to purchase, based on which questions they had answered. The skill acquisition was set in various retail locations: a convenience store called the "Information Emporium" for the information seeking skills, an outdoor street market called the "Communications Market" for the communications skills, and a boutique called the "Hidden Treasures Culture Bazaar" for the cultural competence skills. In each of these environments the player would interact with two characters, one would provide the questions, and one would subsequently sell the skills once the player had amassed enough points by correctly answering the questions. Once the skills have been purchased, they are listed in a skill inventory on the players PDA.

In addition to skills acquired through the various outlets, some cases required the use of a collaborator. Collaborators would be met each time the player entered the "Collaboration Café", a restaurant-like space where various characters would be present. By selecting the characters, the player would get a brief introduction which would include the potential collaborator describing his or her skills. The player would then decide whether these skills might help solve the case at hand. If the player chose, they could take a collaborator's business card and use it later to help solve the case. Players could have up to two business cards for different collaborators simultaneously. Business cards are kept in a section of the players PDA.

Once the player had chosen and acquired the appropriate skills to solve the case at hand, she would return to an office space in the game and use a "drag and drop" feature of the desktop computer to solve the case. If she had chosen the correct skills and collaborator, she would receive a message from the mentor indicating success. If she chose the wrong skills or collaborator, she would receive feedback indicating that the case was not solved. After two unsuccessful attempts to solve the case, the player would get a new case and the unsolved case would return to the pool of cases the player might see again. Successfully solving the case would result in the player receiving a reward in the form of points, which could be spent in another retail setting, the "Bling Boutique". In this space the player could shop for new physical attributes (i.e. hair color or style, eye color, etc) and clothing, jewelry, and accessories.

There is a section of the game world where players can go to display their avatar and see other players and their scores. This is the only part of the game that pits players against each other, and it is not direct competition but rather a comparison of scores and bling.

The elements of the game described above correspond to the essential elements of a game as agreed upon by the design team. The cases are presented in order of difficulty, where the difficulty corresponds to the number of skills and collaborators required. This represents levels of the game. The skills themselves must be earned in the sense that players must correctly answer related questions in order to acquire the skills. This represents new powers. Finally the rewards come as points which can be used to acquire new clothing and physical attributes. This reward system offered visual appeal as well as engaged the players' sense of autonomy as they can choose their own appearance.

USER INTERFACE ELEMENTS

The game consisted of several varieties of characters. The avatar, which the player designed, the proprietors of the various skill shops, collaborators who can help solve the case, and the individuals and families represented in the cases. With the exception of the avatar, all of the non-player characters were drawn by the same artist in the same style. Collaborator narratives were written in a conversational style.

The game world itself was designed as a loop so that the player would never reach a dead end. The loop represented a town, and is composed of photographs of a variety of distinctive local buildings from the campus and surrounding towns that players are likely to recognize. All buildings were renamed to indicate their function in the game,

and minor changes to their appearances were often made. Other outdoor spaces in the game were the result of stitching together various outdoor environments into areas that looked reassuringly familiar to the player, but with slight variations. As the player moved through the world, several store-fronts had active doors that the player could pass through to enter an office, restaurant, or store. Other doors were inactive "place holders", although there is potential for expanding the game world by making any of these inactive doors active and designing a corresponding interior. While outside, the player heard ambient outdoors noises, and each interior had its own distinct soundtrack that corresponded to the environment. The design of the virtual world was driven primarily by the idea that something is fun if it is sensual (in this case visually appealing) and surprising (in this case, the inclusion of recognizable buildings in unfamiliar settings contributes to the surprise). The player's need to amass points by answering questions, and select the correct skill to purchase, represented the element of challenge in the game.

INTEGRATING THE GAME INTO CLASSES

In addition to making the game available on the web, it was integrated as an assignment into a public health class in the Nursing curriculum. Students enrolled in the class were assigned the game, and were expected to complete an in-depth evaluation of the experience as part of the course. The credit they received was for completing the evaluation, not scoring within the game.

As expected, the players were very satisfied with the visual environment of the game. Disappointing to the game's creators was the finding that the game was too difficult for the players. The comments submitted by the student evaluators revealed that they found the interface engaging and stimulating, they appreciated and enjoyed the choices they were able to make in configuring their avatars, and they enjoyed the narratives. They failed, however, to choose the appropriate skills to solve the case. They knew logistically how to solve the cases (i.e. they understood the interface) but they could not make the intellectual choice to pair the appropriate skills and collaborators with the cases.

The most likely explanation for the difficulty of the game lies in the way that the skills are described. When the player amassed enough points through mini-challenge play to acquire a new skill, they must make a choice about which skill is likely to be most useful to the case at hand. The proprietors of the skill shops reveal which skills the player could choose. Each skill included a brief sentence describing when it might be used. Later, when the player was matching their skills and collaborators to the case in order to solve it, they could again see a brief description of the skills. However, players were never able to assimilate the skill as described into their problem solving strategy applied to the case at hand.

Because of time constraints and the terms of the funding, the issue of skill naming has not been resolved. Subsequent games designed under the same grant were much simpler, and would be characterized by purists as exercises rather than true games.

CONCLUSION

This chapter has described some of the design and structural challenges of designing a health literacy game. Designing an educational game is more like creating a work of art than traditional scholarship. It must be informed by literacy in the medium of electronic gaming, as much as by instructional design principles. Ideally the design team should include potential players in order to create an interface that is usable and fun. It is also vitally important for the designers to expose themselves to as many games and opinions about games as possible. We learn as much from people

who say we can't or shouldn't do something as we do from people who claim to know how to do it. Heed the warnings of people who claim that building education into a game "sucks the fun out of it" and try to prove them wrong.

REFERENCES

DiSessa, A. A. (2000). *Changing minds: Computers, learning, and literacy*. Cambridge, MA: MIT Press.

Fabricatore, C. (2000). *Learning and videogames: An unexploited synergy*. Retrieved from www.learndev.org/dl/FabricatoreAECT2000.pdf

Gee, J. P. (2005). Good video games and good learning. *Phi Kappa Phi Forum*, *85*(2), 33–37.

Jenkins, H. (2005). Getting into the game. *Educational Leadership*, *62*(7), 48–51.

Landsberger, J. (2004). Gaming, teaching and learning: An interview with kurt squire. *TechTrends*, *48*(4), 4–7. doi:10.1007/BF02763436

National Library of Medicine. (2000). *Current bibliographies in medicine: Health literacy*. Bethesda, MD: National Institutes of Health, U.S. Department of Health and Human Services. Retrieved from http://www.nlm.nih.gov/pubs/cbm/hliteracy.html

Oblinger, D. (2003). Boomers, gen-xers, millennials: Understanding new students. *EDUCAUSE Review*, (July/August): 37–47.

Oxford english dictionary. (n.d.). New York: Oxford University Press.

Prensky, M. (2001). *Digital game-based learning*. New York: McGraw-Hill.

Recreation. (n.d.). Retrieved April 9, 2009, from http://en.wikipedia.org/wiki/Fun

Squire, K., & Steinkuehler, C. (2005). MEET THE GAMERS. (cover story). *Library Journal*, *130*(7), 38–41.

Steinkuehler, C., & Duncan, S. (2008). Scientific habits of mind in virtual worlds. *Journal of Science Education and Technology*, *17*(6), 530–543. doi:10.1007/s10956-008-9120-8

Chapter 11
The Application of 'Activity Theory' in the Design of Educational Simulation Games

Paul Peachey
University of Glamorgan, UK

ABSTRACT

As you read this text you perform an activity. Activity is literally everything we do and yet we are unaware of most of our operations. In this chapter, I will describe activity through a psychological lens and explain how this relates to the process of learning. The conceptual instrument used for analysis is 'activity theory'; a cultural-historical concept that was formulated in Russia during the 1920s. I will offer suggestions as to how activity theory may be used in the design of computer simulation games directed at education and highlight its conceptual underpinnings. In the latter part of the chapter, I offer possible directions for further research in this field.

INTRODUCTION

Activity is something that the West takes much for granted and yet it epitomizes human life itself. Russian psychologists over the last century have taken the notion of activity more seriously and are accredited for much of the research work in this field. The Russian viewpoint of activity is that it must be driven by a concrete objective and according to Petrovsky (1986), comprises internal (cognitive) and external (behavioural) components. Working with a computer is also an activity. In

fact, it is likely to involve a multitude of activities simultaneously multitasked. It can be argued that the strategic design of human-computer interface (HCI) programs should consider the psychological aspect of the user and application programs designed for education purposes should underpinned with sound pedagogical concepts, which is often not the case: '… educational software has been based on instructionist theories, with the computer performing roles that are traditionally performed by the teacher …' (Sawyer, 2006, p. 29). Bellotti (1988) studied a group of software designers in a number of leading software houses and found that many of these designers were unaware of any research

DOI: 10.4018/978-1-61520-781-7.ch011

in HCI although did concede that many good quality software programs have been developed without the potential benefit afforded by research findings.

Human beings are highly complex animals and the mind remains an enigma. This undermines any attempt to formulate an ideal software package based on theoretical underpinnings. Indeed, there are many sound theoretical underpinnings but only one truth, and adrift in the complexities of the human mind, it is likely to remain elusive.

It is important to acknowledge early on in this chapter that simulation is intended to augment the learning process and is not a substitute for real practice (Bellamy, 1996). One framework that might be considered as an underpinning theoretical base upon which to build a computer simulation program is 'activity theory' (AT). The aim of this chapter is therefore to introduce the concept of AT to designers/ developers of computer games for educational purposes as a viable option in software design in order to provide a sound theoretical pedagogical foundation on which to construct the program. I do not wish to enter epistemological or ontological philosophical debate but simply to introduce a pragmatic option that offers a tangible benefit in the design and development of simulation gaming software for educational purposes.

BACKGROUND ON 'ACTIVITY THEORY'

Activity theory (AT) is a historic-cultural conceptual model that was introduced primarily by the Russian psychologist Vygotsky (1896-1934) and was further developed mainly by Leont'ev (1903-1979) and more recently Engeström, but is influenced by the philosophies of Marx, Engel, Hegel, Kant and Luria. AT is essentially not a theory but a descriptive representation of an activity. AT initially emerged from a totalitarian environment that was highly structured and externally controlled and this powerful cultural antecedent has indelibly permeated the underlying concept. This influence led to Lektorsky's (1999) description of AT as 'one-sided' but the polarization is conceivable given Vygotsky's belief that the development of the mind is profoundly affected by the cultural and societal environment within which it exists.

Activity and Learning

In the West, 'action' is synonymous with 'activity' and the terms are often used interchangeably. Russian psychology suggests a distinct difference in that an activity is a hierarchical construct with action being a subordinate constituent. Operations are found at the next lower level. AT maintains that an activity is broken down into a series of actions which are undertaken consciously by individuals. These actions are facilitated by subconscious, routine motor operations. Repetition of a conscious action will eventually transform into a sub-conscious operation as it becomes *internalized*.

Experiential learning is a keystone in the development of skill-based competences. After some considerable repetition and practice via an interactive computer simulation program, a surgeon's competence transcends from novice level to expert level as the activity of performing a very delicate and intricate operation becomes *second nature*. Although the surgeon may claim that the act of conquering this skill was 'demanding', he accounts only for the explicit learning element. This is metaphorically speaking, the tip of the iceberg because the bulk of the learning was almost certainly implicit and transparent and the surgeon has learned a greater skill than he is aware. The firing of a specific combination of muscle cells in setting the hands at precisely aligned angles and applying carefully defined pressures on the surgeon's tools is a major undertaking. The task would be far too onerous were he to try to learn everything in one effort and mistakes are inevitable, but he calls on his procedural memory, i.e. the knowledge and skill attained previously in his life that is relevant to the task. This memory structure is known as a *schema* (Bartlett, 1932). The surgeon delegates the vast majority of the activity to these pre-learned motor and mental functions: '… [W]hen you learn a new skill you access prior knowledge. Information about a new domain is combined with existing knowledge and recognized to form new knowledge structures' (Preece et al., 1994, p. 164). The positioning of the hands consequently requires only a refinement to this schema. Indeed, the aim of education is to build a catalogue of schemata that the subject may call upon to solve some future real-life problem. It should be acknowledged though that each embedded schema is likely to be out of context to a real problem and hence a degree of creativity is also required. Together, these cognitive skills help to solve the problem whilst also generating a new schema though the experience of the activity.

Education in the West is primarily focused on an expert-learner relationship with a strong emphasis on one-to-one inculcation (McGill & Brockbank, 2004). The Russian pedagogical viewpoint refers to a more relaxed socially oriented epistemological paradigm with learning acquired through interaction and social intercourse. Collective activity is believed by many to have powerful positive ramifications for learning (e.g. Revans, 1980; Rogoff, 2003; Wenger, 1998) as expertise is distributed and shared among the immediate community. Wenger (1998) terms this entity as a 'community of practice':

Over time, this collective learning results in practices that reflect both the pursuit of our enterprises and the attendant social relations. These practices are thus the property of a kind of community created over time by the sustained pursuit of a shared enterprise. It makes sense, therefore, to call these kinds of communities *communities of practice* (p. 45).

AT suggests that does not occur in a vacuum and therefore neither can the process of game design and development. Simulation games are designed and developed with the user in mind and also involves interaction with members of the community of practice within the software firm. The user will also be directly or indirectly engaged in a community of practice and simulation gaming grants this access whilst also providing the tools that defines the individual's role within this community (Lainema, 2009).

Leont'ev (1981) offers a classic anecdote that describes the hierarchical structure of an activity and distinguishes the difference between activity, actions and operations. This example also provides an insight into the efficacy of a community of practice. Leont'ev visualizes the quintessential scenario of a primeval hunt whereby a group of hunters aim to kill game to satisfy their needs for food and clothing. He describes the action of one member of the hunting team whose role is to frighten the game and direct it towards an ambush where the other hunt members lie in wait. He does this by loudly beating on a drum. Leont'ev emphasizes that the action of the beater does not directly satisfy the personal need for food and clothing. The beater's objective differs to the other members who sought to destroy the animal and acquire its meat and skin. Leon'tev describes the beater's activity as the hunt and the frightening of the game is his action. His operation refers to the motor process of banging the drum. The outcome of the activity is the animal's meat and skin. The hunting team comprise specialists each of which brings their own unique expertise collectively to enhance the probability of a successful achievement of the common goal, or in terms of AT, the *object*. The traditional Russian concept of AT is that the object contains within it the motivation, fuelled by a perceived need. In this case, the object was realized by a group of individuals each of which had a specific role in the hunt, but differing personal objectives and operating within their own agreed specified parameters. It is worth noting that each member of this community was aware of his or her role within the practice and applies the synergistic power of the collective knowledge in terms of both the tacit and the explicit. The example also suggests that learning via the community of practice is a natural phenomenon and is activity driven. In each hunt event, further learning has been acquired through personal experience along with the observed actions of the peers operating within the activity.

Activity and learning are synonymous. There is a pervasive assumption that one cannot undertake any conscious activity without acquiring learning (Van Oers et al., 2008). The hunt members will learn both explicitly and tacitly as much from the actions, plans, attitudes and emotions of the peers as from their personal experiences. The process of learning does not operate in a vacuum but within a social milieu (Engeström, 1987; McGill & Brockbank, 2004; Rogoff, 2003; Vygotsky, 1978; Wenger, 1998). The coordination, division of roles, operational planning and so forth were components of a strategy that was formulated on the guidance of a collective pool of knowledge attained from years of experience, observation and instruction by elders.

COMPONENTS OF ACTIVITY THEORY

According to AT, the *subject* is the individual of whom is embedded within the ethos of society, which determines the character and hence the identity of the individual. Vygotsky (1978) maintained that society and the culture within which it lies are not external influences that help to shape the human mind but are generative forces of the mind itself. This relationship is reciprocal as society creates the individual that in turn, creates society. Amidst this socially oriented environment is a plethora of symbolic and physical artifacts that interface people to the external environment. Society along with its artifacts comprises the essence of the outer world. Artifacts are seen as mediating tools that enables the individual to address the object and

may be physical, conceptual or symbolic in form. Contrary to the view that humans may control their lives from the inside, Vygotsky believed that artifacts are tools that enabled humans to control their lives from the outside. Artifacts are modified representations of an earlier form (Cole, 1999) and are a reification of culture. Notably, it is the role of archaeologists to extract the cultural history from relics. Ancient scripts and inscriptions are manifestations of human implicit thoughts that are suspended in time through explicit symbolisation embodied with intent for preservation.

The relationship between the subject and object by means of the artifacts is non-linear as breakdowns occur when the artifacts fail to establish the connection between the subject and the object. The artifact itself might then become the focus of an activity and assume the role of the object. Kaptelinin & Nardi (2006) state that artifacts undergo modification by individuals who adapt them to their special needs. They call this *instrumentalization*. Individuals also need to learn how to operate these artifacts effectively in a process called *instrumentation*: 'Through instrumentalization and instrumentation, that is, the transformations of artifacts and persons, an artifact becomes appropriated and develops into an instrument' (p. 110). The three key components of AT form a triadic relationship as shown in the simple diagram of Figure 1.

Despite the apparent rigid appearance of the classic AT model of Figure 1, it represents an activity that operates within a complex external flux. The model must therefore be highly dynamic and each component interacts and mediates the other two. The subject is internally changed by the activity as learning develops (Kaptelinin & Nardi, 2006). A similar reciprocal relationship occurs between the subject and the mediating artifact and the subject and the object (Kaptelinin, 1996). The object is formulated by the subject but in Russian psychology, this object takes a slightly different meaning than the West is accustomed to: 'The object should not be confused with a conscious

Figure 1. 'Classic' AT model (Vygotsky, 1978, p. 40).

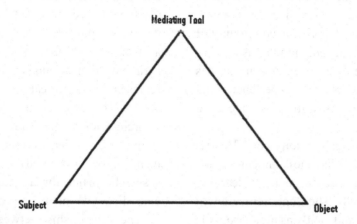

goal or aim. In activity theory, conscious goals are related to discrete, finite, and individual actions; objects are related to continuous, collective activity systems and their motives' (Engeström & Escalante, 1996, p. 360). It is acknowledged that any model cannot be an accurate representation of real life and the classic model of Figure 1 is perhaps far too basic a model to offer an analytical description of an activity given the parameters. Engeström (1987) clarifies the role of AT within a socio-cultural environment in his expanded version as seen in Figure 2.

The expanded AT model of Figure 2 includes additional elements such as the division of labour, rules and community. All are intertwined as indicated by the connecting lines within the model. The added lower trapezium clearly represents the interaction and culture of the social environment which contextualizes AT unyieldingly within communities of practice. In terms of an online virtual game, this community can include up to millions of players from different countries, backgrounds and cultures. In 2007, there were 217 million online gamers (Grabstats, 2009).

One potential obstacle with the collective approach is that it is susceptible to multiple perceptions. Every individual is engaged in a unique combination of communities of practice

Figure 2. 'Expanded' AT model (from 'Perspectives on AT' by Engeström et al., (1999, p. 31). Cambridge: Cambridge University Press.

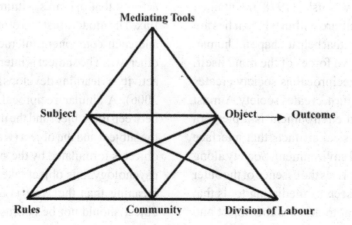

and micro-cultures. Consequently, a common goal between the members of a community of practice might become confused. It is also possible that the subject may not be able to accurately identify the object. Bedny & Meister (1997) suggest that although the subject may be unaware of the operations and even the actions, one must be aware of the object of the activity. In AT the object specifies the motive (Leont'ev, 1978), but these motives will have diverse qualities of meaning and may manifest themselves differently to individuals. Objects are prone to diverse perceptions of importance and meaning and may also be construed by changing circumstances. In terms of Leont'ev's anecdote of the hunt, the association amongst the members may not be as harmonic as the case suggests. Although the outcome is specified by Leont'ev to be that of clothing and food to be shared amongst the members of the hunting group, one may contemplate whether or not the combat is with the animal or with the hunger and cold. Furthermore, some members of the hunt might simply be drawn to the inherent excitement that the hunt affords (this aspect is discussed later in this chapter). Christiansen (1996) metaphorically refers to AT as a prism that reflects activity in 'inner and outer processes'. Christiansen furthers her argument that there are many prisms present in an activity embedded within a community of practice. Identifying the parameters of the activity within a community of practice is problematic and members of the community might have their own personal objectives and agendas that can create tensions and instability. The designer of a computer game may have the personal objective to create a robust application of the highest quality but is frustrated by the need to water down his aspiration because the finance director is focused on budgetary constraints. Holland & Reeves (1996) undertook an ethnographical study of three teams of university students engaged in software engineering and found that each team formulated very different objectives with one team focusing on the development of an efficient

program, another team was primarily concerned with high grades and the third team were occupied in settling internal differences amongst the team members. Moreover, subjects may employ a range of tool options in their pursuit of an object. As Holland & Reeves (op.cit.) point out, mathematic calculations at a grocery store is likely to be different to the mathematical calculations conducted at school. These examples highlight the pressures in terms of identifying the object in the collective social matrix of the community of practice. They also suggest that if the object is shared, the activities, actions and mediating tools are likely to vary and thus cohesion and synergy might be difficult to achieve.

As suggested earlier, AT operates within a flux and is subject to the anomalies of both the human mind and human behaviour. The hierarchical elements of the model are affected by the instability of actions and operations, which both change in position and intrinsic nature. Any state of activity must therefore be temporal and all its components transitional. Kaptelinin & Nardi (2006) indicate that the hunter may experience a state of confusion due to the tension between the threat of starvation and cold and the inherent dangers of the beast. If the animal unexpectedly decides to ferociously attack the hunting team, the object of the activity may very quickly transform from that of killing the animal for the purpose of acquiring food and clothing to the immediate survival of the hunt members. As a consequence, the individual actions and goals of the team members rapidly change and they collectively decide to abandon the hunt activity and flee. This vulnerability suggests that the hunt members are engaged in a constant repetition of cognitive reflection and feedback processes. Indeed, Bedny & Meister (1997) posit that all actions have a loop structure. This mental process of monitoring the circumstances of the immediate situation and reflecting on its outcomes lends itself to the concept of experiential learning (Kolb, 1984). In the case of the hunt, collective as well as individual learning is attained through experience. Having reflected on and critically analysed the activity the hunters might agree on the development of better tools or an improved strategy for the next hunt event.

According to AT, a conscious action, with sufficient practice, becomes internalized and then functions within the subconscious, operational level. Some entity will mediate the process of transformation. A novice learner negotiates the piano keys of an electric piano set in training mode and responds according to the guidance offered by an LCD screen on the instrument. Each time a note appears on the staves, the associated piano key is highlighted and is subsequently depressed by the learner in an external, fully conscious action of concentrated effort. The object is to successfully play the score and in this case, the main mediating tool is the training software program. After some time and considerable practice, the novice pianist develops competence and a degree of expertise as the piano playing becomes an automatic operation. The action of piano playing is transformed to operational level within the hierarchy and although she may still engage with the mediation provided by the virtual trainer, her finger may already be depressing the key the moment a musical note appears on the stave without reference to the trainer. Hence, when the action becomes internalized, the mediating tool may no longer be employed. However, if the pianist then damages a finger, she will need to re-negotiate the process and the operation is raised to action level as she re-structures her pattern of piano playing using perhaps a different finger as a substitute. This is known as a *breakdown* and occurs when an intended action or activity fails in some way. A breakdown might also occur if there is tension between objectives, say, between individuals working collaboratively on the same project. This type of breakdown is classed as a *contradiction*. Breakdowns and contradictions would seem to be unwanted irritations but paradoxically, within the domain of AT, they are a key source of development (Leont'ev, 1978). User errors are breakdowns and

new thinking emerges at the action level until the skill is re-perfected at the operational level (refer to Figure 3).

ACTIVITY THEORY AND SIMULATION

Computer simulation programs can be an effective tool in the generation of knowledge and skill and it is likely that many pilots and passengers owe their lives to the writers of computer simulation software. An animated program that demonstrates the tying of a knot in a rope transcends any written or verbal description. Interactive computer simulation programs afford experiential and incidental learning; something that is impossible to administer within the didactic ambience of a lecture hall.

AT offers a practical underpinning framework for the design of computer simulation games directed at education because first, playing a computer game is an activity and second, AT contains within it a learning mechanism. AT also accommodates objectives, motivation, socio-constructivism and emotion. In an educational simulation program, the objective is to develop the learner to a level whereby in a real life situation, he/she may perform a task at the operational level with minimum error. Bødker (1989) suggests that an individual brings a repertoire of operations to the table (schemata). The activity of engaging in simulation gaming adds to this repertoire. Computer simulation games aimed to appropriate learners with skill and knowledge requires the designer of the application to identify the learning needs of the user and provide the means to maximise the learning opportunities and support the learning process. The application program should therefore be underpinned with a strategy for learning. Attraction in gaming is associated with challenges and hence the game design must include catalysts that stimulate emotion and provide challenges for the player. This means that the objectives that lie within the lower hierarchical levels of activities

Figure 3. Hierarchy of an activity

needs to change by offering new scenarios that will need to be negotiated by the learner. As actions transform into operations, a supply of new challenges should be made available that are set to be within the capability of the individual but are of an appropriate difficulty level. These challenges can instigate a state of concentration and absorption otherwise known as *flow* (Csikszentmihalyi, 1990). Csikszentmihalyi posits that a state of flow incorporates inherent motivation. Knowledge and skill is thus attained on a progressive, incremental basis. Commercial computer games, for example, set levels of difficulty and without these trials the game may be perceived by the player to regress into a mundane irrelevance. Similarly, challenges set at a difficulty level too high for the user may be just as destructive to motivation. Attention is a key learning requirement (McNeil, 2009) and the application should be designed to combat banality. The manipulation of emotion creates its own tacit learning potential through achievement, disappointment, frustration and so forth whilst combating the forces of banality.

The AT expanded model of Figure 4 illustrates the interactivity of the variables in the context of the designer/developer of the computer simulation game within the setting of the software firm. One immediately notices the relative complexities in the endeavour to produce a quality product and the dependence on both other people and associated artifacts. All variables are intertwined in a combined effort to achieve the common goal.

The diagram of Figure 5 applies the AT model in the context of the user. The user might perceive the act of engaging with the simulation program as an isolated affair but the interaction with the external elements is apparent in the model. Indeed, the player is interacting with the software developer albeit displaced in time and space.

In Figure 5, the object of the task, (i.e. to land an aircraft) is merely a test of competence. The learning journey takes precedence and is causal in terms of the output. With learning itself being the objective, the outcome is more relevant to the *means* as opposed to the *end*.

Figure 4. Application of the AT model to a commercial simulation game design in the context of the game designer/ developer.

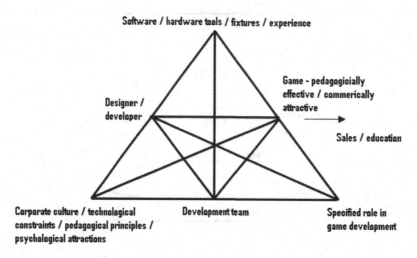

Figure 5. Application of the AT model to a simulation game in the context of the user.

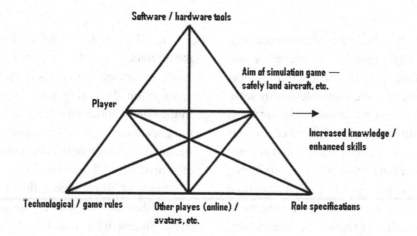

THE 'ZONE OF PROXIMAL DEVELOPMENT'

In terms of AT, challenges will create a shift in level from operation to action and the subject may accordingly employ different mediating tools. At the action level, challenges arise due to the transformation from operation to action within the activity, which in turn demotes the user from expert to novice. This shifting to and fro from action to operation and back again is the nucleus of experiential learning. Contradiction and breakdowns are catalysts that cause the operation to shift to the higher level of an action provoking change in all of the components including the artifact. The subject has attained knowledge from the experience that might result in a correcting behaviour. This shifting of levels is a benefit of AT and relates to a concept devised by Vygotsky (1978) known as the *zone of proximal development* (ZPD). This ZPD gap indicates the current level of knowledge of the learner and the level of knowledge that could be potentially achieved with appropriate guidance from an expert. In terms of the AT model, the expert is the mediator. This mediating instrument may take the form of speech, text within a book, an animation sequence, and so on. All are codified symbolic representations that help transfer tacit thought into explicit objects that are transferable across a medium.

Repetition of the operation is essential for internalization. Engel (1999) posited that neural pathways within the human brain strengthen the more an area of memory is invoked. Bedny & Meister (1997) concurs: 'One can see this in gymnastics, where the gymnast knows the technique, but cannot perform it without extensive practice. Practice turns knowledge into a skill' (p. 308). Once a particular milestone is internalized, another milestone is set by the mediator and the ZPD gap of the learner progressively closes. Engaging with a new application program for the first time calls on a multitude of conscious actions, many of which will slowly transform into operations and the activity of operating the program becomes increasingly less mentally onerous for the learner. During this learning process, the ZPD gap narrows with mediated practice. The learner should be guided along a learning journey by the mediator that affords development of learning at a pace and means comfortable for the learner. The transformation process from externalization to internalization takes time that may involve hours, days or weeks of repetitive practice. An optimum balance needs to be found between operation and action. As actions are internalized, new opportunities for action should replace the old to ensure a sufficient supply that is equal to the pace of transformation. As actions undergo this transformation, the ZPD gap should gradually shrink as progressive learning occurs. One potential problem is that under normal circumstances, the expert will be in a position to identify the parameters of the ZPD of the learner and behave according to these data but it is impossible to accurately determine the ZPD of a user of whom they never meet. This

need not matter in a carefully designed computer program as the code should include levels of difficulty for the purpose of progression and trials for the purpose of feedback. The users' competence will be examined by providing the precondition within the application program that they will need to illustrate sufficient competence within the game tasks before they can be promoted to the next upper level of difficulty. This effectively automates the process of ZPD monitoring.

Although Vygotsky and others relate ZPD to the development of children, adults also have a need to learn. For example, there is still a requirement of the experienced simulation games designer to learn new concepts, technologies, contemporary trends and so forth that are relevant to the task. Adults must therefore also have their own ZPDs to address. Peer learning within the community of practice of the software design firm is one means of addressing this personal ZPD: 'Educators believe that group learning and peer tutoring can offer an effective environment for guiding a child through its ZPD' (Gross 1995, p. 500).

The blueprint of the learning journey for the learner is therefore in the hands of the designers of the computer application program. To be effective in terms of engagement and learning, the computer program must at least contain the following two important elements. First, it must be of an appropriately high quality and second, it must be underpinned with a suitable pedagogy designed to meet specified learning objectives. The blueprint must therefore include an optimal mix of repetitious events and new learning opportunities. Repetition facilitates internalization and learning opportunities manifest themselves in new challenges that develop learning. The needs of the learner should also be considered. In terms of negotiating the ZPD gap, learners will have different intrinsic propensities in addressing the gap.

The internal processes of consolidation, along with contests that are designed to be progressively a little more difficult than previously, provide the key to sustained development. The mediator, such as the expert, should be highly visible at the beginning of the learning journey but stepping back as the learning develops. Addressing the ZPD gap initially entails a high level of external intervention but gradually less afterwards as the learner becomes increasingly competent. This pedagogical approach is known as 'scaffolding' (Wood et al., 1976). Although this approach is primarily directed at children, it may be equally applied to adult learning although mature learners can potentially engage in a self-scaffolding process (Gross, 2005). For example, the learner of the piano as earlier described might require concentrated intervention from the virtual trainer in order to establish how to read the music sheet and associate these symbolic representations to the physical piano keys, but once she acquires a basic understanding, she may provide her own scaffolding structures rendering intervention unnecessary. In a computer simulation application program designed to develop knowledge, the scaffolding may be incorporated within the computer program. The computer software designer interacts with the learner through lines of code, which substitutes the mediation of the expert.

Referring back to Leont'ev's (1978) example of the hunt, it is worth noting that the hunters may engage with the hunt simply for the sense of excitement it affords despite the inherent dangers involved. The object and motive might be less obvious to the participants and the inspiration would be more attributed to the phenomenon of play as opposed to addressing the explicit needs for food and clothing. Bruner et al. (1976) relates play distinctly to learning. This issue of play is highly relevant in the design of simulation games. Indeed, in the eyes of an infant, play is itself a simulation of adulthood. Play is presumably an important attraction for adults otherwise there would be no market for adult sports for example. One potential difference between adult play and

child play lies in the definition of the object. Adult play is usually directed by a conscious goal but the objective in child play might be obscure. In child play, with no clear overarching objective, play must have contained within it an intrinsic natural motivation, which according to Gross (2005) is simple enjoyment. B.F. Skinner's (1974) concept of *positive reinforcement* suggests that a person who engages in a pleasurable experience will want to repeat the experience. Moreover, play lends itself to the concept problem-based learning (PBL), where the traditional teaching concept of *knowledge leading to action* inverts into *action leading to knowledge*.

Piaget (1932) found that children tended to ignore pre-defined rules in play and enforce their own. Moreover, Csikszentmihalyi (1981) posits that the activity of play occurs even outside of the rules of reality itself. Hakkarainen (1999) concurs: '[A]n essential feature of play is its place on the border of two worlds: the narrative world of play and the real world' (p. 232). Kaptelinin & Nardi (2006) features a case concerning the emancipation of an individual entrenched within the virtual environment of an online game. In this study, a player describes his personal experience of being 'let loose' within a virtual game and outlines his pleasure in having the freedom to take or do whatever he wants including even the act of killing. Whereas Engeström's expanded model of AT suggests that the subject complies with cultural and social rules, the virtual game enables the player to circumvent, ignore or break these rules without social penalty. Here, the individual might be realizing his/her natural innate humanistic desires for a high locus of control (Rubin & McNeil, 1983) and not be dictated to by external rules. This point has consequences in terms of addressing the object: 'A pilot may control an aircraft according to the goals that are extrinsically supplied but may be idiosyncratically interpreted' (Bedny & Meister, 1997, p. 9).

DIRECTIONS FOR FUTURE RESEARCH

This chapter focuses on computer simulation games designed for education and not simply computer application programs designed for education. This choice of terminology is deliberate due to the inherent attraction that humans possess in terms of play. This belief is based on a long-held personal predisposition that activity is motivated more by *wanting* to do as opposed to *having* to do; a *pull* rather than *push* ideology. The TEEM report (2001) include the terms stimulation and knowledge in the same sentence:

Games provide a forum in which learning arises as a result of tasks stimulated by the content of the games, knowledge is developed through the content of the game, and skills are developed as a result of playing the game (McFarlane et al. 2001, p. 4).

Challenge and play can merge into a single entity that may provide stimulation in addition to the potential to develop knowledge and skills. The concept of play can be an intrinsically pleasurable experience and through a well designed computer game, learning and development becomes automatic and transparent to the player and is unlikely to be deemed as an obligatory chore.

Furthermore, the application of AT in an online virtual game changes the nature of the concept itself as it finds itself submerged within a vast multicultural global environment. This contemporary socially oriented global environment may be virtual in nature but the people engaged in the game are real and the computer adopts the role as the interfacing communication channel that binds the global mass. This seismic shift in the nature of the community of practice is an interesting phenomenon that offers mouth-watering opportunities for research as does the issue of adult play especially within the domain of computer gaming.

CONCLUSION

Learning derived from an activity is experiential and the societal influence of the AT model infers that activity within the praxis of a community also presents a significant learning opportunity of a socio-constructivist nature. Designing computer simulation games for educational purposes is pedagogically challenging but some understanding as to how people develop their knowledge and skills is paramount in terms of achieving the objective of producing a computer program that is both efficient and effective. AT describes the internalization of conscious actions and offers an explanation as to how knowledge and skill is constructed through the shifting of the hierarchical levels between actions and operations within a defined activity. This movement between levels is the bedrock in learning a skill and internalizing it adequately. The computer game should accommodate this facility within its application and allow learning to develop progressively according to Vygotsky's notion of the zone of proximal development. Careful scaffolding built within the computer program can sustain the learning process and also to retain the motivation of the learner through the intrinsic concept of play. Finally, as technology advances at a breathtaking pace especially in the field of of information and communication technologies (ICT), computer simulation games can only ·improve. Today's cutting edge technology is tomorrow's primitive relic but blueprints for effective computer game design remains indelible and eternal.

REFERENCES

Bartlett, F. C. (1932). *Remembering*. Cambridge, UK: Cambridge University Press.

Bedny, G., & Meister, D. (1997). *The Russian theory of activity: Current applications to design and learning.* London: Laurence Erlbaum Associates Publishing.

Bellamy, R. K. E. (1996). Designing educational technology: Computer mediated change. In Nardi, B. A. (Ed.), *Conscious and consciousness: Activity theory and human-computer interaction* (pp. 123–146). London: MIT Press.

Bellotti, V. (1988). Implications of current design practice for the use of HCI techniques. In D.M.J. & R. Winder (eds.), People and computers IV (pp. 13-34). Cambridge, UK: Cambridge University Press.

Bødker, S. (1989). A human activity approach to user interfaces. *Human-Computer Interaction, 4,* 171–195. doi:10.1207/s15327051hci0403_1

Bruner, J. S., Jolly, A., & Sylva, K. (1976). *Play: Its role in development and evolution.* New York: Penguin.

Christiansen, E. (1996). Tamed by a rose: Computers as tools in human activity. In Nardi, B. A. (Ed.), *Conscious and consciousness: Activity theory and human-computer interaction* (pp. 175–198). London: MIT Press.

Cole, M. (1999). Cultural psychology. Some general principles and a concrete example. In Engeström, Y., Miettinen, R., & Punamäki, R. L. (Eds.), *Perspectives on activity theory* (pp. 232–249). Cambridge, UK: Cambridge University Press.

Csikszentmihalyi, M. (1981). Some paradoxes in the definition of play. In Cheska, A. T. (Ed.), *Play as context.* West Point, NY: Leisure Press.

Csikszentmihalyi, M. (1990). *Flow: The psychology of optimal experience.* New York: Harper & Row.

Engel, S. (1999). *Context is everything: The nature of memory.* London: Freeman.

Engeström, Y. (1987). *Learning by expanding: An activity-theoretical approach to developmental research.* Helsinki: Orienta-Konsultit.

Engeström, Y., Engeström, R., & Karkkainene, M. (1995). Polycontextuality and boundary crossing in expert cognition. *Learning and Instruction, 5*(4), 319–336. doi:10.1016/0959-4752(95)00021-6

Engeström, Y., & Escalante, V. (1996). Mundane tool or object of affection? The rise and fall of the Postal Buddy. In Nardi, B. A. (Ed.), *Conscious and consciousness: Activity theory and human-computer interaction* (pp. 325–373). London: MIT Press.

Grabstats. (n.d.). Retrieved July 7, 2009, from http://www.grabstats.com/statcategorymain. asp?StatCatID=14

Gross, R. (1995). *Psychology: The science of mind and behaviour* (4th ed.). Tonbridge, UK: Greengate Publishing.

Hakkarainen, P. (1999). Play and motivation. In Engeström, Y., Miettinen, R., & Punamäki, R. L. (Eds.), *Perspectives on activity theory* (pp. 232–249). Cambridge, UK: Cambridge University Press.

Kaptelinin, V. (1996). Computer-mediated activity: Functional organs. In Nardi, B. A. (Ed.), *Conscious and consciousness: Activity theory and human-computer interaction* (pp. 45–68). London: MIT Press.

Kaptelinin, V., & Nardi, B. A. (2006). *Acting with technology: Activity theory and interaction design.* London: MIT Press.

Kolb, D. A. (1984). *Experiential learning experience as a source of learning and development.* Upper Saddle River, NJ: Prentice Hall.

Lainema, T. (2009). Perspective making: Constructivism as a meaning-making structure for simulation gaming. *Simulation & Gaming, 40*(1), 48–67. doi:10.1177/1046878107308074

Lektorsky, V. A. (1999). Activity theory in a new era. In Engeström, Y., Miettinen, R., & Punamäki, R. L. (Eds.), *Perspectives on activity theory* (pp. 65–69). Cambridge, UK: Cambridge University Press.

Leont'ev, A. N. (1978). *Activity, consciousness, and personality*. Englewood Cliffs, NJ: Prentice Hall.

Leont'ev, A. N. (1981). *Problems of the development of the mind*. Moscow: Progress.

McFarlane, A., Sparrowhawk, A., & Heald, Y. (2001). *Report on the Educational Use of Games*. Retrieved April 10, 2009, from http://www.teem.org.uk/publications/teem_gamesined_full.pdf

McGill, I., & Brockbank, A. (2004). *The action learning handbook: Powerful techniques for education, professional development & training*. London: Routledge-Falmer.

McNeil, F. (2009). *Learning with the brain in mind*. London: Sage Publications.

Petrovsky, A. V. (Ed.). (1986). *General psychology*. Moscow: Education Publishers.

Piaget, J. (1932). *The moral judgement of the child*. London: Routledge & Keegan Paul.

Preece, J., Rogers, Y., Sharp, H., Benyon, D., Holland, S., & Carey, T. (1994). *Human-computer interaction*. Harlow, UK: Addison-Wesley.

Revans, R. (1980). *Action learning: New techniques for action learning*. London: Blond and Briggs.

Rogoff, B. (2003). *The cultural nature of human development*. Oxford, UK: Oxford University Press.

Rubin, Z., & McNeil, E. B. (1983). *The psychology of being human* (3rd ed.). London: Harper and Row.

Sawyer, R. K. (2006). *The Cambridge handbook of the learning sciences*. Cambridge, MA: Cambridge University Press.

Skinner, B. F. (1974). *About behaviourism*. London: Penguin.

Van Oers, B. (Ed.). (2008). *Learning and learning theory from a cultural-historical point of view*. Cambridge, UK: Cambridge University Press. doi:10.1017/CBO9780511499937

Wenger, E. (1998). *Communities of practice: learning, meaning and identity*. Cambridge, UK: Cambridge University Press.

Wood, D. J., Bruner, J. S., & Ross, G. (1976). The role of tutoring in problem-solving. *Journal of Child Psychology and Psychiatry, and Allied Disciplines, 17*, 89–100. doi:10.1111/j.1469-7610.1976.tb00381.x

Chapter 12
The Learning Toolkit:
The Design, Development, Testing and Dissemination of Evidence-Based Educational Software [1]

Philip C. Abrami
Concordia University, Canada

Robert S. Savage
McGill University, Canada

Gia Deleveaux
Concordia University, Canada

Anne Wade
Concordia University, Canada

Elizabeth Meyer
Concordia University, Canada

Catherine LeBel
Concordia University, Canada

ABSTRACT

In this chapter the authors summarize the design, development, testing, and dissemination of the Learning Toolkit—currently a suite of three highly interactive, multimedia tools for learning. ABRACADABRA is early literacy software designed to encourage the development of reading and writing skills of emerging readers, especially students at-risk of school failure. The authors highlight the important modular design considerations underlying ABRACADABRA; how it scaffolds and supports both teachers and students; the evidence on which it is based; the results of field experiments done to date; and directions for future research, development, and applications. They also present ePEARL and explain how it can be used with ABRACADABRA to promote self-regulation, comprehension and writing. They briefly discuss ISIS-21 the prototype of a tool designed to enhance student inquiry skills and promote information literacy. As an evidence-based toolkit available without charge to educators, the authors believe the suite of tools comprising the Learning Toolkit breaks new ground in bringing research evidence to practice in ways that promote wide scale and sustainable changes in teaching and learning using technology.

DOI: 10.4018/978-1-61520-781-7.ch012

INTRODUCTION

Canada is generally seen as a literate developed nation, with a well-developed and successful education infrastructure. Like all impressions, however, it is important to go deeper and explore the evidence. How well then is Canada really doing in terms of literacy? *PISA 2006: Science Competencies for Tomorrow's World*, reports the results from the most recent PISA survey, focuses on science, mathematics, and reading. The Programme for International Student Assessment (PISA) is a triennial survey of the knowledge and skills of 15-year-olds, and the product of collaboration among participating countries and economies through the Organization for Economic Co-operation and Development (OECD). OECD draws on leading international expertise to develop valid comparisons across countries and cultures. More than 400,000 students from 57 countries, making up close to 90% of the world economy, took part in PISA 2006. The average performance of Canadian students was in the upper quartile on the PISA measures of reading (OECD, 2000, 2006; Statistics Canada, 2004). By itself, these results seem encouraging.

Nevertheless the same reports noted that about 25% of the Canadian students tested performed at or below Level 2. These 15-year-old students encountered basic difficulties in "Locating straightforward information, making low- level inferences of various types, working out what a well-defined part of a text means, and using some outside knowledge to understand it" (OECD, 2000, 2006; Statistics Canada, 2004). Such basic difficulties, played out across the nation, have a significant impact on the economic well-being of all Canadians. Recently the results of national and international surveys—the Adult Literacy and Life Skills (ALLS) survey by Statistics Canada and the Organization for Economic Cooperation and Development (OECD) disseminated by the Canadian Council on Learning (2007)—suggested that almost half of adult Canadians have only low-level literacy skills. The survey established five levels of literacy, with level 3 considered to be the minimum level of skill required in today's society. Results showed that only 58% of Canadians achieved level 3 or above in the category of prose literacy. The ALLS survey was conducted in Canada, the United States, Italy, Norway, Switzerland, Bermuda, and the state of Nuevo León, Mexico. More than 23,000 Canadians took part in the survey that tested prose and document literacy, numeracy, and problem- solving skills. The survey also showed that there has been virtually no improvement in Canada's results since the previous surveys.

Paul Cappon, President and CEO of the Canadian Council on Learning, responded to these findings (2007) by arguing that there is an urgent need to develop a more cohesive approach to ensure that Canadian adults have the literacy, numeracy, and analytical skills they need to reach their full potential. He drew specific attention to the urgent need to understand why our current literacy and learning programs are not succeeding in order to develop more effective approaches.

Is the United States doing better than Canada? The same international research (OECD, 2000, 2006) shows the US fairing worse than their northern counterparts. For example, Finland was the highest-performing country on the science scale, with an average of 563 score points. Six other countries had mean scores of 530 to 542 points: Canada, Japan and New Zealand, and the partner countries/economies of Hong Kong-China, Chinese Taipei, and Estonia. Australia, the Netherlands, Korea, Germany, the United Kingdom, the Czech Republic, Switzerland, Austria, Belgium and Ireland, and the partner countries/ economies Liechtenstein, Slovenia and Macao-China also scored above the OECD average of 500 score points. The United States performed below the OECD average, with a score of 489, ranking 36th out of 57 countries. Less than 10% of American students scored at the highest proficiency levels, contrasted with more than 20% of students in

Finland (PISA results, OECD, http://pisacountry. acer.edu.au/index.php). These results and others emphasize the importance of improving the essential competencies of students and scaffolding support for educators and why we developed the Learning Toolkit, a suite of evidence-based educational software that includes ABRACADABRA, an early literacy tool.

Currently, school is too often a place that disengages learners, focusing more on knowledge transmission than encouraging honest self-assessment and pro-active engagement. In these situations, learning and evaluation may not be meaningful acts of improvement but detached and punitive symbols of failure. As a consequence, the accumulated evidence on student learning has led to recommendations (American Psychological Association, 2008; Conference Board of Canada, 2008) focusing on increasing student activity, meaningfulness, and self-regulation, including the development of strategies for lifelong learning. While students need to develop essential curricular competencies—learning what to learn—they also need to learn better how to learn— developing strategies for mastery in a world where knowledge is increasingly dynamic. Student-centred learning is an approach towards achieving this vision and technology can play an important role as a tool in promoting educational change. Using electronic portfolios may be one way to better engage students and develop their strategies for learning.

An electronic portfolio is a digital container, capable of storing and organizing visual and auditory content, including text, images, video and sound. Electronic portfolios may also be learning tools when they are designed to support a variety of learning processes and are used for assessment purposes (Abrami & Barrett, 2005). Since they are web-based, they provide remote access that encourages anywhere, anytime learning and make it easier for peers, parents, and educators to provide input and feedback.

Electronic portfolios may scaffold attempts at knowledge construction by supporting reflection, refinement, conferencing and other processes of self-regulation, important skills for lifelong learning and learning how to learn. Self-regulation refers to a set of mental behaviours that include monitoring, guiding, and evaluating ones own learning. Students who are self-regulated are cognitively, motivationally, and behaviorally active participants in their own learning process (Zimmerman, 1989, 2000) and thus may demonstrate better academic performance (Rogers & Swan, 2004). The active use of electronic portfolios can contribute to a student's ability to self-regulate their learning and to enhance their meaningful learning of important educational skills and abilities, especially literacy skills (Abrami, Savage, Wade, Hipps, & Lopez, 2008; Meyer, Abrami, Wade, Aslan & Deault, in press; Wade, Abrami & Sclater, 2005). These are the reasons we developed our electronic portfolio tool, ePEARL.

As technology and the Internet become an increasingly pervasive part of everyday life the importance of developing information literacy skills becomes increasingly critical. In fact, the American Library Association considers information literacy skills to be the survival skills of the Information Age. Yet few school curricula specifically address the teaching of these skills. In many cases the teachers lack basic information literacy skills themselves. Severe cutbacks in school library staff and teacher-librarian programs have also contributed to a gap in the teaching of information literacy (Whitehead & Quinlan, 2002). This problem is amplified and exacerbated when students complete homework at home, as parents also lack information literacy skills to help the children with effective research and information evaluation strategies.

Without a systematic approach, the majority of students will continue to construct poor search strategies, retrieve inappropriate material, and incorrectly analyze, synthesize, utilize, problem solve and make decisions based on the information found. Further concerns relate to irresponsible or naïve use of the Internet by students. These weak information literacy skills will follow them into the workplace and into their personal lives and, if uncorrected, will limit the potential of far too many in the Information Age and Knowledge Economy. This overview summarizes our rationale for developing our information literacy tool, ISIS-21.

BACKGROUND

In this chapter we summarize the work we have done to date on evidence-based multimedia for learning and the design, development, testing and dissemination of our suite of tools, the Learning Toolkit (LTK). There are three linked tools that are currently part of the LTK: 1) early literacy software called ABRACADABRA--ABalanced Reading Approach for Canadians Designed to Achieve Best Results for All; 2) a bilingual, learning process electronic portfolio called ePEARL—Electronic Portfolio Encouraging Active Reflective Learning; and the prototype of a information literacy tool called ISIS-21-- Inquiry Strategies for the Information Society in the 21st Century. We outline the design and development of the tools including the evidence used as the basis for their construction. We summarize the research evidence that exists to validate the tools, and we discuss briefly some of the issues involved in dissemination on a wide scale for example, sustainability, and implementation fidelity.

Currently, each of the tools may be used separately or in combination with ePEARL. ePEARL serves as the core of the LTK because of its focus on encouraging the development of student self regulation (Zimmerman, 2000). In ePEARL, students set goals, plan strategies, store versions of work, and collect reflections, peer, teacher, and student feedback. The use of multimedia allows students to store audio recordings of their reading, and collect video images as well as written work. These artifacts are an important supplement to the student comprehension activities in ABRA.

To see demonstration videos and to explore the tools please visit http://doe.concordia.ca/cslp/ under ICT projects.

ABRACADABRA: HELP FOR STRUGGLING READERS

In this section, we outline the developmental history of ABRACADABRA, elaborate important design principles, provide an overview of the tool, highlight some of its gaming elements, and summarize some of the research we have conducted on its effectiveness. Some of the concepts and principles described here also apply to the design, development, testing, and dissemination of ePEARL and ISIS-21, the other tools currently in the LTK.

From the Reading CAT to the Learning Toolkit As our first tool, ABRACADABRA (hereafter referred to as ABRA) has gone through numerous development phases since 2000 and been supported by a variety of external sources. At each turn, we learned something new and overcame a challenge, not the least of which was funding. The initial version, known as the Reading Computer –Assisted Tutor (Reading CAT), was supported by the Chawker's Foundation and through an equipment grant awarded to the CSLP by the Canada Foundation for Innovation that allowed us to establish a new design and development lab for the tool's development.

From the latest research in the area of literacy development, the Balanced Literacy Toolkit (BLTK) emerged as a more complete prototype, combining the best of the Reading CAT and incorporating instructional and professional development modules. With the continued financial support of the Chawkers foundation, VRQ Diva (Valorisation-Recherche Quebec), and Industry Canada, the BLTK morphed into the pilot or alpha version of ABRA. The credit for the name and acronym belong to Mary Ann Evans, a researcher from Guelph University, who penned the title on a napkin during a lunch break at an ABRA Steering Committee meeting.

Through grants awarded by the Norshield Foundation and FQRSC (Province of Quebec) the pilot version of ABRA was tested with first grade students enrolled in a summer program. There were 12 stories and 16 instructional activities across three literacy domains: alphabetics, fluency, and comprehension. Based on evidence gathered from this pilot study, a more comprehensive beta version of ABRA was developed and was tested on a larger scale in Quebec with a sample of nearly 200 students. The beta version of ABRA contained 27 instructional activities and the addition of a writing section. The professional development module also included just-in-time educational videos and information on best English Language Arts practices.

From 2005-2006 further financial support allowed us to modify ABRA into its current form. Through Inukshuk Wireless and Le Ministère de l'Éducation, du Loisir et du Sport (MELS), we further developed the instructional activities that make up this module. This included the addition of five new activities (for a total of 32) and, within the existing activities, the creation of more challenging material using different levels of mastery. A new set of stories was added bringing the total number to 17. In addition, with the help of the Centre de transfert pour la réussite éducatif du Québec (CTREQ), support materials for both teachers and students were developed. Demonstration animations for students were created for each activity. Teachers now have a professional development area that provides them with just-in-time videos for technology integration support, a complete manual on ABRA, and tips for successful English Language Arts practices. The newly developed Assessment, Parent, and Communication modules are also functional as of the January, 2009 release.

Finally, we continue to refine and test ABRA through work funded by research grants. In 2007-2008 the Canadian Council on Learning, the Canadian Language and Literacy Research Network and the Social Sciences and Humanities Research Council funded important aspects of the ongoing ABRA research. As detailed elsewhere, research grants have allowed us to explore the impact of ABRA in field experiments, not only in Quebec but increasingly in a pan-Canadian context and in the Northern Territory of Australia with funding from Telstra.

In its current iteration, ABRA consists of: 1) Instructional Activities (32 alphabetic, fluency, comprehension and writing activities, many at different levels of difficulty and complexity; 17 stories of various genres linked to the activities; and 10 Canadian and Australian stories written by students); 2) Professional Development Materials for teachers (explanations, lesson plans, embedded video teaching vignettes, and printable resource materials); 3) An Assessment Module (where teachers can review student and class performance on instructional activities for any period of time); 4) A Parents' Module (for access to multimedia resources and tips on how to support the use of ABRA in the home); and 5) A Communications Wiki (to encourage teachers and other professionals to share information about learning to read and ways to promote student literacy). Finally, we placed ABRA in the LTK and strengthened the link between it and ePEARL given the natural fit between portfolios and literacy. A screen capture from an ABRA instructional activity is shown in Figure 1.

Balanced literacy Early on in the conceptualization of ABRA, we decided that the pedagogical underpinnings of the software would replicate those contained in programs of Balanced Literacy. Defined as the "radical middle" by Jeanne Chall (1967, 1983) and described by Marilyn Jager Adams (1990), our software would emphasize a harmonious balance between code-emphasis and a literature-rich context. This would allow a child the ability to explore his/her interests by applying a large repertory of strategies that (s)he could access when meaning breaks down (Pressley,

Figure 1. ABRACADABRA instructional activity screen capture

2002). This balanced literacy approach also meant that instructional activities would not be designed outside the context of story texts and vice versa.

<u>Available without charge</u> We also decided from the outset that our software would be adaptive to learners with special needs, promote learning among otherwise struggling and at-risk students, and be widely available at the lowest cost -- especially given the financial situation in many urban and rural schools where literacy rates are poorest. We coined the slogan: "we do not profit from children, but children profit from us," to underscore the notion that the success of our software, first and foremost, is tied to learning outcomes.

To date, all CSLP educational software is available without charge. Face-to-face training for research sites is available without charge and other training is provided on a cost recovery basis. This not-for-profit and philanthropic philosophy is markedly different from commercial software and is one of our greatest commitments, as well as one of our greatest challenges.

<u>Flexible and modular design</u> From the early days of imagining our tools, the CSLP decided it would design the software content in the form of reusable learning objects. This would enable teachers all over Canada, and all over the world, to access a rich pedagogical resource and re-use the instructional components, based on their teaching styles and the needs of their students. This early design philosophy of modularity and reusability, promoted by our grant from Industry Canada, was eventually abandoned in favor of a single, underlying database. However, the legacy of modularity and reusability allowed us to take advantage of technology to design a tool that is not linear in use and not prescriptive of a single approach or method of teaching students to read. The toolkit metaphor aptly describes the notion that our software was intended to be a collection of resources that the teacher could use when, how, and with whom s/he saw fit.

In addition, we consider that to have impact on the literacy problem in Canada and elsewhere, our tools must be easy to use and fit the realities of classrooms. We did not design the LTK to run only on the latest computers or where every schoolchild has unlimited access to technology. Instead, the LTK and its tools are designed for 'the state of the practice, not the state of the art'.

Embedded professional development and support All CSLP educational software includes embedded just-in-time multimedia for professional development and virtual tutorials to help teachers and students start using the tools appropriately and immediately. This embedded support helps insure the tools and their underlying curricular and pedagogical principles and features are used properly. Embedded teacher support also helps reduce the cost of in-service follow-up.

Based on evidence Early on in the development of every tool, we conduct a lengthy needs-analysis where experts in the educational community are surveyed, research is reviewed, and finally, initial design decisions are made. As a research centre, the commitment of the CSLP to evidence-based practice is strong and we used the best evidence to design each version of our software. We also believe in the importance of partnerships to ensure knowledge mobilization for scalability and sustainability—by applying a combination of scholarly expertise and practical wisdom. Finally, we committed ourselves to evidence-proven practice, ensuring that our software does produce the intended impacts on teaching and learning. Several of these studies are summarized elsewhere.

Gaming Elements of ABRACADABRA ABRA uses a number of game features to engage children to read and write and to increase their motivation. Its interactivity draws students in. In each ABRA activity, in addition to the pedagogical experience, children progress towards a goal, according to simple rules. When this goal is reached, students are rewarded with a mini-game. They are then challenged to free a picture caught in seaweed before the time runs out and it vanishes. They experience landing Julie, an ABRA character, on a target with a parachute; they protect a whale from obstacles as they bring it to the ocean; or they light up stars following the sequence they were shown, to name a few examples. At times, the game is at the core of the pedagogical structure of the activities, such as in Word Matching, in which children have to

find cards with similar sounds at the beginning or end of the words.

ABRA's use of characters also gives it a game-like feel. The two main characters, or heroes, a girl and a cat, invite students in a quest to increase their literacy skills. The children can identify with them and can control them in a number of activities, such as in Word Changing. In this activity, students make the girl, Julie, fish the letter needed to change a word into another, and then move her to catch jumping fishes in the mini-game. Secondary characters (a polar bear, a dragon, a Chinese ghost…etc), representing cultural diversity found in Canada, guide the students into the various activities, which take place in different universes, some realistic and others imaginary. Each character has a personal story the children can read or listen to. These stories briefly introduce the universes the students will go into with the guides. Eventually, a larger story will be integrated before each activity, a story reinforcing the purpose and context of what students have to do in each activity. This underlying narrative thread also helps create a gaming experience in ABRA.

The full version of ABRA invites students to choose an avatar that represents them as they login, to personalize the tool. They can see their avatar at the bottom of the ABRA interface, organized as a HUD. They also see the avatars of their teammates, since ABRA encourages collaborative work, a common feature of games. Because of the HUD structure, they have access to the buttons needed to control the activities and the application. In a future version, since the database tracks students performance and usage of the application, an expanded reward system could give them access to a selection of new avatars or mini-games they would unlock as they would progress in their use of ABRA.

Research on Literacy The strongest forms of reading research are those that are both well designed and that have been repeatedly replicated. A good example of this approach is the National Reading Panel report (NRP, 2000, and see also

Pressley, 1998; Pressley, Wharton- McDonald, Allington, Block, Morrow, Tracey, et al., 2001; Taylor, Pearson, Clark, & Walpole, 2000; Savage & Pompey, 2008). In addition, interventions must be comprehensive or balanced. Truly balanced approaches emphasize reading skills such as: phonemic awareness – ability to hear and manipulate individual sounds in spoken language; phonological awareness – ability to relate specific written letter(s) to specific sound(s) (grapheme–phoneme correspondence); fluency – ability to read text effortlessly and expressively; and comprehension – ability to understand and interpret text; and an emphasis on meta-cognition – ability to reflect and regulate knowledge construction. Dozens of studies worldwide have shown these techniques to be effective in improving literacy when used as part of a classroom approach that also includes the fostering of: on- task activities, student self-regulation, connections across curricular themes, and communications between home and school (see e.g., Hall & Harding, 2003 for a review).

We are, therefore, in a position now where we really do know what to do to enhance early literacy. For example, we know that effective preventative reading programs in Grade 1 that involve structured phonics, word recognition, and letter–sound knowledge training that are over- learned and repeatedly connected to the end goal of text reading for meaning, are one of several important elements of balanced literacy approaches. The involvement of explicit attention to fluency and to a host of strategies for understanding and evaluating texts is also critical (e.g., Pressley, 1998). We also know that teachers need support and expert professional development to overcome the challenges of teaching struggling readers (Chambers, Abrami, McWhaw, & Therrien, 2001). Finally, we know generally that the effectiveness of classroom applications of educational software depend on careful attention to instructional design followed by professional development and follow-up support (Abrami et al., 2006).

The next question to address is: what prevents progress in literacy at a national and international level? One key problem is the lack of evidence-based practice in classrooms. One issue that prevents more widespread implementation of evidence-based programs is that such programs are frequently prohibitively expensive. Allington (2004), for example, argued in an influential paper in Educational Leadership, that the costs of current reading programs in the US (some $500,000 per typical school) effectively prevents full literacy for all from ever being achieved. By providing the software at no cost, by embedding professional development within the tool, and by using a model of cost-recovery for face-to-face training, the costs of ABRA ameliorate the expense of implementing an evidence-based reading program.

When students struggle to read, it becomes increasingly important that teachers provide support and guidance for their learning. This increased focus on early literacy best practices and support for students with reading difficulties leads us to converge on the question of teacher preparation and teacher knowledge base of literacy. Despite the knowledge that early interventions for students with reading issues are essential, general education teachers are not prepared adequately for this undertaking (Lyon, 1999; Mather, Bos & Bubur, 2008; National Reading Panel, 2000; Snow et al., 1999). Educators may have little direct instruction in how individuals learn to read, and virtually no information on how to address the learning needs of struggling readers (Fisher, Bruce & Grieve, 2007; Lyon & Moats, 1997). Teachers are found to be unaware of their own knowledge related to literacy practices (Cunnigham et al., 2004), available early literacy programs (Wright, Stackhouse & Wood, 2008), and how technology can support early literacy attainment (Johnston et al., 2008). However, technology can provide both an effective and efficient solution in the form of embedded professional development and just-in-time, scaffolded support.

Finally, the application of evidence about collaborative group-based learning provides another partial solution to the financial problem (see e.g., Abrami et al., 2008; Savage, 2006). Collaborative group-based learning may improve students' literacy and reduces demands on technology since group work is less costly than ubiquitous technology use. In such a context, one might stop and imagine what a massive impact the availability of a flexible, comprehensive, entirely evidence-based intervention program that is entirely free at the point of delivery, would make. What if such a tool also incorporated ongoing professional development, multiple forms of assessment, and recording tools? Such a system could have a significant positive impact on the improvement of national literacy, with far reaching social and economic consequences. ABRA is such a system.

ABRACADABRA Design Methodology The creation of a large application like ABRA is a complex process. The CSLP practices an iterative design and development methodology in which a multidisciplinary team conducts formative evaluation and formal research, works with the community at large for guidance, and designs pedagogically sound tools based on the evidence. See Figure 2. This process culminates in working versions of ABRA and the cycle of research and development begins again. ABRA is an evidence-based tool in at least three senses.

1. The content of ABRA learning activities is derived directly from systematic reviews of evidence about what works in reading and spelling. For example, there is a huge body of evidence that reciprocal teaching techniques involving meta- cognitive skills of prediction, sequencing, and summarizing can improve reading comprehension (e.g., Ehri et al., 2001; Pressley, 1998). These skills are, therefore, integrated in ABRA story elements.

The foundation of the Instruction Module is illustrated in the ABRA research matrix (see Figure 3) as described in Abrami, Savage, Wade, Hipps & Lopez, 2005. The basis of the matrix is the National Reading Panel's 2000 meta-analysis. This analysis examined over 100,000 research studies conducted over 35 years and used the best evidence to summarize the findings and make recommendations regarding the skills necessary to become competent readers. The skill areas are those that beginning readers need to develop, grouped in three major skill categories--Alphabetics, Fluency, and Comprehension—and associated sub-skills.

With our commitment to include the tenets of a Balanced Literacy philosophy, we created a link between stories and activities. The ABRA Research Matrix demonstrates the link between text

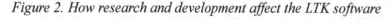

Figure 2. How research and development affect the LTK software

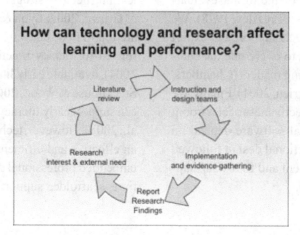

Figure 3. Sample from the ABRACADABRA research matrix for comprehension

Skill Area	COMPREHENSION							
Skill	Prediction	Comprehension Monitoring	Sequencing	Summarizing	Vocabulary	Vocabulary (ESL)	Story Response	Story Elements
Story Titles								
Folk and Fairy Tales								
Little Red Hen	x	x	x	x	x	x	x	x
Dove and the Ant	x	x	x	x	x	x	x	
Three Billy Goats Gruff	x	x	x	x	x	x	x	x
Henny Penny	x		x	x	x	x	x	x
Frogs and the Well	x	x	x	x	x	x	x	x
Poetry								
I Can Move Like A...					x	x		
When I Open My Eyes					x	x	x	
Darryl! Don't Dawdle		x			x	x	x	x
Feelings					x	x	x	
Fiction								
Waterfall	x		x	x	x		x	x
Non-Fiction								
How a Bean Sprouts		x	x		x	x		

from the stories and the activities. It also shows the scope of each activity, defining the various levels and specific content related to each level.

For instance, the Word–Level Sound Discrimination skill is practiced through the activity called Word Counting. This activity has two levels of difficulty, which differ from each other by the number of words the user has to count in a sentence. This activity is linked to multiple stories because the content (words from the stories) is used in the activity. Ultimately, the activities and stories are connected by shared content providing users with contextualized learning experiences.

The approach of constructing and applying evidence matrices are carefully designed for all 17 stories in ABRA and for all 32 text-, word-, and fluency- level activities.

2. ABRACADABRA is based on the experience gained by working with partners and a multi-disciplinary team to develop technological tools. One of the largest and most successful, evidence-based approaches to improving the reading skills of at-risk learners was developed by the Success for All Foundation (SFAF). At the CSLP, we have collaborated actively with SFAF for almost a decade producing numerous software tools to enhance their reading programmes including Alphie's Alley, Team Alphie and Reading Roots Interactive. In addition, we have a team of reading specialists led by Robert Savage including Mary Ann Evans, Linda Siegel, Noella Piquette-Tomei, and Eileen Wood. We have other specialists in educational psychology and technology (Philip Abrami, Ann-Louise Davidson, Richard Schmid), systematic reviews (Robert Bernard), arts education (Ann Patteson, Rena Upitis), special needs learners (Sue Wastie), and aboriginal learners (Genevieve Fox). We have a team of educational partners from across Canada led by Bev White from LEARN (Leading English Education Resource Network) and a team of professionals led by Anne Wade (CSLP Manager and Information Specialist) that includes; Liz Meyer and Gia Deleveaux (project coordinators), Einat Idan and Christine Kelly (instructional designers), Catherine LeBel (Creative Director), and Sebastien Rainville (lead programmer).

3. ABRACADABRA and other LTK tools are developed and improved based upon the CSLP's design principles and evidence

from direct intervention in schools. Our strong belief in evidence-based practice, our guiding design standards (see Table 1), our adherence to ethical responsibilities, and our commitment to working with the community are evident in all stages of this software.

Every year since its launch, we have collected evidence on the usability and effectiveness of ABRA and we continually monitor the research literature to insure we adhere to the principles of best evidence in designing our tool. Our annual ABRA Advisory Board meetings, plus teacher and student interviews and questionnaires, help ensure we understand best how to use the literature from scholars to design and implement our tool. The data on implementation fidelity also tells us how to improve training and professional development to ensure the highest degree of ABRA integration into teaching practices. With the operationalization of the ABRA Assessment Module, educators will be able to track student and class reading performance and the research team will be able to use these trace data as a means to further refine

Table 1. The CSLP Software Design Principles

1. Research
1.1. All aspects of tool development should be based on peer-reviewed empirical research evidence, refined on the basis of research evidence, and then serve as the basis for collecting new evidence about teaching and learning using technology.
1.2. Emphasis should be placed on supporting meaningful motivational and learning outcomes.
1.3. Tool design should consider what is known about the processes and contexts of learning and instruction.
2. Design
2.1. We should strive to achieve the highest standards of excellence and lowest programming, interface, and instructional design error rates in the field of application and use.
2.2. Designs should be appealing and easy to learn and use.
2.3. Tools should be designed to address the specified goals of the target audience.
2.4. To the extent possible, tools should be inclusive and conform to Universal Design Principles.
2.5. Technical support should be readily available and integral where possible.
2.6. Professional Development, with an emphasis on pedagogy, should be readily available and integral where possible.
2.7. Design should emphasize adoption and use by the largest possible audience with a balance between the state of the practice and the state of the art.
2.8. Assumptions about physical (e.g., input devices) and cognitive skills (e.g., memory/attention, problem solving, self-regulation, etc.) interpersonal (e.g., collaboration), and other skills needed to use the tools for learning should be specified by design and validated (e.g., via transfer to novel tasks) either before or during development.
2.9. To the extent possible and appropriate, tools should be flexible and re-usable.
3. Ethics
3.1. The intellectual property is owned by the CSLP unless otherwise specified by contractual agreements with funders.
3.2. All those who made a contribution will receive appropriate recognition.
3.3. Tools should reflect the values of universal human rights by avoiding any form of media that would be seen to unfairly marginalize a segment of our society.
4. Community
4.1. We encourage and support design and development by collaboration among CSLP members with diverse backgrounds and skills.
4.2. Input from the stakeholders should be sought throughout design, development, and testing.
4.3. Tools should be scalable and sustainable with minimal post-production cost.
4.4. Tools should be distributed not-for-profit with a philanthropic purpose in mind.

the tool. Finally, ABRA remains a tool available to researchers interested in exploring issues in literacy development and developing new understandings about reading, technology integration, and knowledge mobilization for example.

ABRACADABRA Research A series of experimental interventions has used randomized control trial (RCT) designs to evaluate the efficacy of ABRA (Abrami et al., 2008: Comaskey, Savage, & Abrami, 2009; Deault, Savage, & Abrami, 2009 in press; Hipps, Abrami, Wade, Savage, & Lopez, 2005; Savage, Abrami, Hipps, & Deault, 2009 in press) in kindergarten and grade 1, using carefully monitored implementations by trained facilitators to carefully study the impact of the tool on student learning.

Our programmatic intervention research work has used two separate RCT studies to evaluate the effectiveness of ABRACADABRA in grade 1 (Abrami et al., 2008; Savage, Abrami, Hipps, & Deault, 2009 in press). We have attempted to carry out experimental trials of ABRA with carefully-monitored implementations by trained facilitators to study the impact of the tool on student learning. In our first research in this domain, we were able to show in a well-designed RCT study, that even a pilot version of ABRACADABRA can produce significant change in literacy in grade 1 (Abrami et al., 2008; Hipps et al., 2005).

Following substantial development of the ABRA tool itself, we completed a further RCT study with n = 144 participants in grade 1 (Savage et al., 2009). We ran an intervention for around 13 weeks in schools during Language Arts classes, with small groups of typically n = 4 children in each group (four groups per class), to evaluate language arts teaching with ABRA against the same classrooms teaching language arts without ABRA. In addition we contrasted two different reading intervention strategies: a so-called 'synthetic phonics' program based upon a highly-structured approach to letter-sound teaching, and focusing on explicit phoneme blending and an 'analytic phonics' program based upon the exposure of

children to words embodying shared rhymes. Contrasts of different phonics programs such as these to establish differential effectiveness have been a recent feature of the reading literature internationally (e.g. Johnston & Watson, 2004). Our results showed statistically significant advantages in standardised measures of key literacy skills of letter-sound knowledge, phonological blending, listening comprehension and reading comprehension only in the ABRACADABRA groups. Intervention effects for listening comprehension reflected one full stanine of improvement, for example, and effects for phonological blending ability were larger still than this. Crucially, the effects were evident at a delayed post-test when children's reading was re-assessed in Grade 2, some eight months after the ABRA intervention had formally closed.

To date, our RCT research showed statistically significant advantages in standardised measures of key literacy skills of letter-sound knowledge, phonological blending, listening comprehension and reading comprehension only in the ABRACADABRA groups. Torgesen (2005) reviewed and aggregated the immediate post-test findings of 14 reading studies to get a mean per hour of intervention received. We have done similarly but for immediate and delayed post-tests; Table 2 shows the effect sizes measured in terms of overall standard score change per hour of intervention received (.23) compared to the mean of the interventions described and analyzed by Torgesen as well as effect sizes by test-type. At immediate post-test, the ABRA students experienced higher effect changes per hour of intervention than Torgesen's mean, except in all comparable measures except reading fluency. There were particularly large effects for blending here. This finding is important because such decoding skills are generally seen as being essential co-requisites to early reading acquisition (e.g. Savage & Carless, 2008; Share, 1995). Crucially, these effects were also evident at a delayed post-test when children's reading was re-assessed in Grade 2, some eight months after the ABRA intervention had formally closed. Here all effect sizes, including that for reading fluency were at least comparable to those of Torgesen's immediate pot-test data. Importantly the effect size for reading comprehension, perhaps the strongest test of reading ability, was larger than those reported in Torgesen's review.

EPEARL: DEVELOPING LITERACY AND SELF-REGULATION SKILLS

This section describes our Electronic Portfolio Encouraging Active Reflective Learning –ePEARL which has been developed by the CSLP in collaboration with our partner LEARN. ePEARL is bilingual (English-French), web-based, student-centred electronic portfolio software, that is designed to support the phases of self-regulation. Developed in PHP using a MySQL database, three levels of ePEARL have been designed for use in early elementary (Level 1), late elementary (Level 2) and secondary schools (Level 3). Features available include: personalizing the portfolio; setting outcome and process goals; creating new

Table 2. Mean Effect Sizes Per Hour of Intervention for All Standardised Measures at Post-Test and Delayed Post-Test In Comparison With Torgesen's (2005) Findings.

Measures (((Standard Scores)	Mean Effect Sizes (Pre-test to Post-test)	Mean Effect Sizes (Pre-test to delayed post-test)	Torgesen's Mean Effect Sizes (Pre-test to Post-test)
Blending Words	.65	.27	.30
Elision	.34	.16	NA
Reading Fluency	-.11	.17	.19
Word Attack	.23	.10	NA
Reading Comprehension	.30	-.03	.19

work; linking to existing work; reflecting on work; sharing work; obtaining feedback from teachers, peers & parents; editing work; saving work under multiple versions and sending work to a presentation folder.

ePEARL's Level 1 is geared to the same audience to whom ABRA is geared – beginning readers and writers. It offers two main features: Reading and Creating. These are presented within the structure of a portfolio environment as students are introduced to basic portfolio processes such as goal setting and reflection. Both the My Readings and My Creations features provide an Index Page where students can quickly review their stored works. From here, they can click on a title or icon to view, edit or delete their work. ePEARL provides a link to ABRA's digital books and illustrations. Each book may be viewed and read from within ePEARL, thereby enabling students to store and monitor their reading progress. It also allows teachers and parents to track their students' or child's reading development. See Figure 4 for a screen capture from ePEARL Level 1.

ePEARL Yearlong Intervention Until recently, evidence on the impacts of electronic portfolios (EPs) on outcomes was sparse. Carney (2005) declared "Electronic portfolios show promise for enhancing learning, but if we fail to critically evaluate our uses of the device, we may find that they will go the way of Papert's Logo turtles and become yet another educational fad—an innovation poorly understood and often implemented in ways contrary to its theoretical underpinnings" (p. 4). Zeichner and Wray (2001) concluded similarly: "Despite the current popularity of teaching portfolios, there have been very few systematic studies of the nature and consequences of their use for either assessment or development purposes" (p.615). Most recently, Barrett (2007) noted that "The empirical research is very limited and focuses more on the development of teaching portfolios than on K-12 student portfolios" (p. 436).

A yearlong non-equivalent pretest-posttest quasi-experiment conducted by Meyer, Abrami,

Figure 4. ePEARL level 1 screen capture

Table 3. CAT-4 data analysis

CAT-4 (N= 296)	Pre-test	Post-test
Control (Mean, SD)	1.95 (.750)	2.05 (.668)
Experimental (Mean, SD)	1.78 (.708)	2.11 (.718)

Wade, Aslan, & Deault (in press) provides exciting new evidence that electronic portfolios, specifically ePEARL, can be used in ways to promote significant gains in children's literacy skills. Participants in this study were from elementary schools (grades 4-6) in Quebec, Manitoba, and Alberta. The constructed response subtest of the Canadian Achievement Test (CAT-4) was administered along with a self-regulation questionnaire in both the fall and the spring. The student questionnaire data showed that students who used ePEARL reported higher levels of some SRL processes, including: setting process goals, listing strategies, using comments from their teacher to improve, and understanding how they are being evaluated, than students who did not use ePEARL. Analyses of the CAT-4 data also showed that students using ePEARL made significant gains in writing skills. Students who were in medium-high implementation classrooms showed significant improvements in content management, which refers to the word choice, sentence structure and conventions of print. See Table 3.

ISIS-21: INFORMATION LITERACY, INQUIRY SKILLS, AND CRITICAL THINKING

With concerns about information literacy in mind, representatives from the CSLP, LEARN and the EMSB School Board in Montreal, Quebec spent 18 months designing, developing and evaluating the first two modules within the ISIS-21 project (Wade, Abrami & MacDonald, 2009). The product--a web-based prototype--is designed to introduce late elementary/early secondary students to selected components (Planning and Searching for Information) of information literacy by guiding them through the inquiry process. See http://grover.concordia.ca/isis/promo/home.php for further information. See Figure 5 for a description of the path that students take within ISIS-21.

Part of the evaluation of the ISIS-21 prototype involved creating a composite "learning" score by merging all the student responses to questions that were related to learning information literacy components specifically addressed within ISIS-21. This score was correlated with the number of hours that students used ISIS-21. We were very pleased to learn that a strong correlation existed (.5) between hours of use with ISIS-21 and the learning of information literacy skills, regardless of enjoyment of the program. Thus, sustained use showed demonstrable transfer of learning. This remains the single most important finding of the evaluation—the strong link between ISIS-21 use and student learning.

LESSONS LEARNED?

We have learned that research on effectiveness alone may be necessary but it is not sufficient to ensure wide-scale adoption and faithful use of evidence-based educational software like the LTK. This is particularly obvious with ePEARL because, even though it is technically simple to use, the underlying student-centred pedagogy presents challenges to both teachers and students. Our approach to exploring teachers' use of ePEARL in their classrooms is grounded in expectancy-value theory which posits that teachers' perceived expectancy of success, combined with their perceived value of technology use, and the perceived cost of technology use, together can explain teachers' varying degrees of motivation to integrate technology in their classrooms (Wozney, Venkatesh & Abrami; 2006).

From our research (Meyer et al., in press) it was clear that teachers who were personally committed to learning how to use ePEARL, and who had administrators and tech personnel who were willing to actively support these initiatives, were able to more regularly and consistently integrate ePEARL in their teaching. On the other hand, teachers who did not personally volunteer for the project or felt as if their administrators and tech personnel weren't providing adequate support were less likely to persist in the face of technical and time constraints.

Figure 5. Illustration of the ISIS-21 research process

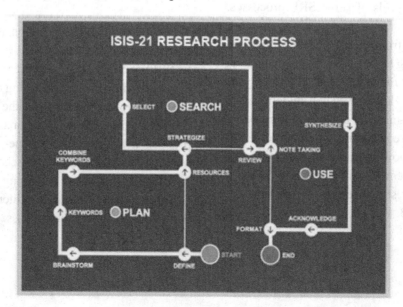

Medium and high implementers of ePEARL reported that it positively impacted on their teaching practice and provided them with valuable pedagogical supports. This is encouraging data as this was part of the intended design of the software. It not only provides structure and support for students as they develop self-regulated learning skills, but it also provides valuable support to teachers who are working to integrate new technologies and student-centred pedagogies in their teaching practice.

On the basis of studying ABRA and ePEARL's use in classrooms over several years (e.g., Abrami, Wade, Pillay, Aslan, Bures & Bentley, 2008), we have learned the following valuable lessons that we think may generalize to the LTK as well as other educational software:

1. The use of the LTK should be a school-based or board- (district-) based initiative. Use of the LTK in one or two classrooms, on an occasional basis will have a smaller impact on the development of literacy and self regulated learning skills.

2. The use of portfolios, in particular, should begin early in students' educational experience and not be short-lived. The processes of self-regulation and approaches to pedagogy that portfolios support require time for younger students to learn and effort for older students to make the transition from traditional, teacher-directed methods.

3. Teachers need to develop facility with student-centred processes embedded in educational software and they should be supported with appropriate professional development.

4. While educational software may provide the means to scaffold teachers and students in portfolio and other processes, and better encourage self-regulation, these tools are not a sufficient condition for change in teaching practices.

5. Students and teachers must believe that the change encouraged by the use of these tools is valued and necessary for authentic, more meaningful learning. The "will" component of self regulated learning is as important as the "skill" component.

With the use of the LTK and its constituent tools—ABRA, ePEARL and ISIS-21-- it is hoped that children will develop self-regulatory behaviors as they become literate and empowered citizens of this information-filled world.

REFERENCES

Abrami, P. C., & Barrett, H. (2005). Directions for research and development on electronic portfolios. *Canadian Journal of Learning and Technology*, *31*(3), 1–15.

Abrami, P. C., Savage, R., Comaskey, E., Silverstone, D., & Hipps, G. (2006). *ABRACADABRA: Evaluation of a balanced text and word-level reading intervention– Winter 2006*. Preliminary findings, June 2006. Centre for the Study of Learning and Performance: Montreal, QC. Retrieved from http://doe.concordia.ca/cslp/ICTABRACADABRA.php

Abrami, P. C., Savage, R., Wade, A., Hipps, G., & Lopez, M. (2008). Using technology to assist children learning to read and write. In Willoughby, T., & Wood, E. (Eds.), *Children's learning in a digital world* (pp. 129–172). Oxford, UK: Blackwell Publishing.

Abrami, P. C., Wade, A., Pillay, V., Aslan, O., Bures, E. & Bentley. (2008). Encouraging self-regulated learning through electronic portfolios. *Canadian Journal on Learning and Technology, 34*(3), 93-117. Retreived April 7, 2009 from http://www.cjlt.ca/index.php/cjlt/article/view/507/238

Adams, M. J. (1990). *Beginning to read: Thinking and learning about print*. Cambridge, MA: MIT Press.

Allington, R. (2004). Setting the record straight. *Educational Leadership, 61*, 22–25.

American Psychological Association. (2008). *Learner centered psychological principles*. Washington, DC. Retrieved September 18, 2008 from http://www.apa.org/ed/lcp2/lcp14.html

Barrett, H. (2007). Researching electronic portfolios and learner engagement: The REFLECT Initiative. *Journal of Adolescent & Adult Literacy, 50*(6), 436–449. doi:10.1598/JAAL.50.6.2

Canada. Statistics Canada. (2004). *Measuring up: Canadian results of the OECD PISA Study*. In P. Bussière, F. Cartwright, & T. Knighton. Ottawa, ON: Statistics Canada. (Cat no. 81-590-XPE, no. 2).

Canadian Council on Learning. (2007). *State of learning in Canada: No time for complacency*. Ottawa, Canada: Report on Learning in Canada.

Carney, J. (2005). *What kind of electronic portfolio research do we need?* Paper presented at the SITE 2conference. Available: http://it.wce.wwu.edu/carney/Presentations/presentations.html

Chall, J. S. (1967). *Learning to read: The great debate*. New York: McGraw-Hill.

Chall, J. S. (1983). Learning to read: The great debate. (Updated ed). New York: McGraw-Hill.

Chambers, B., Abrami, P. C., McWhaw, K., & Therrien, M. C. (2001). Developing a computer-assisted tutoring program to help children at risk learn to read. *Educational Research and Evaluation, 7*(2-3), 223–239. doi:10.1076/edre.7.2.223.3863

Comaskey, E., Savage, R., & Abrami, P. C. (2009). A randomized efficacy study of a web-based literacy intervention among disadvantaged urban kindergarten children. [Special issue on literacy and technology]. *Journal of Research in Reading, 32*(1), 92–108. doi:10.1111/j.1467-9817.2008.01383.x

Conference Board of Canada. (2008). *Education and skills overview*. Ottawa, Canada: Author. Retrieved July 31, 2008 from http://sso.conferenceboard.ca/HCP/overview/Educationskills.aspx

Deault, L. Savage, R., & Abrami, P. C. (2009. (in press). Inattention and response to the ABRACADABRA web-based literacy intervention. *Journal of Research on Educational Effectiveness*.

Ehri, L., Nunes, R. S., Willows, D., Schuster, B. V., Yaghoub-Zadeh, Z., & Shanahan, T. (2001). Phonemic awareness instruction helps children learn to read: Evidence from the national reading panel's meta-analysis. *Reading Research Quarterly, 36*(3), 250–287. doi:10.1598/RRQ.36.3.2

Fisher, B., Bruce, M., & Grieve, C. (2007). *The entry knowledge of Australian preservice teachers in the area of phonological awareness and phonics. Quality of School Education: Senate Standing Committee on Employment, Workplace Relations and Education (No. 172)*. Canberra, Australia: Parliament of the Commonwealth of Australia.

Hall, K., & Harding, A. (2003). A systematic review of effective literacy teaching in the 4 to 14 age range of mainstream school. In *Research Evidence in Education Library*. London: EPPI-Centre, Social Sciences Research Unit, Institute of Education.

Hipps, G., Abrami, P. C., & Savage, R. (2005). ABRACADARA: The research, design development of web-based early literacy software. In Pierre, S. (Ed.), *Développement, intégration et évaluation des technologies de formation et d'apprentissage (DIVA). Innovations et tendances en technologies de formation et d'apprentissage* (pp. 89–112). Montreal, QC: Presses Internationales Polytechnique.

Johnston, R. S., & Watson, J. E. (2004). Accelerating the development of reading, spelling, and phonemic awareness skills in initial readers. *Reading and Writing: An Interdisciplinary Journal, 17*, 327–357. doi:10.1023/B:READ.0000032666.66359.62

Johnston, S., McDonnnell, A., & Hawken, L. (2008). Enhancing outcomes in early literacy for young children with disabilities: Strategies for success. *Intervention in School and Clinic, 43*(3), 210–217. doi:10.1177/1053451207310342

Lyon, G. (1999). *The NICD research program in reading development, reading disorders, and reading instruction*. Washington, DC: National Center for Learning Disabilities.

Lyon, G. R., & Moats, L. C. (1997). Critical conceptual and methodological considerations in reading intervention research. *Journal of Learning Disabilities, 30*(6), 578–588. doi:10.1177/002221949703000601

Mather, N., Bos, N., & Babur, N. (2008). Perceptions and knowledge of preservice and inservice teachers about early literacy instruction. *Journal of Learning Disabilities, 34*(5), 472–482. doi:10.1177/002221940103400508

Meyer, E., Abrami, P. C., Wade, A., Aslan, O., & Deault, L. (in press). Improving literacy and metacognition with electronic portfolios: Teaching and learning with ePEARL. *Computers & Education.* See http://dx.doi.org/10.1016/j.compedu.2009.12.005

National Reading Panel. (2000). *Teaching children to read: reports of the subgroups*. Mahwah, NJ: Lawrence Erlbaum Associates. Retrieved April 7, 2009 from http://www.nichd.nih.gov/publications/pubs_details.cfm?from=&pubs_id=88

Organisation for Economic Co-operation and Development. (2006). *Are students ready for a technology-rich world? What PISA studies tell us*. Paris: OECD Publications.

Organisation for Economic Co-operation and Development. (2007). Pisa 2006: science competencies for tomorrow's world. Volume 1 analysis. Paris: OECD Publications.

Organization for Economic Co-Operation and Developement. (2000). *Knowledge and skills for life: First results from PISA 2000 (Executive summary)*.

Pressley, M. (1998). *Reading instruction that works*. New York: Guilford Press.

Pressley, M. (2002). Effective beginning reading instruction. *Journal of Literacy Research, 34*(2), 165–188. doi:10.1207/s15548430jlr3402_3

Pressley, M., Wharton-McDonald, R., Allington, R., Block, C. C., Morrow, L., & Tracey, D. (2001). A study of effective first-grade literacy instruction. *Scientific Studies of Reading, 5*(1), 35–58. doi:10.1207/S1532799XSSR0501_2

Rogers, D., & Swan, K. (2004). Self regulated learning and Internet search. *Teachers College Record, 106*(9), 804–1824. doi:10.1111/j.1467-9620.2004.00406.x

Savage, R., Abrami, P. C., Hipps, G., & Deault, L. C. (2009. (in press). A randomized control trial study of the ABRACADABRA reading intervention program in Grade 1. *Journal of Educational Psychology*.

Savage, R. S. (2006a). Effective early reading instruction and inclusion: Some reflections on mutual dependence. *International Journal of Inclusive Education: Special Issue, 10*(4-5), 347–361. doi:10.1080/13603110500221495

Savage, R. S. (2006b). Reading comprehension is not always the product of decoding and listening comprehension: Evidence from teenagers who are very poor readers. *Scientific Studies of Reading, 10*(2), 143–164. doi:10.1207/s1532799xssr1002_2

Savage, R. S., & Carless, S. (2008). The impact of reading interventions delivered by Teaching Assistants on Key Stage 1 performance. *British Educational Research Journal, 34*(3), 363–385. doi:10.1080/01411920701609315

Savage, R. S., & Pompey, Y. (2008). What does the evidence really say about effective literacy teaching? *Educational and Child Psychology, 25*, 21–30.

Share, D. L. (1995). Phonological recoding and self-teaching: sine qua non of reading acquisition. *Cognition, 55*(2), 151–218. doi:10.1016/0010-0277(94)00645-2

Snow, C. E., Burns, M. S., & Griffin, P. (Eds.). (1998). *Preventing reading difficulties in young children*. Washington, DC: National Academy Press.

Snow, C. E., & Strucker, J. (1999). *Lessons from preventing reading difficulties in young children for adult learning and literacy (Vol. 1)*. Washington, DC: National Center for the Study of Adult Learning and Literacy.

Taylor, B. M., Pearson, P. D., Clark, K. F., & Walpole, S. (2000). Effective schools and accomplished teachers: Lessons about primary grade reading instruction in low-income schools. *The Elementary School Journal, 101*, 121–165. doi:10.1086/499662

Torgesen, J. K. (2005). Remedial interventions for students with dyslexia: National goals and current accomplishments. In Richardson, S., & Gilger, J. (Eds.), *Research-based education and intervention: What we need to know* (pp. 103–124). Boston: International Dyslexia Association.

Torgesen, J. K. (2005). Recent discoveries from research on remedial interventions for children with dyslexia. In Snowling, M., & Hulme, C. (Eds.), *Presentations and Publications* (pp. 521–537). Oxford, UK: Blackwell Publishers.

Wade, A., Abrami, P. & MacDonald, M. (2008, Feb.). *Inquiry Strategies for the Information Society in the Twenty-First Century (ISIS-21)*. Final report prepared for Inukshuk Wireless. Montreal: Centre for the Study of Learning and Performance.

Wade, A., Abrami, P. C., & Sclater, J. (2005). An electronic portfolio for learning. *Canadian Journal of Learning and Technology, 31*(3), 33–50.

Wade, A., Abrami, P. C., White, B., Baron, M., Farmer, L., & Van Gelder, S. (2008). Information literacy: An essential competency in the twenty-first century. *IFLA School Libraries and Resource Centers Newsletter, 47*, 15–18.

Whitehead, M. J., & Quinlan, C. A. (2002). *Canada: An Information Literacy Case Study*. White Paper prepared for UNESCO, the U.S. National Commission on Libraries and Information Science, and the National Forum on Information Literacy, for use at the Information Literacy Meeting of Experts, Prague, The Czech Republic. Available at: http://www.nclis.gov/libinter/infolitconf&meet/papers/quinlan-fullpaper.pdf

Wozney, L., Venkatesh, V., & Abrami, P. C. (2006). Implementing computer technologies: Teachers' perceptions and practices. *Journal of Technology and Teacher Education, 14*(1), 173–207.

Wright, J., Stackhouse, J., & Wood, J. (2008). Promoting language and literacy skills in the early years: lessons from interdisciplinary teaching and learning. *Child Language Teaching and Therapy, 24*(2), 155–171. doi:10.1177/0265659007090292

Zeichner, K., & Wray, S. (2001). The teaching portfolio in US teacher education programs: what we know and what we need to know. *Teaching and Teacher Education, 17*, 613–621. doi:10.1016/S0742-051X(01)00017-8

Zimmerman, B, J. (1989). A social cognitive view of self-regulated academic learning. *Journal of Educational Psychology, 81*, 329–339. doi:10.1037/0022-0663.81.3.329

Zimmerman, B. J. (2000). Attaining self-regulation: A social cognitive perspective. In Boekaerts, M., & Pintrich, P. R. (Eds.), *Handbook of self-regulation* (pp. 13–39). New York: Academic Press. doi:10.1016/B978-012109890-2/50031-7

ENDNOTES

[1] Funding for the development, testing and dissemination of the Literacy Toolkit has come from multiple sources including: Industry Canada, FQRSC, SSHRC, CCL, CLLRNET, MELS, CTREQ, VRQ, Inukshuk Wireless, the Chawkers Foundation and the Max Bell Foundation.

[2] Philip C. Abrami, Centre for the Study of Learning & Performance, Concordia University, 1455 deMaisonneuve Blvd. W., Montreal, Quebec, Canada H3G 1M8. E-mail: abrami@education.concordia.ca. Website: http://doe.concordia.ca/cslp/

[3] Abrami, Deleveaux, Wade, Meyer & LeBel are at Concordia University; Savage is at McGill University.

Section 3
Using Games in Education

Chapter 13
Games and the Development of Students' Civic Engagement and Ecological Stewardship

Janice L. Anderson
University of North Carolina - Chapel Hill, USA

ABSTRACT

In recent years, researchers and classroom teachers have started to explore purposefully designed computer/video games in supporting student learning. This interest in video and computer games has arisen in part, because preliminary research on educational video and computer games indicates that leveraging this technology has the potential to improve student motivation, interest, and engagement in learning through the use of a familiar medium (Gee, 2005; Mayo, 2009; Squire, 2005; Shaffer, 2006). While most of this early research has focused on the impact of games on academic and social outcomes, relatively few studies have been conducted exploring the influence of games on civic engagement (Lenhart et al, 2008). This chapter will specifically look at how Quest Atlantis, a game designed for learning, can potentially be utilized to facilitate the development of ecological stewardship among its players/students, thereby contributing to a more informed democratic citizenry.

INTRODUCTION

Computer/video games and virtual worlds have emerged as a pervasive influence on American society and culture in a relatively short period of time (Mayo, 2009; Squire, 2006). Students of all ages engage these environments as much or more than they watch television (Buckley & Anderson, 2006; Entertainment Software Association, 2006;

Mayo, 2009; Michigan State University, 2004) which has led researchers to examine motivational factors such as the desire to play, focusing on how computer/video games can be utilized to facilitate student learning in the classroom (Squire, 2006). Computer/video games and virtual worlds have been developed as models for improving the learning environment of students by implementing the types of clear goals and challenges that are presented to students through the gaming platforms, allowing for and challenging students to collaborate creating

DOI: 10.4018/978-1-61520-781-7.ch013

the potential for transforming learning in all types of settings, including schools (Gee, 2003; Shaffer, 2006; Darab et al. 2008; Darab et al., 2007). These virtual environments make it plausible to immerse students within networks of interaction and back-stories which engages them in problem solving and reflection in both real and in-world relationships and identities (Barab, 2008). This type of virtual-engagement represents what Gee (2003) identifies as empathetic embodiment of complex systems, where students develop an understanding of and appreciation for one or more aspects of the context of the virtual worlds in which they are engaged.

Many of the massively multiplayer online games (MMOGs) and multi-user virtual environments (MUVEs) provide students with the opportunity to role play, engaging them in a collaborative processes that facilitates participation and leads to problem solving, hypothesis generation and identity construction (Barab, 2008). These environments allow student players to become engaged in an evolving discourse as members of a community of practice (Barab, 2008; Lave & Wenger, 1991; Squire, 2006). By creating experiences of legitimate peripheral participation (Lave & Wenger, 1991) which emphasize conceptual understanding as a means to address authentic situations (e.g. taking on the role of a scientist, a politician, engineer, etc.), students come to a new way of knowing different from the more traditional, didactic approaches to curriculum and instruction (Barab, Hay, Barnett, & Keating, 2000; Brown, Collins, & Duguid, 1989). By balancing academic content, legitimate peripheral participation, background narratives, and game rules, these virtual worlds can be utilized to support disciplinary-specific learning in content areas such as science, social studies, and civics (Barab, 2008).

Much of the current research has focused on how games and virtual worlds impact academic and social outcomes (e.g. aggression, violence), while relatively little research has been conducted

exploring the impact of games and virtual worlds on civic engagement and society (Lenhart, Kahne, Middaugh, McGill, Evans, & Vitak, 2008). Citizenship, democracy and education are inextricably bound to the life of a nation (Bennett, Wells, & Rank, 2008). Schools work to prepare or help students build tools that enable them to play an active role in society as engaged, educated participants. An educated citizenry will contribute their skills and talents to preserve a democratic society. According to John Dewey (1916), community participation is a key to this maintenance. This community participation consists of individuals united through common interests, goals and ideas, but also allow for "free and full interplay" (Dewey, 1916, p. 83) with those who assert differing viewpoints and perspectives. This is the point of education, to nurture the development of individuals who can think and critically analyze, contributing to a democratic society.

In recent years, post-industrial democracies have acknowledged a crisis in student civic engagement, noting a lack of participation in elections and other traditional civic activities as students mature into adulthood (Bennett, Wells & Rank, 2008). However, while recognizing that students have become disengaged and disconnected from current political practices, most post-industrial democracies have continued to frame their conceptions of citizenship without regard to changing social identities and new and emerging ways of learning, (e.g. gaming, social networking and the internet) among young people (Bennett, Wells, & Rank, 2008). According to the Civic Mission for Schools (Gibson & Levine, 2008), while schools are the main source of civic education today, they fail to account for how students view citizenship roles differently from their parents. This disconnect suggests the need to extend educational methods for citizenship beyond traditional textbooks to include "critical engagement with issues and community involvement" (Bennett, Wells & Rank, 2008, p. 4) in order to fully engage students in becoming democratic citizens.

While technology has been "blamed" for fostering isolation among users, the reality is youth who participate in video/computer game and virtual environments are often actively, and sometimes unknowingly, engaged in new forms of civic life that differs from that of previous generations of non-digital natives like their parents and other adults (Bers, 2008). This type of virtual civic engagement stems from students participation and immersion in a digital culture based on experiential learning and online knowledge sharing with others in their own classrooms and across the globe associated with social networking and digital media (Jenkins, 2006; Bennett, Wells, & Rank, 2008). The emergence and popularity of social networking and media sites such as Facebook©, LinkedIn©, MySpace© and YouTube© provides evidence of this type of virtual civic engagement. As a result, collaborative problem solving and the circular flow of ideas among peers (Jenkins, 2006) is often the norm within this digital native generation. Gaming, likewise, becomes a major component within the range of social activities with a large percentage of youth participation (Lenhart et al, 2008). Multi-user environments provide the opportunity for students to take on the role of producers, as opposed to consumers, of knowledge (Jenkins, 2006; Bers, 2008). Participation in digital environments allows students to explore civic identities by participating in events and discourse related to civic issues in new and unique ways across global communities. This allows students to begin to understand the difficulties that arise from globalization (Bers, 2008).

In recent years, the emergence and growing popularity of the green movement is putting a new emphasis on issues like recycling, composting, and community-based gardening (Biswas et al, 2000) and bringing attention to the size and impact of one's carbon footprint (Weber & Matthews, 2008). With this new interest in ecological stewardship, citizens are becoming increasingly concerned with their impact on the environment, not only in their local communities but across the planet. Through participation in local and digital/virtual environments, youth begin to see a juxtaposition of the worlds; the two worlds are mutually beneficial for learning new skills, so that students take their experiences within the digital environment and transfer them to their local situation where they can work toward long term solutions for environmental and social issues as actively engaged, real-world citizens.

THEORETICAL FRAMEWORK

Contemporary viewpoints of the nature and philosophy of science are rooted in the notion that science is not simply the accumulation of a myriad of facts about the world, but rather it involves the construction of ideas and theories about how the world may be. This view allows for challenges, conflict, and disputes as opposed to common agreement on the nature of science (Giere, 1991; Popper, 1959; Kuhn, 1962). Multi-user, digital environments work to develop these ideas by situating disciplinary content within broader contextual frameworks (Bers, 2008; Sadler, Barab & Scott, 2007; Barab, 2008). According to Papert (1980), the constructivist nature of these environments promotes higher-order learning because they engage the individual in creating personally meaningful artifacts that can benefit and be shared with others within a community. Through this reflection on external objects, internal knowledge is also developed (Papert, 1980).

Quest Atlantis, (QA), builds and expands upon these constructivist principles through the framework of socio-scientific inquiry (Barab, Sadler, Heiselt, Hickey, & Zuiker, 2007). Socio-scientific inquiry engages students in "the process of using scientific methods to interrogate rich narratives about societal issues that have a scientific basis, yet whose solution claims with political, economic and social concerns" (Barab et al., 2007, p. 61). Based upon the three core concepts of narrative engagement ("context"), inscription construction/

deconstruction ("resources") and scientific inquiry ("practice"), *Quest Atlantis* allows students to utilize these core constructs to create compelling solutions to "real world problems." The narrative of the virtual environment contextualizes the scientific content or problem, which, in this study, revolves around why the fish are declining in *Taiga*. Barab and colleagues (2007) see this contextualization as a mechanism to transform student learning from "facts or concepts to be memorized into useful tools to address significant issues" (p. 61).

The inscriptions, or resources, focus on the written or printed objects (e.g. charts, tables, graphs, schemes, diagrams, etc.). These allow the students to demonstrate and represent knowledge, as well as focus on data extrapolated from the larger narrative (Roth & McGinn, 1998). Scientific knowledge is often communicated through these types of simplified representations, or inscriptions, turning them into a conceptual tool that allows students to make sense of the world and creatively solve problems (Barab et al, 2007). The scientific inquiry practices that exist within these gaming and virtual world environments allow students to utilize a dynamic approach towards asking questions, making and testing hypothesis and discoveries, and considering the impact of all possible solutions within the context of the community. *Quest Atlantis* makes use of this socio-scientific inquiry framework to gain insight into how virtual world environments and other computer games are leveraged to address all types of academic content. The focus of this study was analyzing how students learned science content, and developed their own ecological stewardship and civic engagement while engaging with *Quest Atlantis*.

The framework of pedagogical praxis (Shaffer, 2004) utilizes the ideas of situated learning first developed by Brown, Collins, and Duguid (1989); this notion of situated learning was later expanded upon by Lave and Wenger (1991), who begin with the premise that "under the right

conditions, computers and other information technologies can make it easier for students to become active participants in meaningful projects and practices in the life of their community" (p. 1401). Praxis-based educational models, such as digital environments, are designed to encourage experiences where students learn through engagement and participation (Bers, 2008; Shaffer, 2004) as opposed to the more traditional knowledge based models that focus solely on subject specific content. Pedagogical praxis further develops Lave and Wenger (1991) notion of communities of practice by incorporating legitimate peripheral participation (Shaffer, 2004) and Schon's model (1985, 1987) of reflective practice which suggests that one must "think in action" (p. 1402) through these experiences. According to Schon (1985), individuals who make a connection between knowing and doing through reflection are able to "combine reflection and action, on the spot, ... to examine understandings and appreciations while the train is running" (p. 27). Multi-user digital environments provide students with the tools to engage in this form of legitimate peripheral participation where conceptual understanding, in both disciplinary content and practices, in authentic situations is valued.

Citizen models, reflecting global civic and environmental engagement, demonstrate what is described by Westheimer and Kahne as participatory and justice-oriented forms of citizenship. A participatory citizen is actively engaged in his/her community and is working to solve social and environmental problems (e.g. pollution in the rivers). Citizens who take a justice-oriented perspective identify the various social, behavioral, and environmental problems, the structures that perpetuate these problems, and the actions that are needed to change the patterns that contribute to the replication of problems over time (Westheimer & Kahne, 2004).

While commercial games such as *World of Warcraft, SimCity,* and *Second Life* are environments that can potentially nurture the development of ecological stewardship and civic engagement, this study will focus on the use of an educational game, *Quest Atlantis,* developed by education and learning science researchers, to examine how students learn (or do not learn) science content and how interaction with one's environment impacts (or does not impact) the player's sense of ecological stewardship and civic engagement.

This work contributes to a developing body of research that examining the impact of using computer/video games and virtual worlds within educational settings (e.g. Nelson, Ketelhut, Clarke, Bowman & Dede, 2005; Barab et al., 2007; Squire, (2006); Neulight, N. Kafai, Y., Kao, L., Foley, B. & Galas, C. (2007)) It also contributes to the research base on using multi-user virtual environments (MUVEs) through the examination of how students learn science content within the *Quest Atlantis* environment and how they are able to translate these experiences to their own lives, becoming civic and ecological stewards of their communities.

QUEST ATLANTIS

Quest Atlantis (QA), developed at Indiana University, is a multi-user virtual environment that combines strategies used in commercial gaming environments while integrating lessons from educational research on learning and motivation. The immersive gaming environment is designed for students (ages 9-14) to engage in forms of play that allows them to explore social responsibility within the context of both fictional and non-fictional realities while promoting the civic engagement of its participants (www.questatlantis.org). Student engagement is accomplished through a compelling narrative. The back-story focuses on the problems of a mythical world called *Atlantis,* where students encounter issues similar to the challenges faced in their own experiences on Earth. *Atlantis* is described to the participants as a planet experiencing a myriad of social and environmental issues. Students are invited by a group of concerned *Atlantan* citizens to help them solve some of these crucial issues. The story plays out with the 3D world as well as in novels, comic books, and a global community of participants. The game platform provides an immersive context for the students to engage in real-world inquiry through the fictional world, *Atlantis.*

The 3D world provides the platform of engagement for students, who teleport to virtual locations within *Atlantis* to perform educational activities known as *quests,* talk with other students and mentors, and build virtual personae in real-time. The virtual personae, or avatars, can be customized to reflect the student's own identity through their choice of hair and skin color, clothes and other accessories such as hats, glasses and backpacks. Students, through their avatar, respond to *Quests* (developmentally appropriate activities with task descriptions and goals) in order to help the Council of Atlantis solve some of their problems and restore lost knowledge within *Atlantan* society.

Groups of *Atlantans,* known as the Council, are determined to restore *Atlantis* back to its previous magnificence by enlisting the help of student questers from Earth. *Questers* teleport to *Atlantis* via OTAK, the computer designed by the council. Upon entering the *Quest Atlantis* environment, students are free to visit a number of virtual worlds, each with their own unique theme, and council member supporting it (e.g. *Ecology World* with its environmental awareness focus headed by Council Member Lan). Each world is made up of several villages with their own *quests.* The *quests* within the worlds and villages are connected to academic standards, both at the national and state level, and to social commitments such as environmental awareness. Students are invited to bring their own experiences, families, and cultures to help them solve the problems of *Atlantis. Quests* within the world can vary, ranging from simple simulations to complex application problems.

Student *questers* navigate their avatars through the 3D world and interact with other players via a text-based chat window and respond to non-player characters (NPCs) with structured dialogues where they propose solutions and communicate ideas about the problem they are solving. As students complete each quest experience, their final responses/solutions can be typed directly into the game space, or they can upload up to four files, including word processing documents, spreadsheets, presentations, movies, or any other file type. *Quests* are generally assessed by the supervising teacher who assumes the role of a non-player character such as Ranger Bartle in *Taiga,* or Lan, the council member in *Ecology World.* All correspondence about the *quests* is generated by the non-player character/teacher. A teacher can also assign questers to conduct peer reviewing or edits of their fellow classmates. *Questers* access their work and feedback through the 2D window space, which becomes their homepage complete with their electronic portfolios.

While students interacted with their teacher and other non-player characters, there were no internal supports like an intelligent tutor to scaffold students' construction of knowledge. In this study, however, students participants utilized a field notebook, developed by the researcher, to guide their *quests* in *Taiga*. This field notebook provided the students with scaffolds for note-taking as they progressed through *Taiga* and encouraged them to connect their game play to extensions into "real world" experiences and situations.

The focus of this chapter is on *Taiga*, one of the many worlds within *Quest Atlantis. Taiga* is a park located along two water-ways and inhabited by a variety of non-player characters including loggers, tourists, and indigenous farmers. The world also includes a fishing resort and park administration. *Taiga* is designed to help students learn about environmental science concepts such as eutrophication, erosion, water quality indicators and hypothesis testing through their interaction with these virtual characters and data concerning a declining fish population within the park's rivers.

Student *questers* are invited to assume the role of a field investigator helping Ranger Bartle solve his dilemma – the decline of the fish in the river. They begin their narrative immersion by interviewing the various stakeholders/non-player characters found in the park and identifying the possible factors contributing to the decline of the

Figure 1.

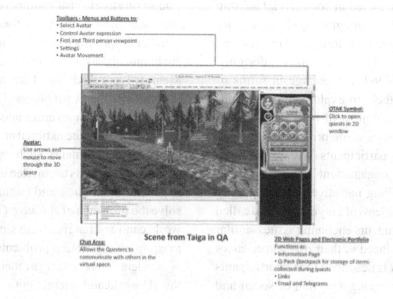

fish population. The non-player characters provide a diverse set of perspectives on the problem of fish decline for the students to analyze.

Students collect water samples, analyze data and formulate a hypothesis that is based upon their understanding of the scientific evidence, along with their analysis of the stakeholder's perspectives of the problem. After proposing an initial solution, students are allowed to travel to the future to see the impact of their ideas on *Taiga*. Depending on their choices, the students will encounter different scenarios that are reflective of their choices. Upon returning to the present, student questers are given the opportunity to revise their solution into a nuanced argument which balances the scientific evidence with a greater understanding of both the political and economical impact on the community. The success of the student within *Taiga* is dependent upon their understanding of 1) water quality indicators such as pH, dissolved oxygen, nitrates and phosphates; 2) the processes of eutrophication and erosion; and 3) the dynamic relationship between the indicators, the processes and the outcomes within the *Taiga* water-ways.

STUDY CONTEXT

Context: School and Students

This study occurred in three fifth grade classrooms (n=50) of two urban schools, Chamberlain Elementary and Edison Elementary, part of the *Northeast Public School System[1]* in the United States. Northeast Public Schools is a large urban district that faces many of the problems plaguing urban centers including poverty, low academic achievement, English Language Learner (ELL) issues, high-risk students, and lack of student engagement. Both schools struggle to meet their annual "Adequate Yearly Progress" (AYP) and are often categorized as being either failing or needs

improvement schools. Both Chamberlain and Edison fall in the "Needs Improvement" category in English Language Arts and "No Status" for Mathematics in the statewide Assessment System used to determine AYP under the federal No Child Left Behind (NCLB) legislation. Neither school met its Annual Yearly Progress (AYP) in English Language Arts. However, Edison met AYP for Mathematics, while Chamberlain did not. Both of these schools have predominately Black and Latino(a) populations, which account for seventy to seventy-five percent of the school populations. Chamberlain is also linguistically diverse with over seventy languages spoken at home.

METHODOLOGY

Data Sources

This study involved a multi-tiered, mixed model approach that allowed for both broad understandings of classroom practices and specific analysis of outcomes. Data were collected from multiple sources reflecting perspectives of the researcher, teachers, and students participating in the *Quest Atlantis* project (Lincoln & Guba, 1985). These sources included both pre- and post- assessments and not only focused on science content, but incorporated or took into account process skills and types of engagement in areas such as ecological stewardship. The data sources included pre- and post- semi-structured interviews of a subset of students (n=20), detailed journal notes of informal and formal conversations between the researcher and students. Other data sources included videotapes interactions of student participation, student products and end-of-project student artifacts (e.g. field notebooks and reports), classroom observations by the researcher, and an archive of online chat dialogues from student interactions within the game.

Data Analysis

Data was triangulated in order to overcome any weakness or intrinsic bias arising from the use of a single data source. An interpretive approach was utilized to analyze the qualitative data sources (Denzin & Lincoln, 2000). The extensive data collected throughout the project provided an in-depth picture of how students re-conceptualized ecological stewardship and engagement over time. Through interaction analysis (Jordan & Henderson, 1995), data were coded by analyzing segments of video that focused on a specific topic of interest (e.g. science content knowledge, ecological stewardship). Further analysis specifically examined the student discourse and actions around ecological stewardship and environmental consciousness during game play, and how the game seemed to support (or not support) their civic engagement within the *Quest Atlantis* virtual environment. Codes that emerged during pre-coding and open coding during implementation were then further collapsed into an axial coding scheme. Additionally, these identified codes served as the foundation for the construction of written cases. Codes were checked for inter-rater reliability by another science education researcher, resulting in a reliability level of 0.8.

What was apparent in the data collection process was that student participation in the *Quest Atlantis* virtual environment represented a fluidity of mutual engagement and disengagement. The social construction of students' knowledge was observed through their interactions with other students and with the game. It therefore became important to look at how students interacted with each other, making known the ideas and strategies they employed within the world to gain entry for their ideas within the community. With respect to technology and other artifacts used to support the students in playing the game, it was important for the researcher to look at how artifacts (e.g. field notebooks and reports) and technology use supported or constrained students' participation in the activity. How were the students occupying space in-world and voicing their ideas? How were these ideas incorporated into problem-solving? Were their ideas translated into practice in the students' own real-world experiences or, if not, could they?

Students in each of the participating classrooms engaged in playing *Quest Atlantis* over 15-20 class periods of 45-60 minutes each. A purposeful sampling of the students was done to reflect the demographics of the school population. An attempt was made to select an equal number of male and female students. Of the students that were interviewed, eight identified as African American (four male, four female), eight were Latino(a) (three male, five female), one Caucasian (male), and two Asian/Pacific Islander (one male, one female).

While the data was extremely rich, this chapter will focus on two students, Rebecca and Keith, who most clearly articulated the impact of playing *Quest Atlantis* on the development of their own ecological stewardship and civic engagement in their communities. Keith was a ten year old Asian/Pacific Islander male student from Edison Elementary while Rebecca was an eleven year old African American female student from Chamberlain Elementary.

FINDINGS/ RESULTS

Through case studies, several themes surfaced that clearly illustrated the ways in which student discourse about notions of ecological stewardship emerged and evolved as students navigated the quests in *Taiga*. First, by playing the game students generally internalized and understood science content knowledge on topics of water quality, ecosystems and system dynamics. The students were also able to supply the researcher with well-developed science content answers while demonstrating a clear understanding of these concepts. While the primary focus of the

Taiga experience was the acquisition of basic science content knowledge on water quality and ecosystems, the conversations and discourse that occurred between students, teachers and researchers demonstrated that the students were also able to offer a more nuanced understanding of how the content they encountered within *Quest Atlantis* was connected to real-world localized water environments.

Secondly, students were able translate the science content and nuanced explanations they learned by playing *Quest Atlantis* to their communities, both virtual and real, whereby giving voice to environmental issues impacting their areas allowing them to begin efforts to solve these problems. These ideas emerged from analysis of both video and audio data collected during the student interviews and in-world experiences. This became particularly evident during the student interviews. The following section will provide further detail about how Keith and Rebecca illustrate these themes.

SCIENCE CONTENT KNOWLEDGE

Analyzing the student responses during these interviews, there was a consistent trend of students moving from vague, non-scientific responses to more nuanced, data driven explanations using precise language and knowledge acquired from the in-world experiences. *Quest Atlantis*, and *Taiga* specifically, appeared to facilitate students' learning of specific science concepts involving water quality and ecosystems within a problem based environment at the fifth grade level. This water quality and ecosystem knowledge was demonstrated through the written assessments where a t-test showed a significance ($p \leq 0.005$) between the paired average (n=50) pre-assessment score of 25 ± 8 and the post-assessment score of 29 ± 8, where r=0.830.[2] More specifically, Keith and Rebecca's scores both improved ten points from pre- to post-assessment, with Keith improving from 24 to 34 and Rebecca improving from 29 to 39.

The water quality and ecosystem knowledge gained by the students from engaging in the virtual environment was then applied to scenarios of their local environments in the interviews. Students applied their new knowledge and demonstrated notions of ecological stewardship and civic responsibility in their responses. For example, during the pre-engagement interviews, students were asked to determine if a particular water source was safe for their families to drink. Nearly all of the students interviewed (18 of 20) indicated that they would "look at it to see if it were clean to drink," and offered no details as to *how* they would "look" to see if this were indeed true. Rebecca's response was indicative of these students:

Researcher: *Imagine that you found out that the river near your house, like the [winding] river was the source of your drinking water. What could you do to make sure the water was safe to drink for you and your family?*

Rebecca: *Well, I can look at the river and see if people are swimming in it…and then look to see if was polluted or something… and to look and see if there is mud and pollution and stuff… and people are swimming in it… then it probably wouldn't be very good to drink out of… but if it were a fresh river and no one was swimming…. there wasn't any pollution and stuff it might be safer to drink…*

Researcher: *So is there anything you might do to see if the water was polluted? How would you know?*

Rebecca: *Like tests or something?*

Researcher: *Yes, are there any tests you might run?*

Rebecca: *You could take a cup and fill it with water to see if its muddy and then I would look to see if there were any things that clean out the water or if they just took the water out of the river....*

In her response, Rebecca focused on people swimming in the river. She talked about pollution, but did not account for the sources of the pollution, nor how she might have worked to eradicate the pollution. Additionally, she did not indicate *how* she would determine if there was pollution beyond taking a sample to analyze. When probed for specifics, the response remained similar - that the water was muddy and therefore polluted.

However, after Rebecca had completed the four quests within Taiga, her answers were different. In the post-engagement interview, Rebecca responded in a much more sophisticated manner with respect to the science content knowledge:

Researcher: *Ok, so let's say that you heard that the [winding] river near your house was where your drinking water came from. What might you do to see if the water was actually safe to drink?*

Rebecca: *Well, first I would get a water sample from the river and test it. The water could be really bad to drink because the water could have like, be like acid, and that wouldn't be very good. I would also test for oxygen and other stuff... it could be... hmmm.... Nitrogen or phosphate or something, you know...kind of like the Mulus [the indigenous stakeholder non-player characters in Taiga] when I played in QA... they had that fertilizer stuff that got in the water...you know, up by that farm area near Norbe.... then the water gets all green and stuff...*

Researcher: *So what kinds of tests do you think you might run?*

Rebecca: *Well.... I'd like to see what is in the water....and like what the pH level was to see if there was acid since that is bad... and turbidity... you know.. the mud and how clear the water is 'cause that makes a difference with the oxygen...*

Rebecca was able to articulate that water quality testing would be central for determining whether the water was safe to drink. Additionally, she was able to identify specific examples (e.g. dissolved oxygen and nitrogen/phosphate testing) and, in several instances, relate it back to her in-world experiences (e.g. the algal bloom from the fertilizer runoff). The types of water quality tests that she identified were the tests that she encountered, learned about and utilized in *Taiga*.

Researchers also asked the students to think about waterways in their own community; if they were polluted and how might this pollution impact living organisms. When questioned about how the students' believed the waterways became polluted, all of the interview participants (n=20) recognized the impact of human activity on the environment through pollutants like boating, factory waste, human pollution and littering. Student responses were consistent between the pre- and post-interviews, however, in post-interview responses, students also addressed the impact of the pollution on food webs and river ecosystems. In the following response, Keith discussed how human activity impacted the turbidity of the river and ultimately, the food chain:

Researcher: *How do you think the river became so polluted?*

Keith: *Well, people litter a lot in the city....and sometimes it gets in the water... and dirt and stuff, when ever they run or do other stuff... maybe cut* *down some trees or something... dirt gets in the water and then the turbidity changes...and you know... the dirt then makes the temperature go up...get hotter...and then the water gets warmer and that is not good...*

Researcher: *So, why is that not good? How does that affect the fish, plants and other animals along the river?*

Keith: *Well... I think that the temperature... it might sorta kill the ecosystem because of how the temperature is... you know the oxygen...it gets messed up and there isn't as much when the temperature is high...so then the fish, they like die...the small fish die, and then the big fish die because they don't have any food anymore...and the food chain is sorta messed up... other animals might not have anything to eat either...*

Like Rebecca before him, Keith's response reflected a nuanced scientific understanding of water quality concepts and, in this instance, dissolved oxygen. This understanding and experience was facilitated through his engagement with the *Taiga* community and reflection in action (Schon, 1985, 1987) on the problems faced by *Taiga*.

CIVIC ENGAGEMENT AND ECOLOGICAL STEWARDSHIP

Examining the context of the students' post-interview responses, what emerged was that students made specific connections between the problems encountered in the virtual world environment and those they saw within their own communities. They began to see themselves as being able to actively engage in community building based upon the in-world experiences in *Quest Atlantis*. For example, during the course of the post-interview, it became evident that Rebecca saw herself as an engaged citizen who wanted to work as a change agent in her local environment. Rebecca's responses reflected that she was not only situating herself as a participatory citizen (Westheimer & Kahne, 2004), but she was beginning to think about the long term impacts of pollution in her community and was therefore moving towards a justice-oriented citizen orientation (Westheimer & Kahne, 2004). She stated:

Rebecca: *.....and if there is no oxygen, then animals like the fish can't live and if there is too much fertilizer and stuff then the water will get all green, with... what is it called... is it algae?*

Researcher: *yes...*

Rebecca: *That would be bad..the water would be dirty and people shouldn't drink out of it at all or they might get sick... so I would want to make sure that I let people know that...and...* **and maybe even get them to help me clean it up so we could use it again***....I like to fish, and if the fish are dead, I can't go fishing....so that's what I would do....*

It was apparent from this brief interlude that Rebecca recognized the need for community action, similar to what she encountered in her *Taiga* experiences, and which demonstrated the type of empathetic embodiment described by Gee (2003). Through her experiences in *Quest Atlantis*, Rebecca came to understand how her participation in a civic community, including virtual communities like *Taiga*, was impacted by her choices and was reflected in the greater global community (Bers, 2008; Shaffer, 2004). This type of participatory citizenship (Westheimer & Kahne, 2004) encouraged community engagement around social and environmental problems, in this instance, impacted the quality of a community waterway. *Taiga* had created an opportunity for pedagogical praxis (Shaffer, 2004) where students, like Rebecca and Keith, were able to participate in communities of practice (Lave & Wenger, 1991) that allowed them to simulate the types of civic and democratic dynamics (Dewey, 1900/1956) that created opportunities for them to both reflect (Schon, 1985, 1987) and act on social and environmental issues.

This participatory citizen perspective emerged again through the conversations with Keith. By understanding the basis of the problems through legitimate peripheral participation (Lave & Wenger, 1991) in the *Taiga* community, students like Keith can begin to examine the structural causes of social and environmental issues and seek solutions. The newly grasped, nuanced scientific knowledge can lead to actions rather than a exhibiting a "divorce between knowledge and action"(Dewey, 1909, 41). Keith through this response demonstrated an understanding of how he moved from this type of participatory citizenship to a more justice oriented citizenship in the example below:

Researcher: *So if the animals don't have anything to eat, what would you do?*

Keith: *Well... ummm...I think I might want to get people not to make pollution...like pick up their trash...and not throw stuff in the water... and maybe not cut down so many trees so that the dirt doesn't get in the water and that way there is oxygen for the fish to breath... and then they can all live too...*

Reseacher: *So how might you do that?*

Keith: *umm...maybe we could get everybody to go down to the river and clean it up....like maybe have a school activity where we do that....or maybe ask my family to help too...*

Keith's response demonstrated participatory citizenship because it reflected a desire to make changes in his environment. However, it also indicated the beginning of a type of justice oriented citizenship because he not only identified the types of behaviors that were contributing to the environmental problem, but he suggested mechanisms for change and solutions to the problem (Westheimer & Kahne, 2004). Both Rebecca and Keith's responses built upon the types of citizenry models that are played out with the *Quest Atlantis* environment. *Quest Atlantis* seeks to engage students within the world, through participation in the community and by proposing solutions that address major environmental issues in ways that can improve the quality of life in their communities over time. By seeing the impact that they made within the virtual environment, students began to make connections and understand how they can use these same types of skills within their own communities, fostering a new sense of ecological stewardship and civic engagement.

DISCUSSION

The underlying story of *Taiga* in *Quest Atlantis* described a society experiencing social and environmental problems. Within this context, students became part of a community of practice (Lave & Wenger, 1991) that was working to solve issues that were similar to the types of problems indigenous to our own society. Building on the Dewey's idea of linking school and society (Dewey, 1900/1956), learning environments such as *Quest Atlantis,* allow students to use the virtual world as a tool to support learning and engagement in epistemologically meaningful projects situated in legitimate "real world" experiences. The advantage of using pedagogical-based praxis models is that the open-ended nature of the environments allow students to have multiple types of experiences within the context of the same world (Bers, 2008; Shaffer, 2004).

In *Quest Atlantis,* and in particular *Taiga*, the underlying message was that students could all work towards solving environmental problems in order to create a better society for both current and future generations. By immersing the students in a high-tech virtual play-space, they acquired not only scientific knowledge, but also an understanding of civic responsibility through their participation in a virtual democratic community (Barab et al, 2007). Through their participation in *Taiga* and its communities of practice within the Atlantan society (Lave & Wenger, 1991), students began to understand the impact of their decisions on the virtual community. They could then apply those lessons to their own communities, recognizing how they could impact local change. This process reflected the framework of Westheimer and Kahne (2004), participatory and justice-oriented citizens.

The *Taiga* missions took on these citizenry models by engaging students with the citizens of *Atlantis*, in order to solve important environmental issues (participatory) and engaged them in proposing solutions that encouraged changes in the behavior and practices of community members. This virtual civic engagement ultimately meant that community problems (e.g. the fish dying in the rivers of *Taiga*) were not perpetuated, but rather eradicated over time (justice oriented). Within the virtual world structure and through the game narrative, students were able to see the impact of their decisions on the *Taiga* community. By participating in this type of decision making within the virtual community, students developed the needed skills including an understanding of the types of questions and action plans needed to create change within their own communities. This was evident in the interviews with Rebecca and Keith, where they not only applied the science content knowledge acquired through their play, but discussed how they could engage their own community to tackle problems of water pollution in local waterways.

Students developed a rich conceptual, perceptual and ethical understanding of the science of water quality through their participation in the narrative of *Taiga*. This allowed them to apply their knowledge to a real-world problem as opposed to simply acquiring scientific facts. Inquiry became the means by which the students engaged with science content and was the tool to solve the environmental problems of *Taiga*. This allowed for an appreciation of the underlying science content and the role that political and economic factors play in scientific decision-making (Barab et al, 2007).

Through the creation of empathetic embodiment (Gee, 2003), students came to understand the unique dynamics and complex systems that are found in within the context of *Taiga*, creating a mechanism for legitimate participation and an understanding of what it means to be an ecological steward within a community of practice (Lave & Wenger, 1991). Through the students' recognition of the need for community action to protect their waterways, they demonstrated the ability to transfer the knowledge gained from their participation to their own communities demonstrating both social responsibility and civic engagement. By creating opportunities for students to become active participants within their communities of practice (Shaffer, 2004; Lave & Wenger, 1991), *Quest Atlantis,* and other virtual worlds and games like it, build on the work of John Dewey (1900/1956;1915), who saw the classroom as a student-centered community of learners.

The collaborative nature of *Taiga* and *Quest Atlantis* is reflective of the type of curriculum that Dewey (1900/1956) envisioned. The larger, global communities afforded by technology, allow students to view the world from broader viewpoint, accounting for a variety of perspectives and solutions to common problems. The knowledge that students construct from these interactions and the proposed solutions as represented in their interviews, demonstrated what Dewey saw as experiential learning, constructed in a social and technological context that is different from traditional epistemologies (Dewey, 1900/1956; Jenkins, 2006; Bers, 2008; Shaffer, 2004). The types of learning and development of ecological stewardship and civic engagement demonstrated by the students in this study confirmed that this type of interactive, virtual world approach could be beneficial when applied to educating students about civic engagement. Part of educating for a democratic society is making sure that students reach their full potential while contributing to the life of a democracy (Martínez Alemán, 2001). It is possible that in contemporary times, being environmentally friendly or ecological stewards, particularly with the emergence of the green movement, is valuable for ensuring a clean environment for many generations. How *Quest Atlantis* and *Taiga* addressed issues of ecological stewardship impacted how students perceived their own ecological and civic responsibilities. The students participating in *Quest Atlantis* environments not only learned about water quality and ecosystems as was demonstrated by their gains in scientific knowledge between pre- and post-assessments, but were able to identify complex problems and phenomenon in their own local waterways suggesting mechanisms for implementing change and their development as an ecological stewards. This suggests that virtual worlds like *Quest Atlantis* can potentially provide inquiry experiences that allow students to engage in experiential learning (Dewey 1900/1956).

IMPLICATIONS AND CONCLUSIONS

There are definite limitations of this study. The study was conducted in three classrooms in just two schools in an urban setting and focused on two students. Despite this snapshot view, this study begins to reveal the potential that this curricular instantiation can have on inquiry based scientific pedagogy and its potential to develop ecological stewardship and civic engagement for

participants. While *Quest Atlantis* and *Taiga* appeared to accomplish this for the two students, as demonstrated by the interviews and the assessments, it was also clear that they could have benefitted from internal scaffolds or supports to help them take on these perspectives and guide them through probing questions. Games or virtual environments that seek to engage students in this manner will need to develop intelligent tutors which prompt students to think about the application of scientific concepts learned during game play to issues in their own communities. Virtual environments, like *Quest Atlantis*, allow students to "do science" in an immersive environment that encourages scientific debate and looks at the broader impacts of the scientific process within communities. Purposefully embedded scaffolds will help to bridge content with community engagement.

The goal of environments such as *Quest Atlantis* is for students to gain an understanding about what it means to participate in a democratic society. By allowing students to gain a sense of civic responsibilities and knowledge about what it means to be a good citizen who cares about the world, the students begin to understand, beyond procedural aspects, what it means to be part of a larger global community. From a theoretical perspective, the pedagogical model of praxis allows one to begin to understand the relationship between activity and learning in context (Shaffer, 2004). By creating learning experiences that immerse students within legitimate science experiences, students begin to internalize scientific ways of knowing allowing them to, in turn, apply knowledge to new contexts and situations. Students participating in *Quest Atlantis* began to recognize their own role in being a voice for issues of the environment that impacted not only the ecosystems, but the larger world. Students acquired a clear understanding of science concepts around water quality, ecosystems and system dynamics. They were also awakened to the roles they played within their own communities and began to make a connection to how they could facilitate change as global citizens of virtual and real worlds.

REFERENCES

Barab, S. A., Hay, K., Barnett, M., & Keating, T. (2000). Virtual solar system: Building understanding through model building. *Journal of Research in Science Teaching, 37*(7), 719–756. doi:10.1002/1098-2736(200009)37:7<719::AID-TEA6>3.0.CO;2-V

Barab, S. A., Ingram-Goble, A., & Warren, S. (2008). Conceptual Playspaces. In Ferdig, R. (Ed.), *Handbook on Research on Effective Electronic Gaming in Education*. Hershey, PA: IGI Global.

Barab, S. A., Sadler, T. D., Heiselt, C., Hickey, D., & Zuiker, S. (2007). Relating narrative, inquiry and inscriptions: Supporting consequential play. *Journal of Science Education and Technology, 16*(1), 59–82. doi:10.1007/s10956-006-9033-3

Bennett, W. L., Wells, C., & Rank, A. (2008). *Young citizens and civic learning: Two paradigms of citizenship in the digital age*. Seattle, WA: University of Washington.

Bers, M. U. (2008). Civic identities, online technologies: From designing civic curriculum to supporting civic engagement. In Bennett, W. L. (Ed.), *Civic Life Online*. Cambridge, MA: MIT Press.

Biswas, A., Licata, J. W., McKee, D., Pullig, C., & Daughtridge, C. (2000). The Recycling Cycle. *Journal of Public Policy & Marketing, 19*(1), 93–105. doi:10.1509/jppm.19.1.93.16950

Brown, J. S., Collins, A., & Duguid, P. (1989). Situated cognition and the culture of learning. *Educational Researcher, 18*(1), 32–42.

Buckley, K. E., & Anderson, C. A. (2006). A theoretical model of the effects and consequences of playing video games. In Vorderer, P., & Bryant, J. (Eds.), *Playing video games: Motives, responses, and consequences*. Mahwah, NJ: Lawrence Erlbaum Associates.

Denzin, N. K., & Lincoln, Y. S. (2000). *The discipline and practice of qualitative research*. In N.K.

Denzin & Y.S. Lincoln (Ed.), *Handbook of Qualitative Research* (2nd ed.). Thousand Oaks, CA: Sage.

Dewey, J. (1909). *Moral Principles in Education*. New York: Houghton Mifflin.

Dewey, J. (1916). *Democracy and Education*. New York: Macmillan.

Dewey, J. (1956). *The Child and the Curriculum*. Chicago: University of Chicago Press. (Original work published 1900)

Entertainment Software Association. (2006). *Essential Facts about the computer and video game industry*.

Gee, J. P. (2003). *What video games have to teach us about learning and literacy*. New York: Palgrave Macmillan.

Gee, J. P. (2005). *Game-like learning: An example of situated learning and implications for the opportunity to learn* [Electronic Version]. Retrieved September 6, 2006 from http://www.academic-colab.org/resources/documents/Game-Like%20Learning.rev.pdf

Gibson, C., & Levine, P. (2003). *The Civic Mission of Schools*. New York: Carnegie Corporation.

Giere, R. (1991). *Understanding Scientific Reasoning* (3rd ed.). Fort Worth, TX: Holt, Rinehardt and Winston.

Jenkins, H. (2006). *Confronting the challenges of participatory culture: Media education for the 21st Century*. Chicago, IL: John D. and Catherine A. MacArthur Foundation.

Jordan & Henderson. (1995). Interaction analysis: Foundations and practice. *Journal of the Learning Sciences, 4*(1), 39–104. doi:10.1207/s15327809jls0401_2

Kuhn, T. E. (1962). *The structure of scientific revolutions*. Chicago: University of Chicago Press.

Lave, J., & Wenger, E. (1991). *Situated learning: Legitimate peripheral participation*. Cambridge, UK: Cambridge University Press.

Lenhart, A., Kahne, J., Middaugh, E., Macgill, A. R., Evans, C., & Vitak, J. (2008). *Teens, Video Games and Civics: Teens' gaming experiences are diverse and include significant social interaction and civic engagement*. Washington, DC: Pew Internet and American Life Project.

Lincoln, Y. S., & Guba, E. G. (1985). *Naturalistic Inquiry*. Newbury Park, CA: Sage.

Martínez Alemán, A. M. (2001). The ethics of democracy: Individuality and educational policy. *Educational Policy*, *15*(3), 379–403. doi:10.1177/0895904801015003003

Mayo, M. J. (2009). Video games: A route to large-scale STEM education? *Science*, *323*, 79–82. doi:10.1126/science.1166900

Michigan State University. (2004). *Children spend more time playing video games than watching TV*. Retrieved from http://www.newsroom.msu.edu/site/indexer/1943/content.htm

Nelson, B., Ketelhut, D., Clarke, J., Bowman, C., Dede, C. (2005, November). Design based research strategies for developing a science inquiry curriculum in a multi-user virtual environment. *Educational Technology*.

Neulight, N., Kafai, Y. B., Kao, L., Foley, B., & Galas, G. (2007, February). Children's participation in a virtual epidemic in the science classroom: Making connections to natural infectious diseases. *Journal of Science Education and Technology*, *16*(1), 47–58. doi:10.1007/s10956-006-9029-z

Papert, S. (1980). *Mindstorms: Children, Computers, and Powerful Ideas*. New York: Basic Books.

Popper, K. (1959). *The logic of scientific discovery*. London: Hutchinson.

Roth, W. M., & McGinn, M. K. (1998). Inscriptions: Toward a theory of representing as social practice. *Review of Educational Research*, *68*(1), 35–59.

Sadler, T. D., Barab, S. A., & Scott, B. (2007). What do students gain by engaging in socioscientific inquiry? *Research in Science Education*, *37*, 371–391. doi:10.1007/s11165-006-9030-9

Schon, D. A. (1985). *The design studio: An exploration of its traditions and potentials*. London: RIBA Publications.

Schon, D. A. (1987). *Educating the reflective practitioner: Toward a new design for teaching and learning in the professions*. San Francisco: Jossey-Bass.

Shaffer, D. W. (2004). Pedagogical praxis: The professional models for post-industrial education. *Teachers College Record*, *106*(7). doi:10.1111/j.1467-9620.2004.00383.x

Shaffer, D. W. (2006). *How Computer Games Help Children Learn*. New York: Palgrave. doi:10.1057/9780230601994

Squire, K. (2005). Changing the game: What happens when video games enter the classroom? *Innovate: Journal of Online Education*, *1*(6). Retrieved from http://innovateonline.info.proxy.bc.edu/index.php?view=article&id=82

Squire, K. (2006). From content to context: Videogames as designed experience. *Educational Researcher*, *35*(8), 19–29. doi:10.3102/0013189X035008019

Weber, C., & Matthews, H. S. (2008). Quantifying the global and distributional aspects of American Household carbon footprints. *Ecological Economics*, *66*, 379–391. doi:10.1016/j.ecolecon.2007.09.021

Westheimer, J., & Kahne, J. (2004). What kind of citizen? The politics of educating for democracy. *American Educational Research Journal, 41*(2), 237–269. doi:10.3102/00028312041002237

ENDNOTES

[1] All names of schools, teachers and students are pseudonyms.

[2] Total score of the assessment was 40 points.

Chapter 14
Quests and Achievements in the Classroom

Matthew Barton
St. Cloud State University, USA

Kevin Moberley
Old Dominion University, USA

ABSTRACT

This chapter discusses how the quest structure and achievement systems so prevalent in popular videogames can help teachers and directors reform their pedagogy. The idea is to give teachers new ways to guide and motivate students, investing them more fully in the course and encouraging them to deeply explore the subject matter. The chapter provides theoretical support for this model as well as practical advice on its implementation.

INTRODUCTION

Instructors who teach first-year university courses often complain that their students are fundamentally unprepared for college. Citing poor study skills and an overall lack of engagement, they claim that students are more concerned with achieving points than mastering the content of the courses. These frustrations frequently surface on the discussion forums of *The Chronicle of Higher Education's* website. In threads titled "Am I a grinch or really unfair?", "Extra Credit?", and "Grade Grubbing Hall of Fame," instructors provide pages of anecdotal evidence that portrays contemporary students as under qualified, uninspired, and unmotivated. As a *chronicle.com* user (2009) asked in a recent forum poll: "It seems as if the current generation expects a high grade for doing the absolute minimum effort. And after encountering the tiniest obstacle, they just quit. Why is this?"

First_year students, for their part, often complain that university instructors have unrealistic expectations. Required to take introductory-level courses that do not appear relevant to their intended majors, they question the usefulness of first-year courses, as well as the ability of instructors to teach the material. Students frequently turn to sites like *Ratemyprofessors.com* to express these misgivings. Given the opportunity to anonymously evaluate professors, they post comments that are as viru-

DOI: 10.4018/978-1-61520-781-7.ch014

lent and as frustrated as those that appear on the *chronicle.com* forums.

Yet despite the tone of this discourse on the part of both instructors and students, there is little concrete evidence to support the assertion that university students are fundamentally unprepared or that university instructors are incompetent. One can argue, in fact, that the opposite is true. Most students are already proficient in a number of academic and non_academic modes of discourse by the time they enter the university. They not only know how to read, write, and conduct research, but often employ these skills socially through e_mail, text_messaging, and social networking sites such as *Facebook* and *Myspace*. Similarly, most instructors are intimately familiar with the forms of academic discourse that are privileged by their universities. They know how to teach students and how to evaluate their performances students based on a number of explicit and implicit criteria.

The difficulty, in this sense, does not lie in the aptitude of students or instructors, but in achieving a sense of what Kenneth Burke (1950 / 1969) describes as "identification" or "consubstantiality" (p. 20): "Identification is affirmed with earnestness precisely because there is division. Identification is compensatory to division. If men were not apart from one another, there would be no need for the rhetorician to proclaim their unity" (p. 22). This task is primarily the responsibility of instructors. Given the authority to choose the material of the course and to evaluate students, instructors must find a common ground that allows them to introduce the forms of discourse that the university demands in such a way that does not alienate students, but builds on the disparate knowledge and skills that they bring to the classroom.

In order to do so, however, instructors must contend with the fact that first-year university courses are rarely structured in a way that promotes learning and communication. One of the chief sources of income for contemporary universities, these courses are often singled out by administrators searching for ways to modernize their faculty and course offerings, while simultaneously slashing budgets and increasing class sizes. While such policies do increase university revenues, they also increase the sense of division between students and instructors. Education, as a result, does appear not as a cooperative endeavor, but as many of the posts on *Ratemyprofessors. com* and on the forums of *chronicle.com* suggest, a matter of "us" versus "them."

The question, then, is how can instructors, working in this precipitous climate, make college courses more fulfilling for students? How can they make their classes more engaging without compromising outcomes or responsible assessment? As James Paul Gee suggests in his 2003 work *What Computer Games Can Teach us about Learning and Literacy,* one intriguing possibility lies in incorporate design principles from popular computer games. This is particularly the case with MMORPGs (Massively Multiplayer Online Role_Playing Games) such as *World of Warcraft.* Highly symbolic spaces that require players to compose themselves through a complex process of reading and writing (Moberly 2008), many MMORPGs present players with challenges that are similar to those faced by instructors of first_year composition: how to introduce new players to the complexities of a gaming environment that might otherwise seem overwhelming, and how to encourage them to prosper within the constraints of these environments.

In this chapter, the authors embark on a quest for better pedagogy, showing how instructors can adapt the quest and achievement systems of popular MMORPGs such as *World of Warcraft* into their classes. Social constructivist in orientation, this chapter not only offers a theoretical understanding of the role that quests and achievements play in contemporary MMORPGs, but uses this understanding to explain how similar structures can serve as a scaffold that helps students master the types of performance that are privileged by contemporary academic discourses communities. This chapter also demonstrates how such a pedagogy can help students better understand how contemporary discourse communities function and therefore recognize that, as active participants in these communities, they have the agency to work to change the conversations that surround them. Although this chapter focuses predominantly on how quests and achievements might supplement first-year composition classes, it is not designed exclusively as a guide to teaching these types of classes. Rather, it uses the example of first-year composition to illustrate the general principles that suggest how a pedagogical system of quests and achievements might be implemented in a number of educational settings.

CONSTRUCTING THE SOCIAL IN THE CLASSROOM AND IN MMORPGS

In his 1984 article, "Collaborative Learning and the 'Conversation of Mankind,'" Kenneth Bruffee rejects the view that thought is an innate human trait whose full expression is hampered by speech or other types of language use. Instead, Bruffee argues that thought is an "artifact of social interaction" (p. 398):

The range, complexity and subtlety of our thought, its power, the practical and conceptual uses we can put it to, and the very issues we can address result in large measure directly from the degree to which we have been initiated into what Oakeshott calls the potential skill and partnership of human conversation in its public and social forum. (p. 399)

This statement has several important implications for the way that knowledge and learning are understood. The most radical is the shift that occurs in the place knowledge is located. If thought is causally related, if not indistinguishable from the conversations in which a particular community

is engaged, it stands to reason that knowledge is also a social endeavor. Thus, if educators are to understand the ways which knowledge is transferred among members of a community—how learning occurs—they must also understand the social context in which particular conversations occur in these communities.

As Bruffee points out, the challenge facing educators is twofold. On one hand, they must induct students into what Richard Rorty (1979) calls the "normal discourse" of the university and their majors. This entails essentially a pedagogy of socialization, in which the classroom becomes a sort of nascent community, an embodiment of academic and professional discourse in microcosm. Encouraged to interact with their peers, students become responsible for the content of the course, and are given the opportunity to practice and master the types of performances that contemporary academic and professional discourse communities privilege.

On the other hand, instructors must also empower students to participate in what Rorty (1979) understands as "abnormal discourse." This entails almost the opposite of the process of socialization described above. Instead of engaging students in conversation, instructors must foreground the fact that conversation is occurring, thereby demonstrating to students that they have the ability and the authority to alter the course of the conversation. Students thus learn that they can challenge the dictates of the discourse and are therefore empowered to experiment with modes of performance that contribute to the generation of new knowledge within the community.

Massively Multiplayer Online Roleplaying Games (MMORPGs) face similar challenges. Structured around a subscription_based profit model, their commercial success depends on their ability to appeal to many different players and play styles in a manner that ensures that their content is not easily exhausted. As T. L. Taylor explains in his 2006 work *Play Between Worlds: Exploring Online Game Culture*, many contemporary

MMORPGs attempt to satisfy these imperatives through a two-pronged strategy. They not only offer players immense, open_ended, and constantly evolving gaming experiences, but supplement these experiences by encouraging players to form communities dedicated to exploring and expanding the possibilities of the games. This double strategy, Taylor claims, ultimately produces a "much broader apparatus, a sociotechnical one, that goes well beyond the artifact contained in the box" (p. 32).

World of Warcraft, for example, presents players with a vast, virtual landscape that is comprised of three distinct continents and a parallel universe, Outland, which was introduced in the "Burning Crusade" (2007) expansion. Divided into distinct geographical regions and populated with a large variety of both friendly and hostile non-player characters (NPCs), this landscape offers players a number of predefined challenges including leveling, exploration, resource gathering, instanced dungeons, and player versus player combat (PVP). *World of Warcraft* also affords players a considerable amount of options when creating and customizing characters. Players can choose from ten distinct races and player classes, each of which embodies a unique approach to the game. They can then further customize these characters by changing their physical appearances, equipping clothing, weapons, and other items, and supplementing their skills and abilities through the game's system of talent trees.

Constructed at the intersection these choices, challenges, conflicts, and opportunities, MMOR-PGs like *World of Warcraft* thus present players with what Roger Caillois (1958/2001) understands as a predominately paidic mode of gameplay—a mode of gameplay that is characterized, in his words, "by an almost indivisible principle, common to diversion, turbulence, free improvisation, and carefree gaiety" (p. 13). While this paidic mode of gameplay ensures the lasting commercial appeal of the games, it can be daunting to new players, especially at the beginning as they struggle to learn the rudiments of controlling their characters and interacting effectively within the complex environments of the games, while simultaneously learning to negotiate the social conventions of interacting other players.

CRITICAL APPROACHES TO QUESTS IN COMPUTER GAMES

As in the first-year classroom, then, MMORPGs like *World of Warcraft* must engage new players in a process of socialization that helps them make the transition from the types of computer games and computer mediated discourses that they are comfortable with to the specific skills and conventions privileged by the MMORPGs. One of the most effective ways that *World of Warcraft* accomplishes this is through its interlocking system of quest narratives. Indeed, as Joseph Campbell (1948/2008) states in his work, *The Hero with a Thousand Faces*, quests are among the oldest forms of narrative. Pointing out quest narratives can be found in the mythological systems of many different cultures, as well as in the work of many contemporary writers, he argues that they are the products of a "nuclear monomyth" that is defined by a tripartite structure: "A hero ventures forth from the world of common day into a region of supernatural wonder: fabulous forces are there encountered and a decisive victory is won: the hero comes back from this mysterious adventure with the power to bestow boons on his fellow man" (23). While it is difficult to substantiate Campbell's claim that quest narratives constitute an archetypical mode of expression that transcends cultural, historical, political, and socioeconomic differences, they are nevertheless ubiquitous in contemporary computer games. Indeed, quest and quest-like structures have become fixtures not only of genres that regularly invoke the conventions of medieval romance such as role-playing games and adventure games, but of real-time strategy games, first-person shooters, driving games and simulations.

Citing this ubiquity, Jeff Howard's 2008 book, *Quests: Design, Theory, and History in Games and Narrative*, offers an interesting study of the role that quests play in contemporary computer games. Searching for a way to reconcile the performative approach to quests advocated by game scholars such as Ragnhild Tronstad (2001) and Espen Aarseth (2004) with the narrative approaches of Campbell and other literary scholars, Howard argues that quests constitute a middle ground between a series of binaries that frequently appear in both new media and literary studies:

- game and narrative
- gaming and literature
- technology and mythology
- and meaning and action (p. xi)

The last binary in this list, "meaning and action," is particularly significant to Howard. Building on Jesper Juul's (2005) claim that "quests in games can actually provide an interesting type of bridge between game rules and game fiction in that the games can contain predefined sequences of events that the player then has to actualize or effect" (p. 17), Howard states that quests can help scholars and game designers better understand how games communicate meaning through the actions they ask players to perform, as well as how players find computer games meaningful. To illustrate this point, Howard demonstrates three principle ways "in which quests can be meaningful" (p. 25). Quests, he states, function to initiate players to the rules and the power structures that constitute the simulated realities of games, they communicate the narrative back-story of the games, and they provide players with opportunities to participate in the larger thematic conflicts that inform the game.

While there is much to be said for Howard's approach to quests, especially his observation that they often function as transitional or liminal structures in computer games, his work ultimately depends on many of the same binaries that he

finds problematic in the work of scholars such as Ragnhild Tronstad (2001) and Espen Aarseth (2004) who favor performative rather than narrative approaches to quests in computer games. Howard, for example, criticizes Tronstad, correctly pointing out that her work is structured around a "false binary between meaning and action" and that it therefore "overlooks the idea that players can enact meaning if the elements of the quest have thematic implications that are revealed through play" (p. 20). Howard, however, invokes a similar binary a few pages later, when he argues that meaning and action are manifested differently when reading a book than when playing a computer game. Although he acknowledges that many postmodern texts privilege interpretive readings, he nevertheless constructs reading as a passive activity in which readers have little or no control over the action that takes place in the texts:

in both postmodern and premodern narratives, the characters' actions for the most part remain the same from reading to reading. Moreover the reader does not have to exert effort to cause these events to occur because they will be narrated no matter what. The reader exerts cognitive and interpretive effort to determine what the actions performed by a character mean after they have occurred (p. 26)

By contrast, Howard constructs play as an active process, writing that "players of quest games must sometimes determine what their actions mean in order to perform them correctly. Their meaning is discovered or created by a player through action, so that the action itself is meaningful" (p. 26).

Yet as many reader-response critics have noted, it is fallacious to argue that events in printed narratives "will be narrated no matter what" (p.26) or that the actions of characters in these texts will occur despite or somehow independently of the presence of the reader. While some texts appear, as Roland Barthes points out (1970/1975) more readerly than others, these texts only appear to contain meaning to the extent that individuals are able to recognize and subsequently produce meaning from their otherwise mute symbols—the words printed on their pages or the pixels fluorescing on the screen. Understood in this sense, reading is not antithetical to play, but, like play, is a socially constructed mode of performance. As with any socially constructed mode of performance, the reader's ability to produce meaning from a text depends on the degree to which she is familiar with and consents to adhere to the discursive practices that define that mode of performance.

If reading and play therefore appear to constitute disparate activities, it is not because the first is passive and the second is active, but because they require individuals to perform in a manner that will produce meaning from the text in question. Howard does not recognize this. As becomes clear in the following passage, he not only locates literary or thematic meaning primarily as the province of the text, but differentiates it from the type of meaning that players produce as they interact with games:

The literary critical sense of "meaning" as a theme of idea conveyed symbolically through a work of literature is an important aspect of meaning in quest games but is only one type of meaning. If a player feels that a quest that she undertakes is a worthwhile expenditure of time and effort rather than an unrewarding chore, then this quest has meaning to the player. (p.25)

Howard, as a result, does not recognize that quests play another role in computer games. As becomes apparent in games like *Katamari Damacy, Neverwinter Nights,* or *Grand Theft Auto IV,* quests work to introduce players to the discursive practices that the games valorize as "normal" or proper play. They show players how to perform basic actions such moving, fighting, and manipulating objects, as well as introduce larger discursive strategies. In doing so, such quests teach players how to produce meaning from the otherwise static environment of the games.

This oversight is especially apparent in Howard's attempts to come to terms with quests in MMORPGs. Writing that MMORPGs "feature a profusion of quests but very little narrative, resulting in constant action that has little meaning" (p. 22), he argues that the quests that MMORPGS offer are unsatisfactory because they deny players what, to Joseph Campbell, is the crucial final function of a quest narrative:

the emphasis on social action over the single-player experience causes the "main-quest" to disappear, resulting in a proliferation of side-quests. These side quests may contribute to an over-arching set of themes. . .. However, the journey of the hero through a series of trials whose completion allow him to bring a meaningful item or insight back to society is often absent. (p. 22)

Howard claims that this is especially the case with *World of Warcraft.* Writing that the theme of the game is "neverending war between racial factions, a bleak scenario that is not particularly conducive to meaningful gameplay" (p. 22), Howard states that if *World of Warcraft's* quests have any meaning at all, it is the "strictly personal satisfaction of possessing a 60th-level character with an expensive suit of enchanted plate mail" (p. 23).

While Howard is correct that *World of Warcraft's* emphasis on racial conflict is problematic, it is difficult to substantiate his claim that the quests in *World of Warcraft* are not meaningful, especially when one recognizes how frequently computer games employ quests to help players make the transition from modes of performance with which they are already familiar (reading, using a keyboard and mouse, etc...) to the more the more specialized modes of performance that constitute gameplay. In this sense, it is not surprising that *World of Warcraft* quest's tend to be less concerned with narrative than action. Nor is it surprising that, as Jill Walker Rettenburg (2008) and Falten Karlson (2008) point out, these quests tend to be highly formulaic and repetitive.

Designed to introduce players to the behaviors, skills, and strategies that the game privileges as "normal" discourse, *World of Warcraft's* quest system not only teaches players the basic mechanics of controlling their characters—how to move, attack, and loot—but directs players to new, more challenging areas of the game, and inspires players to interact with each other. In doing so, the game's quest system works to structure and organize the otherwise paidic content of the game, presenting it to players through a series of short, though interlocking quest narratives. World of Warcraft's quest system thus takes on Roger Caillois characterizes as a ludic role, working, as Caillois writes about the ludus in general, to counter the game's paidic tendencies through "arbitrary, imperative, and purposely tedious conventions, to oppose it still more my ceaselessly practicing the most embarrassing chicanery on it, in order to make it more uncertain of obtaining its desired effect" (p. 13).

QUESTS AND ACHIEVEMENTS IN *WORLD OF WARCRAFT*

Players who create human characters in *World of Warcraft* are greeted by a quest_giver, Deputy Willem, immediately upon entering the game. Standing outside Northshire Abbey and marked with a prominent yellow exclamation point over his head, Willem offers players the first in a series of quests that are designed to introduce the core behaviors that comprise *World of Warcraft's* gameplay—moving, fighting, looting, and manipulating objects. Asking players to seek out a second quest_giver, Marshall McBride, Willem directs players to Northshire Abbey, which stands just behind him. Relatively easy to complete, this quest requires players to simply enter the foyer of the abbey, locate McBride and speak with him. Tin doing so, however, this quest, introduces players to the fundamentals of controlling their characters and interacting with NPCs.

Marshall McBride offers players a second quest. Explaining that "A clan of kobolds have infested the woods to the north," he asks players to slay 10 Kobold Vermin. Slightly more complicated then the first quest, this quest directs players to locate specific NPCs and engage them in combat using their characters' abilities. Since players can loot currency and other items from the corpses of the kobolds they defeat, this quest introduces players to the mechanics of looting and inventory management. Successfully completing this quest unlocks two more quests, one of which requires players to return to slay ten more Kobolds, and the other of which requires them to seek out their class trainers, who grant players additional skills. These quest thus form a quest chain that not only teaches players the fundamentals of controlling and their characters and interacting with the world, but teaches them how to improve their characters through the game's system of class trainers.

World of Warcraft also uses its quest system to direct players to other, more difficult areas of the game. For example, after players have completed most of the quests in Northshire Valley, Marshall McBride offers them the quest "Report to Goldshire," which directs them to seek Marshal Dughan in the town of Goldshire. To complete this quest, players must leave the confines of Northshire Valley and travel south through Elwynn Forest. In the process, they encounter a second quest_giver, Falkhaan Isenstrider, who asks players to deliver a letter to the innkeeper in Goldshire Inn. This journey leads players to a second quest hub, and in doing so, simultaneously introduces them to mechanics of the game's inns and innkeepers.

In addition to introducing players to these core behaviors, *World of Warcraft's* quest system is also designed to introduce players to the complexities of interacting with other players. The most obvious way that it accomplishes this is through a number of group and instance quests that require two or more players to complete. One of the best_known of these quests involves Hogger, a level 11 elite NPC, who terrorizes Southwestern Elwynn forest. With exactly 666 hit points, Hogger presents a difficult challenge for solo players, but is easily defeated when two or more players form a party. As such, the quest prepares players for the type of collaboration that is required to complete the many instanced dungeons scattered throughout the game.

Another way that the quest system encourages players to work together is by requiring items that are only available if crafted by other players. One such quest can be found in the town of Southshore. There, Bartolo Ginsetti offers to craft players a Yeti Fur Cloak in exchange for bringing him a bolt of woolen cloth, fine thread, 10 pieces of yeti fur, and a Hillman's Cloak. Players can easily obtain the thread from trade_good vendors in the game and the 10 pieces of yeti fur from the yetis who dwell in the mountains to the north. However, to obtain the bolt of woolen cloth and the Hillman's Cloak, they must seek out fellow players who have sufficient expertise in tailoring and leather working to craft the items, or buy them through the game's auction house system. In either case, Ginsetti's quest requires players to interact directly or indirectly (economically through the auction house) with other players.

Perhaps the least obvious, though most effective way that *World of Warcraft's* quest system fosters player interaction is through the oftentimes vague or incomplete instructions the quests provide. While many of the game's initial quests give enough information that players can complete them without asking for help, the descriptions that accompany the quests become increasingly vague as players progress. A case in point is a quest to kill Princess, a pig that has been ravaging crops in Elwynn Forest. Obtained from the matron of Stonefield farm, Ma Stonefield, this quest requires players to travel to Brackwell Pumpkin Patch, slay Princess, and bring back her brass collar as proof. Although Stonefield does tell players that the pumpkin patch is located "to the east and beyond the Maclure farm," she does not provide specific directions. Nor does she indicate that the

Brackwell Pumpkin Patch is, in fact, some distance east of the Maclure farm. Since players encounter the quest relatively early on in their progress through the Elwynn Forest zone, at a point when they have not been required to travel significant distances to complete quests, these omissions are significant. Players, as a result, often spend several minutes searching the area just east of the Mcclure farm, which contains several strategically placed, though misleading pumpkin patches before finally asking other players for advice using the game's chat channels. Ma Stonefield's vague directions thus prompt players to collaborate with each other and to pool their knowledge—an activity that, in its most sophisticated iterations, produces the type of knowledge communities that publish and maintain elaborate third party resources about the game such as *wowwiki.com*.

World of Warcraft's quest system, however, is ultimately designed to provide diminishing returns. Indeed, although the game contains upwards of 4000 unique quests that offer players with a number of incentives such as in_game currency, equipment, novelty items, and experience points, its quest system is constructed so that new players are proportionately more likely to benefit from questing than experienced players. This is especially true for players who have reached the level cap. While the quest system offers these players increased monetary rewards for completing quests, they no longer receive experience points. Moreover, the equipment that many upper-level quests reward requires players to dedicate dozens of hours of gameplay to complete very long, and sometimes very complex quest chains. Many players are, of course, willing to keep questing regardless of the size of the payoffs. Yet the rewards for doing so ultimately pale in comparison to those that can be obtained through participating in the more paidic elements of the game such as end_game dungeons and raid instances, PVP battlegrounds, and crafting.

Thus, while *World of Warcraft's* quest system is designed to provide players with a ludic framework that structures their progress through the game, it is not designed to substantially support players after they obtain the level cap. Nor is the quest system designed to inspire players to engage in abnormal discourse—that is, to challenge the constraints of the game in a way that, for better or worse, produces new knowledge about the game and inspires the types of emergent behaviors that provide many MMORPG players with a sense of ownership and accomplishment. *World of Warcraft* had no formal system to reward this type of behavior until the release of patch 3.0.2 in 2008 when it integrated a parallel system of achievements into the game. Patterned after the Xbox Live achievement system that Microsoft released in 2005 with its Xbox gaming console, *World of Warcraft's* system is not simply designed to reward players for reaching predetermined milestones in the game, but as Mary Irwin (2009) writes about achievement systems in general, to provide "incentives for gamers to finish games, try out new features and modes of play, and experiment with the offered tools" (p. 1)—that is, to reward players for innovative or unusual activities that they engage in usually at the upper end of the game.

Indeed, the majority of *World of Warcraft's* achievement are designed so that they are difficult, if not impossible, for low_level players to complete. A case in point is the achievement "To All the Squirrels I've Loved Before," which rewards players 10 achievements points for seeking out the 21 unique critters in the game and performing the "/love" emote on them. While low_level players are apt to encounter many of the critters named in the achievement in entry_level zones, two of them—the "Borean Frog" and the "Steam Frog"—can only be found in the Borean Tundra, a zone intended for level 68 and higher players. Much of the same is true for the followup achievement, "To All the Squirrels Who Shared My Life," which requires players to enter upper_level instanced dungeons in search of critters such as the "crystal spider" to "/love." While it is not inconceivable for low_level players to complete these achieve-

ments—they can solicit the protection of upper level players, for example, as their search for critters leads them into the more dangerous areas of the game—doing so requires them to engage into what is effectively a type of abnormal discourse, adapting the resources that are available to them in a way that the game's designers had, perhaps, not anticipated or encouraged.

World of Warcraft's achievement system is, in this sense, constructed to complement its quest system. Not only is it designed predominantly for upper_level players, but as the two achievements described above illustrate, it is designed to reward a mode of gameplay that is primarily paidic in its emphasis on whimsy, exploration, and on completing tasks that are not tied to specific objectives. The game's achievement system thus encourages retention, compelling players to dedicate their time and resources to earn achievements points through non_standard behaviors that require often require a significant amount of engagement and knowledge about the game. Ultimately, the game's achievement system accomplishes something that its quest system cannot: it rewards players for virtuoso performances—not just for playing "good enough," but for demonstrating mastery of the aspects of the game that the achievement system constructs as significant.

THE QUEST FOR ACHIEVEMENT IN THE CLASSROOM

World of Warcraft's quest and achievement systems work in conjunction to produce many of the learning outcomes that James Paul Gee identifies in his 2003 work *What Video Games have to Teach us about Learning and Literacy.* The game's quest system, for example, is designed to help players construct what Gee describes as a "virtual identity" (p. 54)—a fictional identity that exists in the game as a manifestation of the external "real-world identities" that players assume in relationship to the game. The game's quest system accomplishes this through three principles that Gee argues are crucial for helping students make the transition to the modes of performance that success in the contemporary classroom demands:

1. The learner must be enticed to *try,* even if he or she already has good grounds to be afraid to try.
2. The learner must be enticed to *put in lots of effort* even if he or she begins with little motivation to do so.
3. The learner must *achieve some meaningful success* when he or she has expended this effort. (pp. 61-62)

Understood in this sense, *World of Warcraft's* quest system presents players with a scaffold that allows them to approach the complex problem of how to construct (produce) themselves as characters in the game by engaging in a number of discreet, easily manageable, and repetitive tasks. It further entices players to engage in this multi-tiered process by constantly rewarding them with experience, equipment, in-game currency, and other forms of compensation. Players, as a result, are motivated to continue questing through what Gee understands as the "amplification of input" and the "achievement" principles, which, as he explains, not only mandate that "for a little input, learners get a lot of output" (p. 67), but that "for learners of all levels there are intrinsic rewards from the beginning, customized to each learner's level, effort, and growing mastery and signaling the learner's ongoing achievements" (p. 67).

Although *World of Warcraft's* achievement system is also concerned with documenting players's accomplishments, its larger purpose is to help players develop what Gee identifies as a third type of identity, a projective identity, that represents a player's aspirations for both his or her real and virtual identities. As Gee explains,

A third identity that is at stake is. ... what I will call a projective identity, playing on two senses of the word "project," meaning both 'to project one's values and desires onto a virtual character". ... and "seeing the virtual character as one's own project in the making, a creature whom I imbue with a certain trajectory through time defined by my aspirations for what I want that character to be and become. ... (p. 55)

This becomes immediately clear from the structure of the game's accomplishment menu. Divided into categories such as "Exploration," "Quests," "Player vs. Player," "Reputation," and "World Events," the menu lists individual achievements that are available through battlegrounds, zones, in-game holidays, or other specific areas of gameplay. The achievement menu, however, does not simply display the achievements that players have completed, but more significantly, displays those that remain unfinished. The achievement system thus provides players with concrete goals around which to structure their projective identities. Taken as a whole, it presents an accurate representation of what *World of Warcraft's* designers consider extraordinary behavior in each of the categories of gameplay that the menu identifies.

Yet unlike the menus associated with the quest system, the achievement menu does not provide players with hints or instructions for accomplishing achievements. Players must therefore examine the behaviors that constitute play in the game and revise and experiment with these behaviors until they are able to successfully complete an achievement. In this sense, *World of Warcraft's* achievement system does not simply inspire players towards the sort of abnormal discourse that results in new behaviors, new discoveries, and new knowledge about the game, but as Gee writes about good computer game design in general, forces "players to think about the routinized mastery they have achieved and to undo this routinization to achieve a higher level of skill" (p. 69). By providing players with future goals around which to organize and structure their projective identities, *World of Warcraft's* achievement system rewards players for constructing themselves as ongoing learners and for practicing and testing their skills so that they are always seeking ways to improve their performance.

The quest and achievement systems that MMORPGs like *World of Warcraft* employ thus have the potential to help bridge the gap between the knowledge that first_year instructors possess and the knowledge which students bring to first_year classes. This is particularly the case with first-year composition courses. Traditionally structured around a sequence of major and minor writing assignments, these courses are designed to introduce students to a number of rhetorical skills that, irregardless of their intended majors, will help them participate in the discourse communities that constitute the contemporary university. As such, they often function as the academic equivalent of *World of Warcraft's* Northshire Valley and Elwynn forest zones: small-scale, controlled points of entry into what, to first year students, can otherwise appear to be a vast, overwhelming discursive landscape. Incorporated into these courses, a system of pedagogically_oriented quests and achievements has the potential to help instructors not only establish a metaphorical scaffold that allows them introduce students to the conventions of what, in the context of the university, constitutes normal discourse, but to structure this introduction in a way that is designed to teach students strategies for approaching unfamiliar or intimidating discursive problems in a way that inspires students to excel.

CONSTRUCTING A PEDAGOGICALLY-ORIENTATED QUEST SYSTEM

Jeff Howard (2008) provides a glimpse of the role that quests could play in such a pedagogy. In order to demonstrate how "game design can be taught as an interpretive writing within literature classrooms" (p. 139), Howard describes an assign-ment in which he asks students to produce design documents and quest-based game prototypes based on Thomas Pynchon's novel, *The Crying of Lot 49*. Programmed on a variety of platforms including *NeverWinter Nights'* Aurora Toolset, these prototypes dramatize incidents from the novel as labyrinths and present players with a series of quests that offer interpretative paths through the otherwise tangled narrative landscape. Although this assignment is innovative, especially to the extent that it requires students to express and implement interpretive strategies through game design, Howard does not recognize that the assignment is itself a quest in that it requires students to perform what is essentially the tripartite narrative trajectory that Campbell (ascribes to quests. Indeed, as is the case with many university-level assignments, Howard not only asks students to undertake a task that requires them to engage a difficult subject (Pynchon's novel) through a series of sub-tasks (writing a design document and a prototype quest game), but to return to him with evidence that they have completed the task (the games they have created).

Yet while Howard's assignment provides insight into how university instructors can adapt existing major and minor assignments as quests, it requires students to demonstrate mastery of a number of complex modes of performance and is therefore better suited for the end rather than the beginning of a course. Instructors should, instead, begin by breaking large assignments such as that which Howard proposes into smaller, more manageable tasks—or, to use gaming parlance, into "way points," that students must reach before proceeding forward. These tasks should be designed so that they not only foreground a particular behavior or mode of performance, but help students make a connection to and therefore adapt preexisting behaviors or modes of performance.

For example, first-year college students often have difficulty producing the sophisticated types of thesis sentences that college-level discourse privileges. To help students make this transition, instructors can begin by constructing a series of small, quest-based assignment that, like the initial quests *World of Warcraft's* players encounter in Northshire valley, require students to start by completing a relatively simple task such as composing a thesis statement about an assigned topic. The instructor can then assign a second quest that requires students to find examples of exemplary thesis statements published on the internet. Since many of these examples are often prefaced by instructions that describe how to construct similar thesis sentences, the instructor can assign a third assignment that asks students to produce a brief list of criteria that describes the characteristics which distinguish excellent thesis sentences. Finally, the instructor can ask students to revise the thesis sentences they originally constructed based on these criteria. Through this circular series of quest-like assignments, instructors can not only introduce students to a number of behaviors that are crucial to college-level writing—in this case, drafting, research, evaluation, and revision—but demonstrate how, when taken together, these behaviors can produce an exemplary piece of writing: a thesis sentence that embodies the types of performance that university-level discourse privileges.

It is important to remember, however, that their primary purpose of these initial quests is not to evaluate students, but as in *World of Warcraft*, to introduce a set of core behaviors that students can then use to accomplish more sophisticated modes of performance. As Gee states above, these initial quests should be designed to entice students to participate in course despite their reservations about its content, or, as is often the case with college composition, their anxieties about their ability to perform successfully. This outcome can be easily achieved at the beginning of the course by structuring initial assignments in a way that demonstrates that participating does not require an extraordinary amount of effort or expertise, and that the rewards for doing so potentially outweigh the amount of work required.

These relatively simple and straightforward quest-based assignments can, in turn, serve as the building blocks for more complex modes of performance. Instructors, for example, can use the same process of drafting, research, evaluation, and revision to structure a series of quests that shows students how to develop an introductory paragraph from their thesis sentences, or how to construct topic sentences and body paragraphs. Instructors can also use this process to help students further explore and understand the modes of performance that constitute the core behaviors—how to conduct research and cite sources at the university level, for example, or how to read and evaluate difficult critical sources. The key point is that instructors should not construct these smaller assignments as individual or stand-alone activities, but, as in *World of Warcraft*, approach them as the individual links in larger quest chains that are designed to gradually lead students through the process of completing complex tasks such as a major writing assignment. Conceptualized in this way, these small-scale assignments provide the horizontal boards and vertical ladders of a metaphorical scaffold that not only demonstrates the process through which difficult tasks can be completed, but in doing so, provides students with strategies with which they can complete similar tasks in the future.

If there is a downside to this type of curriculum, it is that quest-based assignments will more than likely generate formulaic, or to use Gee's term, "automized" (p. 70), modes of performance. While this is not necessarily a bad outcome, especially at the beginning of the course as students gain confidence and experience with the modes of performance that the assignments are designed to demonstrate, instructors can encourage students to challenge the content of the course in much of the same way that *World of Warcraft* uses its quest system to challenge players: by gradually assigning fewer quests that provide less explicit instructions and that conversely ask students to engage in larger tasks. Instructors, for example, might structure the second writing assignment as a quest chain that consists of half as many quests. They might also construct the individual quests in the chain so that they not only require students to take on slightly more complicated tasks, but only provide detailed instructions when new material is introduced or when students need additional practice with difficult tasks. Instructors should implement further reductions when constructing the quest chains that constitute subsequent writing assignments so that by the time students reach what is arguably the end-game of the course, the final writing assignment, they are confronted with a single quest—a large assignment that, like the one that Howard proposes, requires them to engage in a number of sophisticated modes of performance, thereby demonstrating that they have internalized and mastered the normal discourse to the extent that they are able to reproduce it without the scaffold afforded by the quest-based assignments.

Instructors can further motivate students through the way they evaluate and reward students for completing quest-based assignments. As mentioned earlier, the purpose of the initial quest-based assignments is to introduce a core set of behaviors that will allow students to successfully complete the remainder of the course. Instructors, as such, should grade initial assignments holistically, assigning students points based on whether or not they complete the quests. As students progress through the course and gain increasing mastery of its underlying discourses, however, instructors can begin to implement more qualitative grading schemes, assigning students points based on how well they complete the assignments. When implemented in conjunction with the gradual reductions in the number and the scope of quest-based assignments discussed above, such an evaluation and reward structure insures that the course is structured in accordance with what Gee understands as the "Regime of Competence Principle" (p. 70)—that is, so that each successive assignment presents students with tasks that are challenging, but not impossible to complete, and

therefore motivates students to engage in a "cycle of automatization, adaption, new learning, and new automatization" (p. 70) which Gee argues is crucial to academic success.

CONSTRUCTING A PEDAGOGICALLY-ORIENTATED ACHIEVEMENT SYSTEM

A pedagogy constructed around the type of quest-based assignments can be made much more effective in conjunction with an achievement system such as that featured by *World of Warcraft*. Indeed, while quests are far more concerned with the journey players undertake, achievements are almost entirely concerned with outcomes. Organized into hierarchical categories and subcategories, they thus present players with a detailed overview of what, to the game's designers, constitutes extraordinary behavior in a number of privileged areas of performance. A pedagogically-oriented achievement system has the potential to fulfil a similar function in the classroom. Established at the onset of the course, it can provide students with a comprehensive, categorical overview that details the types of behaviors that the course privileges and ties these behaviors to specific areas of performance. An achievement system can thus provide students with concrete goals around which to construct their projective identities, encouraging students to work towards ever-greater accomplishments.

Moreover, such a system can foster a sense of community among students. Indeed, in publically recognizing students for exemplary performances, achievements can encourage imitation on the part of other students, or encourage students to work towards achievements for which they are better suited. Similarly, an achievement system can inspire students to work cooperatively to devise strategies through which they can satisfy particularly challenging achievements. As in *World of Warcraft*, where players routinely post guides designed to help others obtain difficult achievements, such behaviors can form the basis of knowledge communities where students work together to teach each other how to flourish in the class.

Paidic in nature, a good achievement system should offer many different ways for students to distinguish themselves, including some that seem (at first) only marginally related to the goals of the course. Yet no matter how irreverent of whimsical, all achievements should work to reinforce the core behaviors around which the quest system is structured, as well as behaviors that are relevant to the academic discourses within which the course is situated, and the larger discourses privileged by the university. An achievement system designed for a first-year composition classroom, for example, might be organized into five basic categories:

a. Primary skills: these include achievements designed to reward excellence in the core behaviors listed earlier—drafting, research, evaluation, and revision—as well as excellence in other important areas such as writing style, grammar, class participation, collaboration, and so forth.

b. Secondary skills: these achievements could extend to skills that are, in a wider sense, regarded as useful and relevant to the course or profession. For a writing class, these might achievements linked to skills like designing document layouts, reading proficiency, familiarity and use of external resources such as the library or the writing center or computer-related skills.

c. Fun achievements: these achievements include silly, satirical, or zany achievements that perhaps poke fun at the course material or achievement system in general. While these may at first seem irrelevant, they can help stimulate interest in the course as long as the subject matter is related. For instance, an achievement might ask students to write a review of a popular song or movie that

imitates the style of a particular author. Another such achievement might ask students to write a series of haikus based on readings or other course materials and e-mail these to the instructor or post these on class discussion forums.

d. Secret achievements: this category includes achievements that are not revealed beforehand, but can be awarded on an ad_hoc basis. Ideally, instructors should inform students that these achievements exist at the onset of the class and should periodically give clues about what accomplishing them entails. Speculation about these achievements can encourage students to perform more diligently and pay more attention to the content of the course.

e. Achievement or meta_skills. This final category includes special awards for earning other achievements. A student might receive an "Achievement_Driven" award for earning twenty lesser achievements, for instance.

As in *World of Warcraft's* achievement system, these categories should be further divided into relevant subcategories that are designed to provide students with an overview of the courses's major areas of concern and its goals. This is especially the case with the first two areas listed above—Primary and Secondary skills—which should ideally be subdivided according to the core behaviors around which the course's quest system is constructed. Instructors should also construct these categories so that there is some amount of overlap between the individual achievements they contain. For instance, each category might contain achievements related to drafting writing assignments. In the primary skills category, such an achievement might consist of asking students to submit unique pre-writing exercises with their drafts. The secondary skills category might contain a similar achievement that rewards students for attending a workshop on pre-writing hosted by the writing center, while the fun achievements category might contain one that asks students to generate their own pre-writing exercise. Likewise, instructors might construct a secret achievement related to pre-writing, and a meta-achievement that requires students to complete an achievement involving pre-writing in each of the categories. Instructors can thus design the achievement system so that its categories not only reinforces the modes of performance around which the class is constructed, but so that the organization of the achievements as a whole helps students understand how these modes of performance are related to each other.

When constructing individual achievements for each category, instructors should follow the advice Mary Jane Irwin offers based on interviews with many different game developers:

- Don't make lame achievements.
- Don't reward failure.
- Don't make them impossible.
- Don't tie them directly to points and high scores. (p. 4)

Indeed, as Irwin argues, achievements that reward plays for performing tedious actions such as "collecting 1,000 baubles" (p. 4) are problematic because they require players to engage in a mode of gameplay that quickly becomes tedious and therefore discourages them from playing. Much of the same can be said for achievement based solely on quantity in a writing class. An achievement, for example, that rewards students for making 100 posts on the course's discussion boards might clog the forums with a glut of poorly constructed posts and also reinforce the view that participating in such forums is pointless. A better achievement might reward students for starting a discussion thread about the course material that inspires a sustained discussion from classmates— an achievement that requires students to not only be conscious of how well they construct their initial posts, but work with other students in the class to insure responses.

Achievements, in short, should be constructed so that they reward quality performances. This does not mean, however, that achievements should be extremely difficult or impossible to achieve. Rather, achievements should be tiered, so that as with the quest system, completing an initial achievement unlocks subsequent achievements that become progressively more difficult. Instructors, for example, might offer students an achievement that requires them to bring a draft of a writing assignment to the writing center. Completing this achievement might unlock a second achievement that requires students to bring the revised draft back to the writing center. This achievement, in turn, could lead to subsequent achievements that require students to complete the same process for the draft of a second and then a third paper. Tiered in this fashion, these achievements serve as stepping stones for what, at the end of the semester, is a very difficult achievement: finding time outside of class to work extensively with tutors at the writing center. Even if students are unable to complete the final, most difficult achievements in the sequence, their tiered structure insures that they are not only rewarded for trying, but are afforded a glimpse of what, to the instructor, constitutes the extremes of that mode of extraordinary performance.

To make achievements more interesting to students, instructors should also give them fun names and descriptions. For instance, an initial achievement that asks students to bring in a typed question about an assigned reading could be could be called "Inquiring Mind," and the last achievement in the sequence could be called "Grand Inquisitor." The description of the achievement should reinforce its value: "You have learned well the importance of sharing knowledge. Without such sharing, there would be no university." Similarly, an achievement for demonstrating mastery of comma use might be called "Dirty Harry Commahan," and its description might read, "Are you feeling lucky, punctuation?" While such titles and descriptions might appear superfluous, they can help accentuate the paidic nature of the achievement system, making it appear fun and challenging, and perhaps a bit irrelevant. Such descriptions can also contribute to what Irwin identifies as the "stickiness" (p. 1) factor of achievements—that is, the titles and descriptions will help students remember the achievements and therefore the content of the class long after the semester is finished.

Although Irwin warns against tying achievements to points and high scores, arguing that, if constructed sensibly, players who have earned all the achievements already have a high score, the question of how to reward students for their achievements is more complicated in educational settings. Indeed, a pedagogical system of achievements should not be designed for students in the top percentage of the class—students who already understand what constitutes excellent or extraordinary performances in academic discourse. Instead, such a system should be designed to show students in the middle and lower percentages of the class what constitutes extraordinary performances and to inspire them attempt such performances on their own terms. Instructors, as such, might consider rewarding students with bonus points for completing achievements, even though doing so can lead to grade inflation. Yet whether or not they tie achievements to points, instructors should publically recognize students for the achievements they complete. At this minimum, this might entail publishing a list of student-earned achievements on the course's website. It might also, however, entail periodically sharing students' work with the class, and, as in *World of Warcraft,* granting students titles as a result of finishing a sequence of achievements.

FUTURE RESEARCH DIRECTIONS

As is the case with many social constructivist pedagogies, building a course around quests and achievement requires instructors to construct themselves as managers, facilitators, or, perhaps more appropriately, as dungeon masters whose role is not to deliver the content of the course wholesale to students through lectures or other traditional means, but to structure the content of the course so that students arrive at an understanding of the subject matter on their own terms. Instructors, as such, not only face the challenge of how to divide a relatively small number of existing major and minor assignments into a significantly larger number of individual quests and achievements, but the significantly more complicated question of how to keep track of the progress of individual students as they move through the system and how to communicate this progress so that students always know their position in relationship to the subject matter of the course. While some of this overhead can be reduced by the way instructors construct quests and achievements, keeping tabs on a class full of students and their progress is a very time consuming and difficult process. One area of concern that needs to be addressed is, therefore, the challenge of book-keeping that accompanies quest- and achievement-based pedagogies.

Contemporary MMORPGS like *World of Warcraft* approach this problem through the use of databases that continually monitor and automatically update information about players as they use the game's interface to interact with its environment. Although instructors in face to face classrooms do not have access to the automation that such interfaces afford, the work of keeping track of the quests and achievements could be greatly simplified if implemented in conjunction with a database or spreadsheet. Such a tool could be especially effective if it could automate the task of displaying students' progress as they move through quest chains and complete achievements. Tied to avatars, maps, or many of the other systems of graphic representation through which MMORPGS like *World of Warcraft* communicate progress and status, such a system could provide a web-based resource that not only allows students to quickly ascertain their own position in relationship to the subject matter of the course, but which allows students to compare their progress with others in the course.

A second, more complicated issue that needs to be addressed in the larger question of how to encourage students to approach the classroom with the enthusiasm that they bring to contemporary computer games. Gee (2003) blames this problem on a public education system that propagates outmoded models of learning through skill-and-drill pedagogies and standardized testing and argues that educators should therefor adapt the learning principles found in contemporary computer games (p. 7). In doing so, Gee positions computer games so that they are proof positive of the Darwinistic power of the marketplace to always self-select the best or most appropriate course. As he explains,

If a game has poor learning principles built into its design, then it won't get learned or played and won't sell well.. .. In the end, then, video games represent a process, thanks to what Marx called the "creativity of capitalism," that leads to better and better designs for good learning and, indeed, good learning of hard and challenging things" (p. 6)

Gee, however, does not consider the alternative view that Louis Althusser advances in his 1968 essay "Ideology and Ideological State Apparatuses"—namely that ideological function of state-sponsored education is not to guarantee the success of every student, but to insure that they receive exactly the amount of ideological conditioning that is appropriate for their socioeconomic background (p. 29). If the education system is broken, in this sense, it is not because it does not work, but because it works too well—because, as Jonathon Kozol (1975/1990) argues, it is an "ice-cold and superb machine" (p. 27) that is in the name of producing "good citizens," subjects students to "twelve years of mandatory self-dehumanization, self debilitation, blood-loss" (p. 27),

Understood in this sense, it is not surprising that many students approach the classroom with suspicion, refusing to see the educational system as anything but coercive and punitive. Indeed, unlike in computer games, where players who perform inadequately can simply restore the game from a save point, failing an assignment or a series of assignments in a university-level class carries serious material consequences. Poor classroom performance, for instance, can significantly lower students' final grades, which might, in turn, cause them to become ineligible for scholarships or other forms of economic assistance. It can also causes student to fail courses, requiring them to dedicate time and resources to retaking them, and in extreme cases, resulting in suspension or expulsion from the university. In the face of such serious economic and ideological strictures, it is not surprising that students refuse to approach classroom activities as fun or playful. In a pedagogical climate where missing a jump or taking a wrong turn can mean substantial economic penalties and months of remediation, many students simply cannot afford the luxury of playing the game this way.

Nor is it surprising that computer games appear to be more educational than schools. Computer games are, after all, products of the twenty-first century culture industry, and are therefore implicated in what, to Theodore Adorno and Max Horkheimer (1944/1972), is a larger, industrial system of cultural production that, like the educational system, functions to mold "men as a type unfailingly reproduced in every product" (p. 127). As they explain,

Something is provided for all so that none may escape; the distinctions are emphasized and extended. The public is catered for with a hierarchical range of mass-produced products of varying quality, thus advancing the rule of complete quantification. Everybody must behave (as if spontaneously) in accordance with his previously determined and indexed level, and choose the category of mass product turned out for his type. (p. 123)

As with other incarnations of the culture industry, computer games thus work to reproduce the means of production—the subjects, or workers, who not only produce the material manifestations of third-stage capitalism (the goods, services, etc...,), but in their relationships with others and society as a whole, produce its ideological manifestations. If computer games thus appear to offer their players a luxury that is denied to them by the classroom and the workplace—the freedom to play at being ideological subjects—their purpose in doing so is not to liberate or to otherwise offer them an escape from the drudgeries of work or education. Constructed in dialog with educational institutions, work, and other sites of social production, they present these drudgeries as natural and inevitable, so that players must construct themselves in relationship to the dominant ideology even as they struggle to escape or otherwise vanquish it. As Adorno and Horkheimer write about earlier incarnations of the culture industry, the result is that

Amusement under late capitalism is the prolongation of work.... mechanization has such power over a man's leisure and happiness, and so profoundly determines the manufacture of amusement goods, that his experiences are inevitably after-images of the work process itself. The ostensible content is merely a faded foreground; what sinks in is the automatic succession of standardized operations. What happens at work, in the factory, or in the office can only be escaped from by approximation to it in one's leisure time. (p. 137)

The challenge of convincing students to approach education enthusiastically is, in this sense, far more complicated than simply constructing the classroom around the strategies that many contemporary computer games successfully deploy. Indeed, if Althusser is correct in stating that the state-sponsored educational systems have replaced the church as the primary ideological institution of capitalism (p. 28), then tackling this challenge not only entails addressing many of the injustices that characterize third-stage capitalism, but dismantling the ideological institutions that train individuals to approach these injustices as natural or inevitable. Such a project would, at the very least, require a substantial reexamination of what, in the context of contemporary education, constitutes "good" learning outcomes. It would probably, also, entail a substantial reexamination of the qualities that Gee and others so unproblematically celebrate as "good" in computer games at the present moment.

CONCLUSION

While the quest- and achievement-based pedagogy described in this chapter is inadequate to this larger project, it nevertheless represents something of a starting point. Indeed, in providing students with a scaffold that is designed to introduce the types of performances that constitutes normal discourse in many contemporary academic settings, such a system has the potential to help students become more conscious of how these discourse communities require them to construct themselves as subjects. This is especially the case if instructors do not present quests and achievements as natural and intuitive, but are careful to draw attention to them at every turn so that as students progress through the course, they understand how the courses underlying pedagogical framework is attempting to socialize them into the normal discourse of the class. By structuring the course in this manner, instructors can not only help students become more aware of the extent to which their experience is structured by the discourse communities in which they are involved, but better understand that the political, economic, and social relationships from which these discourses are constructed are not natural or inevitable, but like much of the roleplaying that takes place in MMORPGS, are socially constructed. Such an awareness might, therefore, lead students to a larger understanding of how knowledge and power is produced and maintained in society, and might empower them to challenge these systems of production, working to address the injustices they encounter through a larger, sustained strategy of abnormal discourse that is considered effective not to the degree that it perpetuates the status quo, but works to change it.

REFERENCES

Aarseth, E. (2004). Quest games as post-narrative discourse. In Ryan, M. (Ed.), *Narrative across Media* (pp. 362–376). Lincoln, NE: University of Nebraska Press.

Adorno, T., & Horkheimer, M. (1972). *The culture industry: enlightenment as mass deception. The dialectics of enlightenment* (Cumming, J., Trans.). New York: Continuum. (Original work published 1944)

Althusser, L. (1971). *Ideology and ideological state apparatuses (notes towards an investigation). Lenin and philosophy and other essays by louis althusser (Ben Brewster, trans.)*. New York: Monthly Review Press. (Original work published 1968)

Barthes, R. (1975). *S/Z* (Miller, R., Trans.). New York: Hill and Wang. (Original work published 1970)

Blizzard Entertainment. (2004/2009). World of warcraft. Irvine, California.

Bruffee, K. A. (1984). Collaborative learning and the 'conversation of mankind'. *College English, 46*(7), 635–652. doi:10.2307/376924

Burke, K. (1969). *A rhetoric of motives*. Berkeley, CA: University of California Press. (Original work published 1950)

Caillois, R. (2001). *Man, play and games* (Barash, M., Trans.). Chicago: University of Illinois Press. (Original work published 1958)

Campbell, J. (2008). *The hero with a thousand faces* (3rd ed.). Novato, CA: New World Library. (Original work published 1948)

Gbrown. (25 May 2009). Generation 'no effort.' why? *Chronicle.com*. Retrieved June 6, 2009 from http://chronicle.com/forums/index.php?topic=60658.0

Gee, J. P. (2003). *What computer games have to teach us about learning and literacy*. New York: Palgrave, Macmillan.

Howard, J. (2008). *Quests: design, theory, and history in games and narratives*. Wellesley, MA: A.K. Peters Press.

Irwin, M. J. (2009). Unlocking achievements: rewarding skill with player incentives. *Gamsutra.com*. Retrieved April 1, 2009 from http://www.gamasutra.com/view/feature /3976/unlocking_achievements_rewarding_.php

Juul, J. (2005). *Half-real: video games between real rules and fictional world*. Cambridge, MA: The MIT Press.

Karlsen, F. (September 2008). Quests in context: a comparative analysis of discworld and world of warcraft. *Game studies, 8*(1). Retrieved June 13, 2009 from http://gamestudies.org/ 0801/articles/karlsen

Kozol, J. (1975/1990). *The night is dark and I am far from home, new* (revised edition). New York: Simon & Schuster.

Moberly, K. (2008, September). Composition, computer games, and the absence of writing. Computers & Composition, 25(3), 284_299.

Rettenburg, J. W. (2008). Quests in world of warcraft: deferral and repetition. In Rettenburg, J. W., & Corneliussen, H. G. (Eds.), *Digital culture, play, and identity: a world of warcraft reader* (pp. 167–184). Cambridge, MA: The MIT Press.

Rorty, R. (1979). *Philosophy and the mirror of knowledge*. Princeton, NJ: Princeton University Press.

Taylor, T. L. (2006). *Play between worlds: exploring online game culture*. Cambridge, MA: The MIT Press.

Tronstad, R. (2001, September). *Semiotic and non semiotic MUD performance*. Paper presented at the 2001 COSIGN conference. Retrieved June 11, 2009 from http://www.cosignconference.org/downloads/papers/tronstad_cosign_2001.pdf

Chapter 15
Modifying Popular Board Games to Illustrate Complex Strategic Concepts:
A Comparison With a Professional Computer Simulation

Scott Gallagher
James Madison University, USA

David Cavazos
James Madison University, USA

Steven Harper
James Madison University, USA

ABSTRACT

Simulations can be powerful tools in helping students learn about strategic management. This chapter discusses the value of simulations in helping to illustrate the importance of contingency, the impossibility of a perfect strategy, planning ahead, and aligning internal resources to external environments in strategic management classes. The authors also discuss the benefits that simulations can offer in going beyond the book and class, being interesting, and the importance of instrumentality in facilitating student learning. This chapter then compares self reported student learning results for each of these variables for two simulations, a professionally packaged simulation and a "home-brewed" one based on a popular board game. The authors expected the professional simulation to do better on every variable except instrumentality. Surprisingly, the "home-brewed" simulation scored better on most of the dimensions. Therefore, they conclude by encouraging management educators to aggressively explore their instincts for simulation learning opportunities.

DOI: 10.4018/978-1-61520-781-7.ch015

INTRODUCTION

Strategic Management (also referred to as Business Policy) courses have typically been used as capstone or integrative reviews in business school curriculum (Kesner, 2001). At the core of strategic management courses is the question of why some firms outperform others (Barney, 1991). Because of their unique place in business schools, strategic management courses have relied on a number of pedagogical tools aimed at integrating, synthesizing, and applying learning objectives. Such tools include case teaching, experiential exercises, field projects, and computer simulations (Kesner, 2001).

One of the biggest challenges of teaching strategic management is conveying to students the difficult nature of firm strategy given the level of uncertainty that surrounds decision-making. Most strategic frameworks such as VRIO, Porter's Five Forces, and Generic Business Level Strategies are not tremendously complex (Porter, 1980; Barney, 1991). The main approach to illustrate these challenges is frequently case discussions. Cases tend to be written as stories with protagonists and antagonists (Liang & Wang, 2004) and as a result case interpretations tend to be biased (Denzin, 1989). For instance, when cases are used whose outcomes are well known, e.g. Enron, it is not uncommon to have students initially dismiss business decisions that have a poor outcome as simply being "bad" or "wrong." As a result, the use of simulations has emerged as a common pedagogical approach to help students understand and appreciate some of the nuances of business strategy. This also can encourage students to achieve higher levels of thinking (Bloom, Hastings, & Medaus, 1971).

Simulations allow difficult concepts like contingency to be vividly illustrated and the challenges of thinking ahead to be applied. Not surprisingly, many have moved to using computer simulations in an effort to enhance student learning (Faria & Wellington, 2004). However, recent changes to a leading strategy computer simulation that constrained students from adding new capacity at their own discretion concerned some of us and motivated a search for alternatives. Two of the authors utilized an alternative computer simulation, Glo-Bus™, while the third customized the venerable Monopoly™ board game to tie it more closely to strategy concepts (Thompson, Stappenbeck, & Reidenbach, 2008). The aim of this study is to examine the merits of each as alternative teaching tools.

We briefly discuss the benefit using simulations in teaching strategic management. This discussion includes brief descriptions of Glo-Bus™ as well as the modified Monopoly™ (hereafter, 487opoly) simulations that we used. We then briefly discuss some key learning aims and our expectations for the relative advantages of the two simulations. Finally, we examine the assessment results from students who participated in both simulations.

BACKGROUND

Simulations

At their core, most strategy classes center on training students to apply frameworks, e.g. Porter's Five Forces, to challenging managerial decisions. At the very least, a good simulation should replicate the environment, e.g. negotiations, uncertainty, and environmental variability, in which strategic decisions are made. A number of scholars have illustrated various uses for simulations in the business classroom. Stephen, Parente, and Brown (2002), for example, discuss the ability of simulations to facilitate student's acquisition of an integrative perspective. The hands-on nature of simulations and their ability to engage students in course content are additionally cited as benefits of simulations as teaching tools (Burke & More, 2003). Moreover, Zantow, Knowlton and Sharp (2005) illustrate how can be conducive to generative learning.

It is clear that simulations offer many advantages. In our case we were primarily interested in four areas whose difficulty is hard to convey in a classroom context: contingency, no perfect strategy, planning ahead, and aligning internal resources with the external environment. Contingency simply refers to the fact that the success of any one strategy is contingent on what others do. If all firms in an industry pursue the same strategy, none of them are likely to break out from the pack and be overly successful. Any simulation will be less complicated than real life, however, it should be impossible for students to derive the key competitive algorithm or develop a perfect strategy that will always prevail. Planning ahead is another obviously important strategic concept that is hard to illustrate in class discussion but can be easily highlighted by a simulation. Finally, most strategy classes revolve around understanding and applying a range of frameworks to make sense of complex external and internal environments in order to help derive a prudent course of action, e.g. a strategy.

Glo-Bus™

Glo-Bus™ is a leading academic business simulation published by McGraw Hill Irwin. It seeks to recreate an industry setting, in this case centered on manufacturing and distributing digital cameras to retailers. As with many other simulations, it involves students making decisions for a discreet, but potentially unknown, number of "rounds", e.g. 6 to 10. Students normally meet in groups to evaluate decisions regarding their advertising levels, distribution outlets, prices, and production levels for their firm as well as the number of cameras to outsource. These variables, along with any environmental variables manipulated per planned economic growth or by the instructor, e.g. changes in demand, interest rates, foreign exchange rates, etc., are then simultaneously resolved by the computer. Computer simulations offer real advantages in regards to instructor time, the range of variables that can be considered, and the complexity of the interactions between those variables.

487opoly[1]

Board games are a common fixture in children's lives. 487opoly takes as its base Hasbro's *Monopoly*™ game. However, the basic rules of this game were modified to include an auction for the sale of all properties, the Chance deck was replaced by a selection of external events, and the Community Chest deck was replaced by a deck of internal strengths that players also bid on to purchase. It remains a board game and the first semester it was used students each contributed 50 cents so the instructor could buy enough copies of *Monopoly*™ for the entire class. The primary modification is that there is only one pawn, it pays any "rent" due to players from landing on their property from the bank, and all properties are sold via an auction. Examples of external events include recessions, anti-trust actions, and environmental rules changes. Examples of internal strengths students can acquire include the ability to hold extra cards, collect extra rent, or build houses and hotels at lower cost. A summary of key changes is included as appendix one, while the complete rules and card text for 487opoly are available upon request from the first author.

EXPECTED TRADEOFFS COMPUTER VERSUS BOARD GAME SIMULATIONS

The kinds of strategic decisions often discussed in strategic management classes are hard to easily model. Even setting up an interesting class discussion often involves students reading cases of several pages in order to convey the array of issues key decision makers faced. When applied to a simulation, recreating this range of complexity potentially requires a huge number of rules and variables that a computer can help resolve.

In thinking about the purpose of simulations in our classes, in addition to reflecting business competition, we identified student learning goals to gain deep understanding of these four key concepts: contingency, no perfect strategy, planning ahead, and the alignment of internal resources with external reality. We were also interested in three helpful aids to learning: instrumentality, interest, and reflecting course content. Finally, we were curious if the simulations helped students understand ideas and issues that went beyond their time attending class or reading the textbook.

Since it attempts to recreate an industry, we expected Glo-Bus™ to perform better in the core areas of contingency, no perfect strategy, planning ahead, and alignment. However, perhaps because of its simplicity, we expected the modified board game to score better on instrumentality. This is simply because in the board game, students resolved their actions in sequence, rather than in "batch processing" as is done in most current computer simulations. Therefore, it is easier for students to see the link between their actions and the outcomes, thereby allowing greater illustration of ideas from the course. The algorithms for the board game are also easily grasped, e.g. roll the dice and move that many spaces, versus a computer program that allocates demand among several different competitors using a sophisticated and unobserved algorithm.

Methodology

A 487opoly "tournament" was used in the spring 2008 semester for three sections of strategic management. The reports from students in these sections were very favorable. However, since these students did not experience both simulations, their feedback could not provide guidance to the faculty of any real advantages or disadvantages of a modified board game versus a computer simulation. However, two summer sections of strategic management were scheduled to use the Glo-Bus™ simulation. Near the conclusion of that simulation, after 7 of 7 turns in one section and 5 of 7 turns in the other, we had the students also play 487opoly. As part of assessment, on the last class day, we had students fill out a brief evaluation form of the two simulations (attached as Appendix

2). 49 students who played both simulations fully filled out these evaluation forms.

We were mainly interested if there was a difference in student evaluations of their learning between the two simulations, as well as their evaluations of our "aids to learning" variables. Therefore, we used a Wilcoxon signed rank sum test. This non-parametric version of the paired sample t-test allowed us to relax the assumption of normality and does not require the differences recorded by students on our likert scale instrument to be interval, only ordinal.

Results

Table 1 presents our results. The difference was computed as board simulation minus computer simulation, with lower numbers indicating a greater preference, so a negative number indicated students thought 487opoly was better while a positive number indicated Glo-Bus was better.

As befitting a complex computer based simulation, students felt that Glo-Bus™ did a better job in reflecting the problems of contingency and preventing the development of a perfect strategy. However, these differences were not statistically significant. We were surprised by the extent that 487opoly outperformed the computer simulation in the areas of thinking ahead and alignment, as well as teaching beyond the class or book. This may be because of the auction system inherent in the board game that provided the opportunity for bidding strategies that are important but often not discussed in strategy classes. Also the face-to-face nature of board games allowed for more negotiations and interaction than is common in computer simulations.

We were additionally surprised to find that the students found the board game so much more interesting than the computer simulation. We suspect this was due to the greater social interaction in 487opoly; the board game revolves around interaction with your rivals in a face to face manner, rather than inputting decisions into a computer program for resolution. As expected,

Table 1. Results from Student Assessment Data

Variable	Mean	Wilcoxian t	P value
Contingency	.122	.724	.473
No Perfect Strategy	.041	.251	.803
Planning/Thinking Ahead	-.449	-1.939†	.058
Alignment of Internal/External	-.388	-1.943†	.058
Simulation Taught Beyond Class/Book	-.388	-1.986†	.053
Interesting	-.918	-4.00**	.000
Reflected Course Content	-.229	-1.245	.219
Simulated Business Competition	-.388	-1.987†	.053
Instrumentality	-.388	-2.032*	.048

$* = < .05; ** = < .01$ and $† = < .1$ levels of significance

Note: Surveys were coded so lower numbers are **better**. The difference was computed 487opoly-Globus, therefore a negative number indicates students' preference for 487opoly while a positive one a preference for Globus.

487opoly did outperform the computer simulation in instrumentality. We surmise this is simply a function of the rules being easy to understand and the absence of any "behind the scenes" resolution by a computer.

SOLUTIONS AND RECOMMENDATIONS

We were surprised at the extent to which a modification to a popular board game could hold its own against a professionally produced educational computer simulation. While we expected it to outperform on the instrumentality dimension, we did not expect it to be preferred in any other areas. We think this is a result of the social interaction, linear (rather than batch) resolution of competitive moves, and novelty. As we noted, a key purpose of a simulation is to have students confront realistic situations, e.g. the trade offs and uncertainty surrounding strategic decisions, without replicating so much context that students become lost. By facilitating social interaction, the modified board game engendered considerable realistic participation that might be lost when entering decisions into a spreadsheet for batch processing by a computer.

One main drawback of the computer simulation is that it can become easy for students to view the next year's projected performance and thus just mechanically make changes to the current round's decision to maximize the forecast results. This feature encourages lower level thinking and frustrates student teams that do not receive the gains they are "promised" in the projections. In this case, the simulation can become a game of numbers. However, student teams that generally tried to understand how their actions fit in the market and mentally simulated the customer's response to their new product offerings, broke out of this lower level thinking and their performance improved. The students must look past the plethora of numbers the simulation provides and use higher levels of thinking and analysis to properly react to the market. However, this change frequently requires instructor encouragement and consulting to allow students to learn more and reduce frustration from the computer simulation.

We in no way view our results as a call to move away from computer simulations. Computer simulations offer several real implementation advantages, especially the fact that the computer acts as an impartial referee and can accommodate a virtually unlimited number of parameters. The computer also frees up considerable time for the professor to engage in consultation and coaching of student teams rather than adjudicating rules disputes. For the sections that utilized 487opoly, that professor had to set aside considerable time to attend and sometimes referee games. This stands in stark contrast to the "hands off" approach professors may take for computer simulations once they are up and running.

Rather, our results show that professors should be encouraged to develop their own customized tools to help convey what they believe are the key ideas from their courses to their students. Simulations have great potential as a teaching tool. The results from our analysis shows that even if the components themselves are crude, a well thought out simulation can be "home-brewed" and still help student learning. Such creations can serve as surprisingly effective compliments to teaching tools such as cases and computer simulations.

REFERENCES

Barney, J. B. (1991). Firm resources and sustained competitive advantage. *Journal of Management*, 7, 99–120. doi:10.1177/014920639101700108

Bloom, B. S., Hastings, J. T., & Medaus, G. F. (1971). *Handbook on Formative and Summative Evaluation of Student Learning*. New York: McGraw-Hill.

Burke, L. A., & Moore, J. E. (2003). A perennial dilemma in OB education: Engaging the traditional student. *Academy of Management Learning & Education*, 2(1), 37–52.

Denzin, N. K. (1989). *Interpretive Biography*. Thousand Oaks, CA: Sage Publications.

Faria, A. J., & Wellington, W. J. (2004). A survey of simulation game users, former-users, and never-users. *Simulation & Gaming*, 35(2), 178–207. doi:10.1177/1046878104263543

Kesner, I. A. (2001). The Strategic Management Course: Tools and Techniques for Successful Teaching. In Hitt, M., Freeman, R. E., & Harrison, J. S. (Eds.), *Handbook of Strategic Management*.

Liang, N., & Wang, J. (2004). Implicit mental models in teaching cases: An empirical study of popular MBA cases in the United States and China. *Academy of Management Learning & Education*, 3(4), 397–413.

Porter, M. (1980). *Competitive Strategy*. New York: The Free Press.

Schumann, P. L., Scott, T. W., & Anderson, P. H. (2006). Designing and introducing ethical dilemmas into computer based business simulations. *Journal of Management Education*, 30(1), 195–219. doi:10.1177/1052562905280844

Stephen, J., Parente, D. H., & Brown, R. C. (2002). Seeing the forest and the trees: Balancing functional and integrative knowledge using large scale simulation in capstone business classes. *Journal of Management Education*, 26(2), 164–193. doi:10.1177/105256290202600204

Thompson, A. A., Stappenbeck, G. J., & Reidenbach, M. A. (2008). *GLO-BUS: Developing Winning Competitive Strategies*. New York: McGraw-Hill/Irwin, Inc.

Zantow, K., Knowlton, D. S., & Sharp, D. C. (2005). More than fun and games: Reconsidering the virtues of strategic management simulations. *Academy of Management Learning & Education*, 4(4), 451–458.

ENDNOTE

[1]   At our college, strategic management's course number is 487.

APPENDIX 1

Summary of Rules for 487opoly

The purpose of 487opoly is to increase the number of investment decisions (and dramatically reduce the role of luck) in a Monopoly™ game in order to illustrate the dynamic and contingent nature of business strategy as well as to illustrate the role of alignment and, to a much lesser extent, corporate strategy.

This game uses the core of a regular Monopoly™ game set but alters many of its rules. Unless otherwise stated below, all the regular rules of Monopoly™ apply. The rules for Monopoly™ can be downloaded at: www.**hasbro**.com/common/instruct/monins.pdf Unless you have played recently, I strongly recommend you review the rules to Monopoly™.

Brief Summary

The full rules are over 6 pages, but most of them are for situations that arise fairly infrequently, here are the key aspects of this game:

- Only one token moves around the board, it pays rent from the bank, players never pay rent.
- Initially, you can only hold a limited number of properties - 5 in a four player game. This limit can be increased by External Events and Internal Strength cards.
- ALL properties are initially sold via an auction. 10 properties are sold before the game begins, the rest are sold as the pawn lands on them.
- Chance is replaced by External Event cards while Community Chest is replaced by Internal Strength cards. Internal Strength cards are auctioned off just like properties.
- You do not have to own all of a color group to build as long as you form an alliance with the other player(s) who own the rest of the color group.
- Alliances are binding, but can be cancelled at any time with a one turn notice.
- The game ends when the bank runs out of money, after about 90 minutes of play, or when two recessions occur back to back. Important: About one in five games end early, be prepared for this!
- You will have two scores in the game. The first is a function of both your total cash and property holdings. The second is a function of the rental income you are positioned to receive.

Appendix 2

Survey Instrument

A. Performance for 487opoly:

How well did your group do in the simulation? (Circle one) Top Half of Class / Bottom Half of Class

Place an X in the box that best represents how you agree with the statements.

Evaluation Area	Strong-ly Agree	Agree	Neu-tral	Dis-agree	Strongly Disagree
1. Contingency – A big problem in strategy is that even if a good strategy can be designed, it is contingent on what others do. If we all go with a low price strategy, then low prices ceases to be a point of distinction in consumers' minds. *487opoly was effective in highlighting contingency*					
2. No Perfect Strategy – As we discussed in class, there is no one perfect strategy. There should be no way to guarantee a "win" in the simulation. *487opoly was effective in highlighting that there was no perfect strategy*					
3. Planning/Thinking Ahead – A good simulation should reward planning out your actions and expectations of others to react to them. **487opoly was effective in rewarding planning.**					
4. Instrumentality – In order to be a useful teaching tool, you have to be able to link your actions with the results of what happened. **487opoly was effective in highlighting instrumentality**					
5. Alignment of Internal and External Strategy – In order for your overall strategy to be effective, you should consider external and internal factors in you planning, implementation, and execution. **487opoly was effective in highlighting alignment**					
6. 487opoly held my interest – it was not boring					
7. 487opoly effectively reflected the course content					
8. 487opoly effectively simulated business competition					
9. Using 487opoly taught me things about in Strategic Management beyond the class or textbook.					

B. Performance for GLO-BUS:

How well did your group do in the simulation? (Circle one) Top Half of Class / Bottom Half of Class
Place an X in the box that best represents how you agree with the statements.

Evaluation Area	Strong-ly Agree	Agree	Neu-tral	Dis-agree	Strongly Disagree
1. Contingency – A big problem in strategy is that even if a good strategy can be designed, it is contingent on what others do. If we all go with a low price strategy, then low prices ceases to be a point of distinction in consumers' minds. *GLO-BUS was effective in highlighting contingency*					
2. No Perfect Strategy – As we discussed in class, there is no one perfect strategy. There should be no way to guarantee a "win" in the simulation. *GLO-BUS was effective in highlighting that there was no perfect strategy*					
3. Planning/Thinking Ahead – A good simulation should reward planning out your actions and expectations of others to react to them. **GLO-BUS was effective in rewarding planning.**					
4. Instrumentality – In order to be a useful teaching tool, you have to be able to link your actions with the results of what happened. **GLO-BUS was effective in highlighting instrumentality**					

5. Alignment of Internal and External Strategy – In order for your overall strategy to be effective, you should consider external and internal factors in you planning, implementation, and execution. **GLO-BUS was effective in highlighting alignment**					
6. GLO-BUS held my interest – it was not boring					
7. GLO-BUS effectively reflected the course content					
8. GLO-BUS effectively simulated business competition					
9. Using GLO-BUS taught me things about in Strategic Management beyond the class or textbook.					

C. Summary:

Based upon what you know about strategic management, GLO-BUS, and 487opoly, what would you recommend for future students to enhance their learning?

Glo-Bus Better No Difference 487opoly Tournament Better

1----------------2-----------------3----------------4-------------------5

Chapter 16
Animated Computer Education Games for Students with ADHD:
Evaluating Their Development and Effectiveness as Instructional Tools

Kim B. Dielmann
University of Central Arkansas, USA

Julie Meaux
University of Central Arkansas, USA

ABSTRACT

Children and adolescents with Attention Deficit Hyperactivity Disorder (ADHD) have difficulty maintaining attention, controlling their activity level, and they typically demonstrate poor interpersonal relationships skills. Because of their challenges, educational performance tends to suffer. Paradoxically, when seated in front of a videogame or computer program they enjoy, the performance of individuals with ADHD becomes similar to non-ADHD peers. The purpose of this chapter is to present a conceptual framework for understanding the factors that affect the outcome of individuals with ADHD, and to demonstrate how instructional design models can be used to guide the design and implementation of animated computer education games as instructional tools for this population. Specifically, the FIDGE model and Gagné's Nine Events of Instruction are evaluated for their contributions to understanding the unique technological needs of the ADHD learner.

INTRODUCTION

Current estimates indicate Attention Deficit Hyperactivity Disorder (ADHD) affects 4% to 12% of U.S. children (Froehlich et al., 2007). Longitudinal studies suggest children who are diagnosed with ADHD continue to have difficulties with organization, time management, impulsive thoughts and actions, stress management, emotional regulation, interpersonal relationships, and academic skills such as reading, studying, and test taking as adolescents and as young adults (Barkley, Fischer, Smallish, and Fletcher, 2006). Children and adolescents with ADHD often struggle in traditional classrooms. Many fidget and have difficulty remaining in their seats, thus causing disruption to the classroom as well as to the child's own education. Even when

DOI: 10.4018/978-1-61520-781-7.ch016

children with ADHD are able to sit quietly, they often require multiple repetition in order to retain information they hear. Most teachers cannot pause to emphasize each individual fact to a child with ADHD while the rest of the class has grasped the material and moved on. As a result, adolescents with ADHD are more likely to drop out of high school and fail to complete college compared to their non-ADHD counterparts. Lower educational achievement often leads to underemployment, poor social adjustment, and decreased overall quality of life. To address these problems, a more engaging and personalized education format is necessary for children and adolescents with ADHD.

According to DuPaul and Stoner (2003), students with ADHD are educated more effectively if multiple mediators (peers, computers, and parents) are involved. They also recommend the intervention strategies be individualized particularly since the ADHD population is heterogenious. According to the Centers for Disease Control and Prevention (September 2, 2005), 56% of all children ages four to 17 years diagnosed with ADHD were taking stimulant medications. Though medication is the most widely used treatment for ADHD, a combination of self-monitoring and self-reinforcement may have longer lasting effects. Barkley, Copeland, and Sivage (1980) found this combination improved task-related attention, academic accuracy, and peer interactions. DuPaul, Rutherford and Hosterman (2008) suggested the use of self-monitoring and self-reinforcement particularly at the secondary level because there are fewer opportunities for this age group for token reinforcement, contingency contracting, or response cost.

Technological advances and the increased availability of technological resources afford most schools the ability to incorporate different types of instructional technology into the classroom. For students with ADHD, educational tools that involve computerized technology offer a wider range of options for learning. The benefits of computerized presentation of information include the use of multiple senses, the breakdown of material into smaller pieces, provision of immediate feedback, and the limitation of unnecessary, distracting features (DuPaul & Weyandt, 2006). According to several studies, children and adolescents with ADHD are more attentive to computerized programs or interventions than to traditional instruction methods (Shalev, Tasal & Mevorach, 2007; Farrace-Di Zinno et al., 2001; Carroll & Bain, 1994). They also seem to respond better to interactive instruction than when they serve in more passive roles as listeners or viewers (Shaw & Lewis, 2005; Klingberg et al., 2005). Shaw, Grayson & Lewis (2005) found students with ADHD performed better and were more engaged by information presented in a game format than by regular computerized instruction. In addition, Farrace-Di Zinno et al. (2001) observed how students with ADHD were more similar to their peers without ADHD with regard to the amount of motor movement and distractability during computer video game play.

According to Fister (1999), computer games can be used for primary learning of different subjects rather than just for review and reinforcement. Ota and DuPaul (2002) evaluated the effects of a game-based math software program on the performance of ADHD students. They found increased math performance, decreased off-task and disruptive behavior, and increased active engagement in the computer-based instruction compared to the traditional classroom lesson. Mautone, DuPaul, and Jitendra (2005) found similar math improvements in ADHD students. Oral reading fluency has also been the target of research using computer-assisted technology with ADHD students. Clarfield and Stoner (2005) found improvements in oral reading fluency and subsequent engagement in the activity when a computer-assisted reading program was used. While data suggest students with ADHD may benefit from the use of computerized educational tools, it is important to understand what and how to appropriately integrate gaming technology into the classroom to improve learning outcomes for these students. In addition, it is imperative educators evaluate the appropriateness of such technology for use with all students. In this chapter, a conceptual framework for understanding the intervening factors that affect outcomes for people with ADHD will be discussed along with models to help educators design and evaluate the quality of computerized games for education purposes.

THE "GAME GENERATION"

Prensky (2001a) describes the most recent generation of children who integrate video games into their daily activities as the "game generation." He also coined the term "Digital Natives" to describe this generation's approach to learning. Digital Natives routinely manage large amounts of information at one time, find alternative ways to acquire knowledge, and seek solutions through different means previously unavailable. Prensky (2001b) compared the digital natives to previous generations, who he named "Digital Immigrants". The primary differences between the groups lie in how they approach learning. Digital natives prefer to multi-task. They prefer to "leap around" as they learn rather than sequentially process information (Prensky, 2001c). According to Prensky (2001c), children of this game generation "have been adjusting or programming their brains to the speed, interactivity, and other factors in the games" (pp.3). This generation of learners has also been referred to as "Generation M" for the group between the ages of 8-18 years who have never known a time without media (Rideout, Roberts, & Foehr, 2005). Other labels given to this generation of learners include "Generation I" to represent the influence of the internet in their lives or "Generation Z" to denote the generation following Generation Y (Schmidt & Hawkins, 2008). Despite their nomenclature, the generation of learners today is vastly different from previous generations. Prensky developed ten cognitive

traits (Table 1) to describe the differences between children of the game generation and children of previous generations.

Twitch speed refers to the fast speed at which the game generation wants information presented. Classroom lectures and independent seatwork that occur at a slower pace can be frustrating and boring to this group who are accustomed to rapid presentation of information. Parallel processing refers to the randomness of responding, such as surfing the internet or completing game challenges in no specific order. The historic rules of reading textbooks and conducting research follow a sequential order and require systematic approaches. The game generation of children can become inattentive and disruptions may result. Graphic representations stimulate the game generation, while reading text may provide little inspiration for learning. The game generation wants to be connected at all times and they often feel as if they are a part of a community of gamers rather than lone players. This sense of interconnectivity can also stimulate negative behavior, such as cheating in school, because of the diffusion of responsibility that accompanies. They are active participants who can impose change on their environments, and can become easily frustrated

Table 1 Differences in cognitive traits between children of the game generation and more traditional learners (Prensky, 2001a).

Game Generation	Traditional
Twitch speed	Conventional speed
Parallel processing	Linear processing
Graphics First	Text First
Random access	Step-by-Step
Connected	Stand alone
Active	Passive
Play	Work
Payoff	Patience
Fantasy	Reality
Technology as friendly	Technology as foe

when placed in an environment where they have no control. Within the game environment, they experience immediate payoff, and many of these activities are fantasy-based. They do not simply use technology as a tool—they are immersed in it as an extension of themselves. Educators who are born of generations past (Digital Immigrants) have to engage the game generation with a different set of tools than what they learned in school (Prensky, 2001a).

Students with ADHD have always used cognitive traits similar to those described by Prensky. Yet, their approaches were viewed as disruptive to the learning environment. Twitch speed was considered hyperactivity and impulsivity. Parallel processing was viewed as disorganization. Connectedness was seen as attention-seeking. Play was considered inattention. Children with ADHD needed more from the learning environment than was available. Now, the needs of the game generation may actually be consistent with the needs of children with ADHD.

Caution has been stressed to adults who are interested in using gaming technology to teach children. There have been negative effects associated with video game use reported in the research. Increased aggression has long been associated with the degree of violence in the game (Gentile & Anderson, 2003; Gentile, Lynch, Linder & Walsh, 2004; Porter & Starcevic, 2007). Gentile et al. (2004) found children who play violent video games are more prone to increased aggression, confrontation with teachers, fights with peers, and decreased academic achievement. However, in a meta-analysis of the effects of violent video-game playing, Ferguson (2007) found no evidence to link playing violent video games with increases in aggression. Additionally, Ferguson et al. (2008) found that when family violence was controlled for, there was no correlational or causal effect of violent video games on aggression. The authors concluded that aggressive personality types and

exposure to family violence were greater predictors of violence than simply exposure to violent video games.

The largest concern associated with video game play seems to be the addictive properties associated with it. Chan and Rabinowitz (2006) found a positive correlation between the amounts of time spent playing video games daily and the number of ADHD symptoms present. Furthermore, Bioulac, Arfi, and Bouvard (2008) found increased addictive tendencies for video games in ADHD children compared to their non-ADHD peers. Results suggest children who play video games for extended periods of time may be prone to more complications and more ADHD symptomology than those who play them less frequently.

Several positive effects from video game play have also been noted. Okagaki and Frensch (1994) found positive effects associated with repeated play of the game Tetris™. Adolescents involved in the study enhanced their visual-spatial and visual reasoning skills through playing the game. They suggested game playing may actually influence performance IQ scores. Ferguson (2007) confirmed these findings and concluded that playing violent video games can actually increase visuospatial cognition. Other positive effects include increased problem-solving, increased motivation, and accelerated learning (eg., de Freitas & Levene, 2004; Garris, Ahlers & Driskell, 2002; Gee, 2003; Hays, 2005).

These benefits could level the playing field for children and adolescents with ADHD. Educators who use gaming technology can more easily accommodate many different types of learners. Games can adjust to the skills and needs of their players, allowing the same product or software to meet the needs of all students. However, before educators adopt the "one size fits all" policy for educational games, they need to understand the specific learning styles associated with the ADHD learner.

ADHD LEARNERS AND EDUCATIONAL GAMES

Mediating Factors that Challenge the ADHD Learner

Students with ADHD have difficulty because their core symptoms of inattention, impulsivity, and hyperactivity affect their ability to manage daily life. ADHD affects the person at three interacting levels: (a) body functions, (b) activities, and (c) participation in society. The impact of ADHD on these three interacting levels is also moderated by environmental and personal factors. A conceptual framework (Figure 1) adapted from the International Classification of Functioning, Disability, and Health (ICF) developed by the World Health Organization identifies how symptoms of ADHD can impede school, social, and home functioning (Ustun, 2007).

The ICF framework provides the basis for understanding the learning and behavioral needs of the students with ADHD.

Intervening Factors:

- *Personal factors* are features of life that are not a part of ADHD but can impact other levels of function. Some personal factors are not amenable to change such as gender, race, social background, familial factors, comorbidity, severity of symptoms, and predominant learning styles. Other personal factors such as knowledge of the disorder and medication use can be affected by intervention. While stimulant medications are effective in decreasing the primary symptoms of ADHD, few adolescents take them routinely (Marcus, Wan, Kemner, & Olfson, 2005). Since games are adaptable to the needs of the individual students, they can be implemented as educational interventions regardless of personal factors. An estimated 30% of students with ADHD have reading or math disabilities (Capano, Minden, Chen, Schachar, & Ickowicz, 2008; Faraone, Biederman, Monuteaux, &

Figure 1. Conceptual framework for ADHD students adapted from the International Classification of Functioning, Disability, and Health Conceptual Model (Ustun, 2006)

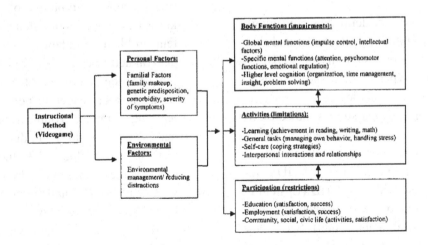

Seidman, 2001). Learning becomes more challenging for this large minority of students. Games can be presented in high text formats (where users must read a substantial amount to complete) and low text formats (where users navigate more through pictures and limited reading) thereby reducing the need for assistance by special educators with reading and comprehension of the material.

- *Environmental factors* consist of physical, social, and attitudinal factors in which people live and conduct their lives (Ustun, 2007). A major focus of ADHD management for young children is modification of the classroom environment in order to improve behavior and performance. Research indicates that during videogame play, hyperactivity and impulsivity decrease for students with ADHD while attention and learning increase (Farrace-Di Zinno et al., 2001). Providing opportunities for integrating videogame technology into the learning environment is a simple way to address the behavioral and academic needs of these students.

Outcome Factors:

- *Body functions* are defined as physiological and psychological functions, and they include the core symptoms of ADHD – inattention, hyperactivity, and impulsivity (American Psychological Association, 2000). Neuroimaging studies indicate differences in the size and activation of the prefrontal cortex during cognitive processing tasks in individuals with ADHD compared to those without ADHD (Epstein et al., 2007; Konrad, Neufang, Hanisch, Fink, & Herpertz-Dahlmann, 2006). Secondary impairments of ADHD, such as verbal and nonverbal working memory, emotional regulation, and behavioral reconstitution

(Barkley, 1997), are also considered body functions according to ICF coding. Behavioral reconstitution is the ability to shape behavior or learn new behavior patterns based on cues provided by models in the environment, and it allows individuals to learn vicariously. According to Barkley (1997), individuals with ADHD have difficulty with behavioral reconstitution. They frequently have to experience the consequences of their own behavior in order to shape new behavior patterns. Videogames can allow the player to become the character in the game; therefore, the player serves as his or her own model for behavior change. Bandura in his social learning theory (1971) emphasizes people can learn by observing a model. Seeing the self successfully perform a skill provides information about how to best perform that skill, strengthens self-efficacy, and reinforces learning.

- *Activities* are defined as the execution of tasks or actions. General activities of daily living are included in this category, such as learning and applying knowledge, general tasks and demands, communication, mobility, self-care, and interpersonal relationships. Symptoms of ADHD are known to cause inconsistency and persistent problems in adaptive functioning for general activities of daily living. Research indicates the symptoms of ADHD significantly impact academic performance and learning. Frazier, Youngstrom, Glutting, and Watkins (2007) conducted a meta-analysis that included 72 studies of academic achievement in children and adolescents with ADHD and found moderate to large discrepancies between achievement scores of those with and without ADHD. Adolescents with ADHD have persistent problems with adaptive communication skills (Clark, Prior, & Kinsella, 2002) as well as difficulties with interpersonal relationships and social situations (Barkley, 2006; Maedgen & Carlson, 2000). Computer technology and virtual reality can be used to create social situations and model interpersonal relationships in order to shape behavior and reinforce learning.

- *Participation* is defined as involvement in life situations, which include education, employment, and community activities. Typically, compared to their peers without ADHD, adolescents with ADHD experience more difficulty moving through and succeeding in educational programs, obtaining and retaining work, and even being involved in community, social, and civic life (Spencer, Biederman, & Mick, 2007). Games that simulate real-world situations could teach these students how to participate by providing them with immediate feedback about their actions without having to expose them to potentially harmful situations.

Students with ADHD need educational opportunities that are purposeful yet fun and engaging. The advancements in gaming technology, as they relate to the instructional environment, are promising. However, the quality, format, and purpose of technological mediums vary widely and it is important to evaluate and select the most appropriate medium for the desired learning outcomes.

EDUCATIONAL GAMES VS. EDUCATIONAL SIMULATIONS

Research differentiates between educational games and educational simulations. According to Price (1990), the purpose of an educational video game is to teach and provide practice. A simulation, on the other hand, has been described as something that mirrors real life and requires

the player to act (Tessmer, Jonassen, & Caverly, 1989, p. 89). According to Gredler (1996), games are typically linear, requiring correct responses before advancing to the next level. Simulations are non-linear, allowing for flexibility in movement within the modules based on decisions made previously. Prensky (2001a) expanded on Gredler's interpretation of games and simulations by suggesting games are viewed as fun, have specific goals, provide structure through rules, and include a competitive component that assumes the player will either win or lose. Using this interpretation, Prensky suggested that simulations can also be games if they are designed as such. He went as far as to say simulations "simulate" reality, which could be boring to the player. By adding game-like components to the simulation (components that are unrealistic), players may enjoy playing and at the same time be able to generalize the skill to an aspect of real life (Prensky, 2001a). Educators must be mindful of these differences when introducing an educational game or simulation into the lesson. A game may be fun with limited learning associated with it. A simulation may have the potential for learning, but it may not be fun. Prensky suggests the best situation may be to give the player real choices, but to "include enough humorous or even outrageous possibilities" to make it fun (Prensky, 2001a). The goal is to keep even the most inattentive and distractible players interested and motivated to continue.

VIDEOGAME PERFORMANCE OF CHILDREN WITH AND WITHOUT ADHD

Research has found mixed results regarding videogame performance of children with ADHD compared to their non-ADHD peers. Continuous Performance Tests (CPT) are typically used to evaluate speed of responding, sustained attention level, motor movements, and executive functioning in individuals with ADHD. These computer-based assessments require individuals to respond to a correct target sequence and refrain from responding to an incorrect target sequence or distractor. People with ADHD are more restless, inattentive, and talkative than their typically developing peers when completing CPTs (Barkley, Grodzinsky, & DuPaul, 1992). In addition, children find them aversive (Smith, Barkley, & Shapiro, 2007). These assessments lack the criteria suggested by Prensky that would engage and motivate the individual during the task. Tannock (1997) conducted an assessment of motor movement in boys with ADHD using the Pacman™ videogame; a two-dimensional, repetitive, restricted player-interface game with a non-variable background, and also found a pattern of restlessness, inattention, and talkativeness compared to boys without ADHD. To paraphrase Prensky, these tasks are not fun and are not based on real-life experiences.

Farrace-Di Zinno et al. (2001) and Lawrence et al. (2002) designed their studies for children with ADHD around an interactive adventure videogame (Crash Bandicoot™, 1996), which requires response inhibition, motor control involving visiospatial skills, and eye-hand coordination skills. The videogame requires the player to negotiate hazards along a jungle path while viewing the journey from the character's perspective. The game depends on the player's ability to move quickly under some circumstances and to refrain from responding when certain hazards are presented. Rolling wheels, killer skunks, snapping plants, and the risk of falling off cliffs are some of the challenges the player faces during the adventure. The player must apply the rules in order to get from the beginning of the path to the end. These tasks mirror real-life skills, but include fun and unrealistic components. Unlike earlier studies involving CPT and Pacman™, the researchers found children with ADHD were more similar to children without ADHD during the interactive adventure videogame. They at-

tributed the variability in results to the differences in the videogame presented to the children. The adventure videogame provided the player with immediate visual and auditory feedback and the responses were self-paced. Children could slow down or speed up the action depending on their individual needs. CPTs and games like Pacman™ are not so adaptable.

EVALUATING INSTRUCTIONAL GAMES AND SIMULATIONS

Instructional development has been the term most used to describe the activities of educators. With the increased need to integrate educational games into the instructional environment, educators are taking on more instructional design responsibilities. Design models help educators understand how to create and evaluate the quality of a game or simulation. Educators can use the design models to understand the needs of ADHD students as well as those of the game generation. One useful design is the FIDGE model (Akilli & Cagiltay, 2006).

FIDGE stands for "Fuzzified Instructional Design Development of Game-like Environments." Ironically, the word *fidge*, or in more current vernacular, *fidget*, means "to move restlessly" or "a condition of restlessness manifested by nervous movements" (American Heritage College Dictionary, 2000). The model was designed to address the eagerness and physical tension associated with the game player. The model is non-linear and includes consideration and evaluation of several components: (a) participants; (b) game-player experience; (c) socio-cultural environment; (d) dynamic elements of the game; (c) change; (e) management; (f) technology; and (g) use. An example of the application of the FIDGE model for educators would be the design of a computer game to teach a concept to elementary students using a simple PowerPoint application.

Figure 2.The eight components of evaluation for computer games or simulations. (Akilli & Cagiltay, 2006) recommend educators evaluate the needs of their learners and the presentation of the game to ensure there is a match before introducing the game to the players

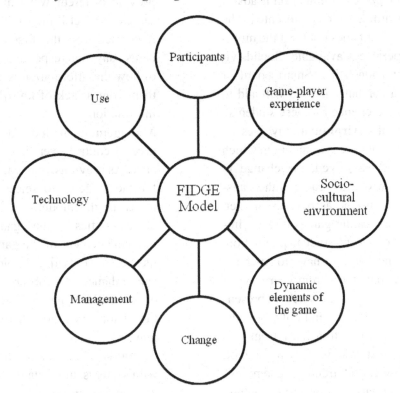

- **Participants** are the users of the game and the experts involved in the development and evaluation of it. The ADHD learner and peers who are members of the game generation are similar, but the added challenge of potential learning disabilities could create a unique set of challenges for educators in the presentation of curricula. One way educators can ensure the needs of the ADHD learner and other subpopulations of learners are included in the curricula is to develop focus groups. Educators may not understand the unique digital needs of the learners, but the learners know what appeals to them. By creating focus groups to help educators choose educational games or simulation material, educators may better understand the needs of the learners. In the example of creating a computer game for teaching the Bill of Rights, educators would first select a heterogeneous group of students from their classes to serve as the focus group. This group would discuss their needs in regards to the learning environment. Such discussions may include what the group identifies as interesting or boring. The responses may differ significantly for the ADHD learner group compared to the non-ADHD counterparts.

- **Game-player experience requires** the need to consider the differences in styles of learning and skill levels of players. Providing multi-sensory experiences can support a diverse group of learners. de Freitas (2004) found that games and simulations can significantly support differentiated learning.

When selecting game-like environments for learning, educators need to ensure the quality of the game or simulation is adaptable to all learning styles represented. The use of PowerPoint does not limit the multi-sensory experiences available. Sound, visual cues and touch if a Smart board or touch screen computer is used will add to the learning experience for these students.

- **Socio-cultural environment** involves an understanding of the environment in which the game will be played, the change in relevance from year to year, and the transfer of skills from one activity to another. Educators are creating games that are important to the current student population, but they do not want to have to re-create these instructional tools from year to year. When developing your PowerPoint presentation, you may need to find links, sounds, or graphics that can transition from one group to the next. It's probably not a good idea to choose current trends as examples.

- **Dynamic elements of the game** include challenge, fantasy, and creativity. Research indicates a similar abnormal brain pattern in creative individuals (Herrmann, 1981; Torrance, 1984) and individuals with ADHD (Hynd, Hern, Voeller & Marshall, 1991). In fact, Shaw (1992) found ADHD children use a magnitude of imagery in problem-solving similar to creative individuals. By including dynamic elements in the games, educators can stimulate not only the attentional needs, but also the creativity needs of the ADHD learner. Integrating video clips, puzzles, or competition into the presentation can enhance the learners' interest in it.

- **Change** refers to requirements for growth and the need for continuous evaluation components built into the game curriculum. As students demonstrate understanding of certain components, the game should provide more advanced curricula. Hyperlinks

within the slides can allow for previous responses to guide future ones. It could also provide different ways of addressing the same construct if the student fails to grasp it correctly on the first try. ADHD students may not respond correctly because of how the information is presented rather than from a lack of knowledge about the information.

- **Management** includes the player's degree of control over time, characters, and pace. As previously stated, the opportunity for the students to select their character increases the modeling effect. Given the characteristics of the "game generation," the management of the game is critical to its success. Providing choice in characters can enhance the observational learning opportunities (making the behaviors of the characters more identifiable with the players).

- **Technology** relates to the compatibility with systems and suitability within the educational environment. Due to budgetary issues, schools face difficulties remaining apace with the most current technological advances. For students to be able to access programs, the programs should be compatible with the technology utilized by the preponderance of schools.

- **Use** refers to the actual implementation of the game. One limitation of this model is a lack of research support for how individuals with challenges in self-regulation (i.e., attention, hyperactivity, or impulsivity) respond to games designed using this model.

Though the FIDGE model was developed for designers of computer games, educators can benefit from understanding its unique instructional design components. Since the thoughts of the game generation and the ADHD learners jump from idea to idea, they require flexibility in approaching their curricula in the same mode. The

FIDGE model can serve as a guide for educators as they prepare their digitally-based instructional materials.

CHOOSING INSTRUCTIONAL GAMES AND DEVELOPING LESSON PLANS FOR THE ADHD LEARNER

Gagné's "Nine Events of Instruction" theory of design development for instructional games (1985) is based on learning and instructional principles. The areas included in the theory are: (a) gaining attention (reception), (b) informing learners of the objective (expectancy), (c) stimulating recall of prior learning (retrieval), (d) presenting the stimulus (selective perception), (e) providing learning guidance (semantic encoding), (f) eliciting performance (responding), (g) providing feedback (reinforcement), (h) assessing performance (retrieval), and (i) enhancing retention and transfer (generalization). The FIDGE model addresses the components developed, whereas the "Nine Events of Instruction" assess how interesting and functional the program will be to its users.

The ADHD learner has difficulty maintaining attention, remaining still and focused, or both. These children can make impulsive decisions, and require additional attention from teachers, staff, and peers. When making choices about ways to present a concept, teachers are trained to consider the needs of the learners. Gagné's Nine Events of Instruction can support teachers' efforts to evaluate these needs when the presentation of material is technology-based. Specific to the ADHD learner, these nine events can target how material should be presented to engage and motivate the student, and assess the mastery of the information:

Event 1: Gain Attention

With any task, gaining the attention of the ADHD learner is critical to the success of the instructional medium. Since inattention is a major challenge for most individuals with ADHD, gaining their attention can be difficult. Gagné suggests adding color or sound to the material that highlights specific information and does not overshadow that which must be learned (Gagné, Briggs, & Wager, 1992). Shaw and Lewis (2005) found children with ADHD demonstrated more on-task behaviors when animated stimuli were presented rather than simple text. Computerized animation can provide a wealth of options for stimulating the attention of these learners.

Event 2: Inform Learners of the Objectives

This event addresses the need to provide a learning map of the material. Ogle (1986) developed the K-W-L instructional design to help learners identify what they already **K**now about the subject, what they **W**ant to learn about the subject, and what they actually **L**earn as they study the material. The development of a graphic organizer helps the learner chart this information. Computer-mediated instruction offers learners a playground where they can attach websites, pictures, sounds, video, and more to their knowledge base about the topic. Titles and topic headings can be presented using *Flash* technology so they stand out to the reader. Informing learners of the objectives can be more interactive, thereby stimulating the interest of individuals with ADHD.

Event 3: Stimulate Recall of Prerequisite Learning

Individuals with ADHD can have difficulty retaining information. According to Barkley (1997), deficits that would impair an individual with ADHD from retrieving previously learned material to solve new problems include those involved in executive functioning. Working memory, activation, arousal, and effort, and complex problem solving are critical to processing new information. Skowronek, Leichtman, and Pillemer (2008) found individuals with ADHD demonstrate strengths in long-term episodic memory. This means when they have to retrieve information based on personal experiences they perform better than average. Attaching meaning to information could enhance the learning for individuals with ADHD. Animated computer education games can allow users to choose a character that represents them. The events can be organized in such a way so they simulate real life experiences, thus improving the chance they will be retained. Zentall, Cassady, and Javorsky (2001) suggest using voice-overs to ask users to recount previous social situations relevant to the material to help improve problem-solving strategies. This strategy capitalizes on the use of sound to maintain attention and episodic memory to enhance retention and recall.

Event 4: Presenting the Content

The presentation of content should vary according to the learning style and age of the user. Learning should be focused on showing the learner how to organize the information in the correct sequence. According to Kataria, Hall, Wong, and Keys (1992), the use of rehearsal, mnemonics, imagery, and organizational strategies can improve retention. The developmental stage of the learner would influence the sophistication of the mnemonics and the detail involved in the imagery. Mayer (1987) suggests that younger children may require support to create the image since they have fewer experiences on which to draw.

Event 5: Providing Learning Guidance

Learning guidance can be provided for the ADHD learner through clearly labeled navigational tools, verbal instructions are repeated throughout the activity, and interactive help menus. The appealing nature of videogames is the technology-driven emphasis rather than staff-driven. More students receive one-on-one learning guidance without requiring more teachers or paraprofessionals to be present. ADHD learners respond to one-on-one instruction where the material introduces the use

of multiple senses, the breakdown of material into smaller pieces, provision of immediate feedback, and the limitation of unnecessary, distracting features (DuPaul & Weyandt, 2006). An example of learning guidance that meets these criteria is the use of interactive case studies where users must experience a scenario familiar to them, problem-solve responses to the scenario, and receive feedback as to their accuracy at the end of the presentation.

Event 6: Eliciting the Performance

Inattention can increase response time. The goal is to get a response to the material so the learner can practice the skill. Teachers may struggle with motivating ADHD learners to start tasks, let alone getting them to complete the tasks. However, we have learned when individuals with ADHD are interested in the material, they are more likely to elicit a response. Opportunities for active learning will increase the likelihood of a response.

Event 7: Providing Feedback

As stated previously, immediate feedback can improve the task performance of ADHD learners (DuPaul & Weyandt, 2006). Furthermore, Codding, Lewandowski, and Eckert (2005) found feedback increased performance when the students actually set their own performance goals. Videogames and other computer education games can allow users to set realistic goals and receive immediate feedback on their performance.

Event 8: Assessing Performance

Any lesson plan should include methods for assessing learning. For ADHD learners these methods should occur frequently and not only assess learning of material, but also assess on-task behavior. Computer education games are capable of tracking responses of the user and adjusting the presentation of material to accommodate the user's specific needs.

Event 9: Enhancing Retention and Transfer

When individuals can take what they have learned and apply it to new situations, learning has taken place. The skills learned during videogame play (planning, organization, problem-solving, adaptability, and processing speed) can easily transfer to other tasks. Since many ADHD learners have deficits in many of these prefrontal activities, it is encouraging that a medium of task presentation can generate skill growth in these areas. A bonus may be lowered levels of hyperactivity and impulsive responding, and increased on-task behavior.

By using Gagné's Nine Event of Instruction, educators can choose computer games that offer the best chance for success in teaching the material to the ADHD learner. They also guide educators in lesson plan development by dividing the lesson into measureable goals; i.e., from preparing the student for learning to generalizing the skills to new material.

FUTURE RESEARCH DIRECTIONS

Animated computer education games developed using the criteria discussed in the FIDGE model is essential. Data suggest a non-linear approach to developing "game-like environments" will suit the specific needs of the ADHD learner. However, the model has not been previously discussed in this context and no research exists to support its use. Instructional games are being developed commercially and by educators for use in their classrooms. Yet, there are no empirical studies that demonstrate whether the games meet the needs of the ADHD learner. Additionally, research to evaluate existing educational games to see if they meet Gagné's criteria for an appropriate instructional tool for ADHD learners is needed. Lesson plan development could also be evaluated to see if learning occurs when the Nine Events of Instruction are followed compared to traditional lesson plan development.

CONCLUSION

This chapter has provided a theoretical framework for understanding the ADHD learner and the importance of using instructional design models to guide educators through the development of appropriate animated computer education curricula for them. Computer gaming technology offers significant promise for the education of individuals with ADHD. The unique challenges of the learner and educators to create a fertile and stimulating environment that individualizes the learning needs of those with ADHD and limits the distractions for non-ADHD students can be daunting. Animated, dynamic elements of computer education games are ripe for meeting those demands. Educators willing to improve their technological skill-sets and integrate computer games into the instructional environment in a purposeful way offer the best chance for the ADHD learner to succeed.

REFERENCES

Akilli, G. K., & Cagiltay, K. (2006). An instructional design/development model for game-like learning environments: The FIDGE model. In M. Pivec (Ed.), Affective and emotional aspects of human-computer interaction game-based and innovative learning approaches (Vol. 1, pp. 93-112). Amsterdam, The Netherlands: IOS Press.

American Heritage College Dictionary (3rd ed.). (2000). Boston: Houghton Mifflin.

Bandura, A., & Barab, P. G. (1971)... *Developmental Psychology, 5,* 244–255. doi:10.1037/h0031499

Barkley, R. A. (1997). Behavioral inhibition, sustained attention, and executive functions: constructing a unifying theory of ADHD. *Psychological Bulletin, 121,* 65–94. doi:10.1037/0033-2909.121.1.65

Barkley, R. A. (2006). Attention-deficit hyperactivity disorder (3rd. ed.): A handbook of diagnosis and treatment. New York: The Guilford Press.

Barkley, R. A., Copeland, A. P., & Sivage, C. (1980). A self-control classroom for hyperactive children. *Journal of Autism and Developmental Disabilities*, *10*, 75–89. doi:10.1007/BF02408435

Barkley, R. A., Fischer, M., Smallish, L., & Fletcher, K. (2006). Young adult outcome of hyperactive children: Adaptive functioning in major life activities. *Journal of the American Academy of Child and Adolescent Psychiatry*, *45*, 192–202. doi:10.1097/01.chi.0000189134.97436.e2

Barkley, R. A., Grodzinsky, G., & DuPaul, G. J. (1992). Frontal-lobe functions in attention-deficit disorder with and without hyperactivity: A review and research report. *Journal of Abnormal Child Psychology*, *20*, 163–188. doi:10.1007/BF00916547

Bioulac, S., Arfi, L., & Bouvard, M. (2008). Attention deficit/hyperactivity disorder and video games: A comparative study of hyperactive and control children. *European Psychiatry*, *23*, 134–141.

Capano, L., Minden, D., Chen, S., Schachar, R. J., & Ickowicz, A. (2008). Mathematical learning disorder in school-age children with Attention-Deficit Hyperactivity Disorder. *Canadian Journal of Psychiatry*, *53*, 392–399.

Carroll, A., & Bain, A. (1994). The effects of interactive versus linear video on the levels of attention and comprehension. *School Psychology Review*, *23*, 29.

Center for Disease Control and Prevention. (2005, September 2). Mental health in the United States: Prevalence of diagnosis and medication treatment for attention-deficit/hyperactivity disorder --- United States, 2003. *Morbidity and Mortality Weekly Report*, *54*, 842–847.

Chan, P., & Rabinowitz, T. (2006). A cross-sectional analysis of video games and attention deficit hyperactivity disorder symptoms in adolescents. *Annals of General Psychiatry*, *5*, 5–16. doi:10.1186/1744-859X-5-16

Clarfield, J., & Stoner, G. (2005). The effects of computerized reading instruction on the academic performance of students identified with ADHD. *School Psychology Review*, *34*, 246–254.

Clark, C., Prior, M., & Kinsella, G. (2002). The relationship between executive function abilities, adaptive behavior, and academic achievement in children with externalizing behavior problems. *Journal of Child Psychology and Psychiatry, and Allied Disciplines*, *43*, 785–796. doi:10.1111/1469-7610.00084

Codding, R. S., Lewandowski, L., & Eckert, T. (2005). Examining the efficacy of performance feedback and goal-setting interventions in children with *ADHD*: A comparison of two methods of goal setting. *Journal of Evidence-Based Practices for Schools*, *6*, 42–58.

de Freitas, S., & Levene, M. (2004). *An investigation of the use of simulations and video gaming for supporting exploratory learning and developing higher-order cognitive skills*. IADIS International Conference in Cognition and Exploratory Learning in the Digital Age, 15-17 December. Lisbon, Portugal.

DuPaul, G., & Weyandt, L. (2006). School-based interventions for children and adolescents with attention-deficit/hyperactivity disorder: enhancing academic and behavioral outcomes. *Education & Treatment of Children*, *29*, 341–358.

DuPaul, G. J., Rutherford, L. E., & Hosterman, S. J. (2008). Attention-deficit/hyperactivity disorder. In Morris, R.J., & Mather, N. (Eds.), Evidence-based interventions for students with learning and behavioral challenges (pp. 42). New York: Routledge.

DuPaul, G. J., & Stoner, G. (2003). ADHD in the schools: Assessment and intervention strategies (2nd ed.). New York: Guilford.

Epstein, J., Casey, B. J., Toney, S. T., Davidson, M. C., Reiss, A. L., & Garrett, A. (2007). ADHD and medication-related brain activation effects in concordantly affected parent-child dyads with ADHD. *Journal of Child Psychology and Psychiatry, and Allied Disciplines, 48,* 899–913. doi:10.1111/j.1469-7610.2007.01761.x

Faraone, S. V., Biederman, J., Monuteaux, M. C., & Seidman, L. J. (2001). A psychometric measure of learning disability predicts educational failure four years later in boys with attention deficit hyperactivity disorder. *Journal of Attention Disorders, 4,* 220–230. doi:10.1177/108705470100400404

Farrace-Di Zinno, A., Douglas, G., Houghton, S., Lawrence, V., West, J., & Whiting, K. (2001). Body movements of boys with attention deficit hyperactivity disorder (ADHD) during computer video game play. *British Journal of Educational Technology, 32,* 607–618. doi:10.1111/1467-8535.00229

Ferguson, C. J. (2007). The good, the bad, and the ugly: A meta-analytic review of positive and negative effects of violent video games. *The Psychiatric Quarterly, 78,* 309–316. doi:10.1007/s11126-007-9056-9

Ferguson, C. J., Rueda, S. M., Cruz, A. M., Ferguson, D. E., Fritz, S., & Smith, S. M. (2008). Violent video games and aggression: Causal relationship or byproduct of family violence and intrinsic violence motivation? *Criminal Justice and Behavior, 35,* 311–332. doi:10.1177/0093854807311719

Fister, S. (1999). CBT fun and games. *Training Magazine, 36*(5), 68–70.

Frazier, T., Youngstrom, E., Glutting, J., & Watkins, M. (2007). ADHD and achievement: Meta-analysis of the child, adolescent, and adult literatures and a concomitant study with college students. *Journal of Learning Disabilities, 40,* 49–65. doi:10.1177/00222194070400010401

Froehlich, T. E., Lanphear, B. P., Epstein, J. N., Barbaresi, W. J., Katusic, S. K., & Kahn, R. S. (2007). Prevalence, recognition, and treatment of attention-deficit/hyperactivity disorder in a national sample of U.S. children. *Archives of Pediatrics & Adolescent Medicine, 161,* 857–864. doi:10.1001/archpedi.161.9.857

Gagné, R. M. (1985). The conditions of learning and theory of instruction (4th ed.). New York: Holt, Rinehart and Winston.

Gagné, R. M. Briggs. L., & Wager, W. (1992). Principles of instructional design. Fort Worth, TX: Harcourt Brace Jovanovich.

Garris, R., Ahlers, R., & Driskell, J. E. (2002). Games, motivation, and learning: A research and practice model. *Simulation & Gaming, 33,* 441–467. doi:10.1177/1046878102238607

Gee, J. P. (2003). What video games have to teach us about learning and literacy. New York: Palgrave Macmillan.

Gentile, D. A., & Anderson, C. A. (2003). Violent video games: The newest media violence hazard. In D.A. Gentile (Ed.), Media violence and children. Westport, CT: Praeger Publishing.

Gentile, D. A., Lynch, P., Linder, J., & Walsh, D. (2004). The effects of violent video game habits on adolescent hostility, aggressive behaviors, and school performance. *Journal of Adolescence, 27,* 5–22. doi:10.1016/j.adolescence.2003.10.002

Gredler, M. E. (1996). Educational games and simulations: A technology in search of a (research) paradigm. In D.H. Jonassen (Ed.), Handbook of research for educational communications and technology (pp. 521-539). New York: Macmillan.

Hays, R. T. (2005). The effectiveness of instructional games: A literature review and discussion. Technical Report for the Naval Air Center Training Systems Division: Orlando, FL.

Herrmann, N. (1981). The creative brain. *Training and Development Journal, 35*(10), 10–16.

Hynd, G. W., Hern, K. L., Voeller, K. K., & Marshall, R. M. (1991). Neurobiological basis of Attention-Deficit Hyperactivity Disorder (ADHD). *School Psychology Review*, *20*, 174–186.

Kataria, S., Hall, C. W., Wong, M. M., & Keys, G. F. (1992). Learning styles of LD and NLD ADHD children. *Journal of Clinical Psychology*, *48*, 371–378. doi:10.1002/1097-4679(199205)48:3<371::AID-JCLP2270480316>3.0.CO;2-F

Klingberg, T., Fernell, E., Olesen, P., Johnson, M., Gustafsson, P., & Dahlström, K. (2005). Computerized training of working memory in children with ADHD- A randomized, controlled trial. *Journal of the American Academy of Child and Adolescent Psychiatry*, *44*, 177–186. doi:10.1097/00004583-200502000-00010

Konrad, K., Neufang, S., Hanisch, C., Fink, G. R., & Herpertz-Dahlmann, B. (2006). Dysfunctional attentional networks in children with attention deficit/hyperactivity disorder: Evidence from an event-related functional magnetic resonance imaging study. *Biological Psychiatry*, *59*, 643–651. doi:10.1016/j.biopsych.2005.08.013

Lawrence, V., Houghton, S., Tannock, R., Douglas, G., Durkin, K., & Whiting, K. (2002). ADHD outside the laboratory: boys" executive function performance on tasks in videogame play and on a visit to the zoo. *Journal of Abnormal Child Psychology*, *30*, 447–462. doi:10.1023/A:1019812829706

Maedgen, J., & Carlson, C. (2000). Social functioning and emotional regulation in attention deficit hyperactivity disorder subtypes. *Journal of Clinical Child Psychology*, *29*, 30–42. doi:10.1207/S15374424jccp2901_4

Marcus, S., Wan, G., Kemner, J., & Olfson, M. (2005). Continuity of methylphenidate treatment for attention-deficit/hyperactivity disorder. *Archives of Pediatrics & Adolescent Medicine*, *159*, 572–578. doi:10.1001/archpedi.159.6.572

Mautone, J. A., DuPaul, G. J., & Jitendra, A. K. (2005). The effects of computer-assisted instruction on the mathematics performance and classroom behavior of children with ADHD. *Journal of Attention Disorders*, *9*, 301–312. doi:10.1177/1087054705278832

Mayer, R. (1987). Educational psychology: A cognitive approach. Boston: Little, Brown.

Ogle, D. (1986, February). K-W-L: A teaching model that develops active reading of expository text. *The Reading Teacher*, *39*, 564–570. doi:10.1598/RT.39.6.11

Okagaki, L., & Frensch, P. A. (1994). Effects of video game playing on measures of spatial performance: Gender effects in late adolescence. *Journal of Applied Developmental Psychology*, *15*, 33–58. doi:10.1016/0193-3973(94)90005-1

Ota, K. R., & DuPaul, G. J. (2002). Task engagement and mathematics performance in children with attention-deficit hyperactivity disorder: Effects of supplemental computer instruction. *School Psychology Quarterly*, *17*, 242–257. doi:10.1521/scpq.17.3.242.20881

Porter, G., & Starcevic, V. (2007). Are violent video games harmful? *Australasian Psychiatry*, *15*, 422–426. doi:10.1080/10398560701463343

Prensky, M. (2001a). "Simulations": Are they games? In Digital game-based learning (pp. 210-220). New York: McGraw-Hill.

Prensky, M. (2001b). Digital natives, digital immigrants. *Horizon*, *9*(5), 1–6. doi:10.1108/10748120110424816

Prensky, M. (2001c). Digital natives, digital immigrants, Part II: Do they really think differently? *Horizon*, *9*(6), 1–8. doi:10.1108/10748120110424843

Price, R. V. (1990). Computer-aided instruction: A guide for authors. Pacific Grove, CA: Brooks/Cole Publishing Company.

Rideout, V., Roberts, D.F., & Foehr, U.G. (March, 2005). *Media in the lives of 8-18 year olds*. A Kaiser Family Foundation Study.

Schmidt, L., & Hawkins, P. (July 15, 2008). Children of the tech revolution. *Sydney Morning Herald*. Retrieved July 25, 2009 from http://www.smh.com.au/news/parenting/children-of-the-tech-revolution/2008/07/15/1215887601694.html

Shalev, L., Tsal, Y., & Mevorach, C. (2007). Computerized progressive attentional training (CPAT) program: Effective direct intervention for children with ADHD. *Child Neuropsychology, 13*, 382–388. doi:10.1080/09297040600770787

Shaw, G. A. (1992). Hyperactivity and creativity: The tacit dimension. *Bulletin of the Psychonomic Society, 30*, 152–160.

Shaw, R., Grayson, A., & Lewis, V. (2005). Inhibition, ADHD, and computer games: The inhibitory performance of children with ADHD on computerized tasks and games. *Journal of Attention Disorders, 8*, 160–168. doi:10.1177/1087054705278771

Shaw, R., & Lewis, V. (2005). The impact of computer-mediated and traditional academic task presentation on the performance and behaviour of children with ADHD. *Journal of Research in Special Educational Needs, 5*, 47–54. doi:10.1111/J.1471-3802.2005.00041.x

Skowronek, J. S., Leichtman, M. D., & Pillemer, D. B. (2008). Long-term episodic memory in children with Attention-Deficit/Hyperactivity Disorder. *Learning Disabilities Research & Practice, 23*, 25–35. doi:10.1111/j.1540-5826.2007.00260.x

Smith, B. H., Barkley, R. A., & Shapiro, C. J. (2007). Attention-deficit/hyperactivity disorder. In E.J. Mash, & R.A. Barkley, (Eds.), Assessment of childhood disorders, (4th ed.), (pp. 100-101). New York: Guilford Press.

Spencer, T.J., Biederman, J., & Mick, E. (2007). Attention-deficit/hyperactivity disorder: diagnosis, lifespan, comorbidities, and neurobiology. *Journal of Pediatric Psychology, 6, Special issue: Attention-deficit/hyperactivity disorder*, 631-642.

Tannock, R. (1997). Television, videogames, and ADHD: Challenging a popular belief. *The ADHD Report, 5*, 3–7.

Tessmer, M., Jonassen, D. H., & Caverly, D. (1989). Non-programmer's guide to designing instruction for microcomputers. Littleton, CO: Libraries Unlimited.

Torrance, P. E. (1984). The role of creativity in identification of the gifted and talented. *Gifted Child Quarterly, 28*, 153–156. doi:10.1177/001698628402800403

Ustun, T. B. (2007). Using the international classification of functioning, disease and health in attention-deficit/hyperactivity disorder: Separating the disease from its epiphenomena. *Ambulatory Pediatrics, 7*(1S), 132–139. doi:10.1016/j.ambp.2006.05.004

Van Cleave, J., & Leslie, L. K. (2008). Approaching *ADHD* as a chronic condition: Implications for long-term adherence. *Psychiatric Annals, 38*, 35–42. doi:10.3928/00485713-20080101-05

Zentall, S. S., Cassady, J. C., & Javorsky, J. (2001). Social comprehension of children with hyperactivity. *Journal of Attention Disorders, 5*, 11–24. doi:10.1177/108705470100500102

Chapter 17
Adult Learning and Virtual Worlds Simulations

Michele D. Estes
James Madison University, USA

Randell Snow
James Madison University, USA

ABSTRACT

This chapter will explore conditions for meaningful adult learning and explain how virtual environments and in-world simulations enable or discourage the development of intellectual skills in adults. Adult learners possess particular characteristics that should influence instructional designs. Issues that affect learning in the real-world are also found in the virtual world. Particular problems of cognitive and cultural dissonance in the virtual environment, finding and creating meaningful simulations, and protecting the fidelity of authentic simulations in a public space are discussed. Recommendations and future research directions are provided.

ADULT LEARNING AND VIRTUAL WORLDS SIMULATIONS

This chapter will explore conditions for adult learning and explain how virtual environments and in-world simulations enable or discourage meaningful adult learning. To describe adult learning we will consider what is known about the learner, learning process, meaningful contexts for learning, and concepts important to adult educators (Kiely, Sandmann, & Truluck, 2004). We will situate adult learning in the context of the Second Life virtual

world and in-world simulations that respond to the underlying theories, practices, and issues of contemporary adult learning.

BACKGROUND

Adult Learning

Kiely, Sandmann, and Truluck (2004) describe the theoretical and practical facets of adult learning as a "vast territory" (p. 19) deserving of a conceptual framework that is both useful and holistic. Adding to an earlier framework proposed by Merriam and

DOI: 10.4018/978-1-61520-781-7.ch017

Cafarrella (1999), the authors offer a four-lens approach for understanding the theory and practice of adult learning that considers process, learner, educator and context.

Learning is a lifelong process. It is not limited to childhood, for "if no biological mechanism operates to set the limits of development, then it should go on throughout life" (Driscoll, p. 213). The process of adult learning is interactive, reflective, dialogical, experiential, and even transformational (Kiely, Sandmann, and Truluck, 2004). It does not contradict stages of learning that occur earlier in life (Brookfield, 1995) although adult learners do have unique traits that should be considered when designing virtual learning experiences.

Malcolm Knowles (1970) differentiated pedagogy, "the art and science of teaching children," (p. 40) from andragogy, "the art and science of helping adults learn" (p. 43). Andragogy is grounded in the belief that adult learners tend to be independent and self-directed. With years of experience adult learners possess expertise and a wealth of knowledge that should be recognized respectfully, and used as a basis for constructing new knowledge. He described adult learners as having a sense of immediacy for practical knowledge as one might have in the workplace, and an instrinsic motivation for knowledge that supports adult social roles (Knowles, 1980; Knowles, et. al, 1984; Merriam and Cafarella, 1999).

Throughout the twentieth century technology has played a key role in allowing adults access to college course work and degree programs at home and in the workplace. The demands for distance learning, and the options for delivery, are growing. Busy adults are well suited for learning through innovative delivery technologies given the intrinsic motivation and just-in-time learning needs we experience. Modern technologies like virtual worlds and in-world simulations extend our capabilities as learners and educators because they offer immersive experiences, transform reality, and enable self-directed and social learning.

Meaningful learning can be addressed with innovative technologies given thoughtful instructional design. For instance, an instructor in Second Life chose to allow students to self-assess. Students typed chat responses to questions while sitting on mushrooms, and received instant feedback as their mushroom raised or lowered in height for correct or incorrect responses. The assessment was motivating, engaging and self-explanatory given the physical experience of movement in-world. Virtual world simulations are well-suited for experiential and transformational learning theories. Issues of learner preference, personal philosophy, power, and diversity will continue to contextualize the adult learning experience (Kiely, Sandmann, and Truluck, 2004) and the approach and response by educators will be important.

Virtual Worlds Simulations

Second Life, a virtual environment designed for adults and popularized by the general public since its inception in 2003 (Rosedale, 2007), currently maintains a strong user-base with nearly one million residents logging in during the thirty days prior to the writing of this chapter (economic statistics available at http://secondlife.com/statistics/economy-data.php). It was not designed specifically for educational purposes and it is unclear how many educators are using the virtual environment for the purpose of teaching and learning (Kelton, 2008). The significant presence of educators in-world is evident (Harris, Lowendahl, and Zastrocky, 2007) though, with hundreds of institutions represented in searches, educational listservs (ex. Second Life for Educators or SLED and Second Life for Resarchers or SLRL), at least one educational social network heavily populated by Second Life members (ie. ReZEd in Ning), and journals like the Journal of Virtual Worlds Research where educational applications of Second Life are often mentioned.

Within the Second Life virtual world are simulations that resemble real and imagined scenarios constructed by its members. According to Clark and Mayer (2007) simulations may be operational or conceptual. Operational simulations exhibit high fidelity to the actual task scenario and are designed for near transfer of skills. The College of North West London, for instance, built a heating, air conditioning and ventilating (HVAC) operational simulation in Second Life where learners control the parameters of a central heating system (such as water flow, power to the boiler, and time delay) to generate various outcomes. The controls appear when the user attaches a heads-up display, or HUD, to their avatar. The heads-up display is a feature that helps orient the avatar and enables specific interactivity. The HVAC system simulation supports critical skills practice in a safe environment. The HUD facilitates interactivity that enables a meaningful learning experience for the adult learner who is self-directed and problem-centered. Gredler (2003) uses the phrase *symbolic simulations* to group laboratory-research simulations and systems simulations in which the learner manipulates the events as an external force but is not inherently a part of the system itself, as in this HVAC example.

Conceptual simulations call for the learner to apply principles that underlie ill-defined problems. In other words, they prompt interaction and guide the learner to respond to scenarios that vary with circumstance. For adult learners, conceptual simulations may relate to the workplace. Examples include but are not limited to providing client support, solving financial problems, teaching students in the classroom, and diagnosing and responding to patient problems. In the conceptual simulation, the learner is «one of the functional components» (Gredler, 2003, p. 573) of the experience. At Imperial College London Postgraduate Medical School in Second Life, the Infusion Device Training Simulator is an example of a conceptual simulation that involves diagnosis. At the onset of the simulation, a note card is given to the learner with prerequisite expectations and a brief description of what is to come. The avatar

acquires the skin of a male or female nurse, enters the changing room and changes clothing, scrubs hands, enters the ward and alerts the departing nurse of their arrival. Finally, the learner begins a training simulation that allows full control over a problem-solving scenario involving an ailing patient. Survival of the patient is dependent upon the learner. Immediate feedback is provided as in an authentic context, particularly through hospital equipment readings. At the end of the experience, a performance summary is given to the learner. By touching a phone on the wall, the learner may choose to send a summary of their performance to a researcher at the sponsoring institution. Conceptual simulations are designed to facilitate far transfer through discovery learning and problem solving (Clark and Mayer, 2007). They are ideal for practice with systems that are too costly or too dangerous for initial hands-on practice. They are experiential and situated in a "complex evolving scenario" (Gredler, 2003, p. 574).

ISSUES, CONTROVERSIES, PROBLEMS

Although most learning organizations are exploring virtual worlds in practice or research (The Horizon Report, 2008, p. 8), the potential of virtual worlds for adult learning remains largely unrealized. Adults are far less likely to visit virtual worlds than teens (Lenhart, 2008) despite the popularity of public virtual environments like Second Life. The dissonance between what is known and what is the innovation is still something to be reckoned with (Rogers, 2003); and there are challenges for adults who seek meaningful learning experiences through in-world simulations.

Cognitive and Cultural Dissonance

Whitney (2006) found that senior executives may be particularly resistant to virtual training simulations, questioning the tool, its effectiveness, and its application before ever entering the virtual environment. Individuals seek to resolve feelings of dissonance, or inconsistencies in prior knowledge and innovative ideas, by moving through stages of decision-making. If there are no perceived personal or professional advantages of an innovation; if it seems incompatible or too complex; if it is not easily observed or cannot be tried in a low-stakes environment initially, then adoption is not likely. Perceptions of these characteristics are good indicators of adoption decisions (Rogers, 2003). Unfortunately, the media has sensationalized some aspects of public virtual worlds that cause potential members to reject the technology without ever trying it out (Kelton, 2008). For example, de Freitas (2009) reported that many adults were introduced to the existence of virtual worlds through a well-publicized divorce resulting from a virtual affair. In my own graduate teaching, students have presented that argument to abdicate the use of Second Life for course work. Adult learners have deeply-rooted beliefs and attitudes that contextualize the learning experience. Educators must recognize the opportunity created by cognitive dissonance, and work to overcome rejection of innovations that may in fact lead to meaningful learning experiences.

The norms and strategies of avatars in the social, virtual environment may instill a sense of dissonance in newcomers to Second Life. For this reason, new account subscribers may opt to join an in-world community of people who speak the same language and share common interests. As avatars move beyond their homogenous community there are in-world tools to assist with language barriers. One tool, for example, the X-Lang HUD, translates an avatars chat messages into a variety of languages and allows the avatar to interpret other languages spoken via chat. The HUD may be purchased in-world, from the Codeee Nishi Store.

Fromme (2003) describes modern day as a new media culture that is driven largely by children who grew up with it; and who therefore possess informal computing experiences that exceed that of their teachers. This generational tension presents inconsistencies in the educational values, attitudes, conceptual understandings, and actions of children and adults. The new media culture brings with it at least two problems relevant to this chapter. One is the incorrect association of innovations with concepts with which adults are already familiar. Adults who lack a good conceptual understanding of virtual worlds, for instance, often confuse them with games (Kelton, 2008). Unlike games, there are no specific rules about functioning in the virtual world of Second Life. The virtual context is built by its members with no particular strategy or competition involved. Preconceived notions about games may deter adults who do not value play, particularly in relation to education (Rieber, 1996). A second problem is improper recognition of innovation value. The educational value of simulations, for example, may not be readily apparent to teachers even though the technology enables complex concepts to be taught at early ages (Gagne, et. al., 2005; Rieber, 2004). Children and adult learners are not likely to adopt virtual worlds for the same reasons. When making an innovation-decision, adults are likely to draw on their own life experiences and perceptions.

Finding and Creating Meaningful Simulations

For what reasons might virtual worlds be perceived as advantageous for adult learning? Gagne, Wager, Golas, and Keller (2005) discuss principles of instructional design in relation to five learned capabilities that are: intellectual skills, cognitive strategies, verbal information, attitudes, and motor skills. The Second Life virtual world is most inherently supportive of intellectual skills development. The three-dimensional environment supports the understanding of complex concepts and problem solving strategies that enable near and far transfer of skills to the adult workplace. For example, underlying rules and principles of the HVAC and Infusion Device Training simulations described earlier can be tested under a variety of conditions with little risk. An overview of the Second Life U. S. Navy's Undersea Warfare Center can be found at http://rezedhub.ning.com/video/us-navys-undersea-warfare. The solution sensitivity analysis portion of the high fidelity simulation is a good example of how the virtual world and advanced scripting allow for the visual demonstration of learned intellectual skills.

Although Second Life technology affords development and demonstration of intellectual skills, "…what you do with it [Second Life] is up to you" (Rymaszewski, et. al., 2007). Philip Rosedale is the Linden Lab Founder and CEO. His company created Second Life, and the vision was for a co-constructed, rapidly-changing and dynamic world that resembles the fantasies and realities of first life. The evolving technology and co-constructed nature of in-world experiences presents at least two significant problems for educators. Meaningful in-world simulations are difficult to find and a challenge to create.

In-world searches may be conducted from the Edit menu in Second Life. The user can limit the search to Places for example, and then by a category such as Education. To visit the HVAC simulation you could conduct this type of restricted search, using "College of North West London" as your search term. Of the parcels listed as hits, you would teleport to the one that is described as having "Plumbing Gas H & V student courses." The search process is still a bit involved, given the technology and the variety of search terms that may be entered into the system by members who are developers. Should you teleport to the island of interest in this case, your avatar must navigate up (by flying), right, and around a bulletin board to find the simulation. It shares a platform in the sky with a drum set. It is likely the developers of this simulation were not concerned with making it easily accessible. In fact, many educational simulations are embedded in a discreet location within the island or parcel of interest. Fortunately,

there are some techniques developers can use to make simulations more evident.

A search for "Imperial College of London" yields no results. By removing "of" or searching only for one word in the phrase, I am able to locate the Imperial College London Postgraduate Medical School in Second Life. Although the location of the Infusion Device Training Simulator is not immediately clear after teleporting to the island, there are helpful cues. First a note card is automatically offered to my visiting avatar. The note card gives instruction for participating in digital tours and using a teleporter to transport my avatar to key locations that I select.

Careful entry of search data and some knowledge of what you seek are important. A search by simulation name is not possible. Instead, you must know the name submitted for the parcel on which the simulation exists. There are two ways to rediscover quality simulations in Second Life. Once you find a location of interest, choose "create landmark here" from the World menu. Landmarks are stored in your inventory for retrieval later. The landmark allows the avatar to teleport directly to the parcel of interest without first conducting a search. To make an in-world location accessible from the Internet you can create a SLURL, or in-world link. The SLURL address is composed of the text "http://slurl.com/secondlife/islandname/coordinates" followed by the x, y, and z coordinates of the island location. The SLURL for the International Society for Technology in Education (ISTE) is as follows: http://slurl.com/secondlife/ISTE Island/86/58/30. By clicking on a SLURL, the user can log into the Second Life client software application to go directly to the intended destination.

Simulations may reside anywhere on land, in the sky, or beneath the ocean. The co-constructed virtual environment warrants flexible search tools. Shortcuts like teleporters, landmarks and SLURLs are invaluable for the busy self-directed learner, and for the adult educator who seeks to reduce complexity and increase trialability (Rogers, 2003) of the innovation.

There is a second reason why quality simulations are difficult to locate. Effective simulations are a challenge to create (Rieber, 1996). In Second Life, developers must own land or have building rights. Building tools are accessible from the View menu in Second Life. As a novice developer, one can construct and position textured three dimensional objects. Expert developers can use the proprietary Linden Scripting Language (LSL) to animate objects, construct heads up displays (HUDs) that enhance sensory and interactive experiences, and integrate multimedia. Expert developers who are, or who collaborate with, subject matter experts and instructional designers have the tools available in Second Life to create high fidelity simulated experiences.

Protecting the Fidelity of Simulations

Collaboration is an effective use of simulation and virtual reality (Gagne et. al., 2005). In businesses, virtual teams are formed to solve problems at a distance through the use of technology (Davis and Bryant, 2003; Junemann and Lloyd, 2003; Lipnack and Stamps, 1999). The term *social capital* refers to the cooperative and mutually beneficial relationship among team members who are interdependent and who possess shared values and trust. If the process is positive, employees will be motivated to collaborate in the future (Lipnack and Stamps, 1999). In postsecondary education, adult education often mimics real-life experience in order to address the sense of immediacy for practical information that supports our social roles. In the workplace and in the classroom there is an expectation that adult learning will involve professionalism and respect.

Although the tools for developing realistic simulations in public virtual worlds do exist, the fidelity of the experience can be compromised by members outside of the organization unless security measures (such as making the experience off-limits) are imposed. In a study at San Jose State, a faculty member found that 73% of the fourteen students enrolled in an immersive environments college course in Second Life reported that they had encountered avatars unaffiliated with the institution whose disruptions made the virtual class "less enjoyable" (Haycock and Kemp, 2008, p. 93).

Griefers are people who attack, harass, or intentionally disrupt the activities and normalcy of others in Second Life (Diehl and Prins, 2008; Gaimster, 2008; Prentice, 2008; Haycock and Kemp, 2008). Research on real-world personal space, the effect of time on non-verbal communications, the stimulation of sensory perceptions, kinesics, vocalics, physical appearance, and the use of real-world artifacts is related to in-world avatar behaviors (Gibbons, 2009). In-world attacks take many forms, including but not limited to surrounding others with particles and/or offensive artifacts. An overwhelming number of particles can overload another's graphics system to slow or stop their computer. Another technique is to animate or freeze other avatars.

Victims of in-world offenses should right click on the griefer, select *abuse report* and follow instructions. Copy any communications with the offender to a note card, take a snapshot, and send with the report. Offenders can also be ejected and/or banned from a parcel by the land owner. Gibbons (2009) proposes that the nexus of human and avatar is real and that the human should be held accountable for real-world psychological and other damages.

SUMMARY

Learning is a lifelong and multi-faceted process that is supported by a variety of delivery technologies. Innovative technologies like virtual worlds simulations may or may not be readily embraced even if the affordances create conditions favorable for meaningful adult learning. By recognizing the value of in-world simulations for adult learning, educators can proactively address an inevitable dissonance experienced by students new to virtual worlds like Second Life.

The Second Life virtual world is best suited for fostering intellectual skills development. Complex concepts and problem solving strategies are two examples of intellectual skills that can be directly transferred into the adult workplace. Locating high quality simulations in Second Life is a challenge because the in-world search process is involved and does not always yield useful results. The number of high quality simulations for education is limited because of the technical expertise required for scripting. Even with the proper content knowledge, and technical and design skills, the fidelity of real-world simulations is at risk. Griefing counteracts the mutually respectful context of adult learning and encourages the "closing off" of educational simulations to the general public.

SOLUTIONS AND RECOMMENDATIONS

Virtual world simulations are well-suited for encouraging strategic thinking, and this cognitive skill is expected of learners who use modern technologies (Gagne et. al., 2005). Adult educators should move learners from understanding *what* (conceptual expertise), to understanding *why*, in an effort to develop theoretical expertise (Driscoll, 2005). Incorporating a virtual world like Second Life into adult education may increase opportunities for meaningful learning.

Adult educators may resolve cognitive and cultural dissonance by becoming skilled in the operation of virtual worlds simulations and generating an awareness of its application to real-world scenarios that influence the thinking and motivation of adult learners. In the context of Second Life where there is no inherent mission or goal, learners should be encouraged to take advantage of communications tools and specific strategies and simulations.

Locating meaningful, educational simulations can be a challenge. Using short-cuts like landmarks and SLURLs can help organize the experience for students. By developing an expertise in Linden Scripting Language educators can create original simulations that stimulate intellectual skills development. If technical expertise is not possible, novice developers should take advantage of in-world freebies and customizable scripts. Unfortunately, the challenges of searching for, developing, and organizing useful in-world experiences for adult learning may present significant problems in sustaining use of the innovation.

Disruptions to the learning context will negatively influence the fidelity of in-world simulations. To avoid griefing, instructors may make particular parcels off-limits to the general public. Another solution is to post signs and distribute note cards to visitors with behavior policies. When establishing a virtual space, the owner may also specify whether or not mature content is allowable. This information serves as a query limiter in searches for in-world places, and may be a deterrent for griefers.

Kelton (2008) described the value of virtual worlds using the analogy of a lawnmower. The lawnmower may prove useful for homeowners and at the same time useless to those who rent an apartment. How valuable are virtual worlds simulations for adult learning? The answer lies within the self-directed adult learner who, if new to virtual worlds, will move through an innovation-decision process that may or may not result in its adoption. Adult learning is an "emotional, social, physical, cognitive, and spiritual kaleidoscope" (MacKeracher, 1996, p. 3) that should be nurtured by an educator who is informed of the functions of the innovation that encourage and discourage meaningful learning.

FUTURE RESEARCH DIRECTIONS

Even though adults are far less likely to visit virtual worlds than teens (Lenhart, 2008), the affordances of virtual worlds do support meaningful adult learning. One widely perceived characteristic of adult learners is that learners are self-directed, seeking out learning experiences for their own betterment. To make use of this trait, adult educators create learner-centered designs in which the role of the instructor is that of a facilitator. Hiemstra (2006) has suggested that the exploratory nature of modern technologies will make self-directed learning the default learning strategy in the near future. The tenets of self-directed learning should be studied in the context of virtual worlds. Does the nature of Second Life, for example, promote meaningful self-directed learning or simply give the learner more control? By what means do we measure the effectiveness of self-directed learning in open, virtual environments? What are the roles of instructor and avatar in the virtual environment?

In a study conducted by researchers at the University of Texas, the affordances of the Second Life virtual world were found to support experiential learning processes in a graduate interdisciplinary communications course (Jarmon, Traphagana, Mayratha, and Trivedia, 2009). Without real-world constraints learners were able to construct an alternate reality through collaborative, project based activities that stimulated active learning and engagement. More research is needed to document the process of successful, sustained collaboration in public environments like Second Life. Additionally, studies of project based learning could result in useful data about how learners who are novice developers demonstrate intellectual skills mastery in the virtual world.

Multisensory experiences enhance learning (Chittaro and Ranon, 2007). Andreano, et. al. (2009) tested the effects of auditory cues on brain function in a virtual reality experience and found that a combination of visual and auditory stimuli, as opposed to just auditory cues, triggered "higher cognitive processes" (p. 312). How can instructional designs take advantage of multisensory experiences in virtual worlds to foster intellectual skills relevant to the workplace? Perhaps with further study we will know how the various forms of adult learning are supported by the affordances of virtual worlds simulations, and how the design of virtual worlds may evolve to better support adult education.

REFERENCES

Abrams, C. (2007). *Factors to consider when selecting virtual worlds for international markets.* Gartner Report No. G00153506.

Andreano, J., Liang, K., Kong, L., Hubbard, D., Wiederhold, B. K., & Wiederhold, M. D. (2009). Auditory Cues Increase the Hippocampal Response to Unimodal Virtual Reality. *Cyberpsychology & Behavior, 12*(3), 309–313. doi:10.1089/cpb.2009.0104

Brookfield, S. (1995). Adult Learning: An Overview. In A. Tuinjman (ed.), *International Encyclopedia of Education*. Oxford, UK: Permamon Press. Retrieved July 24, 2009, from http://stephenbrookfield.com/by_sb.html

Chittaro, L., & Ranon, R. (2007). Web3D technologies in learning, education and training: Motivations, issues, opportunities. *Computers & Education, 49*, 3–18. doi:10.1016/j.compedu.2005.06.002

Clark, R., & Mayer, R. (2007). E-learning and the science of instruction: Second edition. San Francisco: Pfeiffer.

Davis, D. D., & Bryant, J. L. (2003). Influence at a distance: Leadership in global virtual teams. *Advances in Global Leadership, 3*, 303–340. doi:10.1016/S1535-1203(02)03015-0

De Freitas, S. (2009). Serious games. *Adults Learning, 20*(7), 26–27.

Diehl, W. C., & Prins, E. (2008). Unintended outcomes in Second Life: Intercultural literacy and cultural identity in a virtual world. *Language and Intercultural Communication, 8*(2), 101–118. doi:10.1080/14708470802139619

Driscoll, M. (2005). Psychology of Learning for Instruction, (3rd Ed.). Boston: Pearson Education.

Fromme, J. (2003). Computer games as a part of children's culture. *The International Journal of Computer Game Research, 3*(1). Retrieved July 30, 2009 from http://gamestudies.org/0301/fromme/

Gagne, R. M., Walter, W. W., Golas, K., & Keller, J. (2005). Principles of instructional design: Fifth edition. Belmont, CA: Wadsworth.

Gaimster, J. (2008). Reflections on interactions in virtual worlds and their implication for learning art and design. *Art. Design & Communication in Higher Education, 6*(3), 187–199. doi:10.1386/adch.6.3.187_1

Gibbons, L. J. (2009). Law and the Emotive Avatar. *Vanderbilt Journal of Entertainment and Technology Law, 11*(4), 899–920.

Gredler, M. E. (2003). Games and simulations and their relationships to learning. In D. Jonassen (Ed.), Handbook of research for educational communications and technology, (2nd Ed.), (pp. 571-581). Mahwah, NJ: Lawrence Erlbaum Associates.

Harris, M., Lowendahl, J. M., & Zastrocky, M. (2007). *Second Life: Expanding higher education e-learning into 3-D.* Gartner Report No. G00149847.

Haycock & Kemp. (2008). Immersive Learning Environments in Parallel Universes: Learning through Second Life. *School Libraries Worldwide, 14*(2), 89–97.

Hiemstra, R. (2006). More than three decades of self-directed learning: From whence have we come? *Adult Learning*, 5–8.

Jarmon, L., Traphagana, T., Mayratha, M., & Trivedia, A. (2009). Virtual world teaching, experiential learning, and assessment: An interdisciplinary communication course in Second Life. *Computers & Education, 53*(1), 169–182. doi:10.1016/j.compedu.2009.01.010

Junemann, E., & Lloyd, B. (2003). Consulting for Virtual Excellence: Virtual teamwork as a task for consultants. *Team Performance Management: An International Journal, 9*(7/8), 182–189. doi:10.1108/13527590310507435

Kelton, A. J. (2008). Virtual Worlds? «Outlook Good». *EDUCAUSE Review*, (September/October), 15-22. Retrieved July 30, 2009, from http://net.educause.edu/ir/library/pdf/ERM0850.pdf

Kiely, R., Sandmann, L. R., & Truluck, J. (2004). Adult learning theory and the pursuit of adult degrees. *New Directions for Adult and Continuing Education, 103*, 17–30. doi:10.1002/ace.145

Knowles, M. S. (1970). The Modern Practice of Adult Education: Andragogy vs. Pedagogy. New York: Association Press.

Knowles, M. S. (1980, August). My Farewell Address...Andragogy - No Panacea, No Ideology. *Training and Development Journal*, 48–50.

Knowles, M. S. (1980). The Modern Practice of Adult Education: from Pedagogy to Andragogy: Second edition. New York: Cambridge Books.

Knowles, M. S. (1984). The Adult Learner: A Neglected Species (3rd Ed.). Houston, TX: Gulf.

Knowles, M. S., & Associates. (1984). Andragogy in action: Applying modern principles of adult learning. San Francisco: Jossey-Bass.

Lenhart, A. (2008). *Pew Internet Project Data Memo*. Retrieved from http://www.pewinternet.org/pdfs/PIP_Adult_gaming_memo.pdf

Lipnack, J., & Stamps, J. (1999). Virtual teams: The new way to work. *Strategy and Leadership, 27*(1), 14–19. doi:10.1108/eb054625

Lloyd, J., Persaud, N., & Powell, T. E. (2009). Equivalence of Real-World and Virtual-Reality Route Learning: A Pilot Study. *Cyberpsychology & Behavior, 4*(12), 423–427. doi:10.1089/cpb.2008.0326

MacKeracher, D. (1996). Making Sense of Adult Learning. Toronto: Culture Concepts.

Merriam, S. B., & Caffarella, R. S. (1999). Learning in Adulthood: A comprehensive guide, (2nd Ed.). San Francisco: Jossey-Bass.

Prentice, S. (2008). *Using virtual worlds as a communications channel*. Gartner Report No. G00160043.

Rieber, L. P. (1996). Seriously considering play: Designing interactive learning environments based on the blending of microworlds, simulations, and games. *Educational Technology Research and Development, 44*(2), 43–58. doi:10.1007/BF02300540

Rieber, L. P. (2004). Microworlds. In D. Jonassen (Ed.), Handbook of research for educational communications and technology: Second edition, (pp. 583-603). Mahwah, NJ: Lawrence Erlbaum Associates.

Rodriquez, F. G., & Nash, S. S. (2004). Technology and the adult degree program: The human element. *New Directions for Adult and Continuing Education, 103*, 73–79. doi:10.1002/ace.150

Rogers, E. M. (2003). Diffusion of innovations (5th ed.). New York: Free Press.

Rosedale, P. (2007). Forward. In Rymaszewski, M. Wagner, J. A., Wallace, M., Winters, C. Ondrejka, C., Batstone-Cunninghan, B., & Second Life citizens. Second Life: The official guide. Hoboken, NJ: John Wiley & Sons, Inc.

Rymaszewski, M., Wagner, J. A., Wallace, M., & Winters, C. Ondrejka, C., Batstone-Cunninghan, B., & Second Life citizens (2007). Second Life: The official guide. Hoboken, NJ: John Wiley & Sons, Inc.

Schmelter, A., Jansen, P., & Heil, M. (2009). Empirical evaluation of virtual environment technology as an experimental tool in developmental spatial cognition research. *The European Journal of Cognitive Psychology, 21*(5), 724–739. doi:10.1080/09541440802426465

The New Media Consortium & EDUCAUSE Learning Initiative. (2008). *The Horizon Report: 2008 Edition*. Stanford, California. Retrieved March 15, 2009, from http://www.nmc.org/pdf/2008-Horizon-Report.pdf

Whitney, K. (2006). Simulations in Management Education. Chief Learning Officer, (pp. 48-51).

Chapter 18

Using Commercial–Off–the–Shelf Video Games to Facilitate Habits of Mind:
Spore™ in the Seventh Grade Life Science Classroom

Michael A. Evans
Virginia Tech, USA

ABSTRACT

The purpose of this chapter is to provide a theoretically based argument for using commercial-off-the-shelf (COTS) video games to teach life science topics in the seventh grade science classroom. Specifically, the game Spore™, a turn-based strategy game, will be examined as a potential tool and environment for cultivating knowledge building and model-based reasoning. Though the diversity in methods of the reasoning processes are great and varied, researchers believe that "scientists' work involves building and refining models of the world" (Lehrer & Schauble, 2006, p. 371). The argument forwarded is that Spore™, contextualized by purposeful efforts of instructors and researchers, may facilitate the development and refinement of scientific habits of mind and computational thinking. An exploratory case study derived from an overview of five sections of a seventh grade life science course (n=85), where a two-week lesson on evolutionary biology was significantly revised, illustrates opportunities for and challenges to incorporating COTS games into formal middle school science classroom.

INTRODUCTION

Although there is a long historical national debate regarding school reform in America, many are now suggesting that digital media could be leveraged to improve middle school education, particularly with increased emphasis in four core areas referred to as STEM topics – *science, technology, engineering,* and *mathematics.* A case in point are the efforts spurred by the MacArthur Foundation, which in 2006 launched a five-year $50 million digital media and learning initiative to develop and investigate emerging communication and computational technologies in the lives of youth, both inside and outside of school[1]. A specific media type – *digital video games* – has recently garnered significant

DOI: 10.4018/978-1-61520-781-7.ch018

attention within this new agenda. As Shaffer, Squire, Halverson, and Gee (2004) argue: "Video games are a powerful new medium with potential implications for schooling" (p. 14).

Thus, the purpose of this chapter is to provide a theoretically based argument for using commercial-off-the-shelf (COTS) video games to teach life science topics in the seventh grade classroom. In particular, Spore™, a turn-based strategy game, will be examined as a potential tool and environment for cultivating knowledge building and scientific habits of mind. Though the diversity in methods of the reasoning processes associated with habits of mind are great and varied, researchers believe that "scientists' work involves building and refining models of the world" (Lehrer & Schauble, 2006, p. 371). The argument is that a commercial game such as Spore™ may facilitate the development and refinement of *syntactic* and *emergent* models of reasoning if properly contextualized with strategies, tools, accommodations, and assessments. Syntactic models summarize the essential functions of a system and map relationships while emergent models require predictions and implications of dynamic systems – a critical aspect of scientific inquiry and discovery.

To place games such as Spore™ in proper context, COTS games can be evaluated from two perspectives - as a polished artifact (much like film or textbook) being brought in from the outside (exogenous) or as an emergent artifact (much like a discussion board or wiki) developed from within the classroom (endogenous). Richard Halverson (2005) explains this simple dichotomy as follows. *Exogenous games* are easy to create but "not intrinsically related to the learning content." Exogenous games are often "off-the-shelf" titles such as Civilization™ that were built for entertainment purposes and thus require much innovation and time on the part of the teacher to locate appropriate places in the curriculum for use. *Endogenous games* "seek to simulate relevant practices of the target environment in the structure of the game" (Halverson, 2005, p.

2). The value of endogenous games is that they are designed with a specific subject domain and curriculum in mind. Thus, the adoption of these titles may be more likely as there are clear ties to teaching objectives. The argument put forth in this chapter is that the distinction is not as clear as one might first assume. Moreover, the availability of endogenous games is far exceeded by exogenous titles. A case in point is Spore™: though certainly developed as a form of entertainment, the title has features unlike comparative titles, which will be described in more detail below. A simple example for now is that the game is based on the idea of being "massively, single player," meaning that sharing and exchange are built into game play though not mandatory if one chooses. The ability to connect with other players through a feature called the *Sporepedia* (a dynamic encyclopedia of creations contributed by the global network of players that can be annotated, freely exchanged, and commented on by others), and thus introduce an unknown variable into game play may allow for modifications that lend to unprecedented instructional treatments if placed in the hands of creative teachers and enthusiastic students motivated to innovative learning. It is in these ways that the distinction between exogenous and endogenous games may begin to break down, becoming more problematic, more complex and thus worthy of further investigation.

With this potential in mind, science teachers and educational researchers are beginning to contemplate the importance of digital video games in the classroom. Although the *how* of learning in these environments is well documented, the *what* is still elusive. That is, the issue of transfer remains one of the most sought after explanations in the games-for-education literature. Critics of digital game-based learning point out that an insufficient number of rigorous, empirical studies have begun to resolve the transfer issue. Consequently, a logical next step is to explore what knowledge and strategies might be learned (and, subsequently, transferred) in these complex digital environments.

For the current illustrative case study the focus is on evidence of model-based reasoning occurring within game play.

This chapter will combine a theoretical base, examining the use of an exogenous game, Spore™, to scaffold model-based reasoning in the seventh grade science classroom while providing preliminary empirical data (in the form of an illustrative case study) that may lead to practical classroom implications. Areas to be addressed that could benefit teachers include:

1. Science classrooms and game play as knowledge-building environments;
2. Using games and simulations to promote scientific habits of mind & computational thinking;
3. Adapting games and simulations to individual learner needs (cognitive, social, physical), focusing on issues of adaptability and differentiation;
4. Integrating games and simulations into/across existing curricula, exploring single or cross-curricular topics.

Although the above points will receive due attention, it may serve better to introduce Spore™ first to orient the reader and lay a foundation for subsequent argument as to the feasibility of incorporating it into the formal life sciences classroom.

Spore™: A Turn-Based, Massive Single Player Strategy Game

Spore™ a turn-based, massive single player strategy game developed by Maxis and designed by Will Wright, the creator of the Sims™ franchise. Based loosely on the theory of panspermia (which claims that the origins of life on earth were deposited by a meteor containing the "seeds" for evolution) Spore allows a player to control the development of a species from its beginnings as a simple cell organism, through development to an intelligent and social creature, to interstellar exploration as a war-faring society. The game allows micro-control of mutation and growth as the player creates and guides its own creature through five stages of evolution. Beginning in the Cell Stage, the player is a microscopic simple cell creature that must survive in a shallow pool and then through primordial ooze. From the beginning, a player must decide to be an herbivore or a carnivore. Mutations occur through the collecting DNA by swimming through treacherous waters and avoiding being eaten by competing predators. As the player earns more DNA, evolution continues until the Creature Stage is reached. To allow for micro-control of traits, a game creator editor allows a player to customize the avatar, buy more parts using DNA points, and showcase creations online through Sporedeia. Being about development and growth, the creatures brain continues to grow as more DNA is collected, sentience is achieved and learning to befriend other species of friendly animals that co-exist on the planet is integral to game play in the Creature Stage. A dramatic shift occurs in the Tribal Stage as culture, custom, ritual, and socialization take priority. The player's tribe lives in their own village and is responsible for harvesting or hunting for food, keeping away danger in the form of vicious creatures or competing tribes, and, of course, strengthening the position by increasing the population of the tribe. The next evolutionary step takes one to the Civilization Stage, where the player is responsible for designing a community and government. The goal in this stage is to either befriend or concur competing cities and defeat errant creatures. Once successful, the player is presented with the Space Stage to travel within and beyond a home galaxy. By collecting artifacts and completing missions assigned by friendly planets, the player can procure weapons and engage in diplomacy to secure the home planet. At this point of the game, there is potentially an infinite combination of episodes that can be played endlessly. Greater detail on game objectives and mechanics can be found on numerous walkthroughs online[2].

Science Classrooms & Game Play: Knowledge Building Prerequisites

Games and simulations are part of a growing entertainment and educational market, where increasing amounts of advertising dollars and effort are spent marketing games to the 8-18 target demographic. Consequently, given the cultural relevance and pervasiveness of this technology, games are becoming a topic of increasing interest in educational circles. A significant question revolves around how games can effectively be integrated into curriculum to promote learning and the construction of knowledge. The means by which commercial-off-the-shelf (COTS) games and simulations can help foster and facilitate collaborative learning environments might be labeled game-enhanced knowledge-building prerequisites (Marsh & Evans, in press).

This section begins with a discussion of what knowledge construction and knowledge-building communities are and why they may be a valid pursuit in attempting to include games and simulations in the middle school science curriculum. Knowledge construction has been defined as "the deliberate part of learning [which] consists of making connections between mental entities that already exist; new mental entities seem to come into existence in more subtle ways that escape conscious control… This suggests a strategy to facilitate learning by improving the connectivity in the learning environment, by actions on cultures rather than on individuals" (Kafai, 2006, p. 39; Papert, 1993, p.105). As new forms of knowledge are learned, they build on structural foundations. This process is accomplished through "actions on cultures," or through collaborative activity. Knowledge-building communities have been defined as "the classroom community [that] works to produce knowledge – a collective product and not merely a summary report of what is in individual minds or a collection of outputs from group work" (Scardamalia & Bereiter, 1993-1994, p. 270). Knowledge-building communities place value

on what has collectively been learned and how these learning environments push the boundaries of learning further than ones that focus on individual work. Participation is valued over simple knowledge acquisition (Barab & Roth, 2006, p. 3-4). Exemplars of this type activity occur within inquiry-based disciplines such as science or history, interestingly areas that have garnered much attention in the digital-game based literature. An illustrative example might be that if one scientist discovered how a given enzyme could be used to cure a given a virus (for example, swine flu), another scientist would not necessarily attempt to "discover" the same thing. He or she may attempt to replicate the work, but for accepted procedures of verification, not to find something new. The first scientist's work is an addition to the body of knowledge we call "science." It is a contribution to the knowledge-building community, which then sets about the task of verifying, further evaluating, and appropriating that knowledge for other uses and further advancement of the field.

There are two different aspects to games (Gee, 2007, p. 27-28). One is the game itself, or the internal view. The other is the social network that surrounds the game play, or the external view. Gee (2007), for example, calls this social network an affinity group (p.27). Others refer to these as affordance networks (Barab & Roth, 2006, p. 4). A game-facilitated knowledge-building community exists when a game [the internal view] and its reciprocal social network [the external view] are wrapped around an educational topic for the collective purpose of knowledge construction.

It is imperative for a teacher to master this first aspect of the game he or she is using in the classroom. The teacher must know the title, understand where inaccuracies may exist in the game [as compared to real life], and develop ways to address these. It is perhaps of even greater importance to develop the second aspect of the game – the affordance network or affinity group. A student playing a game like Civilization IV in a history class may learn different facts about history, learn how to play the game itself, and even learn how to learn. The social network that stems from the game play is where knowledge construction is going to take place and where the lessons learned in the game play are going to tie into the curriculum. Decentralized, open knowledge building forums allow for elimination of turn-taking problems, opportunities for peer commentary and review, and for individuals from different entry points to all contribute to discussion in meaningful ways (Scardamalia & Bereiter, 1993-1994, p. 278). In this social community that surrounds the game play, students can contribute to a collective body of knowledge that will not only advance their knowledge of how to play (for example) Civilization IV, but also how it relates to topics of world history. Each player will make different decisions regarding their own civilizations and these decisions and the results that stem from them can open up a wide discussion in an

affordance group. Teachers can also bring students back to the curriculum by wrapping a dialogue around how the game situates events in history or why certain things might have happened one way in the game and another in real life.

Game-facilitated knowledge-building communities foster individual student reflection and independent while advancing a cumulative body of knowledge (Scardamalia & Bereiter, 1993-1994, p. 279). While many would push back and argue that such a focus on the collective would cause individual results to suffer, there is little evidence to support that claim (Scardamalia & Bereiter, p. 281). To the contrary, these types of communities tend to foster deeper learning and motivate students to achieve beyond what they might have individually in a classroom without games or game-facilitated knowledge-building communities.

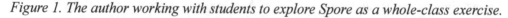

Figure 1. The author working with students to explore Spore as a whole-class exercise.

Using Games & Simulations to Promote Scientific Habits of Mind & Computational Thinking

Computational thinking requires abilities to identify, analyze, and evaluate ill-structured, complex problems in STEM domain areas. Middle school is a critical milestone in the United States education system as students are introduced to scientific habits of mind and advanced forms of mathematics, including algebra, statistics, and probability. Computational thinking requires appropriate cognitive development as well as properly matched instructional opportunities to form in the minds of young learners. Whereas existing classroom strategies may be robust to engage students in opportunities to come in contact with complex abstract ideas and procedures, there is insufficient opportunity to engage in more realistic scenarios to observe, manipulate, and test variables in scientific and mathematical domains. This is where simulations and games may have significant impact on learning. When learners interact with models and simulations, they are able to "empathize" with the previously abstract concepts and principles and make public their attempts to understand.

Subsequently, a digital game-based pedagogy would emphasize knowledge building, collaboration, and mediation by technology and digital artifacts. By using models, simulations, digital game interfaces, structures, and mechanisms, learners might engage in scientific inquiry and develop habits of mind as they encounter ill-structured, complex problems in a game or simulation environment. Although the learning theory that guides this instructional orientation may be labeled " social constructivist" broadly speaking, more specifically this perspective is grounded in a combination of situated cognition, collaborative learning, and distributed intelligence. That is, teachers and researchers work in collaboration so that students are able to approach a habit of mind where it is as if they can "act like scientists, health experts, and decision makers" (situated cognition), while also emphasizing that learning, and thus cognitive development, is an inherently social activity - it is the construction and sharing of private cognitions in a public sphere (demonstrating knowledge through action) that is at the heart of collaborative learning and distributed intelligence. Another way to phrase this is that focus is on knowledge building - making understandings public with the intent of having a positive effect on common well being, creating artifacts to demonstrate this process and progress (Evans, in press). It was these requirements that led to the selection of Spore as a platform and environment to instigate desired scientific habits of mind and computational thinking.

Adapting Spore to Individual Learner Needs - Adaptability and Differentiation

As noted earlier, educational researchers and practitioners are beginning to understand the importance of models, simulations, and games in the classroom. Although the how of learning in these environments is known, the *what* is still elusive (Squire, 2006). Therefore, the logical next step in this area of investigation is to determine what can be learned in advanced digital game-based learning environments. The goal of the reported project was to explore an exogenous game that allowed teachers and students to interact with and traits and DNA of simple cell and increasingly complex creatures to observe effects predicted by current scientific understanding of evolutionary biology (See Table 1 for examples and non-examples of scientific understanding). The interactions were bound by instructional goals to teach middle school students scientific inquiry, and thus instill habits of mind, in the area of evolutionary biology.

The intervention used Spore to establish a digital game-based learning environment to promote knowledge building, habits of mind, and computational thinking. The following design principles

267

Table 1. Expert Log for cell stage of Spore.

Directions: You have two challenges as you play! Your *first* challenge is to find ways that SPORE shows examples of evolution and ways that does not show examples of evolution. Your *second* challenge is to create a creature throughout the game that has several features that demonstrate adaptations to its environment. In order to show that you have met these two challenges, you will create an "expert log". Below is an outline of what to include in your log. You will complete a log for each stage of Spore.	
Part A Cell Stage:	
This is the part where you will list parts of the game that are examples of evolution and parts that are non-examples of evolution. Create a chart like the one below and fill in as many examples on each side as possible. In order to get an A, you will need to list 6 examples of each. For a B, you will list 5 examples. For a C, you will list 3 examples. As you fill out your chart, think about the following topics:	
For examples of Evolution: 1. List where SPORE began and compare this to where scientists believe life began. 2. Is SPORE unicellular or multicellular? How is this like evolution? 3. In the beginning of the game, how did SPORE end up on Earth? 4. When does change occur in an organism during the game? How is this like evolution? 5. How is SPORE identified and described during the game. How is this like what scientists do when studying organisms from the past? 6. How is a timeline used during the game? What does a timeline have to do with evolution?	For non-examples of Evolution: 1. How does the creature earn a new part? How is this different from evolution? 2. How are new parts found and made available? How is this different from evolution? 3. What happens when a creature dies? How is this unlike evolution? 4. How is the movement of SPORE to land unlike evolution? 5. Does evolution occur every generation like in SPORE? 6. Does an organism loose DNA when acquiring a new trait?

were incorporated to serve needs of accountability, adaptability, and differentiation:

- The design of game play will aim at improving abilities for problem solving, reasoning, predicting, collaborating, communicating, planning, and resource managing
- The game will enable cooperative and competitive play modes so that teachers can use the game to implement a collaborative teaching environment
- To engage players, there will be a novel story and challenge design to create a sense of urgency, enhancing the immersive quality of the game
- The game will establish a series of missions/levels, designed in a scaffolded fashion: For students, design will enable them to grasp the basic path of evolutionary processes, game play and interfaces through introductory and tutorial missions; For teachers, design will allow implementation in a flexible in-class schedule using the short tutorial missions to get immediate

teaching outcomes; teachers will encourage students to explore more complex missions after school.

The full lesson plan developed by the teacher, in response to the requirements above, can be found in Appendix A. Taking this instructional artifact as a reference, one can see how the teacher attempted to integrate the game into familiar classroom practices while leveraging the potential of the game.

Integrating Games & Simulations Into Curricula, Exploring Cross-Curricular Topics

Digital games and simulations may be tools that help facilitate knowledge-building around topics in the formal classroom. Nevertheless, they cannot simply be purchased one weekend and brought into the classroom on a Monday with any hope for successful implementation. Integrating games into the classroom involves a great deal of work on the part of teachers and researcher should success be a target (Charsky & Mims, 2008). A teacher interested in creating a game-facilitated knowledge-building community will need to begin by knowing the title he or she is using inside and out. Titles like Spore, and other turned-based strategy games such as Civilization IV, might be considered open-ended simulation games (Squire, 2008, p. 170-172). These games allow for many trajectories that a player can take in playing the game. In a sense, each player can play his or her own game. While this can be advantageous in some ways, it is not in a classroom setting. Time is a commodity for teachers and allowing students to play a game like Spore for an hour with no direct purpose could be considered a waste of time. Both Spore and Civilization can be saved at different points in the game. A feature like this allows a teacher to have students play a specific part of the game and allows open-ended games like the two above-mentioned titles to become feasible in a classroom setting.

To attempt to effectively integrate an exogenous digital game title into the classroom requires careful preparation on the teacher's part. To prepare students to engage intellectually with what was designed as an entertainment vehicle necessitates laying a foundation of scientific knowledge. In the case of the middle school classroom studied for this chapter, the teacher ensured that students had a firm grasp of the following relevant concepts and principles related to evolutionary biology:

1. Scientists believe that the first organisms on Earth lived in the ocean.
2. Scientists believe that the first organisms on Earth were prokaryotic and lived in the ocean floor.
3. Changes in a species occur through mutations in DNA that happen in a sperm or egg cell.
4. All mutations in DNA that occur in sperm or egg cells result in a change in the phenotype of the offspring.
5. An example of natural selection would be if an organism had a mutation in its DNA that occurred before birth, was born with a superior phenotype, and then survived to reproduce and pass on its new trait.
6. A mutation in DNA in a sperm or egg cell always results in a positive change in the organism.
7. A mutation in DNA in a sperm or egg cell may cause a change in the phenotype that cannot be seen.
8. An organism can acquire new traits as it increases the amount of DNA throughout its lifetime.
9. An organism can learn new skills during its lifetime and then pass those skills on to offspring through DNA.
10. In sexual organisms, mating has to occur for natural selection to occur.
11. If a species has traits that are not suitable to survival in its environment, then it is likely to go extinct.
12. Scientists have named and described organisms from the past. They have created timelines that show changes in species over time.
13. A timeline showing the evolution of an organism may include aspects such as: changes in phenotype, social behaviors, and eating habits.
14. Evolution of a species occurs every generation.
15. In general, evolution occurs slowly.
16. Scientists believe that species evolve gradually. For example, organisms that first moved to land were crawling insects or amphibious creatures.
17. Evolution of an organism results in an increase in the size of its brain.
18. Organisms have to learn a skill in order to possess it.
19. Phenotype is influenced both by genotype and the environment.

20. Successful evolution of an organism may lead to extinction of another living in the same habitat. This is part of the natural selection process.
21. Organisms get smarter as they evolve.
22. Migration is a part of evolution because it can lead to speciation.
23. Many factors in an environment may lead to migration.

Once the class as a whole had reviewed these ideas as a whole, they were prepared to play the Cell Stage of Spore. To facilitate scientific habits of mind and direct students to determine the scientific validity of incidents encountered during game play, students were instructed to refer to their Expert Log (Table 1).

As students played the Cell Stage, in this case on iPod Touches to allow for a one-to-one computing experience, they were to complete the Expert Log. Figure 2 illustrates the effort placed into this lesson by one student, Kelly.

Below are additional comments from the teacher as she reflected on using Spore, justifying choices made to provide a scientifically sound, yet motivating, experience for students.

Using games and simulations to teach or reinforce important or difficult standards of learning for all science. Spore can be used to reinforce many important concepts included in state and national standards, which includes investigating and understanding that organisms change over time. During the game, students can observe and investigate key components of these standards such as variations in offspring causing changes in successive generations, and changes in the environment that cause changes in species. Students often need to see demonstrations of how natural selection, adaptations, and extinction affect a species. The game, along with instruction that scaffolds material presented in Spore, was an excellent method by which such demonstrations can occur. One of the essential skills dictated in the standards is for students to use simulations

Figure 2.

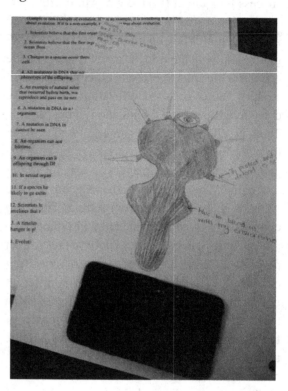

in order to demonstrate selection of a trait in a species. Spore also was an excellent avenue by which to conduct a simulation. Without the game, simulations for teaching evolution have often been difficult to design or were not sufficiently engaging in previous attempts.

Designing, developing, and using games and simulations in the classroom. Each student was provided a handout (Table 1) designed to provide a bridge between the game, and the key concepts to be learned. This handout prompted students to complete tasks such as: 1) drawing the creature with the adaptations that have occurred, 2) responding to parts of the game that contradicted concepts learned (such as the absence of random DNA mutations as the catalyst for chances in a species), and 3) responding to parts that exemplified evolution (such as life starting in the ocean). Students would need to pause throughout the game to add responses to the handout, and guided through direct instruction when students were getting off task or misconceptions were identified. Also, for gifted students, there was a component of the handout that allowed these students to go beyond what was covered in class and demonstrate further understanding.

Adapting games and simulations to individual learner needs (cognitive, social, physical), focusing on issues of adaptability and differentiation. By allowing each student to play the game at his or her own pace, the teacher promoted differentiation. Also, students were provided materials to provide focus on key concepts of evolution during game play, and as a way for them to be assessed on their understanding of how the game illustrated, or not, key concepts. Students had different levels by which they were able to extend their understanding of key concepts, working individually to allow for adaptability to individual levels of ability. Socially, students could bring together their thoughts and discoveries about the game, as well as feel a sense of competition when building and documenting their evolving creatures. This was viewed as an excellent motivator. Physically, the game demanded that students take part in activities on the screen on the iPod Touches, and thereby kept them engaged.

Reflection and Discussion: A Teacher's Perspective

Spending over 20 hours to learn the mechanics and intricacies of a game as complex as Spore, plus the time to revise and re-write a lesson plan, is not an easy task for a seventh grade science teacher with five sections to teach a day. Ms. Brookings was convincingly impressed by the potential of the title to invest such effort for the benefit of her teaching and student learning. Upon completion of the pilot intervention, she reflected on the project in the following ways.

1. Using games and simulations to teach or reinforce important or difficult standards of learning in science

Pre-intervention justification: Spore can be used to reinforce many important concepts included in LS.14, which includes investigating and understanding that organisms change over time. During the game, students can observe and investigate key components of LS.14 such as variations in offspring causing changes in successive generations, and changes in the environment that cause changes in species. Students often need to see demonstrations of how natural selection, adaptations, and extinction affect a species. The game, along with instruction that scaffolds material presented in Spore, is an excellent method by which such demonstrations can occur. One of the essential skills dictated in LS.14 is for students to use simulations in order to demonstrate selection of a trait in a species. Spore also is an excellent avenue by which to provide a simulation. Without the game, simulations for teaching evolution are difficult to design or are often not engaging.

Post-intervention reflection: Spore without question was engaging. With the scaffolding provided by the directions for the expert log, students were able to identify examples of what they had previously learned in the unit. Students found it easier to identify was incorrect than to synthesize information about what was missing. Students often needed to be prompted during discussion to fill in what was absent in the game. This was accomplished through questions posed by the teacher, and by students sharing their ideas. Such sharing and prompting makes it difficult to assess whether students could create the log completely on their own. A multiple-choice pre-test and post-test will be used in the future in addition to the expert log. Certainly, students learned through processing the simulation presented, cooperatively sharing ideas.

2. Designing, developing, and using games and simulations in the science classroom

Pre-intervention justification: Each student will need a handout that is designed to provide a bridge between the game, and the key concepts that they must learn. This handout would ask the student to complete tasks such as: drawing the creature with the adaptations that have occurred, responses to parts of the game that contradict concepts learned (such as the absence of random DNA mutations as the catalyst for chances in a species), and responses to parts that do exemplify evolution (such as life starting in the ocean). Students would need to pause throughout the game to add responses to the handout, and it would be guided through direct instruction. Also, for gifted students, there also needs to be a component of the handout that allows students to go beyond what is achieved in class and demonstrate further understanding.

Post-intervention reflection: The handout was instrumental for the creation of student expert logs. Pausing during the game was also a necessary component, which helped students record thoughts before they were forgotten. It also allowed opportunities for students to share ideas and for the instructor to provide verbal prompts to give aspects of the game on which students should focus. Equally important with pausing was the prevention of the "gaming zone", where students would lose focus and become only focused on the game itself. The differentiated version for the gifted students did not prove to be useful. It was too abstract, even for the most gifted. This would be more suited to high school level. There was still opportunity for differentiation because students could take their log notes to various levels of cognition. For instance, some logs included the most concrete examples whereas others were extremely complex.

3. Adapting games and simulations to individual learner needs (cognitive, social, physical), focusing on issues of adaptability and differentiation

Pre-intervention justification: By allowing each student to play the game at their own pace,

the instructor is allowing differentiation to take place in the class. Also, students will need to be provided materials that will be used to provide focus on key concepts of evolution during the game, and as a way for them to be assessed on their understanding of how the game illustrates, or does not illustrate the concepts. Students will have different levels to which they are able to extend their understanding of key concepts, so working individually can allow for adaptability to individual levels of ability. Socially, students can bring together their thoughts and discoveries about the game, as well as feel a sense of competition when building their evolving creature. This is an excellent motivator. Physically, the game demands that students take part in activities on the screen, and is thereby keeps them engaged.

Post-intervention reflection: The competition component was not built into the lessons. Students worked cooperatively to build their logs and there was not enough exploration time to create much competition. Also, students needed their own computers for this to be truly useful. With regard to motivation, it was always present in the room during the lessons. However, some students who took their logs home to complete them, never submitted them for evaluation. For the students lacking motivation, the logs needed to be completed in class to guarantee their success.

4. Integrating games and simulations into/ across existing curricula, exploring single or cross-curricular topics

Pre-intervention justification: Spore is an excellent extension activity after the unit on Evolution is taught. It would need to take place after students have mastered the basic concepts so that they are able to identify non-examples of evolution during the game. It also can be used to exemplify symbiotic relationships as the creature makes allies that help in hunting (LS.9).

5. Making games modifiable for practice and assessment, discussing the need for embedded assessment

Pre-intervention justification: The handout is a method by which students can be assessed. This would be a performance-based assessment, both accounting for the responses that the student provides on papers, as well as completion to a certain point in the game. Students will need to submit their handout for assessment.

Post-intervention reflection: Students were evaluated using performance assessment. They created an "expert log" where they documented examples of evolution in the game as well as non-examples. 100% attainment of the goal was demonstrated if students had 7 examples and 7 non-examples that were: logical, accurate, and pertained to at least one of the skill objectives. Students surpassed expectations and also referred to examples and non-examples that were not defined in the objectives. Many of these were clever, logical, and accurate and were therefore accepted. Students who are accustomed to simply memorizing information were often shocked by the low grade and feedback on their first log. They learned to analyze and synthesize and improved their performance for the second log.

6. Exploring how games and simulations will alter teaching, learning, and assessment and what needs to be done to meet these challenges

Pre-intervention justification: The biggest challenge will be in keeping students focused on the lesson objectives, instead on just the mechanics of the game. Students are not accustomed to using OTS games in the Science classroom and will most likely approach the game as they normally do at home, just for fun. Their normal approach is not necessarily academic and productive. So, thought will need to be put into the materials and conversation that are part of the lesson as students play the game. One necessary component of the lesson will be to have students pause the game every few minutes and to discuss how what they have seen relates to evolution and to give time and guidance pertaining to filling out the handout.

Post-intervention reflection: Students were focused with very few exceptions. All students were engaged in discussion. A few were reluctant to write all their thoughts down, with written language being a barrier for their success. Often, students gave the instructor their idea, and then the instructor helped him/her word their thought for the log. This scaffolding was a way to take the knowledge that they possessed, and assist them with demonstrating this knowledge on paper.

7. Professional development needs of teachers who want to design and use games and simulations in the classroom

Pre-intervention justification: Time to work on the handout and to continue play testing. This will require a minimum of 20 hours. A substitute needs to be provided to allow for the 20 hours. (This cannot take place after school, but could take place one day per week, etc.)

Post-intervention reflection: A module of materials can be constructed that gives provides sequence for the lessons. It would also be helpful to provide a workshop were demonstration could be given of how to lead discussion during the formation of the expert logs. During the SPORE lessons, students required direction from the instructor regarding which aspects of the game on which to focus, models of how to critique part of the game and formulate a response, and correction if discussion headed down an unproductive pathway.

CONCLUSION

In this chapter, an argument has been made for the use of Spore, a COTS video game, in the seventh grade science classroom. The purpose was to provide theoretical grounding and practical strategies that might be adopted by others. Moreover, through the exploratory case study, where an actual middle school teacher made the attempt to incorporate a COTS game into existing curriculum, it may have been demonstrated that the distinction between exogenous and endogenous games is not so obvious. What might be said is that there is a potential merging of these two terms in a product such as Spore, particularly where access is granted to modifications of game mechanics through APIs and content. Speaking of which, Spore as a commercial product has certainly come under critique by digital rights advocates and scientists. The former concerns the digital rights management constraint imposed by the publishers, which, unintentionally, resulted in Spore being the most widely distributed game title via unauthorized peer-to-peer networks. In an era where open educational resources are becoming the norm, one cannot take this point lightly. In terms of content, Spore has also been criticized as being "unscientific."[3] The argument is that the game violates known scientific principles from evolutionary biology, sociology, and astrology (to name a few) in the service of entertainment. A rejoinder to this criticism notes that a potentially unfounded assumption is that teachers and students are insufficiently sophisticated to notice these discrepancies. [4] Hopefully, the brief case provided in this chapter begins a more intense cycle of investigating the effects of COTS games in the formal science classroom, from upper elementary to lower high school.

Enthusiasm for exogenous, commercial-off-the-shelf game titles, and endogenous, curriculum-driven game titles will not likely soon abate. Consequently, it is the best interest of educational researchers and practitioners to continue to criti-cally and empirically explore stated benefits of learning with these complex, model-based digital environments. In this chapter, we have taken a recently released title, Spore, which has received an unusually diverse range of criticism from both the entertainment and scientific sectors regarding issues to include digital rights management and scientific validity. From the experience of a single classroom study, lasting the length of a two-week lesson plan, we have attempted to portray one of the first published accounts of using Spore to teach evolutionary biology. From the initial analysis, sufficient evidence exists to suggest that with careful preparation, guidance, accommodation, and assessment, exogenous games have a place in the middle school science classroom. Future work lies ahead to determine the range of possibilities of this title and to explore more rigorously the effects of Spore in the classroom.

REFERENCES

Barab, S., Thomas, M., Dodge, T., Carteaux, R., & Tuzun, H. Making learning fun: A game without guns. *Educational Technology Research and Development*, *5*(1), 86–107.

Barab, S. A., & Roth, W. (2006). Curriculum-baed ecosystems: Supporting knowing from an ecological perspective. *Educational Researcher*, *35*(5), 3–13. doi:10.3102/0013189X035005003

Bohannon, J. (2008). Flunking Spore. *Science*, *322*(5901). Retrieved January 11, 2009 from http://www.sciencemag.org/cgi/content/full/322/5901/531b

Charsky, D., & Mims, C. (2008). Integrating commercial off-the-shelf video games into school curriculums. *TechTrends*, *52*(5), 38–44. doi:10.1007/s11528-008-0195-0

Driscoll, M. P. GLE: Grade level evaluation: Ensuring academic success. *Psychology of Learning for Instruction*. Boston: Allyn & Bacon.

Edelson, D. C., Gordin, D. N., & Pea, R. D. (1999). Addressing the challenges of inquiry-based learning through technology and curriculum design. *Journal of the Learning Sciences, 8*(3/4), 391–450. doi:10.1207/s15327809jls0803&4_3

Evans, M. A. (in press). Mobility, games, and education. To appear in the *Handbook of Research on Educational Games.*

Gee, J. P. (2003, 2004). Good Video Games and Good Learning. Retrieved April 27, 2009 from http://www.academiccolab.org/resources/documents/Good_Learning.pdf

Gee, J. P. (2007). What video games have to teach us about learning and literacy. New York: Palgrave Macmillan.

Gee, J. P. (2008). Learning and games. In K. Salen (Ed) The Ecology of Games: Connecting Youth, Games, and Learning (pp 21-40). Cambridge, MA: The MIT Press.

Kafai, Y. B. (2006). Constructionism. In R. K. Sawyer (Ed.), The Cambridge Handbook of the Learning Sciences (pp. 35-46). Cambridge, UK: Cambridge University Press.

Papert, S. (1993). The children's machine: Rethinking school in the age of the computer. New York: BasicBooks.

Pellegrino, J., & Scott, A. (2004). *The Transition from Simulation to Game-Based Learning.* Retrieved March 8, 2008 from http://www.learningarchitects.net/files/Transition_from_Sims_to_Games.pdf

Salen, K. (2008). Toward an Ecology of Gaming. In K. Salen (Ed) The Ecology of Games: Connecting Youth, Games, and Learning (pp 1-17). Cambridge, MA: The MIT Press

Scardamalia, M., & Bereiter, C. (1993-1994). Computer support for knowledge-building communities. *Journal of the Learning Sciences, 3*(3), 265–283. doi:10.1207/s15327809jls0303_3

Shaffer, D. W., Squire, K. R., Halverson, R., & Gee, J. P. (2004). *Video Games and the Future of Learning* Retrieved March 10, 2008 from http://www.academiccolab.org/resources/gappspaper1.pdf

Squire, K. (2006). From content to context: Videogames as designed experience. *Educational Researcher, 35*(8), 19–29. doi:10.3102/0013189X035008019

Squire, K. (2008). Open-ended video games: A model for developing learning for the interactive age. In K. Salen (Ed.), The ecology of games: Connecting youth, games, and learning (pp. 167-198). Cambridge, MA: The MIT Press.

Summit on Educational Games. (2006). Retrieved January 23, 2008 from http://www.fas.org/gamesummit/Resources/Summit%20on%20Educational%20Games.pdf

Wing, J. M. (2006). Computational thinking. *CACM Viewpoint, 49*(3), 33–35.

ENDNOTES

[1] MacArthur Foundation Digital Media and Learning Competition: http://www.dmlcompetition.net/

[2] A personal favorite is provided by the media review site, IGN: http://guides.ign.com/guides/735340/index.html

[3] Flunking Spore: http://www.sciencemag.org/cgi/content/full/322/5901/531b

[4] In Response to "Flunking Spore" (Part 2): http://www.learninggamesnetwork.org/content/response-flunking-spore-part-2

APPENDIX A.

Excerpt from lesson plan revised to accommodate Spore.

Day One

Spore Lesson Plan
  Goals:

- To assess the student's knowledge previous to the use of SPORE as a tool to extend their knowledge about evolution
- To activate the knowledge that students have about evolution prior to the SPORE lessons
- To introduce SPORE and the challenge that students will be faced with as they play the game

  Objectives and Correlated SOLs:

- Students will individually complete the retest based on prior knowledge
- In small groups, students will take turns listing what they know about the following topics: What is evolution? What are the ways that evolution takes place? What evidence exists for evolution? What is an example of variations in a specific population that have taken place through evolution? LS.14a, LS.14b, LS.14c
- Students will demonstrate both individually, then as a group that they can identify examples and non-examples of evolution. LS.14a-c
- Students will listen to and watch an introduction of the SPORE game, and hear the challenge that they will have as they play the game

  Materials:

- Pretest
- Large poster paper with a question for each group (ex: what is evolution)
- Handout: examples and non-examples of evolution
- SPORE introduction and explanation of the challenge (PowerPoint)

  Teaching Strategies:

- *Warm-up:* Do you thing that students can learn from playing a video game? Why do you think so?
- *Review and Introduction:* Students will work in a small group to each take a turn writing something they know that is written on a large poster size sheet taped to the wall. Students can assist each other but each student will have to write their own response. Groups will share their responses and afterwards, students will write one thing they learned from another group after the groups have shared. This will be their exit pass at the end of class.
- *Pre-assessment:* Students will complete a pretest about evolution

- *Independent Practice and cooperative learning:* Students will individually identify examples and non-examples of evolution. They will then share answers as a class, correcting any on their sheet that are incorrectly marked.
- *Direction Instruction:* Students will watch a PowerPoint about evolution. They will also be introduced to how they will use the game in order to learn about evolution. They will be told they will be the "evolution expert" who will identify parts the game that exemplify evolution as well as parts that do not.

Chapter 19

"Click, You're It!":
The Role of Gaming in the K-12 Educational Setting

Karen Kellison
James Madison University, USA

George Font
James Madison University, USA

ABSTRACT

Video games are serious work for today's students. 93% of the K-12 population plays video games on a regular basis. Educators are now pressed to determine the appropriate integration of this technology into the pedagogy of K-12 classrooms. Research indicates that there are positive effects from playing serious video games, those that aim to teach something. Students are motivated and engaged during such game play. Some speculate that players are using and developing cognitive brain capabilities that have been dormant. The question is whether or not these games, if adequately designed, will teach more than just the skill of playing the game. This chapter takes a look at the evolution of play and games in K-12 education and then seeks to define serious computer games in terms of positive design elements and integration techniques for K-12 classrooms. In conclusion, a research agenda that moves educational gaming forward is explored.

INTRODUCTION

Take a peek into a middle school classroom. Students are excitedly adding large numbers in their heads. They are reading and sharing information. They are providing peer support to those who do not understand. And the teacher, while present, is not providing content information. Rather a peer-to-peer network of sixth graders mediates the learning experience and important content to be mastered.

Many contemporary educators might say this embodies a vision of how we want students to learn in the 21st century - in a motivating, challenging, and supportive environment. Yet it is extremely difficult to create this dream scenario in the real world. What is the 'magic' in this classroom? Perhaps the students in this scenario are high achievers or somehow 'gifted' at learning? Not at all. In fact, this group of 12 middle schools students has more detention referrals among them than their grade level at large. Most are academically challenged

DOI: 10.4018/978-1-61520-781-7.ch019

and lagging behind grade level in subjects such as math and reading. Yet they are engaged, supportive, and they are learning! The sad twist to this story is that they are playing a popular strategy game, Bakugan. It is not considered educational and does not rate time during the school day. It has been 'safely' relegated to after-school, a common theme to the use of games in our k-12 educational system today. A great deal has been made recently about teaching 21st century skills, including those needed to make the best use of rapidly changing technologies and those that lead to the ability to innovate. These 'soft skills' are now considered the most important natural resources in our global high-tech world. The purpose of this chapter is to briefly review the theoretical and historical foundations of using play and games in learning and to explore the relevance of this foundation in the design and use of educational video games for K-12 students today.

BACKGROUND

Play and Learning

"Play is the work of children." This quote has been attributed to many, from Piaget to Dr. Spock to Captain Kangaroo, but few educators in early childhood would argue with its foundational assumption: Play can be very serious work for the young child. In play, children engage in many kinds of activities, such as practice, sharing, pretending, and negotiating rules. All of these types of play allow children to increase their ability to deal with cognitive, social, and emotional issues, as well as develop physical skills (Fromberg 2006). Play is an iterative and collaborative process whereby children negotiate the play scenarios and seamlessly enter into and exit out of the activities. Not just about fostering social and emotional competence, play also contributes to the cogni-

tive development of children, by providing a safe environment for exercising executive skills such as strategic planning, self-regulation, symbolism, designing constructions, and organizing the play with rules.

While few will dispute the importance of play in the development of children, what about in the classroom? Do we think of school as work or does play still have value? Play loses its appeal as a necessary part of learning when children reach school. "The common sense tendency is for people to define play as the opposite of work" (Rieber, 1996, p.43). In order to understand the role of play in learning, it is important to look at the defining attributes of play. What are the specific attributes of play that make it such a valuable and time-tested tool in learning? Klopfer, Osterweil, & Salen (2009) list the following "freedoms" as attributes of play

- freedom to fail – failure is not an 'end', but a way of learning - doing things that don't work out the first time and using this 'failure' to move toward mastery.
- freedom to experiment – the ability to experiment and construct varying scenarios that can be tested and modified.
- freedom to fashion identities – identity is not a fixed thing, but rather part of the 'play'. By trying on various identities, children begin to define themselves.
- freedom of effort – research shows that children alternate between intense and relaxed play. Adult intervention tends to raise the expectation of uniform effort and thus disqualifies the activity as play.
- freedom of interpretation – this is a challenge for those who look for games to provide a standardized context for learning, as play is always subject to the individual, social, and cultural motivations of the player.

Serious Games - Play, With a Purpose

It is important to note that these descriptions of play are not at odds with game playing. While games often have rules, much of the game involves questioning rules and testing strategies. Games are purposeful – fun with an end in mind. Those that specifically aim to teach something have been termed 'serious games.' Effective instructional design in both traditional and serious game environments is driven by how learners are connected to the content and each other. Given this, one of the greatest strengths of using games for learning is that they are excellent tools for connecting learners to knowledge, key concepts, facts, and processes in a way that is fun and purposeful. What makes games so engaging and motivating for students? What is it about the game environment that encourages a feeling of empowerment, where the player will continue with a belief that success is possible, even after numerous 'failures'? Educators should be asking these questions, as they are directly related to positive learning environments. In fact, to explore these questions about how the powerful features of digital games can be harnessed for educational purposes, the Federation of American Scientists, the Entertainment Software Association, and the National Science Foundation co-sponsored a historic event in October of 2005. The Summit on Educational Games brought together over 100 experts to discuss ways to bring the research, development, and deployment of serious games to the forefront of United States' education and policy agenda. A key finding was the essential difference between games for education and games for entertainment. "Educational games must be built on the science of learning" (2006, p. 5).

Both Keller (ARCS model) and Gagne (Nine Events of Instruction) have provided a theoretical foundation for the instructional design of successful serious games. "The ARCS model is a problem solving approach to designing the motivational aspects of learning environments to stimulate and sustain students' motivation to learn" (Keller, 1987). Gagne's (1987) model is a ladder of learning events that is similar to the approach taken in serious game design - that is, to create a system of levels whereby successfully completing the mission of one level provides access to the next level. However, the engagement that happens in serious game playing demonstrates that there is not a hierarchy of events, but rather these events are more like threads that are woven in and out of the learning experience. Common game elements that can be compared to the elements of these theoretical approaches to instruction are those of scenario and problem setup (attention); challenge and choices (stimulus); prompting and eliciting action/decision (guidance/confidence and challenge); outcome and success/failure screens (feedback, assessment) demonstrate this. Additionally, Prensky (2007) coined what he terms 'rules of engagement' for creating the best learning environments in educational games.

- Goals – must be engaging and internalized by students as their own.
- Decisions – must be required, frequent, and important to reaching the goals.
- Discussion – both during and after the experience.
- Emotional Connection – story development, sight, sound, and motion.
- Cooperation & Competition – careful balancing of these two forces is crucial.
- Personalization – meeting students at precisely their own level.
- Review – immediate feedback and reflection
- Iteration - periodic revision based on the players' experiences and feedback
- Fun – absolutely critical for engaging the 'net generation.'

However, there are foundational elements of good instruction that appear to be consistently missing from most present day educational game design. When comparing general game design methods, Gunter, Kenny, & Vick (2007) found that Gagne's step 3 (stimulate recall) and step 9 (accommodate retention and transfer) are generally lacking in most game designs. Learning theory attests to the importance of the transfer and application of knowledge to new situations as part of the process. This is where computer-based serious games that are well designed can fill the void.

Using Serious Video Games in K-12

While the teaching profession understands theories of learning and what makes a positive learning environment, it is also recognized that meeting the needs of individual learners is quite challenging. Gaining attention, presenting challenges, instilling confidence, and creating a short feedback loop are all admirable goals (and theoretically sound), but next to impossible on a daily basis with each individual student. The way each of us learns is as different as our DNA and our needs are ever changing, depending on the goals of the instruction and existing schema relative to the content and context. This is a very tall order for even the most seasoned educator. Perhaps this is why educators continue to look for the 'silver bullet', that one approach or technology that will reach everyone, even when this simply does not make sense.

Serious games, a term used to denote games that use instructionally sound pedagogy to teach, are beginning to emerge as a viable option for the K-12 classroom, but not without skeptics and naysayers. While many would agree that most games teach something - many computer games in education are designed such that students are not empowered to make important decisions and take actions that truly change the course of the game. Even when 'levels' are used, as they are often in entertainment-based video games, often nothing new is learned or carried forward from one level to the next. Gunter et al. (2007) proposed that the key to creating a successful serious game is to embed content-based interaction and choices

that require players to implicitly and naturally learn the desired content in order to advance. The 'level-design' must take into account the use and reuse of the academic content in new circumstances (transfer of learning) to the extent that it is internalized and naturalized. Associated with critical choices, another positive element of video games is that they can take into consideration learner characteristics. If well designed, such a game can make adjustments when the learner struggles, by giving hints and encouragement that individualize the experience each and every time the game is played.

Moving Past the Frivolous Notion of Games

Glickman's (1984) historical review of play in public schools clearly shows how play has been viewed either as a valuable instructional cornerstone or as frivolous and nonproductive, depending on the political agendas of the time. The use of computer games in education can be traced back to about 1984, when Math Blaster (Davidson) was created for the then new innovation in schools, the Apple II personal computer. Since that time, the technology and students who use it have changed considerably. Today's educational computer games must be more than entertainment. They must be firmly anchored in pedagogical principles and must not only engage but teach, something that has been missing from most educational games to date. Unfortunately, much of computer-based educational game design has been largely driven by traditional educational approaches. They are generic in context so that they can be used in several different learning situations, much like textbooks have been for some time. These games have been developed by teachers or textbook publishers and simply 'smell too much like school' (Lim, 2008). Such games are often a replication of drill and practice activities already taking place in the classroom.

Gee, already known for discourse analysis work, declared video games good learning machines with good design principles (Gee, Hawisher, & Slefe, 2007). He described video games as not only creating a learning process, but also creating one that players are willing to immerse themselves in for hours. He likened games to life, a domain that you slowly learn to make sense of and navigate in. The learning experience in a video game allows mistakes without real consequences, and encouragement to continue trying. Video games are not a waste of time or effort, but instead offer superior opportunities for critical learning and problem solving.

MIT's "Education Arcade" explores the educational potential of video games. In "Moving Learning Games Forward", Klopfer et al. (2009) assert that those who believe in using these games in education usually start with the same basic assumptions. They observe that those who play the games typically develop persistence, risk-taking, attention to detail, and problem solving skills that would be desired in most school settings. Moving beyond this initial level of interest, he divides those interested in using games in education into two basic camps. There are those that advocate for the use of game-based learning who see this as a basis for 21st century skills and who see schools as stuck in a 19th century approach to learning. Certainly it appears that a participatory culture of social networking, user generated content, and student driven learning is not reflected in most current school structures. Those in this camp see important learning as taking place outside of school and would place serious video games in the afterschool environment, much like the opening scenario of this chapter.

In contrast, the opposing camp sees a value in educational gaming to the extent that it can be used in traditional school settings. There are obstacles to this approach that must be addressed, not the least of which include the teacher's need to cover material, the lack of infrastructure for these technologies, and unfamiliarity with games (a generational disconnect). Ke (2008) found that the application of external classroom goal structures influences the efficacy of educational computer games. In addition to these institutional obstacles, this group must also wrestle with the objections of parents, teachers, and administrators who see games as 'play' in a context that cannot possibly lead to serious learning. If, as Lev Vygotsky, the Russian psychologist, informs us, "a child's greatest achievements are possible in play – achievements that tomorrow will become his average level of real action and his morality (1933)," there may be no more important method for learning. The resulting question must be phrased not as 'whether or not to use video games?' but rather 'when and how will serious video games facilitate purposeful learning in school?'

New technologies are first condemned, soon afterward though, the walls that separate learning and fun, work and play begin to tumble like Humpty Dumpty. Video games are beginning to enter the world of education slowly, and may soon become part of the school curriculum as research is showing them to have considerable educational value. The choice is clear. Either we bury our heads in what was, or realize video games are not going away any time soon (Gee, 2003, 2007).

Cognitive Characteristics of a New Generation

From a practical standpoint, the profile of learners has changed. Of our 53 million K-12 students, 51 million of them (or 93%) play video games (Etuk, 2008). More important to our discussion than the sheer numbers is the approach used to 'teach' in these games. They violate the traditional 'teacher-learner' model we have embraced in education for centuries. These games come with very little in the way of 'instruction' manuals or tutorials. If they did, one might venture a guess that they would go unread. When children pick up a new video game, they know very little about the game. It is not important to know all about the games rules, the interaction, the problems to solve. Their perception of the game evolves from a game to learn, to a game to play, to a game with strategies - all the while being supported and guided by the game itself. An important feature of the video game is that it includes a self-regulation system, that is, a set of rules that adapt the game and its contents to the user's level. The aim is to avoid frustration and boredom. And there must be something to this approach as players willingly enter the gaming environment – investing 40 to 60 hours (the standard amount of time a game plays), accepting that there will be much to learn, excited about the learning, and with the belief that, once the rules are mastered, success will be theirs.

The educational gaming literature continues to point to learner characteristic as an essential component that moderates games' efficacy. Some speculate that player/learners who have grown up watching fast-paced TV, commercials, and now playing video games for entertainment may have a developed a new set of cognitive characteristics (Prensky & Thiagrajan, 2007). Kenny (2009) suggests that these characteristics do not represent new human potential, but rather these are areas of our mental capability that have always existed but were not previously developed. In the 'use it or lose it' vain, these latent characteristics have come to the forefront because of their continued use in this new generation of learners. Characteristics that have been attributed to the 'games generation' are: a preference for multimedia sources; a need for random access (influenced by the non-linear approach of games and the Internet); a need to interact with their peers and actively participate in the learning process; lack of patience with experiences that do not have obvious payoff; and a "just in time" view of learning – information is retrieved when needed and disposed of until it is needed again. These attributes point to differences in how learners acquire knowledge both in and outside of school.

Video games are a vast resource waiting to be tapped. That sounds good, but what is real, how much is hype? Much of the negative feedback is focused on aggression and social maladjustment due to video game playing (Provenzo, 1991). Some early research concluded children's behaviors could be negatively modified by exposure to video games (Schutte, Malouff, Post-Gorden, & Rodasta, 1988; Irwin & Gross, 1995). Other research (Anderson & Ford 1986; Calvert & Tan 1994; Graybill, Kirsch, & Esselman 1985) suggested that video games may cause an increase in violent thoughts or feelings. Schutte et al. (1988) found increased violent play in children who played violent games compared to those who played nonviolent games. Conversely, Graybill, Strawniak, Hunter, & O'Leary (1987) found no increases in violent thoughts in children who played violent video games. So what is the scoop? Been to the mall lately? Have you noticed that video game arcades are places where gamers rendezvous, display substantial skills, and socialize away from parental control (Michaels, 1993)? Today, video games are competing successfully with other media for students' attention because gaming is second nature to children (Foreman, 2004).

Changing the Culture and Practice of 'School'

The rather obvious difference between games and traditional schooling is that good games always involve play, and schooling rarely does. Pressure from students who want more engagement in their learning, and the need to move toward more 21st century skills and approaches that work with technology will hopefully drive a change in the culture and practice of 'school'. The prevalent instructional paradigm in K-12 education is fundamentally different than that proposed for serious educational video games. These games are based on challenge, reward, and discovery, in contrast to segmented instructional blocks and standardized strategies prevalent in today's K-12 education. According to the findings from the Summit on Educational Games, "effective use of games is likely to be limited until educational institutions are willing to consider significant changes in pedagogy and content, and rethink the role of teachers and other educational professionals" (p.6).

In the meantime, we must be cognizant of not just the content, but also the context of video game use. Critics view games as activities that cut into time practicing relevant content, rather than being another form of learning and practice. In a study done by Ramani & Siegler (2008), youngsters from low-income backgrounds who were exposed to a simple board game that involved counting produced large and lasting gains in their understanding of numbers. However, there are researchers who oppose this narrow view of video games suggesting that it is not the content, skills and attitudes relative to educational purposes that is important but rather the structural characteristics of the video game that encourage the higher level, problem solving skills that are applicable to all content areas of learning. The concept of no-fault problem solving, where players are allowed to fail, fault-free and are given several chances to get the right solution, fosters creativity and inventiveness, but does not fit will with traditional educational practices. We certainly are not doing a very good job of keeping our students engaged in learning, particularly after setbacks and failures. The perception that there is a freedom to fail is a powerful element in the design of effective educational video games.

Evolving Research Agenda

21st Century video gaming is a maturing medium in our global high-tech world. (Squire, 2003). Although not the first of its kind, "Joystick Nation" (Herz, 1996) and "Digital Game-Based Learning" (Prensky, 2000) were there earlier, Gee's "What Video Games Have to Teach Us About Learning" (2003), was the first 'for real' academic book with an aura of authority. The literature still varies widely and remains inconclusive. Some studies conclude that video games are socially damaging, others discuss benefits (Turkle, 1984; Postman, 1986). There is research showing no evidence that video games result in negative effects (Gibb, Bailey, Lambirth, & Wilson, 1983). There is research indicating that video games are not addictive (Egli & Meyers, 1984), and research finding that heavy video game use does not lead to mental disorders or delinquency (McClure & Mears, 1986). Some studies (Bowman, 1982, Bracey, 1992, Driskell & Dwyer, 1984) focused on deriving principles from traditional action ("twitch") games, others on adventure, sports, strategy, role-playing games, as well as hybrid games of multiple genres (Appleman & Goldsworthy 1999; Saltzman 1999).

A criticism specific to video games research is that it often involves research done by the actual game developers. When researchers conduct studies of the games they build, they of course expect success. Those who advocate the use of games in education carry an enthusiasm and advocacy that has been accused of clouding the research process. In writing this chapter, numerous interviews and discussions of educational gaming by the developers themselves were located. One example is educational video gaming entrepreneur, Ntiedo Etuk. As it turns out, Etuk founded the company Tabula Digita in 2004 and has been immersed in disseminating his educational video game software into the nation's school systems. He states that Tabula Digita is focused on creating games that engage and boost achievement, and provides his own research and that of University of Central Florida to back up this claim. He asserts that the Tabula Digita DimensionM suite of products caused test scores on the Orange Co, Florida benchmark exams to more than double. That is quite a claim, however one is well into his educational gaming article (2008) before realizing the connection. Some games researchers believe that the only effective way to study video games is in the natural, informal environment of play. This is in direct competition with the methods of accountability in today's political arena – whereby funding sources, government, and parents want formal and easily understood learning environments. Many would say this is not conducive to exploring the value of video games. This has led gaming companies to design chiefly for the 'after-school' market, where such informal learning environments are encouraged.

Attributes of Quality Video Game Environments for Children

The simplest video games contain a complex set of properties. We all know that children quickly develop an understanding of the concept of a game at developmentally appropriate levels. It is as though the game concept plays a special organizing role in cognition, not unlike a story schema. Video games also shift the balance of information processing from verbal to visual. These games emphasize spatial and symbolic imagery, attributes that remain unchanged no matter the learning task or content area (Subrahmanyam & Greenfield, 2001.) Video games are built on a set of design principles and these principles stem from the fundamental learning principles that cognitive theory has validated (Gee, 2003; Gee, Hawisher, & Selfe, 2007). Gee's 36 Principles, which we will not deal with in particular, are pretty heady stuff claiming that video games lend themselves well to transference; in other words, you can transfer what you learn in video games to other contexts (Williamson & Gee, 2006). In a well-designed game, gamers learn new skills and see the consequences of their knowledge as scores climb or fall. Winning and losing are real experiences with strong emotional implications, and also a big part of the attraction of video games.

No denying it, there is something exciting about video games. They are interactive, never lose patience, and are second nature to today's students who often play in groups, and share experiences. And the positive excitement may have something to do with the fact that much of video gaming is situated in social and cultural spheres that are in many ways more important than the game itself. Students learn to interact with technology and each other early, developing technological literacy

(Subrahmanyam & Greenfield 1998). There is substantial antidotal evidence that video game playing often leads to an interest with technology in general (Herz, 1997; Subrahmanyam & Greenfield, 1998). Although regularly blamed for being time-wasters requiring little or zero intellectual capacity, research reveals that gaming not only offers meaningful and challenging learning environments, but promotes the development of cognitive skills and engaging learning opportunities (Prensky & Thiagrajan, 2007). Educators need to see video games as a new, amazing resource not as a menace.

Many of the currently available computer games for K-12 have targeted science education. It may be that the inquiry-oriented, process-approach to learning science has just lent itself well to the positive attributes of gaming. Real-world problems in science are all around us and do not have to be contrived. The scientific process almost always involves collecting bits of information and then synthesizing these into a 'truth' for the sake of solving the problem. It is understood that there is likely no 'one right answer' to the problem and value is placed on the inquiry process. An example that relates to the biosciences is "Eco-Quest," an adventure video game designed to teach the importance of environmental ethics. Certainly a hot topic today in K-12 education, this game includes two topics. The first encourages the player to explore various ecosystems and the creatures provide information on how to avoid pollution. The second game requires that the player cure a disease affecting rainforest residents. The National Science Foundation has funded several such scientific inquiry video games, including "QuestAtlantis" and "RiverCity." This problem solving approach has also found its way into serious video games devoted to history and social studies. Muzzy Lane's "Making History" is described as a strategy game where players lead real nations through the World War II years. The "Civilization" series (Hasbro) has been described as a strategy game but criticized for perpetuating the American myths of how empires are built or destroyed (Kapell, 2002).

Classroom Environments that Support Learning Games

The use of video games and traditional K-12 instructional methods has come into conflict. Truth is, from the start, gaming was viewed as a menace to instructional efforts. Why? Maybe something as simple as what Grand Master McLuhan said, "every new technology necessitates a new war" (McLuhan & Fiore, 1968). Well, make no mistake, the tide has changed. There is nothing less than a full-blooded learning paradigm shift happening right now. The challenge is for 21st Century teachers to rethink teaching; to stop skilling-and-drilling, and multiple-choice testing students to oblivion. Students are not learning how to think as much as learning how to memorize. What they are learning outside school is not being replicated inside it (Silvern & Williamson,1987). The best video games encourage players to achieve mastery of one level, only to have to regain that mastery in the next, forcing adaptation and evolvement. When students play video games they experience a much more powerful form of learning than when they are in class.

Perhaps the answer lies not in having an either/or division of camps as described by Klopfer et al. (2009) but in using serious video games as an integral part of the learning environment in K-12 education. The appropriate and authentic integration of technology, from using videos to using computers, is an on-going theme in the literature. Simply 'using' a technology does not place it in a position to make a difference in teaching and learning. Too often word processors are used to 'type up' a paper that has already been written or videos are shown to keep students occupied. Serious video games challenge K-12 educators to examine their use in terms of real learning. Calling these 'game-anchored' lessons, Simpson & Clem (2008) describe a pilot curriculum built

around a commercial video game. These lessons are guided by the teacher, but give the students the opportunity to use the video game as a simulation to apply concepts they were learning in class. Through analyzing student journals, they determined that the students viewed the game as a social and shared experience, thus reinforcing what has been said about a change in learner characteristics and demands.

The blending of the video game atmosphere and the classroom experience may be possible, as long as educators keep in mind the tentative nature of the true 'play' experience. Remembering that too much adult intervention changes the game into work, if not careful, the structuring and teacher involvement suggested by some will begin to look and smell 'like school.' Charsky and Mims (2008) suggest that a teacher wishing to use a video game in learning must first learn everything about the game. That's quite a tall order, considering the limited time teachers have and the complex nature of these video games. In fact, these games are constructed such that players do not have to know everything about the game in order to be successful and it may even be next to impossible to know it all. There are programmed twists and turns that are completely dependent on the decisions of the player. The game is devised to be different each time it is played. That's one thing that makes it a 'game.'

The context and structure of the game may be just as important as the 'content.' Bowman (1982), for example, compared gamers engaged in states of flow, with students in traditional school environments. Then, suggested that educators use video games as a model for improving learning environments, by providing clear goals, challenging students, allowing for collaboration, using criterion based assessments, giving students more control over the learning process, and incorporating novelty into the environment. 'Game flow' is also described as a state of optimal experience whereby, a person is so engaged in activity that self-consciousness disappears, and time becomes distorted (Csikszentmihalyi, 1990); in other words, a state of intense concentration, where previously difficult tasks become easy, and whatever you are doing becomes pleasurable. Not too surprisingly, well-designed video games are especially good at maintaining this flow state in players (Squire, 2003).

The use of video games allows teachers and learners to simulate rich multimedia learning experiences that might otherwise not be possible. The use of video games is meant to allow learners to become immersed in authentic environments, giving teachers an opportunity to create real-world learning situations, tasks, and problems. Remember, it must first be a game, and only then, a teacher. The old tell and test method has failed because the world and learner have changed. There are no longer many people denying that intrinsic motivation is lacking in education. Intrinsic motivation is what promotes desire for reoccurrence of the experience and motivates learners to engage in activities with which they have little or no previous experience. Attempting to 'diagnose' the fundamental problems of public education today, Christensen states that 'motivation is the catalyzing ingredient for every successful innovation' (2008, p.7) and he goes on to relate this to learning. Bottom line: When we enjoy learning, we learn better.

FUTURE RESEARCH DIRECTIONS

Plagued by comparison groups that don't compare, either with student characteristics or teacher influences, educational research, especially with regard to activities involving technology, has fallen prisoner to the 'no significant difference' phenomenon. Research in the realm of educational video games is no exception. Enthusiasm for educational video games is tempered by the lack of empirical evidence that clearly establishes improved learning outcomes for game-based activities. Video games seem to promote significantly more positive atti-

tudes toward learning (Ke, 2008) but qualitatively do not significantly surpass pencil and paper drills in promoting cognitive performance. While not unexplored territory, research into the educational significance of serious video games is lacking. Researchers are scattered over many disciplines and share little except the interest in exploring the educational value of games. Clark (2007) suggests one remedy to this situation is that more valid and reliable tests of learning and motivation should be implemented in research designs.

Findings from the Summit on Educational Games (2006) indicate that a more robust program of research and experimentation is needed. Private sector investment in such a program will continue to be lacking because of the exploratory nature and uncertain return on this development. They suggest that the potential market is fragmented because some 16,000 K-12 school districts in the United States are unwilling to abandon textbooks and traditional materials and are reluctant to invest in unproven or unchartered territory. Educational game researchers suggest finding the areas of intersection in engineering, philosophical theory, and learning theory and using this as a focus and driving force for new educational games research. This could help contribute to the establishment of a common research language. In turn, this may also help researchers define what exactly is to be considered a 'serious game' and move research past games that do not encourage cognitive engagement.

As we begin to realize and value informal opportunities to learn, serious video games may find their way into our classrooms and into 21st century learning. Speak Up 2007, conducted by Project Tomorrow (2008), found that over 64% of students in grades K-12 play online and/or electronics based games regularly and on average across all grades, K-12 students are playing games approximately 8-10 hours a week. However the number one use of technology to facilitate student learning cited by teachers was assigning homework or practice work (51%). More than half of students in grades 3 through 12 believe educational gaming would help them learn, yet only 16% of teachers, 15% of administrators and 19% of parents are on board. Clearly, we have some work to do in this area.

While much has been made regarding 'game flow' in the playing of commercial video games, those video games that aim to teach are trying to convey knowledge, as well as the skill of learning to play the game. Measuring the player's skill at playing the game does not adequately measure the acquisition of content knowledge. However, knowledge attainment should be viewed as an enjoyable and desired outcome of playing serious video games. Transference of knowledge has always been the elusive brass ring for education. Therefore, tools to measure this outside of game skill must be developed and used as part of the evaluation of serious video games. Various scales are finding their way into the research (Fu, Su, & Yu, 2009; Liu & Lin, 2009) and may be a step in the right direction, however these still rely heavily on learner opinions and game design in terms of skill, rather than application of content knowledge.

Additionally, moving away from a one-student/ one-screen approach can provide the opportunities for adult guidance and peer interaction that are still missing in most educational video games. Of course, this all requires a break from the didactic classroom model. Educators are now realizing the role that 'informal' learning plays for adults and thus, isn't it realistic to imagine that K-12 students can also benefit from a more constructivist approach to learning? Students today are able to seek out information and content from many sources, not just from the teacher/expert. It is worth investigating the potential of peer support networks for learning and how serious gaming can provide a safe and organized means of doing this. Perhaps the issue is that the adults just don't have the capacity for designing such video games. Marc Prensky sees students as the next generation of designers and creators of educational computer games. "The next generation of educational games – the games that will truly engage and teach students – is likely to come from the minds of other students, rather than from their teachers. And it is likely that learners will relate to these games, and learn from them, in a way that is not happening today." (Prensky, 2008, pp.1004-1005)

The Horizon Report (2008) identifies video game play as one of the seven metatrends that continue to affect teaching and learning and that this is evolving to include virtual worlds, augmented reality, and massive multiplayer modes. An emerging trend that is worth exploration is that of haptic computing, which adds the sense of touch to the experience. Nintendo's Wii platform has brought on an initial awareness of this approach. Such input devices, by activating a sense of touch, hold potential to involve those learners who may have been out of reach in the past. In addition, Wii has provided a holistic view of video games as environments that require movement and player engagement.

CONCLUSION

Greenfield (1984) calls video games the first medium to combine visual dynamism with an active, participatory role. The secret of video games is their underlying architecture, hard enough at every point, just doable. Tapscott (2009) says gamers want to be users, not just viewers or listeners. Active not passive absorbers of knowledge, Murray (1997) refers to this as agency, the satisfying power to take meaningful action and see the results of our decisions and choices. When students do not pay attention in school, it is not because they cannot, it is because they choose not to. That is an important distinction. Students' brains are antithetical to traditional ways of learning. This is at the root of many tensions. Linear thought processes that once dominated educational systems now get in the way of learning. No technology should become an end in itself, especially not outdated ones (Withrow,

2004). Video games are a vast resource waiting to be tapped. Go play.

REFERENCES

Anderson, C., & Ford, C. (1986). Affect of the game player: Short-term effects of highly and mildly aggressive video games. *Personality and Social Psychology Bulletin, 12*(4), 290–402. doi:10.1177/0146167286124002

Appleman, R., & Goldsworthy, R. (1999). The juncture of games & instructional design: Can fun be learning? Presentation made at the 1999 annual meeting of the Association of Educational Communications and Technology, Houston, TX.

Bowman, R. (1982). A Pac-Man theory of motivation: Tactical implications for classroom instruction. *Educational Technology, 22*(9), 14–17.

Bracey, G. (1992). The bright future of integrated learning systems. *Educational Technology, 32*(9), 60–62.

Calvert, S., & Tan, S. (1994). Impact of virtual reality on young adults' physiological arousal and aggressive thoughts: Interaction versus observation. *Journal of Applied Developmental Psychology, 15*(1), 125–139. doi:10.1016/0193-3973(94)90009-4

Charsky, D., & Mims, C. (2008). Integrating commercial off-the-shelf video games into school curriculums. *TechTrends, 52*(5), 38–44. doi:10.1007/s11528-008-0195-0

Christensen, C., Horn, M., & Johnson, C. (2008). *Disrupting class: How disruptive innovation will change the way the world learns.* New York: McGraw Hill.

Clark, R. (2007). Learning from serious games? Arguments, evidence, and research suggestions. *Educational Technology, 47*(3), 56–59.

Csikszentmihalyi, M. (1990). *Flow: the psychology of optical experience.* New York: Harper Perennial.

Driskell, J., & Dwyer, D. (1984). Microcomputer videogame based training. *Educational Technology, 24*(2), 11–15.

Egli, E., & Meyers, L. (1984). The role of video game playing in adolescent life: Is there reason to be concerned? *Bulletin of the Psychonomic Society, 22*, 309–312.

Etuk, N. (2008). Educational gaming: From edutainment to bona fide 21st century teaching tool. *MultiMedia & Internet @Schools, 15*(6), 10-13.

Federation of American Scientists. (2006). *Findings and recommendations from the Summit on Educational Games: Harnessing the power of video games for learning. October 25, 2005.* Washington, DC: Author.

Foreman, J. (2004). Video game studies and the emerging instructional revolution. *Innovate: Journal of Online Education, 1*. Retrieved from http://www.innovationonline.info/index.php?view=article&id=2

Fromberg, D., & Bergen, D. (2006). *Play from Birth to 12.* New York: Routledge.

Fu, F., Su, R., & Yu, S. (2009). EGameFlow: a scale to measure learners' enjoyment of e-learning games. *Computers & Education, 52*, 101–112. doi:10.1016/j.compedu.2008.07.004

Gagne, R. (1987). *Instructional Technology Foundations.* Hillsdale, NJ: Lawrence Erlbaum Assoc.

Gee, J. P. (2003). *What video games have to teach us about learning and literacy.* New York: Palgrave Macmillan.

Gee, J. P., Hawisher, G., & Selfe, C. (2007). *Gaming lives in the twenty-first century: Literate connections*. New York: Palgrave/Macmillan.

Gibb, G., Bailey, J., Lambirth, T., & Wilson, W. (1983). Personality differences between high and low electronic video game users. *The Journal of Psychology, 114*, 159–165.

Glickman, C. (1984). Play in public school settings: A philosophical question. In Yawkey, T. D., & Pellegrini, A. D. (Eds.), *Child's play: Developmental and applied* (pp. 255–271). Hillsdale, NJ: Lawrence Erlbaum Associates.

Graybill, D., Kirsch, J., & Esselman, E. (1985). Effects of playing violent versus nonviolent video games on the aggressive ideation of aggressive and nonaggressive children. *Child Study Journal, 15*(3), 299–205.

Graybill, D., Strawniak, M., Hunter, T., & O'Leary, M. (1987). Effects of playing versus observing violent versus nonviolent video games on children's aggression. *Psychology: A Quarterly Journal of Human Behavior, 24*(3), 1-8.

Greenfield, P. (1984). *Mind & media: The effects of television, video games & computers*. Cambridge, MA: Harvard University Press.

Gunter, G., Kenny, R., & Vick, E. (2007). Taking educational games seriously: using the RETAIN model to design endogenous fantasy into stand-alone educational games. *Educational Technology Research and Development, 56*, 511–537. doi:10.1007/s11423-007-9073-2

Herz, J. (1997). *Joystick nation. How videogames ate our quarters, won our hearts, and rewired our minds*. Princeton, NJ: Little Brown & Company.

Irwin, R., & Gross, A. (1995). Cognitive tempo, violent video games, and aggressive behavior in young boys. *Journal of Family Violence, 10*, 337–350. doi:10.1007/BF02110997

Kapell, M. (2002). Civilization and its discontents: American monomythic structure as historical simulacrum. *Popular Culture Review, 13*(2), 129–136.

Ke, F. (2008). Computer games application within alternative classroom goal structures: cognitive, metacognitive, and affective evaluation. *Educational Technology Research and Development, 56*, 539–556. doi:10.1007/s11423-008-9086-5

Keller, J. M. (1987). Development and use of the ARCS model of motivational design. *Journal of Instructional Development, 10*(3), 2–10. doi:10.1007/BF02905780

Kenny, R. (2009). Evaluating cognitive tempo in the digital age. *Educational Technology Research and Development, 57*, 45–60. doi:10.1007/s11423-007-9035-8

Klopfer, E., Osterweil, S., & Salen, K. (2009). Moving learning games forward: obstacles, opportunities, and openness. *The Education Arcade*. Cambridge, MA: Massachusetts Institute of Technology. Retrieved April 2, 2009 from: http://www.educationarcade.org/

Lim, C. (2008). Spirit of the game; empowering students as designers in schools. *British Journal of Educational Technology, 39*(6), 996–1003. doi:10.1111/j.1467-8535.2008.00823_1.x

Liu, E., & Lin, C. (2009). Developing evaluative indicators for educational computer games. *British Journal of Educational Technology, 40*(1), 174–178. doi:10.1111/j.1467-8535.2008.00852.x

McClure, R., & Mears, F. (1986). Videogame playing and psychopathology. *Psychological Reports, 59*, 59–62.

McLuhan, M., & Fiore, Q. (1968). *War and peace in the global village*. New York: Bantam.

Michaels, J. (1993). Patterns of video game play in parlors as a function of endogenous and exogenous factors. *Youth & Society, 25*(2), 272–289. doi:10.1177/0044118X93025002005

Murray, J. (1997). *Hamlet on the holodeck: The future of narrative in cyberspace.* New York: The Free Press.

New Media Consortium. (2008). *The 2008 horizon report.* Retrieved from New Media Consortium web site: http://wp.nmc.org/horizon2008/

Paley, V. (2004). *A child's work: The importance of fantasy play.* Chicago: University of Chicago Press.

Postman, N. (1986). *Amusing ourselves to death: Public discourse in the age of show business.* New York: Penguin USA.

Prensky, M. (2000). *Digital game-based learning.* New York: McGraw Hill.

Prensky, M. (Interviewee). (2007). *The rules of engagement.* [video file]. Interview with Sisomo on 20 January 2007. Retrieved from Sisomo web site: http://sisomo.com/interviews/Marc-Prensky.htm

Prensky, M. (2008). Students as designers and creators of educational computer games: Who else? *British Journal of Educational Technology, 39*(6), 1004–1019. doi:10.1111/j.1467-8535.2008.00823_2.x

Prensky, M., & Thiagrajan, S. (2007). *Digital game-based learning.* New York: McGraw Hill.

Project Tomorrow. (2007). *Speak up 2007 for students, teachers, parents & school leaders - selected national findings.* Retrieved December 10, 2008 from http://www.tomorrow.org/docs/National%20Findings%20Speak%20Up%202007.pdf

Provenzo, E. (1991). *Video kids: Making sense of Nintendo.* Cambridge, MA: Harvard.

Provenzo, E. (1992). What do video games teach? *Education Digest, 58*(4), 56–58.

Ramani, G., & Siegler, R. (2008). Promoting broad and stable improvements in low-income children's numerical knowledge through playing number board games. *Child Development, 79*(2), 375–394. doi:10.1111/j.1467-8624.2007.01131.x

Rieber, L. (1996). Seriously considering play: Designing interactive learning environments based on the blending of microworlds, simulations, and games. *Educational Technology Research and Development, 44*(1), 43–58. doi:10.1007/BF02300540

Saltzman, M. (Ed.). (1999). *Game design: Secrets of the sages.* Indianapolis: Brady.

Schutte, N., Malouff, J., Post-Gorden, J., & Rodasta, A. (1988). Effects of playing videogames on children's aggressive and other behaviors. *Journal of Applied Social Psychology, 18*(5), 454–460. doi:10.1111/j.1559-1816.1988.tb00028.x

Silvern, S., & Williamson, P. (1987). The effects of video game play on young children's aggression, fantasy and prosocial behavior. *Journal of Applied Developmental Psychology, 8*, 453–462. doi:10.1016/0193-3973(87)90033-5

Simpson, E., & Clem, F. (2008). Video games in the middle school classroom. *Middle School Journal, 39*(4), 4–11.

Squire, K. (2003). Video games in education. *International Journal of Intelligent Simulations and Gaming, 2*(1).

Subrahmanyam, K., & Greenfield, P. (1998). Computer games for girls: What makes them play? In Cassell, J., & Jenkins, H. (Eds.), *From Barbie to Mortal Combat: Gender and computer games.* Cambridge, MA: MIT Press.

Subrahmanyan, K., & Greenfield, P. (2001). The impact of computer use on children's and adolescent's development. *Journal of Applied Developmental Psychology, 22*(1), 7–30. doi:10.1016/S0193-3973(00)00063-0

Tapscott, D. (2009). *Grown up digital: How the net generation is changing your world.* New York: McGraw Hill.

Turkle, S. (1984). *The second self: Computers and the human spirit.* New York: Simon and Schuster.

Vygotsky, L. (1933). *Play and its role in the mental development of the child.* Retrieved from http://www.marxists.org/archive/vygotsky/works/1933/play.htm by *Psychology and Marxism Internet Archive (marxists.org).*

Williamson, D., & Gee, J. P. (2006). *How computer games help children learn.* New York: Palgrave Macmillan. McGraw Hill.

Withrow, F. (2004). *Literacy in the digital age: Reading, writing, viewing, and computing.* Lanham, MD: Scarecrow Education.

Chapter 20
Video Games in Education:
Opportunities for Learning Beyond Research Claims and Advertising Hype

P.G. Schrader
University of Nevada, USA

Kimberly A. Lawless
University of Illinois, USA

Hasan Deniz
University of Nevada, USA

ABSTRACT

There has been an abundance of writing about video games[1] in education. Characteristic of a young field, much of this work is theoretical and not necessarily based on data (de Freitas, 2006). Classroom integration strategies rely on researchers' arguments, anecdotal evidence, and teachers' pragmatism. Unfortunately, video games are often created for profit and to entertain, leaving many additional issues to consider (i.e., marketing, effectiveness, etc.). Researchers' arguments combined with video games' widespread popularity and potentially spurious advertising may leave teachers confused or misinformed. To exemplify this issue, this chapter contrasts the salient properties of a commercial game (Spore), an immersive context with game-like features (Quest Atlantis), and a pedagogically based immersive context (GlobalEd 2). Specifically, the authors describe the educational and technological affordances of three contexts, the limitations associated with each, and the necessary yet pragmatic steps involved in their classroom use.

INTRODUCTION

Video games have become both a national and international phenomenon. In the United States, nearly all students (97%) report that they play some form of electronic game (i.e., computer, web, por-

table, or console; Pew Internet and American Life Project, 2008). By virtue of this popularity, games given rise to new industries including professional gaming, sale of digital resources, and game-for-pay industries in Europe, North America and even Asia (Bailey, 2006; Dibbel, 2007; Jiminez, 2007). Sales figures reached $21.3 billion in 2008 (Ault, 2009) and continue to show strong signs of growth, even

DOI: 10.4018/978-1-61520-781-7.ch020

in an economic recession (Pham, 2009). The commercial appeal and success of video games is often used as part of an argument promoting the use of video games as learning tools.

However, industry professionals are commonly interested in creating entertaining games that provide a significant and often sustainable source of revenue (e.g., subscription models). By contrast, educators and researchers are committed to understanding and leveraging the educational attributes of games. These two goals are not always aligned. Researchers espouse the educative properties of games (e.g., Gee, 2003; Schrader & McCreery, 2007; Squire, 2006; Steinkuehler, 2006; Young, Schrader, & Zheng, 2006). However, developers do not necessarily leverage the current knowledge base when creating games even though researchers' arguments are abundant, convincing, and pervasive.

The popularity of games combined with the many arguments associated with their use in classrooms may have unfortunate outcomes. For example, these "experts" in the field may persuade teachers to adopt games-based learning tools without due and careful consideration. Other, more skeptical educators may remain unsure about the effectiveness of games as learning tools. Regardless, there is little information about effective strategies or approaches to utilizing games in classrooms. Without empirical guidance, these emphatic claims about video games in education and the associated decisions to bring them into classes may be premature.

As is common in new fields, there are few studies to guide educators. The studies that exist document a wide array of helpful outcomes, including positive influence on motivation and reinforcement (Malouf, 1987; Millar & Navarick, 1984), spatial ability (Greenfield, Brannon, & Lohr, 1994; Subrahmanyam & Greenfield, 1994) and the development of complex motor skills (Day, Arthur, & Gettman, 2001; Mane, Adams, & Donchin, 1989). Moreover, several authors have postulated that games can also further skills

in terms of communication (Steinkuehler, 2004; Squire, 2003), collaboration (Schrader & McCreery, 2007; Squire, 2006), and problem solving (Gee, 2003; Young et al., 2006).

However, it is clear that researchers must continue to examine video games as learning tools. Unfortunately, the development of new technology frequently outpaces academic understanding of those tools in education. In extreme cases, games designed and promoted around content may lead to undesired consequences. For example, *Spore* is a game designed around the concept of evolution, but play is likely to reinforce misconceptions, rather than promote scientific understanding (Bean, Sinatra, & Schrader, 2009). Given that there is a large market for all video games, developers may rush to create educational titles so they may attempt to capitalize on market trends. As a result, arguments in the literature extolling the virtues of games may not align with the affordances present in contemporary video games.

Fortunately, many of these issues can be resolved if researchers and educators are capable of moving beyond discourse extolling the virtues of educational gaming and toward the meaningful incorporation of immersive contexts into curricula. In service of this idea, this chapter describes the salient technological and educational affordances of three starkly contrasting environments that vary in terms of their ludic characteristics. Specifically, the attributes of a commercial game, a game-like immersive context developed for education, and an immersive pedagogical space are compared (*Spore*, *Quest Atlantis*, and *GlobalEd 2*, respectively). More importantly, this analysis provides a framework to examine the meaningful integration of video games in education. In the process, we expose an unfortunate inability for *Spore* to directly support disciplinary objectives as well as the compromises made by *Quest Atlantis* and *GlobalEd 2* in order to create salient and accessible game-based instructional interventions. Ultimately, we examine implications for educators, researchers, and designers.

Games in Education

Any discussion involving video games and their use in education typically involves notions of fun, popularity, and engagement. There is little question that games are entertaining. Specifically, they offer students a way to engage in flow (see Csikszentmihalyi, 1991), feel a diminished sense of self, and pursue a pure sensory experience that is of the moment and devoid of hyper-intellectualism (Brown & Vaughan, 2009). Sales statistics also indicate that consumers' have an insatiable appetite for video games, yielding more than 50 billion dollars in revenue for 2008, even in an economic recession (Ault, 2009; Pham, 2009). Video games are also highly engaging, a characteristic that interests educators (Schrader, Young, & Zheng, 2006).

However convincing, the views that games are fun, popular, and engaging do not necessarily justify their use in education. Technology integration is a complex endeavor that requires knowledge of the technology itself, the content, and the unique pedagogies involved (TPACK; Archambault & Crippen, 2009; Colbert et al., 2008). From this view, educational theory and research should inform the decision and strategies associated with the classroom integration of video games.

Admittedly, few challenge the notion that video games are fun and popular. However, there has been more than 25 years of discussion about motivation and video games (Bowman, 1982; 2007; Malouf, 1987; Millar & Navarick, 1984). Bowman (1982) described the ways that *Pac-Man* and the surrounding ethos provided both intrinsic and extrinsic rewards, resulting in high levels of motivation to play the game. Bowman (2007) later reprised these views and asked if the focus should be on facilitating motivation or if researchers should focus on ways to remove barriers that inhibit motivation (e.g., policy, practice, morale, etc.). Although motivation is an important issue in general and video games may provide motivating elements (see Gee, 2003; Squire, 2006; Young et al., 2007), there are many other ways in which video games are thought to have an impact on learning and learning environments.

A scan of the literature will reveal that educational research associated with games falls into a few specific categories. One major approach encompasses research linked to the outcomes or consequences associated with playing games, whether or not those outcomes are positive. For example, researchers have examined the nature of gender and identity as a result of game play. Kafai (1996) documented that boys and girls prefer different levels of competition in games, the latter showing a preference for single player and/or cooperative-style games. According to others, the technological gender gap is exacerbated by the fact that males often design games for other males (Canada & Brusca, 1991; Kafai, 1996) and the depiction of women in games is often negative (i.e., women portrayed in a subordinate role, unrealistic, or anatomically inaccurate; Children Now, 2000).

Another outcome often associated with video games is the apparent likelihood that some games, and other media, promote aggression and hostility. Specific examples include the Virginia Tech and Northern Illinois campus shootings. In both cases, critics and opponents claimed that video game play was directly responsible for the tragic events. Specifically, Jack Thompson, a former Florida attorney and opponent of violent video games, argued that games like *Counter Strike*, a realistic first-person game involving shooting and strategy, were to blame for the incidents (Benedetti, 2007).

These anecdotal arguments tend to inflame the public and invite a "moral panic" that is not founded in evidence (Ferguson, 2008). Researchers who examine aggressive aspects of games and their impact on hostility, aggressive behaviors, and cognitions may fuel this panic (Anderson & Bushman, 2001; Gentile, Lynch, Linder, & Walsh, 2004; Webber, Ritterfeld, & Mathiak, 2006). However, Ferguson argues that more than a decade of research fails to establish a link, causal or otherwise, between violent video games and violent crimes, like school shootings.

In addition to their potential link to aggression, video games have been criticized for their addictive nature (Fisher, 1994; Griffiths & Dancaster, 1995) and association with inactivity and obesity (Vandewater, Shim, & Caplovitz, 2004). These issues have become more visible to the public for two key reasons, video games are more popular than ever and they are also much more involved, dynamic, and immersive. Overall, contemporary video games require a significant investment of time to accomplish obstacles and objectives. In some cases, video games require significant amounts of money.

For some, playing video games comes at a different type of cost. In one severe case, a 28 year old South Korean man died of heart failure caused by dehydration and starvation after 50 consecutive hours of game play (BBC News, 2005). Because of this, several video game addiction resources have emerged (e.g., http://www.video gameaddiction.net/, http://www.video-game-addiction.org/). However, there are no clinical criteria to diagnose video game addiction (i.e., distinguishable from a compulsive disorder) and the behaviors exhibited by "addicts" are neither consistent nor are they necessarily linked to addictive traits (Wood, 2008).

In general, it seems that games' meteoric rise in popularity has invited many negative perceptions and "media panic" associated with them. Because of these issues, individuals like Jack Thompson have attempted to demonize video games. However, several researchers report positive consequences of playing games. For example, Green and Bavelier (2003; 2007) found that video game players have: 1) enhanced attention resources, 2) better enumeration, and 3) better perceptual attention over space and time with respect to information presented on a screen. These findings align with earlier results (Greenfield et al., 1994; Subrahmanyam & Greenfield, 1994). Researchers

have also documented other positive outcomes associated with Attention Deficit-Hyperactivity Disorder (Lawrence et al., 2002; Shaw, Grayson, & Lewis, 2006) and the inhibition of eye-poking behavior (Kennedy & Souza, 1995).

Although this perspective may be informative for certain constituencies (e.g., military training of visual acuity), other researchers have argued that video games are more than technologies to bring about a change (i.e., cognitive or behavioral residue; see Salomon, Perkins, & Globerson, 1991). Researchers have also discussed the way individuals interact *with* video games and *within* video game contexts (Schrader, 2008). In the first case, players form intellectual partnerships with the systems and algorithms in the games. The interactions with the system allow players to off-load considerable cognitive burden onto the game itself while allowing them to address more complex ideas. For example, it is not necessary for *World of Warcraft* (*WOW*) players to heed the statistical enhancements gained by donning different equipment. Rather, players make changes to their characters and observe the outcome in a trial and error fashion (Schrader & McCreery, 2007).

As a context for interaction and learning, video games and their encapsulating culture have significant implications for education. By way of an avatar, a digital persona by which the player experiences the virtual world, players interact with objects, creatures, and other players within virtual spaces like Massively Multiplayer Online Games (MMOGs) and Multi-User Virtual Environments (MUVEs). The degree of interaction and the technological capabilities of contemporary environments are the topic of considerable interest. Several authors postulate that games can be used to promote communication (Steinkuehler, 2004; Squire, 2003), collaboration (Schrader & McCreery, 2007; Squire, 2006), and problem solving skills (Gee, 2003; Young et al., 2006).

Whether viewed as intellectual partners or immersive contexts, video games are most accurately described as ideological experiences (Squire, 2006). With or within them, players can interact with the environment and/or each other in purposeful ways (Gee, 2003; Squire, 2006; Young et al., 2006). Accordingly, game developers' and instructional designers' roles involve constraining the affordances of the game (i.e., control users' ability to act on and interact with the environment). This directs the experience and promotes learning. Combined with appropriate teaching strategies, students could be guided toward a common learning objective.

Using this approach, Squire and Durga (2008) leveraged *Civilization III* as a historical simulation. They describe an iterative process in which students played and replayed different eras in the game. This repetition allowed students to extrapolate salient principles across eras (e.g., major world powers typically have a) natural resources and b) multiple coastlines). Although commercially designed games do not typically leverage educational content, some pedagogical models are in place to do so.

Collectively, these arguments inform practice in key ways; they indicate what to avoid as well as what to target. The literature highlights several warnings about video games in education. From these lessons, it is clear that teachers must decide whether or not the content of a video game is appropriate (e.g., gender, violence, etc.) or even useful in the classroom (e.g., on-domain). Similarly, teachers should evaluate games based on their potential to influence learning in desired ways (e.g., learning gains, problem solving, communication, etc.).

To properly evaluate a video game, educators must examine the technological properties of the game itself; after all, not all games are created to be equal. Overall, the nature and complexity of video games has increased since their initial development in the late 1940's and early 1950's (Winter, 2008). Since that time, emerging tech-

nologies like graphics processors (e.g., NVidia, ATI), human interfaces (e.g., Nintendo Wii), networking technologies (e.g., Xbox Live™), and distribution philosophies (e.g., OnLive™), have and continue to drastically change players' experiences. Although this may be obvious to players and technologists, each video game represents a distinct set of affordances.

The relative uniqueness of modern digital games results in a vast landscape of experiences, with nearly limitless forms, genres, classes, and delivery methods. Video games like *Mario Brothers* allow users to interact in a fantasy world, following a somewhat linear storyline (Squire, 2006). By contrast, players who subscribe to WOW interact with millions of other players in a dynamically evolving world with no clear end (Schrader & McCreery, 2007). For players, this represents a rich selection of titles to play and enjoy. However, educators are responsible for evaluating these games and their technological and educational affordances. Each distinct capability aligns with a unique set of educational goals, activities, and assessment issues. Specifically, each innovation adds layers of complexity to an already complex task: technology integration.

While games' potential to entertain and promote motivation factored into teachers' dispositions, educators must also consider content, curriculum, and learning objectives (Archambault & Crippen, 2009; Schrader et al., 2006). On a broad scope, integration should be contextualized within the general literature, research, and arguments about video games in education. On a practical level, educators should examine the technological properties as they interact with content, curriculum, and pedagogy. Unfortunately, the numerous arguments about video games combined with the multitude of available technological affordances may be overwhelming for educators who seek to carefully and intentionally integrate games in education.

Affordances and Integration

The term "*affordance*" refers to the relationship between the latent properties of an object (or environment) and the capability for an agent to act upon those properties (Gibson, 1986). For example, a traditional wooden table affords a human many different things, including a flat surface for writing or sitting. In a less obvious way, a wooden table can also be burned, provide safety or shelter during a storm, or even turned on its side to make a goal for a game. Although the properties of the table may be latent, an affordance is dependent upon the agent's capacity to perform the action. Said another way, the agent does not necessarily need to perceive the possibility of an action, but the action must be possible (e.g., a child may dance on a table while a fish cannot).

With respect to technology, affordances are the technological functions or properties of a tool as they interact with a user's capability to perform actions. Adobe's Photoshop, a digital photo-editing tool, is a good example of a program that affords much more than the average user perceives. For example, the application permits sophisticated levels of post-production image editing. This includes altering the color of the image, its sharpness, and digital size. Some users may even know how to combine images in different ways (e.g., putting someone's head on a different body). However, Photoshop also allows users to overlay a 3D wireframe onto a 2D image. The combination makes it possible to add features like shadows, edits, and other changes that are consistent with the new 3D model. Because Photoshop is so complex, affordances like these are often overlooked.

In classrooms, teachers must understand two distinct aspects of technology. They must be aware of the technological capabilities of tools and they must address how those affordances influence learning (i.e., pedagogical affordances). For example, video production software like iMovie allows users to create and refine digital video. Throughout the process, users implement transition effects, customize audio, and select distribution models. On a cognitive level, students must identify and select appropriate media, evaluate and organize information on a timeline, and edit all content to communicate their perspective. Interactions like these represent a sophisticated degree of learning. As a result, educators may target those specific pedagogical affordances in their instruction (i.e., selection, identification, organization, etc.). Teachers bear the responsibility of identifying a tool's affordances and evaluating whether or not those affordances are appropriate to instruction (i.e., able to support educational objectives).

Unfortunately, this may not be an easy task with respect to video games. In a pragmatic sense, there are many challenges associated with video games in education. Relative to the number of lessons they may serve, the cost of video games is high, especially when multiple copies must be purchased. In most cases, video games also require high-powered computers with fast video processors, which is not typical of educational computer labs. Literature about video games also indicates that learning in such environments is time-intensive, which is a luxury in most educational settings that are constrained by national testing, class size issues, and formalized procedures. Time must be allotted to training as well, since video games require a certain amount of skill to play. Students and teachers must practice if they do not possess the requisite experience. Ultimately, teachers must also strike a balance between the learning experiences and local accountability requirements.

Once the logistical constraints have been mitigated or addressed, teachers must clearly delineate the educational objectives (i.e., content, process, etc.) and how they can maximize the technological affordances to meet those objectives. Specifically, they must determine how each game's properties interact with learning. In some games, 3D immersive environments may foster exploration and inquiry. In others, the capacity for multiplayer interaction may support problem solving. Something as simple as automatically recording information in a chat log might even mitigate cognitive load and allow players to pursue other goals without focusing on memorizing or recording events in the game.

However, video games vary widely in their content and their affordances. Unless one spends a great deal of time playing games, it would be difficult to identify the many, distinct technological affordances. Further, video game content does not necessarily align with educational objectives in an obvious way; there are no step-by-step instructions for using games in classrooms. As a result, teachers are left to combine the arguments in the literature with the marketing promises offered by developers. Unfortunately, marketing and reality are not always the same. Specifically, the video game *Spore* allows players to "create and guide your creature through five stages of evolution" (p 1., Electronic Arts, 2008). In reality, *Spore* is more likely to reinforce misconceptions and non-scientific views of evolution than it is to promote learning (Bean et al., 2009).

When well understood, researchers have documented it is possible to leverage the inherent affordances of video games to promote desired outcomes or learning. Subrahmanyam and Greenfield (1994) examined a video game in which the user controls a marble through a virtual obstacle course. Attempts at the course were timed and involved cliffs, ramps, bumpers, and worms that caused the marble to fall. Falling or failing the time limit ended the turn. The game, *Marble Madness*, was selected because game play involved "the spatial skills of guiding objects, judging speeds and distances of moving objects, and intercepting objects" (p. 19). In this way, Subrahmanyam and Greenfield leveraged the spatial affordances of Marble Madness to significantly increase performance of dynamic spatial skills in both boys and girls, though effects were concentrated on participants who scored low pretest measures.

Although this study reflects a cognitive residue

model of learning from technology (Salomon, Perkins, & Globerson, 1991), the example also demonstrates the role of affordances in promoting or achieving an educational objective. Specifically, Subrahmanyam and Greenfield (1994) developed an intervention based on previous findings and a tool that exhibited an appropriate set of affordances pertaining to a desired outcome. By following this approach, teachers might similarly integrate video games in education. However, teachers must rectify the many messages in the literature, the complexity of contemporary video games, and the marketing efforts that may result in a misperception of affordances (Gibson, 1996).

Even though it is necessary to identify and leverage affordances for the purpose of integrating video games in education, this process is far from obvious. Further, the initial impressions of a video game do not necessarily align with the actual affordances. For example, *GlobalEd 2* is far from inviting in terms of its visual appeal. It is designed for learning while its ludic properties are secondary. As such, the context promotes high levels of learning, but also happens to be engaging and meaningful. Similarly, *Spore* was advertised to be a game in which players experienced evolution, leading educators to believe such claims. Unfortunately, this fallacy becomes clear only by playing the game.

To elucidate the process and concretize the issues, the remaining sections of this chapter examine three separate contexts that vary in terms of key affordances. The first example was designed to be fun and is graphically appealing (i.e, *Spore*). In terms of education, *Spore* has also been advertised as an experience in evolution. The second game shares some of the properties of *Spore* (e.g., 3D immersion, interactivity in a virtual world, etc.), but is a game-like context designed for education (i.e., less of a focus on fun). Specifically, *Quest Atlantis* has been designed as a complete, situated experience to address scientific content. The third environment is distinct from the others because it does not contain sophisticated graphics or models and it was designed to promote learning as a principal goal. Specifically, *GlobalEd 2* employs an interactive text-based interface to facilitate an engaging pedagogical space rather than entertain players. *GlobalEd 2* was selected specifically because it is not a game in the traditional sense and therefore illustrates important contrasts to other contexts.

Each environment was selected because it varies in terms of affordances associated with educational game design. The systems were developed with different goals and exhibit unique educational and technological affordances as a result. More importantly, the variety among these three environments provides an ideal spectrum to examine the process of technology integration. For example, these environments vary along a ludic spectrum as well as their technological capabilities. Although the natural affordances of each environment differ, they all have educative potential. As such, they provide an opportunity to highlight educators' decisions as they relate to these environments.

Spore

Description

Spore is a graphically rich video game created by designer, Will Wright. Wright is best known for his work on games like *Sim City* and *The Sims*. Developed commercially by Maxis, these games are also considered to be icons of the simulation genre. In *Spore*, users control an organism as it develops, through five distinct stages of evolution. Each stage is unique and employs different algorithms and game mechanics. Further, stages are defined by their the appropriate frame of reference characterized by the sentience of the organism. The game begins in a liquid environment in which the player controls a cell that is microscopic and unaware. From there, the organism increases in awareness and complexity and matures through the creature, tribe, civilization, and space stages.

Spore was developed commercially and the main purpose of the game is to entertain. All interactions within the game and consequences of playing the game are the result of this principal objective.

During the cell stage, the player selects the major attributes of the cell, including size and diet (i.e., carnivore or herbivore). By interacting (i.e., swimming) through the environment, the organism collects DNA points by eating meat or organic matter. In the same way, the cell collects organic parts that allow it to become more complex. For example, once enough DNA points are accumulated, the organism can call a mate and the user can change the creature's parts (i.e., eyes, mouth, fins, etc.). DNA points also indicate a threshold of complexity and size. Once a specific number of DNA points are collected, the organism "evolves" legs and leaves the liquid environment.

On land, the primary activity returns to eating and collecting genetic material. However, the creature can also befriend other creatures using social skills (e.g., singing, dancing, posing). By contrast, the player can also cause the creature to attack others in the environment and attempt to dominate them via aggression (e.g., biting, striking, spitting). DNA points are awarded either for eliminating or befriending a different species and once sufficient DNA points have been accumulated, the player can use parts to alter their creature. This is accomplished via sexual reproduction, a process that involves calling a mate, entering the reproduction screen, and manipulating creature's characteristics (e.g., number of limbs, type of mouth, eyes, etc.). Upon leaving this screen, offspring are immediately produced and reflect all of the changes made by the player.

Once the creature has advanced a pre-defined number of times, it enters the tribal phase. At this point, it no longer evolves on a biological level. The tribal phase and two subsequent phases involve the development of socialization skills in a tribe, a civilization, and an intergalactic empire. Players create buildings, manipulate resources, and control space ships as their creature continues to advance.

Similarly, the remainder of game play involves interacting with other species and civilizations so the player's civilization can advance. The final objective in the game is to defeat an evil empire (i.e., Grox) and conquer/control the known galaxy. Although all five stages of *Spore* are entertaining, the first two phases are more relevant to science learning by virtue of their relationship to Darwinian evolution. As a result, these will serve as the focus of discussion.

Affordances

Technological. Although movement during the cell stage is constrained to two axes, *Spore* is a commercially developed, 3D immersive environment. As a result, players control their creatures as they navigate through an expansive landscape. Further, the graphics afford a variety of information not common in other games. Specifically, developers use a level of graphic 'zoom' to convey the sentience and complexity of the player's organism. For example, a field of view that is cloudy with elements on a microscopic scale is consistent with a single celled organism, unaware of their world on a planetary scale. Upon growing more complex, the visual field increases on the screen and the frame of reference 'zooms out' to include items on a larger scale. To represent this well, developers spent a great deal of time and energy refining the graphics of the immersive world.

Spore leverages graphics and motion to communicate other important information and aspects of the game. In addition to sentience, scale, and complexity, *Spore* uses a 3D immersive world to represent a creature's location as it navigates throughout the space. Because the game is primarily visual, graphics also communicate the nature of interaction with other species. For example, aggressive creatures adopt different stances, move in defensive positions, and generally behave in threatening ways. By contrast, social or friendly species sing, dance, and communicate with graphic icons above their heads. The visual field

is combined with sound, and using this information, the player is informed of the environmental constraints and can execute the appropriate action or change.

In addition to graphics, there are many underlying mechanics the player experiences via a dynamic feedback loop. For example, during the cell stage, players cause the organism to swim through the environment, the speed and accuracy of which can be modified using genetic parts. The graphics communicate distance, occlusion, and other visual affordances. However, cell movement is constrained by approximations of fluid dynamics, collision models, and Newtonian physics. For example, if a player's cell is caught in current, they move more slowly. As with the real world, these models have consequences. Specifically, a player may leverage this affordance to escape an attack while another may not and get killed by an attacking cell as a result.

Similarly, the creature stage obeys many real-world models. During this stage, creatures move around on a planet, interacting with other species and objects (e.g., trees, shrubs, cliffs, etc.). Each interaction is governed by appropriate Newtonian mechanics, such as gravity, collision, mass, and inertia. For example, a creature runs downhill faster than they are able to run up a steep slope. Similarly, adding wings to a creature allows them to experience acceleration due to gravity as well as the force of wind currents. Like the cell stage, players who understand and leverage these affordances enjoy an advantage. They can flee, attack, or generally facilitate their personal in-game goals.

Socially, *Spore* employs a unique set of affordances. Unlike many games today, *Spore* is not a typical MMOG or MUVE. Specifically, *Spore* does not allow players to interact with each other directly. Rather, players interact with the artifacts created by others. In other words, players control a creature of their own design as it interacts with creatures designed by other players in the *Spore* community. Although player-to-player contact does not take place in the game, the community is expansive, rich, and highly interactive.

Considered an integral aspect of the game, the online community that encapsulates *Spore* affords a variety of communication strategies and levels of interaction. For example, all of the creatures, buildings, and vehicles that have been created in the game are linked to a player's unique account. The *Spore* network allows players the opportunity to rate each other's creations, comment on them, or download them. Once downloaded, they can be used in their own game or modified however the player chooses. In this way, players can participate in the game and observe the artifacts of play without being actively logged in.

Learning. Because *Spore* was created commercially and for entertainment purposes, the content does not necessarily align with disciplinary objectives. *Spore* conveys the idea that members of a species do not stay the same and they can change over time, an idea that is consistent with Darwinian evolution. However, researchers suggest that people tend to think about biological content in personal ways that enable them to function in and make predictions about the everyday world (Evans 2001; Poling & Evans, 2002; Sinatra, Brem, & Evans, 2008). Unfortunately, there are at least three ways in which *Spore* may reinforce or promote the development of non-scientific thinking. Specifically, the underlying technological affordances may reinforce three major biases: the essentialist, teleological, and intentionality constraints (Bean et al., 2009; Sinatra, et al., 2008).

According to an essentialist view, organisms' traits and qualities are intractable and cannot change. Specifically, those adhering to this bias are unable to accept the generational development of a species. Evolution in *Spore* acts on individuals within a species rather than populations. Further, leveraging the game's speed to accurately playing geologic time (i.e., billions of years) would slow the game considerably. As a result, players do not observe genetic variability over time or even within that species. Rather, *Spore* affords play-

ers the opportunity to completely redesign their creature in a single session. As such, it transforms into a completely new creature in a single step. In the process, *Spore* masks the nature of variation and randomness, the process of natural selection, and geologic time and may promote non-scientific views of evolution.

Another potentially undesirable learning affordance originates from the fundamental nature of video games in general as it relates to the teleological constraint. By design, video games are goal oriented. Systems are created to allow players to experience phases, levels, and achievements. Using DNA points, *Spore* players advance through stages and dominate their immediate environment. Implicit in this process is a goal to "win" the game of evolution. However, this aligns with a very problematic belief that evolution is goal-directed (Kuhn, 1970). The idea that organisms change their characteristics to better fit their environments (i.e., the teleological constraint) is communicated by *Spore*, but is in direct conflict with Darwinian views of evolution.

The third misconception associated with *Spore* is the intentionality bias. This originates from the fundamental design of *Spore*. Specifically, users design their organisms and the player maintains complete control over the outcomes of reproduction or play. In the reproduction screen, players select genetic parts or components, combine them, and manipulate the settings to produce the desired creature. Environmentally, players determine how their creatures' interact in the world by selecting the creature's path, behaviors, and responses to environmental constraints. These technological affordances reduce the notion of randomness, natural selection, and evolution to a misconception of control by some intelligent agent.

Spore has been developed to entertain players and has not been designed to teach disciplinary content. Although teachers may be seduced by marketing promises (i.e., participating in evolution), the naturally occurring learning affordances of *Spore* may reinforce non-scientific views rather than promote scientific learning. As a result, potential users of this game should consider these points in order not confuse major ideas of Darwinian evolution with the ideas of change and design presented within *Spore*.

Although it may be problematic to use *Spore* as an educational game to teach about evolution, there are a few ways teachers can modify the broad educational context to promote learning. For example, teachers can alter the pedagogical context to directly target the misconceptions prevalent in *Spore*. Students could reflect and argue what is inherently wrong with the evolution models in the game. Similarly, *Spore* can serve as an authentic assessment to document students' understanding of evolution. In this way, students could play *Spore* and then criticize the embedded scientific models based on their understanding of Darwinian evolution.

Another way to promote learning with *Spore* is to examine the sub-mechanics inherent to the game. While principles of evolution are not accurate, *Spore* may serve as a simulation environment for students to experience the models of physics and other science concepts. This could be achieved through repeated trials as has been done with *Civilization III* (Squire & Durga, 2008) or by comparing the models in *Spore* with other simulation environments (Bean et al., 2009). In either case, teachers promote a deep and broad understanding of how models succeed and fail. According to Jonassen (2006), this approach is an ideal way to develop understanding of the world around us.

Quest Atlantis

Description

Quest Atlantis (QA) is an educational, multi-user virtual environment (MUVE) that leverages various components of commercial MMOGs as part of its overall design (Barab, Thomas, Dodge, Carteaux & Tuzun, 2005). Development for QA began in 2001 as a result of funding from the National Science Foundation. Unlike *Spore*, QA was designed to provide a learning environment while taking advantage of game-like properties of immersive contexts. The overarching goal in QA is to help the citizens of Atlantis save their city from impending extinction. The key components of QA are: 1) a 3-D persistent, virtual world; 2) educational lesson plans and curricular units; 3) a narrative storyline; and, 4) a globally distributed community of participants (Barab, Arici, & Jackson, 2005; Barab, et al., 2007).

The QA interface, referred to as the OTAK, is a 3D immersive environment, comprised of multiple worlds. Each world is further divided into villages that are organized around central themes (e.g., urban ecology, water quality, astronomy, weather). Within these worlds, students, who range in age from 9 to 14 years old, collaborate with other players, mentors, and non-playing characters to complete "quests." In a quest, students participate in simulated experiences that are socially and academically significant. These include environmental studies, researching other cultures, interviewing community members, and developing action plans. To complement the work online, virtual activities are paired with tasks that take place in the classroom. Depending on the number of students and the sophistication of the learning tasks, the timeframe for quests ranges from one hour to one week. Individual quests are linked together within unit plans. A unit plan is a two-week curricular module comprised of five to eight quests focused around a common topic (e.g., water quality, environmental awareness).

Central to the design of QA is the narrative storyline. This narrative is presented by a virtual group of young activists in Atlantis, the Council, who communicate with participating children and help scaffold their activities (Barab, Sadler, et al., 2007). The storyline is more than simple background information to induce player "buy-in." Rather it is used to establish continuity among the QA elements. It is interwoven through all elements of the QA experience and delivered across multiple on and off-line media (e.g., through an introductory video, novel and comic book). For example, the information gained from quests enable students to provide feedback to the governing council of Atlantis regarding ways they may stave off environmental disaster (Barab, Arici, & Jackson, 2005).

Like *Spore*, the QA community extends beyond the scope of the online context (Barab, Thomas, Dodge, Carteaux, & Tuzun, 2005). To participate in QA, children between must be registered online with a QA Center (i.e., participating elementary schools and after-school programs). Within the on-line contexts, each player controls a single avatar. Each avatar is connected to a child's account as part of their QA participation. This avatar functions like the creature in *Spore* and by manipulating its actions, QA participants navigate within the virtual worlds and interact with each another. Off-line, students meet face-to-face at QA centers and participate in extension activities designed to supplement online experiences. During the sessions at the QA centers, students collaborate and develop strategies to solve or complete particular quests.

Affordances

Technological. Compared to the graphics, algorithms, and other technologies in *Spore*, QA is not advanced. However, QA is considerably more interactive and immersive. The QA context is immersive, and leverages characteristics of 3D virtual worlds, such as the ability to navigate within the graphic space, virtually navigate from village to village, and see bird's eye as well as omnibus views of the environment. In addition, QA afford students the opportunity to customize their own avatars as representations of their online persona. As such, avatars only allow users to act on the virtual environment. In situ, students extend their sense of self into the virtual space and even begin to develop a virtual identity.

The virtual worlds created within QA provide opportunities to interact in 21st century "third spaces" (see Steinkuhler, 2005). While these environments were designed to leverage ludic properties of games, the main purpose of QA is to influence learning. Specifically, the design intent for QA was linked to education and educational objectives. As a result, significantly less capital was provided for the rendering of the graphics and student interactions. Further, QA was developed several years ago. In a technological sense, it is not as realistic or graphically sophisticated as many of the MMOGs available on the commercial market. The quality of images, sound, and other mechanisms are not as sophisticated as those present in *Spore*. However, QA was designed as a learning tool with game-like features. As a result, this neither detracts from the overall experience of interacting with the QA system nor does it fail the overall goal, situated content learning.

Another notable difference between *Spore* and QA is the degree to which players interact with each other. QA is designed to promote interaction with characters in the environment, other users, and facilitate learning and development in the game. These features include synchronous chat, an email system, personal web pages, and other spaces for reflection. Similar to *Spore*, QA affords the opportunity to meaningfully change the virtual landscape. Students can build virtual structures (e.g., homes or offices) for their characters and furnish these structures with objects (e.g., paintings, furniture, etc.) (Tuzun, 2006). The ability to personally influence and create a portion of the virtual world increases a sense of ownership and further develops the virtual culture of the game space. Not only do these features add opportunities for interaction within the system, they also model characteristics present in many commercial MMOGs.

Research has shown that students find the technological affordances of QA to be highly motivating (Barab, Arici, & Jackson, 2005). Data have illustrated that the majority of participants' engagement is attributed to the resources, structures, and overall aesthetic that contributes to QA environment (Tunzun, 2006). However, the complexity of the system has also proven difficult for some learners (Lim, Nonis & Hedberg, 2006). Data from this study indicated that engagement with the system was often hindered by the overly complex 3D environment, students' difficulty with language used within system interactions, and their lack of computer competency for QA tasks.

Learning. Unlike *Spore*, QA is positioned as a multi-disciplinary environment for learning. Originally, QA was conceived as a means for students to engage in ethnographic-type inquiry related to understanding cultural history. Further, it was intended to provide an avenue to examine their findings from multiple social perspectives. Over time, the system evolved and additional disciplinary content was added. This enables students to explore interactions across domains like science and math within a socially responsive context.

Currently, academic domains are encapsulated within the various QA worlds and the villages that comprise them. For example, the science world engages students in a set of quests to ascertain the reasons behind a failing water-based ecosystem within Atlantis. Students must virtually collect samples around the park, take them to a lab within the game to be analyzed, and interpret the results. From this work, students develop a rationale for the problem and craft a potential solution. Researchers have documented student gains in 'social perspective adoption.' Specifically, QA appears to impact student views concerning the environmental and economic impacts of science as well as proximal and distal science content learning (Barab, Sadler, Heiselt, Hickey & Zuiker, 2007).

Unlike *Spore* that is a game designed to entertain, QA bases interactions upon a social responsiveness model (i.e., actions influenced by interaction among players). As a result, QA places content learning in the traditional academic sense as an important, but secondary outcome (Barab, Dodge, Thomas, Jackson & Tuzan, 2007; Barab, Sadler, Heiselt, Hickey & Zuiker, 2007). Although researchers have argued that 21st century citizens benefit from this socio-scientific approach to integrated learning (Borgman et al., 2008; NRC, 2006), it takes time. Specifically, learning develops at a much slower pace than alternative pedagogical approaches focused specifically on content demands. Further, researchers documented only small content gains relative to the time spent playing QA (Lim, Nonis, & Hedberg, 2006). They also indicated that a teacher could have addressed the same content in about one and half hours using a traditional lecture format that took several sessions to develop via game play. This is an important issue in an era of standardized testing and accountability.

However, the nature of learning is very different with respect to each approach (i.e., lecture vs. QA). QA outcomes extend far beyond traditional academic content and the experiences are retained better. The complexity of the environment and the emphasis on collaboration extend learning to higher order skills. These benefits emerge directly from the interactions designed into QA or leveraged from commercial gaming contexts. For example, students can cooperate and disperse the workload associated with particular quests across players in the game. This can be informal or they can form a "guild" and work together in a more formalized way. In QA, students utilize chat and email functions to scaffold experiences for one another and to negotiate co-constructed meanings of game related concepts. Ultimately, students recommend actions to the Council of Atlantis that must be taken in order to save their world. QA provides a clear mechanism for developing skills that will empower the workforce of tomorrow.

GlobalEd 2

Description

GlobalEd 2 makes use of an Internet-based communication system and a web-based research environment to link classrooms of students, otherwise isolated from one another by physical distance and socio-economic boundaries. *GlobalEd 2* was developed as part of a research initiative funded by the Institute of Education Sciences. As a result, *GlobalEd 2* leverages an immersive pedagogical space that does not share the same technological characteristics of *Spore* or QA.

During the course of a semester, *GlobalEd 2* leverages synchronous (e.g., chat) and asynchronous communications (e.g., forums) to provide a collaborative, simulation environment. Simulations are 5 weeks in duration and are embedded within the curriculum. These simulations span multiple, physical settings, with approximately 12-15 different classrooms of students assigned a unique country. The selected countries vary in terms of economic development, geographical representation, political structures, and centrality to the science issues being discussed in a given simulation scenario. This provides an opportunity for high school students to experience global science issues from different perspectives (i.e., geographic, economic, and cultural).

Each simulation consists of three components: 1) the problem scenario; 2) the resources and materials for the students and teachers; and 3) the 'issue area' details within the simulation. The problem scenario contains background information about global problems that are described in future terms. Specifically, the simulation takes place six months in the future to reduce interference from current events. Each problem scenario contains specific scientific details that require the participating countries to take some form of science policy action. The resources and materials for each simulation consist of documents, data, and links to websites pertaining to various scientific concepts involved in the problem scenario. Each classroom may also access country-specific, scientific policy resources. These materials and resources are used during two phases of the project: Research phase and Interactive Simulation phase. Specifically, students use these materials to interpret findings and provide scientifically valid evidence for their positions.

In addition to the problem scenario, there are four major issue areas within each simulation. These issue areas (e.g., global health, human rights, etc.) allow students to group into smaller, collaborative units. In these groups, students prepare for the simulation and engage in the negotiations within the class and across classes. These four issue areas are consistent across all the classrooms in the simulation. This consistency allows students from one issue area to communicate with their counterparts in another classroom. Each *GlobalEd 2* country must develop their national position in collaboration across these four issue areas, so that multiple perspectives on the scientific policies will be considered. In essence, by working across these four *GlobalEd 2* issue areas, students are immersed in a learning environment where natural science and social science knowledge and concepts are seamlessly integrated.

Participation in the simulation requires the classrooms/countries to collaboratively resolve a science related, real world, socio-political problem through the development of "multinational" agreements, or global accords. Thus, students, participating as scientific advisors for their assigned countries, need to understand the underlying scientific concepts related to these issues. In this role, they must subsequently develop an understanding of how those concepts can be applied, negotiated and potentially resolved in the simulated international political arena. Students also need to be able to communicate these understandings to the others participating in the simulation during the negotiation process.

Affordances

Technological. By contrast to *Spore* and *Quest Atlantis*, the technological affordances of *GlobalEd 2* are quite rudimentary. For example, students interact with each other during their multinational deliberations via a text-based interface. An Oracle-based communication system affords students the ability to craft email-like messages with attachments as well as participate in synchronous communications similar to instant messaging. As such, there is no movement around a "virtual world" and no visual representations for "virtual avatars."

Students within *GlobalEd 2* simply identify themselves as "China's environmental negotiator" or "Brazil's economic negotiator." Further, these identities are developed by virtue of the content and tone of their communications as students represent their countries. A benefit to the relative anonymity of these identities is the ability for educators to hold some factors in the educational context neutral (e.g., personal appearance, gender, race, and verbal communication abilities). As a result, teachers are able to reduce the probability of stereotyping and resultant discrimination.

While *Quest Atlantis* provides internal links and references to material and *Spore* is encased in numerous fan-sites, support sites, and similar resources, the research environment in *GlobalEd 2* takes the form of a researcher-created portal to online information. This organized set of links pertains to scientific issues and country related policies relevant to the simulation scenario. Although avatars are not used, human simulation moderators (or "Simcon") act as a virtual teacher/ facilitator while students interact with each other in an active learning classroom. The Simcon oversees all aspects of the learning process and helps students think critically about the complex problem-based learning environment. Specifically, the Simcon monitors the flow of messages, using technology tools, between teams and facilitates scheduled web-based multilateral conferences

and assures that simulations do not devolve into simple game playing.

Although *GlobalEd 2* does not involve the same degree of technological enhancements when compared to *Spore* or *Quest Atlantis*, the lack of sophisticated bells and whistles does not impede student's motivation or desire to engage within the system. Research examining the outcomes of students participating within GlobalEd simulations illustrates that such simulations are highly motivating (Brown, et al., 2003). More importantly, researchers have documented significant increases in academic self-efficacy, technological self-efficacy, and content area interest as a result of participation in GlobalEd simulations (Boyer et al., 2009; Mayall, 2002).

Learning. In terms of disciplinary content, *GlobalEd 2* is linked to the national standards in science, social studies and language arts. Students participating in a GlobalEd simulation are first expected to understand the important scientific principles related to the simulation scenario and, second, to recognize how these issues relate to the countries participating in the simulation. In the process, students begin to see the synergistic connections between human systems (communities and government leading to decision-making and policies) and the biosphere of natural sciences (which impacts and is impacted by human actions), allowing them to gain a deep understanding of the inherent interactions between social sciences and natural sciences.

Moreover, the *GlobalEd 2* environment provides an invaluable venue for students to practice written communications in science within a real world context and to an authentic audience that will respond and urge revision and reevaluation of both content and written argument. During the course of a single simulation, an average of approximately 1000 messages of varying length (asynchronous and synchronous combined) are exchanged online among issue area groups and countries in general. Data analysis of simulation communications indicates that over 50% of all communications exchanged during any particular simulation is shaped as formal scientific argumentation. This genre of writing has been highlighted as a critical area for development among today's students (NRC, 1996; 2006; NAS, 1998), yet receives disappointingly little direct attention in traditional science curricula (Keys, 1998).

Beyond the development of content area knowledge among participants, the *GlobalEd 2* pedagogical approach also addresses and nurtures the "soft skills" required of 21st century citizens. These include social perspective taking, collaboration and negotiation skills, problem-solving and leadership abilities (North American Council for Online Learning & the Partnership for 21st Century Skills, 2006). GlobalEd directly addresses these issues by placing the science education process within the socio-political context of an Internet-based international negotiation simulation program. Succinctly, GlobalEd requires students to understand science problems and issues in sophisticated ways (specifically water and climate change issues and problem sets) while at the same time they are required to make international decisions on those topics. Thus, as simulated national decision-makers, they must negotiate and make science policy decisions on these issues in an effort to develop leadership for policies on these vital transnational environmental issues. Research on GlobalEd has isolated positive outcomes in terms of increased social perspective taking (Gehlbach, et al., 2008), decision-making (Boyer, et al., 2008; negotiation (Boyer, et al., 2009) and leadership (Johnson, Brown, Lima, Boyer, & Hudson, 2006).

DISCUSSION AND IMPLICATIONS

As noted, judicious integration of technology relies on the interaction of practitioners' knowledge of tools, knowledge of content, and knowledge of pedagogy (Archambault & Crippen, 2009; Colbert et al., 2008). Each of these categories is

informed by current views in the literature as well as teachers' experiences and expertise with technology. Without an appreciation of the literature, an understanding of the tools, and a disposition to use them, teachers adopt a pragmatic approaches based on prior experiences (Schrader, et al., 2006). Unfortunately, research indicates that the majority of teachers experienced video games as a reward for behavior, such as completing an assignment early (Schrader, et al., 2006; Selfe & Hawisher, 2004). This contrasts with the pedagogies and benefits of video games described in the literature (e.g., context for learning, simulation, etc.).

It follows that a mindful and judicious implementation of video games begins with the definition of instructional objectives (Baek & Choi, 2008; Gros, 2007; O'Brien, Lawless, & Schrader, in press) but continues with a pedagogical marriage between those objectives and the attributes of learning tools involved. For example, single-player games do not permit communication among players in the same game. Although social learning is not always an instructional approach, it would be fruitless to target contextualized, communication-based problem solving using a system that does not afford communication within the experience. By contrast, single-player games have many other useful characteristics (e.g., can be saved, often portable, re-playable, etc.) that can be useful to educators.

Throughout the process, teachers face challenges associated with the quantity and variety of video game titles, perceptions of their educative value, and/or marketing efforts that promote games in a light that fails to meet expectations (i.e., *Spore*). Any single issue may lead practitioners to adopt conceptual inconsistencies or misunderstandings about video games and their application in education. From all of this, it is also clear that educators bear the burden of understanding the tools they use as well as the nature in which they use them.

In the examples listed here, each environment was designed with a distinct purpose. Further, each system exhibits a unique set of affordances. *Spore* is highly advanced in a technological sense and employs significantly more ludic affordances. By contrast, *GlobalEd 2* is impoverished graphically but provides an engaging learning environment. The relevance of these examples does not strictly stem from their similarities or differences, but rather from the manner in which teachers intentionally leverage the existing affordances of these systems. From these comparisons, one might conclude that there is a "correct" set of affordances when using any type of video game in classrooms. However, this is far from correct. The main task is to identify and make use of the technological and learning affordances of games, regardless of their source.

In particular, teachers should determine the content first and then develop appropriate instructional objectives. Once the objectives are established, they should review the literature and identify a pairing between the potential and the specified objectives. A pairing of this sort will allow teachers to identify an appropriate game that aligns with their expectations and educational goals. However, they must examine the technological and educational affordances of the video game. Specifically, they must consider whether or not it is possible to leverage the affordances in service of learning. If this is possible, then the last step is to provide instruction and evaluate the results. By carefully examining the affordances, the similarities, and the differences across these contexts, the educative implications of each become clear. Ultimately, the process is applicable and useful for all educators who seek to look beyond research claims and marketing hype toward the informed and judicious integration of video games.

Although this process may seem obvious, the interactions among the technological and learning affordances within a dynamic educational context are highly complex. Further, these affordances are the result of a negotiation among design constraints. Game developers must balance an implicit notion of fun with the educational merit of a video game. In most commercial examples, disciplinary content is secondary to enjoyment and pleasure. In most educational examples, fun and engagement is a byproduct of the context. Developers face the daunting task of maximizing the technological elements of video games alongside the educational affordances. Further, they must accomplish this without losing the intangible element of fun.

A video game created commercially with stunning graphics like *Spore* may not possess the same potential for learning as a text-based pedagogical space designed around disciplinary content, such as *GlobalEd 2*. As a result, educators and developers must work together to produce immersive video game contexts that provide affordances that maximize learning and fun. Each context described here was designed for different reasons and demonstrates distinct technological and educational attributes. As a result, each environment supports different educational uses and pedagogical approaches. The marriage between what developers produce and what educators do with those tools should not be one filled with obstacles.

REFERENCES

Anderson, C. A., & Bushman, B. J. (2001). Effects of violent video games on aggressive behavior, aggressive cognition, aggressive affect, physiological arousal, and prosocial behavior: A meta-analytic review of the scientific literature. *Psychological Science, 12*(5), 353–359. doi:10.1111/1467-9280.00366

Archambault, L., & Crippen, K. (2009). Examining TPACK among K-12 online distance educators in the United States. *Contemporary Issues in Technology and Teacher Education, 9* (1). Retrieved from http://www.citejournal.org/vol9/iss1/general/article2.cfm

Ault, S. (March 19, 2009). Video game revenue climbs 10% in February. *Video Business*. http://www.videobusiness.com/article/CA6645368.html

Baek, Y., & Choi, S. (2008). Implications of Educational Digital Game Structure for Use in Formal Education Settings. In K. McFerrin et al. (Eds.), Proceedings of Society for Information Technology and Teacher Education International Conference 2008 (pp. 1613-1619). Chesapeake, VA: AACE.

Bailey, C. (2006). China's full-time computer gamers. *BBC News*. Retrieved from http://news.bbc.co.uk/2/hi/business/5151916.stm

Barab, S. A., Dodge, T., Thomas, M., Jackson, C., & Tuzun, H. (2007). Our designs and the social agendas they carry. *Journal of the Learning Sciences, 16*(2), 263–305.

Barab, S. A., Sadler, T., Heiselt, C., Hickey, D., & Zuiker, S. (2007). Relating narrative, inquiry, and inscriptions: A framework for socio-scientific inquiry. *Journal of Science Education and Technology, 16*(1), 59–82. doi:10.1007/s10956-006-9033-3

Barab, S. A., Thomas, M., Dodge, T., Carteaux, R., & Tuzun, H. (2005). Making learning fun: *Quest Atlantis*, a game without guns. *Educational Technology Research and Development, 53*(1), 86–107. doi:10.1007/BF02504859

Bean, T., Sinatra, G., & Schrader, P. G. (2009). *Spore: Spawning Evolutionary Misconceptions*. Unpublished manuscript.

Benedetti, W. (2007). *Were video games to blame for massacre? Pundits rushed to judge industry, gamers in the wake of shooting*. Retrieved from http://www.msnbc.msn.com/id/18220228/

Bowman, R. (1982). A "Pac-Man" theory of motivation: Tactical implications for classroom instruction. *Educational Technology, 22*(9), 14–16.

Bowman, R. (2007). How can students be motivated: A misplaced question? *Clearing House (Menasha, Wis.), 81*(2), 81–86. doi:10.3200/TCHS.81.2.81-86

Boyer, M. A., Urlacher, B., Hudson, N. B., Janik, L., Niv-Solomon, A., Brown, S. W., & Ioannou, A. (2009). Gender and negotiation: Some experimental findings. *International Studies Quarterly, 53*, 23–47. doi:10.1111/j.1468-2478.2008.01522.x

Brown, S., & Vaughan, C. (2009). *Play: How it Shapes the Brain, Opens the Imagination, and Invigorates the Soul*. New York: Avery.

Brown, S. W., Boyer, M. A., Mayall, H. J., Johnson, P. R., & Meng, L. (2003). The GlobaEd project: Gender differences in a problem-based learning environment of international negotiations. *Instructional Science, 31*(4-5), 255–276. doi:10.1023/A:1024677708501

Canada, K., & Brusca, F. (1991). The technological gender gap: Evidence and recommendations for educators and computer-based instruction designers. *Educational Technology Research and Development, 39*(2), 43–51. doi:10.1007/BF02298153

Children Now. (2000). *Girls and Gaming: A Console Video Game Content Analysis*. Oakland, CA: Children Now.

Colbert, J. A., Boyd, K. E., Clark, K. A., Guan, S., Harris, J. B., & Kelley, M. A. (2008). *Handbook of Technological Pedagogical Content Knowledge (TPCK) for Educators*. New York: Routledge.

Csikszentmihalyi, M. (1991). *Flow: The Psychology of Optimal Experience*. New York: Harper Perennial.

Day, E. A., Arthur, W., & Gettman, D. (2001). Knowledge structures and the acquisition of complex skill. *The Journal of Applied Psychology, 85*(5), 1022–1033. doi:10.1037/0021-9010.86.5.1022 de Freitas, S. (200 6). Learning in Immersive Worlds: A Review of Game Based Learning. *JISC.* Retrieved July 31, 2006, from http://www.jisc.ac.uk/media/documents/programmes/elearning_innovation/gaming report_v3.3.pdf

Dibbell, J. (2007). The life of the Chinese gold farmer. *New York Times.* Retrieved from http://www.nytimes.com/2007/06/17/magazine/17lootfarmerst.html?pagewanted=print

Entertainment Software Association. (2006). *Essential Facts about the Computer and Video Game Industry.* Retrieved January 11, 2007, from http://www.theesa.com/facts/index.php.

Evans, E. M. (2008). Conceptual change and evolutionary biology: A developmental analysis. In Vosiandou, S. (Ed.), *International Handbook of Research on Conceptual Change.* New York: Routledge.

Ferguson, C. J. (2008). The school shooting/violent video game link: Causal relationship or moral panic? *Journal of Investigative Psychology and Offender Profiling, 5,* 25–37. doi:10.1002/jip.76

Fisher, S. (1994). Identifying video game addiction in children and adolescents. *Addictive Behaviors, 19*(5), 545–553. doi:10.1016/0306-4603(94)90010-8

Gee, J. P. (2003). *What video games have to teach us about learning and literacy.* New York: Palgrave/St. Martin's.

Gehlbach, H., Brown, S.W., Ioannou, A., Boyer, M.A., & Hudson, N., & Niv-Solomon, A.et al. (2008). Increasing interest in social studies: Social perspective taking and self-efficacy in stimulating simulations. *Contemporary Educational Psychology, 33,* 894–914. doi:10.1016/j.cedpsych.2007.11.002

Gentile, D. A., Lynch, P. J., Linder, J. R., & Walsh, D. A. (2004). The effects of violent video game habits on adolescent hostility, aggressive behaviors, and school performance. *Journal of Adolescence, 27,* 5–22. doi:10.1016/j.adolescence.2003.10.002

Gibson, J. J. (1986). *The Ecological Approach to Visual Perception.* Hillsdale, NJ: Erlbaum.

Green, C. S., & Bavelier, D. (2003). Action video game modifies visual selective attention. *Nature, 423,* 534–537. doi:10.1038/nature01647

Green, C. S., & Bavelier, D. (2007). Action-video-game experience alters the spatial resolution of vision. *Psychological Science, 18*(1), 88–94. doi:10.1111/j.1467-9280.2007.01853.x

Greenfield, P. M., Brannon, C., & Lohr, D. (1994). Two-dimensional representation of movement through three-dimensional space: The role of video game expertise. *Journal of Applied Developmental Psychology, 15,* 87–103. doi:10.1016/0193-3973(94)90007-8

Griffiths, M. D., & Dancaster, I. (1995). The effect of type A personality on physiological arousal while playing computer games. *Addictive Behaviors, 20*(4), 543–548. doi:10.1016/0306-4603(95)00001-S

Gros, B. (2007). Digital games in education: The design of games-based learning environments. *Journal of Research on Technology in Education, 40*(1), 23–38.

Harper, E. (2006, September). World of Warcraft hits 7 million subscribers. *Joystiq.* Retrieved January 11, 2007 from http://www.joystiq.com/2006/09/07/world-of-warcraft-hits-7-million-subscribers/

Jiminez, C. (2007). The high cost of World of Warcraft. *BBC News.* Retrieved from http://news.bbc.co.uk/2/hi/technology/7007026.stm

Johnson, P. R., Brown, S. W., Lima, C. O., Boyer, M. A., & Hudson, N. (2006, April). *GlobalEd: A comparison of leadership in FTF and CMC environments*. Poster presented at the AERA conference, San Francisco, CA.

Jonassen. (2006). *Modeling with Technology: Mindtools for Conceptual Change*. Columbus, OH: Pearson.

Kafai, Y. B. (1996). Electronic play worlds: Gender differences in children's construction of video games. In Kafai, Y., & Resnick, M. (Eds.), *Constructivism in Practice: Designing, Thinking, and Learning in a Digital World* (pp. 97–123). Mahwah, NJ: Erlbaum.

Kennedy, C. H., & Souza, G. (1995). Functional analysis and treatment of eye poking. *Journal of Applied Behavior Analysis*, *28*(1), 27–37. doi:10.1901/jaba.1995.28-27

Kuhn, T. S. (1970). *The structure of scientific revolutions* (2nd ed.). Chicago: University of Chicago Press.

Lawrence, V., Houghton, S., Tannock, R., Graham, D., Durkin, K., & Whiting, K. (2002). ADHD outside the laboratory: Boys' executive function performance on tasks in video game play and on a visit to the zoo. *Journal of Abnormal Child Psychology*, *30*(5), 447–462. doi:10.1023/A:1019812829706

Lim, C., Nonis, D., & Hedberg, J. (2006). Gaming in a 3D multiuser virtual environment: Engaging students in science lessons. *British Journal of Educational Technology*, *37*(2), 211–231. doi:10.1111/j.1467-8535.2006.00531.x

Malouf, D. B. (1987). The effect of instructional computer games on continuing student motivation. *The Journal of Special Education*, *21*(4), 27–38. doi:10.1177/002246698802100406

Mane, A. M., Adams, J. A., & Donchin, E. (1989). Adaptive and part: Whole training in the acquisition of a complex perceptual-motor skill. *Acta Psychologica*, *71*, 179–196. doi:10.1016/0001-6918(89)90008-5

Mayall, H. J. (2002). *An Exploratory/Descriptive Look at Gender Differences in Technology Self-efficacy and Academic Self-efficacy in the GlobalEd Project*. Unpublished dissertation, University of Connecticut.

Millar, A., & Navarick, D. J. (1984). Self-control and choice in humans: Effects of video game playing as a positive reinforcer. *Learning and Motivation*, *15*, 203–218. doi:10.1016/0023-9690(84)90030-4

National Academy of Science. (1998). *Teaching About Evolution and the Nature of Science*. Washington, DC: National Academy Press.

News, B. B. C. (2005). S Korean Dies After Games Session. Retrieved from http://news.bbc.co.uk/2/hi/technology/4137782.stm

NRC. (1996). *National science education standards*. Washington, DC: National Academy Press.

NRC. (2006). *America's Lab Report: Investigations in High School Science*. Washington, DC: National Academy Press.

O'Brien, D. A., Lawless, K. A., & Schrader, P. G. (in press). A taxonomy of educational games: Genres and applications. In Baek, Y. K. (Ed.), *Gaming and Classroom-Based Learning: Digital Role Playing as a Motivator of Study*. Hershey, PA: Information Science Reference.

Pew Internet and American Life Project. (2008). *Teens, Video Games, and Civics*. Pew Internet and American Life Project. Retrieved April 29, 2009 from http://www.pewinternet.org/~/media/Files/Reports/2008/PIP_Teens_Games_and_Civics_Report_FINAL.pdf.pdf

Pham, A. (2009, March 20). Video game revenue jumps 9% in February. *Los Angeles Times*. Retrieved from http://www.latimes.com/business/la-fi-cotown-games20-2009mar20,0,6765213.story

Poling, D., & Evans, E. (2002, March). Why do birds of a feather flock together? Developmental change in the use of multiple explanations: Intention, teleology and essentialism. *The British Journal of Developmental Psychology, 20*(1), 89. doi:10.1348/026151002166343

Salguero, R. A., & Moran, R. M. (2002). Measuring problem video game playing in adolescents. *Addiction (Abingdon, England), 97*, 1601–1606. doi:10.1046/j.1360-0443.2002.00218.x

Schrader, P. G. (2008). Learning *in* technology: Reconceptualizing immersive environments. *AACE Journal, 16*(4), 457–475.

Schrader, P. G., & McCreery, M. (2007). The acquisition of skill and expertise in massively multiplayer online games. *Educational Technology Research & Development*. Retrieved October 10, 2007 from http://www.springerlink.com/content/n2496u376825u512/

Selfe, C. L., & Hawisher, G. E. (2004). *Literate Lives in the Information Age: Narratives On Literacy From the United States*. Mahwah, NJ: Erlbaum.

Shaw, R., Grayson, A., & Lewis, V. (2006). Inhibition, ADHD, and computer games: The inhibitory performance of children with ADHD on computerized tasks and games. *Journal of Attention Disorders, 8*(4), 160–168. doi:10.1177/1087054705278771

Sherry, J. (2001). The effects of violent video games on aggression: A meta-analysis. *Human Communication Research, 27*(3), 409–431.

Squire, K. (2003). Video games in education. *International Journal of Intelligent Simulations and Gaming, 2*(1). Retrieved January 27, 2006 from http://cms.mit.edu/games/education/pubs/IJIS.doc

Squire, K., & Durga, S. (2008). Productive gaming: The case for historiographic game play. In Ferdig, R. E. (Ed.), *Handbook of Research on Effective Electronic Gaming in Education (Vol. I)*. Hershey, PA: Information Science Reference.

Squire, K. D. (2006). From content to context: Video games as designed experiences. *Educational Researcher, 35*(8), 19–29. doi:10.3102/0013189X035008019

Steinkuehler, C. A. (2004). Learning in massively multiplayer online games. In Y. B. Kafai, W. A. Sandoval, N. Enyedy, A. S. Nixon, and F. Herrera, (ed.), *Proceedings of the Sixth International Conference of the Learning Sciences*, (pp. 521-8). Mahwah, NJ: Erlbaum.

Steinkuehler, C. A. (2005). The new third place: Massively multiplayer online gaming in American youth culture. *Tidskrift Journal of Research in Teacher Education, 3*, 17–32.

Steinkuehler, C. A. (2006). Why game (culture) studies now? *Games and Culture, 1*(1), 97–102. doi:10.1177/1555412005281911

Subrahmanyam, K., & Greenfield, P. M. (1994). Effect of video game practice on spatial skills in girls and boys. *Journal of Applied Developmental Psychology, 15*, 13–32. doi:10.1016/0193-3973(94)90004-3

Tuzun, H. (2006). Egitsel bilgisayar oyunlari ve bir örnek: *Quest Atlantis* (Educational computer games and a case: *Quest Atlantis*). *Hacettepe Universitesi Egitim Fakültesi Dergisi, 30*, 220–229.

Vandewater, E. A., Shim, M., & Caplovitz, A. G. (2004). Linking obesity and activity level with children's television and video game use. *Journal of Adolescence, 27*(1), 71–85. doi:10.1016/j.adolescence.2003.10.003

Webber, R., Ritterfeld, U., & Mathiak, K. (2006). Does playing violent video games induce aggression? Empirical evidence of a functional magnetic resonance imaging study. *Media Psychology, 8,* 39–60. doi:10.1207/S1532785XMEP0801_4

Winter, D. (2008). *Welcome to PONG-Story: The Site of the First Video Game.* Retrieved from http://www.pong-story.com/intro.htm

Wood, R. T. A. (2008). Problems with the concept of video game "addiction": Some case study examples. *International Journal of Mental Health and Addiction, 6,* 169–178. doi:10.1007/s11469-007-9118-0

Young, M. F., Schrader, P. G., & Zheng, D. P. (2006). MMOGs as learning environments: An ecological journey into *Quest Atlantis* and the Sims Online. *Innovate, 2* (4). Retrieved March 20, 2006, from http://www.innovateonline.info/index.php?view=article&id=66

ENDNOTE

[1] For the purpose of brevity, we use the term video game and games to include computer games, home console systems, stand-alone arcade systems, and the myriad of handheld options.

Chapter 21
Benefits of Video and Eye Toy Gaming for Children with Autism

Nava Silton
Fordham University, USA

Ann Higgins D'Alessandro
Fordham University, USA

ABSTRACT

The purpose of this chapter is to illustrate how video games, which incorporate eye toy technology, can be utilized to teach social learning to children with autism directly through video modeling and multimedia social story interventions and indirectly through engaging typically developing students with educational video games that increase their sensitivity, knowledge, and behavioral intentions when interacting socially with children on the spectrum and with other disorders, as well. The popular medium of gaming is designed to enhance the appeal of rote instruction for children and their families as well as to create tools that improve a child's ability to generalize learned social and adaptive skills. Moreover, these tools will offer richer research methodologies for tracking and understanding important micro-developmental changes in daily and weekly interpersonal skills development among both typical and atypical children.

INTRODUCTION

The purpose of this chapter is to illustrate that video and eye toy gaming can be used to enhance the social learning of children with autism directly through video modeling and multimedia social story interventions and indirectly through engaging typically developing students with educational videos that increase their **sensitivity**, knowledge,

and **behavioral intentions** when interacting socially with children with autism, and perhaps other disorders as well. We suggest that it is important to develop typical children's positive attitudes and intentions toward peers with disabilities. Research has shown that this can be accomplished through video which has the power to influence a person's perception and subsequent behavior in other situations, for instance, in moderating the development and use of stereotypes regarding race (Givens & Monahan, 2005; Ward, Hansbrough, & Walker,

DOI: 10.4018/978-1-61520-781-7.ch021

2005). Thinking creatively about the power of gaming to enhance development and social interactions among typical and atypical children, as specifically illustrated here for children with autism, will help bring interventions for atypical children into the 21st century as well as allow the development of much richer research methodologies for tracking and understanding important micro-developmental changes in daily and weekly interpersonal skills development.

Specifically in this chapter we address how video games which involve eye toy gaming, can be used as a teaching tool for children with autism to enhance the appeal of rote instruction for children and their families as well as create tools that can enhance a child's ability to generalize learned social and adaptive skills. An eye toy refers to a small low resolution camera used in video games to capture "players" and insert them directly into the onscreen game. Eye toy technology could be utilized to employ "video self modeling" (VSM), i.e., giving children with autism the ability to capture their own desirable behaviors on-screen. Additionally, we suggest that using video and eye toy gaming as an educational tool enhances the **sensitivity** and skills of typically developing children, enabling them to feel more at ease and competent with their atypical peers. These themes of the appeal of the educational tool, of the generalizability of key skills learned through the video tool, and of the sensitivity of others to children with autism are woven throughout the chapter. The rationale for particularly intervening with children on the autism spectrum will be tackled by delineating the high prevalence of autism today, the characteristic deficits associated with autism, the pervasive effect of autism on the family unit, the stigmatization of behavioral disabilities such as autism in both the school and social environment and the particular affinity children with autism appear to have for computers, mechanical toys and visual mediums. The potential of video modeling, video self modeling, and social stories to overcome limitations and expand current educational tools for autism will then be addressed to show

how video games incorporating eye toy gaming can enhance both typical and atypical children's sensitivity and social skills. Finally, the chapter will close by speculating how a theory pertaining to our bio-evolutionary roots may lend further support to the effectiveness of video and eye toy gaming for teaching generalizable skills and by suggesting further routes towards utilizing video and eye toy technology.

We perceive video games featuring eye toy gaming as transformative instruments in the future education of all children due to its interactive nature which allows ideas and skills to meet each child where he is, and not to demand equal skill levels required for reading, writing, and arithmetic. Promoting and keeping young children with behavioral disabilities more "on track" with individualized but social experiences may be the best educational tool possible for them and the richest education possible for typical children. Thus the specific goals of this chapter are twofold: one, to present a strong case that video games can be successfully used to enhance the social learning of children with autism, and two, to demonstrate that these same techniques can be used to heighten the sensitivity and social skills of typically developing children when they interact with each other and with their atypical peers.

BACKGROUND

Epidemiology of Autism

Autism identified by Kanner in 1943, is a life-long neuro-developmental disorder which begins in infancy and is characterized by impairments in everyday living skills, social skills, communication, and language, and by the presence of repetitive, obsessive behaviors, and rigid, and focused interests (Silton, 2009; Volkmar & Pauls, 2003). Deficits in everyday living and social skills and communication, language vary along a continuum from mild to severe, thus children receive diagnoses along the autism spectrum.

Autism is the nation's fastest growing serious developmental disorder and has reached epidemic proportions over the last few years. Diagnoses are rapidly increasing from about 10% to 17% per year (Autism Speaks, 2006). Moreover, **autism spectrum disorders (ASDs)** and behavior disorders surpassed the number of individuals with mental handicap in 2000 with a prevalence of 22% and 25%, respectively, according to an application distributed to families of children with a severe disability (Nessa, 2004). The most recent statistics on ASDs suggest that **autism spectrum disorders**, account for more diagnoses than childhood cancer, AIDS and diabetes combined (CNN Report, 2007).

Some researchers hypothesize that this rise is due to increased awareness of autism spectrum disorders in the medical community and to a wider spectrum of what constitutes autism spectrum disorders. Researchers continue to deliberate over the causes for autism and over the causes for increasing rates of the disorder. Since autism is often diagnosed between eighteen months and two to three years of age, various researchers used to implicate Thimerisol, a compound composed of 49.6 percent mercury present in the measles, mumps and rubella (MMR) vaccine, as a primary cause for autism (Blaxill, Redwood, & Bernard, 2004). Overall, the research has largely refuted the Thimerisol hypothesis. Some think that diagnosis shifting is the principal cause for increased reported rates of the disorder. However, critics of this proposal have posited that diagnosis shifting would likely cause declines in rates of reported mental retardation and speech and language delays, but no differences have thus far been reported (Newschaffer et al., 2005). Although the etiology, pathophysiology and genetic transmission of autism are controversial and still mostly unknown, autism may best be perceived as a heterogeneous disorder, resulting from multiple genetic and environmental factors, which are often exacerbated by neurologic, cytogenetic, neurotransmitter, and immunologic abnormalities (Hollander et al., 1999). Since children with autism show no physical signs of having a disorder, their often peculiar, repetitive, and asocial behaviors are misunderstood, and are often perceived as under their control, when in fact such behaviors are not. A report of one family's experience echoes anecdotes of other families; a child's autistic behaviors combined with a public lack of knowledge and misunderstanding lead to stigmatization of the child and his/her parents (Oizumi, 1997).

At Particular Risk for Rejection and Stigmatization

Sensitivity programming is a particularly worthy endeavor since in addition to the high incidence and prevalence of autism spectrum disorders, children with autism are at particular risk for rejection and stigmatization by peers. It is important to specifically explore why typical peers of children with autism may find it particularly challenging to interact with a child on the autism spectrum and why children with autism may be classified as unpopular in the classroom. A variety of intervention studies are designed to address the deficits of unpopular children (those with poor social skills), since studies have noted that particular types of behaviors, personality, and physical features (e.g. aggression, hyperactivity, social withdrawal) evoke negative reactions from peers (Juvonen, 1992). Previous research suggests that typical children identify aggressive, hyperactive, or socially withdrawn peers as deviant from others and therefore typical peers are more likely to reject children who display these behaviors (Juvonen, 1991).

Despite their typical appearance, children with autism often display severe and disruptive antisocial behaviors, self-destructive acts, inappropriate public behaviors, and tantrums which frequently lead to stigmatization (Gray, 1993). This combination of a typical physical appearance and highly disruptive behavior often also stigmatizes parents of children with autism and is typically met with hostile, insensitive and negative reactions from the public, given their lack of understanding and knowledge of autism (Gray, 1993). Despite findings that aggressive children are actively disliked and rejected, while shy children and those with disabilities are simply disliked and neglected rather than actively rejected (Juvonen & Weiner, 1993), children with autism may suffer from both having a disability and showing disability-related aggression.

In a recent study, children with autism were most highly stigmatized by the public when they produced behaviors such as leaning back and moaning, having a temper tantrum or crying for no evident reason; failing to conform to social norms. Interestingly, however, children with autism were rated less harshly when parents were told of the child's autism diagnosis (Chambres & Vasingle, 2008).

Children with autism spend little time socializing with peers, make and accept fewer initiations, and spend more time playing alone than typically developing children (Koegel, Koegel, Frea, & Fredeen, 2001). Unfortunately, children with autism's lack of effective social interaction skills further exacerbate their maladaptive behaviors and poor peer outcomes. Frea (1995) suggests that inadequate social skills affect development by 1) increasing behavior problems that arise from a lack of social interaction skills, 2) increasing the likelihood of maladaptive behavior in later life, and 3) reducing the positive developmental support and learning opportunities available in successful peer relationships (Disalvo & Oswald, 2002; Frea, 1995). Children with autism are at an increased risk for these adverse consequences given their inability to imitate and comprehend social nuances related to joint play activities and to interpret social initiations by other children. Social skills require the ability to relate to others in a reciprocally reinforcing manner and to adapt social behaviors to a variety of contexts (Schopler & Mesibov, 1986). Unable to relate spontaneously and flexibly to others, children with autism cannot effectively participate in social reciprocity. Thus, while individuals with autism appear to desire social interaction, they are lacking the

necessary skills to partake in it (Scott, Clark & Brady, 2000).

The research suggests that even children with mild delays are less accepted as playmates than their typical peers (Hames, 2005). These children express peer-related social skills deficits beyond what would be expected from their developmental age and, as a result, are selected less frequently as friends by their peers (Hames, 2005; Guralnick et al., 1996). Thus those who possessed greater recognition of the deficits of a child with disabilities were more likely to suggest that the child with disabilities would have fewer friends. These results were apparent even in children whose siblings possessed a disability (Hames, 2005).

Difficult Features of Having a Sibling with Autism

There are mixed findings as to whether or not siblings of individuals with disabilities are at greater risk for psychological maladjustment than typically-developing children or whether they glean some advantages from their situation (Burton & Parks, 1994). However, due to the deeper complexity, unpredictability, variability and ambiguity of symptoms of ASD, siblings are thought to exhibit different patterns of strengths and limitations than siblings of children with other disabilities (Verte, Roeyers, & Buysse, 2003).

With respect to the adverse consequences of having a sibling with autism, siblings of children with autism are more predisposed to internalizing disorders, externalizing disorders, adjustment problems and issues with peer relationships than children with typical siblings (Guite, Lobato, Kao, & Plante, 2004). Significant factors which may relate to these psychological difficulties include the sibling's gender, age, birth order and the type and severity of the handicap, caretaking responsibility, parental adjustment and the potential effect of the child with disability on the sibling's future (Konstam, Drainoni, Mitchell & Houser, 1993). Parents report greater stress (Bagenholm & Gillberg, 1991) and greater concern for siblings than siblings report for themselves. Younger and male siblings reported higher scores on the *Sibling Perception Questionnaire* (SPQ) than older kids; perhaps older siblings are further removed from the acute crises related to the diagnosis or strategies for coping may improve over time (Guite et al., 2004). Similarly younger siblings exhibited more behavioral problems due to attention-seeking while their older counterparts were more capable of adapting: helping older children achieve a more positive self-concept and better social skills (Verte, Roeyers & Buysse, 2003). For instance, siblings of children with high functioning autism (HFA), chiefly those between the ages of 6 and 11, exhibited more internalizing and externalizing problems compared with children in the control group (Verte et al., 2003).

Moreover, negative reactions to having a sibling with a disability principally revolved around feelings of bitterness and resentment due to the additional attention given to the disabled individual and to guilt that they felt for being healthy (Bangenholm & Gillberg, 1991). Finally compared to parents of typical children and children with differing disabilities, siblings of children with autism were more averse in their view of their sibling relationship, more concerned about the future, had fewer words to describe their sibling's condition, felt they could not confide in family members, had more issues with their sibling breaking their things and felt lonelier than siblings of control children (Bagenholm & Gillberg, 1991). In addition to siblings, parents of children with autism experience particularly heightened stress in contending with a child with developmental disabilities in the home.

Video gaming might prove to be an effective method by which to improve children with autism's behavior in the household. This would allow their typical siblings to be involved in their learning process and to potentially view them in a more positive light, thereby helping to reduce any feelings of bitterness or resentment.

Parents' Heightened Distress and Parental Interest in Media's Assistance

Parents of children with autism suffer more stress than parents of non-disabled children and parents of children with a host of other disabilities (Bouma & Schweitzer, 1990; Holroyd & MacArthur, 1976; McKinney & Peterson, 1987). For instance, parents of children with autism reported more depression, social isolation and less parenting competence, marital satisfaction, and family adaptability than parents of typical or Down syndrome children (Bouma & Schweitzer, 1990). In a study of 26 mothers of children with autism, 24 mothers of children with attention deficit and hyperactivity disorder (ADHD) and 24 mothers of typically developing children, mothers of children with autism showed higher levels of psychological symptomatology, higher parenting stress, poorer perceptions of their family environment and their ability to parent siblings, and higher perceptions of internalized problems of siblings than mothers of ADHD and typically developing children (Oizumi, 1997).

Parents and Children's Educational Programming

Parents, in addition to children, are frequent consumers of children's educational programming. A video tool which can build social skills development into the programming and offer a greater visibility of autism in children's educational programming may help society and children better understand and interact with children on the autism spectrum and therefore both directly and indirectly alleviate some of the undue burdens and stress levels with which children with autism and their parents contend. Children's educational programming and gaming are mass-media vehicles through which to teach key social skills to children with autism and to reduce the stigmatization of typical children towards children with disabilities by teaching typical children sensitivity and positive social interactions with children on the spectrum. Knowledge and sensitivity training on disabilities for parents in general would be useful, but parents of children with autism and other less visible disabilities may especially appreciate efforts towards integration. Moreover, video is not only a mass-media vehicle, but one that has been addressed along with computer games, mechanical toys and alternative visual mediums as being preferential tools for teaching children with autism much needed social-emotional-based skills.

Capitalizing on Children with Autism's Affinity for Mechanical Games and Visual Mediums

The interest of individuals with autism in regular patterns and order relates closely to their preferences for computer games, mechanical toys, and math puzzles (Barakova et al., 2007). Computer games must be flexible enough to adapt to the personal data, world and belief system of a child with autism (Schaba et al., 2005). Mechanical toys offer repetitively moving parts, the feeling of being in control and predictability, all of which are key ingredients that make mechanical toys an appealing medium for children on the spectrum.

Barakova et al. (2007) sought to capitalize on children with autism's preferences for regular patterns, order and mechanical toys by creating an intelligent toy which uses cubes, changing colors and emergently changing behavior to stimulate communication and other underdeveloped behaviors and social skills of children on the autism spectrum. The researchers encouraged exploratory behavior, awareness of self and turn-taking through an affordable, universal, stimulating, interactive and intelligent toy. Barakova et al. (2007) discovered that children with autism had a strong preference for spending free time on games rather than on strictly educational programs. Additionally, the authors learned that games for children on the spectrum should not be over-stimulating (they

should focus on one sense at a time), should be structured and logical and should encourage novel behavior or the incorporation of another individual into the game (Barakova et al., 2007).

A variety of studies have sought to capitalize on the affinity and success of computer games and mechanical toys with children on the spectrum by utilizing these forms as mediums through which to teach emergent behaviors and important social skills: two clear impairments of children with autism. Barakova et al. (2007) introduced the notion of a multi-agent system—a system comprised of multiple autonomous parts with the following criteria: each agent has an incomplete ability to solve problems independently, no global system control, decentralized data and asynchronous computation. These systems offer self-organization and development of complex behaviors despite following simple rules. One or more rules constitute a relationship to the other agents—multiple agents system-which expresses emergent behavior. This organization parallels the communication among individuals with their own communication systems, complex patterns, norms and rules. These multi-agent systems are likely to be appealing to individuals with autism due to the patterning, structure and the opportunity for full and direct control over the system.

Schaba et al. (2005) introduces an interactive model based on a multi-agent system between children with autism and a system taking expert directions. It affords the analysis of children's behavior via their actions. The "expert" defines an individualized activities plan which is a series of educational games catered to children with autism. Finally, the "expert" is able to observe the user's particular actions via camera, touch screen, mouse or keyboard and thus to interface with the user and the activities of the protocol to help rehabilitate specific behaviors of the user. This proposed Autism Project was geared at employing a User Observation Agent (UOA) to observe the child's actions through behaviors and through words describing behavior. The software/hardware FaceLab, however, measures three-dimensional representations of the face and the orientation of the gaze (Schaba et al., 2005).

In addition to the use of multi-agent systems to appeal to the structure, patterning and control preferences of children with autism, researchers have proposed employing Kismet and Robota dolls in an effort to teach imitation and further social-emotional skills via preferred mediums to children on the spectrum. Kismet is a humanoid face which creates expressive social interactions with "human caretakers," with the hope of generalizing social relationships between the robot and human (Schaba et al., 2005). The Robota Doll is a 45 cm high humanoid robotic doll designed as an interactive toy to determine how a human could teach a robot to utilize imitation, speech and gesturing skills. Robota can react to touch through its body which is composed of electronic boards and motors that drive the arms, legs and head (Billard, 2003). Robota has a serial link connected to a PC, which can apply speech synthesis and the video processing of data to copy the outward and sideways movements of the users' arms and head when the individual sits directly across from it.

Dautenhahn & Billard (2002) utilized Robota to stimulate social interaction skills including eye gaze, touch, and imitation skills in children with autism, who struggle with establishing proper eye-contact, social interaction, social communication, and imaginative skills and rarely participate in interactive games. Imitation plays an integral role in the acquisition of social cognition and communication skills, allowing an infant to establish bonds with others (Dautenhahn & Billard, 2002; Nadel et al., 1999). Some researchers suggest that individuals with autism struggle with imitation while others suggest that they are capable of partaking in immediate imitation of familiar actions (Robins et al., Rogers and Pennington, 1991; Hammes and Langdel, 1981). Nadel (1999) discovered a significant correlation between imitation and positive social behavior suggesting that imitation is predictive of social capabilities in individuals with autism. Moreover, individuals with autism demonstrated improved social re-

sponsiveness when their own actions were being imitated (Dautenhahn & Billard, 2002; Dawson and Adams, 1984).

The researchers initially utilized a camera system to fully analyze the arm movements of the children to ensure that Robota could imitate the child and to encourage the children to imitate Robota. The study was conducted with children between the ages of 5 to 10 from the Enhanced Provision unit of Bentfield Primary School in Essex, UK. The robot was connected to a laptop and laid atop a table against a wall at the side of the room. Two cameras were placed in the room; one to observe the area in front of the robot and children when addressing the robot and the other behind the robot, in an attempt to observe the facial expressions of the child during their interaction with the robot. Sessions were typically fewer than three to five minutes in duration and children were placed into one of three setups. In Setup A, children observed a "dancing robot" in a box, moving to prerecorded music in order to familiarize the children with the robot. In Setup B, the robot was removed from the box and the carer demonstrated how to move the robot and actively encouraged the child to play with the robot. This "puppeteer robot" was manned by the investigator, who ensured that the robot was accurately imitating the child's arm, leg and head movements, even when the child was not facing or close to the robot. In Setup C, the children were not given any encouragement or instructions, but the robot in "puppeteer mode" would respond to even subtle movements of the child and introduced role-switching and a simple imitation game. The researchers evaluated the following behaviors: eye gaze towards the robot, touching the robot, direct, delayed or attempted imitation of the robot, and the child's proximity to the robot (Dautenhahn & Billard, 2002).

The results suggest that the children significantly increased their scores for proximity, eye gaze and imitation over the course of the intervention. With respect to social interaction skills and turn-taking, the children demonstrated more frequent interactions with the adults in the room either via the robot or separately. Overall, the children utilized the robot as a mediator, or as an object of shared attention with their teachers and were able to include the investigators and carers into their worlds (Dautenhahn & Billard, 2002).

ISSUES AND LIMITATIONS

Based on the high prevalence of **autism spectrum disorders** and the pervasive effect of autism on the family unit, on peers and on other key microsystems of the child with autism's life, this chapter addresses two principal limitations in the current intervention literature: 1) the failure of video interventions to successfully promote positive **behavioral intentions**, **attitudes** and **sensitivity** of typical children towards children with autism and 2) the need for further therapeautic tools to effectively teach appealing and generalizable social skills to children with autism. The following section highlights these limitations and the subsequent section provides ideas for initial solutions to these obstacles by consulting video modeling, video self monitoring, and social stories literature.

Limitations of Video Interventions Promoting Sensitivity

While numerous studies have employed video technology to teach about a particular disability in the hopes of teaching typical children how to be more sensitive and accepting of children with special needs, few of these video interventions have proven fruitful. Video interventions have either been characterized as harmful (Siperstein & Bak, 1980; Swaim & Morgan, 2001), unhelpful (Friedrich, Morgan, & Devine, 1996) or minimally helpful (Campbell, Ferguson, Herzinger, Jackson, & Marino, 2004) for increasing the sensitivity and positive behavioral intentions of typical children towards children with disabilities. Thus, a successful paradigm for a sensitivity training video

tool is needed, since the potential of programming has not been adequately tapped. A video tool which would promote sensitivity of typical children towards children with autism could achieve three aims: 1) prevent the ostracism of peers with autism and promote the interest of typical peers in interacting with them, 2) enhance the social and empathic development of typical children by exposing them to peers with differing needs, and 3) offer children with autism more social skills training by encouraging typical children to interact with them.

Limitations of Therapies in Teaching Children with Autism Appealing and Generalizable Skills

While a video sensitivity training tool may indirectly promote the social skills development of children with autism, a variety of therapies are geared towards directly teaching children with autism valuable social-emotional skills. A number of behavioral therapies have shown success in teaching children with autism how to effectively function in everyday life and how to participate to a greater extent in family life, schooling, and socializing with peers. However, treatments are not yet successful in fully teaching complex behavior sequences necessary for positive interactions and the development of true friendships. Current therapies, of which Applied Behavior Analysis (ABA) is one of the most common, impose severe time demands on the child and family. While somewhat successful, ABA may be tedious for the therapist and unappealing, repetitive or aversive for the child client with autism. Moreover, the generalizability and usefulness of what is taught may be limited. One-on-one therapy may not adequately prepare children with autism for the fast-paced and fast-changing world of social relationships characteristic of three to 10 year-olds.

These two limitations or boundaries will be addressed in the following section. The failure of information from previous video interventions to improve the reactions of typical peers towards children with autism will be considered and alternative forms of information will be introduced to try to enhance the efficacy of these video tools. Moreover, more appealing modes of teaching social and life skills through multimedia forms to children with autism will be discussed rather than relying on behavioral methods which may be unappealing and may lack generalizability.

SOLUTIONS

Tackling Boundary 1: Video-Based Sensitivity Training

Prior studies have attempted to promote positive behavioral intentions and cognitive attitudes of typical children towards children with physical disabilities (Morgan, Biebrich, Walker & Schwerdtfeger, 1998; Sigelman, 1991), obesity (Bell & Morgan, 2000), Tourette's syndrome (Friedrich, Morgan and Devine, 1996), autism (Swaim & Morgan, 2001) and other disabilities through a video medium. All of the aforementioned studies, which presented descriptive information about children with autism, appeared harmful, neutral or minimally helpful at improving typical peers' positive intentions and attitudes towards children with disabilities. **Descriptive information**, based on Heider's (1958) cognitive consistency theory, offers information relating to the similarities between a child with a disability and his/her typical peer. The notion is that typical peers will be more accepting and more interested in socially interacting with a peer with disabilities, if he/she appears similar to the typical peer.

To expand upon descriptive information, Campbell et al. (2004) added explanatory information to descriptive information in order to determine if explanatory information would help promote more positive intentions and attitudes of typical students towards peers with autism. **Explanatory information**, which is based on the social attribution theory (Kelley, 1967; Heider, 1958), offers causal information about a

disorder. Including **explanatory information** is partially based on research suggesting that typical peers will be more accepting and will show more positive intentions towards children with autism if they believe children with autism possess low responsibility for their disorder (Juvonen, 1992). In contrast, if typical peers attribute high levels of responsibility and blame to their peers with autism for their condition, typical peers are more likely to show anger and more negative intentions and attitudes towards children with autism (Juvonen, 1992).

Campbell et al. (2004) discovered that adding **explanatory information** to **descriptive information** increased the positive attitudes of younger children towards children with autism. Despite the success, however, of combining explanatory and descriptive information for younger children (third and fourth graders), older children (fifth graders) failed to show a significant increase in positive behavioral intentions towards children with autism following the combined video information. An earlier study demonstrated the same trend for age. In a sample of 184 younger (third and fourth grade) and older (fifth and sixth grade) elementary school children, Bell and Morgan (2000) found that younger children assigned less blame, gave higher ratings to, and expressed more willingness to engage in academic activities with an on-screen target child with obesity than older children. These findings are in line with studies suggesting that **cognitive attitudes** towards individuals with disabilities appear to become more negative as children progress from childhood to adulthood (Ryan, 1981). Thus, **sensitivity** interventions show promise, but further research is needed to determine how best to teach disability awareness, sensitivity and positive attitudes to older, typical children.

To improve upon the descriptive and explanatory information used in previous video interventions, Silton (2009) conducted a random assignment, experimental study by incorporating peer strategies and strengths information to demonstrate the additive benefit of presenting alternative forms of video-based information to enhance typical children's knowledge, positive **behavioral intentions** and **cognitive attitudes** towards children on the autism spectrum. Silton (2009) based her use of **peer strategy information** on social learning theory (Bandura, 1977), which suggests that individuals will learn behaviors if the behaviors are properly modeled and reinforced, and self-fulfilling prophecy (Rosenthal, 1963), which suggests that a perceiver's expectations & behavior will provoke the responses of others. Rather than solely relying on descriptive and explanatory information, Silton (2009) believed a more hands-on interactive approach, whereby typical peers could be taught actual **peer strategies** to contend with the odd or repetitive behaviors of children with autism may enhance typical peers' positive intentions or interest in interacting with peers on the autism spectrum. These **peer strategies** were created based on successful studies relating to peer networks (Disalvo & Oswald, 2002), pivotal response training (Pierce & Schreibman, 1995), peer-mediated interaction (Goldstein et al., 1992) and peer mentors (Odom & McConnell, 1993; Strain & Odom, 1986).

Moreover, Silton (2009) asserted that incorporating **strengths information**, rather than solely relying on deficit-based information on autism, may inspire typical peers to learn more about their peers with autism. Silton (2009) based her inclusion of strengths information on the affect/effort theory (Rosenthal, 1963), which suggests that more positive expectancies will encourage greater affect and effort.

If a typical peer perceives that a child with autism possesses special strengths or abilities rather than solely possessing deficits, the typical peer may exert more effort in attempting to socially interact or in getting to know his peer on the autism spectrum. Additionally, a previous study suggested that offering strengths and preference information about children with autism coupled with peer strategies information, greatly enhanced the social initiations and responses of both the typical peers and the peers with autism, alike (Owen

& Deschryver, 2004). Savant abilities, superior and perceptual abilities and a special connection to animals were all highlighted in the strengths information section of her study.

The findings in the Silton (2009) study suggested that adding peer strategies was especially useful for enhancing typical children's **behavioral intentions** as measured by the Shared Activities Questionnaire (SAQ; Morgan et al., 1996), a behavioral intentions measure, while strengths information appeared to be minimally helpful in increasing typical children's **cognitive attitudes** towards children with autism as assessed by the Adjective Checklist (ACL; Silperstein, 1980, Silperstein & Bak, 1977). Both peer strategies and strengths information appeared helpful for enhancing the knowledge typical children have of children with autism. Each video tool in the study was distinctively created to incorporate descriptive and explanatory information and these two alternative forms of information, peer strategies and **strengths information**: Video 1 (AUT-D+E [Autism-descriptive + explanatory]; descriptive and explanatory information), video 2 (AUT-D+E+ Peer Strategies; descriptive, explanatory and peer strategies information), video 3 (AUT-D+E+ Strengths; descriptive, explanatory and strengths information) and video 4 (AUT-D+E+ Peer Strategies + Strengths; descriptive, explanatory, peer strategies and strengths information). Thus, the partial success of these alternative forms of video-based information, suggest that previous video-based sensitivity interventions may be enhanced through the incorporation of alternative forms of video-based information.

In addition to these encouraging findings, Silton (2009) uncovered an intriguing and unanticipated finding in the process of creating the video tools for her sensitivity study. The actors in her videos, those assuming the roles of the male and female target children with autism and those playing the peers of the target children with autism, appeared to develop a significant interest in autism over the course of producing the video tool. The actors asked a plethora of questions and were anxious to practice their new skills with a child on the spectrum. Silton (2009) suggested that rather than solely focusing on sensitivity, future research could track changes in knowledge, intentions, attitudes, empathy and self-concept of the actors in the process of the video creation from time 1 (prior to the video creation) to time 2 (following the video creation). With the continued use, appeal and success of video and digital media with children (Blumberg & Ismailer, 2008), video interventions which encourage children to play the role of an individual with a disability or the sensitive peer of an individual with a disability, may be particularly powerful in enhancing the interest and sensitivity of typical elementary and middle-school aged children towards children with autism and other disabilities. Thus, it is important to review how best to teach social and life skills to children with autism through video both to directly teach children with autism hallmark social-emotional skills, and to determine how best to both enhance the sensitivity of typical children towards children with autism and how to benefit typical children in the video-making process.

Tackling Boundary 2: Video Modeling, Self Modeling and Social Story Interventions

Video modeling and video self modeling have recently been introduced as potential tools which may be more successful for teaching complex social behaviors by offering flexibility and appeal, which are necessary for positive social interactions. As developmental psychologists, we want to stress how important it is that children with autism socialize with typically developing peers as a condition for their own development. We suggest that video technologies can improve upon current therapies, especially Applied Behavior Analysis (ABA), by creatively addressing the issues of stigmatization, the lack of appeal of varying therapies for child clients, and the lack of generalizability or usefulness of the learned behaviors for success in social interactions. In addition, we

see the great potential of using video technologies educationally to enhance the sensitivity and social abilities of typically developing children and to promote the interaction of typically-developing peers with social-emotionally challenged peers, in order to address issues of stigmatization and generalizability.

Video Modeling and Video Self Monitoring

Video modeling produces a wide range of social, communication, and academic benefits for children with disabilities (Sturmey, 2003). Based on Bandura's (1977) observational learning and modeling theory, video modeling should enhance children's communication skills and decrease problem behaviors by encouraging them to model behaviors of those around them (Charlop-Christy & Daneshvar, 2003). Video modeling has been utilized to teach and improve upon a variety of play, social and life skills. Teaching imaginative play skills among three play categories including a tea party, shopping and baking helped children with autism rapidly learn complex verbal and motor sequences from video modeling tapes without the use of error correction procedures or experimenter-reinforced contingencies (D'Ateno, Mangiapanello, & Taylor, 2003). Perspective-taking skills, skills that are often absent or deficient in children with autism, were also successfully taught through video modeling (Charlop-Christy & Daneshvar, 2003). Moreover, recent studies at Indiana University suggest that video modeling may help improve the social skills and activities of daily living skills (ADLs) of children and adolescents with autism: chiefly their functional skills, followed by their social communication and behavioral functioning skills (Bellini & Akullian, 2007). Finally, Model Me Kids, an organization headed by Susan Klein, attempts to disseminate video modeling on a broader scale, by producing video-modeling based teaching tools for children with autism, Asperger syndrome, Pervasive Developmental Disorder-Not Otherwise Specified and Nonverbal Learning Disorder. While these videos appear to effectively break down social-skills into digestible segments, they may benefit tremendously by exploring the field of digital media and gaming.

Video self modeling (VSM) takes observational learning and modeling a step further by affording individuals the opportunity to observe and then act on their own behaviors. VSM includes imitation of one's desirable behaviors captured on videotape, edited, and played back. While over 150 articles on VSM have been published utilizing thirty years of Bandura's modeling research, VSM has only recently been used to aid children with autism with language and social-communication skills. Several studies show the effectiveness of video and VSM in enhancing vocabulary (Zihni & Zihni, 1995), imaginative play (D'Ateno, Mangiapanello & Taylor, 2003), spontaneous request behaviors (Wert & Neisworth, 2003) and perspective-taking skills (Charlop-Christy & Daneshvar, 2003).

Interventions employing video self monitoring (VSM) have been used with children on the autism spectrum and have been found to be effective for those children who already had established preferences for video (Scherer, Pierce, Paredes, Kisacky, Ingersoll, & Schreibmen, 20001). While the aforementioned study and others report positive findings for small samples of children with autism, Bellini and Akullian (in press) conducted a meta-analysis of video modeling featuring 23 studies with a total of 73 participants. The median number of intervention sessions was nine; results showed rapid changes in target social skills, more often positive but sometimes negative. The rapidity of the change suggests that video monitoring and VSM are potent therapeutic and educational strategies. In addition, their results showed that both video monitoring and VSM are effective for improving social skills of young children with autism when interacting with adults. Bellini, Akullian, and Hopf (2007) conducted an intervention study which involved presenting VSM videos to

two preschool children with autism. The preschool children were challenged to watch themselves in peer interactions without adult prompting. Videos were created in the context of the preschool over three days with the teacher prompting both the child with autism and his peers. Videotapes were then edited, and the teacher and all ineffectual interactions were removed. Involving typical peers, rather than solely relying on teachers to model appropriate social interactions, affords children with autism a natural context for learning, since it precludes the further steps needed to transfer learning to interactions with peers (DiSalvo & Oswald, 2002; Rogers, 2000). The intervention occurred almost daily for four weeks (total 17 days). After each child viewed his own video, he was introduced to thirty minutes of unsupervised play, which was observed by the researchers. No prompts were given during the observation periods. Both children increased their social engagement from baseline lows of 3 and 6% to highs of 43 and 24% during the observation phase which was maintained when VSM stopped for the two following weeks. The teacher's reaction to the ease of implementation and effectiveness of VSM was very positive. As we stress, Bellini et al (2007) point to the negative effects of social isolation on the overall development of young children with autism.

The results of this study, rapid changes in social engagement with young children and the ease of the intervention, point the way to viewing VSM as an educational as well as a treatment tool—to blurring the lines between treatment and education allowing children with autism to be truly educated in the same classrooms as their typically developing peers. Firstly, blurring these lines decreases stigmatization and secondly, creating an intervention tool which effectively increases social engagement in the complex situation of unsupervised play, demonstrates remarkable generalizability and flexibility of skill use with different people (children in the classroom) for a rather extended amount of time (30 minutes).

Nikopoulos and Keenan (2007) conducted research that specifically examined the relationship of successful social engagement including initiation with the number of social interactions included on videos made for four six and seven year old children with autism in the context of their school. The videos depicted a 10 year-old child with learning difficulties initiating a sequence of social activities that he and an adult engaged in together. Videotapes, about thirty seconds long, demonstrated initiation and three behaviors built up from one to three as well as a sequence of three novel behaviors. Intervention sessions were five minutes in which the child viewed the videos and then imitated the behaviors and initiated a social activity he saw with his own teacher. The videos were created and intervention sessions were conducted in the same room with the same toys and chairs. Both a generalizability session with a typical 11 year-old peer and one and two month maintenance sessions were held. Similar to the previous study, this study showed rapid positive changes in 9 to 24 sessions. Video modeling effectively built novel skill sequences using three behaviors sequences which were not targeted in previous training. Although the children initiated less than they imitated, when they did initiate, the levels of genuine reciprocal play increased substantially. Moreover, these levels generalized to another peer and were maintained in long-term follow-up sessions. In addition to demonstrating that education can serve as treatment, this study also demonstrates that children with autism learn to learn, a hallmark for successful adaptive learning. The children's effectiveness for modeling the sequence of novel behaviors shows that they used the video as a learning tool over time.

Video modeling and VSM draw on the visual strengths often seen in children with autism (Tissot & Evans, 2003). For instance, children with autism were found to have an islet of ability on a visual, Embedded Figures Task compared to individuals with mental retardation and typical controls (Shah & Frith, 2006). Despite these visual strengths, however, a recent study noted that children with autism exhibit abnormal patterns of social visual pursuit since they tend to focus on mouths, bodies, and objects rather than on the eye region of an individual's face, the key location for inputting social messages. Thus, the amount of time fixated on mouths and objects rather than on the eye region of the face are strong predictors of the individual with autism's degree of social competence (Klin et al., 2002). The video modeling procedure we will employ in this proposal will attempt to capitalize on the visual strengths and preferences of individuals with autism while also encouraging them to focus on the most socially valuable region of the face, the eye region. Videos do not require prior training nor do they demand prerequisite skills, especially language or picture-to-picture or picture-to-object correspondence abilities. Individual studies and a meta-analysis provide evidence that children with autism seem to: a) find this form of treatment or education appealing and enjoyable, b) learn more complex behaviors, c) initiate social interactions, albeit at rather low frequencies, d) use the skills they learned with peers in unsupervised play, and e) learn rapidly with videos. Together, these results strongly suggest that children with autism can learn to learn - the hallmark of adaptive successful learning and living - and that video modeling and VSM are potent forces for opening the social world to children with autism, helping them get on track and stay on track developmentally. Despite the effectiveness of video self modeling (VSM), employing VSM for observational learning has yet to reach the mass video and gaming market.

Multimedia social stories are another form of effective instruction which could be more successfully produced on the mass-market. Hagiwara, Myles & Smith (2002) developed a multimedia story by employing HyperCard [supTM] (Apple Computer, 1994) software. This program utilized a book-like format, which contained a text of social stories; videos of participants' actions corresponding to social story sentences; audio with read aloud sentences utilizing a synthesized computer voice; and a navigational button for use by the participants. The researchers thus utilized computer technology and a film of participants in action to teach children with autism social-emotional skills. Gray (1994), Gray and Garand (1993), and Swaggart et al. (1995) suggested that social stories are one method to teach children with developmental disabilities appropriate social behaviors and interactions in order to enhance their success in academic and work settings. This instructional technique is thought to ease the confusion of verbal instructions and social interactions for individuals with autism (Gray & Garand, 1993) through the use of icons or symbols connected to short sentences in a small book format. Icons aid students in recognizing stories because previous research suggests that many students with autism are visual learners. A **social story** elucidates social situations in terms of relevant cues and identifies appropriate responses for individuals to make. The typical framework of a social story is comprised of two to five sentences that are (a) descriptive, including information about the setting, participants and actions, (b) directive, including statements concerning appropriate behavioral response, (c) perspective, describing feelings and reactions of others in the targeted situation, and (d) control, offering analogies with similar actions and responses utilizing nonhuman subjects (Gray, 1994; Gray & Garand, 1993). In short, specific guidelines for writing social stories include the "who, what, when, where and why," of a given situation (Lorimer, 2002).

The method of multimedia social story interventions elaborates social situations in terms of relevant cues and appropriate responses. Studies show the benefits of written social story interventions (Gray & Garand, 2001; Lorimer, 2002) as well as multimedia social story interventions (Hagiwara et al., 1999) for promoting social behavior and decreasing tantrum behaviors of children with autism. Since the latter study was the first of its kind in the special education literature and since a small sample size was utilized, this section describes ways to improve current research methodologies and designs by generating video

or gaming-based multimedia social story interventions. While Gray and Garand (2001) advised that social stories be presented on a single piece of paper without the use of visual stimuli, social stories coupled with icons, and gaming features can offer visual support to enhance comprehension.

Hagiwara, Taku, Myles and Smith (1999) demonstrated the potential additional benefits of presenting **a multimedia social story** intervention rather than solely relying on a written social story intervention for young children with autism. Unfortunately, while only one of the three children in their study generalized their improved social behavior across environments, each child in the study benefited in some substantial way from the multimedia social story intervention. Potential reasons for the variability of children's results are likely due to the variability in the duration of the intervention, individual differences among participants, the nature of the target behaviors, consistency in educational environments and differing levels of enthusiasm for viewing the multimedia social story program. Since this study was the first of its kind in the special education literature and since such a small sample size was employed, there is clearly room for improvement of both the methodology and design of the multimedia social story intervention, itself (Hagiwara, Taku, Myles, & Smith, 1999).

In a more recent study, Lorimer (2002) utilized social stories in an ABAB single-subject design to reduce precursors to tantrum behavior in a home setting with a five-year old child with autism. Tantrums occurred five of seven times in the initial baseline period, whereas tantrums decreased on the sixth and seventh day with the introduction of social stories and returned to two to three times per day when the social stories were removed. When the social stories were reintroduced, the child's precursor trends toward tantrum behavior again showed a downward trend (Lorimer, 2002). Thus, the use of social stories, has clearly demonstrated some utility in both aiding with social behavior and decreasing tantrum behaviors in children with autism.

The following theory-based proposals reveal initial steps towards developing successful video modeling, video self-modeling and multimedia social-story-based tools with significant gaming features, in order to best maximize the visual, video, computer and mechanical preferences of children on the autism spectrum. Silton, the first author, is currently in the process of developing the following gaming tools.

FUTURE RESEARCH DIRECTIONS

Future research should consider the alternative forms of information which may enhance the success of video and gaming tools in promoting the sensitivity of typical children towards children with autism and various ways in which to make video modeling, self modeling and social story tools more appealing and successful in teaching social, play and daily living skills to children with autism. Silton (2009) is currently embarking on the following video game proposal, which is an attempt to offer appealing and effective video tools for transmitting key social and life-skills information to children with autism.

Pre-game Setup and Background

The child player with autism is paired with a typical sibling or peer player. Please note: If no other player is available, the child with autism can select a playmate from the video game to serve as his/her model. Each child selects a video game character from a list of characters. Following his/her selection, a digital camera situated above the TV screen will take a head shot of each participant. The head shot will then be superimposed on the video game character so that each participant will view him or herself on the screen, albeit with a cartoon character body. This self-shot will allow for video self modeling to take effect. The entire game sequence will thus utilize video modeling and video self modeling as a rudimentary form of learning. Additionally, multimedia social stories will form the backdrop of this video game series since children with autism and their typical peers will be accomplishing a variety of activities of daily living (ADLs) (Levels 1-3) and social-emotional skills (Levels 4-5) through social stories in a multimedia, video game format.

The intention during the game is to have the typical child start the game first and have the child with autism follow. This will hopefully accomplish two goals. First, the child with autism will be able to practice modeling by seeing what the typical child does and imitating it. Moreover, by playing the game along with the child with autism, the typical child might learn to foster sensitivity towards his or her atypical counterpart; better appreciating the strengths and limitations of a child on the spectrum. Ideally, the game would be played in a virtual reality style so that both children would actively perform the necessary tasks while simultaneously visualizing themselves on screen. In this sense, not only is the child with autism able to accomplish video-modeling by imitating his or her model, but he is also able to perform self-modeling since he can view himself on-screen as well. If the virtual reality task is too difficult to perform each child will, alternatively, simply click on the screen with a mouse to lead their character into performing the necessary tasks.

LEVEL ONE

Level 1A

Level 1A entails the child preparing himself for a typical day. The ultimate goal is to leave the house on time to catch a bus to school. Level 1A involves rising from bed and performing tasks in the bathroom (such as voiding, brushing one's teeth and washing one's face). After exiting the bathroom and successfully, performing all of the necessary tasks, both children would advance to Level 1B. It is important to note, however, that the children can only advance to the next level if **both** of them successfully complete the tasks of Level 1A.

Level 1B

In this Level, the children must dress themselves correctly for a day at school. They must select appropriate undergarments, shirt, pants, socks and shoes from a drawer or closet in a bedroom. If the child selects an inappropriate garment, the article of clothing will automatically be removed from the character's body and will be returned to the drawer from which is was taken. The child will then have to select the correct item. This will be repeated until both children select appropriate and complete outfits to wear to school. Once both children leave their bedroom dressed properly, they will advance to level 1C. For less advanced players with autism, an option could be to have a pre-selected outfit for the child, which the child is only required to click onto his character's body and the child need not select his own outfit.

Level 1C

This is the final stage of the first level. Now that the children have dressed themselves they must proceed downstairs to eat breakfast, take their school bag and find their bus to school outside. As in level 1B, this level could also have multiple options, depending on the level of functioning of the child with autism. For those children on a lower level of functioning, breakfast could be prepared in advance and the child would simply have to eat it with the appropriate utensils. For those children who are higher functioning, the task could involve pouring a bowl of cereal with milk along with a glass of orange juice and, as with the previous option, eating it with the correct utensil. In either case, the child would be required to place his dirty dishes properly in the sink, grab his backpack and lunchbox for school and proceed to the door and to the school bus waiting outside. As in the other levels, the children can only suc-

cessfully proceed to Level 2, if **both** children complete Level 1C.

LEVEL TWO

Level 2A

In the beginning of Level 2A, both players will appear in a supermarket. The game begins by challenging the participants to locate shopping carts to begin their grocery shopping. The players are then given a list of items which they have to purchase. Each item has an icon to denote in picture-form what the item is. For instance, individual pictures of an apple, a juice, a cereal box and vegetable will appear on their list. Each time an item is appropriately selected and placed into the shopping cart, the character will receive a check on his/her shopping list. Once all of the four grocery items are selected, the children can proceed to Level 2B.

Level 2B

The players, who have now selected all of their grocery items, are ready to wait in line to purchase their items. In Level 2B, each character will find himself in an empty check-out line. He will have to wait until the cashier is ready. Each character has a wallet in his pocket with one, five and ten dollar bills and with a few coins. Once the cashier gives the total cost of the item, the character must select the correct number of bills to purchase his grocery items. Those who are at a lower level of functioning can simply click on the help button which will visually display the exact bills and coins that are required. Children who are more high-functioning can select the proper bills with no visual support. Once the items are correctly purchased, the characters can proceed to Level 3.

LEVEL THREE

Level 3A

Level 3A prepares the child for post-school activities. Similar to Level 1C, the player will have to prepare for another meal of the day. For those children on a lower level of functioning, dinner could be prepared in advance and the child would simply have to eat it with the appropriate utensils. For those children who are higher functioning, the task could involve setting the table in the appropriate fashion, ensuring that they have a protein, carbohydrate and vegetable on their plate. The player will receive a beverage option and three levels of food icons: protein (meats, fish), carbohydrates (rice, pasta) and vegetables (peas/carrots, salad) and will have to ensure that one item from each category is placed on his/her plate. The child will then proceed to eat his/her virtual food with the appropriate utensils. The child would then be required to place his dirty dishes properly in the sink. The child could then proceed to Level 3B.

Level 3B

Players have the option of selecting a bath or shower for Level 3B. The player will select undergarments, pajamas and a towel from a drawer set which will clearly label these items in written and picture form. The player will then remove his upper and lower garments and prepare for his bath or shower. A meter will note the heat of the water. The player will choose the appropriate temperature and will select the proper bathroom items for use. The player will select the shampoo for his hair and soap for his body. The game will break the body into three parts; the upper, middle and lower parts of the body. The player will be required to comprehensively wash all three areas of his/her body. Once this is accomplished, the player can turn off the water and use the towel he selected to dry himself off. He can then select the undergarments and then pajamas. Players who

have successfully washed (bathed or showered) and dressed in undergarments and pajamas can proceed to Level 3C.

Level 3C

Finally, the player is ready for bedtime. Bedtime preparations will require that the child brush his teeth, pour himself a cup of water for the night, select a book and cuddle up in bed for the night. The player will need to appropriately accomplish each aspect of toothbrushing, from selecting a toothbrush and toothpaste from the cabinet, to placing the toothpaste on the toothbrush and brushing in the appropriate places for one minute. A clock on-screen will denote when "one minute" has elapsed. The player will then rinse his mouth out, clean and then dry his toothbrush and place both the toothbrush and toothpaste back into the cabinet. Once he has accomplished toothbrushing, he will pour himself a cup of water for the night and will select a book from a large bookshelf for the night. Once he selects a book, he will enter his bed and place the covers over his body for a good nights' sleep.

LEVEL FOUR

Level 4 (A Variety of Emotion Recognition Scenarios)

Level 4 introduces a variety of scenarios involving emotion recognition skills. The players are required to label which emotions would be most relevant to a variety of scenarios. For instance, if a child receives an "A" on a paper, the player will be required to click on the happy/elated smile icon. A child, who is poked fun of in-class, will most likely click on the "embarrassed/blushing icon." A child who has lost a game might select a "sad/muted icon." Finally, a child who unexpectedly views a large animal may click on the "startled/fear icon." Level 5 affords the child an opportunity to accurately recognize and utilize appropriate emotional reactions to common life events. Emotion recognition impairments account for a large percentage of the hallmark social deficits most apparent in autism spectrum disorders.

LEVEL FIVE

Level 5 (5A-Classroom, 5B-Lunchroom, 5C-Playground):

Level 4 places the players in the classroom, in the lunchroom or in the playground at school. Level 4 not only involves activities of daily living, but social interactions the child with autism will experience in the school environment. The player must appropriately contend with a variety of situations in the school environment in order to progress to Level 5. Again, he is capable of modeling the social behaviors of his typical peer, sibling or alternatively a character he selects on the game to gain an initial notion of how to manage these social situations.

Take Home

The appeal of computers, mechanical toys and video games for children on the spectrum make this proposed video game product an especially exciting venture. This video game product will capitalize on the strength and success of imitation, modeling, self-modeling and multi-media social story interventions to create an engaging and interactive virtual atmosphere wherein children on the spectrum can learn key activities of daily living (ADL) skills, and key social interaction and emotion recognition skills for use both within the home and school environments. The boon of including a typical peer and/ or sibling into the gaming environment offers two further levels of learning, whereby the child with autism can model key social-emotional and daily living skills from his typical peer or sibling and his typical peer or sibling can gain key knowledge, sensitivity and tolerance skills towards his peer on the autism spectrum.

In considering the efficacy of a video game which employs aspects of video modeling, video self modeling and multimedia social story interventions, it is useful to determine: a) whether or not viewers with autism, who are imitating proper social skills and behaviors, will repeat these behaviors in the future and b) whether or not the typical players, who are modeling the proper social skills and behaviors, will show increased social skills and sensitivity and understanding about the disorder, due to their modeling. Do the encouraging and positively-reinforcing external cues present in the video game after passing each level, help children with autism internalize these emotional experiences? Would video games incorporating these modeling and self-modeling features help viewers with autism generalize activities of daily living or express overt facial expressions, which would then translate into more internalized experiences of emotions? Do the typical players modeling appropriate, initial behaviors in the video game, gain further social skills from this modeling and take a greater interest in peers with autism, who may be less capable of exercising typical social skills and behaviors?

With respect to sensitivity videos, if players (who are selected to display positive social skills) are encouraged to demonstrate positive behaviors and to smile and show encouragement while they are interacting with the target on-screen child with autism, is it plausible that these reactions would generalize towards their treatment of actual children with autism? Would the expressive output of facial movements they employed to model behaviors and to exhibit positive behaviors, sensitivity, and tolerance towards the on-screen child with autism translate into a transformation in their true inner emotional experiences and autonomic responses towards real or in-vivo children with autism? Following the creation and implementation of the proposed video game, significant research studies will ensue to answer the aforementioned inquiries.

CONCLUSION

Typical peers and children with autism may significantly benefit from both observing and modeling proper behaviors and interactions through a gaming medium. Creating video modeling or game-based sensitivity tools may enhance typical children's actual reactions towards children with autism through practicing effective peer strategies to utilize with children on the autism spectrum. Additionally, knowledge of potential **strengths** of children with autism may increase their effort and willingness to interact and spend time with children on the autism spectrum.

Children with autism may benefit from increased social exposure if typical peers are more willing and eager to socially interact with them and may appreciate increased tolerance and understanding of typical peers towards some of their disorder-based struggles. Additionally, children with autism may benefit directly from gaming based on video modeling, video self modeling and multimedia social story interventions. Learning and observing proper social, play and life skills in an appealing manner, rather than solely relying on rote behavioral therapies which lack generalizability, may help children with autism advance their social-emotional skills, the key hallmark deficit in autism.

If the research community could effectively utilize this contemporary video game tool to disseminate their research-based findings in an effective and appealing manner, many more individuals, families and peers affected by autism and other disorders, could benefit tremendously from this technology. These tools could help promote tolerance and learning in an engaging way and would thus benefit schools and families, who are educating and raising typical and atypical children, alike. Moreover, these tools would offer much richer research methodologies for tracking and understanding important micro-developmental changes in daily and weekly interpersonal skills development among both typical and atypical children. We must all foster sensitivity and understanding in our children and we must galvanize each other to pull our precious peers, siblings and family members with autism out of their lonely corners.

REFERENCES

Adelmann, P. K., & Zajonc, R. (1989). Facial efference and the experience of emotion. *Annual Review of Psychology*, *40*, 249–280. doi:10.1146/annurev.ps.40.020189.001341

Autism Speaks. (2006). Retrieved December 2, 2006, from, http://www.autismspeaks.org

Autism Speaks. (2007). Retrieved September 9, 2007, from, http://www.autismspeaks.org

Bagenholm, A., & Gillberg, C. (1991). Psychosocial effects on siblings of children with autism and mental retardation: a population-based study. *Journal of Intellectual Disability Research*, *35*(4), 291–307.

Bandura, A. (1977). *Social Learning Theory*. Englewood Cliffs, NJ: Prentice Hall.

Barakova, E., van Wanrooij, G., van Limpt, R., & Menting, M. (2007) Using an emergent system concept in designing interactive games for autistic children. Interaction Design and Children. In *Proceedings of the 6th international conference on Interaction design and children*, (pp. 73-76).

Bell, S. K., & Morgan, S. B. (2000). Children's attitudes and behavioral intentions toward a peer presented as obese: Does a medical explanation for the obesity make a difference? *Journal of Pediatric Psychology*, *25*, 137–148. doi:10.1093/jpepsy/25.3.137

Bellini & Akullian, J. (2007). A meta-analysis of video modeling and video self-modeling interventions For children and adolescents with ASD. *Exceptional Children*, *73*, 261–228.

Blaxill, M. F., Redwood, L., & Bernard, S. (2004). Thimerosal and autism? A plausible hypothesis that should not be dismissed. *Medical Hypotheses, 62*, 788–794. doi:10.1016/j.mehy.2003.11.033

Blumberg, F., & Ismailer, S. (2008). *Children's Problem Solving During Video Game Play. Fordham University, Aug. 17*. Boston Convention and Exhibition Center.

Bouma, R., & Schweitzer, R. (1990). The impact of chronic childhood illness on family stress: a comparison between autism and cystic fibrosis. *Journal of Clinical Psychology, 46*(6), 722–730. doi:10.1002/1097-4679(199011)46:6<722::AID-JCLP2270460605>3.0.CO;2-6

Burton, S.L. & Parks, A Personal author, compiler, or editor name(s); click on any author to run a new search on that name.L. (1994). Self-Esteem, Locus of Control, and Career Aspirations of College-Age Siblings of Individuals with Disabilities. *Social Work Research, 18*(3), 178–185.

Cable News Network (CNN) Report. (2007).

Campbell, J. M., Ferguson, J. E., Herzinger, C. V., Jackson, J. N., & Marino, C. A. (2004). Combined descriptive and explanatory information improve peers' perceptions of autism. *Research in Developmental Disabilities, 25*, 321–329. doi:10.1016/j.ridd.2004.01.005

Chambres, P., Auxiette, C., Vansingle, C., & Gil, S. (2008). Adult attitudes toward behaviors of a six-year old boy with autism. *Journal of Autism and Developmental Disorders, 38*(7), 1320–1327. doi:10.1007/s10803-007-0519-5

Charlop-Christy, M. H., & Daneshvar, S. (2003). Using video modeling to teach perspective taking to children with autism. *Journal of Positive Behavior Interventions, 5*(1), 12–21. doi:10.1177/10983007030050010101

D'Ateno, P., Mangiapanello, K., & Taylor, B. A. (2003). Using video modeling to teach complex play sequences to a preschooler with autism. *Journal of Positive Behavior Interventions, 5*(1), 5–11. doi:10.1177/10983007030050010801

Dautenhahn, K., & Billard, A. (2002) Games Children with Autism Can Play With Robota, a Humanoid Robotic Doll. Proc. 1st Cambridge Workshop on Universal Access and Assistive Technology (CWUAAT). In S. Keates, P.J. Clarkson, P.M. Langdon & P. Robinson (eds.), *Universal Access and Assistive Technology*. London: Springer-Verlag.

Davidson, R. J., Ekman, P., Saron, C., Senulius, J., & Friesen, W. V. (1990). Approach-withdrawal and cerebral asymmetry: Emotional expression and brain physiology I. *Journal of Personality and Social Psychology, 58*, 330–341. doi:10.1037/0022-3514.58.2.330

Dickson, K. L., Walker, H., & Fogel, A. (1997). The relationship between smile type and play type during parent–infant play. *Developmental Psychology, 33*, 925–933. doi:10.1037/0012-1649.33.6.925

Dimberg, U. (1982). Facial reactions to facial expressions. *Psychophysiology, 19*, 643–647. doi:10.1111/j.1469-8986.1982.tb02516.x

DiSalvo, C. A., & Oswald, D. P. (2002). Peer-mediated interventions to increase the social interaction of children with autism: Consideration of peer expectancies. *Focus on Autism and Other Developmental Disabilities, 17*(4), 198–207. doi:10.1177/10883576020170040201

Duchenne, G. B. (1990). *The mechanism of human facial expression or an electro-physiological analysis of the expression of emotions* (Cutherbertson, R. A. (Trans. Ed.)). New York: Cambridge University Press. (Original work published 1862)

Duclos, S. E., & Laird, J. D. (2001). The deliberate control of emotional experience through control of expressions. *Cognition and Emotion, 15*, 27–56. doi:10.1080/0269993004200088

Ekman, P., & Friesen, W. V. (1982). Felt, false, and miserable smiles. *Journal of Nonverbal Behavior, 6*, 238–252. doi:10.1007/BF00987191

Ekman, P., Levenson, R. W., & Friesen, W. V. (1983). Autonomivic nervous system activity distinguishes among emotions. *Science, 221*, 1208–1210. doi:10.1126/science.6612338

Fernández-Dols, J. M., & Ruiz-Belda, M. A. (1995). Are smiles a sign of happiness? Gold medal winners at the Olympic Games. *Journal of Personality and Social Psychology, 69*, 1113–1119. doi:10.1037/0022-3514.69.6.1113

Frea, W. D. (1995). Social-communicative skills in high-functioning children with autism. In Krogel, R. L., & Koegel, L. K. (Eds.), *Teaching children with autism: Strategies for initiating positive interactions and improving learning opportunities* (pp. 53–66). Baltimore: Brookes.

Friedrich, S., Morgan, S. B., & Devine, C. (1996). Children's attitudes and behavioral intentions toward a peer with Tourette's syndrome. *Journal of Pediatric Psychology, 21*, 307–319. doi:10.1093/jpepsy/21.3.307

Givens, S., & Monahan, J. (2005). Priming Mammies, Jezebels, and Other Controlling Images: An Examination of the Influence of Mediated Stereotypes on Perceptions of an African American Woman. *Media Psychology, 7*(1), 87–106. doi:10.1207/S1532785XMEP0701_5

Goldstein, H., Kaczmarek, L., & Pennington, R. (1992). Peer-mediated intervention: Attending to, commenting on, and acknowledging the behavior of preschoolers with autism. *Journal of Applied Behavior Analysis, 25*(2), 289–305. doi:10.1901/jaba.1992.25-289

Gray, C. A., & Garand, J. D. (1993). Social stories: Improving responses of students with autism with accurate social information. *Focus on Autistic Behavior, 8*(1), 1–10.

Gray, D. E. (1993). Perceptions of stigma: The parents of autistic children. *Sociology of Health & Illness, 15*, 103–120. doi:10.1111/1467-9566.ep11343802

Guite, J., Lobato, D., Kao, B., & Plante, W. (2004). Discordance Between Sibling and Parent Reports of the Impact of Chronic Illness and Disability on Siblings. *Children's Health Care, 33*(1), 77–92. doi:10.1207/s15326888chc3301_5

Guralnick, M. J., Connor, R. T., Hammond, M. A., Gottman, J. M., & Kinnish, K. (1996). The peer relations of preschool children with communications disorders. *Child Development, 67*(2), 471–489. doi:10.2307/1131827

Hagiwara, T., & Myles, B. S. (1999). A multimedia social story intervention: Teaching skills to children with autism. *Focus on Autism and Other Developmental Disabilities, 14*(2), 82–95. doi:10.1177/108835769901400203

Hames, A. (2005). How younger siblings of children with learning disabilities understand the cognitive and social implications of learning disabilities. *European Journal of Special Needs Education, 20*(1), 3–19. doi:10.1080/0885625042000319052

Heider, F. (1958). *The Psychology of Interpersonal relations*. New York: Wiley. doi:10.1037/10628-000

Hess, U., Kappas, A., McHugo, G. J., Lanzetta, J. T., & Kleck, R. E. (1992). The facilitative effect of facial expression on the self-generation of emotion. *International Journal of Psychophysiology, 12*, 251–265. doi:10.1016/0167-8760(92)90064-I

Hollander, E., DelGiudice-Asch, G., & Simon, J. (1999). B lymphocyte D8/17 and repetitive behaviors in autism. *The American Journal of Psychiatry*, *156*, 317–320.

Holroyd, J., & MacArthur, D. (1976). Mental retardation and stress on the parents: a contrast between Down syndrome and childhood autism. *American Journal of Mental Deficiency*, *4*, 431–436.

Juvonen, J. (1991). Deviance, perceived responsibility and negative peer reactions. *Developmental Psychology*, *27*, 672–681. doi:10.1037/0012-1649.27.4.672

Juvonen, J. (1992). Negative peer reactions from the perspective of the reactor. *Journal of Educational Psychology*, *84*, 314–321. doi:10.1037/0022-0663.84.3.314

Juvonen, J., & Weiner, B. (1993). An attributional analysis of students' interactions: the social consequences of perceived responsibility. *Educational Psychology Review*, *5*(4), 325–345. doi:10.1007/BF01320222

Klin, A., Warren, J., Schultz, R., & Volkmar, F. (2002). Visual fixation patterns during viewing of naturalistic social situations as predictors of social competence in individuals with autism. *Archives of General Psychiatry*, *59*(9), 809–816. doi:10.1001/archpsyc.59.9.809

Konstam, V., Drainoni, M., Mitchell, G., Houser, R., Reddington, D., & Eaton, D. (1993). Career choices and values of siblings of individuals with developmental disabilities. *The School Counselor*, *40*(4).

Lorimer, P. A., Simpson, R. L., Myles, B. S., & Ganz, J. B. (2003). The use of social stories as a preventative behavioral intervention in a home setting with a child with autism. *Journal of Positive Behavior Interventions*, *4*(1), 53–60. doi:10.1177/10983007020040019

Nessa, N. (2004). National Statistics: The health of children and young people, (pp. 1- 20).

Newschaffer, C. J., Falb, M. D., & Gurney, J. G. (2005). National autism prevalence trends from United States special education data. *Pediatrics*, *115*(3), 277–282. doi:10.1542/peds.2004-1958

Odom, S. L., McConnell, S. R., & Chandler, L. K. (1993). Acceptability and feasibility of classroom-based social interaction interventions for young children. *Exceptional Children*, *60*, 226–236.

Oizumi, J. J. (1997). Assessing maternal functioning in families of children with autism. *Dissertation Abstracts International Section B: The Sciences and Engineering*, *57* (7-B), 5720.

Pierce, K., & Schreibman, L. (1995). Increasing complex social behaviors in children with autism: Effects of peer-implemented pivotal response training. *Journal of Applied Behavior Analysis*, *28*, 285–295. doi:10.1901/jaba.1995.28-285

Rosenthal, R. (1963). On the social psychology of the psychological experiment: the experimenter's hypotheses as unintended experimental results. *American Scientist*, *51*, 268–283.

Schopler, E., & Mesibov, G. B. (Eds.). (1986). *Social behavior in autism*. New York: Plenum Press.

Scott, J., Clark, C., & Brady, M. (2000). *Students with autism: Characteristics and Instruction programming*. San Diego, CA: Singular.

Sehaba, K., Estraillier, P., & Lambert, D. (2005). Interactive Educational Games for Autistic Children with Agent -Based System. *Lecture Notes in Computer Science*, *3711*, 422–432. doi:10.1007/11558651_41

Shah, A., & Frith, U. (2006). An islet of ability in autistic children: a research note. *Journal of Child Psychology and Psychiatry, and Allied Disciplines*, *24*(4), 613–620. doi:10.1111/j.1469-7610.1983.tb00137.x

Silton, N. (2009). *Fostering knowledge, positive intentions and attitudes of typical children towards children with autism.* Unpublished doctoral dissertation, Fordham University, USA.

Siperstein, G. N., & Bak, J. (1980). Improving children's attitudes toward blind peers. *Journal of Visual Impairment & Blindness*, 132–135.

Sturmey, P. (2003). Video technology and persons with autism and other developmental disabilities. *Journal of Positive Behavior Interventions, 5*(1), 3–4. doi:10.1177/10983007030050010401

Swaim, K. F., & Morgan, S. B. (2001). Children's attitudes and behavioral intentions toward a peer with autistic behaviors: Does a brief educational intervention have an effect? *Journal of Autism and Developmental Disorders, 31*(2), 195–207. doi:10.1023/A:1010703316365

Verte, S., Roeyers, A., & Buysse, A. (2003). Behavioral problems, social competence, and self-concept in siblings of children with autism. *Child: Care, Health and Development, 29*(3), 193–205. doi:10.1046/j.1365-2214.2003.00331.x

Volkmar, F., & Pauls, D. (2003). Autism. *Lancet, 362*(9390), 1133–1141. doi:10.1016/S0140-6736(03)14471-6

Ward, L., Hansbrough, E., & Walker, E. (2005). Contributions of Music Video Exposure to Black Adolescents' Gender and Sexual Schemas. *Journal of Adolescent Research, 20*(2), 143–166. doi:10.1177/0743558404271135

Wert, B. Y., & Neisworth, J. T. (2003). Effects of video self-modeling in spontaneous requesting in children with autism. *Journal of Positive Behavior Interventions, 5*(1), 30–34. doi:10.1177/1098300 7030050010501

Zihni, F., & Zihni, F. (1995). *The AZ method: The use of video techniques to develop language skills in autistic children.*

ADDITIONAL READING

Elder, J. (2006). *Different like me: My book of autism heroes.* London: Jessica Kingsley Publishers.

Farber, B. (1963). Interaction with Retarded Siblings and Life Goals of Children. *Marriage and Family Living, 25*(1), 96–98. doi:10.2307/349015

Garrison-Harrell, L., Kamps, D., & Kravits, T. (1997). The effects of peer networks On social-communicative behaviors for students with autism. *Focus on Autism and Other Developmental Disabilities, 12*(4), 241–256. doi:10.1177/108835769701200406

Gonzalez-Lopez, A., & Kamps, D. M. (1997). Social skills training to increase social interactions between children with autism and their typical peers. *Focus on Autism and Other Developmental Disabilities, 12*, 2–14. doi:10.1177/108835769701200101

Gotthelf, C., & Peel, T. (1990). The Children's Television Workshop goes to school. *Educational Technology Research and Development, 38*(4), 25–33. doi:10.1007/BF02314642

Gottlieb, J., & Gottlieb, B. W. (1977). Stereotypic attitudes and behavioral intentions toward handicapped children. *American Journal of Mental Deficiency, 82*, 65–71.

Gould, L.J., & Corey, M. Social desirability in children: an extension and replication. *Journal of Consulting and Clinical Psychology, 33*-128.

Grandin, T. (1995). *Thinking in Pictures: My Life with Autism.* New York: Doubleday.

Grandin, T., & Johnson, C. (2005). *Animals in translation.* New York: Scribner.

Grossman, F. K. (1972). *Brothers and sisters of retarded children: An exploratory study.* Syracuse, NY: Syracuse University Press.

Gutner, T. (2004). Special needs, crushing costs. *Business Week, Issue 3885.*Klein, E.B., Haddon, M. (2003). The Curious Incident of the Dog in the Night-time. United Kingdom: Jonathan Cape.

Haring, T. G., & Breen, C. G. (1992). A peer-mediated social network intervention to enhance the social network intervention to enhance the social integration of persons with moderate and severe disabilities. *Journal of Applied Behavior Analysis, 25*, 319–333. doi:10.1901/jaba.1992.25-319

Harper, D. C. (1999). Social psychology of differences: Stigma, spread, and stereotypes in Childhood. *Rehabilitation Psychology, 44*, 131–144. doi:10.1037/0090-5550.44.2.131

Harris, M. J., Milich, R. C., Corbitt, E. M., Hoover, D. W., & Brady, M. (1992). Self-fulfilling effects of stigmatizing information on children's social interactions. *Journal of Personality and Social Psychology, 63*, 41–50. doi:10.1037/0022-3514.63.1.41

Hayden-Thomson, L., Rubin, K. H., & Hymel, S. (1987). Sex preferences in sociometric choices. *Developmental Psychology, 23*, 558–562. doi:10.1037/0012-1649.23.4.558

Hick, J. (1977). *Evil and the God of Love*. San Francisco: Harper and Row.

Iavaraone, A., Patruno, M., Galeone, F., Chieffi, S., & Carlomagno, S. (2007). Brief report: error pattern in an autistic savant calendar calculator. *Journal of Autism and Developmental Disorders, 37*, 775–779. doi:10.1007/s10803-006-0190-2

Jones, E. E. (1990). *Interpersonal Perception*. New York: W.H. Freeman.

Kamps, D., Gonzalez-Lopez, A., Potucek, J., Kravits, T., Kemmerer, K., & Garrison-Harrell, L. (1998). What do the peers think? Social validity of integrated programs. *Education & Treatment of Children, 21*, 107–134.

Kamps, D. M., Kravitz, T., Gonzalez-Lopez, A., Kemmerer, K., Potucek, J., & Harrell, L. G. (1988). What do peers think? Social validity of peer-mediated programs. *Education & Treatment of Children, 21*, 107–134.

Kelley, H. H. (1967). Attribution Theory in Social Psychology. In D. Levine (Ed.), *Nebraska Symposium on Motivation, 1967*. Lincoln: University of Nebraska Press.

Maccoby, E. E., & Jacklin, C. N. (1987). Gender segregation in childhood. In Reese, E. H. (Ed.), *Advances in child development and behavior* (Vol. 20, pp. 239–287). New York: Academic Press.

Maras, P., & Brown, R. Effects of different forms of school contact on children's attitudes toward disabled and non-disabled peers. *The British Journal of Educational Psychology, 70*(3), 337–351. doi:10.1348/000709900158164

McEvoy, M. A., & Odom, S. L. (1987). Social interaction training for preschool children with behavioral disorders. *Behavioral Disorders, 12*, 242–251.

Morgan, S. B., Biebrich, A. A., Walker, M., & Schwerdtfeger, H. (1998). Children's willingness to share activities with a physically handicapped peer: Am I more willing than my classmates? *Journal of Pediatric Psychology, 23*(6), 1998. doi:10.1093/jpepsy/23.6.367

Morgan, S. B., & Wisely, D. W. (1996). Children's attitudes and behavioral intentions toward a peer presented as physically handicapped: A more positive view. *Journal of Developmental and Physical Disabilities, 8*, 29–42. doi:10.1007/BF02578438

Mottron, L., Dawson, M., Soulieres, I., Hubert, B., & Burack, J. (2006). Enhanced perceptual functioning in autism: an update, and eight principles of autistic perception. *Journal of Autism and Developmental Disorders, 36*(1), 27–43. doi:10.1007/s10803-005-0040-7

Myles, B. S., Simpson, R. L., Ormsbee, C. K., & Erikson, C. (1993). Integrating preschool children with autism with their normally developing peers: Research findings and best practice recommendations. *Focus on Autistic Behavior, 8*, 1–18.

Nabors, L. A., & Larson, E. R. (2002). The effects of brief interventions on children's playmate preferences for a child sitting in a wheelchair. *Journal of Developmental and Physical Disabilities, 14,* 403–413. doi:10.1023/A:1020339004125

Newacheck, P. W., Inkelas, M., & Kim, S. (2004). Health services use and health care Expenditures for children with disabilities. *Pediatrics, 114,* 79–85. doi:10.1542/peds.114.1.79

Notbohm, E. (2005). *Ten Things Every Child with Autism Wishes You Knew.* Arlington, Texas: Future Horizons.

Owen-Deschryver, J. S. (2004). Promoting social interactions between students with Autism and their peers in inclusive school settings. *Dissertation Abstracts International Section A: Humanities and Social Sciences, 64(9-A),* 3246.

Rice, M. L., Huston, A. C., Truglio, R., & Wright, J. (1990). Words from "Sesame Street": learning vocabulary while viewing. *Developmental Psychology, 26*(3), 421–428. doi:10.1037/0012-1649.26.3.421

Roeyers, H. (1996). The influence of nonhandicapped peers on the social interactions of children with a pervasive developmental disorder. *Journal of Autism and Developmental Disorders, 26,* 303–320. doi:10.1007/BF02172476

Rogers, S. J. (2000). Interventions that facilitate socialization in children with autism. *Journal of Autism and Developmental Disorders, 30,* 399–409. doi:10.1023/A:1005543321840

Rosenbaum, P. L., Armstrong, R. W., & King, S. M. (1988). Determinants of children's attitudes toward disability: A review of the evidence. *Children's Health Care, 17,* 1–8. doi:10.1207/s15326888chc1701_5

Rosenthal, R. (1963). On the social psychology of the psychological experiment: The experimenter's hypotheses as unintended experimental results. *American Scientist, 51,* 268–283.

Rosenthal, R. (1989). Experimenter expectancy covert communication and meta-analytic methods. Address delivered to the 97th annual convention of the American Psychological Association, New Orleans.

Rossi, P. H., Lipsey, M. W., & Freeman, H. E. (2004). *Evaluation: A Systematic Approach* (7th ed.). Thousand Oaks: Sage Publications.

Ruble, L. A., Heflinger, C. A., Renfrew, J. W., & Saunders, R. C. (2005). Access and service use by children with autism spectrum disorders in medicaid managed care. *Journal of Autism and Developmental Disorders, 35,* 3–13. doi:10.1007/s10803-004-1026-6

Ryan, K. M. (1981). Developmental differences in reactions to the physically disabled. *Human Development, 24,* 240–256. doi:10.1159/000272685

Schreibman, L., O'Neill, R. E., & Koegel, R. L. (1983). Behavioral training for siblings of autistic children. *Journal of Applied Behavior Analysis, 16,* 129–138. doi:10.1901/jaba.1983.16-129

Serbin, L. A., & Sprafkin, C. (1986). The salience of gender and the process of sex-typing In three-to-seven year-old children. *Child Development, 57,* 1188–1199. doi:10.2307/1130442

Sigelman, C. K. (1991). The effect of causal information on peer perceptions of children with a pervasive developmental disorder. *Journal of Applied Developmental Psychology, 12,* 237–253. doi:10.1016/0193-3973(91)90014-U

Siperstein, G. N., & Bak, J. (1977). *Instruments to measure children's attitudes toward the handicapped: Adjective Checklist and Activity Preference List.* Unpublished Manuscript, University of Massachusetts, Boston.

Siperstein, G. N., & Chatillion, A. C. (1982). Importance of perceived similarity in Improving children's attitudes toward mentally retarded peers. *American Journal of Mental Deficiency, 86*(5), 453–458.

Stephens, C. E. (2005). Overcoming challenges and identifying a consensus about autism intervention programming. *International Journal of Special Education, 20*(1), 35–49.

TheHarvard Brain. (Spring 2000) An interview with Temple Grandin. *Vol. 7.*http://www.hcs.harvard.edu/~husn/BRAIN/vol7-spring2000/grandin.html.

Voeltz, I. M. (1980). Children's attitudes toward handicapped peers. *American Journal of Mental Deficiency, 84,* 455–464.

Waltz, M. (1993). Chapter 9 of Pervasive Developmental Disorders: Finding a Diagnosis and Getting Help. O'Reilly & Associates. Retrieved October 2, 2007, from, http://oreilly.com/medical/autism/news/social_skills.html

Weiner, B. (1993). On sin versus sickness: A theory of perceived responsibility and social motivation. *The American Psychologist, 48,* 957–965. doi:10.1037/0003-066X.48.9.957

Wisely, D. W., & Morgan, S. B. (1981). Children's ratings of peers presented as mentally Retarded and physically handicapped. *American Journal of Mental Deficiency, 86*(3), 281–286.

Chapter 22
Gaming and Simulation:
Training, and the Military

Sheila Seitz
Windwalker Corporation, USA

Courtney Uram
James Madison University, USA

ABSTRACT

The purpose of this chapter is to provide a brief summary of the military's use of gaming and simulation to accomplish training. Historically, the military has been a forerunner in the exploration of training techniques that incorporate aspects of games and simulations. Training tools emerge in various gaming formats such as simulations, edutainment, commercial-off-the-shelf games (COTS), and serious games. To develop training in the form of games or simulations, elements of instructional design must be considered to include learning objectives, game play, and feedback. Emerging technologies provide possible solutions to training challenges such as achieving affective learning domain objectives and the portability of training. The military, as an early adapter of games and simulation, continues to forge the way by integrating gaming and simulation, instructional design, and emerging technologies to achieve the ever growing demands of training.

INTRODUCTION

Gaming and the military have a long tradition together, beginning with the use of toy figures within sandbox representations, progressing to complex board games requiring complex analytical skills, and evolving into current use of sophisticated computer models, gaming engines, and high definition 3-D graphics to create virtual worlds of combat.

DOI: 10.4018/978-1-61520-781-7.ch022

The military has historically used technology to "maximize the efficiency and effectiveness of all their activities, training and education." (Fletcher, 2009, p. 72). Current training tools include a wide range of application of technologies. Simulators, sophisticated machines relying on computational models to mimic the actual experience of soldiers, assist to train in various tasks such as driving a truck, steering a ship, flying an airplane, or shooting a weapon. Games are created to encourage thought and practice in decision making from simple tasks to more complex work of war planning. When simulation is combined with elements of gaming, opportunities emerge to encourage effective training with the unique audience of learners found in the military.

The military considers each member a lifelong learner. This core principle presents many challenges to the development of training and becomes accentuated in the development of games and simulations. Specifically is the challenge of reaching today's military audience of Soldiers, Sailors, Marines, and Airmen; mostly made up of young adult males. (Watkins & Sherk, 2008). They are members of what is known at the Net Gen, the generation cohort who came of age with the evolution of the internet and exponential growth of technology's role in society. For this military audience, "Learning is participatory; knowing depends on practice and participation. Digital resources enable experiential learning—something in tune with Net Gen preferences. Rather than being told, Net Geners would rather construct their own learning, assembling information, tools, and frameworks from a variety of sources." (Oblinger & Oblinger, 2005). The military has responded with various methodologies to include games and simulations, serious games, Commercial-off-the-shelf (COTS) computer games, and Massive Multiplayer On-line Games (MMOG). This chapter discusses the success and challenges of these methodologies, identifies critical aspects of instructional design when developing games for military training, and suggests emerging technologies be examined as new methodologies in the military training field.

History of Gaming in the Military

Roberts (1976) noted that gaming as training was "often used to train military officers" (p. 3). Games found in the military took many forms and emerged as effective methods for training. Chessboards acted as terrain maps and chessmen as soldiers. Sand tables with miniature models to represent armies gave leaders the ability to visualize battles and play out possible scenarios. The Prussians instituted the practice of wargaming around 1824, with the American military adapting wargaming for training later that century. William McCarty Little admired the value of wargaming and ensured that it became a significant part of the curriculum at the newly established U.S. Naval War College in Rhode Island. (Gray, 1995).

Eventually, terrain maps and wooden blocks replaced chessboards and chessmen as civilization progressed. By World War II, wargaming marked an immense turning point for training and development. War games were something used by all super powers (Roberts). The simulation that occurred during the game process was treated as a training technique and evolved into paper based exercises that integrated mathematical algorithms to model elements of warfare such as movement and attrition (Smith, n.d.).

During the 1950's the Rand Corporation used ideas that emerged during the evolution of simulation training and war gaming to create a board game. Building upon their research and the ideas of Clark Roberts, the project resulted in:

"the formalization of the playing board with a gridded overlay to manage movement and engagements; the use of a Combat Results Table to formalize the results of the battle, the incorporation of terrain types that influence combat activities; a turn-based play mechanism; and the use of dice to add random outcomes to the battle" (Smith, n.d.,).

With the onset of the computer age, the abilities of wargaming as training grew exponentially.

A presentation by Hilton G. Weiner at the 35th National Meeting of the Operations Research Society of America in 1969 (Weiner, 1969), examined the trends of the time in regards to military gaming. He likened the games with "confrontational analysis" (p. 1) and identified the ability of computers to advance the technique. Specifically, he noted that computers allowed greater detail in simulation and provided accelerated bookkeeping skills. These advancements furthered abilities of time-sharing, multi-agency and standardization. However, he felt that while phenomena of warfare such as machines and munitions could be captured in the war games, much work was needed to capture the other phenomena of motivation, morale, and miscalculation (p. 5). He called for further research in the improvement of understanding the phenomena and increasing the ability to model them.

The use of wargaming in training continued to evolve throughout the 1970s and at the beginning of the 1980's, an emphasis was placed on combining the best features of war gaming and analytic modeling to build strategic analysis for existing threats of nuclear warfare. Building upon RAND's expertise in these areas, the US Defense Department supported the efforts of the Rand Strategy Assessment Center (RASC) which guided much of the research and advancement in the area of training and war gaming throughout the decade. (Davis & Winnefeld, 1983). Davis (1986) called for the need to create computer programs that were transparent yet able to explain the decision that occurred during the simulations of wargaming. While much advancement was made with the now familiar Red and Blue Agents programs (Schwabe & Wilson, 1990), the end of the decade and the Cold War would bring new demands to the field.

Throughout the 1990's, investigators of wargaming as a training technique recognized in numerous studies the need to advance the models driving the artificial intelligence with the computer programs and increase the ability to share data across those institutions engaged in the field. (Bennett, 1993, Hillestad, Bennett, & Moore, 1996, and Davis, Bigelow, & McEver 2001). As mentioned by Bankes (1991), many of the models did not adequately reflect the new requirements of warfare, a shift from the force on force of the Cold War to more of contingency based operations known as Military Operations Other Than War (MOOTW) (Joint Publication 3-07, 1995).

Yet, the focus of wargaming as a training technique remained that of increasing understanding as opposed to outcome based performance, i.e. winning the war. (Schwabe, 1994).

Today, games and simulations function as military recruiting tools (Zyda, 2005), educational learning tools (Gredler, 2004; Gee 2003), and corporate training tools to foster learning in professional, corporate, or adult education. As for the military specifically, games and simulations are teaching tools at all levels of education (Babus, Hodges, & Kjonnerod, 1997). Collective and individual training designs benefit from the critical thinking and flexibility encouraged by games and simulations. These learning tools address many objectives: rehearsing behaviors, teaching skills to troops, and assisting policy makers in evaluating, identifying, and improving protocol.

Current regulations within the military identify distributed learning as a key to facilitating continuing education programs (AR 370-1, 2007). Included within distributed learning are various forms of gaming and simulation described as interactive multimedia instruction, computer aided instruction, simulation, and interactive training technology (including stand-alone and on-line games.) Training commands are encouraged to leverage "distributed–learning concepts, when cost efficient and effective training will result." (p.15)

The military possesses a rich history of training and education to draw upon as it continues to develop and implement games and simulations as viable training tools. Central to this effort is the ability to consider the learner, more specifically the range of learners that exist in the military, when designing games and simulations for training. As noted by Klopfer, Osterweil,& Salen (2009): "Lastly, it is important to acknowledge that games and learning has a history that predates the advent of modern video games…This history has taught us several important things, not the least of which is that players determine how they learn." (p.8).

Range of Gaming within Training

The study of gaming within the military is somewhat confounded by the wide range of definitions that exist to explain what is and is not consider a game. As noted by Klopfer, Osterweil, and Salen (2009), "…perceptions of what games are (are or aren't) continue to cast a heavy shadow over the games and learning space." (p.7). The range of games considered for training, to include occurrences within the military, are games, simulations, serious games, COTS games, and massive multiplayer online games (MMOGs). Perhaps the best approach in examining games within military training is suggested by Caspian Learning (2008), "…it is more useful to look at the general literature placing these terms in their cultural context." (p. 14).

Games and Simulations

Games and simulations have unique characteristics that differentiate them from each other (Kirkley & Kirkley, 2004; Prensky, 2001; Ricci, Salas, & Cannon-Bowers, 1996). Games are defined by Gredler (2004) as "competitive exercises in which the objective is to win and players must apply subject matter or other relevant knowledge" (p. 571). Simulations conversely are "open-ended evolving situations with many interacting variables" (p. 571). Understanding games paves the pathway for recognizing the structures, standards, and techniques found in simulations (Aldrich, 2004). Mike Zyda, a professor of gaming at the University of Southern California and a key contributor to the successful game, *America's Army*, explains that, "The definition of games is story, art and software." (Federation of American Scientists, 2006; Zyda, 2005). The primary difference, when considering military applications, may be found in the purpose or application of the game.

While it is important to understand that games and simulations differ in many aspects; they often share an important commonality. Each works to foster experiential learning (Gredler, 1996). Within this model of learning, elements such as reflection and debriefing are significant (Thatcher, 1990; Kriz, 2003). If the context of the game or simulation is primarily to construct a story whose intent for learning is to encourage game play for entertainment, it remains a game albeit with learning requirements. The game may employ experiential learning as an element, perhaps a motivator. However, the game would not be classified as an "instructional game". According to Tennyson and Jorczak (2009), "Instructional games have specific learning outcomes as primary goals." (p. 5).

A helpful comparison of games and simulation within the military is found with *America's Army* and *DARWARS Ambush*. *America's Army* is a game that was developed specifically for the purpose of recruiting new soldiers by the U.S. Army. The game takes the form of a first person shooting perspective and role plays the life of a soldier. While some military units have used the game for training, its primary purpose and design is to attract young men who enjoy gaming and may gain an interest in the U.S. Army while playing. *DARWARS Ambush* is a simulation game that simulates a vehicular movement (patrol) within a combat environment. The purpose of simulation is to train multiple people within an immersive environment how to react to possible ambushes when part of a vehicular patrol. While *DARWARS Ambush* evolved from a stand-alone, single player simulation to the current version of an immersive environment that changes based on lessons from the actual combat environment and involves multiple players, its primary training purpose persists.

The military's success with games and simulations may be found in the wide variety and continuous adaptations that are applied as training needs increase and diversify. At the National Defense University, gaming and simulation have been combined to create learning environments which foster analytic skills and enable the process of concept validation leading to doctrine development. (Joint Forces Quarterly, 2009). To do so, one must consider that, "useful analytical environment in which to identify and weigh policy options and needs is the goal of good game design. (McCown, 2005). Flexibility and adaptability can be found in projects such as the development of various leadership games noted in the work of Iuppa and Borst (2007). During these projects, developers experimented with the balance of computer modeling for simulation and the interplay of human actors with virtual avatars to achieve training objectives. Over time, they found what worked and did not work was based on its appropriateness toward implementing the training objective.

Challenges with games and simulations are most exemplified in selection of the appropriate instructional delivery to meet the training objective. Choosing an advanced technological tool simply because it is available does not guarantee effective training. Investigations into simulators (computer generated environments to replicate the actual skill which the learner must perform) supports this; as Yardley (2003) states that in training, one must consider if the technology is, "… appropriate for increasing the use of simulation and strategies for purchasing and implementing simulators." This finding emerged as he studied the Navy's desire to balance training which normally occurred at sea with the possibilities of what could be done while ships are in port.

DARWARS and America's Army are motivating examples of the diverse goals which can be achieved through games and simulation. The military continues to lead the way in developing the possibilities both within training goals and outside of the goals, such as analytical analysis, recruiting, and doctrine development. However, more research is needed to determine what learning outcomes can be systematically achieved by the use of individual and multiplayer games to train adult participants in acquiring knowledge and skills while sustaining the ability of games to provide intense and engaging experiences (O'Neil & Perez, 2009).

Serious Games

When applied in a non-entertainment realm, gaming and simulation technology results in serious games (Zyda, 2005). According to Susi, Johannesson, and Backlund (2007), the term serious games have been defined, but no true definition of what it actually is exists. Taken as a whole, Susi, Johannesson, and Backlund's (2007) interpretation of serious games from present research is defined as "digital games used for purposes other than mere entertainment" (p. 2). Serious games emerged from research within the military training field. Observing great potential for other occupational training, the Woodrow Wilson Foundation funded the Serious Games Initiative (www.seriousgames.com). Serious Games "…are characterized by their specificity and applicability for particular work-related purposes." (Klopfer, Osterweil,& Salen, 2009, p.21).

The 1980's decade marked the time when serious games, which often take the form of simulations and games in electronic formats, were used throughout the military (BinSubaih, Maddock & Romano, 2009). As described earlier, these electronic wargaming formats would use computer modeling and data capabilities to create simulation centers where soldiers would gather to analyze and fight wars against the computer. The goal was a performance oriented outcome where the decisions were analyzed and evaluated rather than simply trying to "beat" the computer. As computing ability grew, so did the complexity and effectiveness of these serious games to achieve training.

Not until 2002 were serious games recognized by other organizations. The Serious Games Initiative furthered interest in serious games beyond the military. This form of gaming was distinguished by its purpose "to train people for tasks in particular job". (Klopfer, Osterweil,& Salen, 2009) The serious game industry, described as flexible and adaptable, has developed into a $20 million dollar market (Van Eck, 2006). The military invests most heavily in the serious games market. (BinSubaih, Maddock & Romano, 2009).

Serious games cover a wide range of training opportunities for the military. These include: tactical experience, ambush, rifle range, foreign language and culture, leadership, post traumatic stress disorder and obstacle courses (BinSubaih, Maddock & Romano, 2009). Sawyer and Smith (2008) created a taxonomy to capture the range and application of current serious games development efforts. Within the taxonomy, military training is identified as "defense" and examples such as games for health (rehabilitation and wellness) and games for training (solider support) are recognized.

One example of a serious game endeavor by the military that models the type of electronic games commercial and civilian entities are interested in is that of games developed for dismounted infantry leaders. (Beal, 2006). The project included three games to teach leadership skills at different organizational levels experienced by infantry leaders. Successes of these serious games included the ability to represent realism and fidelity to the actual combat environment due in large part to the involvement of subject matter experts early on and throughout the development of the games. The learners also valued the opportunity to learn desired leadership skills; the findings found this factor to be more important than ensuring the games were fun and entertaining.

Challenges in implementing these serious games involved capturing feedback for a high level of required cognitive skills in an artificial intelligence model. The participants expressed the need for feedback from a human instructor vital to their learning. Continuing to improve models and consolidative representation, especially in such a dynamic combat situation, is one goal of the Modeling and Simulation Center Information Analysis Center (Henninger, 2009).

Also of interest was the finding that although the participants were of the digital native generation, not all found the technology to be intuitive

or familiar. (Beal, 2006). Ensuring a serious game is navigable without interfering with learning is an important task of the developer. As pointed out throughout this chapter, stating clear training objectives for the games was critical.

Given the high cost of creating in-person training to address the skills at the center of serious games objectives, makes this genre of game a center piece for further research and investigation. As computing ability allows the fidelity of the experience to increase, it cannot be considered a panacea for all training. However, its effectiveness and potential justify development to continue, especially as training budgets are high visible targets both in military and corporate budget scenarios. The military's contribution to serious games is significant; yet the influence of the military within body of research for serious games and training must be acknowledged and addressed. National education and workforce development goals may differ, generating more varied requirements from research. (Federation of American Scientists, 2006).

Commercial-Off-The-Shelf (COTS) Games

Current markets of COTS games include a plethora of titles that carry a military theme. A small sample of these games include: *Call of Duty, Close Combat: First to Fight,* and *Full Spectrum Warrior.* Because these titles are COTS, it is safe to assume the primary purpose of their development was not training but rather entertainment. However, the military's National Simulation Center at Fort Leavenworth, Kansas, endorses the use of these games as training tools, validating their potential in preparing soldiers for combat situations. In their publication, *Commander's Guide to Games for Training,* (2006), it is noted, "Games can provide an alternative training environment at a lower cost. The tradeoff is a reduction in fidelity." (p.5).

The success of COTS development can be partially attributed to the investment of the entertainment industry in the wargame genre. As noted by Macedonia (2000), "The military cannot afford to ignore advances in industry, where the graphics systems for game consoles and personal computers have nearly doubled their performance every nine months for the last five years." While the fidelity, which is the ability of training to recreate the actual environment where the task must be performed such as the war zone for the military, is decreased by moving from a realistic environment to a virtual world, the savings in terms of both fiscal and time cannot be ignored.

Another element contributing to the success of COTS in military training is that of providing a training environment familiar to the target audience. (Ford, Barlow & Lewis, n.d.). Many soldiers today grew up alongside the internet and are quite comfortable using the technology for the purpose of learning. COTS provide a motivating environment through its natural design of engagement. If soldiers are aware of the training purposes with COTS, they may overcome the outcome based orientation (play to win) and focus on the feedback given by the game to grow in understanding of their personal skill development.

The primary challenge in using COTS as a training tool is achieving the goals of training. "COTS gaming systems do not generally have the assessment components that are critical for effective training." Hussain and Ferguson, (2005). This finding is shared by O'Neill and Perez (2009), "There is general consensus in our community that learning with interactive environments, such as games and simulations, is not effective when no effective instructional measure or support is added." The communities these authors refer to are the developers of games and simulation for training and adult education purposes. While few would dispute that learning occurs while gaming, the challenge for adapting COTS for military training is in achieving the specificity of the learning goal and the requirement to measure training effects to justify critical resources. Other challenges such as licensing fees and use of appropriate technologies to achieve training also exist.

To balance the evident worthiness of COTS for training with the need to ensure the targeted learning is achieved within training, it would be helpful for future training developers to provide policy and guidelines in this area, "Subject to the evaluation and trialing of games, the policies and practices for the effective use of games must be produced." (Ford, Barlow & Lewis, n.d.)

Massive Multiplayer Online Games (MMOGs)

Massive multiplayer online games (MMOGs) are another type of gaming medium the military is exploring. MMOGs offer collaboration and sharing of knowledge, skills, and values with other players both inside and outside of the game (Gee, 2003). MMOGs encourage individuals to think as a team and "make soldiers to think critically about their surroundings and enhance their situational awareness" (Curtis, Thomas & Ritter, 2008).

In their attempt to create elements of military training that address changing tactics of asymmetric threats, Fu and et.al (2007) investigated the use of MMOGs in developing and distributing training demonstrations. While training demonstrations exist in many forms to address different objectives, Fu, et.al, focused on 2-D animated representations with the intent to achieve procedural knowledge objectives. They used MMOG in the development of the demonstration, seeking synchronous feedback from soldiers currently implementing tactics in the war zone who provided current and relative data. The format of a 2-D animated representation provided a familiar training format for the target audience of soldiers. While the training demonstration did not attempt to achieve all training requirements, it proved worthy of development to provide one type of training tool within a toolkit of training sources.

Challenges with MMOGs and use in military training include security, cost, synchronous participation and connectivity of the technology. Because applications of MMOGs involve real time interactions between avatars driven by actual soldiers, knowledge exchanged should be shielded from possible enemy actors. This requires similar security measures used with existing military networks; the unique requirement of 2-D virtual world representations further implicates current challenges in this area. (Axe, 2008). While significant cost savings can be realized with MMOGs by reducing the logistical requirements of bringing soldiers and equipment together to train, the cost to develop realistic virtual representations must be carefully managed. The success of using MMOGs in the development of the training demonstration relied on synchronous participation of soldiers. Saving logistical costs in moving soldiers to a central place to train and away from the war zone is one advantage of MMOGs application; however, bandwidth and connectivity have persisted throughout the current decade as challenges for the military. The advantage of MMOGs may be lost to the lack of connectivity and bandwidth required.

Despite these challenges, the benefits of MMOGs and the possibilities in developing future training remain worthwhile. As noted in a research study of wargaming and distributed learning (Van der Hulst, Muller, & Roos, 2008), "…decision making can only be mastered by repeating the task as many times as possible in a controlled yet relevant reality, combined with intensive reflection upon one's own performance." MMOGs demonstrate promise in providing training avenues of relevant reality and the ability to access reflection and feedback.

Key Factors when Implementing Games as Training

Objectives

The first task in designing games for training is to ask, "What task(s) do I want the learner to perform after completing this training?" This is especially relevant for military training: "Clearly defined training objectives are critical to training effectiveness. Training game developers should define specific training objectives before software development begins." (Beal, 2006).

In their study of military training, Fletcher and Chatalier (2000) clarify the role of objectives:

"Training objectives are most often expressed in terms of what students can do (skills), what they must know (knowledge), and/or the attitudes they must possess after they finish the instruction. In training, the objectives can be derived directly from the skills and knowledge required to perform a job. In the absence of these objectives, relevant, systematic design, development, implementation, and evaluation of the instruction is unlikely". (p.14).

By nature, objectives must be measurable. Within a gaming context, determining if low level cognitive skills such as knowledge or comprehension are achieved is a simple task. Multiple gaming elements have been created to move game play along by requiring the measurement of learning and provide designers many options. While developed for game play, these elements prove useful in evaluating learning. Simulation training designers have developed strategies allowing the measurement of higher level cognitive skills such as analysis and synthesis.

However, measuring affective skills such as motivation and attitudinal change is much more difficult. One strategy is to integrate decision points within the training and record the action of the learner. Choices are aligned to objectives and measure whether the desired outcome is met. Yet, this is only one strategy; if more games are to be developed for training purposes, designers will need multiple approaches to achieve any affective behavioral goals. Writing measurable, sound objectives to attain affective performance learning goals continues to be a significant factor to creating successful training tools.

Game Play

A key characteristic of games is often referred to as "game play". Rollings and Adams (2003) define game play as, "one or more causally linked series of challenges in a simulated environment." Associated with this description are terms such as: competition, story, and reward. Game play provides a strong link between games and learning. "The promise of games is that we can harness the spirit of play to enable players to build new cognitive structures and ideas of substance." (Klopfer, Osterweil,& Salen, 2009).

Yet, the goal to build cognitive structures is not always the game developer's goal. This is where design goals for games that are to be used in military training differ from those of commercial game developers. Commercial games are primarily concerned with game play and interweave learning and game play to motivate the user to continue. A fine balance between failure, which is expected, and advancing forward, which is desired, is often described as key to a successful commercial game:

"The secret of a videogame as a teaching machine isn't its immersive 3-D graphics, but its underlying architecture. Each level dances around the outer limits of the player's abilities, seeking at every point to be hard enough to be just doable. In cognitive science, this is referred to as the regime of competence principle, which results in a feeling of simultaneous pleasure and frustration--a sensation as familiar to gamers as sore thumbs." Gee (2008, p.67).

Games designed for military training may engage in the interweaving of learning and game play, however, the primary purpose of training drives design not game play. As mentioned with serious games, most applications of games and simulations within the military motivate the user by providing the expected training within the experience of playing the game. While studying cadets who played a COTS game for training purposes, researchers reported that, "We found

that leaders who are serious about using games for training want to use them to learn leader tasks and skills; they are less motivated to use them for fun." (Beal, 2006, p.8).

The challenge for developers of military training games becomes in implementing game play within instructional design of a game whose purpose is training. If successfully accomplished, this can increase learner motivation with a positive effect in meeting performance outcomes. The developer's challenge is to work with instructional designers to integrate elements of game play that create desired effects of motivation without interfering or distracting from the training goals of the game.

Iuppa and Borst (2007), in developing story based simulation for the military, identified elements of game play that can assist in achieving training goals. These include: navigation (allowing the learner to move around within the game and create a "sense of agency"); purpose (if the learner understands purpose of game play then becomes motivated to participate in the simulation); and competition (which can be with other people or factors such as a clock). The authors also state that narratives "afford the opportunity for learners to acquire tacit knowledge and leadership skills through anecdotes." (p.60)

Feedback

In order to achieve the balance of game play (failure and success); the game design must be able to prevent the player from experiencing too much failure. Various types of feedback exist for this function, the most predominant tool being game hints or clues. While these tools occur in a subtle manner (between scene transitions or as an optional navigational button), they become critical in assisting the player to advance within the game. The player thus learns through feedback.

Instructional design principles for adults state the importance of feedback within effective training. Lieb (1991) noted that adult learners often require specific knowledge, or feedback, regarding their learning to meet training objectives. The most common form of feedback is to provide correct answers to exam questions. Other techniques include visual clues that represent the correct information and compare against the information the learner generated. In analyzing the feedback, the learner comes to understand the knowledge and can apply it within the training task.

Many leaders in the military find that a key to the success of military training is the inclusion of feedback to the soldiers during and after a training event. The feedback is provided in a formal process known as the After Action Review (AAR). Unique to this process is that the soldiers generate the critique of the learning themselves, facilitated by the instructor or observer as opposed to the instructor or observer solely providing comments. Research has documented the difficulty in integrating feedback, "Modeling the human cognitive skills required for effective feedback during mission execution and critical thinking during after-action reviews has proven very difficult...to incorporate into stand-alone training games." (Beal, 2006, p.8)

Since many games and simulations are implemented without instructors or facilitators, it is important design the game or simulation to include AARs. According to software developers, Virtual Heroes (2008):

"These data points (AAR) accomplish several critical goals. First, they ensure congruity between instructional and game design; learning objectives are now measureable outcomes. Second, AARs translates to clear return on investment for organizations who select learning based game products. Third and arguably most importantly, in this virtual world, objectives translate to behavioral goals." (p.5).

To link these critical elements of objectives and feedback, a variety of game play tools have been created to target specific aspects of learning. Developers at Virtual Heroes are focusing on integrating biofeedback data to learners while they engage

in a simulation (2008). This technique is similar to an athlete that might monitor their heart rate while exercising, adjusting their actions in accordance with their goals. Another technique found in the simulations that Iuppa and Borst (2007) describe simply provides text based feedback to the player based on the decision they made during the game play. The feedback includes whether the decision was correct or not, a review of the decision made, and an explanation of how the decision is related to the desired training objective. These examples model the spectrum of technology within games that can be implemented to provide feedback, an essential element of effective training.

Emerging Technologies and Military Training

As the military continues to develop the use of games and simulations to meet their training mission, challenges continue to arise. Two specific challenges that appear to persist are: (1) achieving affective domain objectives and (2) portability. In searching for solutions, an examination of emerging technologies is useful.

Achieving Affective Domain Objectives

One key to effective training mentioned in this chapter is to identify measurable objectives, to include those for the affective domain. Traditionally these objectives would measure learners' motivation, attitude, values, and other affective descriptors with instruments such as questionnaires, surveys, or indicator instruments. Training that centers around affective domain objectives may rely on intangible actions such as the informal learning that occurs when learners communicate with each other regarding the training content. To achieve these objectives can be challenging; emerging technologies may offer some solutions.

While emerging technologies encompasses hardware and software products, this discussion of affective domain objectives is focused on specific Web 2.0 tools. Web 2.0 internet technologies, such as social networking tools, blogging and virtual worlds are emerging as parallel opportunities for learning in addition to serious games and simulations. Moreover, the technologies are proving to be particularly effective training tools for the military.

Social networking sites, such as *MySpace, Facebook* and *LinkedIn* provide a location on the web where people can interact with each other to form and support relationships. These sites include e-mail and instant messaging and encourage the user to generate their own content to display and share. The U.S. Army has incorporated this concept to some extent with its *Army Knowledge Online* (AKO) program. AKO is a central location on the World Wide Web for soldiers to utilize many services, among them the ability to dialogue with each other through the use of discussion forums. Topics on these discussion forums are generated by soldiers and by moderators, chosen for their subject matter expertise.

Considering social networks for integration with games in designing training programs reveals much potential. "Social networks themselves may also be powerful learning tools. ... social networking application supports the game, but is not a game itself." (Klopfer, Osterweil,& Salen, 2009, p.14). Utilizing a social networking tool within a training program with affective domain objectives has many advantages, including the ability to support soldiers with communication tools that are familiar and appealing, especially when they are isolated by their mission or location. Social networking tools can also facilitate the dialogue required for successful implementation of this type of training.

The challenges of implementing such a social network include the ability to mitigate the risk of soldiers' confidentiality and maintaining high quality moderators who facilitate dialogue and ensure program integrity. Developer's must also consider how to create game play that calls for so-

cial networking tools while remaining focused on learning objectives. However, the ability of social networking tools to assist in achieving affective domain objectives cause them to be worthy of further investigation and experimentation within training programs.

Blogs are web-based platforms for hosting discussions around specific topics. These types of dialogues have long existed in electronic platforms, primarily within e-mail exchanges or on discussion forum boards. However, the structure of blogs has emerged as the preferred form by users of electronic communication methods (Brogan, 2008). Blogs often adapt guidelines such as e-mail policies to avoid abuse of the tool. Among the many advantages of blogs are that they increase trust while building a collaborative environment. Since blog postings are permanent, they build a wealth of collective knowledge. Participants tend to avoid posting information that is false because of the audience's ability to question and hold authors accountable. Promoting blogs may send a message to soldiers that they are trusted to share; censorship becomes the exception rather than the rule.

The military has had mixed experience with blogs. Many soldiers have posted their own experiences within a blog format for the world to read. Due to concerns of compromised information unintentionally reaching the enemy, policies were established to mitigate the risk. Soldiers continue to share their stories online in blogs; however, content must be screened by leadership to ensure that sensitive information is not being compromised. The military as an enterprise hosts public affairs (PA) sponsored blogs which are considered a tool in the PA mission. Discussion forums continue to be the primary dialogue tool within training realms.

By adding blogs as a tool within a training program that is primarily dealing with affective domain objectives, developers expand the program's ability to reach a variety of learners. Also, learners' can gain a sense of ownership not only of their learning, but as part of the training program itself. Combining these aspects with a gaming format may prove to be powerful strategies to achieve challenging training goals.

Virtual world is a term often used to describe a 3-D computer simulated environment where people interact via an avatar. The extent to which content is mostly generated by the users is unique to virtual worlds. (Rezed.org, 2008). Virtual worlds are an example of a term described by Dede (2007) as a MUVE, an acronym for Multiuser Virtual Environment. In his research, Dede explores MUVEs as a possible format for schools in the future. Virtual worlds and MUVEs are relatively new (*Second Life* began in 2003). They share many attributes of serious gaming formats, yet little data exists regarding these formats as a viable training tool. Many large corporations and universities are exploring the potential of MUVEs and virtual worlds for educational purposes.

The military is exploring the use of virtual worlds. The U.S. Army teamed with commercial entities to launch five pilot projects in 2008. (U.S. Army, 2008) The pilots focus on various training venues to include information models for wounded soldiers, collaboration between representatives of several different federal agencies, and preparation of new recruits with virtual drill sergeants and recruiters. Forterra Inc., a commercial creator of virtual worlds, supported the U.S. Army in an endeavor to fill training gaps existing for deploying units (McCaskill, 2005). Testing of a prototype demonstrated that virtual worlds can support a wide range of military training audiences with relevant experiences based upon current combat conditions at multiple levels of warfare.

For the military, virtual worlds can enable those soldiers who share a common interest in the subject matter of the training to dialogue and extend learning beyond the training content presented in a standalone version. Osmotic conversation is that information which flows in the background hearing of members so that they may pick up relevant bits as though by osmosis.

(Merriam-Webster, 2008). It is a tool that may assist in achieving affect domain objectives. In *Second Life*, members have the ability to be in a large group, yet eaves drop on the conversations which are occurring in the background. The informal nature of osmotic communication can be realized within the virtual world format. *Second Life* uses a tool called "spatial audio" defined as the moving of an avatar away from another avatar that allows side conversations, which is impossible within traditional telephone conferences. While the military is exploring the use of virtual worlds in many aspects such as recruiting, conferencing and training based on primarily cognitive domains, it may also consider expanding exploration of virtual technology to affective domain centered training.

A model for utilizing gaming as an integrator of formal and informal learning emerged during an attempt to create a conceptual plan to deliver an alcohol and substance abuse prevention training model grounded in persuasion theories for the military. The current face-to-face training relies on the instructor's ability to manage active resistance by the students, facilitate respectful collaboration and move students toward personal behavioral change. The model is structured around a series of activities that provide formal learning (dissemination of information) and informal learning (students sharing their personal experiences, views and perceptions). Often it is interactions and conversations that occur between the students participating in the training that becomes the most influential component in moving students toward change.

Traditional models of e-learning typically begin with an underlying structure for disseminating information. Layers of interactivity are added throughout the training to engage and motivate the learner thus improving their retention, comprehension and ability to apply the information presented. Elements of the alcohol and substance abuse prevention training easily converted to this format; however, lost in the translation were the affective elements, such as the student interactions and conversations which are necessary in applying persuasion theories. Web 2.0 internet technologies demonstrate the potential to achieve the affective elements. The challenge is how to integrate e-learning and Web 2.0 technologies to create an effective training model; and a possible solution may be gaming. Through gaming, the core element of the training model is able to deliver information while simultaneously engaging the affective domains with Web 2.0 internet technology components.

Current efforts in the realms of military training reveal a model shift from traditional instructor-led training to more diverse, multiple-delivery type systems centered on the student. Included in these systems are gaming platforms such as simulations and scenario-based gaming. By positioning the game as a central platform for the alcohol and substance abuse prevention training, the student is afforded the opportunity to control the learning situation and become motivated to achieve the objectives set forth in the training tasks. The model described is currently in development; it remains to be seen whether developers will create a training program with the ability to achieve affective domain objectives.

Portability

The military approach to training is to define objectives for student outcomes and the requirements for the training program, then devise alternative approaches to satisfy them. (Fletcher & Chatelier, 2000). The military's focus on distributed learning evolved from multiple goals; however, a significant factor is the ability to deliver individual training that is effective, yet saves money and time – limited resources of the military.

Emerging technologies such as streaming video, virtual worlds, file compression, and various communication tools advance the ability of the military in meeting its distributed learning goals. Most games retain the trait of portability; they can be delivered to the learner in almost any location via electronic methods. This feature has become critical as the military continues long-term combat operations in remote locations.

Web 2.0 applications provide the military with scalable and sustainable tools that are adaptable when delivering the program anywhere, anytime, for anyone. A technological advantage of current virtual worlds such as *Second Life*, is the small memory space on a computer that is needed; most of the program is streamed via internet to avoid cumbersome updates and large data requirements.

Designing training that combines gaming and simulation with emerging technologies takes advantage of tools to meet affective domain objectives and utilizes applications that meet distributed learning goals of portability while possibly reducing costs and time requirements. Reflected in research is the ability of distributed learning to conserve resources (Prensky, 2001). Future investigations should focus on the ability to measure effectiveness of these programs with learners and ensure that training design focuses on its primary purpose to assist the learner in building and developing skills.

CONCLUSION

"Games can play a number of roles in learning, but they are most effective as learning environments when they have well-integrated instructional guidance and/or instructional support." (Munro, 2009) This is a fact the military not only recognizes but embraces as they attempt to expand their ability to deliver training anywhere, anytime for anyone. The varieties of games that exist provide multiple opportunities for learning, but it is important to identify what the games were designed for (learning versus entertainment) before establishing expectations for the game player. Developers of military training must understand the desired outcomes and ensure that sound instructional design is incorporated. The key factor for selecting training tools should focus on appropriateness rather than technological features or efficiently priced deliveries. Emerging technologies appear promising when creating games that require a blend of informal and formal learning and are primarily focused on affective domain objectives. Technological issues such as portability become more significant to a military engaged in persistent high operational tempos.

Fletcher (2003) suggests that those concerned with military training change the paradigm within current development arenas; "We should start building -- design drives science more than science drives design." Designing training environments that may employ technologies yet to be developed may inform the direction and future of distributed learning, both for the military and the fields of training and education.

REFERENCES

Aldrich, C. (2004). *Simulators and the future of learning: An innovative (and perhaps\revolutionary) approach to e-learning*. San Francisco: Pfeiffer.

U.S. Army. (2007). *Army Regulation 350-1: Army Training and Leadership Development*.

Army, U. S. (2008). Army exploring virtual worlds. *Training and Doctrine Command*. Retrieved from The Army website www.army.mil/standto/archive/2008/11/21/

Axe, D. (2008, August 4). *Is the Army's virtual world already here?* Retrieved from Wire.com Web site: http://www.wired.com/danger-room/2008/08/more-mmog/

Babus, S., Hodges, K., & Kjonnerod, E. (1997). Simulations and institutional change: Training US government professionals for improved management of complex emergencies abroad. *Journal of Contingencies and Crisis Management*, *5*(4), 231–233. doi:10.1111/1468-5973.00061

Bankes, S. C. (1991). *Methodological Considerations in Using Simulation to Assess the Combat Value of Intelligence and Electronic Warfare. Technical Notes N-3010-A*. RAND Corporation.

Beal, S. (2006, March). *Using games for training Army leaders: Newsletter of the U.S. Army Research Institute for Behavioral and Social Sciences 16(1)*. Retrieved from http://www.hqda.army.mil/ari/pdf/NewsLtr_Vol16_03_06.pdf

Bennett, B. W. (1993). Flexible Combat Modeling. *Simulation & Gaming*, *24*, 2. doi:10.1177/1046878193242005

BinSubaih, A., Maddock, S., Romano, D. (2009). *Serious games for the police: Opportunities and challenges*. Special Reports & Studies Series at the Research & Studies Center (Dubai Police Academy).

Bonk, C. J., & Dennen, V. P. (2005). *Massive Multiplayer Online Gaming: A Research Framework for Military Training and Education. Technical Report 2005-1*, Department of Defense of the USA.

Brogan, C. (2008, October). *Re: Community and social media* [Internet]. Message posted to: http://www.chrisbrogan.com/

Caspian Learning. (2008). *Defence Academy Serious Games Report*. [White paper]. Retrieved http://www.caspianlearning.co.uk/MoD_Defence_Academy_Serious_games_Report_04.11.08.pdf

Command Arms Center, National Simulation Center. (2006). *Commander's guide to games for training*. Retrieved from the Advanced Distributed Learning Community of the U.S. Department of Defense Website http://adlcommunity.net/mod/data/view.php?d=38&advanced=0&paging=&page=1

Curtis, C. K., Thomas, K. M., & Ritter, J. (2008). Interactive gaming technologies and air force technical training. *Journal of Interactive Instruction Development, 20*(3), 17–23.

Davis, P. K., Bankes, S. C., & Kahan, J. P. (1986). *A new methodology for Modeling National Command Level Decision making in War Games and Simulations.* Technical Report R3290, RAND Corporation.

Davis, P. K., & Winnefeld, J. (1983). *The Rand Strategy Assessment Center. Technical Report-R2945.* RAND Corporation.

Dede, C. (2007). Planning for neomillennial learning styles. *EDUCAUSE.* Retrieved, from http://net.educause.edu/ir/library/pdf/EQM0511.pdf.

Federation of American Scientists. (2006). *Summit on Educational Games* [White paper]. Retrieved from Federation of American Scientist, Washington, DC: http://www.fas.org/gamesummit/

Fletcher, J.D. & Chatelier. (2000). *An overview of military training* (Office of Under Secretary for Defense (P&R) (Readiness and Training. No. BE-2-1710). Washington, DC: Institute for Defense Analysis.

Fletcher, J. D. (2009, January). Education and training technology in the military. *Science, 323*, 72–75. doi:10.1126/science.1167778

Ford, Barlow & Lewis, (n.d.). *An initial analysis of the military potential of COTS games.* Retrieved from Australian Defence Force Academy Web Site: www.siaa.asn.au/get/2391114970.pdf

Fu, D., Jensen, R., Ramachandran, S., Salas, E., Rosen, M., Upshaw, C., et al. (2007). *Authoring Effective Demonstrations.* Technical Report TR2007-01. San Mateo, CA: Stottler Henke.

Gee, J. P. (2003). *What video games have to teach us about learning and literacy.* New York: Palgrave/Macmillian.

Gray, W. (1995). *Playing War: the Applicability of Commercial Conflict Simulations to Military Intelligence Training and Education. DIA Joint Military Intelligence College.* Washington, DC: Bolling Air Force Base.

Gredler, M. E. (1996). Educational games and simulations: A technology in search of a (research) paradigm. In Jonassen, D. H. (Ed.), *Handbook of research for educational communications and technology* (pp. 521–539). New York: Macmillan.

Gredller, M. E. (2004). Games and simulations and their relationships to learning. In Jonassen, D. H. (Ed.), *Handbook of research on educational communications and technology* (2nd ed., pp. 571–581). Mahwah, NJ: Lawrence Erlbaum Associates.

Henninger, A. (2009). On uncertainty. *The Modeling and Simulation Center Information Analysis Center Journal, 4*(1), 2.

Hillestad, R. J., Bennett, B., & Moore, L. R. (1996). *AF Modeling for Campaign Analysis: Lessons for the Next Generation of Models: Executive Summary. Technical Report – MR-710.* RAND Corporation.

Iuppa, N., & Borst, T. (2007). *Story and simulations for serious games: Tales from the trenches.* Boston: Focal Press.

Joint Forces Quarterly. (2009). Gaming the 21st century: what to game? *Joint Forces Quarterly, 53*(2), 141–142.

Kirkley, S. E., & Kirkley, J. R. (2004). Creating next generation blended learning environments using mixed reality, video games and simulations. *TechTrends, 49*(3), 42–89. doi:10.1007/BF02763646

Klopfer, E., Osterweil, S., & Salen, K. (2009). *Moving learning games forward: obstacles, opportunities, & openness* [White paper]. Retrieved from Massachusetts Institute of Technology: http://education.mit.edu/papers/MovingLearningGamesForward_EdArcade.pdf

Kriz, W. C. (2003). Creating effective learning environments and learning organizations through gaming simulation design. *Simulation & Gaming, 34*, 495–511. doi:10.1177/1046878103258201

Lieb, S. (1991). *Principles of adult learning* [White paper]. Retrieved from Honolulu Community College Web site: http://honolulu.hawaii.edu/intranet/committees/FacDevCom/guidebk/teachtip/adults-2.htm

Macedonia, M. (2000). *Entertainment technology and virtual environments for military training and education.* Retrieved from the Educause Website net.educause.edu/ir/library/pdf/ffp0107s.pdf

McCaskill, L. (2005). Internet based lessons learned project provides first hand assistance prior to deployments. *REDCOM Magazine,* Winter, 2005-2006.

McCown, M. (2005). Strategic gaming for the national security community. *Joint Forces Quarterly, 39*(4), 34–39.

Michael, D., & Chen, S. (2006). *Serious games: Games that educate, train, and inform.* Boston, MA: Thomson Course Technology.

Munro, A. (2009). Software support of instruction in game contexts. In O'Neil, H. F., & Perez, R. (Eds.), *Computer games and team and individual learning* (pp. 3–20). Amsterdam, The Netherlands: Elsevier Ltd.

O'Neil, H., & Perez, R. (2009) *Computer games and team and individual learning.* Amsterdam, Netherlands: Elsevier Ltd. osmotic. (2008). *Merriam-Webster online dictionary.* Retrieved July 16, 2008, from http://www.merriam-webster.com/dictionary/osmotic

Oblinger, D., & Oblinger, J. (2005). Is it age or IT: first steps toward understanding the net generation. In D. Oblinger & J. Oblinger (Eds.), *Educating the net generation* (p. 2.1-2.19). Educause. Retrieved from Educause Web site: www.educause.edu/educatingthenetgen/

Prensky, M. (2001). *Digital game-based learning.* New York: McGraw-Hill.

RezEd.org. (2008, June). Re: What are virtual worlds? Message posted to http://www.rezed.org/forum/topic/show?id=2047896%3ATopic%3A7218

Ricci, K. E., Salas, E., & Cannon-Bowers, J. A. (1996). Do computer-based games facilitate knowledge acquisition and retention? *Military Psychology, 8*(4), 295–307. doi:10.1207/s15327876mp0804_3

Roberts, N. (1976). Simulation gaming: A critical review. Cambridge, MA: Lesley College and Massachusetts Institute of Technology. (ERIC Document Reproduction Service No. ED 137165)

Rollings, A., & Adams, E. (2003). *Andrew Rollings and Ernest Adams on Game Design.* Retrieved from GameDev.net Web site: http://www.gamedev.net/reference/design/features/rollingsadams/

Schwabe, W. (1994). *An Introduction to Analytic Gaming.* Technical Paper P-7864, RAND Corporation.

Schwabe, W., & Wilson, B. (1990). *Analytic War Plans: Adaptive Force-Employment Logic in the RAND Strategy Assessment System (RSAS). Technical Notes N-3051-NA.* RAND Corporation.

Smith, R. (n.d.). *The long history of gaming in military training*. Retrieved from the U.S. Army Program Executive Office of Simulation, Training, and Instrumentation, Orlando, FL, Website http://www.peostri.army.mil/CTO/FILES/RSmith_LongHistory_SG40.pdf

Susi, T., Johannesson, M., & Backlund, P. (2007). *Serious games: An overview*.

Technical Report HS-IKI-TR-07-001, University of Skövde.

Tennyson, R., & Jorczak, R. (2009). A conceptual framework for empirical study of instructional games. In O'Neil, H. F., & Perez, R. (Eds.), *Computer games and team and individual learning* (pp. 3–20). Amsterdam, The Netherlands: Elsevier Ltd.

Thatcher, D. C. (1990). Promoting learning through games and simulations. *Simulation & Gaming, 21*, 262–273. doi:10.1177/1046878190213005

U.S. Department of Defense. (1995). *Joint Publication 3-07: Joint publication for operations other than war*.

Van der Hulst, A. Muller, T.J., & Roos, C.I. (2008). *Handling serious gaming, Job Oriented Training*. Technical Report TNO-DV 2008 A340. Netherlands.

Van Eck, R. (2006). Digital game-based learning: It's not just the digital natives who are restless. *EDUCAUSE Review, 41*(2), 1–16.

Virtual Heroes. (2008). *Serious Game Conceptualization as a Learning Objectives-Driven Process* [White paper]. Retrieved from Virtual Heroes of North Carolina Website http://www.virtualheroes.com

Watkins, S., & Sherk, J. (2008). Who serves in the U.S. military? *Center for Data Analysis*. Retrieved from National Defense Industry Association Web Site: http://www.ndia.org/Divisions/Divisions/SOLIC/Documents/Content/ContentGroups/Divisions1/Special_Operations_Low_Intensity_Conflict/CDA%20-%20Who%20Serves%20in%20the%20Military%209-17-08.pdf

Weinger, H. (1969). *Trends in Military Gaming*. Technical Paper P-4173, RAND Corporation.

Yardley, R. J., Thie, H., Schank, J. F., Galegher, J. R., & Riposo, J. L. (2003) *Use of simulation for training in the U.S. Navy Surface Force*, Technical Report MR-1770-NAVY, RAND Corporation.

Zyda, M. (2005). From visual simulation to virtual reality to games. *Computer, 38*(9), 25–32. doi:10.1109/MC.2005.297

Chapter 23

Design–Researching Gamestar Mechanic:
Integrating Sound Learning Theory into a Game about Game Design

Ivan Alex Games
Michigan State University, USA

ABSTRACT

This chapter presents the results of a three-year design research study of Gamestar Mechanic, a multiplayer online role-playing game designed to teach middle school children to think like designers by exposing them to key practices behind good computer game production. Using discourse-based ethnographic methods, it examines the ways in which the multimodal meaning representations of the language of games (Gee, 2003) provided within Gamestar Mechanic, have helped learners think and communicate in increasingly sophisticated ways with and about game design. It also examines the implications of these language and literacy skills for other areas of players' lives, as well as for the improvement of the game as a learning environment over time.

INTRODUCTION

This chapter presents the results of a three-year design research study of *Gamestar Mechanic*, a project's whose goal has been to produce, deploy, and assess a game-based learning environment intended to foster the adoption by middle school children of a designer mindset. Such a mindset involves a set of language and literacy skills involving digital media that a growing number of scholars recognize as fundamental to learners in the 21st century (New

London Group, 1996; Perkins, 1995; diSessa, 2002; Partnership for 21st Century Skills, 2006). The game aims to achieve its curricular goals through an online multiplayer role-playing game experience that places learners in the role of game designers (Games, 2008; Salen, 2007).

The chapter begins by presenting the background of the project, its initial aims and the learning theory upon which it was built. It then presents the design research methodology used in its production, and discusses how the core findings in each of three research phases contributed to its improvement as a game-based learning environment. It concludes

DOI: 10.4018/978-1-61520-781-7.ch023

with a discussion of its implications for learners outside of games, and for educational practice.

Background: The Aims and Learning Theory behind a Game about Making Games

Since it's inception, the core objective of Gamestar Mechanic has been to effectively blend sound learning science theory and good game design principles into a pedagogical intervention. The goal for this intervention would be to help learners from traditionally underserved groups within the U.S. (e.g. minorities, girls), engage with digital technology and develop 21st century language and literacy skills.

Gamestar Mechanic research builds on two decades of educational research involving games for learning. It builds upon the works of scholars such as Seymour Papert, Yasmin Kafai, and other early constructionists (Papert and Harel, 1991; Kafai, 1995), who explored the potential of children designing interactive media using computer-based tools such as the Logo language to foster computer-programming and math skills. It has been substantially informed by recent literacy research involving multimodal systems of meaning representation beyond traditional print literacy (e.g. multiliteracies, New London Group, 1996; new literacies, Knobel and Lankshear, 2006; computational literacy, diSessa, 2002). It also builds on the more recent sociocultural research on games and learning, which proposes that playing and designing videogames can help children develop skills in areas such as language and literacy (Gee, 2003), history (Squire, Giovanetto, Devane, and Durga, 2005), and scientific and professional thinking practices (Steinkuehler, 2005; Shaffer, 2006).

In addition, in order to design the game, the development teams have adopted numerous lessons learned from previous attempts at using game design for learning in both formal and informal environments, many of which also generated theoretical frameworks that have informed its development over the years (see Hayes and Games, 2008 for a full review of the research)

Playing Gamestar Mechanic: Gamestar Mechanic is, in a nutshell, a game about making games, where players learn to think and communicate like designers by playing, building, and sharing computer games, in a flash-based online environment. The game narrative places players in the role of *game mechanics,* in a fantasy world where people have discovered how to encapsulate well-designed games, and harness their energy to fuel their life-support systems. However, over time different philosophies and approaches to making the "best games" have emerged, and groups specialized in specific game types –schools of gaming- formed. Different philosophies have brought with them rifts between members of different schools, and people got so involved in them that knowledge of how to make high yield games was lost.

As a consequence, the factories that once produced high-energy games have fallen into disrepair, the games they made but ghosts of what they used to be. Unfortunately, the schools have reacted to the energy crisis by adopting more radical postures, and require all their members to strict adherence to their philosophy. Players enter the world by choosing avatars, characters that represent new recruits of one of the schools of gaming, and who strive to become true mechanics by learning the core principles of game design espoused by their school (Figure 1).

According to Gee (2003), a central way in which games can encourage powerful learning experiences is by allowing players to take on and play with different *identities*, and explore their possibilities within the virtual world of the game. In role-playing games such as *World of Warcraft*, In Gamestar Mechanic, the narrative serves precisely the purpose of situate the players' decisions in ways that encourage the negotiation between their *real world identity*—and the *virtual identity* of their avatar, with the goal of generating a *projective*

Figure 1. Examples of Gamestar Mechanic Avatars

Chronox Altair

The strange gamers and mechanics of Chronox Altair worship speed above everything else.

Jurors of Constant

The Jurors are the oldest and most influential of the Schools of Gaming, focused on the rules.

Karakuri

The Karakuri are more interested in chaos, randomness, unpredictability, and bending or breaking the rules.

identity, -a hybrid identity where players learns to think and act like the virtual identity they role-play-, and where the powerful learning germane to modern videogames often occurs.

Players advance in status within the game by exploring the factories, within which they discover locations containing *game jobs.* These involve playing, designing, documenting and repairing games. Players are free to choose the types of jobs they wish to specialize in, thus giving individuals with different learning strengths, skills, and preferences, multiple paths to advancement in their learning (Gee, 2003 P. 108). As they successfully complete jobs, players are rewarded with game creatures (e.g. heroes and enemies), pre-designed with specific qualities and behaviors. Mechanics' creatures are stored as a collection within their *toolbox,* a web-based game editor where they can be dragged from a palette into a play area, and brought to life by flicking a switch from edit to play mode (Figure 2 screenshot a).

Learning Theory behind the Game Curriculum: Jobs are built on a learning-through-design approach, informed by a broad body of literature on design-based pedagogies, that have been especially fruitful in areas such as computer science and engineering education (Papert and Harel, 1991; Kolodner, et. al. 1996). At the centre of these pedagogies lies placing learners in a position where they must make (or redesign) something – whether a new structure, device or the solution to a problem – in order to gain and demonstrate their knowledge. In Gamestar Mechanic, players demonstrate proficiency in game design by making their own games, repairing broken games or proving that existing games are functional by having other mechanics play and critique them.

In conjunction, the system of components and activities that constitute Gamestar Mechanic (playing, constructing, repairing and sharing games), are set up with the specific intention of promoting the appropriation by learners of a game designer Discourse (Gee, 1996; 2005). D/discourse theory (or big and small d, discourse theory), construes the notion of *Discourse* as a term that builds upon Wittgenstein's "lifeworld" (1953), to encapsulate the ways of doing, being, thinking, talking and participating that define a person's identity as a member of a specific community, in this case a community of designers. People demarcate these identities for others through instances of language used in context, or *discourse,* through which they situate the meaning of identities, activities, tools and institutions, constructing an immediate reality for others in communication.

The game scaffolds players into the Discourse of game design through key principles defined in the job specifications required for successful completion of each job. These specifications provide the specialist language terms germane to game design intended to help children think about their games in more nuanced ways. Screenshot b) in Figure 2 gives an example of a job specifications screen. In this specific job, the core principle to be learned is that every game must have a reachable goal or it is not a game.

Figure 2. Job requirements screenshot, toolbox screenshot

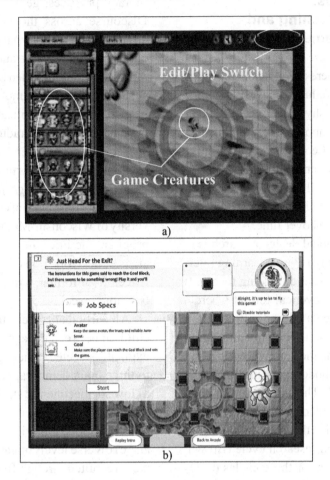

As the specs also show, this win condition should be designed using an avatar creature and a goal block, hence situating the meaning of "game goal" in the context of Gamestar Mechanic. Learning, in this context, takes place as players iteratively design and redesign their games in order to meet the specifications, and for every step in the right direction they take, the game provides them with visual feedback, pacing a checkmark on the specification covered.

However, adopting an identity as a game designer–the hallmark of a Discourse- cannot occur in a vacuum. The practices of designers just like those of other communities are only legitimized when others who share the same interest and activity recognize them as valid (Gee, 2005). To accomplish this, the game frames the jobs and their outcomes within a robust online community of mechanics, using a multiplayer role-playing game model. This way, game jobs may require players to share their games with others, and to either critique or defend a design in a public forum called the Game Alley, a site where every game made public by a mechanic can be played by others.

While Gamestar Mechanic is a game intended to promote a game designer Discourse, its central purpose as a learning tool is not to train professional game designers. Rather, by immersing students in key activities and practices of game design, it is intended to act as an *epistemic game* (Shaffer, 2006) that encourages learners to think and communicate like game designers do.

Research Methods: Designing, Researching and Assessing the Game

The studies reported here were conducted using discourse-based design ethnography. This method mixes design ethnography (Barab, et. al. 2004), and discourse-based ethnography (Steinkuehler, 2005), with the goal of constructing a narrative that provides a "thick description" (Geertz, 1976) of the overall language and literacy learning ecology of the game, through the lens of participants' communication practices over time.

The goal of educational design research is to implement and gradually refine a learning intervention that integrates sound learning theory. It does so by following a cyclical format where a learning theory is articulated and reified into a version of the intervention. The implementation is then tested in an authentic learning setting, and assessed through methodologies matching the questions being asked. The insights from each test are then used to produce a refined version of the theory, and to redesign the intervention before beginning a new design research cycle (Brown, 1992). The ultimate goal of these cycles of design and research is to produce an ideal learning intervention built upon robust theory of its effects in authentic settings.

This paper reports the findings of the first three year-long cycles of design research with Gamestar Mechanic using the format suggested by Collins, Joseph and Bielazyc (2004) for reporting design research. The narrative is organized according to three year-long phases termed pre-alpha, alpha and beta, labels used widely in the field of software design that mark turning points in the evolution of the game. For each phase, it reports specific information on the learning environment's goals and components, and how the insights obtained informed the redesign of the next.

The narrative in each section places emphasis upon two types of insights so as to to articulate trends in participant thinking, language, and literacy practices, germane to a game designer Discourse across the different cycles. These are: a) insights about participants' thinking and communication about and with the knowledge representations provided by Gamestar Mechanic, across the different game design workshops, and b) insights on the implications of these changes for the redesign and gradual improvement of the subsequent phase's version of the game, its curriculum, and its supporting learning theory.

Participant Demographic Information: The three phases took place at computer labs at the University of Wisconsin-Madison, and at after-school program facilities in the Madison-Milwaukee areas. The workshops followed a seven-week, fifteen-hour format, which gathered for just over two hours weekly.

All participants recruited were middle school children between the ages of twelve and sixteen, explicitly selected to the degree possible according to three main demographic variables of interest: a) low socioeconomic status, b) membership to a traditionally underserved group regarding technology education (minorities, girls, rural children), and c) diverse levels of gaming experience. They were recruited through flyers announcing a mini game design workshop for children posted in public areas, after-school programs, libraries, and community centers in the Madison-Milwaukee Wisconsin area, and their demographics pre-screened using a background interview.

As much as possible, considering the samples were incidental, the resulting group was diverse, with approximately equal distributions in gender and ethnicities, which included African American, Asian American, Hispanic, and Caucasian. Table 1 provides a summary of participant distributions in each research cycle.

To stimulate the formation of a community of mechanics with a variety of levels of experience represented, five professional game designers were recruited for the length of the project. These professionals worked for both from Gamelab and external companies, and agreed to become players

Table 1. Gamestar Mechanic project workshop formats and participant distributions.

Cycle	Pre-alpha (Fall 2006-Spring 2007)	Alpha (Summer 2007-Fall 2007)	Beta (Spring 2008-Summer 2008)
Workshop and Format	• Two 6-hour mini-workshop focus groups during the fall • 15-hour after-school workshop format gathering 2 1/2 hours a week for 7 weeks during the spring	• Two 15-hour after-school workshop formats, gathering 5 hours daily for 3 days in the Summer, and 2 1/2 hours a week for 7 weeks during the fall	• Two 15-hour workshop formats, gathering for 2 1/2 hours a week for 7 weeks in the spring, and 3 hours a day for 5 days in the summer
Participant Distribution	• For the focus groups, 6 males and 6 females between 5th and 8th grades. • For the workshop 2 males and 3 females between 6th and 8th grades	• For the summer workshop, 15 participants, all male between 6th and 9th grades. For the fall workshop, 20 participants were involved, between 5th and 8th grade	• For the spring workshop, 10 participants, 5 male 5 female between 6th and 8th grade • For the summer workshop, 6 participants, all female between 6th and 9th grade

• 5 professional designers participated as advanced players through the project

who would interact with students in the online community. Their Discourse practices served as reference against which to assess changes in the children's practices.

Documentation Methods: In order to document changes in participants' thinking, language, and literacy practices in the context of Gamestar Mechanic, the researcher designed a pre and post workshop assessment protocol consisting of two parts. These were first, a game design literacy concepts interview, consisting of a series of questions aimed at assessing their thinking on the nature of games and game design. Questions such as "what are the minimum parts something should have to be a game?" and "what are the main activities of a game designer while making a game?" were typical in this section.

Second, a think aloud interview conducted with participants as they completed three game jobs requiring them to play, fix, design and critique a game. Questions during this interview were aimed at assessing their meaning production process, and typical ones were 'why did you choose that creature?" and "do you identify any problems with this game?" were typical in this interview. Both the interviews and think aloud protocols were video recorded and screencast using the Camtasia Studio screen capture software. This resulted in over 20 hours of digital video showing the participants' behavior in parallel with their actions in the computer screen.

During the workshop sessions, the researcher took on the role of an advanced player, and documented the students' practices through a) participant observations, b) field notes, and c) over 60 hours of digital video and screencasts of their play activities, and d) digital copies of their game designs and related documentation stored in a server.

Data Analysis: For the analysis of the language samples collected throughout the workshops, the study relied on Discourse Analysis (Gee, 2005). The method examines language-in-use through the lens of seven building tasks of language, categories that help code utterances according to the situated meanings that people intend to express with them. They are (1) *significance*, using language to make certain things more relevant than others, (2) *activities*, using language to get recognized as engaging in a certain activity, 3) *identities*, using language to get categorized as enacting a certain role or identity, 4) *relationships*, using language to signal a sort of relationship between two people, 5) *politics*, using language to convey a perspective on the distribution of social goods, 6) *connections*, using language to highlight the relationships between two incidents or concepts, and 7) *sign systems*, privileging certain ways of communicating through symbols over others. Through these seven tasks, people's utterances help demarcate the identities of people, tools, activities and institutions, hence construing reality for others in their immediate context.

The researcher transcribed the video data collected in the workshop sessions and assessments prior to coding them using Transana (Woods, 2003), a video analysis tool that synchronizes the video and audio tracks of a recording with a transcript, thus facilitating the analysis substantially.

Fieldwork: Refining Theory and Design based on Phase Insights

This section reports these findings of each project phase by concentrating on (a) those constructs that emerged from each cycle and that were consistent across different workshops, and (b) how these findings informed changes to the game and its supporting theory on subsequent cycles. For quick reference, Table 2 summarizes the features of the

Table 2. Summary of game components, learning outcomes and limitations in each design research phase

Cycle	Pre-alpha (Fall 2006-Spring 2007)	Alpha (Summer 2007-Fall 2007)	Beta (Spring 2008-Summer 2008)
Game Components	• Early prototype consisting of a rudimentary online version of the toolbox with a limited creature set (22 creatures), and a paper-based version of the game design curriculum.	• Toolbox implementing more polished artwork, elements of the storyline. • Extended creature set (62 creatures) and the ability to modify creature behaviors, level rules, level look and feel, and digital game documentation. • Extended version of the game design curriculum implementing best practices and lessons learned from the pre-alpha cycle.	• Expanded creature set for the toolbox (100+ creatures), adds an online version of the curriculum in the form of game jobs inside the factory, complemented by paper-based jobs, and provides the web infrastructure to make games public in order to share and discuss game designs with other users. • Paper versions of teacher-driven game jobs available for flexibly adaptable curriculum.
Learning and Literacy Outcomes	• Strong participant engagement in designing their own games • Use of specialist game design concepts such as "challenge" to guide design strategies • Design in the form of a "material dialog", leading to cycles of hypothesis postulation, testing and refinement of the game form and function • Evolution of an understanding of games as complex systems of components (the design grammar of the language of games)	• A larger creature lexicon translated into more sophisticated player designs • Cycles of design, testing, and redesign of the game now guided by the introduction of an "ideal player" as a co-constructor of meaning through interaction. • The semantics of the language of games gained influence in player's minds through the concept of "player engagement" as a goal for design. • Players developed a more self-critical stance towards their own designs.	• Shift from thinking of games as representational objects to communicational ones. • Recruiting the specialist terms of the Discourse of game design to discuss games. • Practice of literacy skills such as narrative and argumentation in the discussion forums.
Limitations requiring changes	• Limited expressive capacity due to small number of creatures and fixed behaviors • Game needed to provide more facilities to design original games • Discourse theory needed to consider the multimodal nature of the specialist language of games	• Little understanding of the appropriateness of certain design patterns over others. • Narrow and self-centered understandings of specialist language terms and design practices. • Too much flexibility in configuring game creature behaviors led to confusion about their role in different design patterns.	• Overemphasis of Gamelab's particular philosophy of game design in jobs and narrative, at the expense of others available in the world. • Insufficient integration between the game narrative, the game's scoring system, and the activity of game critique.

game in each phase, and the core outcomes of that phase in terms of learning benefits for children, and its limitations and changes that were required as a result.

The Pre-Alpha Phase

The initial phase of research into the educational effectiveness of Gametar Mechanic took place between December 2006 and May 2007 with the intention of assessing two things. First, whether the game would produce a lethal mutation and be perceived too much as school or whether it would engage players for extended periods. Second, to do an initial assessment of the player's language and literacy practices with a prototype version of the game.

Pre-Alpha Phase Goals and Game Components: The prototype consisted of a) an early version of the *toolbox* with a limited set of crea-

tures and fixed behaviors, b) paper based *creature profiles* that would allow players to compare their descriptions and make decisions as to which to use in their games, c) a rudimentary version of the *game design curriculum* within the narrative and jobs in the form of paper-based narrative storyboards, and d) a *game label* format where players would write the description and instructions for their games. Figure 3 shows an example of each of these components. Their purpose was to simulate as completely as possible the overall experience of playing Gamestar Mechanic. Because the game in meant to be a reification of learning theory, this prototype would allow the researcher to conduct initial empirical tests of some key theoretical questions.

In order to structure the workshop around jobs, the game relied on a set of job templates provided by Gamelab with the prototype storyboards. These templates were short texts that

Figure 3. Components of the Gamestar Mechanic Prototype

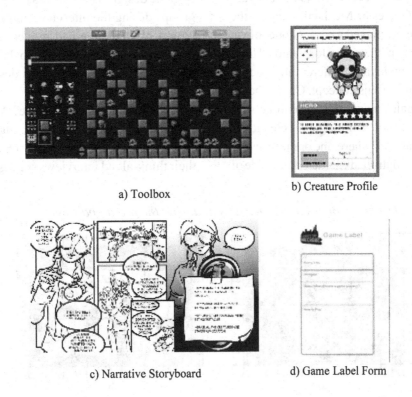

a) Toolbox

b) Creature Profile

c) Narrative Storyboard

d) Game Label Form

described the requirements of the specific job the children needed to complete. They organized jobs according to three categories: a) *play jobs* –where players needed to win a game previously designed, b) *repair jobs* –where they had to identify and fix a problem with a dysfunctional game-, and c) *design jobs* – where they had to design a game from scratch within constraints specific to the Discourse.

Phase Findings: In this cycle it became evident that even a rudimentary version of the game was able to hold the young students' attention for extended periods even among those children with little gaming experience, calming my concerns about possible lethal mutations. More importantly, the extended version of the workshop during this time showed that for most students, the form of literacy that emerged was substantially focused on developing a systems-based notion of games and game design, a perspective that has been recognized as a fundamental skill for 21st century learners.

Consistently across every workshop in every phase, for new Gamestar Mechanic players the concept of challenge played a cornerstone role in guiding their design strategies for games. However, males and females took different approaches and interpretations of this concept. On one hand, the designs of males tended to concentrate substantially on the shoot 'em up genre, characterized by design patterns where one or more avatar creatures (player-controlled characters, left side of screenshot a, Table 2) capable of shooting, would be confronted with a large number of enemies in relatively open spaces (right side, screenshot a). During the interviews, statements from boys such as "I need to add more enemies to make it more challenging" suggest that at this point, their model of a challenging game was associated to the number of enemies an avatar had to defeat in order to win.

In contrast, the designs of females were guided by a different notion of challenge, one that placed decision-making at its center. In their designs, organizing space in maze-like spaces played a key role in creating game mechanics that required guiding their avatars to a goal by making strategic decisions about possible enemy movements (screenshot b, Figure 4).

However, also consistent across workshops was the observation that toward the end of a research cycle, the notion of challenge of both groups became more complex, and their designs suggested a more sophisticated thought process of game design. The discourse of both participant groups during the interview suggested that their notion of challenge had moved into a systems perspective, that necessitated balancing multiple variables in order to achieve a desired form and function in the game.

What promoted this change? As previous research with Gamestar Mechanic suggests (Games, 2008), the discourse of participants throughout their think-aloud interviews suggests that change

Figure 4. Typical designs by males a) and females b) during the pre-alpha stage

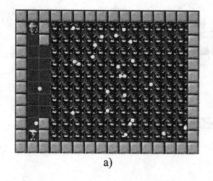
a)

b)

Figure 5. The material dialog

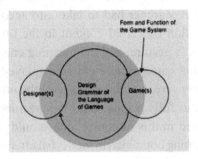

was influenced by Gamestar Mechanic itself through an interaction (or rather, several interactions) that Games terms the material dialog. This dialog places the players and toolbox as interlopers of sorts, attempting to produce a game model resulting from a negotiation between a mental model the designer intends to communicate in the game, and the grammatical relationships between the affordances perceived in the tools, creatures and functionality available in the toolbox (Figure 5).

The following transcript of an interview with Tec (an avatar name), a male participant during the pre-alpha phase workshops, which gives a typical

example of how this dialog helped participants recruit all these components in design strategies guided by more complex notions of challenge than the one above. This exchange took place in the context of Tec wanting to make a game where the avatar (a player-controlled creature, marked 1 in Figure 6 screenshot a) had to traverse a maze of concrete blocks in order to reach a goal block (marked 2, screenshot a), while avoiding or destroying the enemy characters patrolling the corridors (marked 3, screenshot a).

Tec's statement in line T1 comes just as he pressed the switch to enter play mode, making the game begin to function. As his statements in T2 and T3 indicate, the outcome (Gamestar Mechanic's response) did not reflect his intended game model. In T3 he indicates that this model would have had enemies moving in many directions, making it harder for the player to avoid them. However, in this version of the toolbox, the strong enemy characters he had chosen were designed to only move horizontally.

The sophistication of his design strategy, and its relationship to challenge, became evident after the researcher probed for his next design steps

Figure 6. Two stages and transcript of Tec's game design interview

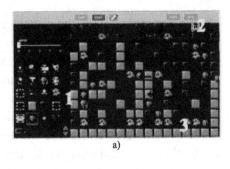 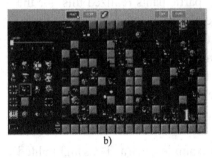

a)   b)

Stanza 1:
T1: Wanna see if it (.) works (presses the play button on the toolbox, game system begins to work).
T2: Not how I planned it
T3: I thought they were gonna move all over (points at some of the enemies, as indicated on screen d, who are just moving back and forth on a horizontal pattern in screenshot d)
R1: What do you think happened here?
T4: I think...
R2: What sprite would you trade those guys for I guess?
T5: I guess I'll trade them for the red characters (referring to the shooter enemy sprite indicated on screen e)
T6: so that I make it (.) a little more challenging
T7: But I'd have to put more, like times(.) times two since these go away so easily (referring to the shooter enemy sprite)
T8: So now I have to get rid of all these guys I just put (deletes all the old enemies and replaces them with shooter enemies)
T9: So, 16 (.) hmmm, 32, am I right?
T10: And now (presses play and the game begins, with the new enemies now shooing and moving all over the screen as shown in screen f)
T11: Oh my god! They're going so fast! And I'm not moving at all!

in lines R1 and R2. He decided to replace the strong enemy characters shooter enemies (labeled 1 in screenshot b) that, while having the ability to move in all directions, also differed from the strong ones in that they could take only half of the damage from the player's gun before being destroyed. His redesign strategy anticipated this issue (Line T7), and compensated for this problem by replacing every strong enemy removed for two weak ones, suggesting his view of challenge involved a certain number of potential shots an avatar might have to fire in the game (Line T7 and T9). However, lines T10 and T11 show how when he pressed play, Gamestar Mechanic kept the material dialog going, since the new function of the system showed him that these enemies moved faster than the strong ones, thus starting a new cycle of hypothesis testing.

Phase Limitations and Implications for Redesign: While it was clear that the early prototype fostered a promising systems level perspective on participants about their games (their design grammar), it was evident that the limited availability of features and creatures was detrimental to its expressive potential. This would also limit the sophistication of the players' Discourse, games, and text production in the game, as well as the potential long-term engagement of students with the game. The participants realized this, for the researcher received many requests for more ability to manipulate the behaviors of game components, as well as for more creatures available for designs. Hence, the main goal for the alpha phase would be to make such extended functionality available, to allow students more expressiveness through their games.

Numerous examples such as Tec's highlighted a fundamental insight about the guiding theoretical framework of the game and its associated research agenda that emerged in this phase. As the transcript shows, in his attempt to situate the meaning of his utterances, Tec did not rely on discourse in the traditional sense of the word (referring to mostly verbal utterances). Instead, to understand his true

communicational intention in an utterance like T1, the researcher had to take into account the conjunction of verbal content in the utterance, with Tec's gesture, and the meaning encoded in the visual game representation displayed on the computer screen at the moment of the utterance. Hence, to fully do justice to the meaning being expressed in this utterance, one should think of the meaning contained in the verbal utterance and the visual elements of the game not as separate representations, but rather as a multimodal system of complimentary representations meant to construct an emergent meaning.

The implications of this insight were crucial for the studies thereon, for the Discourse Analysis from this phase had to become a truly multimodal form of analysis, examining situated language through the building tasks not as a verbal descriptor of games, but rather using the tasks to examine games as a language constructions in and of themselves. The systemic perspective fostered on students at this point, seen as a multimodal literacy practice, amounted to learning the grammar of a new language, what Gee terms the *design grammar* of the specialist language of games (2003).

The Alpha Phase

In the summer of 2007, the game design team at Gamelab released the alpha version of Gamestar Mechanic. This version implemented improvements based on the insights from the pre-alpha phase in the form of a toolbox with an extended creature set, as well as tools for the player to modify character and game system behavior. Once the theoretical framework examined games as products of mutimodal language patterns, it became evident that more creatures would function in this language in the same way an expanded lexicon would in verbal language. The hope was that it would extend players' expressive capacity and yield more sophisticated and nuanced designs and literacy practices.

In this version, the game job curriculum was still paper-based, however, it addressed the issue of creature variety with two important features, as the following section explains.

Phase Goals and Game Components: Figure 7 shows screenshots that demonstrate the alpha toolbox features. First, it made sixty-two creatures available to players, as opposed to the twenty-two available in the prototype (screenshot a). Second, creatures not only had default looks and behaviors that differentiated them from each other, but the new toolbox introduced the ability to modify their behaviors, and the look and feel of the game through configuration panels. This expanded players' ability to express game ideas with an exponentially larger variety of interactions (screenshot b).

Phase Findings: As expected, the introduction of a larger lexicon of the language of games through an extended creature set led to more sophisticated and complex player game designs. Designs in this phase began to explore genres outside the dominant maze and puzzle games designed in the pre-alpha. Games such as platformers (jumping games), and games that mixed multiple mechanics (e.g. shooting and jumping, or solving a spatial maze puzzle by avoiding contact with patrolling enemies) became much more common.

A key finding resulted from putting this phase's observations in context with those of the pre-alpha. Between these two phases, it became evident that over time and interaction with the game, players developed sophisticated design strategies and

understandings of their games by attempting to communicate interaction goals to an idealized player (Games, 2008).

These expressions were commonly guided by attempts to construct models of what Gee (2003) calls a *projective idenity* for such a player. This would be an identity that emerged as a result of a player "stepping into the shoes" of a virtual identity being proposed by the designer in the game. Professional designers commonly foster the negotiation of a projective identity by framing the possible actions players can take in the game in ways that make them meaningful, and which lead to an increased investment and engagement in the game on the player's part (Freeman, 2004).

This became especially evident in player's conversations about designs they had completed either after design jobs or after making original games in the toolbox during the alpha and beta phases. In these conversations, connections between game creatures and possible player identities guided design strategy more strongly than in the alpha, by requiring the participants to "step into the shoes" of a player playing their games.

An interactive design think-aloud conducted him toward the end of the alpha phase exemplifies this point, and shows how semantic attributions drove a strategic approach to the design of more complex interactions in games. This semantic activity was particularly evident when players engaged in "post-mortems", activities of reflection about designs they had previously completed.

Figure 7. Components of the alpha build

a) extended creature set　　　　　　　b) creature profile and behaviors

In this sample, Marc, a participant in the alpha stage workshops explained to the researcher his favorite part of a game previously designed. The questions posed for him were aimed at leading him to reflect on his game design process. A key aspect that differentiated his explanation of design strategy at this stage versus during the pre-alpha phase was that as the transcript in Figure 8 suggests, instead of being guided by predictions of the form and function of the game, the actions that conformed his strategy were guided by predictions of the possible actions (and reactions) of a player during play.

What is most interesting in this analysis is found in lines M2-M5. In them, Marc implies a hypothesis of the way he would expect a player to react to the design decisions he implemented in this *level* (a specialist language term that denotes a section of a game bounded by spatial or temporal limits) of his game.

Since in Gamestar Mechanic it is possible to make levels that span an area larger than the computer screen, Figure 8 shows the particular section of the level he was referring to during this reflection. The way he designed this section, the player character would enter this screen through the bottom right section of the screen (the vertical tunnel-like section surrounded by rocky blocks), and then attempt to get to the next level section by making his character jump from cloud to cloud in the section indicated with the number 1. In line M2 Marc's utterance predicts that if "the player" were to fall below the line of clouds at the bottom of Figure 8, he or she would experience an undesirable level of frustration by falling to the bottom of the level, which is several screens below this section.

What these utterances show is that Marc was beginning to think self-critically about his design, and about the possible ways in which a player might interpret it. This critical view of his game was not based on simple conjecture, but rather was the result of a dialogic interaction with himself as lines M6 and M7 indicate, in the form of a semantic negotiation of meaning with an ideal player. This observation resulted in a new construct for the theoretical framework that would guide the design of the next phase, which I term the ideal player dialog, as Figure 9 shows.

Also important in this transcript is the fact that Marc relied on another important tool within the game designer Discourse to situate the meaning of his design and think about it, and that is *player engagement* (Rollings and Adams, 2003 P. 6;

Figure 8. Marc's level section and interview transcript during the ideal dialog interview

Stanza 1
R1: So what was your favorite part when you made this game?
M1: Umm…all the ideas, putting them into one (scrolls the level to a particular section where the avatar can jump from cloud to cloud across the sky, below is a platform of clouds for the avatar to fall into as shown in Figure 3)
Stanza 2
M2: …and since I don't wanna make the gamer too mad at me
M3: so that's why I put those down there (points to the platform of clouds labeled 1)
M4: so in case he falls they got this (points to a cloud just above the platform labeled 2)
M5: and they can get back up there.
R2: Ok, so instead of just having to just float through those clouds
R3: they can actually fall down there (points to the long platform of clouds at the bottom of the screen labeled 3) and don't have to go all the way down to the bottom of the level?
M6: Yeah (.) cause when I played this I fell down a lot
M7: and was like ugh, I don't really want to play this anymore.

Rouse, 2001 P.6; Salen and Zimmerman, 2003 P. 312). Gee (2003) has argued that it is precisely their ability to elicit extended player engagement that makes games powerful learning platforms.

In lines M6 and M7, Marc took advantage of the organizational function of this concept, and used it to structure his thinking about design strategy in terms of the emotional responses of a player with his design. Mental exercises such as this one are important affordances of Gamestar Mechanic, for they have provided players through-out the workshops with an important literacy skill that applies to either print or digital media. Thinking in function of an "audience" for their games, allows them to maintain coherence in a design process involving many variables (e.g. the creatures, the space they formed, possible player actions and reactions, multiple screens not visible all at once).

Phase Limitations and Implications for Redesign: To this point most of these reflective ideas of students about their designs were guided by the players' own initiative and conceptions regarding the identity of an ideal player. This was reflected in the use of specialist language terms in ways that were narrowly defined according to each individual's interpretation. Thus, it was common to see players talk about good games being challenging because they were very difficult to win, regardless of whether this was true or not for other people playing their games. There was very little sharing or consensus among players regarding what would make better or worse games, and most games would go untested by anyone but their designer.

This led to several problems. First, the production of many dysfunctional designs with unclear mechanics or using creatures ineffectively, but that participants were convinced others would understand and like. Second, facile and poorly thought arguments about the relative worth of others' games were common when players engaged in jobs requiring critiquing games.

Figure 9. The ideal player dialog

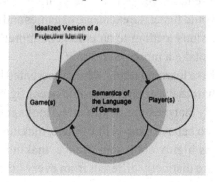

The researcher's observations during this stage suggested that while the scaffolding system built into the game contributed to the learning limitations of the game in this phase. Jobs primarily fostered design practices by giving feedback to players as to whether specific requirements had been satisfied, measured through the presence or absence of certain creatures (and configurations of creatures) in the play area. In practice, this translated into players understanding good Gamestar Mechanic games as those that had all the required components and interactions, but they had little notion of how appropriate these would be in what kinds of games, for no *appreciative system* (Gee, 2003) was furthered by the game. Implementing the game scaffolding thus had been a conscious design decision by the developers of Gamestar Mechanic, since while interpreting the structural aspects of a complete game is a relatively straightforward computational task, interpreting those emergent properties of a "good game" is beyond most computer systems today.

However, a central principle within Discourse theory and the game-based learning theories built upon it (Gee, 2003) is that learning is a function of the degree to which a person adopts meaning production practices considered authentic by the members of a community. Hence, these observations made it very clear that in for learners to adopt the practices of an authentically represented a game designer Discourse, it was imperative that in subsequent versions of the game, mechanics that would foster the exchange of games and game discussions leading to an emergent appreciative system take a more central role.

These learning issues were exacerbated by the fact that creature behaviors could be configured so flexibly that creatures with distinct looks could be made to behave exactly like others, making some designs highly confusing. Hence, making every creature distinctly different from every other one in look and behavior became a core goal for the next implementation of the game as a result.

The Beta Phase

In the Spring of 2008 the developers Gamelab completed the final research version of the game. In this phase, the game brought a much stronger emphasis to the "multiplayer role-playing" aspect. It did so by integrating expanding the toolbox with over 100 configurable creatures, delimiting their behaviors so they would be clearly different from each other, and integrating them into a game narrative set within an online social network website. This made it possible for players outside specific workshop contexts to interact with others more directly, playing and discussing their games.

Phase Goals and Game Components: The beta version of the game addressed the lack of mechanisms for an emergent appreciative system by implementing the role-playing aspect of the game through a web-based community model resembling spaces such as Facebook or Myspace. The community is framed in the context of the overall game narrative, where players must choose an avatar that enters the virtual world as a member of one of the six available "schools of gaming" (Figure 1). Up to the time of writing, the Gamestar Mechanic design team and research teams put a strong emphasis in enriching the narrative so that all the play and design activities in the game are made meaningful within it. The goal of the schools of gaming is for all players' (through their virtual identities) to be introduced

to their school's initial appreciative system, and in this way learn to judge the relative worth of their games according to its parameters.

This version of the game now integrated the job curriculum and the narrative into a flash-based virtual world representing the factory. The factory is divided into six different sections, each of which belongs to an individual school of gaming. When the game begins, most of these areas are covered in steam and inaccessible to the player, as a result of the broken machinery that now fails to produce energy for lack of a supply of well-designed games. In explorable areas, the game implemented zones called "arcades" where players could find all the jobs available for completion. Choosing a job tied the decision into the game narrative, giving the player actions meaning through creature rewards and through recognition of their status in the community of designers by game characters.

This version also first implemented the game alley, a shared space where mechanics could engage in discussions about games and game design. They now had the option to publish their games in the alley, where each public game would be assigned a commentary and discussion forum. Using these, players could now leave feedback and critique for games' authors, and use a rating scale to contribute a score to a rolling average representing the community's perception of the game's relative worth.

Phase Findings: With the introduction of richer storyline and the community tools in the game, the workshops now placed a stronger emphasis on the role of social exchange in game design. With this shift, there was also a shift in the discourse of players and the ways in which they used design patterns not only to think about their games, but also to communicate through them. This move was particularly evident in the amount of specialist language concepts used by players in the texts associated to their games. Most games made in earlier phases either did not have labels or when they did, they tended to be very succinct and loosely tied to the game mechanics and player identities they commonly discussed in their interviews. An example of a typical label up to this point read: "What you do in my game is try to get to the bottom right corner without getting hit", a label that loosely recruits the concepts of rules and goal for the game, but does not communicate any of the actual mechanics or actions that a player should take to actually play the game, assuming that a potential player will interpret the game like the author does.

In contrast, in the beta phase I began to see a clear trend from using games for mostly representational purposes to using them for more communicational ones by recruiting more aspects of the game designer Discourse to convey their intended play model to real players. This was evidenced by a more sophisticated use of written language during play, as the example of a game and label (Figure 10) by Pekenya, a female participant in this phase exemplifies.

In this label, Pekenya not only recruited the notion of game goal to articulate her thoughts on the game, but also used references to the game's actual components to clarify to potential players how they must reach it. She began by using the phrase "get to the goal" in the label, suggesting she somehow saw the goal as being achievable in a spatial form. Her design confirmed this notion, as she has put a goal block in the game (labeled 4 in the screenshot above), that gives the player a winning message when all game conditions have been met and the avatar comes in contact with it. She then explicitly stated the two preconditions the player must complete to do this, collect all items (referring to the point creatures, labeled 1) and kill all enemy creatures (labeled 3). Her last sentence in the label, also suggests to players that the enemies will be fast, suggesting that they will present some form of motion that may harm the avatar.

A factor that contributed to this increased sophistication in the labels was that with the communicational function emphasized in the multiplayer game model, the labels no longer were just ways

Figure 10. Discussion forum for a Pekenya's published game

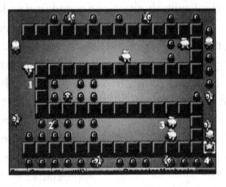

Game Label
"Game Title: Trickey.
Goal: You must collect all the items in order to get to the goal. But you must also kill all the enemies in order to get the items, but watch out, there [sic] fast"

Game Comments

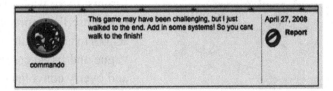

for players to represent game ideas for themselves, but rather became potential initiators of dialogs with other players, mediated by the games. This insight suggested a new change in the theoretical model that should guide the design of the game in the future, as this dialog with real players had the role of helping learners gain awareness of the appreciation others would give to their designs, as well as of the pragmatic value (in terms of solving design issues or creating particularly fun game experiences) given to different design features by the community (Figure 11).

Many instances of this dialog became evident particularly in the commentary forms associated with different games during this phase, as the sample commentaries to Pekenya's game show. A player nicknamed commando realized that even though the game might pose a challenge, it was too easy to find a loophole through which to avoid confronting enemies or picking coins altogether and still finish, meaning that her stated label preconditions, while adequate in theory, were not implemented in the actual game. He suggested she add some systems creatures, which would tie the coin, and enemy creatures as preconditions to the goal, giving her (and the whole mechanic community) a new set of tools to think with about future redesigns.

As this example also shows, these changes in the positioning of designers, players and games into a system of communication, brought with them a new set of thinking and language prac-

Figure 11. The real player dialog

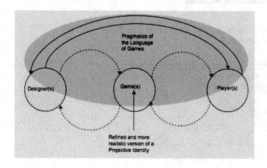

tices with them, for by becoming mediators of a dialog, games became a digital medium for learners to practice skills such as evidence-based argumentation and narrative, fundamental to learners in today's academic and professional world (Steinkuehler, 2005; Seely-Brown, Denning, Groh, & Prusak, 2004).

Phase Limitations and Implications for Redesign: An issue observed in this phase was that even when the community features emphasized the development of an appreciative system, in practice the value systems set forth by the schools were emphasizing Gamelab's notions of good game design at the expense of incorporating important language and concepts used to evaluate the worth of games in the real world. For example, traditional genres such as platformers, shoot 'em ups, or racing games are terms generally used to categorize games and serve as the basis for many critiques in professional gaming media. However, these genres were scantly used as part of the narrative or job specs in Gamestar Mechanic.

This was problematic for two reasons. First, it was effectively blocking many players' previous gaming Discourse from helping them develop the game design Discourse furthered by the game. Second, it was leading to localized appreciative systems that were mishmash between perspectives furthered by the game, and perspectives players brought from without, limiting the effectiveness of practices such as argumentation. Hence, a goal for the further refinement of the game should be to integrate a broader swath of specialist language used in authentic ways into the narrative and jobs, and implement mechanisms to further consistent appreciative systems in the shared spaces of the game.

Another problem was that within the discussion forums, there was very little incentive for players to use the appreciative system of their own school to critique other's games, leading to many vague and facile comments left for some games and overly convoluted ones for others. Hence, a tighter integration between the game narrative, the status of mechanics in the game and community, and the game discussion activities would be necessary to increase the game's educational effectiveness in the future.

Discussion and Implications for Learning and Instruction beyond Game Design

The purpose of this chapter was to document at the overall project level the evolution of the game-based learning environment and its learning theory over the last three years, as well as to discuss the strengths and limitations observed by the researcher on the ways in which Gamestar Mechanic might help students develop core language and literacy skills regarded as necessary for learners in the 21st century.

The findings shown here represent those general trends that emerged from an analysis (and in later phases re-analysis) of data across the different phases of the project, regarding those aspects of the game designer Discourse that players appropriated as a result of playing the game.

The core finding of this work is that when children play Gamestar Mechanic, they learn to gradually develop communicational competence using a form of language that integrates not only specialist verbal terms germane to game design, but also the multimodal representations intrinsic to computer games – the language of games. They learn to do so by gradually learning the grammatical, semantic and pragmatic functions that this language can serve for making games through the three dialogs, and using them to communicate ideas to other players in a community centered on game design.

The findings also suggest that through games made in Gamestar Mechanic, players can learn to think and use literacy practices involving complex systems, by learning the grammatical relationships between creatures through the solution of design problems. Using these systems as tools to think with, players can learn not only to analyze designs

articulated by others, but also to articulate their own versions of problems and solutions, a skill deemed fundamental to participating in the joint effort to address today's complex issues (Partnership for 21st Century Sikills, 2002).

They suggest that through the construction of patterns of creatures, players can express increasingly complex ideas, and understand these systems as a function of interactions with other people developing a sense of "audience" as an active participant in the meaning-making process of design, that is fundamental in activities such as academic writing (Bereiter and Scardamalia, 1987), and other forms of professional communication.

The findings also show how the community features of Gamestar Mechanic can place players in the sort of active, critical roles necessitated by most knowledge communities and so seldom taught in schools today (Gee, 2004). Using the systems they construct as communicational tools, students can finally recruit aspects of their previous experience formerly considered as trivial, in authentic activities of peer review, knowledge negotiation and critique that resemble in many ways those enacted by scientists and academics in many "serious settings".

Perhaps more importantly, these findings echo Gee's (2003) notion that the sort of learning practices taking place in out of school contexts are now more in tune with the needs of work and life in the 21st century than those practiced in most schools today. Nevertheless, the extensive use of traditional literacy within Gamestar Mechanic also shows that the sort of knowledge being constructed in game design still necessitates basic skills such as reading and writing, currently emphasized in schools. With this in mind, a research agenda that explores the potential of a game like Gamestar Mechanic to bridge the Discourses of learning in and out of school might be the timely thing to do, as it could lead to beneficial outcomes to educators and learners alike.

REFERENCES

Bereiter, C., & Scardamalia, M. (1987). *The psychology of written composition*. Mahwah, NJ: Lawrence Erlbaum Associates.

Brown, A. L., & Campione, J. C. (1994). Guided discovery in a community of learners. In McGilly, K. (Ed.), *Classroom lessons: Integrating cognitive theory and classroom practice* (pp. 229–270). Cambridge, MA: MIT Press.

Collins, A., Joseph, D., & Bielaczyc, K. (2004). Design research: Theoretical and methodological issues. *Journal of the Learning Sciences, 13*(1), 15–42. doi:10.1207/s15327809jls1301_2

diSessa, A. (2002). *Changing minds: Computers, learning, and literacy*. Cambridge, MA: MIT Press.

Freeman, D. (2004). *Creating emotion in games*. San Francisco, CA: New Riders.

Games, I. A. (2008). Three Dialogs: a framework for the analysis and assessment of twenty-first century literacy practices, and its use in the context of game design within Gamestar Mechanic. *E-learning, 5*(4), 396–417. doi:10.2304/elea.2008.5.4.396

Gee, J. P. (1996). *Social linguistics and literacies: Ideology in discourses*. New York: Routledge.

Gee, J. P. (2003). *What video games have to teach us about learning and literacy* (1st ed.). New York: Palgrave Macmillan.

Gee, J. P. (2004). *Situated Language and Learning: A Critique of Traditional Schooling*. New York: Routledge.

Gee, J. P. (2005). *An introduction to discourse analysis*. Abingdon, UK: Routledge.

Geertz, C. (1973). *The Interpretation of Cultures*. New York: Basic Books.

Hayes, E., & Games, I. A. (2008). Making computer games and design thinking: A review of current software and strategies. *Games and Culture, 3*(1), 309–332. doi:10.1177/1555412008317312

Kafai, Y. B. (1995). *Minds in play: Computer game design as a context for children's learning*. Mahwah, NJ: Lawrence Erlbaum Associates, Inc.

Kolodner, J. L., Crismond, D., Gray, J., Holbrook, J., & Puntambekar, S. (1998). Learning by design from theory to practice. In *Proceedings of the International Conference of the Learning Sciences*, (pp. 16–22).

New London Group. (1996). A pedagogy of multiliteracies: Designing social futures. *Harvard Educational Review, 66*(66), 60–92.

Papert, S., & Harel, I. (1991). *Situating constructionism. Constructionism*. Norwood, NJ: Ablex.

Partnership for 21st Century Skills. (2002). *Learning for the 21st Century*. Tucson, AZ: Partnership for 21st Century Skills. Retrieved March 1st, 2009 from http://www.21stcenturyskills.org/index.php?option=com_content&task=view&id=29&Itemid=185

Perkins, D. N. (1986). *Knowledge as Design*. Hillsdale, NJ: Erlbaum.

Rollins, A., & Adams, E. (2003). *Andrew Rollins and Ernest Adams on game design*. Indianapolis: New Riders.

Rouse, R. (2001). *Game Design: Theory and Practice*. Plano, TX: Wordware Publishing.

Salen, K. (2007). Gaming literacies: A game design study in action. *Journal of Educational Multimedia and Hypermedia, 16*(3), 301–322.

Salen, K., & Zimmerman, E. (2003). *Rules of play: Game design fundamentals*. Cambridge, MA: MIT Press.

Seely-Brown, J., Denning, S., Groh, K., & Prusak, L. (2004). *Storytelling in Organizations: Why Storytelling is Transforming 21st Century Organizations and Management*. Burlington, MA: Elseiver.

Shaffer, D. W. (2006). *How Videogames Can Help Children Learn*. New York: Palgrave McMillan. doi:10.1057/9780230601994

Soloway, E. (1998). No one is Making Money in Educational Software. *Communications of the ACM*, *4*(12), 11–15. doi:10.1145/269012.269014

Squire, K. D., Giovanetto, L., DeVane, B., & Durga, S. (2005). From users to designers: Building a self-organizing game-based learning environment. *TechTrends*, *49*(5), 34–42. doi:10.1007/BF02763688

Steinkhueler, C. (2005). Cognition and literacy in massively multiplayer online games. In D. Leu, J. Corio, C. Lankshear & C. Knobel (Eds.), *Handbook of research on new literacies*. Mahwah, New Jersey: Erlbaum. Retrieved October 18, 2006, from http://website.education.wisc.edu/steinkuehler/papers/ SteinkuehlerNEWLIT2005

Wittgenstein, L. (1953). *Philosophical Investigations*. Malden, MA: Blackwell Publishing.

Chapter 24
Second Life as a Tool for Engaging Students Across the Curriculum

Kathryn E. Stevens
James Madison University, USA

S.E. Kruck
James Madison University, USA

Jeremy Hawkins
James Madison University, USA

Suzanne C. Baker
James Madison University, USA

ABSTRACT

Second Life (SL) is a virtual world that possesses great potential as an innovative teaching tool. SL not only allows users to meet, interact, and collaborate in a virtual space, but also to create their own learning environments. This chapter explores how virtual worlds such as Second Life can be used to enhance the overall educational experience of both traditional and distance education students. We describe applications of SL to teaching diverse classes in art history and museum studies, business, and psychology, and to community building across the university. In general, our experiences with using SL have been positive, and our students report enjoying the creativity and flexibility of SL as well as the opportunity for social interaction in the virtual world. We provide recommendations to those considering the use of SL.

INTRODUCTION

The digital world is one constructed of information. It is a frequent complaint that the dilemma facing students today is no longer in locating facts but in determining their value. As a result many colleges and universities have adapted by teaching their students critical and empathetic thinking skills and no longer emphasize memorization of factual information. For instance, the mission of statement of James Madison University (JMU) is not to teach

DOI: 10.4018/978-1-61520-781-7.ch024

its students specific data, but to *prepare* them to be educated and enlightened citizens who can lead productive and meaningful lives. In other words, we want our students to be able to assess new situations, to interact successfully with them, and finally to reflect and to learn from their experiences. Inherent in their success is an ethical evaluative component that we believe will guide them at a personal and global level.

For this method of education to be effective, instructors need to understand the new generation of students. Frequently dubbed Generation Y or the Millennial Generation, these students were born between the early 1980s and the mid-1990s. Computers and the Internet have always been a part of their world. They tend to embrace new digital forms of communication, using instant messaging, text and twitters to connect frequently with their peers. Because of this familiarity with technology, Second Life (SL) can be a strong educational tool for students.

SL is a virtual world that came on-line in June 2003. It is owned by Linden Lab located in California, USA but is used by people all over the world. Unlike many virtual worlds or computer games such as Sims Online and World of Warcraft, SL is envisioned and created by its users. This fundamental difference is reflected in the Linden Lab's slogan for SL, "Your World, Your Imagination" (www.secondlife.com). Also unlike many other virtual realities, SL is not a game, although it shares many characteristics with Massively Multiplayer Online Role Playing Games (MMORPGs). There are no conflicts that must be resolved, no rules of game-play, and no requirements for progressing ("leveling") in SL. Since there is no "object of the game" users are free to use the virtual SL world however they wish. Rather than a space for engaging the storyline of a game, SL is more accurately thought of as a space for social interaction. As of spring 2009, statistics indicate that approximately one million users from all over the globe log in to SL during a typical thirty-day period. It is this multicultural social

aspect of SL that makes it particularly suited to the innovative uses generated by educators.

In SL users create an avatar, or a character that represents them in the virtual world. Avatars interact by chatting, using text or voice to communicate with others in their general vicinity or instant messaging to communicate privately or with others in different locations. Avatars travel through the virtual world by walking, flying, or teleporting from place to place. Unlike most other virtual worlds, SL users may make their avatar anything they can imagine. The basic creation tools allow users to change the apparent height, weight, age, and gender of their avatar. Avatar shapes may be manipulated to appear as animals, futuristic robots, or any number of inanimate objects.

We have found this creation of a digital self to be an important aspect of SL for most users. It is common for an introductory session to focus specifically on avatar creation and image manipulation, regardless of the planned agenda. Many people are simply unwilling to continue tutorials about how to use the world until they are satisfied with their appearance. It is also not uncommon for users to select or to create avatars that are dissimilar from their appearance in the physical world, preferring instead to experience SL as an avatar that may be of the opposite gender, older or younger age, or more or less attractive.

It has already been noted that a major distinguishing feature of SL is that users create most of the content. Current estimates suggest that less than one percent of all objects found in SL were created by Linden Lab (Boellstorff, 2008). Because of this freedom, SL is home to a tremendous diversity of environments. Some areas seek to recreate parts of the physical world, such as ancient Rome or a New York City street. Other sections of SL reflect the creativity of their owner or are personal interpretations of science fiction or fantasy worlds.

Since SL is not a game that involves specific rules or requirements, what do people do with their avatars in SL? SL is primarily a space for social interaction. Residents may join social groups, special interest groups, or support groups. Common group activities include academic lectures, dances, musical performances, philosophical discussions, spiritual services, and even bingo. Many users develop friendships, and spend time with acquaintances visiting virtual parks, gardens, or museums. It is not uncommon for these relationships to deepen and to successfully cross over into the physical world.

SL hosts numerous virtual campuses which have been created by university faculty and students. For example, De Lucia, Francese, Passero, & Tortora (2009) describe building a virtual campus in SL and evaluating its effectiveness as a learning environment. Because Linden Lab offers a fifty percent educational discount on private island purchases for non-profit or educational organizations, SL is a low-cost way to establish a presence in a virtual world. Some universities such as Princeton have chosen to recreate their actual campus in SL, using it as an alternative venue for classes and lectures. Others have elements of real life and fantasy, such as the SL campus of Vassar College that houses virtual recreations of the Sistine Chapel from Italy, the main building from their physical campus, and Castle Vassar that exists only in SL.

There is increasing interest on the part of educators in the possibilities of using virtual worlds in teaching (Warburton, 2009). Although we used SL in our classes, other virtual worlds also exist and have shown promise in educational settings (e.g. *Active Worlds,* Dickey, 2005; Peterson, 2006; *Whyville,* Neulight, Kafai, Kao, Foley, & Galas, 2007). Educators have begun exploring how SL can be used to enhance learning in a diverse array of fields, including media studies (Herold, 2009), operations management (Lee, 2009), communication (Jarman, Traphagen, & Mayrath, 2008), health education (Boulos, Hetherington, & Wheeler, 2007), archaeology (Edirisingha, Nie, Pluciennik, & Young, 2009), and computer science (Esteves, Fonseca, Morgado, & Martins, 2009).

SL also offers interesting possibilities for learning through role play. This potential is enhanced by the ability to design environments in SL, and to create avatars whose appearance can be changed in appropriate ways to augment the experience. Several islands in SL are built around the concept of educational role-play, such as the virtual hospital owned by Imperial College London where medical students may practice game based learning in respiratory medicine. Walker (2009) incorporated role playing in SL in a counseling skills and techniques course which was conducted online. Students created avatars and practiced their counseling skills in a virtual counseling facility.

Many of these early reports of the use of SL are preliminary in nature. However, these early studies point to some of the benefits (and potential problems) of using SL in teaching. SL can be an effective means of engaging students in the learning experience. For example, 100% of the students in a communication class reported that SL enhanced their learning in the course, and increased their engagement with the course material (Jarman, Traphagen, & Mayrath, 2008). However, many students in the course also reported that SL was not easy to use, and that they had technical problems. Perhaps most importantly, students evaluated SL negatively when they did not see a connection between learning goals and the use this technology (e.g. Cheal, 2009; Herold, 2009). These early studies, while preliminary, indicate that instructors should be mindful to design experiences in SL that are explicitly related to learning objectives, and should be prepared to provide the necessary scaffolding to help students benefit from this technology.

As instructors and student development professionals, our interests focus on the use of SL in engaging students, and in how SL can be leveraged to provide a space for social interaction across the university community. Several characteristics of SL make it a particularly useful tool in these contexts. As we noted above, SL functions primarily as a space for social interaction of all kinds, making it useful for many types of learning experiences, both formal (such as delivering a content-based lecture) and more informal (discussion, collaborative projects). Also, because SL users create the content of the virtual world, there is potential for the creation of new learning environments, and for student-student and student-faculty collaboration in creating their own environments for learning and social interaction (e.g. see Salmon, 2009). SL's flexibility means that it is a tool that can potentially be used to engage students in learning across a wide range of disciplines.

In the rest of this chapter, we discuss our use of SL in teaching classes in art history and museum studies, business, and psychology, and our efforts to design a virtual campus that facilitates the creation of community online.

Creating a University Community in Second Life

Jeremy Hawkins

Today, there is a great emphasis given to the sense of community on a college or university campus. Considerable effort is put into fostering environments in which students are engaged and have a sense of belonging both in and out of the classroom. In SL, a strong sense of community is equally as important to students, particularly those who fall into the category of distance learners (students primarily taking online courses), as it is to the students living and learning on our real world campuses.

Distance education (DE) has a unique set of hurdles to overcome in order to provide a quality learning experience. Specific problems that have been documented as a result of these hurdles include high dropout rates, feelings of isolation, issues with procrastination, and poor motivation (e.g. Bernard, de Rubalcava, St-Pierre, 2000). The asynchronous delivery of information in traditional DE and Internet based courses leads

to an understandable disconnect for many students. They lack the basic social structures and supportive frameworks that exist in traditional classrooms to promote effective learning (Redfern & Naughton, 2002). There are opportunities for collaboration and shared discovery that arise in the social times before and after classes that simply do not exist in DE courses. In his writing on asynchronous learning networks, Wegerif (1998) notes that "forming a sense of community, where people feel they will be treated sympathetically by their fellows, seems to be a necessary first step for collaborative learning. Without a feeling of community people are on their own, likely to be anxious, defensive and unwilling to take the risks involved in learning" (p. 48).

The Internet provides a rich environment for the formation of community (Haythornthwaite, 2007; Tanis, 2007). Participants in online communities report the formation of strong social ties with other community members. Online virtual worlds might further enhance this sense of community, by providing visual cues that contribute to a feeling of presence, or a sense of "being there" with another person (Steinkuhler & Williams, 2006). As Steinkuhler and Williams (2006) point out, online virtual worlds have the potential to function as "third places;" social spaces outside home and the workplace that enable social connections between individuals. The structure and tools offered in SL afford us the ability to create the type of community in which students can thrive and be successful.

Part of the beauty of SL is that certain conventional definitions do not apply. Here, a classroom is not required to be a room full of desks facing a lectern. It can be located in the middle of the woods, under the ocean's surface, in the heart of a volcano, or hidden amongst the clouds. While it is not necessary for a virtual campus to have buildings and sidewalks, there is an argument to be made in favor of adhering to some of these traditional constructs in a visually-based virtual environment. In short, it provides a sense of familiarity and comfort. This can be especially important for users who are not adept at navigating in a virtual world.

Even though a community in SL doesn't need to revolve around any set location, we felt it was important to provide members of our virtual JMU community with a home base or a starting off point for exploration. Unlike most Internet based courses that use systems such as Blackboard to deliver and receive content and provide means of communication, SL provides a sense of physical place, a virtual location that can literally be plotted on a map.

You can build a virtual campus that has academic buildings, student unions, performance venues, and even green spaces. This allows students a chance for socialization and interaction outside of the classroom setting, helping to foster those personal relationships that are essential to creating a healthy and functional community, and, as studies have shown, are integral to improve learning (Berge & Collins, 1995). The actual design and construction of the virtual campus is an excellent opportunity for collaboration between students, faculty, and staff.

The main JMU virtual campus is anchored by replicas of two of the most well-known and recognizable buildings from its real-world counterpart,

Wilson Hall and ISAT (Integrated Science and Technology building). Wilson Hall is the central building on JMU's historic bluestone quad. The building in SL functions much like the actual Wilson, providing a space for large meetings and events. ISAT provides virtual classroom space that can be customized to suit the needs of the instructor. In planning out our virtual campus, we thought it was important to have these identifiable structures to help connect the SL campus with the actual JMU campus. This approach is mirrored by a fair number of the colleges and universities that have established a presence in SL, and helps to tie in the virtual community with the physical one.

One of the more powerful community building tools available in SL is the resident-made group. Users in SL are free to join together and create unique groups associated with common interests and purposes. In order to set their in-world home location to the JMU campus, a resident has to be a member of the JMU group. Being a member of this group also gives them rights to build on the campus and to send out messages to other members. Groups come with highly effective communication tools, allowing for quick and efficient dissemination of information and subsequent feedback. We have subdivided the JMU group into students, faculty and staff, and alumni,

Figure 1. Wilson Hall on the SL JMU Campus with Duke Dog, the university mascot

Figure 2. ISAT building on the SL JMU campus

providing a degree of separation that allows for quick identification and enhances the overall sense of belonging to the community.

Traditions and myths are an important component of any campus culture. We decided to bring some of these real-world traditions, myths, and "rites of passage" to our SL campus to further enhance that feeling of inclusion. The hidden tunnels under the Quad, the ghost in the Wilson Hall cupola, and the JMU kissing rock are just a few of the notable bits of campus legend we've incorporated. It is our hope that as students take on a more active role in the creation and maintenance of the virtual campus, that even more of these traditions are recognized and included, and that a few new ones might take root in this evolving media.

The student union on our virtual campus serves as a casual meeting place for students to gather and engage with one another. There is a stage full of musical instruments that avatars can play, a room for viewing student-created videos, and a small bookstore offering JMU t-shirts and other branded items. The question of how to go about obtaining a t-shirt is one of the first questions we hear when introducing others to SL. This demonstrates a desire on behalf of the user to display an affiliation with the campus and its culture.

The student union is an important symbol on our virtual campus, one that signals our institution's student-centered approach to higher education and commitment to the entire collegiate experience, both in and out of the virtual class.

The authors of this paper teach a diverse array of courses in three different disciplines: art history and museum studies, business, and psychology. In the sections below we describe how SL has been used in our classes. We also discuss how SL can be used to extend the University community.

Teaching About Past Cultures: Art History and Museum Studies Applications

Dr. Kathryn E. Stevens

SL is the perfect tool for teaching past cultures. First, it has the virtue of being non-destructive of archaeological sites or artifacts. Second, while it cannot reproduce the experience of physically being present at a location, it is a considerably less expensive and less dangerous alternative to world travel. Third, because the virtual world is so easily modified by users, interaction with the past can be controlled to provide a specific experience that cannot be gained through the traditional use of

Figure 3. Faculty and student avatars play music and dance at the JMU Student Union

two-dimensional visual aids. Virtual worlds allow students to be engaged in learning auditorially, visually, and experientially.

I became interested in SL because I am passionate about the past and wanted to spark a similar interest in my students. I had tried to use tools such as Google Earth to convey a sense of presence for sites such as the Great Pyramids of Giza or the Pantheon in Rome, but with little success. The pan-and-zoom feature seemed to blur, rather than augment the distance between sites, and seeing specific details was impossible with current technology. It also failed to interpret the past. What I wanted was a time-machine where instead of showing flat painted reconstructions of sites or describing them in great and perhaps mind-numbing detail for the students in the classroom, they could instead walk around and through the structures in the landscape for themselves. When we studied Neolithic structures like Stonehenge or Avebury, I wanted the students to try and apply theories, then make informed decisions about their validity. And secretly, I wanted the students to experience a "eureka" moment while learning about a life-style different from their own.

SL has been worthwhile investment for me as an educator. It took time to learn how to build but now I can quickly create virtual learning environments centered on the ancient world for the students, such as a recreation of Stonehenge circa 1500 BCE, located in the SL JMU's Cultural Arts Museum. Because it is such a famous site, most students come to this lecture believing they already understand the use of the structure. In class we discuss popular conceptions of Stonehenge as well as the archaeological data surrounding its creation and use. Then the students go in-world to experience the site on their own.

In the case of Stonehenge, this virtual visit is almost better than the real world one. Unless you apply well in advance and have academic credentials, it is very difficult to actually walk among the stones themselves. Most visitors are relegated to a walkway several meters from the site and peer at the stones through their cameras. And of course, the site has suffered much damage since its last ancient use around 1500 BCE, missing key components that would indicate its probable use. In my SL recreation, the students walk along the procession pathway from the Avon River and pass through the henge and ditch built of chalky soil. Once they are inside the outer ring and see the large sarsen stone horseshoe, they begin to understand how architectural structures create sacred space set aside from the everyday world. And since they are progressing through

Figure 4. Stonehenge recreated on the SL JMU museum site showing the winter solstice alignment

space, they begin to understand why the winter solstice is more important for this archaeological site than the summer solstice.

Part of the academic joy of SL is that it is a *virtual* world. The students understand before and during their visit that this is a recreation, an interpretation. It is apparent to them that everything that exists there I have placed for a reason, and so they pay attention to it. They are also appropriately skeptical. For the first time they pause to ask the fundamental question, "How do you know?"

In many cases the students can visit SL sites beyond the JMU virtual campus and my classroom. Seeing different versions of the same archaeological site encourages students to compare and to contrast them. Most SL builders and academics are very friendly and like to talk about their work with interested people. From this conversational interaction they get a bit of insight into a professional world from which they are usually separated, and so they start to buy into it themselves. I have come to understand that the reasons students might not care about academic debates and advances have little to do with their emotional or intellectual ability and everything to do with feeling included.

As the director of JMU's permanent cultural and art collection, I also teach museum studies. Again SL is a perfect venue for this discipline

because the museum is *all* about interpretation. Every one of the students in these classes wants to curate exhibits. They have already bought into the importance of history and want to share their insights and experiences with others. However, as with most museums, in the physical world we have limited money and space. In the SL virtual world, I have lots more space and probably as much money as students will ever need to create their show.

It is easy to import images, or textures, of our physical world collection and create a virtual collection in SL. Unlike object use or display in the physical world, virtual use of the collection does not harm the object. My museum studies students can progress through all the exhibit phases they would when creating an exhibit for a museum in the real world. They are placed in groups where they create exhibit proposals that include an intended audience and message. Each group selects a member to research and write display text, one to create a design scheme, one to produce educational materials, and one to craft the perfect display venue. At the end of the semester each group presents its completed exhibit to the class. During this presentation they also discuss the process, talking about the various problems they encountered through each phase and how they arrived at solutions.

Figure 5. A student created exhibit on display in the SL JMU museum

My students for the most part have enjoyed SL. It exists beyond their classroom and as such they can share their work with their family and peers. They can document their exhibits with digital photographs and include them in their portfolios. As most collections and museums develop a virtual presence, their SL experience is also something they wish to include on their resumes. But as their instructor, the most important thing the students come away with is the understanding of the need for meticulous detail-oriented work in the museum world and the absolute necessity of good team work. They get this in spades using SL for my class projects.

Business Uses and Applications

Dr. S. E. Kruck

I have used SL in a graduate Management Information Systems (MIS) course for over three years in four course sessions. Prior to making the SL assignment each semester, I have the students read current articles about business use of virtual worlds (see our suggested readings). We then discuss these readings in class before I give each of them two brief descriptions about SL, one positive and one negative. It is at this point that I demonstrate

SL for them on the overhead projector, showing them how to move through virtual space and to interact with other avatars.

To address some of the learning outcomes in many MIS courses, assignments were created to include e-business, systems development, virtual work, and IT planning (Wagner, 2008). The first year SL was included, I developed an assignment that gave students two options. They could either complete a simple scavenger hunt in SL or they could research and write a paper on SL and Linden Lab. Because I was still new to SL and was learning about the fluidity of the virtual world I felt that this assignment would allow both the students and I to learn more about the potential of virtual worlds. Of the nineteen students enrolled in the course the first semester, nine participated in the scavenger hunt while the other ten students opted for the paper. When I inquired about the paper choice, most indicated that their computer did not have the required graphics card or they had a dial-up connection.

The SL scavenger hunt required students to take document their activities using the SL camera feature. This camera allows the viewer to frame the intended image and then send a snapshot to his or her email account or save it to the computer's hard drive. The students needed to use the SL search engine to locate a variety of uses in SL. For instance, they needed to identify repositories of shared information used by SL residents or to show their interaction with other avatars. They needed to visit business sites in SL, like IBM, and use the tools developed there to build a real world computer that could then be delivered to them, should they wish to purchase it. The alternative paper required students to research Linden Lab itself. They needed to document its growth as well as discover information on SL users. Most important was the task to understand how real world businesses were using SL to market their products or to train their employees. Informal feedback from students found positive feedback on both options for the assignment. However, the students that participated in the scavenger hunt were more engaged in the discussion of SL business applications than were those who only researched and wrote.

The second year increased the virtual component of the scavenger hunt and included more course related activities. In addition, instead of requiring a specific location, such as a computer manufacture, the assignment was more open ended. There were a total of twenty-eight students in the class with twenty-six participating in the scavenger hunt. Students again had positive comments. Upon inquiry, the two students who had not chosen to explore SL itself did so because of limited computer graphics ability or because of a slow Internet connection.

The third year, Fall 2008, a second assignment was added that include creating objects in-world. After students worked through a basic building tutorial, they needed to create a simple chair to demonstrate their competence. This aspect of the project was only possible because JMU had invested in creating a virtual campus. Part of the JMU virtual island is dedicated for building exercises that allow students and faculty to be as creative and as much a part of the SL campus as they wish. In the future, programming in SL will be added to enrich the course by providing more

lifelike and industry relevant learning (Dreher, Reiners, Dreher & Dreher, 2009).

Two sections of the graduate MIS course were taught that year. The first section had twelve students and eight worked within SL. The second section was structured differently, however. It was learner-centered and allowed the students to pick and choose among a number of assignments; therefore, SL was not required in any form. However, eight of the eleven students in this section decided to work within SL. The second assignment was available only to this group of students. Of the eight that completed the SL project, four learned how to build and completed the chair project. All participating students enjoyed exploring SL and the building exercise and had positive comments about the experience.

Using SL to Increase Student Engagement: Psychology Applications

Dr. Suzanne C. Baker

I used SL to enhance student opportunities in an advanced psychology course, specifically, a course in animal behavior taught to junior and senior psychology and biology majors. The course is taught online during the summer and in a traditional face-to-face format during the regular academic year. The online class is conducted asynchronously; students and faculty do not meet in real time. I felt that SL might be particularly useful in the online class as a way of increasing student engagement and the sense of social presence (Edirisingha et al, 2009; Omale, Hung, Luetkehans, & Cooke-Plagwtiz, 2009).

Students in the online course were provided with instructions for installing SL and creating an avatar, and with tips and guidelines for using SL and for navigating in the virtual world. In addition, an experienced student was available to serve as a "Second Life guide" for students in the class who wanted help with SL. My goal in using SL in this class was to provide students with opportunities to meet with me, since there were no face-to-face meetings of the class. I held virtual office hours and student appointments in SL. Office hours were scheduled at various times during the course. During these hours, I was available at the virtual campus in SL to meet with students to discuss course content. Fewer than 10% of the students in the course (three students out of a class of thirty-five) chose to meet with me in SL. Although this was a very small number of students, this was comparable to the percentage of students that meet with me during face-to-face courses. In end-of-semester student evaluations, the primary reason that students gave for not meeting with me during virtual office hours was that they did not need help with course content. The students who did use SL were very positive about the experience. They reported that they enjoyed the opportunity to interact with each other and with the instructor. This may indicate that SL was successful in facilitating a sense of social presence for these students.

In the face-to-face course, students have attended lectures and other SL events relevant to course content. For example, students were able to attend a lecture on manatee behavior and conservation given at the SL site for the Nature Publishing Group. Students received extra credit for attending the lecture, just as they would have if they attended a relevant on-campus lecture or event. Qualitative feedback from nine students who attended the lecture (15% of the class) indicated that students' experiences were mostly positive. Student comments stressed the convenience of being able to attend lectures and other events in SL, and they also reported that they enjoyed interacting with other class members while in the virtual world. A small number of students reported having technical problems, but this was the only negative aspect students mentioned. Although I do not have directly comparable data, the percentage of students attending this SL lecture was higher than the typical percent that attend "real world"

events for extra credit. This is probably due to the convenience of SL; students could log on from home, their laptop, or any computer lab on campus. In addition, the students suggested other potential uses of SL, including holding online class when weather prevented students from getting to campus, and using SL for meetings for students working on group projects.

In addition to its potential role in teaching and learning, SL provides a rich platform for psychology researchers and students interested in issues such as self-presentation and social interaction in virtual worlds (see Bainbridge, 2007; Yee & Bailenson, 2007). For example, researchers can examine whether people create avatars that are similar to their "real world" selves (Messenger et al, 2008), and can examine how social interaction in the virtual world is similar to, and differs from, interaction in the "real world."

INCORPORATING SL INTO THE CLASSROOM: SUGGESTIONS

Having taught several workshops for faculty and students, as well as presenting SL to a variety of community groups, we have several suggestions for anyone considering use of this virtual world for educational purposes. Baker, Wentz, & Woods (2009) and McVey (2008) also provide suggestions for the use of SL in teaching.

First, we recommend that educational institutions invest in virtual property. Small plots of land on educational islands can be rented for a nominal fee. This will provide you and your students with a home base from which to work. It allows instructors to teach in an area under their control and provides room for students to build.

One of the most important steps before taking students into SL is to prepare them for the virtual world. Many students are aware of SL from media coverage. However, if they have not been in-world SL, they may not understand the richness and diversity of the culture. Just as study abroad students go through an orientation session before traveling to another country, we encourage at least a lecture that discusses the SL virtual world. Some professors have found that the use of an SL "buddy" can reduce the first-time disorientation that some students experience. Students, like instructors, vary in their comfort level with technology, and some students will need extra support when learning to use SL.

Advanced preparation is an important aspect to successfully teaching with SL. Again, we compare it to leading a study-abroad session. Things change quickly in SL just as they do in the physical world. Log in before you work with your class to verify that there are currently no technical problems in-world. Be aware of the weekly SL rolling restarts of regions and try to schedule activities around them. Realize that SL is a world in which unexpected things sometimes happen. If you are relaxed and able to calmly deal with any situation, your students will generally follow your example.

We are frequently asked about the dangers of SL. Certainly students should be reminded of Internet security issues and warned against providing information to casual acquaintances in SL, just as in the real world. However, given adherence to typical social and password security, students are much safer in SL than they are in many real life situations. For instance, in SL if a student finds himself or herself in an uncomfortable situation, all he or she has to do is to teleport to a safe location, such as a "home" SL campus. If a student is subjected to unwanted comments, it takes but a simple click to mute an offending party. Most importantly, in SL the avatar is under the control of the owner who operates the computer keyboard. No one can animate another's avatar without specific permission.

The most important, overarching recommendation we would make is that instructors should carefully consider the learning objectives for their course, and whether SL (or a similar virtual world) is the right tool to use to accomplish their objectives. Preliminary studies have indicated the potential of SL, but they also show that students respond negatively when the connection between their virtual world experiences and what they are supposed to be learning is not clear.

While SL is not a game, our experiences suggest that it can be an engaging learning environment for students. Be willing to try new things and your students will enjoy the learning experience as much as you will. Most of all, understand that SL is a virtual world created by its users. In an educational context, this means that the classroom can be anything that the instructor can imagine and build. Then, that classroom becomes part of a shared reality in which all types of students may interact with each other, with their instructor, and with the world.

REFERENCES

Bainbridge, W. S. (2007). The scientific research potential of virtual worlds. *Science*, *317*, 472–476. doi:10.1126/science.1146930

Baker, S. C., Wentz, R. K., & Woods, M. M. (2009). Using virtual worlds in education: Second Life as an educational tool. *Teaching of Psychology*, *36*, 59–64. doi:10.1080/00986280802529079

Berge, Z., & Collins, M. (1995). Computer-mediated communication and the online classroom in distance learning. *Computer-Mediated Communication Magazine*, *2*(4), 6–13.

Bernard, R. M., de Rubalcava, B. R., & St-Pierre, D. (2000). Collaborative online distance learning: Issues for future practice and research. *Distance Education*, *2*(2), 260–277. doi:10.1080/0158791000210205

Boellstorff, T. (2008). Coming of Age in Second Life: An anthropologist explores the virtually human. Princeton and Harvard: Princeton University Press.

Boulos, M. N. K., Hetherington, L., & Wheeler, S. (2007). Second Life: An overview of the potential of 3-D virtual worlds in medical and health education. *Health Information and Libraries Journal, 24,* 233–245. doi:10.1111/j.1471-1842.2007.00733.x

Cheal, C. (2009). Student perceptions of a course taught in Second Life. *Innovate: Journal of Online Education, 5*(5). Retrieved July 27, 2009, from http://www.innovateonline.info/index.php?view=article&id=692

De Lucia, A., Francese, R., Passero, I., & Tortora, G. (2009). Development and evaluation of a virtual campus on Second Life: The case of SecondDMI. *Computers & Education, 52,* 220–233. doi:10.1016/j.compedu.2008.08.001

Dickey, M. D. (2005). Three-dimensional worlds and distance learning: Two case studies of Active Worlds as a medium for distance education. *British Journal of Educational Technology, 36,* 439–451. doi:10.1111/j.1467-8535.2005.00477.x

Dreher, C., Reiners, T., Dreher, N., & Dreher, H. (2009). Virtual worlds as a context suited for information systems education: Discussion of pedagogical experience and curriculum design with reference to Second Life. *Journal of Information Systems Education, 20*(2), 211–224.

Edirisingha, P., Nie, M., Pluciennik, M., & Young, R. (2009). Socialisation for learning at a distance in a 3-D multi-user virtual environment. *British Journal of Educational Technology, 40,* 458–479. doi:10.1111/j.1467-8535.2009.00962.x

Esteves, M., Fonseca, B., Morgado, L., & Martins, P. (2009). Using Second Life for problem-based learning in computer science programming. *Journal of Virtual Worlds Research, 2* (1). Retrieved July 29, 2009 from https://journals.tdl.org/jvwr/article/view/419/462

Haythornthwaite, C. (2007). Social networks and online community. In Joinson, A. M., McKenna, K. Y. A., Postmes, T., & Reips, U.-D. (Eds.), *The Oxford Handbook of Internet Psychology* (pp. 121–137). Oxford: Oxford University Press.

Herold, D. K. (2009). Virtual education: Teaching media studies in Second Life. *Journal of Virtual Worlds Research, 2* (1). Retrieved July 27, 2009 from https://journals.tdl.org/jvwr/article/view/380/454

Jarman, L., Traphagan, T., & Mayrath, M. (2008). Understanding project-based learning in Second Life with a pedagogy, training, and assessment trio. *Educational Media International, 45,* 157–176. doi:10.1080/09523980802283889

Lee, P. D. (2009). Using Second Life to teach operations management. *Journal of Virtual Worlds Research, 2* (1). Retrieved July 29, 2009 from https://journals.tdl.org/jvwr/article/view/431/464

McVey, M. H. (2008). Observations of expert communicators in immersive virtual worlds: Implications for synchronous discussion. *ALT-J. Research in Learning Technology, 16,* 173–180.

Messinger, P. R., Ge, X., Stroulia, E., Lyons, K., Smirnov, K., & Bone, M. (2008). On the relationship between my avatar and myself. *Journal of Virtual Worlds Research, 1*(2), 1–17.

Neulight, N., Kafai, Y. B., Kao, L., Foley, B., & Galas, C. (2007). Children's participation in a virtual epidemic in the science classroom: Making connections to natural infectious diseases. *Journal of Science Education and Technology, 16,* 47–58. doi:10.1007/s10956-006-9029-z

Omale, N., Hung, W.-C., Luetkehans, L., & Cooke-Plagwitz, J. (2009). Learning in 3-D multiuser virtual environments: Exploring the use of unique 3-D attributes for online problem-based learning. *British Journal of Educational Technology*, *40*, 480–495. doi:10.1111/j.1467-8535.2009.00941.x

Peterson, M. (2006). Learner interaction management in an avatar and chat-based virtual world. *Computer Assisted Language Learning*, *19*, 79–103. doi:10.1080/09588220600804087

Redfern, S., & Naughton, N. (2002). Collaborative virtual environments to support communication and community in internet-based distance education. *Journal of Information Technology Education*, *1*(3), 12.

Salmon, G. (2009). The future for (second) life and learning. *British Journal of Educational Technology*, *40*, 526–538. doi:10.1111/j.1467-8535.2009.00967.x

Steinkuhler, C. A., & Williams, D. (2006). Where everybody knows your (screen) name: Online games as "third places.". *Journal of Computer-Mediated Communication*, *11*, 885–909. doi:10.1111/j.1083-6101.2006.00300.x

Tanis, M. (2007). Online social support groups. In Joinson, A. M., McKenna, K. Y. A., Postmes, T., & Reips, U.-D. (Eds.), *The Oxford Handbook of Internet Psychology* (pp. 139–153). Oxford: Oxford University Press.

Wagner, C. (2008). Learning experience with virtual worlds. *Journal of Information Systems Education*, *19*, 263–266.

Walker, V. L. (2009). 3D virtual learning in counselor education: Using Second Life in counselor skill development. *Journal of Virtual Worlds Research*, *2*(1). Retrieved July 27, 2009 from https://journals.tdl.org/jvwr/article/view/423/463`

Warburton, S. (2009). Second Life in higher education: Assessing the potential for and barriers to deploying virtual worlds in learning and teaching. *British Journal of Educational Technology*, *40*, 414–426. doi:10.1111/j.1467-8535.2009.00952.x

Wegerif, R. (1998). The social dimension of asynchronous learning networks. *Journal of Asynchronous Learning Networks*, *2*(1), 34-49, Retrieved April 8, 2009 from http://www.sloan-c.org/publications/jaln/v2n1/pdf/v2n1_wegerif.pdf.

Yee, N., & Bailenson, J. (2007). The Proteus Effect: The effect of transformed self-representation on behavior. *Human Communication Research*, *33*, 271–290. doi:10.1111/j.1468-2958.2007.00299.x

ADDITIONAL READING

Business Week, 15.

Cameron, F., & Kenderdine, S. (Eds.). (2007). *Theorizing digital cultural heritage: A critical discourse*. Cambridge, Massachusetts: The MIT Press.

Genocchio, B. (2008, March 12). Flying avatars admire the artwork. *The New York Times*, p. 36.

Guest, T. (2007). *Second lives: A journey through virtual worlds*. New York: Random House.

Hanson, M. (2006). *Bodies in code: Interfaces with digital media*. London: Routledge.

Jones, C. (Ed.). (2006). *Sensorium: Embodied experience, technology, and contemporary art*. Cambridge, Massachusetts: The MIT Press.

Kreijns, K., Kirschner, P. A., Jochems, W., & van Buuren, H. (2007). Measuring perceived sociability of computer-supported collaborative learning environments. *Computers & Education*, *49*, 176–192. doi:10.1016/j.compedu.2005.05.004

Livingstone, D., & Kemp, J. (Eds.). (2006). *Proceedings of the Second Life Education Workshop at the Second Life Community Convention*. University of Paisley. Retrieved April 6, 2009 from http://www.simteach.com/SLCC06/slcc2006-proceedings.pdf.

Ludlow, P., & Wallace, M. (2007). The Second Life Herald: The virtual tabloid that witnessed the dawn of the metaverse. Cambridge, Massachusettes: The MIT Press.

Mansfield, R. (2008). *How to do everything with Second Life*. New York: McGraw Hill.

McGonigal, J. (2009, March/April). Museums as happiness pioneers. *Museum*, *88*, 48–53.

Ondrejka, C. (2008). Education unleashed: Participatory culture, education, and innovation in Second Life. In Salen, K. (Ed.), *The ecology of games: Connecting youth, games, and learning* (pp. 229–251). Cambridge, MA: The MIT Press.

Popper, F. (2007). *From technology to virtual art*. Cambridge, Massachusetts: The MIT Press.

Schroeder, R. (Ed.). (2002). *The social life of avatars: Presence and interacton in shared virtual environments*. London: Springer-Verlag.

Schroeder, R., & Axelsson, A.-S. (Eds.). (2006). *Avatars at work and play: Collaboration and interaction in shared virtual environments*. London: Springer-Verlag.

Second Life hosts a dedicated education page at http://slife.com/education

Tech Special Report: "Virtual Life". *Business Week*. Retrieved April 13, 2009 from

Tribune Business News, 1.

Wagner, A. J. (2008, May 5). Special Report "Second Life Marketing: Still Strong"

Walsh, C. (2007, April 14). If One Life's Not Enough, Try A 2nd One. *Knight Ridder*

Waters, J. K. (2009). A 'Second Life' For Educators. *T.H.E. Journal*, *36*(1), 29–34.

www.businessweek.com/technology/special_reports/20070416virtuallife.htm?campaign_id=rss_daily

Chapter 25
Collaborative Online Roleplay for Adult Learners

Paul Pivec
Deakin University, Australia

Maja Pivec
University of Applied Sciences, Austria

ABSTRACT

Game-based learning has gained popularity in schools and has been proposed for adult education, both at Universities and in the corporate training sector. Games are becoming a new form of interactive content and game playing provides an interactive and collaborative platform for learning purposes. Collaborative learning allows participants to produce new ideas as well as to exchange information, simplify problems, and resolve the tasks. Context based collaborative learning method is based on constructivist learning theory and guides the design of the effective learning environments. In this environment the teacher or trainer becomes the active partner, moderator and advisor of the educational process, not just a repository of the information importing his or her own knowledge to a passive learner as in traditional education. Learners bring their prior skills and knowledge to the classroom community. The trainer structures learning situations in which each learner can interact with other learners to develop new knowledge and fashion their own needs and capacities. Knowledge is generated from experience with complex tasks rather than from isolated activities like learning and practicing separately. Skills and knowledge are best acquired within the context. This helps the learners easily to transfer learning from classroom to "real life" and back, or information from one subject to another. Therefore this method requires that the trainer and learners play nontraditional roles such as interaction and collaboration with each other within the educational process. The classroom drops the physical boundaries and becomes a goal-oriented platform dedicated to learning. Online role-play scenario platforms offers an environment where trainers can define their own role-playing scenarios and provide the opportunity for learners to apply factual knowledge and to gain experience through the digital world. Trainers can define new games or adopt and modify sample games without any programming skills. Some platforms provide a variety of communication means within the scenarios; players can communicate with the use of multimedia discussion forums, text and voice chat modules, as well as

DOI: 10.4018/978-1-61520-781-7.ch025

through multi-user video conferencing. These platforms foster participation in problem-solving, effective communication, teamwork, project management, as well as other soft skills such as responsibility, creativity, micro-entrepreneurship, corporate culture, and cultural awareness. They are designed for use as a supplement to normal in-class teaching and corporate training, but it is also possible to be used independently from a class course. The constructivist design required for successful Game-Based Learning will be discussed and a model is provided to display how Game-Based Learning occurs in a collaborative online environment. This chapter will present example scenarios and highlight resources available to interested teachers and trainers.

INTRODUCTION

Many studies have investigated the learning aspects of computer games and how they can be used for teaching skills and knowledge. Pillay (2003) studied groups of children playing computer games and their subsequent ability to complete instructional tasks. *"The findings suggest that playing recreational computer games may influence performance on subsequent computer-based educational tasks"* (p.1). This suggests that either cognitive ability has been increased while playing computer games, or the focus and motivation for completing subsequent computer-based tasks has been enhanced. In an extensive literature review on educational multiplayer games, McGrenere (1996) summarised two studies measuring the success of using computer technology for learning. McGrenere findings were similar to those of Butler (1988), who concluded that by using games for learning:

1. the time to learn information is reduced;
2. performance is increased through greater interest;
3. learners are motivated to participate; and
4. learner attendance is increased.

McGrenere (1996) suggested that computer *"games and simulations can be equally as good or better than traditional teaching"* (p.19). Many educators and researchers agree with McGrenere and argue that video games have the potential to enhance learning (Malone, 1981; Ramsberger et

al., 1983; Malone & Lepper, 1987; Donchin, 1989; Thomas & Macredie, 1994; Ruben, 1999). Some state that the characteristics of electronic games create an immersive environment, focusing the player's attention and potentially increasing the uptake of knowledge (MacMahan, 2003; Paras & Bizzocchi, 2005; Gentile, 2005; Kearney, 2006). What is generally accepted, is that the game environment, electronic or otherwise, can provide the motivation necessary to invoke a persistent re-engagement by the player, thereby improving the chances of the desired learning outcomes to occur (Garris, Ahlers, & Driskell, 2002; Kearney & Pivec, 2007).

Several major reports that have been commissioned on the topic of educational games (Entertainment and Leisure Software Publishers Association, 2006; Federation of American Scientists, 2006; Facer, Ulicsak, & Sandford, 2007; Project Tomorrow, 2008) have implied that video games teach skills that relate to education and these skills transfer to business. They call for educational institutions at all levels to embrace the games community. These reports cite publications such as Menn (1993), who argues that only 50% of what is watched is learnt, yet 90% of what is experienced is mastered. Levy and Murnane (2004) conclude that although learning often focuses only on topics such as math and literacy, soft skills like communication, collaboration, and problem solving are not taught, and these are skills that industry requires. Klopfer (2008) advocates educational games as a method for teaching soft skills by allowing the players to experience learning through role-play and games. This teaching approach is based on constructivist learning theory and Game-Based Learning is situated in the constructivist arena for both academic institutions and industry.

Game-Based Learning for Academic Achievement

There are different beliefs *if, how, why* and *when* learning takes place while playing games. Wainess (2007) advocates that games do not foster learning at all, cognitive skills nor knowledge acquisition, and it is purely the context in which they are used that stimulates any learning to take place. Garris et. al. (2002) argue that learning occurs only after reflection and debriefing, and the game characteristics and instructional content are paramount in allowing this to happen. Shaffer (2006) partially agrees and states that the virtual worlds created by such games allow players to take action within the game and then reflect on this action, both during and after play.

Commercial video games are known for creating social environments and cult followings surrounding the game play, the character attributes, and player's abilities. Surveys (Facer, Ulicsak, & Sandford, 2007; Project Tomorrow, 2008) suggest a difference in the perceived learning outcomes of Game-Based Learning. Both teachers and students believed that computer skills are enhanced by utilizing games in the classroom, but where the teachers perceive the value to be in the uptake of declarative knowledge, the students believe the value is more affective learning, i.e. social skills.

Knowledge based skills are defined within this model as declarative, procedural, strategic knowledge. Declarative knowledge being facts and data that are required to complete a task or to perform well within the task and these would be provided by the game or system feedback. Procedural knowledge is required to know how to approach the task and subsequently complete

it. This could be referred to as knowing how to apply the declarative knowledge to a given situation. Strategic knowledge is the reasoning behind the task and how the task could be achieved in a different or more creative way. Each of these skills is achieved through repetition and reflection, but with many fast action video games, it is facilitated through reflection-in-action. This occurs throughout the game cycle and within each level. As skills and abilities are attained, players advance through the game and increments their knowledge. Players often do this without being aware of the process and this is where the teacher, as trainer, can highlight the meta-cognitive skills utilized. However, both the above-mentioned surveys found that there is a generation gap of technical knowledge with teachers rarely playing or even having knowledge about video games and the learners being well versed in the technology.

Referring to the model of Game-Based Learning *(Figure 1)*, we can show where the different types of learning occur by means of the macro and micro game cycles. The model includes the player reflection within the game, during play and between levels. The skill-based learning appears to comfortably fit within the micro game cycle or levels within the game. For example, Rosser et al., (2007) found that the playing of commercial action games improved the surgical skills of laparoscopic physicians and decreased their error rate. There was no documented debriefing session for Rosser's study and it is assumed that the development of technical or motor skills occurs within the game itself.

Simulations vs. Role Play Games

Salen and Zimmerman (2003) define games as systems where a player engages in conflict regulated by a defined set of rules and the result is a defined outcome. They argue that while games and role-plays share the key features that define them both as games, they are different in one critical respect; role-plays do not always have a

Figure 1. Recursive loops of game-based learning. (Kearney & Pivec, 2007)

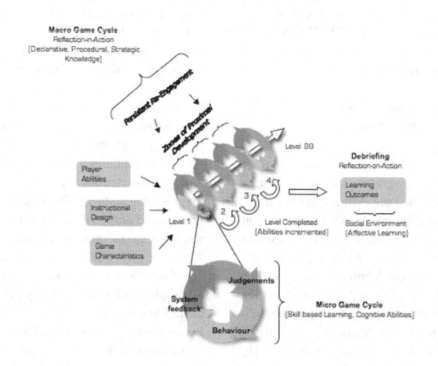

defined outcome. However, Salen and Zimmerman concede that this depends on the framework or platform that provides the role-play. They suggest that where a game and a role-play overlap is that they are systems requiring players to interact according to a set of rules in a contest or in conflict (Salen & Zimmerman 2003).

Kelly (2005) argues that simulations have an enormous impact on education and many products such as Microsoft's "*Flight Simulator*" are in fact simulations and neither games nor role-plays. Linser (2008) suggests that for pedagogical purposes, a role-play is closer to a simulation than a game. Linser argues that with the acquisition of real world knowledge, and the understanding and skills acquired by the player, a role-play is designed as an attempt to simulate processes, issues and conditions that exist in the real world.

In the model of Game-Based Learning shown in *figure 1*, the inclusion of instructional design is a critical element of the game to enable the

achievement of the learning outcomes. Akilli (2007) argues that while game designers need to improve their instructional design and equally, instructional designers need to give more attention to game design principles, there is a lack of guideline documentation supporting this area of pedagogy.

Linser (2008) concludes by stating that while he considers role-play as a simulation, given the right environment and delivery platform, a role-play can include all the engagement, immersion, and motivation that are inherent in the game environment. Fortugno and Zimmerman (2005) agree and suggest that teachers and trainers do not yet understand the use and potential of games and most games to not include sound pedagogical principles in their design.

Guidelines for Educational Game Design

There are specific educational domains where Game-Based Learning concepts and approaches have a high learning value. These domains are interdisciplinary topics where skills such as critical thinking, group communication, debate and decision-making are of high importance. Such subjects, if learned in isolation, often cannot be applied in real world contexts. To create a successful e-learning opportunity, the 14 learner-centered psychological principles defined by the American Psychological Association (APA) should be considered. They are grouped in 4 areas and listed as:

- Cognitive and Metacognitive Factors
  1. Nature of the learning process.
  2. Goals of the learning process.
  3. Construction of knowledge.
  4. Strategic thinking.
  5. Thinking about thinking.
  6. Context of learning.
- Motivational and Affective Factors
  7. Motivational and emotional influences on learning.
  8. Intrinsic motivation to learn.
  9. Effects of motivation on effort.
- Developmental and Social Factors
  10. Developmental influences on learning.
  11. Social influences on learning.
- Individual Differences
  12. Individual differences in learning.
  13. Learning and diversity.
  14. Standards and assessment.

(Learner-centered psychological principles revised, 1996)

Educational technologists advocate the shift from instructor-centered to learner or learner-centered approaches (constructivism). Learner-centered pedagogy looks at what the learners need to learn, what their learning preferences are, and what is meaningful to them in their specific environment. E-Learning provides opportunities for learning materials, tasks, and activities to fit individual learning styles and preferences. Networks of learning information, such as digital libraries and e-learning platforms, are also available to motivate learner interests and spark ideas. Online role-play fits within this realm and can be defined and equaled with collaborative e-learning.

Salmon (2002) proposed the design of a collaborative e-learning process that includes a five-stage framework, which is helpful and useful for any e-trainer that builds online courses. In the first stage an e-trainer designs (1) access and motivation of the participants. Online socialization of the learners (2) is then reached. By using the results of these two steps the e-trainer organizes the next processes: (3) the information exchange, then (4) knowledge construction and as a benefit - the development of knowledge (5). An important note is that without successful processes in the first two stages there is no possibility for successful development in the last stages.

Cummings (2000) defines the sequence of steps to conduct a successful virtual debate as follows:

1. The Instructor selects controversial topic with input from class.
2. The Instructor divides class into subtopic pairs.
3. The Instructor assigns subtopic pairs.
4. Critics and defenders post initial positions.
5. The Learners review all initial position statements.
6. The Learners reply to at least two position statements with comments or questions.
7. Each learner rebuts opposing initial statement or individual in his/her pair.
8. Based on a review of all statements, comments, and questions, learners formulate personal positions.

9. The Learners post personal position statements in private forums.

By mapping these steps in a game-based e-learning environment, debating as a part of a role-play would look like:

1. a) With the narration the Instructor sets a scene i.e. a context of the situation and introduces the debate topic.
   b) The Instructor selects controversial topic (with or without input from learners, as preferred).
2. The Instructor divides class into teams (2 or more) based on the topic scenario.
3. The Instructor defines and assigns player roles or the learners choose their own.
4. a) Each Player/Learner researches its role.
   b) Subsequently the Learner posts initial position statements from the viewpoint of their role.
5. The Learners review all initial position statements of each team.
6. The Learners each take a position within their team based on their individual role.
7. The Learners research and discuss, post statements and provide input to private team forums.
8. a) Based on a review of all statements, information, and questions, learners formulate individual positions based on their roles and within their teams.
   b) Team leaders summarize the team position via chat and/or videoconference and confront other teams with their arguments and proposed options.
9. a) The Team leaders post team position statements in public forums.
   b) Learners responsible for specific topics debate with other team/s via chat and/or videoconference.
10. The Instructor or team leaders decide if an agreement has been reached, who has won or if a win-win agreement was elaborated.

Critics suggest that an e-learning platform cannot be compared with a game, as it does not include the extensive graphical environment that game players have come to expect. However, Pivec (2009) concluded that the majority of players perceive compelling game-play as more important than rich graphics. Jenkins (2007) argues that game players see past the eye candy of modern games and look for the affordances that allow them to progress through the objectives. With mapping of e-learning debate activities to a role-play game-based environment we have shown that interaction and participation can be activity rich, inspiring and very intense. Hence a game-based e-learning platform can provide an environment that takes advantage of the motivational and immersive properties of games, yet with the features and facilities of an e-learning system.

Considerations for Online platforms

Online role-plays can be achieved without using a purpose built platform. Scenarios can be played using email, online forums, and Video conferencing software such as Skype. However, these applications will have limitations that may impact on the learning outcomes of the game. *Table 1* shown below, compares some of the features that need to be considered for an online collaborative role-play.

The Training Room platform (2009) offers an environment where trainers can define there own on-line role playing scenarios and provide the opportunity for learners to apply factual knowledge and to gain experience through the digital world. Trainers can define new games or adopt and modify sample games without any programming skills. The platform provides a variety of communication means within the scenarios; players can communicate with the use of discussion forums, text and voice chat modules as well as through multi-user video conferencing. An important feature of this product is the collaborative learning design, which allows participants to exchange information as

Table 1. Online role-play platform comparison.

	Freely Available S/W				Purpose Built Platforms		
	Email Only	Open source Forum	Email & Forum	Email, Forum, & Skype	UWA Simulation Builder	Fablusi™	The Training Room™
Online Administration Tool					✓	✓	✓
Allow Learners to customize roles						✓	✓
Anonymity of Learners						✓	✓
Collaboration between Teams	✓				✓	✓	✓
Separate Role communications		✓	✓	✓	✓	✓	✓
Role Specific Access Rights					✓	✓	✓
Role Specific Resources	✓		✓	✓	✓	✓	✓
Team Specific Resources					✓	✓	✓
Audio/Video Resource upload							✓
Multimedia Resource Library							✓
Multiple Meeting Places						✓	✓
Private Communication between Roles	✓		✓	✓	✓	✓	✓
Private Chat by invitation				✓		✓	✓
Always available Team Chat Rooms							✓
Always available Public Chat Room							✓
Audio/Video Chat				✓			✓
Audio/Video Conferencing							✓
Public Multi-user Whiteboard							✓
Team Multi-user Whiteboard							✓
Separate Debriefing Area		✓	✓	✓	✓	✓	✓
Online logs for Debrief session		✓	✓	✓	✓	✓	✓
Online Feedback for Learners							✓
Online Feedback for Trainers							✓
Modification of Scenario during Game	✓	✓	✓	✓	✓	✓	✓
Modification of Roles during Game	✓	✓	✓	✓	✓		✓
Automated Timer for Game phases							✓
Role Assessment Tools						✓	✓
Team Assessment Tools						✓	✓
Multiple Games with Same Scenario						✓	✓
Customization for reuse						✓	✓
Database of Learners for future Scenarios							✓
Online repository for Scenario Sharing							✓
Personalized Scenario Creation (by Contract)						✓	✓

A Collaborative e-Learning Platform

well as to produce ideas, simplify problems, and resolve the tasks. In this product, the trainer can be an active partner, trainer and advisor of the educational process, or take a passive role and just observe.

The trainer or instructor defines the overall game theme either by selecting an already existing theme or creating a new one. Playing time can fluctuate from several days to many weeks and depends from the difficulty of the theme and basic skills of the learners. The overall game theme can be seen as setting the scene of the role-play. Game flow and various stages of the game are presented to the players in the form of an introduction. The introduction can be based on narration and extended with a variety of multimedia material e.g. clips of news reports, interviews, newspaper articles, public opinion polls, and similar. In the game, basic stages can be distinguished as follows: (i) introduction to the game and role assignment, (ii) teamwork: team preparation and research time, (iii) general discussion, (iv) player feedback, and (v) discussion of the game in the debriefing room. All rooms are presented in the form of a multi-user Flash based system and allow for access from any computer with an internet connection and browser software.

In order to play a game, learners are assigned into or form several teams. Each learner can also select a particular role within a team which the can build upon and teams are able to communicate by entering the team rooms for discussions, text chat or audio/video. Each team has to create a strategy for the discussion. Each member of the team takes a subject that he/she is responsible for. Because each team has to discuss all proposed subjects, to encourage the participation and share responsibility within the team, each player is responsible for at least one subject. This player will prepare arguments for the discussion of the defined subject in the Virtual Conference Room. Every player of the team has to participate actively in a preparation for the discussion at least for one subject, preferably for more. The trainer defines

the duration of teamwork i.e. time necessary for preparation for the Virtual Conference, as well as the time allowed for each discussion.

During the teamwork phase, players develop a game strategy, collect and select valuable information and prepare for argumentation. Teams communicate and exchange information in the Team Space (Team Forum, Virtual Conference, Content Library, Player Profile). The consultant, i.e. team member responsible for the particular subject, posts a position statement on the subject and all relevant collected information into the Content Library of the Team Room. The Content Library caters for audio and video postings as well as URL bookmarking. When the search for information is completed, the team has to organize a Team common session. This session enables learners to discuss all the problems of each subject and have all information for argumentation (for the case that they choose that only one will be speaker and argue their positions in General discussion, or if any of the learners will be unable to attend discussion). At the end of the team preparation time, teams have to present their final point of view within the game platform and outline their general position.

The next phase of the game starts with allocation of the weight factors: defining the importance of each of the subjects and balancing it with the win chances. Each team has to decide which subjects are more important for them and what percentage they wish to allocate on the chance of achievement. Each team will allocate a percentage to three or more subjects depending on the scenario. This must be done within a specified time. All game time limits are displayed within the game status panel of the screen. During the game, the percentage weighting to each of the subjects can be seen by the players, but the players do not see the allocation of other teams. The trainer has all the information about allocated weighting factors of all teams.

During the general discussion, all teams meet in a Virtual Conference Room to discuss subjects within a given time. Discussions can be moderated or freeform. The platform automatically includes a bad words filter and a player kick/ban facility for the trainer if needed. The aim of discussion is to reach an agreement on each subject or goal within the scenario. In a moderated scenario, the role of a trainer is to formalize the reached agreement and to support the constructive discussion. In a free form scenario, the tutor takes a passive role. The team's score is based on whether or not agreement was reached in their favor in each topic and what percentage factor they allocated to that topic. More than one team can win the game depending on how the scenario is structured and if the trainer permits a win-win situation.

A general discussion is followed by detailed feedback from each player and debriefing is carried out within the team, and by the trainer in the Virtual Debriefing Room. Other team members provide feedback of each player's performance. The debriefing should also provide some general feedback on issues like information gathering, discussion, argumentation, consensus and some theme related issues related to consensus that has been achieved. The trainer also receives logs of player participation, along with archived forums and content libraries if requested.

Considerations for Scenario Design

There are some aspects that need to be considered when designing a collaborative role-play scenario.

1. Are there clearly articulated learning objectives within the scenario? What will be the learning outcomes from this scenario and is it obvious to the learner, what they are expected to have learnt at the end of the game? Learning objectives should always be clearly stated to avoid any confusion by the learner. Keep the number of learning outcomes small. A suggested number would be less than five for each scenario.

2. Are there clearly definable goals that can be solved? Does the learner know what is expected of them within the game and are the defined goal achievable? If the goals are too difficult, the learner will give up, or might have substantial problems at the beginning, yet if they are too easy, they will get bored and wont take the activity serious. The goals must be set to achieve the learning objectives but also be targeted at the correct level for the learner abilities.

3. Are both the learning objectives and scenario goals achievable within the given timeframe? If the game is to be played over a long period of time, it might be difficult to keep the interest of the learner. However, when the game is scheduled for a shorter period, it has to be verified that the goals and objectives are structured accordingly and are achievable within the timeframe. Can the play be divided into smaller periods of game time without losing the momentum for the learner?

4. Is the storyline able to be described adequately for the players? Often when creating a scenario, the author will have a clear picture in their head of how it all fits together, but this is sometimes difficult to transfer to the players. Feedback from the players early in the game will often tell the trainer if they understand what is to be achieved. If this is unclear, the trainer has to be able to modify or alter the scenario after the game has started by introducing new information or by changing the goals. Learners should not be allowed to fail because of misunderstanding.

5. Is there additional resource and research information available to the players? Characters, situations, and events need to be able to be researched or have additional material that the learner can access during the timeframe of the game. This can be done as an individual or group task. The research activity is one of the elements that promotes

learning within a role-play scenario.

6. Are there sufficient roles within each team for individuality and equal opportunity to participate? In any group of learners, there will always be those who lead and those who follow. Care should be taken to allow the followers opportunity to participate and contribute in discussions and activities within the scenario. Defined roles within the scenario should always have a specific purpose related to the outcome.

7. Can the workloads of players be adequately balanced? For assessment purposes, the workloads of each learner need to be balanced. If there is to be unequal workloads, individual assessment should be considered, but this will create additional work for the trainer. Workloads should be considered when creating player roles and expectations clearly stated regarding player participation.

8. Does the scenario allow for cross-team collaboration and is this desirable? Multi-player scenarios focus on collaboration within each team and often will allow for collaboration between the teams. Does the platform utilized allow for this and does it fit within the theme of the story? Will it enhance or detract from the learning outcomes? Is there a mechanism for preventing cross-team collaboration if it is decided to be undesirable? These questions should be asked while choosing the environment.

9. Does each team have sufficient power within the scenario to achieve the stated objectives? Each of the teams should have opportunity to excel within their role but there should also be equal barriers put in front of each, to ensure that the challenge is adequate. If all teams/learners perform well, a win-win situation should be allowed.

10. Is the scenario re-usable? Considerable work goes into creating a well-structured scenario. Thought should be given to opportunities to reuse the scenario for other learners. This

may not be possible if it is too tightly aligned with current events.

Additional guidelines and activities related to introducing Game-Based Learning as a supplement to traditional teaching methods, can be found in Pivec and Pivec (2008).

Collaborative Scenario Examples

As with all scenarios, storylines may be fictitious, the places, items, and/or concepts should be real. This allows the players to research the background and learn factual knowledge about the included topics.

- **Scenario One:** Project Management with an influence of Cultural Sensitivity.
- **Learning Goals:** Risk assessment and problem solving.
  - Working in multi-cultural environments.
  - Achieving project goals within given constraints.

This scenario is based on four teams, each with four or more players: (i) Team one will play as the administration or funding organization. This could be someone like UNESCO or the European Commission; the choice is up to the trainer but should fit within the environment of the players and enable them to relate to the situation. This team has provided the (ii) Team two, an educational institution, with a grant i.e. specified sum of money to deliver an educational syllabus to a remote part of a country that has neither electricity nor technology. However, the course to be delivered is based on technology and it is not feasible to re-develop the content within the given timeframe. Hence Team two has contracted (iii) Team three to deploy and install the computer systems with generators and satellite networking, team three being a technology company. However, as happens often in the commercial sector, Team three under bid the contract and does not have sufficient funds to deliver within the allocated budget.

To make matters more complicated, (iv) Team four is representing the indigenous people (choose a culture relevant to the learners environment) who will receive the technology and hence the education. Although they welcome the attention and the chance for their young people to learn, their elders require the correct protocols to be followed. This will lengthen timelines and further compound the budget problems. The funding commission (Team one) also requests publicity of the project, something that the indigenous people are opposed to.

Each team, except Team four, must have a leader, a finance administrator, a technology expert, and a cultural liaison. Other roles can be created to fit the particular setting, for example, a travel consultant, an educational specialist, a historian, etc. Team four will have a group of elders each with a specific mandate depending on the culture chosen. They may also have several young people who have returned from the city with an appreciation of business and technology, but also retain a respect for the views of the elders and their own culture.

The objective of the game is to find solutions for the following goals.

- To install all technology within budget and time.
- To deliver the funded educational syllabus (and fulfill other obligations as per contract).
- To abide by the cultural needs of the indigenous people.
- To provide the publicity requested by the commission.

The trainer may also add additional goals. Teams are permitted to allocate a defined number of points to only three of the four goals. If solutions are found and are acceptable to all teams participating in the conference, an agreement is reached and points for given for the particular goal under discussion. If solutions to all goals are agreed, then all teams get maximum points and all teams win.

For a longer and more in depth game, a real budget should be provided with specific hardware, software, and defined educational syllabus. Travel costs could be estimated and the scenario should be made as close to reality as possible. This allows for actual research and declarative knowledge to be learned by the players.

- **Scenario Two:** Problem solving within Cultural Issues.
- **Learning Goals:** Different cultures have different needs and beliefs.
  - Opinions and actions are based on history and previous experiences.
  - Concerns from all participants are equally important.

This storyline is fictitious, the places, and concepts are set in the future. However, the characters are based on popular science fiction television and movie themes, which also allows the players to research background information from many of the cult websites available.

The suggested teams would be the Shadows and the Narn, both from the Babylon 5 series created by Joseph Michael Straczynsk, the Vulcans from the Start Trek series created by Gene Roddenberry, and the Guardians, characters from Doctor Who produced by BBC Televison. It should be noted that this scenario and any other others using copyrighted characters should be provided freely and for educational use only. All references made to fictional characters does not imply ownership and all copyrights remain with the original creators.

The storyline is as follows: It is the year 1637AE (After Enlightenment). Peace and tranquility for all known life forms is possible, although there was still much work to be done within some distance galaxies. The ability to travel through hyperspace had long since joined galaxies from each corner of the known Universe, and ruling Federations had been disbanded in favor of an overseeing Moderation. This body of trainers was called the EU (Enlightened Universe) and it resided in a unique space entity called the Pooling Area – a space within hyperspace where time itself stood still and time could be changed without a paradox occurring. The Role of the EU is not to govern, but to host negotiations between life forms and seek resolutions. Membership to the EU was voluntary, but as it resided within the Pooling Area, the notion that the EU could alter events within time to meet their goals of Peace, commanded the ultimate respect.

The Pooling Area was originally inhabited by an ancient alien life known as the Shadows. With the destruction of their home planet Z'ha'dum, they sought refuge within hyperspace and vowed to seek revenge for their plight. However, war is outlawed and the Shadows now play host to the EU but have no seat on the board of Moderation. After a lifetime of oppression and subsequent war, occupation, and destruction of their homeworld, the Narn seek EU help with the re-creation of their solar system. Centuries of terraforming have made little progress and although strictly against the EU constitution, the Narn seek assistance through the changing of events within time.

The Vulcans, originally affiliated with the United Federation of Planets, joined the EU early in its conception. With their strong views on ethics and desire for universal peace, the Vulcans believed that they were needed to add a calming influence to all negotiations. Although not a distrustful race, they did have misgivings with the presence of the Shadows within the Pooling Area. The Guardians were also early members of the EU. Although still affiliated with the Council of Guardians, these lifeforms are Anthropomorphic and as such are seen to have supernatural powers. The Council of Guardians believes their role to be to balance out the forces of the universe by using either chaos or through the manipulation of time.

The Narn have requested the EU to alter time and allow the destruction of their homeworld to have never occurred. They have successfully lobbied the Guardians to back their quest and allow this one-time use of un-constitutional powers within the Pooling Area. However, the Shadows mistrust the Narns, as they believe them to be responsible for the destruction of their home planet Z'ha'dum, although they have little proof of this.

The Vulcans posses the knowledge of Genesis, an instant terraforming process which would be an answer to the Narns request, however their strong ethics and belief in allowing the passage of time to heal such issues, prevent them from using this technology. A feeling of mistrust exists between all parties and this is borne from differing cultural beliefs and historic events. However, none of the players are willing to act against the consensus of the EU. The Vulcans and the Guardians are ruling members of the EU. Neither the Shadows nor the Narn have a seat on the board of Moderation but both have a claim in the process of resolution.

Negotiations within the Pooling Area occur within a computation program called The Training Room. All participants adopt the form of Humans, a long since extinct species of humanoid. Each of the participating lifeforms will have a team of players that will present their case and lobby the other teams to achieve a consensus. All four teams will take an equal role in this negotiation. Each member of a team will adopt a role and state their case based on that role and within the team. The team leader will summarize the team's position and present this as a position statement for the start of negotiations.

Cultural differences and ethical values will need to be allowed for and some concessions may need to be considered by each participant and by the team as a whole. The Goals of the game are as follows:

- To preserve the EU constitution by not using the Pooling Area to alter events in time.
- To respect the ethics and cultural views of all participants.
- To address all perceived injustices occurring in the past.
- To resolve the request from the Narn to restore their homeworld.
- To allow the Shadows a seat on the board of Moderation.

FUTURE RESEARCH DIRECTIONS

It is envisaged that by the time this chapter is published, an online repository of reusable scenarios will have been created. Scenarios will be organized into categories promoting topics and learning outcomes for various subjects. Topics such as project management, cultural issues, workplace conflicts, event planning, crisis resolution, environmental issues, and scientific ethics will be covered.

A trial role-play course related to game industry with international participation is scheduled for late 2009, early 2010. The goals of the course are to introduce the video game industry to learners and are based on creating an educational video game concept. The course environment will depict a real life situation, where collaboration in international teams of people with various knowledge and cultural background is necessary. Innovative ideas have to be developed within certain requirements and resource constrains.

CONCLUSION

Games for learning, or serious games as they are often called, vary from single player to multiplayer games. Different types of games have different sets of features that have to be considered in respect to their application for education. For declarative knowledge, features such as content, assessment ability, and the scaffolding of levels along with time constraints, are all very important. To acquire skills, games must be session based, where atten-

tion is paid to creating an immersive environment, this enabling an enhanced learning. In the area of decision-making and problem solving, games should be narrative based where chance is a factor, accurate in the problem descriptions, with background knowledge of the content being vital to successful completion. Role-play games and simulations provide ideal and safe environments for learning and gathering experience. If learning is defined as the acquisition of knowledge or skills through experience, practice, or study, and learning outcomes are the knowledge, skills and abilities that the learner will possess following the learning experience, then scenario based role-play games can be successfully used as supplement to traditional teaching.

The application of collaborative role-play for learning provides an opportunity for learners to apply acquired knowledge and to experiment, get feedback in form of consequences thus getting the experiences in the "safe virtual world". In interdisciplinary learning domains where skills such as critical thinking, debating and decision-making, i.e. ability to work, communicate and achieve set goals in teams are in the foreground, Game-Based Learning concepts and approaches have a high learning value.

When choosing appropriate environment for game-based e-learning, it is important to support multiple modes of communication and collaboration within and outside the groups. The environment should also foster structured reflection and allow the learner to take responsibility for participation thus promoting learning.

REFERENCES

Akilli, G. K. (2007). Games and Simulations: A new approach in Education? In Gibson, D., Aldrich, C., & Prensky, M. (Eds.), *Games and Simulations in Online Learning: Research and Development Frameworks* (pp. 1–20). Hershey, PA: Information Science Publishing.

Butler, T. J. (1988). Games and simulations: Creative educational alternatives. *TechTrends*, (September): 20–24. doi:10.1007/BF02771190

Cummings, J. A. (2000). *Debate in the virtual classroom*. Unpublished manuscript, Indiana University at Bloomington, Bloomington, IN.

Donchin, E. (1989). The learning strategies project. *Acta Psychologica, 71*, 1–15. doi:10.1016/0001-6918(89)90002-4

Entertainment and Leisure Software Publishers Association. (2006). *Unlimited Learning; Computer and Video Games in the Learning Landscape*. Retrieved from http://www.elspa.com/assets/files/u/unlimitedlearningtheroleofcomputerand-videogamesint_344.pdf

Facer, K., Ulicsak, M., & Sandford, R. (2007*)*. Can computer games go to school? In *Emerging technologies 2007, BECTA*. Retrieved May 12, 2007 from www.becta.org.uk

Federation of American Scientists. (2006, October 25th). Harnessing the Power of Video Games for Learning. In *Proceedings of the Summit on Educational Games*, Washington DC.

Fortugno, N., & Zimmerman, E. (2005). *Learning to Play to Learn - Lessons in Educational Game Design*. Retrieved 8 July 2008, from http://www.gamasutra.com/features/20050405/zimmerman_01.shtml

Garris, R., Ahlers, R., & Driskell, J. E. (2002). Games, motivation, and learning: A research and practice model. *Simulation & Gaming, 33*(4), 441–467. doi:10.1177/1046878102238607

Gentile, D. A. (2005). *The psychology behind video games as excellent teachers: A dimensional approach*. Paper presented at the 91W EMS/Department of combat medical training education conference, San Antonio, TX.

Jenkins, H. (2007). Keynote presented at the Games in Action Conference, Gothenburg, Sweden.

Kearney, P., & Pivec, M. (2007). Recursive loops of game based learning. *In Proceedings of World Conference on Educational Multimedia, Hypermedia and telecommunications* 2007 Vancouver BC, Canada, 2007, (pp. 2546 – 2553).

Kearney, P. R. (2006). Immersive environments: What can we learn from commercial computer games. In Pivec, M. (Ed.), *Affective and emotional aspects of human-computer interaction: Emphasis on game-based and innovative learning approaches*. Amsterdam: IOS Press BV.

Kelly, H. (2005). Games, cookies, and the future of education. *Issues in Science and Technology, 21*(4), 33–40.

Klopfer, E. (2008). *Augmented Learning; Research and Design of Mobile Educational Games*. Cambridge, MA: The MIT Press.

Learner-centered psychological principles revised. (1996). *Newsletter for Educational Psychologists, 19*(2), 10.

Levy, F., & Murnane, R. (2004). *The New Division of Labor: How Computers are Creating the Next Job Market*. Princeton, NJ: Princeton University Press.

Linser, R. (2008) The Magic Circle – Game Design Principles and Online Role-Play Simulations. In *Proceedings of World Conference on Educational Multimedia, Hypermedia and telecommunications 2008* Vienna, Austria, 2008, (pp. 5290 - 5297).

MacMahan, A. (2003). Immersion, engagement, and presence: A method for analysing 3-d video games. In Wolf, M. J. P., & Perron, B. (Eds.), *The video game theory reader* (pp. 67–86). New York: Routledge.

Malone, T. W. (1981). What makes video games fun? *Byte, 6*(12), 258–277.

Malone, T. W., & Lepper, M. R. (1987). *Aptitude, learning and instruction iii: Cognitive and affective process analysis*. Hillsdale, NJ: Lawrence Erlbaum Associates.

McGrenere, J. (1996). *Design: Educational Electronic Multi-player Games – A Literature Review*. Technical Report 96-12, the University of British Columbia. Retrieved on 27 June 2003.http://www.cs.ubc.ca/nest/egems/papers/desmugs.pdf

Menn, D. (1993) Multimedia in Education: Arming Our Kids For the Future. *PC World, 11*(October).

Paras, B., & Bizzocchi, J. (2005). Game, motivation, and effective learning: An integrated model for educational game design. *Digital Games Research Association 2005 Conference: Changing views- worlds in play, Vancouver, 16 - 20 June 2005*. Vancouver, Canada: Digital Games Research Association.

Pillay, H. (2003). An investigation of cognitive processes engaged in by recreational computer game players: Implications for skills of the future. *Journal of Research on Technology in Education, 34*(3), 336–350.

Pivec, M., & Pivec, P. (2008). Designing and implementing a game in an educational context. In Pivec, M., & Moretti, M. (Eds.), *Discover the Pleasure of Learning - Guidelines on Game-Based Learning*. Pabst.

Pivec, P. (2009). Presentation at the Game-Based Learning Conference, London.

Project Tomorrow. (2008). *Speak Up 2007 for Students, Teachers, Parents & School Leaders Selected National Findings - April 8, 2008*. Retrieved from http://www.tomorrow.org/docs/National Findings Speak U 202007.pdf

Ramsberger, P. F., Hopwood, D., Hargan, C. S., & Underhill, W. G. (1983). *Evaluation of a spatial data management system for basic skills education. Final phase 1 report for period 7 october 1980– 30 april 1983*. Alexandria, VA: Human Resources Research Organization.

Rosser, J. C., Lynch, P. J., Cuddihy, L., Gentile, D. A., Klonsky, J., & Merrell, R. (2007). The impact of video games on training surgeons in the 21st century. *Archives of Surgery, 142*(2), 181–186. doi:10.1001/archsurg.142.2.181

Ruben, B. D. (1999). Simulations, games, and experience-based learning: The quest for a new paradigm for teaching and learning. *Simulation & Gaming, 30*, 498–505. doi:10.1177/104687819903000409

Salen, L., & Zimmerman, E. (2003). *Rules of Play, Game Design Fundamentals* (pp. 80–94). Cambridge, MA: The MIT Press.

Salmon, G. (2002). E-tivities: the key to active online learning. *American Philosophy of Science, 24*, 148–156.

Shaffer, D. W. (2006). *How video games help children learn*. New York: Palgrave Macmillan. doi:10.1057/9780230601994

The Training Room. (2009). Retrieved February 29, 2009, from http://www.gamedesigncampus.com

Thomas, P., & Macredie, R. (1994). Games and the design of human-computer interfaces. *Educational Technology, 31*(2), 134–142.

Wainess, R. (2007). The potential of games & simulations for learning and assessment. In *2007 CRESST Conference: The Future of Test-based Educational Accountability*, Los Angeles, CA.

ADDITIONAL READING

Kearney, P., & Pivec, M. (2007). *Immersed and how? That is the question.* Gothenburg, Sweden: Games in Action.

Pivec, M. (Ed.). (2006) Affective and emotional aspects of human-computer interaction; Game-Based and Innovative Learning Approaches. Vol.1: The Future of Learning (IOS Press, 2006), ISBN 1-58603-572-x

Pivec, M., & Moretti, M. (Eds.). (2008) Discover the Pleasure of Learning - Guidelines on Game- Based Learning. Pabst Vrlg. ISBN 978-3-89967-521-4

Pivec, M., & Pivec, P. (2008a). Playing to Learn: Guidelines for Designing Educational Games. Proceedings of *World Conference on Educational Multimedia, Hypermedia and telecommunications 2008* Vienna, Austria, 2008, pp. 3247 - 3252

Pivec, M., & Pivec, P. (2009) Misconceptions about being Digital. Chapter in Zheng R. (Ed.): Adolescent Online Social Communication and Behavior: Relationship Formation on the Internet. (In press, 2009)

Pivec, P., & Pivec, M. (2008b) Games in Schools. Commissioned report for Interactive Software Federation of Europe (ISFE) by the European Commission (EC). Retrieved November 30, 2008, from http://www.isfe.eu/

Chapter 26
ExerLearning®:
Movement, Fitness, Technology and Learning

Judy Shasek
ExerLearning

ABSTRACT

ExerLearning® provides parents, educators and others with a solid background of the direct connection between regular, rhythmic aerobic activity, balance, eye-foot coordination and academic success. We can increase students' fitness while simultaneously increasing their academic success. Activity breaks have been shown to improve cognitive performance and promote on-task classroom behavior. Today's exergame and related computer technology can seamlessly deliver activity without over-burdening busy teachers in grades K-12. Activity isn't optional for humans, and our brain, along with its ability to learn and function at its best, isn't a separate "thing" perched in our heads. The wiring, the circulation, the connection between mind and body is very real. The brain is made up of one hundred billion neurons that chat with one another by way of hundreds of different chemicals. Physical activity can enhance the availability and delivery of those chemicals. Harnessing technology to that activity is the ExerLearning solution.

READING, WRITING AND EXERGAMES?

Our lifestyles have become ever more sedentary with screens – television, computer and video game – being used for leisure, entertainment, communication, information and a pervasive social-networking culture. With only so much time in the school day it's tough to fit in physical activity, balance training and fitness to counter "screen" time. Research has been done by many independent and university researchers over the past decade. There is adequate evidence on the positive benefits of physical fitness on academic success and cognitive skills. We developed specific ExerLearning strategies that can tap into computer and game technology to easily become an integral part of the school environment.

DOI: 10.4018/978-1-61520-781-7.ch026

What is ExerLearning? It is a technology-delivered intervention that interrupts the sedentary practice of learning and classroom procedure. ExerLearning challenges sitting, a desk and conventional computer input devices as the default – or the best – route to cognitive skill development and academic success. According to Dr. John Ratey, author of "Spark – The Revolutionary New Science of exercise and the Brain" says, "Darwin taught us that learning is the survival mechanism we use to adapt to constantly changing environments." ExerLearning adds physical activity known to enhance the workings of the brain to learning.

- ExerLearning can be delivered by technology
- ExerLearning can be led and managed by students
- Technology delivered solutions like exergames and computer peripherals that require standing, balance and rhythmic movement improve students' fitness while simultaneously increasing their academic success.
- ExerLearning meets the needs of the most challenged, challenging or diverse learners without requiring teachers to write additional lesson plans
- ExerLearning sessions should occur for approximately 10 minutes every few hours.

Over-scheduled teachers and over-scheduled school days beg the question, "When will we have time to add 15-45 minutes of daily – or even weekly – physical activity? Preparing healthy, active children for life has taken a backseat to preparing the K-12 student for standardized tests. Educators have been mandated to address both the fitness **and** the test-score issues, but they need help.

Key Concept: In order to add more activity to the learning environment we can tap into technology that can add exactly the sort of physical activity students need and deliver it simultaneously with core content. ExerLearning tackles fitness and academic goals simultaneously-while saving teachers' time – and Districts' money. ExerLearning engages the very students we target while harnessing computer technology to consistently deliver any time any where rhythmic, aerobic activity.

There is an endless list of factors that impact a student's academic achievement. Among those, maybe the one least understood is the impact of regular physical activity. Throughout the development of ExerLearning concepts and practices, research on the benefits of regular rhythmic, aerobic and balance activity has been explored. Today's brain-scanning tools and a sophisticated understanding of biochemistry have led researchers to realize that the mental effects of exercise are far more profound and complex than they once thought.

"Exercise optimizes the brain and the person for learning. It creates the right environment for all of our 100 billion nerve cells up there. Exercise promotes the growth of new brain cells more than anything else we know," says Dr. Ratey. Ratey cites studies showing that exercise promotes the growth of new cells in the hippocampus, an area in the brain associated with memory and learning.

That's just the beginning. This chapter will weave facts and findings from brain research, innovative PE programs, unique peripherals that tie technology to physical activity and solid academic research on learning and test success. Our goal is to provide a solid overview of ExerLearning's potential in K-12 learning environments. Why did we coin the term, ExerLearning? As we work with educators, students, parents and wellness/learning advocates in dozens of states and hundreds of school Districts, we have found that having a vocabulary to explain this ground-breaking work is very important.

ExerLearning allows educators to reach academic goals while integrating aerobic exercise, balance, eye-foot coordination and agility to the learning environment. Physical activity does not have to be restricted to the gym. We love PE and welcome all a school can deliver. Budgets and philosophies differ across the country and there is no denying that we are not meeting PE mandates even in the 44 states where they have been set. Until adequate budgets, schedules, time and resources are allocated so educators can offer students daily, regular physical activity sessions ExerLearning can be a technology-delivered solution. Educators can choose ExerLearning interventions that deliver students prepared to learn via cost and time-effective choices. There is a wide array of products and programs that can provide ExerLearning.

No matter what a school District's stance on standardized testing, it is time for most test-prep practices to get a boost. An extraordinary amount of time and budget dollars are invested in test-prep materials and practices that, sadly, leave many students in a constant of failure. Our current efforts at raising performance for the 30% most challenged and challenging of our students remains frustrating for all. We hope to provide the case for meeting them where their needs and learning style intersect:

- Provide movement during academic work right at the computer using educational software and learning games already integrated in a school's curriculum. Many exergames and FootGaming™ via the FootPOWR™ peripheral can do that.
- Decrease negative behaviors and increase attendance (28% on average – teacher reporting)
- Prepare the brain to learn via the very process and physical development the brain was meant to experience during cognitive tasks

How Can a Teacher Add Exerlearning to the Regular Classroom Environment?

Exergames are video games that use exertion-based interfaces to promote physical activity, fitness, and gross motor skill development. Wii FIT and Wii Sports, Dance Dance Revolution stations, balance balls instead of chairs, FootPOWR computer peripherals instead of the conventional mouse, game cycles and similar exergames can all deliver physical activity that our brains need. The unique aspect of these unusual learning tools is that they consistently deliver endless customizable, compelling, fun and multi-level activity via technology.

In a classroom, students want to play the exergames. The built-in "fun-factor" is useful for teachers. In a very short time students can be taught a summary of brain research connecting physical activity to many benefits deemed valuable by students. Once the students realize that the exergame is not simply a reward for work completed or a diversionary toy, they respect it in new ways.

The next step is for teachers to take the time to develop a set of expect behaviors around the use of the exergames. An effective strategy has been used through a student-led ExerLearning program, Generation FIT, in more than 200 schools over the past five years (http://www.generation-fit.com). The 30% most challenged or challenging students are trained to lead and manage peers in groups of 2-3 using the exergame available in class. Leadership, providing a valuable service, the actual impact of the exergame practice and the understanding of related brain research all serve to positively impact these targeted students.

The student mentors rotate to the exergame stations in a classroom as it suits the teacher. Ideally, the students will enjoy one or more 10-15 minute

ExerLearning breaks throughout the school day. Before a particularly difficult assignment, at the completion of a contracted amount of work, or when frustration, stress or other negative emotion threatens to undermine a student's best learning an ExerLearning session can be assigned.

When exergames or unique activity-driven peripherals are added to the classroom the novelty may attract attention from non-participating students. Consistent adherence to expected behaviors is important. In most cases students who need a consequence for unacceptable behavior around the exergaming activity will change quickly when their ExerLearning break is cancelled and they are positioned at the end of the student rotation.

Why Add ExerLearning to the Regular Classroom Environment

Physical activity enhances a student's ability to pay attention. According to Charles Hillman and Darla Castelli (2009), professors of kinesiology and community health at the Neurocognitive Kinesiology Laboratory at Illinois, "physical activity may increase students' cognitive control -- or ability to pay attention -- and also result in better performance on academic achievement tests." The goal of the study was to see if a single acute bout of moderate exercise was beneficial for cognitive function in a period of time afterward.

For each of three testing criteria, researchers noted a positive outcome linking physical activity, attention and academic achievement. Study participants were 9-year-olds (eight girls, 12 boys) who performed a series of stimulus-discrimination tests known as flanker tasks, to assess their inhibitory control. Following the acute bout of walking, children performed better on the flanker task. They had a higher rate of accuracy, especially when the task was more difficult. Along with that behavioral effect there were changes in their event-related brain potentials (ERPs) – in these neuroelectric signals that are a covert measure of attentional resource allocation.

In an effort to see how performance on such tests relates to actual classroom learning, researchers next administered an academic achievement test. The test measured performance in three areas: reading, spelling and math. The researchers noted better test results following exercise. The following should bring smiles to the faces of hard-working teachers concerned about reading achievement and scores.

"When we assessed it, the effect was largest in reading comprehension," Hillman said. In fact, he said, "If you go by the guidelines set forth by the Wide Range Achievement Test, **the increase in reading comprehension following exercise equated to approximately a full grade level.**"

It's not easy for busy teachers to add physical activity required for this type of benefit. Harnessing technology to deliver easily quantified and measured activity data, we suggest ExerLearning. Computer and console delivered exergames can be a valuable learning tool, particularly the easy-to-implement FootPOWR computer peripheral. It makes good sense to harness software and computers already in the classroom for integrating physical activity into the curriculum.

Fit to Learn?

According to a CDC survey (2003), only 3.8 percent of elementary schools, 7.9 percent of middle schools and 2.1 percent of high schools provide daily physical education. A study published in the 2007 issue of Health Economics stated that daily P.E. for high school students declined from 41.6 percent in 1991 to 28.4 percent in 2003. (The survey did not have statistics for middle and elementary schools.)

- 22 percent of schools don't require kids to take any P.E.
- Nearly half -- 46 percent -- of high school students were not attending any P.E. classes when surveyed by the CDC.

In more than 44 states, mandates to provide more physical education are being flouted due to lack of time, space, or competition from academic requirements. Research indicates again and again that schools that don't offer enough P.E. are "cheating" children. *Active Living Research* (ALR) a national program of the Robert Wood Johnson Foundation in an article called, "Active Education" (2007) found that, although more than one-third of U.S. children and teens are considered overweight or obese, schools are increasingly replacing physical education with academic coursework in their push to improve standardized test scores.

However, the report points out that decreased P.E. time is not associated with improved academic performance. In fact, the report indicates:

- Children who are physically active tend to perform at higher levels in the classroom and on standardized tests.
- In addition, active students exhibit fewer behavior problems and better concentration skills.

According to Jerry Gabriel (2001), a "growing body of research [suggests] that physical activity is integral to keeping cognitive processes working on all valves" (p.3). Current educational practices were developed in the early 19th century well before any of the brain research existed. It's time for a change.

On average, the PE mandate requires 150 minutes per week for all elementary students and 225 for middle and high school students. The budgetary support for this mandate spans "not enough" to "next to nothing." Some schools have stretched the "physical activity" point so far that they count the time children use to move from class to class – calling it 30 minutes per day and their fulfillment of the mandate. The impetus for doing that is as understandable as it is pathetic. Sometimes there seems to be no other viable solution.

What are over-scheduled, busy teachers to do? Our reply is, empower tomorrow's fitness and tech-leaders today. Make use of the time, energy and expertise of your students now. Budgets are tight and such increases are not being funded or enforced as needed. Teachers are busy and the school day is already over-scheduled. Technology tools and unique peripherals like the FootPOWR pads can enhance computer technology while saving teachers time and delivering valuable physical activity to students. The concepts behind ExerLearning are ones that we can wrap our minds around. We can begin to connect the dots on strategies that make good sense for lots of students, especially the most challenged and challenging ones.

What if You Knew That Physical Activity Actually Enhanced Academic Success?

While the sedentary habits of our youth are conclusively adding to the overweight crisis, we argue that not including regular and daily physical activity breaks also short-changes the **productivity, focus and chance for academic success we're working so hard to deliver**. Consider this: **exercise and balance- activity practice has been shown to directly improve students' cognitive development and academic achievement.** This adds a new dimension to the rationale we hold when we define "what is learning?"

The greatest limitation to the addition of physical activity to the learning environment is over-scheduled and over busy teachers. School schedules are full and test-prep takes preference in terms of time and scheduling. The recent development of the FootPOWR pad, a computer peripheral that can do anything a mouse can do, add activity simultaneously with learning outcomes and seamlessly integrates into the classroom.

What's a FootPOWR Peripheral?

FootPOWR pads look like the dance mats conventionally used in dance video games. The similarity ends there. Added FootPOWR microcontrollers turn the dance mat into a computer peripheral that can do anything a mouse can do. You simply plug the pad into the computer USB port, stand on the pad and move your feet to move the cursor. Suddenly many existing educational software games and hundreds of other software can become physical activity and balance generating interactive tools for your students. By re-inventing the computer "controller" from a mouse or keyboard used while sitting, to a dance-mat type tool that requires rhythmic activity and balance we can positively and easily impact learning and the needs of diverse learners.

Evidence that physical activity affects the brain in ways that improve learning has been mounting from the fields of molecular, cognitive, behavioral, and systems neuroscience, psychology, and directly from field studies performed in schools. That information inspired the development of Generation FIT over five years and led to the development of the FootPOWR pad. Teachers need easy to use tools that deliver results. Schools need fitness tools that can be obtained via reading, math, Title I and technology budgets when PE budgets are not enough. Bridging budgets to deliver physical activity right on the classroom makes sense for both learning and health outcomes.

Imagine how well an educator can do what he or she does best teaching and facilitating in a learning environment - when all students are *prepared to learn both mentally and physically.* ExerLearning breaks throughout the day can deliver exactly that. When students in the ExerLearning program called, Generation FIT, (http://www.generation-fit.com) lead and managed the use of exergames during the learning day we found that participants:

- reduced absenteeism by 28%
- Increased leisure reading
- Reduced negative behaviors, frustration and improved mood
- Gained confidence and social/teamwork skills

Programs like Generation FIT and FootGaming which deliver physical activity for a healthy body *and mind* are crucial, especially for the most challenged learners. The mind-body connection is well-known and widely noted. Time and time again research has proven that children who are physically fit score higher on standardized math and English tests than do their less fit peers.

A study, led by Virginia R. Chomitz, PhD (2009), found a significant relationship between physical fitness and academic performance. She and her team examined the test scores of over 1,000 children enrolled in grades 4 to 8 for the 2004 to 2005 academic year. Looking at two sets of figures—the MCAS test (Massachusetts Comprehensive Assessment System test) and physical fitness tests—Chomitz and her fellow researchers found that the likelihood of passing the academic tests improved as the number of fitness tests increased, even when controlling for gender, race/ethnicity, and socio-economic status.

How Can Educators Inject More Sensorimotor Experience Into the Regular Classroom, in After School Programs and at Home?

In times of diminishing financial resources, educators must make hard choices.

- Do dance, recess, exercise breaks and physical education belong in the budget? Are they frills or fundamentals?
- When classroom teachers are over-scheduled and busier than ever is there time for movement, exercise and dance in the regular classroom learning environment?
- We need to invest in test prep strategies, reading interventions, behavior modification and meeting the needs of students with diverse learning styles?
- Students must acquire content and technology skills via increased time interacting with 'screens" – how can we add the

physical activity and fitness factors they need to best succeed?

Physical Education, Daily Activity and Learning

As mentioned earlier in this chapter, an astonishingly high percent of K-12 American students do not participate in a daily physical education program. That is not the case at Naperville Central High School (NCHS) where PE4Life founder, Phil Lawler, and Paul Zientarsky have re-invented the process of preparing students to learn. According to Zientarsky (2007), "In our department, we create the brain cells. It's up to the other teachers to fill them up." Go ahead, read that again. It's *powerful* stuff. Research meets reality under the heroic leadership of Phil Lawler and Paul Zientarsky in the Naperville, IL school district.

Results and Outcomes

- Students are more focused and energized in class
- Increased confidence and engagement in the learning process
- Test scores improve
- Students and teachers have an understanding of the physiology, brain research and kinesiology behind the effects – and that made all the difference!

NCHS LRPE = MIND and BODY CONNECTION Learning Readiness Physical Education (LRPE) was designed based on research indicating that students who are physically active and fit are more academically alert and experience growth in brain cells or enhancement in brain development; NCHS pairs a PE class that incorporates cardiovascular exercise, core strength training, cross lateral movements and literacy and math strategies with literacy and math classes that utilizes movement to enhance learning and improve achievement.

LRPE students have experienced notable gains in their reading ability and comprehension as well as improvement in math and other courses. Starting their day with physical workouts seems to be "waking up" their brains. The study incorporated in this project is providing the justification for expanding the program so many more students can experience the improvements and achievements of the original group.

Naperville Central High has embraced the premise of ExerLearning with full support of Reading, Math and PE teachers, District budgets and parents. Such a comprehensive program did not happen overnight and every school may not be ready for such an investment just yet. FootGaming is one way to test the waters, so to speak. It could move your students toward the sort of gains made by the LRPE students in Naperville.

Research and recent "Learning Readiness PE" (LRPE) classes at Naperville Central High (IL) indicate that physical activity can impact student performance enough to elevate test scores. "We're putting kids in P.E. class prior to a classes that they struggle in and what we're doing is we're finding great, great results," said Paul Zientarski, who helps run LRPE program at Naperville Central High School. The program was started in response to research showing a link between exercise and increased brain function. He says that he has seen the results.

"Kids who took P.E. before they took the math class had **double the improvement** of kids who had P.E. afterward," Zientarski, explained. (P. Zientarski, personal communication, May, 2009). Naperville Central High School has embraced the idea that working out helps a child learn. There you can find exercise equipment, including Foot-POWR peripherals, in some classrooms.

"Their bodies are moving and their brains are thinking and they're engaged - not sitting still trying to memorize something," said Maxyne Kozil, a reading teacher, who believes that kids learn best when they're moving. An example of this is having a student work on her vocabulary while standing on balance boards. "They say having to balance actually helps them to concentrate even better," Kozil said.

It is time for our test-prep practices to get a boost. Our current efforts at raising performance for the 30% most challenged and challenging of our students remains frustrating for all. We hope to provide the case for meeting these students where their needs and learning style intersect:

- Provide movement during academic work right at the computer using educational software, interactive peripherals that require physical activity and exergames
- Provide leadership and collaborative practice for students in need of confidence and social skills
- Decrease negative behaviors and increase attendance (28% on average-teacher reporting)
- Prepare the brain to learn via the very process the brain was meant to experience during cognitive tasks

Do Physical Activity and Physical Education Interfere With Academics?

In many states physical education is done away with because "academic classes" are considered more important. Importance being "you get what you measure" and we measure reading and math scores far more than fitness and wellness choices our students make. A two year study in San Diego that examined standardized test scores revealed that students having a physical education class outperformed those that did not (1992). Researchers have demonstrated that physical activity improves brain function, elevates mood, and promotes learning. Exercise improves blood flow to the brain and spurs cell growth, leading some to compare the brain to a muscle which performs best when the body exercises.

Teachers and administrators are working harder than ever to provide what each student needs to be a successful learner while making the most of skills, aptitudes and learning styles. A variety of funding sources for academics, including No Child Left Behind (NCLB) are being used to their maximum. But are we impacting the students who need it most by implementing strategies that shift the paradigm of what "test prep" and learning look like? Unless regular physical activity breaks are included in the learning environment we are shortchanging cognitive success, focus and productivity.

Activity Breaks Can Improve Cognitive Performance and Classroom Behavior.

As referenced time and again in this chapter, many studies involving elementary students, regular physical activity breaks during the school day may enhance academic performance. Introducing physical activity has been shown to improve cognitive performance and promote on-task classroom behavior. During our field testing of Generation in Central Oregon elementary schools we found that students exhibited significantly more on-task behavior and significantly less fidgeting on days with a scheduled activity break than on non activity days. This isn't just a case of a distracting insertion of random "playtime." Short activity breaks during the school day can improve students' concentration skills and classroom behavior.

Judy Shasek, author of this article and developer of Generation FIT and FootGaming, discovered that students as young as age 8 are eager to learn exactly *why* regular aerobic activity and balance practice helps a brain to be more productive, to increase BDNF and neurotransmitters and to help them focus. During field studies, we used a simple PowerPoint slideshow called, "Brainy Stuff" (2009). With it and others created by students, hundreds of students have shared complicated brain research with peers and teachers. For many struggling students it is a major relief to understand why learning is often such a struggle and how they can do something that actually **enjoy** to increase their academic success (and often their behavior). Many challenged learners are relieved to discover that their lack of "sit still and focus" is linked to a real, physical and brain-driven need to move on a regular basis throughout the learning day. Once we harness technology to deliver that movement practice in an orderly and seamless manner everyone is happier

What Does the Research Say?

A cross-sectional study conducted in 2002 by the California Department of Education demonstrated a strong association between physical fitness and academic performance. Using the Fitnessgram®, a six-faceted measure of overall physical fitness, and students' grades on the SAT-9 state standardized test, nearly one million students in grades five, seven, and nine were evaluated. The consistent finding: not only did those with higher levels of physical fitness score higher on the SAT-9, but there was a positive linear relationship between the number of fitness standards achieved and academic achievement. This result held for boys and girls in both math and reading, but was most pronounced in math. The same study found:

- Ten minutes of rhythmic aerobic exercise before a cognitive task (like reading or math) resulted in better success at that task
- Students who did 10 minutes of rhythmic aerobics before a standardized test, did up to 25% better at that test than students who received 20 minutes of test-specific tutoring.
- School-age children who have a higher level of aerobic fitness processed information more efficiently

Even when time allocated to other subjects is reduced, shifting more curricular time toward physical activity does not negatively affect aca-

demic achievement. In one such study (2003), a reduction of two-hundred forty minutes per week of class time, replaced with increased PE, led to higher scores on standardized math examinations. As we review studies that assessed the association between physical activity and academic outcomes among school-aged children, we conclude that there is evidence to suggest that short term cognitive benefits of physical activity during the school day adequately compensate for time spent away from other academic areas" According to Dr. Debbye Turner Bell (2009), researchers are finding that exercise can do more than keep you fit; it can also make you smarter.

"Exercise in many ways optimizes your brain to learn," said Dr. John Ratey (2008), a clinical associate professor of psychiatry at Harvard Medical School in Boston, author of "Spark." Exercise improves circulation throughout the body, including the brain, Ratey explains. Exercise also boosts metabolism, decreases stress and improves mood and attention, all of which help the brain perform better, he said.

"The brain cells actually become more resilient and more pliable and are more ready to link up," he says. It's this linking up that allows us to retain new information. Much of the research on the specific effects of exercise on neurons has been done in the lab. But studies in people also are backing physical activity as a way to keep the brain healthy and our minds sharp.

The research is profoundly relevant to today's health and fitness crisis. At the same time the fitness-overweight dilemma is growing, funding for programs like physical education in schools are being reduced or eliminated. Kids are spending an average of 5.5 hours a day in front of a screen of some sort.

With ExerLearning programs integrated right in classrooms and computer labs, such activity is easy to integrate into the regular school day, not only in structured Physical Education classes. When neurons fire together they "wire together." If we already don't include words like glutamate, serotonin, norepinephrine and dopamine when we talk about learning, hopefully we soon will. ExerLearning students as young as age eight easily banter about, "increasing neurotransmitters," "sending oxygen to your brain," and BDNF as "Miracle Gro" for the brain as reasons they lead their peers in regular sessions of FootGaming and other "exergames." The very students who struggle to read at the second grade level in sixth grade, most readily absorb the ExerLearning philosophy and practice. ExerLearning programs aim to deliver many of those important outcomes for teachers and schools with limited time or budget – right now.

Mandated PE Minutes

As we mentioned earlier in this chapter, more than 44 states have mandated 150 minutes of weekly physical activity for grades K-5 and 225 minutes weekly for grades 6-12. In almost every case, no additional budget, teachers or time is added to the school program. What's a busy teacher to do when presented with this challenge? Schedules are already full and teachers are already over-extended with responsibilities and measurable outcomes in the "academic" areas. We propose that ExerLearning can help support the mandates while providing exactly the sort of physical activities kinesthetic learners and the 30% most challenged students need.

The very students who wiggle, act out, collect repeated absences and are consistently disengaged, perform best with more technology. These kinesthetic learners seem married to their "screens" and eagerly spend upwards of three hours a day playing video games. These same very challenging students could provide the solution to the over-busy teacher and not enough physical activity in the learning environment. Technology that can deliver physical activity at the same time students spend working on reading and math software in a computer lab is readily available. Not only can students gain valuable "learning time" by moving as they learn – they will gain a good measure of the mandated activity minutes.

Much research has been done to quantify the physical activity afforded by such an intervention – at little more cost that a high quality mouse. For example, consider this study, "Energy Expenditure of Sedentary Screen Time Compared With Active Screen Time for Children"(2006).

SUMMARY: The team examined the effect of activity-enhancing screen devices on children's energy expenditure compared with performing the same activities while seated. Their hypothesis was that energy expenditure would be significantly greater when children played activity-promoting video games, compared with sedentary video games. Energy expenditure was measured for 25 children aged 8 to 12 years, 15 of whom were lean, while they were watching television seated, playing a traditional video game seated, watching television while walking on a treadmill at 1.5 miles per hour, and playing activity-promoting video games.

They found that energy expenditure more than doubles when sedentary screen time is converted to active screen time. Sitting in front of a television, video game, or computer screen has been associated consistently with low levels of physical activity. Weekly screen time for children is as high as 55 hours/week, and the average home in the United States has a television on for 6 hours per day. Although many programs have attempted to separate children from the screen, these activities are highly valued and children are resistant to relinquishing them. An alternative approach is to examine whether sedentary screen time can be converted into active screen time. This is exactly what ExerLearning via FootGaming was created to do – and to do right in the home or classroom.

CONCLUSIONS. Energy expenditure more than doubles when sedentary screen time is converted to active screen time. This is the strategy upon which ExerLearning is built.

ExerLearning helps teachers by harnessing technology to the *physical activity and balance*

practice need for optimal brain function. Walking on two feet is very difficult. It takes a lot of balance, coordination, synchronization and timing of muscles. It takes a tremendous amount of motor control to be able to do that. It takes constant output from the brain and constant feedback to the brain. When we are in an upright position these receptors constantly fire back to the brain. They stimulate the brain. It appears that as humans stood in an upright position or as we became more and more upright, our brain grew larger and larger in response to this constant stimulus of gravity. Our goal in ExerLearning and its various intervention games and tools is to increase the amount of time students spend standing, moving and balancing under the influence of gravity *while they are learning*.

Decreased stimulation from postural muscles to cerebellum and brain, anything that takes us away from standing and being upright, will affect our brain in an adverse way. It will slow down the temporal processing speed of the brain, or parts of the brain, with resulting "clumsiness" and cognitive developmental delays. ExerLearning's foundation is solidly built upon the need to get students out of the desk or chair and working in an upright, standing position. Simply standing is not very inviting to most of us. Technology allows teachers add the playful fun of "exergames" accessed by controllers that require standing, movement and balance.

Balance – The ExerLearning Bonus Benefit

Everyone knows the five basic senses; seeing, hearing, taste, smell and touch. But there are other senses that are not as familiar including the sense of **movement (vestibular), and sense of muscle awareness (proprioception)**. Unorganized sensory input creates a traffic jam in our brain making it difficult to pay attention and learn. To be successful learners, our senses must work together in an organized manner. This is known as **sensory integration**. The foundation for sensory integration is the organization of tactile, **proprioceptive and vestibular input.** A person diagnosed with ADD or ADHD, due to their difficulty paying attention, may in fact have an immature nervous system causing sensory integration dysfunction. This makes it difficult for him/her to filter out nonessential information, background noises or visual distraction and focus on what is essential. There is a direct relationship between sensory integration, learning and attention.

ExerLearning technology tools, consisting of exergames and activity driven computer peripherals like the FootPOWR pad, provide the development of the vestibular sense. By providing technology delivered activities that provide balance practice students become prepared to learn. **The vestibular sense is important for development of balance, coordination, eye**

Table 1.

What does ExerLearning™ Do?	How does that happen?
ExerLearning opens up a direct channel to the brain/mind-	The mind becomes a sponge: absorption, processing, integration, retention, cognition (i.e. LEARNING) all improve.
ExerLearning gets the brain pumping	By getting the heart pumping.
The brain is muscle that can be developed through physical training	Just like the heart the brain can be strengthened via physical training.
ExerLearning adds physical movement	Utilizing the mind-body connection
ExerLearning optimizes the learning environment for diverse learners	Harnesses technology to deliver rhythmic physical activity and valuable fitness factors to the learning process
ExerLearning allows neurogenesis: growth of new brain cells	Exercise enables more blood and proteins to enter the brain

control, attention, being secure with movement, emotional security and some aspects of language development. Disorganized processing of vestibular input may be seen when someone has difficulty with attention, coordination, following directions, reading (keeping eyes focused on the page or board) or eye-hand coordination.

Ironically, the cerebellum, an area of the brain most commonly linked to movement turns out to be a virtual switchboard of cognitive activity. The first evidence of a linkage between mind and body originated decades ago with Henrietta Leiner and Alan Leiner (1997), two Stanford University neuroscientists. Their research began what would eventually redraw "the cognitive map"

The Leiners' work centered on the cerebellum, and they made some critical discoveries that spurred years of subsequent research. First, the cerebellum takes up just one-tenth of the brain by volume. But it contains over half of all its neurons. It has some 40 million nerve fibers, 40 times more than even the highly complex optical tract. Those fibers not only feed information from the cortex to the cerebellum, but they feed them back to the cortex. If this was only for motor function, why are the connections so powerfully distributed in both directions to all areas of the brain? In other words, this subsection of the brain -- long known for its role in posture, coordination, balance, and movement -- *may be the ExerLearning hub.*

Students who tip back on two legs of their chairs in class often are stimulating their brain with a rocking, vestibular-activating motion. While it's an unsafe activity, it happens to be good for the brain. We ought to give students more activities that let them move safely while practicing balance skills. Busy teachers may have difficulty planning interventions such as those but when technology and exergames are selected for classroom use students get the balance practice they need. Such interventions, ExerLearning at its best, can change the world of learning for struggling students.

In one field study using dance mat video games with a fourth grade class, an autistic student whose entire left side was affected by cerebral palsy, participated as a program mentor for 10-20 minutes per day using the dance mat changed his balance, coordination, social engagement and enthusiasm for PE. Studies done by neuroscientist Eric Courchesne (1995) of the University of California have shown that autistic children have smaller cerebellums and fewer cerebellar neurons. Courchesne says the cerebellum filters and integrates floods of incoming data in sophisticated ways that allow for complex decision making. Once again, the part of the brain known to control movement is involved in learning. Movement and learning have constant interplay.

Some of the decline in physical activity is due to schools' implementation of strategies designed to improve achievement outcomes. But the theory that spending more time learning academics in the classroom will lead to higher test scores and grades has not been proven. The more brain research is explored the more crucial physical activity proves to be for cognitive tasks. In other words, allotting too little time to physical activity may undermine the goal of better performance, while adding time for physical activity may support improved academic performance.

Children who participated in a Generation FIT-ExerLearning peer mentoring program were absent 25% fewer days than the control group.

This is a key measure and critical for decision makers in schools at local and District levels. Absenteeism costs Districts $9-$20 per student per day. In a field study done during the 2004-2005 school year at Vern Patrick Elementary (Redmond, OR), fourth graders who used Generation FIT ExerLearning peer mentoring program were absent fewer days, even during flu season, than they had been in the Fall quarter before the program was begun. They were absent 25% fewer days than other fourth graders not participating in increased daily physical activity. This caught the attention of teachers (more time in class meant more time to make an impact on the student) and District budget staff.

Health is not the only reason children miss school. The most challenged and most disengaged students find numerous and creative ways to be absent. We discovered that many students that fit such a profile made the most improvement in both attendance and engagement in the learning process after being trained as Generation FIT ExerLearning peer mentors and leaders. **Ask any teacher the ramifications of these two changes on the lowest performing students.**

With Districts budgets already tight it would pay to create a preliminary estimate of the potential impact of physical inactivity and related health factors on school funding. The *Executive Summary: Healthy Children, Healthy Schools* predicts the loss in large cities could be $28 million in New York, Chicago could forfeit $9 million and Los Angeles an estimated $15 million. So, obviously, we want our children to get and stay active!

In nine states (California, Idaho, Illinois, Kentucky, Mississippi, Missouri, new York, Tennessee and Texas) collectively serving more than one-third of all students in the US, state funding for schools is determined using the Average Daily Attendance (ADA) methodology. In other words, public education dollars in these states are determined not by how many students are enrolled, but by how many actually show up at school. Student absenteeism can therefore have a negative impact on the school's bottom line. Data from The Finance Project, a nonprofit policy research and technical assistance group, demonstrate how absenteeism can be a significant problem for school budgets. These data suggest that a single-day absence by one student costs a school district in these states anywhere between $9 and $20.

While these figures seem small, they add up quickly. An estimated 16 percent of youth are overweight to a degree that affects their health. One study found that severely overweight students miss (using the median number) one day per month or nine days per year.[1] This type of absentee rate among overweight students in a student population with average prevalence of overweight could lead to a potential loss of state aid of $95,000 per year in an average size school district in Texas, and $160,000 per year in an average California school district.

In the Vern Patrick Elementary study, additional reasons for decreased absenteeism emerged from anecdotal reporting from both students and their parents. Student mentors who managed the day to day operation of the Generation FIT ExerLearning program gained ownership of the technology-delivered game activity. Their foray into ExerLearning included a leadership/peer mentoring piece that changed their attitudes about school attendance and their engagement in the learning process when they were at school. Increased daily attendance by students who were among the most challenged learners were part of the dramatic 25 percent improvement in attendance over the quarter prior to their program participation. Parents reported that students refused to miss school for any reason on the days they were scheduled to use the dance mats and mentor their peer-team.

A Summary- What Happens When We Exercise?

When humans exercise, the body-brain goes into a homeostatic state, balancing brain chemicals, hormones, electricity, and system functions. When the body-brain is out of balance because of poor nutrition and lack of physical activity, the student is not in a good learning state. Movement, physical activity, and exercise change the learning state into one appropriate for retention and retrieval of memory, the effects lasting as much as 30-60 minutes depending on the student. Studies show that just 10 minutes of rhythmic aerobic activity prior to a cognitive task improves academic success.

Physical Activity Provides Enriched Environments

Physical activity in a positive social setting creates an environment conducive for learning.

Being Active Grows New Brain Cells

Aerobic activity releases endorphins, the class of neurotransmitters that relax us into a state of cortical alertness. Exercise also tends to raise levels of glucose, serotonin, epinephrine, and dopamine, chemicals that are known to balance behavior.

Aerobic Fitness Aids Cognition

Researchers found that subjects who were the most aerobically fit had the fastest cognitive responses, measured by reaction time, the speed that subjects processed information, memory span, and problem solving.

Exercise Triggers BDNF

Exercise triggers the release of BDNF a brain-derived neurotropic factor that enables one neuron to communicate with another. (Kinoshita 1997) Students who sit for longer than twenty minutes experience a decrease in the flow of BDNF. Recess and physical education is one way students can trigger sharper learning skills.

Cross Lateral Movement Organizes Brain Functions

Crossing the midline integrates brain hemispheres to enable the brain to organize itself. When students perform cross lateral activities, like dance, sport and most play, blood flow is increased in all parts of the brain making it more alert and energized for stronger, more cohesive learning.

Eye Tracking Exercises and Peripheral Vision Development Helps Reading

One of the reasons students have trouble with reading is because of the lack of eye fitness. When students watch screens their eyes lock in constant distant vision and the muscles that control eye movement atrophy. In video games that provide screens with ever changing patterns and whole-body response to those screens, as in Red Octane's "In the Groove" dance games, eye tracking and expectation skills, peripheral vision are all improved

Balance Improves Reading Capacity

The vestibular and cerebellum systems (inner ear and motor activity) are the first systems to mature. These two systems work closely with the RAS system (reticular activation system) that is located at the top of the brain stem and is critical to our attentional system. These systems interact to keep our balance, turn thinking into action, and coordinate moves. Games and activities that stimulate inner ear motion like Red Octane's "*In The Groove*," are useful in laying the foundation for learning.

Exercise Reduces Stress

Movement can foster self-discipline, improve self-esteem, increase creativity, and enhance emotional expression through social games like FootGaming.

Movement Can Help Reinforce Academic Skills For All Students.

Eighty five percent of school age children are natural kinesthetic learners (Hannaford). Sensory motor learning is innate in humans. Teachers who incorporate kinesthetic teaching strategies reach a greater percentage of the learners. Kinesthetic learners do best while touching and moving. Kinesthetic learners tend to lose concentration if there is little or no external stimulation or movement. To integrate this style into the learning environment educators integrate creative strategies like:

- Using activities that get students up and moving
- Use activities that include music or rhythm
- Give frequent brain breaks that include activity and moving

REFERENCES

Action for Health Kids. (2003). Retrieved from http://actionforhealthykids.org

Courchesne, E. (1995, February). An MRI study of autism: The cerebellum revisited. *Journal of Autism and Developmental Disorders*, *25*(1), 19–22. doi:10.1007/BF02178164

Dietz W.H., Bandini L.G., Morelli J.A., Peers K.F., Ching P.L. Effect of sedentary activities on resting metabolic rate. *American Journal of Clinical Nutition*, *59*, 556–559.

Generation Fit. (2007). [Video File]. Video posted to http://www.generation-fit.com

Lanningham-Foster, L., Jensen, T., Foster, R. C., & Redmond, A. B. (2006, December). Energy expenditure of sedentary screen time compared with active screen time for children. *Pediatrics*, *118*(6). doi:10.1542/peds.2006-1087

Leiner, A. C., Leiner, H., & Noback, C. R. (1997). *Cerebellar Communications with the Prefrontal Cortex: Their Effect on Human Cognitive Skills*. Palo Alto, CA: Channing House.

Maloney, A. (2007). *Generation-Fit, a Pilot Study of Youth in Maine Middle Schools Using an "Exer-learning" Dance Video Game to Promote Physical Activity During School*. Retrieved from http://clinicaltrials.gov/ct2/show/NCT00424918

Ratey, J. (2008). *Spark: The revolutionary new science of exercise and the brain*. New York: Little, Brown and Company.

Sallis, J. F., Hovell, M. F., Hofstetter, C. R., & Barrington, E. (1992). Explanation of vigorous physical activity during two years using social learning variables. *Social Science & Medicine*, *34*, 25–32. doi:10.1016/0277-9536(92)90063-V

Schwimmer, J. B., Burwinkle, T. M., & Varni, J. W. (2003, April 9). Health-related Quality of Life of Severely Obese Children and Adolescents. *Journal of the American Medical Association*, *289*.

Shasek, J. (2009). *Brainy Stuff* [PowerPoint slides]. Retrieved from http://www.slideshare.net/invenTEAM/brainy-stuff-1078097

Shepard, R. J. (1997). *Curricular Physical Activity and Academic Performance*. Pediatric Exercise Science.

Turner Bell, D. (2009, March). *Exercise Gives The Brain A Workout, Too*. Retrieved from http://www.cbsnews.com/stories/2009/01/30/earlyshow/health/main4764523.shtml

Chapter 27

Designing Serious Games for People with Dual Diagnosis:
Learning Disabilities and Sensory Impairments

David J. Brown
Nottingham Trent University, Clifton Campus, UK

Penny Standen
University of Nottingham, UK

Lindsay Evett
Nottingham Trent University, Clifton Campus, UK

Steven Battersby
Nottingham Trent University, Clifton Campus, UK

Nick Shopland
Nottingham Trent University, Clifton Campus, UK

ABSTRACT

This chapter is concerned with the potential of serious games as effective and engaging learning resources for people with learning and sensory disabilities. This is considered, followed by detailing of a suitable design methodology and its application, description of a range of types of games that have been successfully developed for this target group, and an explication of accessibility guidelines. Future development in this area is discussed, and it is concluded that there is great potential in the wide range of possible areas of research into, and development of, serious games for supporting people with learning and sensory disabilities, which would contribute greatly to their inclusion in society.

DOI: 10.4018/978-1-61520-781-7.ch027

INTRODUCTION

This chapter deals with the participation of people with disabilities in the design of serious games and their potential as effective and engaging educational tools for this target audience. Aspects of developmental and cognitive psychological theories are reviewed and it is suggested that serious games are valuable educational media for people with learning disabilities and sensory impairments. These theoretical aspects are complimented by practical perspectives via a discussion of the outcomes of two current European projects to design serious games to develop employment related skills in people with both learning disabilities and sensory impairments (deafness). Finally, a set of design guidelines is presented for this target audience that synthesise heuristics from a variety of sources including existing guidelines and past related projects.

THE POTENTIAL OF SERIOUS GAMES IN SPECIAL EDUCATION

In the UK around 25 people in every thousand have mild or moderate intellectual disabilities and about four or five per thousand have severe intellectual disabilities (Department of Health, 2001). Many have additional impairments in the form of difficulties with mobility or fine motor control and additional sensory impairments. For the most disabled of these help will always be needed with almost every aspect of daily living, yet even those who are more able will still need a degree of support to achieve the things the rest of society takes for granted. According to the 2001 Department of Health White Paper, people with intellectual disabilities are amongst the most socially excluded and vulnerable groups in Britain, and this is unlikely to differ in other countries. Very few have jobs, live in their own homes or have real choice over who cares for them. Today, the majority no longer live in institutions but in the family home and, although their individual needs will differ, there is an expectation that they will achieve greater independence and greater inclusion in society (Department of Health, 2001). The intention of current policy is to enable them to have as much choice and control as possible over their lives, be involved in their communities and to make a valued contribution to the world at work.

However, in order to achieve these aims, their education needs to equip them with appropriate skills. The Tomlinson Report (Tomlinson, 1997) highlighted the need to provide courses which taught independent living and communication skills and this need has been reiterated by others (National Development Group for the Mentally Handicapped, 1977). For people with intellectual disabilities, computer based learning has a huge contribution to make. According to Hawkridge & Vincent (1992), it enables pupils to take charge of their own learning. Pupils with intellectual disabilities will find stimulation through 'enjoyable repetition' and a gradual increase in level of challenge: "Words like 'handicapped' and 'disabled' imply dependence and powerlessness: with computers, learners can be less dependent and more capable." (Hawkridge & Vincent 1992, p. 25). Blamires (1999) argues that enabling technology provides access to educational opportunities and life experiences, and facilitates engagement with knowledge and people: "Speech, pictures, words, and animation can be combined in interactive ways to structure concepts to suit the level of understanding of learners and their interests." (p. 1). Thus it facilitates alternative methods of supplying information which may help this group of people grasp more complex concepts. This is of particular importance for learners who may have a poor grasp of language and its abundance of visual opportunities makes it particularly suitable for those with little or no hearing.

Interactive software encourages active involvement in learning and gives the user the experience of control over the learning process (Pantelidis,

1993). This is especially important for people with intellectual disabilities who are often perceived as being passive. Learners can work at their own pace. They can make as many mistakes as they like without irritating others (Salem-Darrow 1996) and the computer will not tire of the learner attempting the same task over and over again, nor get impatient because they are slow or engrossed in particular details (Cromby et al, 1996).

A recent development in educational software is to recognise the value of learning through playing computer or video games: serious games. For recent reviews see the Futurelab website (Futurelab, 2009). Originally, the majority of the research on computer games focused on the negative aspects (Elgi & Meyers 1984). Pivec (2007) makes the point that while it is widely recognised that games have an important role in early learning, as education becomes more formal, games tend to be seen as just an "unserious activity" (p. 387). However, more recently their positive aspects have been documented. In a review of both the positive and negative effects of playing videogames, Griffiths (2004) describes the role of videogames in cognitive rehabilitation, for example in perceptual disorders, conceptual thinking, attention, concentration and memory in patients with brain damage following stroke or trauma.

In addition to the advantages outlined above in using computer based learning, one of the primary advantages of games in learning is their ability to engage the learner voluntarily in sufficient repetitions of the activities to ensure learning takes place (Pivec, 2007). This is what Garris et al (2002) termed persistent reengagement, where the player returns to the task unprompted. Evidence of the motivational power of computer game playing can be found in a report by Standen et al (2006a) of a study to design a new navigational interface for people with intellectual disabilities. The users in this study needed to use the device regularly over a period of eighteen months in order to complete a baseline evaluation and to test each version of

the prototype. Retention was easily achieved by allowing them to play computer games specifically designed for the study.

A second characteristic to be exploited in serious games is the immediate feedback they can provide so that an activity is easily linked with a learning outcome, in Pivec's (2007) words: "the debriefing process between the game cycle and the achievement of the learning outcomes" (p. 388). Finally, games can be structured with different levels of challenge. One of the primary functions of tutoring, according to Wood, Bruner & Ross (1976), is to allow the learner to make progress by initially providing scaffolding, for example by controlling those elements of the task that are initially beyond the beginner's capability. As the beginner becomes more familiar with elements of the task and develops the ability to carry it out independently the tutor intervenes less. The secret is to ensure a balance between success and challenge and the different levels that can be built into games to provide this.

There is now a body of evidence on the positive effects of computer game playing that has implications for the introduction of serious games into education. Green & Bavelier (2003) found that playing action video games can give a person the ability to monitor more objects in their visual field and do so faster than a person who does not play such games. In their most recent study, Green & Bavelier (2007) found a causative relationship between action video game playing and increased spatial resolution of visual processing. In order to explore whether game playing might have benefits for people with intellectual disabilities, Standen et al (2006b) assessed the effect of playing a switch controlled computer game with a time limit for responses on choice reaction time. They found a significant decrease in choice reaction time in the intervention group compared to the control group who, for the same amount of time, played a game with no time limit. In a later study, Standen, Rees & Brown (2009) investigated whether computer games may give people with intellectual disabilities the opportunity to practice the underlying components of decision making, a skill with which they can experience difficulties. After repeated sessions playing a Tetris like game, the intervention group showed a significant improvement in two paper based tests of decision making. The increase observed in the control group failed to reach significance.

DESIGNING GAMES FOR PEOPLE WITH LEARNING DISABILITIES AND SENSORY IMPAIRMENTS

Positive outcomes of the participation of people with disabilities in research and development of serious games have been demonstrated (e.g., Buhler, 2001; Brown et al, 2005). Combining established guidelines on user-centred design (i.e., INUSE (Daly-Jones et al, 1999) and USERfit (e.g., Poulson et al, 1996; Poulson & Waddell, 2001)) with contemporary human-computer interaction and product design research has produced a user sensitive design methodology for application to serious games (USDM; Battersby et al, 2004).

USDM is a six stage, iterative, design process:

1. Understand and Specify the Context of Use
2. Specify User and Organisational Requirements
3. Technology Review
4. Produce Concept Designs and Prototypes
5. Carry out a User-Based Assessment
6. Modify designs on the basis of the assessment outcomes

This approach has been used in a number of projects, and specifically the GOAL (Game On accessible Learning) and GOET (Game On Extra Time) EU Leonardo projects. Both aim to develop serious games to teach employment skills to people with a wide range of disabilities, includ-

ing learning disabilities and sensory impairments (deafness). Stage 1 was carried out in both these cases. Participants trialled a range of existing serious games aimed at this target audience as part of this process to identify their limitations to further inform design requirements. Disabilities included sensory impairments (deafness), severe learning disabilities (including Down's Syndrome and Williams Syndrome), and learning difficulties (including Autism and Dyslexia). There was a range of IT experience from limited or little to good. Computer facilities and support staff varied. All of the responding trainers and tutors confirmed that the content specification of the serious games should encompass basic skills, personal development and work preparation.

Specifying user and organisational requirements involves considering each of the outcomes of the user context analysis and considering how they each affect the design requirements of the serious games to be developed. For example, as our analysis of user characteristics revealed a high degree of users with severe learning disabilities and deafness then a corresponding design requirement is that alternative and augmented communication systems should be the primary mode of communication within the games, and that there should be alternatives to text understandable by our target population. Other design requirements have been derived from existing design requirements relevant to our target population, for example designing interactive media for people with Dyslexia (Brown et al, 2002; Evett et al, 2006; and see section 5). In a modification from the existing USDM process the third step – the technology review was combined with the second, where a review of existing and good practice serious games was considered by the project design group and used to inform the set of design requirements for the serious games in this project.

A consolidated set of design requirements was derived from these processes and the next stage – producing concept designs and prototypes – began by considering how each could be met by a specific design feature. These features were then represented on a set of conceptual design storyboards. The project design group used their multivariate experience to judge the best configuration of these design features matching the design requirements derived earlier in the USDM. Implementation of these designs led to the development of 6 prototype serious games, which are currently in the process of iterative user based assessment and modification (steps 5 and 6 of the USDM).

THEMES IN GAMES BASED LEARNING FOR PEOPLE WITH LEARNING DISABILITIES AND SENSORY IMPAIRMENTS

The influence of some of the current themes in games based learning on the development of the serious games developed in the GOAL and GOET projects are now considered.

Modding

Many young people with disabilities are experienced in playing contemporary computer and video games, and have an expectation to do so with such games being part of popular culture which they aspire to being part of, and not marked out as being apart from. A 'modding' approach was therefore taken to simulate the activities of the first days at work for our target audience. 'The process of manipulating computer games beyond their original purpose to produce and share new content with other players (known as game modding) has evolved' (Bates et al, 2008, p.3). The Source Engine (Valve Corporation) was chosen to develop the 'Work Induction Tour' for the GOAL and GOET projects. This engine is the same as used to develop the Half Life 2 game. It allows the use of closed captions (a major accessibility plus) and the character models are realistic. It is important that the context is realistic for people with learning disabilities who are often termed 'concrete thinkers'.

Figure 1 shows part of the user's work induction.

Figure 1. An interaction as part of the user's work induction.

Accessibility

In designing serious games for our target audience accessibility is paramount, and game features should include signing tracks, closed captions and audio tracks as alternatives to text (Brown et al, 2009a). Closed Captions 'typically display a transcription of the audio portion of a program as it occurs (either verbatim or in edited form), sometimes including non-speech elements' (Wikipedia, 2009). The 'Work Induction Tour' developed for the GOAL and GOET projects introduce our target audience to their first days at work via a 'mod' created using the Source Engine. The closed captions within the Source Engine are similar to television subtitles, but also include other sounds like doors opening, as well as voice subtitles. Closed captions have been added to the Work Induction Tour using the 'GCFscape' tool that enables browsing through the GCF files that are utilized by Steam for game content storage (Valve Developer Community, 2008). Additionally a signing track has been loaded into an additional layer in the DVD created from the tour (in this case British Sign Language). These alternatives to text should ensure that people with a learning disability and additional deafness can access the information offered to them in the tour.

Location Based Games

There are approaches which integrate location based experiences within games that are relevant to education (Benford, 2005). An application where such an approach might be particularly useful for our target audience is in route planning and rehearsal (Brown et al, 2009b). Developed on the Android Operating System for mobile devices (Android, 2009), 'Route Mate' combines games based learning and location based services to help our target audience to Plan (setting starting location, end location, key landmarks along the route) and Practice (select an existing route, route status – late or alarms for divergence from route,

overall time for arrival) routes. The third mode challenges users to correctly identify the next landmark (and its function or purpose) they are approaching whilst carrying out one of their own created routes using the location sensitivity of the system. The user does so by selecting the correct graphic image from a larger range of landmark and function images. In doing so this game promotes the gradual learning of a complex route by breaking it down into a series of smaller components (journeys between key landmarks) and rehearsing and successfully completing these before the next stage is attempted. Figure 2 shows a screen from the Plan Mode in setting up a new route. Using a mobile device means that the system can be used en route, will be popular with the target groups, and contribute to their sense of inclusion.

Personalisation and User Created Content

As a future trend in online learning researchers have recognised the increasing role of user created content in higher education, representing a new form of contribution and an increasing trend toward authorship that is happening at almost all levels of experience (Horizon Report, 2007). The roles of user created content and personalisation might be at least as important in special education, where students are often disengaged and disaffected from learning especially if they feel their opinions are often over looked (if ever sought in the first place) and not valued. An ability to personalise their learning materials and be involved in creating content could go someway in redressing the balance. The serious games developed for the GOAL and GOET projects offer many opportunities for personalisation and user created content.

Route Mate can be personalized via the 'take picture' function using the phone's digital camera which automatically loads in the system's Use Mode. Pictures of key landmarks can be taken and symbols used to personalise the function of

Figure 2. Planning a new route

each of these landmarks. These location-based reminders can help prompt important actions that must be taken in the course of a journey (Figure 3), and are used in the location sensitive games challenging users to correctly identify their next important landmark. The 'My Appearance' game challenges users to carry out their daily hygiene and getting ready for work routines when selecting a variety of wake up times. The game can be personalised in many ways including alarm settings, times to carry out daily hygiene routines, gender and character selection (Figure 4).

Scalability

In designing serious games for people with learning disabilities and additional deafness a wide range of abilities is encountered although all may be considered to have a disability. It is important therefore to build scalability into any serious games developed, to cope with the wide range of educational and sensory abilities of such a target audience. This can be done using game features such as difficulty levels. Cheese Factory is a Tetris-like game which challenges users to match portions of falling cheeses to make whole shapes, thus replicating the early stages of teaching percentages, fractions and decimals. Initial game options include a difficulty bar to set the speed of the falling cheeses from a 7 point scale, whilst the 5 game levels progress to increasingly more complex fractions and, in later stages, amorphous shapes so the users are simply matching fractions without the additional guidance of the corresponding shape (Figure 5).

Escapology is a simple word game that challenges users to guess the correct word associated with a related clue to release the magician. Our target audience is highly sensitive to text based educational content so a question editor has been provided to allow tutors to create and edit content in these games. This feature allows the content to be scaled to any educational level, and presented in alternative ways to match individual learning needs (e.g., syntax of the text can be changed to reflect that of some signing systems such as BSL).

Figure 3. Personalisation of location based games

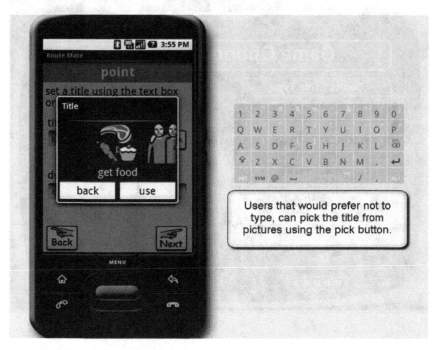

Figure 4. Personalisation of game variables in My Appearance

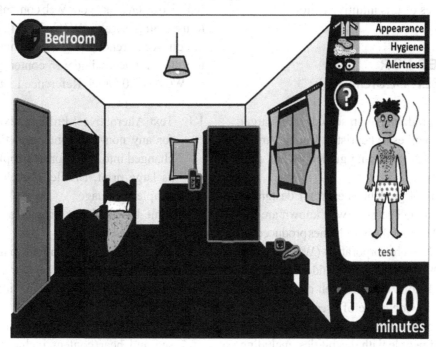

Figure 5. Scalability in Cheese Factory

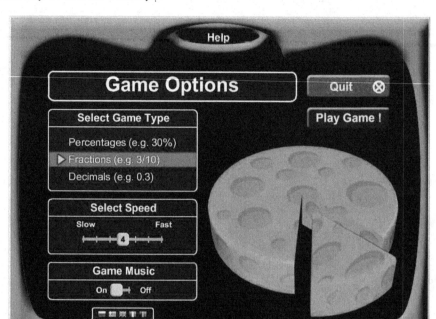

It provides an intuitive interface (iconic rather that textual) that enables review, editing, addition and deletion of question content. Figure 6 shows some of the interfaces of this intuitive editor.

GUIDELINES FOR ACCESSIBLE DESIGN

A set of design guidelines is presented for this target audience that synthesise heuristics from a variety of sources including existing guidelines and past related projects.

Various sets of guidelines exist for designing accessible content. The most well known are the Web Content Accessibility Guidelines produced by the World Wide Web Corporation (W3C WCAG 1.0 and 2.0, 1999, 2008a). These guidelines consist of recommendations to make web content more accessible for a wide range of users: "Following these guidelines will make content accessible to a wider range of people with disabilities, including blindness and low vision, deafness and hearing loss,

learning disabilities, cognitive limitations, limited movement, speech disabilities, photosensitivity and combinations of these. Following these guidelines will also often make your Web content more usable to users in general." (W3C, 2008a). The WCAG 2.0 quick reference list gives the main principles to follow for accessible web content:

WCAG 2.0 Quick Reference List

1.1 Text Alternatives: Provide text alternatives for any non-text content so that it can be changed into other forms people need, such as large print, Braille, speech, symbols or simpler language.

1.2 Time-based Media: Provide alternatives for time-based media.

1.3 Adaptable: Create content that can be presented in different ways (for example simpler layout) without losing information or structure.

1.4 Distinguishable: Make it easier for users to see and hear content including separating foreground from background.

Figure 6. Editing educational content in Escapology

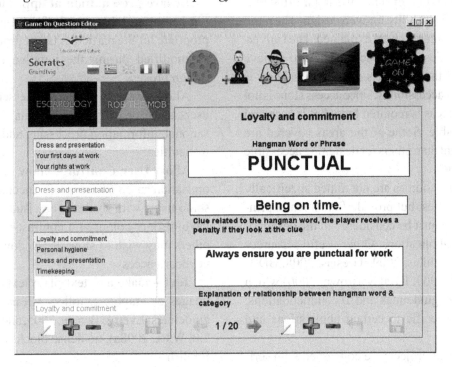

2.1 Keyboard Accessible: Make all functionality available from a keyboard.

2.2 Enough Time: Provide users enough time to read and use content.

2.3 Seizures: Do not design content in a way that is known to cause seizures.

2.4 Navigable: Provide ways to help users navigate, find content and determine where they are.

3.1 Readable: Make text content readable and understandable.

3.2 Predictable: Make Web pages appear and operate in predictable ways.

3.3 Input Assistance: Help users avoid and correct mistakes.

4.1 Compatible: Maximize compatibility with current and future user agents, including assistive technologies. (W3C, 2008b)

These main principles are applicable to all multi-media systems, although there may be differences in emphasis depending on purpose and content. They are consistent with the main points of the various other sets of guidelines which exist. An important source of relevance to the current applications is the general approach of Universal Design (Universal Usability, Inclusive Design, Design for All), in particular the Universal Usability approach proposed by Horton (2006). This approach aims to "provide for diversity through design rather than accommodation" (Horton, 2006, p xvi). This approach focuses on facilitating and enabling users, whoever they are, to succeed in carrying out their aims when using information technology. Universal Design is becoming more widespread, and is partly driven by the need to conform to disability equality laws which are ever more common around the world (e.g., the UK's Disability Discrimination Act, DDA, 2005; in the US, Section 508, 2006). It is important to note that improving accessibility of materials can and does improve accessibility for all users (DRC, 2004; Brown et al, 2002; Evett et al, 2006).

Horton (2006) considers the main principles for Universal Usability for web design. The main areas for consideration are explained. The Universal Usability design approach and how to achieve it in each of these areas is detailed. Usability is stressed over accessibility, since access alone is not enough – access is required but what is accessed must be usable. Some of the areas covered are more relevant than others for designing accessible serious games.

These two sources are not aimed specifically at serious games, but provide fundamental principles which must be considered in the design of the current applications. Other useful resources exist (e.g., TechDis, 2009; Tiresias, 2008; BDA, 2008; NLN, 2003; Evett & Brown, 2006) which give general guidelines and recommendations, sometimes specific to certain applications and disabilities.

The current projects are concerned with serious games to support employment for a wide range of user groups with various learning and sensory (deafness) disabilities. While accessibility is achievable in the major web formats (HTML and XML), it is more problematic with other formats, such as Flash and Java, and off the shelf games engines. The situation is improving in later versions of these formats, but remains an issue. However, most of the main principles can be followed. Mobile systems have their own usability issues, and the Android Operating System has good potential for accessible design. USDM has informed the design of the current systems so that they are usable by the range of user groups in the project, and building accessibility into their design facilitates this process.

From consideration of the main resources (i.e., W3C 1999, 2008a; Horton, 2006), and various other notable resources (as above), a set of design guidelines for accessible serious games has been distilled. These guidelines focus on the aspects which are important for the design of accessible serious games:

Ensure presentation at appropriate speed – it is essential that speed of presentation is appropriate for the particular target group, and may be modified during the iterative user-centred design process

Allow users to go back – essential for all users, and especially those who may have organisational, information processing and/or memory difficulties

Allow User Control – allow for user customisation based on user preference; for example, some users with dyslexia or visual impairment have distinct colour and contrast requirements, others may wish to slow things down, or to use keyboard access

Text – make any text plain text (rather than images or graphics), follow Clear Text for All guidelines (Evett & Brown, 2005, and see WCAG 2.0, W3C, 2008a), no dense blocks of text, plain English

Text Alternatives: Provide text equivalents for non-text content, including auditory and visual components, so that it can be changed into other forms people need, such as Braille, speech, symbols, other languages including sign language

Colour – never convey information by colour alone

Contrast – ensure sufficient contrast so that it is easier to distinguish items, both visual and auditory (cf. WCAG 2.0, W3C, 2008a)

Navigable – help users navigate, find content and know where they are: by placing navigation information in the same place (usually at the top) and ensuring that it is consistent and simple, using maps when appropriate, using home and back buttons, providing context and orientation information

Maintain organisation – instructions, buttons, clearly displayed and in the same place (often at top) throughout presentations

Links – use unique and informative text descriptions for any hyperlinks (never click here!)

Use accessibility features – HTML/XML have inherent accessibility features (e.g., alt text, long desc) which should always be used, other formats (e.g., Java, Flash, Games environments) are not necessarily accessible, although this is improving with more recent versions having accessibility features, which should be used; provide alternatives where possible

Design simply – in simple layouts, it is relatively easy to draw attention to important features and differences; in more complex layouts it becomes harder to highlight features, thus making presentations even more complex

Use fallbacks – provide alternatives, provide equivalent content as accessible html when possible and design for graceful transformation (such as reflowing)

Robust – make systems consistent and error free, provide appropriate error messages and error catching

Aim for compatibility with assistive technologies – e.g., screenreaders, text-to-speech, zoom features

Allow keyboard access – ensure the system can be controlled from the keyboard and not just by using the mouse

Seizures – do not include elements that are known to cause seizures, for example by having elements that flash or have particular spatial frequencies

FUTURE RESEARCH DIRECTIONS

There may be opportunities for our target audience to benefit in future from the use of Massively Multiplayer Online Games (MMO) and Virtual Worlds. MMO games bring many players together in activities that are collaborative, competitive, goal-oriented, and narrative driven, whilst Virtual Worlds are also multiuser but not in themselves games (Horizon Report, 2007, p.25). It is the social and collaborative aspects of learning that these spaces afford which is both exciting to people with learning disabilities and sensory impairments and

potentially alarming to their parents or caregivers. Obviously controls are needed, but with these in place, new learning spaces can be created that are the natural successors to the offline virtual environments that were successfully developed for the education of people with learning disabilities in the 1990's (Cromby et al, 1996).

Mobile devices offer great potential as platforms for serious games for learning and support. The mobile-based location games described in this paper demonstrate this. They support inclusion. There is a growing incidence of users accessing web-based systems, which have been designed for the PC, on mobile devices. This is encouraged by the rise in use of phones with large screens and additional functionality, such as the iPhone and the Google phone, and other multi-purpose mobile devices such as the Nintendo DSi and Wii devices. The small screens of mobile devices require additional user interface considerations, and it is becoming ever more necessary to consider this in initial design, along with accessibility considerations. It is not too difficult to foresee that soon mobile devices will be truly multi purpose (not just phones with Personal Digital Assistant (PDA) and Global Positioning System (GPS) functionality, but also with e-books, music, speech input and output, pointing and remote access devices etc; most mobiles have a mix of some of these applications, but the mix is becoming ever greater). Some applications are designed for the PC and some for mobile devices, but many need to be functional on both, and this must be considered during the design process. There are particular issues to consider when designing for mobile devices (e.g., see Ballard, 2007) and these must be considered in the design of many applications. Interestingly, features with assistive functions are becoming ever more available for such devices (e.g., screen-readers, e.g., Mobile Speak, Code Factory, 2009; Android, BlindWikia, 2009; Text-to-speech, e.g., Nokia, 2009a; GPS and mapping applications, e.g., Nokia, 2009b; accessible mobile interfaces, e.g., Kane et al, 2008, Mukherjee, 2008; talking iTunes, Apple, 2009a) often because of demand from general users and facilitated by the ease of application development (e.g., iPhone apps, Apple, 2009b; Android, Android, 2009).

CONCLUSION

This chapter has explained the potential of serious games for people with learning disabilities and additional hearing impairments. It has detailed a design methodology and described how this has resulted in the creation of a number of varied serious games which have been successfully developed for this target audience. Accessibility guidelines have been developed and described. Future developments have also been considered. Overall, there is great potential in the wide range of possible areas of research and development into serious games for supporting people with learning and sensory disabilities, which would contribute greatly to their inclusion in society.

ACKNOWLEDGMENT

The GOAL (UK/07/LLP-LdV/TOI-009) and GOET (UK/08/LLP-LdV/TOI/163_181) projects have been funded with support from the European Commission.

REFERENCES

W3C. (1999). *Web Content Accessibility Guidelines 1.0, W3C Recommendation 5.5*. Retrieved July 7, 2007, from www.w3.org/TR/1999/WAI-WEBCONTENT-19990505, W3C

W3C. (2008a). *Web Content Accessibility Guidelines (WCAG) 2.0, W3C Recommendation 11 December 2008*. Retrieved May 4, 2007, from http://www.w3.org/TR/WCAG20/

W3C. (2008b). *How to Meet WCAG 2.0: A customizable quick reference to Web Content Accessibility Guidelines 2.0 requirements (success criteria) and techniques*. Retrieved May 4, 2007, from http://www.w3.org/WAI/WCAG20/quickref/

Android (2009). *Android*. Retrieved May 5, 2009, from http://www.android.com

Apple. (2009a). *VoiceOver, the talk of the music world*. Retrieved May 5, 2009, from http://www.apple.com/uk/ipodshuffle/voiceover.html

Apple. (2009b). *iPhone3G – 35,000 apps. and counting*. Retrieved May 5, 2009, from http://www.apple.com/iphone/

Ballard, B. (2007). *Designing the Mobile User Experience*. Sussex, UK: WileyBlackwell. doi:10.1002/9780470060575

Bates, M., Brown, D. J., Cranton, W., & Lewis, J. (2008, November). *Playing to win: motivation for teaching and learning in today's gaming culture*. Paper presented at Interactive Technologies 08, Nottingham Trent University, Nottingham, UK.

Battersby, S., Brown, D. J., Standen, P. J., Anderton, N., & Harrison, M. (2004). Design, development and manufacture of novel assistive and adaptive technology devices. In P. M. Sharkey, R. McCrindle & D. Brown (Eds.), *Proceedings of the Fifth International Conference on Disability, Virtual Reality and Associated Technologies* (pp.283-290), Oxford, UK.

BDA. (2008). British Dyslexia Association Dyslexia Style Guide. Retrieved May 5, 2009, from http://www.bdadyslexia.org.uk/extra352.html

Benford, S. (2005). Future Location-Based Experiences. *JISC Report*. Retrieved from www.jisc.ac.uk

Blamires, M. (Ed.). (1999). *Enabling Technology for Inclusion*. London: Paul Chapman Publishing.

BlindWikia. (2009). *Android Accessibility*. Retrieved May 6, 2009, from http://blind.wikia.com/wiki/Open_Letter_Initiative#Android_Accessibility

Brown, D., Evett, L., & Lawton, J. (2002). Accessible web based multimedia for use by people with learning disabilities. In [Derby, UK: British Computer Society.]. *Proceedings of the International Conference of Assistive Technology, 2002*, 72–85. doi:10.2469/cp.v2002.n4.3218

Brown, D. J., Battersby, S., & Shopland, N. (2005). Design and evaluation of a flexible travel training environment for use in a supported employment setting. *International Journal of Disability and Human Development, 4*(3), 251–258.

Brown, D. J., McHugh, D., & Sik Lanyi, C. (2009b, in press). Combining location based services with games based learning approaches in assistive technology. In *Proceedings of AAATE 2009*.

Brown, D.J., Shopland, N., Battersby, S., Tully, A., & Richardson, S. (2009a. (in press). Game On: Accessible Serious Games for Offenders and those at Risk of Offending. *Journal of Assistive Technology*.

Buhler, C. (2001). Empowered participation of users with disabilities in R&D projects. *International Journal of Human-Computer Studies, 55*(4), 645–659. doi:10.1006/ijhc.2001.0489

Cromby, J. J., Standen, P. J., & Brown, D. J. (1996). The potentials of virtual environments in the education and training of people with learning disabilities. *Journal of Intellectual Disability Research, 40*, 489–501. doi:10.1111/j.1365-2788.1996.tb00659.x

Daly-Jones, O., Bevan, N., & Thomas, C. (1999). *INUSE: Handbook of User-Centred Design*. Serco Usability Services, National Physical Laboratory.

Department of Health. (2001). *Valuing People: a new strategy for learning disability for the 21st century*. London: HMSO.

Disability Discrimination Act. (2005). *HMSO*. Retrieved March 23, 2006, from http://www.opsi.gov.uk/acts/acts2005/20050013.htm

Disability Rights Commission. (2004). *The Web: Access and Inclusion for Disabled People*. Retrieved May 8, 2009, from http://www.equalityhumanrights.com/en/publicationsandresources/Pages/webaccess.aspx?k=The%20Web:%20Access%20and%20Inclusion%20for%20Disabled%20People

Elgi, E. A., & Meyers, L. S. (1984). The role of video game playing in adolescent life; is there a reason to be concerned? *Bulletin of the Psychonomic Society, 22*, 309–312.

Evett, L., & Brown, D. (2005). Text formats and web design for visually impaired readers – Clear Text for All. *Interacting with Computers, 17*, 453–472. doi:10.1016/j.intcom.2005.04.001

Evett, L., Brown, D., Smith, P., & Hibberd, R. (2006). Cleaning up the environment – Accessible PowerPoint Presentations. In *Proceedings of NTU 6th Annual Learning and Teaching Conference* (pp. 26-44). March 2006. Nottingham, UK: Nottingham Trent University.

Factory, C. (2009). *Mobile Speak for Symbian OS*. Retrieved May 7, 2009, from http://www.codefactory.es/en/products.asp?id=24

Futurelab. (2009). *Futurelab – Innovation in Education*. Retrieved May 7, 2009, from http://www.futurelab.org.uk/

Garris, R., Ahlers, R., & Driskell, J. E. (2002). Games, motivation and learning. *Simulation & Gaming; An Interdisciplinary Journal of Theory. Practice and Research, 33*(4), 43–56.

Green, C. S., & Bavelier, D. (2003). Action video game modifies visual selective attention. *Nature*, *423*, 534–537. doi:10.1038/nature01647

Green, C. S., & Bavelier, D. (2007). Action-Video-Game Experience Alters the Spatial Resolution of Vision. *Psychological Science*, *18*(1), 88–94. doi:10.1111/j.1467-9280.2007.01853.x

Griffiths, M. (2004). Can videogames be good for your health? *Journal of Health Psychology*, *9*(3), 340–343. doi:10.1177/1359105304042344

Hawkridge, D., & Vincent, T. (1992). *Learning Difficulties and Computers*. London: Jessica Kingsley.

Horton, S. (2006). Access by Design: A Guide to Universal Usability for Web Designers. Berkeley, CA: New Riders. Retrieved January 3, 2009, from http://universalusability.com/index.html

Kane, S. K., Bigham, J. P., & Wobbrock, J. O. (2008). Slide Rule: Making mobile touch screens accessible to blind people using multi-touch interaction techniques. In *Proceedings of the ACM SIGACCESS Conference on Computers and Accessibility (ASSETS '08)*. New York: ACM Press. Retrieved May 5, 2009, from http://students.washington.edu/skane/sliderule/

Mukherjee, W. (2008). Nokia plans to design handsets for disabled. *The Economic Times*. Retrieved May 5, 2009, from http://economictimes.indiatimes.com/Nokia_plans_handsets_for_disabled/rssarticleshow/3830729.cms

National Development Group for the Mentally Handicapped. (1977). *Day Services for Mentally Handicapped Adults*. London: Department of Health and Social Security.

NLN. (2003). *Paving the Way – Developing standards for e-learning*. National Learning Network. Retrieved May 14, 2008, from http://www.nln.ac.uk/?p=Using

Nokia. (2009a). *Text-to-speech*. Retrieved May 6, 2009, from http://blind.wikia.com/wiki/Open_Letter_Initiative#Android_Accessibility

Nokia (2009b). Nokia maps application. Retrieved May 6, 2009, from http://www.nokia.co.uk/get-support-and-software/navigation

Pantelidis, V. S. (1993). Virtual reality in the classroom. *Educational Technology*, 23–27.

Pivec, M. (2007). Editorial: Play and learn: potentials of game-based learning. *British Journal of Educational Technology*, *38*(3), 387–393. doi:10.1111/j.1467-8535.2007.00722.x

Poulson, D. F., Ashby, M., & Richardson, S. (1996). USERFIT: A Practical Handbook on User-Centred Design for Assistive Technology. Brussels: TIDE European Commission, ECSC-EC-EAEC.

Poulson, D. F., & Waddell, F. N. (2001). USERFIT: user centred design in assistive technology. In Nicholle, C. A., & Abascal, J. (Eds.), *Inclusive Guidelines for HCI*. San Francisco: Taylor and Francis.

Report, H. (2007). *Trends in Online Learning*. The New Media Consortium.

Salem Darrow, M. (1995). Increasing research and development of virtual reality in education and special education: what about mental retardation? *VR in the Schools*, *1*(3), 1–7.

Section 508. (2006). *Assistive technology resource*. section508.gov. Retrieved July 7, 2007, from http://www.section508.gov/

Standen, P. J., Brown, D. J., Anderton, N., & Battersby, S. (2006a). A systematic evaluation of current control devices used by people with intellectual disabilities in non-immersive virtual environments. *Cyberpsychology & Behavior*, *9*(5), 608–613. doi:10.1089/cpb.2006.9.608

Standen, P. J., Karsandas, R., Anderton, N., Battersby, S., & Brown, D. J. (2006b). An evaluation of the use of a switch controlled computer game in improving the choice reaction time of adults with intellectual disabilities. In P. M. Sharkey (Ed.), *Proceedings of the sixth International conference on Disability, Virtual Research and Associated Technology,* (pp. 285-291).

Standen, P.J., Rees, F., & Brown, D.J. (2009. (in press). Effect of playing computer games on decision making in people with intellectual disabilities. *Journal of Assistive Technologies.*

TechDis. (2009). Accessibility Essentials Series. *JISC TechDis*. Retrieved January 16, 2009, from http://www.techdis.ac.uk/index.php?p=3_20

Tiresias. (2008). *Checklists*. Retrieved January 3, 2009, from http://www.tiresias.org/research/guidelines/checklists/index.htm

Tomlinson, J. (1997). Inclusive learning: the report of the committee of enquiry into the post-school education of those with learning difficultles and/or disabilities, in England 1996. *European Journal of Special Needs Education, 12,* 184–196. doi:10.1080/0885625970120302

Valve Developer Community. (2008). *GCFScape*. Retrieved March 2, 2008, from http://developer.valvesoftware.com/wiki/GCFScape

Wikipedia contributors. (2009). *Closed captioning*. Wikipedia, The Free Encyclopedia. Retrieved May 8, 2009, from http://en.wikipedia.org/w/index.php?title=Closed_captioning&oldid=288518912

Wood, D. J., Bruner, J. S., & Ross, G. (1976). The role of tutoring in problem solving. *Journal of Child Psychiatry and Psychology, 17,* 89–100. doi:10.1111/j.1469-7610.1976.tb00381.x

Compilation of References

Aarseth, E. (2004). Quest games as post-narrative discourse. In Ryan, M. (Ed.), *Narrative across Media* (pp. 362–376). Lincoln, NE: University of Nebraska Press.

Abrami, P. C., & Barrett, H. (2005). Directions for research and development on electronic portfolios. *Canadian Journal of Learning and Technology, 31*(3), 1–15.

Abrami, P. C., Savage, R., Comaskey, E., Silverstone, D., & Hipps, G. (2006). *ABRACADABRA: Evaluation of a balanced text and word-level reading intervention–Winter 2006*. Preliminary findings, June 2006. Centre for the Study of Learning and Performance: Montreal, QC. Retrieved from http://doe.concordia.ca/cslp/ICTAB-RACADABRA.php

Abrami, P. C., Savage, R., Wade, A., Hipps, G., & Lopez, M. (2008). Using technology to assist children learning to read and write. In Willoughby, T., & Wood, E. (Eds.), *Children's learning in a digital world* (pp. 129–172). Oxford, UK: Blackwell Publishing.

Abrami, P. C., Wade, A., Pillay, V., Aslan, O., Bures, E. & Bentley. (2008). Encouraging self-regulated learning through electronic portfolios. *Canadian Journal on Learning and Technology, 34*(3), 93-117. Retreived April 7, 2009 from http://www.cjlt.ca/index.php/cjlt/article/view/507/238

Abrams, C. (2007). *Factors to consider when selecting virtual worlds for international markets*. Gartner Report No. G00153506.

Abt, C. (1968). Games for Learning. In S. Boocock & E. Schild (Eds.), Simulation Games in Learning. Beverly Hills, CA: Sage.

Action for Health Kids. (2003). Retrieved from http://actionforhealthykids.org

Adams, E. (2005). *Educational Games Don't Have to Stink!* Retrieved 31 January, 2009, from http://www.gamasutra.com/features/20050126/adams_01.shtml

Adams, M. J. (1990). *Beginning to read: Thinking and learning about print*. Cambridge, MA: MIT Press.

Adelmann, P. K., & Zajonc, R. (1989). Facial efference and the experience of emotion. *Annual Review of Psychology, 40*, 249–280. doi:10.1146/annurev.ps.40.020189.001341

Adorno, T., & Horkheimer, M. (1972). *The culture industry: enlightenment as mass deception. The dialectics of enlightenment* (Cumming, J., Trans.). New York: Continuum. (Original work published 1944)

Akilli, G. K. (2007). Games and Simulations: A new approach in Education? In Gibson, D., Aldrich, C., & Prensky, M. (Eds.), *Games and Simulations in Online Learning: Research and Development Frameworks* (pp. 1–20). Hershey, PA: Information Science Publishing.

Akilli, G. K., & Cagiltay, K. (2006). An instructional design/development model for game-like learning environments: The FIDGE model. In M. Pivec (Ed.), Affective and emotional aspects of human-computer interaction game-based and innovative learning approaches (Vol. 1, pp. 93-112). Amsterdam, The Netherlands: IOS Press.

Alberti, J. (2008). The game of reading and writing: How video games reframe our understanding of literacy. *Computers and Composition, 25*, 258–269. doi:10.1016/j.compcom.2008.04.004

Aldrich, C. (2004). Simulations and the Future of Learning: An Innovative (and Perhaps Revolutionary) Approach to e-Learning. San Francisco: John Wiley & Sons, Inc.

Allen, B., Otto, R., & Hoffman, B. (2003). Media as Lived Environments: The Ecological Psychology of Educational Technology. In D. Jonassen (Ed.), Handbook of Research on Educational Communications and Technology. Mahwah, NJ: Lawrence Erlbaum Associates, Inc.

Allington, R. (2004). Setting the record straight. *Educational Leadership, 61*, 22–25.

Althusser, L. (1971). *Ideology and ideological state apparatuses (notes towards an investigation). Lenin and philosophy and other essays by louis althusser (Ben Brewster, trans.).* New York: Monthly Review Press. (Original work published 1968)

Alvermann, D. E. (2002). Effective literacy instruction for adolescents. *Journal of Literacy Research, 34*(2), 189–208. doi:10.1207/s15548430jlr3402_4

Alvermann, D. E., & Heron, A. H. (2001). Literacy identity work: Playing to learn with popular media. *Journal of Adolescent & Adult Literacy, 45*(2), 118–122.

American Heritage College Dictionary (3rd ed.). (2000). Boston: Houghton Mifflin.

American Psychological Association. (2006, March). Multitasking- switching costs. *American Psychological Association Online.* Retrieved February 24, 2009 from ttp://www.psychologymatters.org/multitask0306.html

American Psychological Association. (2008). *Learner centered psychological principles.* Washington, DC. Retrieved September 18, 2008 from http://www.apa.org/ed/lcp2/lcp14.html

Anand, V. (2007). A study of time management: The correlation between video game usage and academic performance markers. *Cyberpsychology & Behavior, 10*(4), 552–559. doi:10.1089/cpb.2007.9991

Anderson, C. A., & Bushman, B. J. (2001). Effects of violent video games on aggressive behavior, aggressive cognition, aggressive affect, physiological arousal, and prosocial behavior: A meta-analytic review of the scientific literature. *Psychological Science, 12*(5), 353–359. doi:10.1111/1467-9280.00366

Anderson, C. A., & Dill, K. E. (2000). Video games and aggressive thoughts, feelings, and behavior in the laboratory and in life. *Journal of Personality and Social Psychology, 78*(4), 772–790. doi:10.1037/0022-3514.78.4.772

Anderson, C., & Ford, C. (1986). Affect of the game player: Short-term effects of highly and mildly aggressive video games. *Personality and Social Psychology Bulletin, 12*(4), 290–402. doi:10.1177/0146167286124002

Anderson, J. R., Corbett, A. T., Koedinger, K. R., & Pelletier, R. (1995). Cognitive tutors: Lessons learned. *Journal of the Learning Sciences, 4*, 167–207. doi:10.1207/s15327809jls0402_2

Anderson, L. W., & Krathwohl, D. R. (Eds.). (2001). A taxonomy for learning, teaching and assessing: A revision of Bloom's Taxonomy of educational objectives: Complete edition. New York: Longman.

Anderson, L. W., Krathwohl, D. R., Airasian, P. W., Cruikshank, K. A., Mayer, R. E., Pintrich, P. R., et al. (2000). A Taxonomy for Learning, Teaching, and Assessing: A Revision of Bloom's Taxonomy of Educational Objectives (2nd ed.). Boston: Allyn & Bacon.

Anderson, P. H., & Lawton, L. (1997). Demonstrating the learning effectiveness of simulations: Where we are and where we need to go. *Developments in Business Simulation & Experiential Exercises, 24*, 68–73.

Anderson, P., H. & Lawton, L. (2009). Business Simulations and Cognitive Learning. *Simulation & Gaming, 40*(2), 193–216. doi:10.1177/1046878108321624

Andreano, J., Liang, K., Kong, L., Hubbard, D., Wiederhold, B. K., & Wiederhold, M. D. (2009). Auditory Cues Increase the Hippocampal Response to Unimodal Virtual Reality. *Cyberpsychology & Behavior, 12*(3), 309–313. doi:10.1089/cpb.2009.0104

Android (2009). *Android.* Retrieved May 5, 2009, from http://www.android.com

Ang, C. S., Zaphiris, P., & Mahmood, S. (2007). A Model of Cognitive Loads in Massively Multiplayer Online Role Playing Games. *Interacting with Computers, 19*(2), 167–179. doi:10.1016/j.intcom.2006.08.006

Apple. (2009a). *VoiceOver, the talk of the music world.* Retrieved May 5, 2009, from http://www.apple.com/uk/ipodshuffle/voiceover.html

Apple. (2009b). *iPhone3G – 35,000 apps. and counting.* Retrieved May 5, 2009, from http://www.apple.com/iphone/

Appleman, R., & Goldsworthy, R. (1999). The juncture of games & instructional design: Can fun be learning? Presentation made at the 1999 annual meeting of the Association of Educational Communications and Technology, Houston, TX.

Apter, M. (1991). A Structural Phenomenology of Play. In J. Kerr & M. Apter (Eds.), Adult Play: A Reversal Theory Approach. Amsterdam: Swets & Zeitlinger.

Archambault, L., & Crippen, K. (2009). Examining TPACK among K-12 online distance educators in the United States. *Contemporary Issues in Technology and Teacher Education, 9* (1). Retrieved from http://www.citejournal.org/vol9/iss1/general/article2.*cfm*

Argyris, C., & Schön, D. (1978). Organizational Learning: A Theory of Action Perspective. Reading, MA: Addison-Wesley.

Army, U. S. (2008). Army exploring virtual worlds. *Training and Doctrine Command.* Retrieved from The Army website www.army.mil/standto/archive/2008/11/21/

Ault, S. (March 19, 2009). Video game revenue climbs 10% in February. *Video Business.* http://www.videobusiness.com/article/CA6645368.html

Autism Speaks. (2006). Retrieved December 2, 2006, from, http://www.autismspeaks.org

Autism Speaks. (2007). Retrieved September 9, 2007, from, http://www.autismspeaks.org

Axe, D. (2008, August 4). *Is the Army's virtual world already here?* Retrieved from Wire.com Web site: http://www.wired.com/dangerroom/2008/08/more-mmog/

Babus, S., Hodges, K., & Kjonnerod, E. (1997). Simulations and institutional change: Training US government professionals for improved management of complex emergencies abroad. *Journal of Contingencies and Crisis Management, 5*(4), 231–233. doi:10.1111/1468-5973.00061

Baek, Y., & Choi, S. (2008). Implications of Educational Digital Game Structure for Use in Formal Education Settings. In K. McFerrin et al. (Eds.), Proceedings of Society for Information Technology and Teacher Education International Conference 2008 (pp. 1613-1619). Chesapeake, VA: AACE.

Bagenholm, A., & Gillberg, C. (1991). Psychosocial effects on siblings of children with autism and mental retardation: a population-based study. *Journal of Intellectual Disability Research, 35*(4), 291–307.

Bailey, C. (2006). China's full-time computer gamers. *BBC News.* Retrieved from http://news.bbc.co.uk/2/hi/business/5151916.stm

Bainbridge, W. S. (2007). The scientific research potential of virtual worlds. *Science, 317,* 472–476. doi:10.1126/science.1146930

Baker, S. C., Wentz, R. K., & Woods, M. M. (2009). Using virtual worlds in education: Second Life as an educational tool. *Teaching of Psychology, 36,* 59–64. doi:10.1080/00986280802529079

Ballard, B. (2007). *Designing the Mobile User Experience.* Sussex, UK: WileyBlackwell. doi:10.1002/9780470060575

Ballard, D., Hayhoe, M., Pook, P., & Rao, R. (1997). Deictic Codes for the Embodiment of Cognition. *The Behavioral and Brain Sciences, 20,* 723–742.

Bandura, A. (1977). *Social Learning Theory.* Englewood Cliffs, NJ: Prentice Hall.

Bandura, A. (1997). Self-Efficacy: The Exercise of Control. New York.

Bandura, A., & Barab, P. G. (1971)... *Developmental Psychology, 5,* 244–255. doi:10.1037/h0031499

Bankes, S. C. (1991). *Methodological Considerations in Using Simulation to Assess the Combat Value of Intelligence and Electronic Warfare. Technical Notes N-3010-A.* RAND Corporation.

Barab, S. A., & Roth, W. (2006). Curriculum-baed ecosystems: Supporting knowing from an ecological perspective. Educational Researcher, 35(5), 3–13. doi:10.3102/0013189X035005003

Barab, S. A., Arici, A., & Jackson, C. (2005). Eat your vegetables and do your homework: A design-based investigation of enjoyment and meaning in learning. *Educational Technology, 65*(1), 15–21.

Barab, S. A., Dodge, T., & Ingram-Goble, A. (2006). *Conceptual play spaces: A 21st Century pedagogy.* Paper presented at the Annual Meeting of the American Educational Research Association, Chicago, IL.

Barab, S. A., Dodge, T., Thomas, M., Jackson, C., & Tuzun, H. (2007). Our designs and the social agendas they carry. *Journal of the Learning Sciences, 16*(2), 263–305.

Barab, S. A., Hay, K., Barnett, M., & Keating, T. (2000). Virtual solar system: Building understanding through model building. *Journal of Research in Science Teaching, 37*(7), 719–756. doi:10.1002/1098-2736(200009)37:7<719::AID-TEA6>3.0.CO;2-V

Barab, S. A., Ingram-Goble, A., & Warren, S. (2008). Conceptual Playspaces. In Ferdig, R. (Ed.), *Handbook on Research on Effective Electronic Gaming in Education.* Hershey, PA: IGI Global.

Barab, S. A., Sadler, T. D., Heiselt, C., Hickey, D., & Zuiker, S. (2007). Relating narrative, inquiry and inscriptions: Supporting consequential play. *Journal of Science Education and Technology, 16*(1), 59–82. doi:10.1007/s10956-006-9033-3

Barab, S. A., Sadler, T., Heiselt, C., Hickey, D., & Zuiker, S. (2007). Relating narrative, inquiry, and inscriptions: A framework for socio-scientific inquiry. *Journal of Science Education and Technology, 16*(1), 59–82. doi:10.1007/s10956-006-9033-3

Barab, S. A., Thomas, M., Dodge, T., Carteaux, R., & Tuzun, H. (2005). Making learning fun: *Quest Atlantis*, a game without guns. *Educational Technology Research and Development, 53*(1), 86–107. doi:10.1007/BF02504859

Barab, S., & Squire, K. (2004). Design-Based Research: Putting a Stake in the Ground. *Journal of the Learning Sciences, 13*(1), 1–14. doi:10.1207/s15327809jls1301_1

Barakova, E., van Wanrooij, G., van Limpt, R., & Menting, M. (2007) Using an emergent system concept in designing interactive games for autistic children. Interaction Design and Children. In *Proceedings of the 6th international conference on Interaction design and children,* (pp. 73-76).

Barkley, R. A. (1997). Behavioral inhibition, sustained attention, and executive functions: constructing a unifying theory of ADHD. *Psychological Bulletin, 121,* 65–94. doi:10.1037/0033-2909.121.1.65

Barkley, R. A. (2006). Attention-deficit hyperactivity disorder (3rd. ed.): A handbook of diagnosis and treatment. New York: The Guilford Press.

Barkley, R. A., Copeland, A. P., & Sivage, C. (1980). A self-control classroom for hyperactive children. *Journal of Autism and Developmental Disabilities, 10,* 75–89. doi:10.1007/BF02408435

Barkley, R. A., Fischer, M., Smallish, L., & Fletcher, K. (2006). Young adult outcome of hyperactive children: Adaptive functioning in major life activities. *Journal of the American Academy of Child and Adolescent Psychiatry, 45,* 192–202. doi:10.1097/01.chi.0000189134.97436.e2

Barkley, R. A., Grodzinsky, G., & DuPaul, G. J. (1992). Frontal-lobe functions in attention-deficit disorder with and without hyperactivity: A review and research report. *Journal of Abnormal Child Psychology, 20,* 163–188. doi:10.1007/BF00916547

Barney, J. B. (1991). Firm resources and sustained competitive advantage. *Journal of Management, 7,* 99–120. doi:10.1177/014920639101700108

Barr, P., Noble, J., & Biddle, R. (2007). Video Game Values: Human-Computer Interaction and Games. *Interacting with Computers, 19*(2), 180–195. doi:10.1016/j.intcom.2006.08.008

Barrett, H. (2007). Researching electronic portfolios and learner engagement: The REFLECT Initiative. *Journal of Adolescent & Adult Literacy, 50*(6), 436–449. doi:10.1598/JAAL.50.6.2

Barthes, R. (1975). *S/Z* (Miller, R., Trans.). New York: Hill and Wang. (Original work published 1970)

Bartle, R. (1997). Hearts, Clubs, Diamonds, Spades: Players Who Suit MUDs. *The Journal of Virtual Environments, 1*. Retrieved February 25, 2009, from http://www.brandeis.edu/pubs/jove/HTML/v1/bartle.html

Bartle, R. A. (1996). *Hearts, Clubs, Diamonds, Spades: Players who suit muds.* Retrieved April 14, 2009, from Richard Bartle's webpage: http://www.mud.co.uk/richard/hcds.htm

Bartle, R. A. (2003). Designing Virtual Worlds. Indiana: New Riders Publishing.

Bartlett, F. C. (1932). *Remembering.* Cambridge, UK: Cambridge University Press.

Bates, M., Brown, D. J., Cranton, W., & Lewis, J. (2008, November). *Playing to win: motivation for teaching and learning in today's gaming culture.* Paper presented at Interactive Technologies 08, Nottingham Trent University, Nottingham, UK.

Battersby, S., Brown, D. J., Standen, P. J., Anderton, N., & Harrison, M. (2004). Design, development and manufacture of novel assistive and adaptive technology devices. In P. M. Sharkey, R. McCrindle & D. Brown (Eds.), *Proceedings of the Fifth International Conference on Disability, Virtual Reality and Associated Technologies* (pp.283-290). Oxford, UK.

Baum, M. (2006). Soft News goes to war: public opinion and American foreign policy in the new media age. Princeton, NJ: Princeton.

Bayman, P., & Mayer, R. (1988). Using Conceptual Models to Teach BASIC Computer Programming. *Journal of Educational Psychology, 80*(3), 291–298. doi:10.1037/0022-0663.80.3.291

BDA. (2008). British Dyslexia Association Dyslexia Style Guide. Retrieved May 5, 2009, from http://www.bdadyslexia.org.uk/extra352.html

Beal, S. (2006, March). *Using games for training Army leaders: Newsletter of the U.S. Army Research Institute for Behavioral and Social Sciences 16(1).* Retrieved from http://www.hqda.army.mil/ari/pdf/NewsLtr_Vol16_03_06.pdf

Bean, T., Sinatra, G., & Schrader, P. G. (2009). *Spore: Spawning Evolutionary Misconceptions.* Unpublished manuscript.

Beck, U. (1986). Risikogesellschaft. Auf dem Weg in eine andere Moderne. Frankfurt/M, Germany: Suhrkamp.

BECTa. (2006). *Computer Games in Education: Findings Report.* Retrieved 19 February, 2008, from http://partners.becta.org.uk/index.php?section=rh&rid=13595

Bednar, A. K., Cunningham, D., Duffy, T. M., & Perry, J. D. (1992). Theory into practice: How do we link? In Duffy, T. M., & Jonassen, D. H. (Eds.), Constructivism and the technology of instruction: A conversation, (pp. 17-34). Hillsdale, NJ: Lawrence Erlbaum.

Bedny, G., & Meister, D. (1997). *The Russian theory of activity: Current applications to design and learning.* London: Laurence Erlbaum Associates Publishing.

Bell, S. K., & Morgan, S. B. (2000). Children's attitudes and behavioral intentions toward a peer presented as obese: Does a medical explanation for the obesity make a difference? *Journal of Pediatric Psychology, 25,* 137–148. doi:10.1093/jpepsy/25.3.137

Bellamy, R. K. E. (1996). Designing educational technology: Computer mediated change. In Nardi, B. A. (Ed.), *Conscious and consciousness: Activity theory and human-computer interaction* (pp. 123–146). London: MIT Press.

Bellini & Akullian, J. (2007). A meta-analysis of video modeling and video self-modeling interventions For children and adolescents with ASD. *Exceptional Children, 73,* 261–228.

Bellotti, V. (1988). Implications of current design practice for the use of HCI techniques. In D.M.J. & R. Winder (eds.), People and computers IV (pp. 13-34). Cambridge, UK: Cambridge University Press.

Benedetti, W. (2007). *Were video games to blame for massacre? Pundits rushed to judge industry, gamers in the wake of shooting.* Retrieved from http://www.msnbc.msn.com/id/18220228/

Benford, S. (2005). Future Location-Based Experiences. *JISC Report.* Retrieved from www.jisc.ac.uk

Benjamin, W. (1991a). Über den Begriff der Geschichte. In R. Tiedemann & H. Schweppenhäuser (Eds.), Walter Benjamin. Gesammelte Schriften in 7 Bänden, (Vol. 2, pp. 691-704). Frankfurt/M, Germany: Suhrkamp-Verlag.

Benjamin, W. (1991b). Eduard Fuchs, der Sammler und Historiker. In R. Tiedemann & H. Schweppenhäuser (Eds.), Walter Benjamin. Gesammelte Schriften in 7 Bänden, Vol. II.2, 465-505, Frankfurt/M, Germany: Suhrkamp-Verlag.

Bennett, B. W. (1993). Flexible Combat Modeling. *Simulation & Gaming, 24,* 2. doi:10.1177/1046878193242005

Bennett, W. L., Wells, C., & Rank, A. (2008). *Young citizens and civic learning: Two paradigms of citizenship in the digital age.* Seattle, WA: University of Washington.

Bente, G., & Fromm, B. (1997). Affektfernsehen: Motive, Angebotsweisen und Wirkungen. Opladen, Germany: Leske und Budrich.

Bereiter, C., & Scardamalia, M. (1987). *The psychology of written composition.* Mahwah, NJ: Lawrence Erlbaum Associates.

Berge, Z., & Collins, M. (1995). Computer-mediated communication and the online classroom in distance learning. *Computer-Mediated Communication Magazine, 2*(4), 6–13.

Berger, P. L., & Luckman, T. (1966). *The Social Construction of Reality.* New York: Doubleday.

Bergeron, B. (2006). Developing Serious Games. Hingham, MA: Charles River Media.

Bernard, R. M., de Rubalcava, B. R., & St-Pierre, D. (2000). Collaborative online distance learning: Issues for future practice and research. *Distance Education, 2*(2), 260–277. doi:10.1080/0158791000210205

Bers, M. U. (2008). Civic identities, online technologies: From designing civic curriculum to supporting civic engagement. In Bennett, W. L. (Ed.), *Civic Life Online.* Cambridge, MA: MIT Press.

Betz, J. A. (1995). Computer games: Increases learning in an interactive multidisciplinary environment. *Journal of Educational Technology Systems, 24,* 195 205. doi:10.2190/119M-BRMU-J8HC-XM6F

Bevc, T. (2005). Kulturgenese als Dialektik von Mythos und Vernunft. Ernst Cassirer und die Kritische Theorie. Würzburg, Germany: Verlag Königshausen & Neumann.

Bevc, T. (2006). Affirmation des Bestehenden. Konstruktion von Politik und Gesellschaft in Computerspielen. *Telepolis,* 07.12.2006. Retrieved March 1, 2009, from http://www.heise.de/tp/r4/artikel/24/24129/1.html

Bevc, T. (2007a). Konstruktion von Politik und Gesellschaft in Computerspielen? In T. Bevc (Ed.), Computerspiele und Politik. Zur Konstruktion von Politik und Gesellschaft in Computerspielen (pp. 25-54). Münster, Germany: Lit Verlag.

Bevc, T. (2007b). Political Education via Video Games? In D. Remeny (Ed.), *Proceedings of the European Conference on Game Based Learning. 25-26. 10. 2007 in Paisley, Scotland* (pp. 27-34). Reading.

Bevc, T. (2008). Gesellschaft und Geschichte in Computerspielen. *Einsichten und Perspektiven,* 1/2008, 50-59. Retrieved March 10, 2009 from http://www.km.bayern.de/blz/eup/01_08/4.asp

Bevc, T. (2009). Visuelle Kommunikation und Politik in Videospielen: Perspektiven für die politische Bildung? In K. Thimm (Ed.), Das Spiel - Muster und Metapher der Mediengesellschaft? (pp. 169-190). Wiesbaden, Germany: VS Verlag.

Bevc, T., & Zapf, H. (Eds.). (2009). Wie wir spielen, was wir werden. Computerspiele in unserer Gesellschaft. Konstanz, Germany: Universitätsverlag Konstanz.

Biermann, R., & Fromme, J. (2009). Identitätsbildung und politische Sozailisation. In: T. Bevc & H. Zapf (Eds.), Wie wir spielen, was wir werden. Konstanz, 113-138.

BinSubaih, A., Maddock, S., Romano, D. (2009). *Serious games for the police: Opportunities and challenges.* Special Reports & Studies Series at the Research & Studies Center (Dubai Police Academy).

Bioulac, S., Arfi, L., & Bouvard, M. (2008). Attention deficit/hyperactivity disorder and video games: A comparative study of hyperactive and control children. *European Psychiatry, 23*, 134–141.

Biswas, A., Licata, J. W., McKee, D., Pullig, C., & Daughtridge, C. (2000). The Recycling Cycle. *Journal of Public Policy & Marketing, 19*(1), 93–105. doi:10.1509/jppm.19.1.93.16950

Bixler, B. (2006). *Games and Motivation: Implications for Instructional Design.* Paper presented at the 2006 NMC Summer Conference.

Blamires, M. (Ed.). (1999). *Enabling Technology for Inclusion.* London: Paul Chapman Publishing.

Blaxill, M. F., Redwood, L., & Bernard, S. (2004). Thimerosal and autism? A plausible hypothesis that should not be dismissed. *Medical Hypotheses, 62*, 788–794. doi:10.1016/j.mehy.2003.11.033

Blind Wikia. (2009). *Android Accessibility.* Retrieved May 6, 2009, from http://blind.wikia.com/wiki/Open_Letter_Initiative#Android_Accessibility

Blizzard Entertainment. (2004/2009). World of warcraft. Irvine, California.

Bloom, B. S. (1956). Taxonomy of Educational Objectives, Handbook I: The Cognitive Domain. New York: David McKay Co Inc.

Bloom, B. S., Hastings, J. T., & Medaus, G. F. (1971). *Handbook on Formative and Summative Evaluation of Student Learning.* New York: McGraw-Hill.

Blumberg, F., & Ismailer, S. (2008). *Children's Problem Solving During Video Game Play. Fordham University, Aug. 17.* Boston Convention and Exhibition Center.

Bødker, S. (1989). A human activity approach to user interfaces. *Human-Computer Interaction, 4*, 171–195. doi:10.1207/s15327051hci0403_1

Boellstorff, T. (2008). Coming of Age in Second Life: An anthropologist explores the virtually human. Princeton and Harvard: Princeton University Press.

Bohannon, J. (2008). Flunking Spore. Science, 322(5901). Retrieved January 11, 2009 from http://www.sciencemag.org/cgi/content/full/322/5901/531b

Bonanno, P., & Kommers, P. A. M. (2005). Gender differences and styles in the use of digital games. *Educational Psychology, 25*(1), 13–41. doi:10.1080/0144341042000294877

Bonk, C. J., & Dennen, V. P. (2005). *Massive Multiplayer Online Gaming: A Research Framework for Military Training and Education.* Technical Report 2005-1, Department of Defense of the U.S.A.

Boocock, S., & Schild, E. (Eds.). (1968). Simulation Games in Learning. Beverly Hills, CA: Sage Publications.

Boot, W. R., Kramer, A. F., Simons, D. J., Fabiani, M., & Gratton, G. (2008). The effects of video game playing on attention, memory, and executive control. *Acta Psychologica, 129*, 387–398.

Boulos, M. N. K., Hetherington, L., & Wheeler, S. (2007). Second Life: An overview of the potential of 3-D virtual worlds in medical and health education. *Health Information and Libraries Journal, 24*, 233–245. doi:10.1111/j.1471-1842.2007.00733.x

Bouma, R., & Schweitzer, R. (1990). The impact of chronic childhood illness on family stress: a comparison between autism and cystic fibrosis. *Journal of Clinical Psychology, 46*(6), 722–730. doi:10.1002/1097-4679(199011)46:6<722::AID-JCLP2270460605>3.0.CO;2-6

Bowman, R. (1982). A Pac-Man theory of motivation: Tactical implications for classroom instruction. *Educational Technology, 22*(9), 14–17.

Bowman, R. (2007). How can students be motivated: A misplaced question? *Clearing House (Menasha, Wis.), 81*(2), 81–86. doi:10.3200/TCHS.81.2.81-86

Boyd, G. M. (1983). *The Use of Heuristics Based on Frank's Political-Value Triangle for the Analysis and Design of Legitimate Educational Games.* Paper presented at the International Conference on Cybernetics, Namur, Belgium.

Boyer, M. A., Urlacher, B., Hudson, N. B., Janik, L., Niv-Solomon, A., Brown, S. W., & Ioannou, A. (2009). Gender and negotiation: Some experimental findings. *International Studies Quarterly, 53*, 23–47. doi:10.1111/j.1468-2478.2008.01522.x

Bracey, G. (1992). The bright future of integrated learning systems. *Educational Technology, 32*(9), 60–62.

Bransford, J. D. L., B. A., & Crocking, R. R. (1999). How People Learn: Brain, Mind, Experience, and School. Washington, DC: National Academic Press.

Bredemeier, M., & Greenblat, C. (1981). The Educational Effectiveness of Simulation Games: A Synthesis of Findings. *Simulation & Games, 12*(3), 307–332. doi:10.1177/104687818101200304

Brogan, C. (2008, October). *Re: Community and social media* [Internet]. Message posted to: http://www.chrisbrogan.com/

Brookfield, S. (1987). Developing Critical Thinkers: Challenging Adults to Explore Alternative Ways of Thinking and Acting. San Francisco: Josey-Bass Inc.

Brookfield, S. (1995). Adult Learning: An Overview. In A. Tuinjman (ed.), *International Encyclopedia of Education*. Oxford, UK: Permamon Press. Retrieved July 24, 2009, from http://stephenbrookfield.com/by_sb.html

Brown, A. L., & Campione, J. C. (1994). Guided discovery in a community of learners. In McGilly, K. (Ed.), *Classroom lessons: Integrating cognitive theory and classroom practice* (pp. 229–270). Cambridge, MA: MIT Press.

Brown, D. J., Battersby, S., & Shopland, N. (2005). Design and evaluation of a flexible travel training environment for use in a supported employment setting. *International Journal of Disability and Human Development, 4*(3), 251–258.

Brown, D. J., McHugh, D., & Sik Lanyi, C. (2009b, in press). Combining location based services with games based learning approaches in assistive technology. In *Proceedings of AAATE 2009*.

Brown, D., Evett, L., & Lawton, J. (2002). Accessible web based multimedia for use by people with learning disabilities. In [Derby, UK: British Computer Society.]. *Proceedings of the International Conference of Assistive Technology, 2002*, 72–85. doi:10.2469/cp.v2002.n4.3218

Brown, D.J., Shopland, N., Battersby, S., Tully, A., & Richardson, S. (2009a. (in press). Game On: Accessible Serious Games for Offenders and those at Risk of Offending. *Journal of Assistive Technology.*

Brown, E., & Cairns, P. (2004). *A grounded investigation of game immersion*. Paper presented at the Conference on Human Factors in Computing Systems.

Brown, J. S., Collins, A., & Duguid, P. (1989). Situated Cognition and the Culture of Learning. *Educational Researcher, 18*, 32–42.

Brown, S. W., Boyer, M. A., Mayall, H. J., Johnson, P. R., & Meng, L. (2003). The GlobaEd project: Gender differences in a problem-based learning environment of international negotiations. *Instructional Science, 31*(4-5), 255–276. doi:10.1023/A:1024677708501

Brown, S., & Vaughan, C. (2009). *Play: How it Shapes the Brain, Opens the Imagination, and Invigorates the Soul*. New York: Avery.

Brozo, W. G., & Young, J. P. (2001). Boys will be boys, or will they? Literacy and masculinities. *Reading Research Quarterly, 36*(3), 316–325. doi:10.1598/RRQ.36.3.4

Bruckman, A., & Resnick, M. (1995). The mediamoo project constructionism and professional community. *Convergence, 1*(1), 94–109.

Bruffee, K. A. (1984). Collaborative learning and the 'conversation of mankind'. *College English, 46*(7), 635–652. doi:10.2307/376924

Bruner, J. S. (1960). The Process of Education. Cambridge, MA: Harvard University Press.

Bruner, J. S. (1961). The act of discovery. *Harvard Educational Review, 31*(1), 21–32.

Bruner, J. S., Jolly, A., & Sylva, K. (1976). *Play: Its role in development and evolution*. New York: Penguin.

Buckley, K. E., & Anderson, C. A. (2006). A theoretical model of the effects and consequences of playing video games. In Vorderer, P., & Bryant, J. (Eds.), *Playing video games: Motives, responses, and consequences*. Mahwah, NJ: Lawrence Erlbaum Associates.

Buhler, C. (2001). Empowered participation of users with disabilities in R&D projects. *International Journal of Human-Computer Studies*, *55*(4), 645–659. doi:10.1006/ijhc.2001.0489

Burke, K. (1969). *A rhetoric of motives*. Berkeley, CA: University of California Press. (Original work published 1950)

Burke, L. A., & Moore, J. E. (2003). A perennial dilemma in OB education: Engaging the traditional student. *Academy of Management Learning & Education*, *2*(1), 37–52.

Burton, S.L. & Parks, A Personal author, compiler, or editor name(s); click on any author to run a new search on that name.L. (1994). Self-Esteem, Locus of Control, and Career Aspirations of College-Age Siblings of Individuals with Disabilities. *Social Work Research*, *18*(3), 178–185.

Business Week, 15. www.businessweek.com/technology/special_reports/20070416virtuallife.htm?campaign_id=rss_daily

Butler, T. J. (1988). Games and simulations: Creative educational alternatives. *TechTrends*, (September): 20–24. doi:10.1007/BF02771190

Cable News Network (CNN) Report. (2007).

Caillois, R. (1958). Les jeux et les hommes. Paris: Gallimard.

Caillois, R. (2001). *Man, play and games* (Barash, M., Trans.). Chicago: University of Illinois Press. (Original work published 1958)

Calvert, S., & Tan, S. (1994). Impact of virtual reality on young adults' physiological arousal and aggressive thoughts: Interaction versus observation. *Journal of Applied Developmental Psychology*, *15*(1), 125–139. doi:10.1016/0193-3973(94)90009-4

Cameron, F., & Kenderdine, S. (Eds.). (2007). *Theorizing digital cultural heritage: A critical discourse*. Cambridge, Massachusetts: The MIT Press.

Campbell, J. (2008). *The hero with a thousand faces* (3rd ed.). Novato, CA: New World Library. (Original work published 1948)

Campbell, J. M., Ferguson, J. E., Herzinger, C. V., Jackson, J. N., & Marino, C. A. (2004). Combined descriptive and explanatory information improve peers' perceptions of autism. *Research in Developmental Disabilities*, *25*, 321–329. doi:10.1016/j.ridd.2004.01.005

Canada, K., & Brusca, F. (1991). The technological gender gap: Evidence and recommendations for educators and computer-based instruction designers. *Educational Technology Research and Development*, *39*(2), 43–51. doi:10.1007/BF02298153

Canada. Statistics Canada. (2004). *Measuring up: Canadian results of the OECD PISA Study*. In P. Bussière, F. Cartwright, & T. Knighton. Ottawa, ON: Statistics Canada. (Cat no. 81-590-XPE, no. 2).

Canadian Council on Learning. (2007). *State of learning in Canada: No time for complacency*. Ottawa, Canada: Report on Learning in Canada.

Capano, L., Minden, D., Chen, S., Schachar, R. J., & Ickowicz, A. (2008). Mathematical learning disorder in school-age children with Attention-Deficit Hyperactivity Disorder. *Canadian Journal of Psychiatry*, *53*, 392–399.

Carney, J. (2005). *What kind of electronic portfolio research do we need?* Paper presented at the SITE 2conference. Available: http://it.wce.wwu.edu/carney/Presentations/presentations.html

Carroll, A., & Bain, A. (1994). The effects of interactive versus linear video on the levels of attention and comprehension. *School Psychology Review*, *23*, 29.

Carroll, J.M. (Ed.). (1998). Minimalism Beyond the Nurnberg Funnel (Technical Communication, Multimedia and Information Systems). Cambridge, MA: MIT Press.

Caspian Learning. (2008). *Defence Academy Serious Games Report.* [White paper]. Retrieved http://www.caspianlearning.co.uk/MoD_Defence_Academy_Serious_games_Report_04.11.08.pdf

Cassirer, E. (1996). Versuch über den Menschen. Eine Philosophie der Kultur. Hamburg, Germany: Felix Meiner Verlag.

Castronova, E. (2006). Synthetic worlds: the business and culture of online games. Chicago: The University of Chicago Press.

Cavazos-Kottke, S. (2005). Tuned out but turned on: Boys' (dis)engaged reading in and out of school. *Journal of Adolescent & Adult Literacy, 49*(3), 180–184. doi:10.1598/JAAL.49.3.1

Center for Disease Control and Prevention. (2005, September 2). Mental health in the United States: Prevalence of diagnosis and medication treatment for attention-deficit/hyperactivity disorder --- United States, 2003. *Morbidity and Mortality Weekly Report, 54,* 842–847.

Chall, J. S. (1983). Learning to read: The great debate. (Updated ed). New York: McGraw-Hill.

Chambers, B., Abrami, P. C., McWhaw, K., & Therrien, M. C. (2001). Developing a computer-assisted tutoring program to help children at risk learn to read. *Educational Research and Evaluation, 7*(2-3), 223–239. doi:10.1076/edre.7.2.223.3863

Chambres, P., Auxiette, C., Vansingle, C., & Gil, S. (2008). Adult attitudes toward behaviors of a six-year old boy with autism. *Journal of Autism and Developmental Disorders, 38*(7), 1320–1327. doi:10.1007/s10803-007-0519-5

Chan, P., & Rabinowitz, T. (2006). A cross-sectional analysis of video games and attention deficit hyperactivity disorder symptoms in adolescents. *Annals of General Psychiatry, 5,* 5–16. doi:10.1186/1744-859X-5-16

Chandler, M. A. (2009, January 4). More and more, schools got game. *The Washington Post,* (pp. C1-C4).

Charlop-Christy, M. H., & Daneshvar, S. (2003). Using video modeling to teach perspective taking to children with autism. *Journal of Positive Behavior Interventions, 5*(1), 12–21. doi:10.1177/10983007030050010101

Charsky, D., & Mims, C. (2008). Integrating commercial off-the-shelf video games into school curriculums. *TechTrends, 52*(5), 38–44. doi:10.1007/s11528-008-0195-0

Cheal, C. (2009). Student perceptions of a course taught in Second Life. *Innovate: Journal of Online Education, 5*(5). Retrieved July 27, 2009, from http://www.innovateonline.info/index.php?view=article&id=692

Cheetham, G., & Chivers, G. (2001). How Professionals Learn in Practice: An Investigation of Informal Learning Amongst People Working in Professions. *Journal of European Industrial Training, 25*(5), 247–292. doi:10.1108/03090590110395870

Chen, S., & Michael, D. (2005). *Proof of learning: Assessment in serious games.* Retrieved on December 10, 2008 from http://www.gamasutra.com/features/20051019/chen_01.shtml

Cherney, I. D. (2008). Mom, let me play more computer games: They improve my mental rotation skills. *Sex Roles, 59,* 776–786. doi:10.1007/s11199-008-9498-z

Children Now. (2000). *Girls and Gaming: A Console Video Game Content Analysis.* Oakland, CA: Children Now.

Chittaro, L., & Ranon, R. (2007). Web3D technologies in learning, education and training: Motivations, issues, opportunities. *Computers & Education, 49,* 3–18. doi:10.1016/j.compedu.2005.06.002

Christensen, C., Horn, M., & Johnson, C. (2008). *Disrupting class: How disruptive innovation will change the way the world learns.* New York: McGraw Hill.

Christiansen, E. (1996). Tamed by a rose: Computers as tools in human activity. In Nardi, B. A. (Ed.), *Conscious and consciousness: Activity theory and human-computer interaction* (pp. 175–198). London: MIT Press.

Chute, R., & Miksad, J. (1997). Computer assisted instruction and cognitive development in preschoolers. *Child Study Journal, 27*(3), 237–254.

Clarfield, J., & Stoner, G. (2005). The effects of computerized reading instruction on the academic performance of students identified with ADHD. *School Psychology Review, 34,* 246–254.

Clark, C., Prior, M., & Kinsella, G. (2002). The relationship between executive function abilities, adaptive behavior, and academic achievement in children with externalizing behavior problems. *Journal of Child Psychology and Psychiatry, and Allied Disciplines, 43*, 785–796. doi:10.1111/1469-7610.00084

Clark, R. (2007). Learning from serious games? Arguments, evidence, and research suggestions. *Educational Technology, 47*(3), 56–59.

Clark, R. E. (1983). Reconsidering research on learning from media. *Review of Educational Research, 53*(4), 445–459.

Clark, R. E. (1994a). Media will never influence learning. *Educational Technology Research and Development, 42*(2), 21–29. doi:10.1007/BF02299088

Clark, R. E. (1994b). Media and method. *Educational Technology Research and Development, 42*(3), 7–10. doi:10.1007/BF02298090

Clark, R., & Mayer, R. (2007). E-learning and the science of instruction: Second edition. San Francisco: Pfeiffer.

Clarke, J., & Dukas, G. (2009). Studying the potential of virtual performance assessments for measuring student achievement in science. Presentation at AERA 2009, San Diego, CA.

Clay, R. A. (2009, February). Mini-mulitaskers. *Monitor on Psychology*. February 24, 2009, from http://www.apa.org/monitor/2009/02/multitaskers.html

Coates, J. (2003). *Generational learning styles*. River Falls, WI: Lern Books.

Cocking, R. R., & Greenfield, P. M. (1996). Effects of interactive entertainment technologies on children's development. In P.M. Greenfield & R.R. Cocking (Eds.), Interacting with Video (pp. 3-7). Norwood, NJ: Ablex Publishing.

Codding, R. S., Lewandowski, L., & Eckert, T. (2005). Examining the efficacy of performance feedback and goal-setting interventions in children with *ADHD*: A comparison of two methods of goal setting. *Journal of Evidence-Based Practices for Schools, 6*, 42–58.

Colbert, J. A., Boyd, K. E., Clark, K. A., Guan, S., Harris, J. B., & Kelley, M. A. (2008). *Handbook of Technological Pedagogical Content Knowledge (TPCK) for Educators*. New York: Routledge.

Cole, M. (1999). Cultural psychology: Some general principles and a concrete example. In Engeström, Y., Miettinen, R., & Punamäki, R. L. (Eds.), *Perspectives on activity theory* (pp. 232–249). Cambridge, UK: Cambridge University Press.

Collins, A., Joseph, D., & Bielaczyc, K. (2004). Design research: Theoretical and methodological issues. *Journal of the Learning Sciences, 13*(1), 15–42. doi:10.1207/s15327809jls1301_2

Colt, H. G., & Crawford, S. W., & III, O. G. (2001). Virtual Reality Bronchoscopy Simulation*: A Revolution in Procedural Training. *Chest, 120*(4), 1333–1339. doi:10.1378/chest.120.4.1333

Comaskey, E., Savage, R., & Abrami, P. C. (2009). A randomized efficacy study of a web-based literacy intervention among disadvantaged urban kindergarten children. [Special issue on literacy and technology]. *Journal of Research in Reading, 32*(1), 92–108. doi:10.1111/j.1467-9817.2008.01383.x

Command Arms Center, National Simulation Center. (2006). *Commander's guide to games for training*. Retrieved from the Advanced Distributed Learning Community of the U.S. Department of Defense Website http://adlcommunity.net/mod/data/view.php?d=38&advanced=0&paging=&page=1

Conference Board of Canada. (2008). *Education and skills overview*. Ottawa, Canada: Author. Retrieved July 31, 2008 from http://sso.conferenceboard.ca/HCP/overview/Educationskills.aspx

Cooper, S., Dann, W., & Pausch, R. (2000). *Alice: A 3D tool for introductory programming courses*. In Proceedings of the 5th Annual CCSC Northeastern Conference 2000, Ramapo, NJ.

Cope, B., & Kalantzis, M. (2000). Multiliteracies: Literacy, learning, and the design of social futures. London: Routledge.

Courchesne, E. (1995, February). An MRI study of autism: The cerebellum revisited. *Journal of Autism and Developmental Disorders, 25*(1), 19–22. doi:10.1007/BF02178164

Crawford, C. (1984). The art of computer game design. Berkeley, CA: Osborne/McGraw-Hill.

Crawford, C. (2005). Chris Crawford on Interactive Storytelling. Berkeley, CA: New Riders.

Crawford, G. (2005). Digital gaming, sport and gender. *Leisure Studies, 24*(3), 259–270. doi:10.1080/0261436042000290317

Creemers, B. P. M. (1994). The Effective Classroom. London: Cassell.

Cromby, J. J., Standen, P. J., & Brown, D. J. (1996). The potentials of virtual environments in the education and training of people with learning disabilities. *Journal of Intellectual Disability Research, 40*, 489–501. doi:10.1111/j.1365-2788.1996.tb00659.x

Crookall, D., Oxford, R. L., & Saunders, D. (1987). Towards a reconceptualization of simulation: From representation to reality. *Simulation/Games for Learning, 17*, 147-171.

Csikszentmihalyi, M. (1981). Some paradoxes in the definition of play. In Cheska, A. T. (Ed.), *Play as context*. West Point, NY: Leisure Press.

Csikszentmihalyi, M. (1990). *Flow: the psychology of optical experience*. New York: Harper Perennial.

Cummings, J. A. (2000). *Debate in the virtual classroom*. Unpublished manuscript, Indiana University at Bloomington, Bloomington, IN.

Curtis, C. K., Thomas, K. M., & Ritter, J. (2008). Interactive gaming technologies and air force technical training. *Journal of Interactive Instruction Development, 20*(3), 17–23.

D'Ateno, P., Mangiapanello, K., & Taylor, B. A. (2003). Using video modeling to teach complex play sequences to a preschooler with autism. *Journal of Positive Behavior Interventions, 5*(1), 5–11. doi:10.1177/10983007030050010801

Daly-Jones, O., Bevan, N., & Thomas, C. (1999). *INUSE: Handbook of User-Centred Design*. Serco Usability Services, National Physical Laboratory.

Dautenhahn, K., & Billard, A. (2002) Games Children with Autism Can Play With Robota, a Humanoid Robotic Doll. Proc. 1st Cambridge Workshop on Universal Access and Assistive Technology (CWUAAT). In S. Keates, P.J. Clarkson, P.M. Langdon & P. Robinson (eds.), *Universal Access and Assistive Technology*. London: Springer-Verlag.

Davidson, R. J., Ekman, P., Saron, C., Senulius, J., & Friesen, W. V. (1990). Approach-withdrawal and cerebral asymmetry: Emotional expression and brain physiology I. *Journal of Personality and Social Psychology, 58*, 330–341. doi:10.1037/0022-3514.58.2.330

Davis, D. D., & Bryant, J. L. (2003). Influence at a distance: Leadership in global virtual teams. *Advances in Global Leadership, 3*, 303–340. doi:10.1016/S1535-1203(02)03015-0

Davis, P. K., & Winnefeld, J. (1983). *The Rand Strategy Assessment Center. Technical Report- R2945*. RAND Corporation.

Davis, P. K., Bankes, S. C., & Kahan, J. P. (1986). *A new methodology for Modeling National Command Level Decision making in War Games and Simulations*. Technical Report R3290, RAND Corporation.

Dawson, C. R., Cragg, A., Taylor, C., & Toombs, B. (2007). Video Games Research to improve understanding of what players enjoy about video games, and to explain their preferences for particular games. London: British Board of Film Classification (BBFC).

Day, E. A., Arthur, W., & Gettman, D. (2001). Knowledge structures and the acquisition of complex skill. *The Journal of Applied Psychology, 85*(5), 1022–1033. doi:10.1037/0021-9010.86.5.1022

de Freitas, S. (200 6). Learning in Immersive Worlds: A Review of Game Based Learning. *JISC*. Retrieved July 31, 2006, from http://www.jisc.ac.uk/media/documents/programmes/elearning_innovation/gaming report_v3.3.pdf

De Freitas, S. (2009). Serious games. *Adults Learning, 20*(7), 26–27.

de Freitas, S., & Levene, M. (2004). *An investigation of the use of simulations and video gaming for supporting exploratory learning and developing higher-order cognitive skills.* IADIS International Conference in Cognition and Exploratory Learning in the Digital Age, 15-17 December. Lisbon, Portugal.

De Lucia, A., Francese, R., Passero, I., & Tortora, G. (2009). Development and evaluation of a virtual campus on Second Life: The case of SecondDMI. *Computers & Education, 52*, 220–233. doi:10.1016/j.compedu.2008.08.001

Deault, L. Savage, R., & Abrami, P. C. (2009. (in press). Inattention and response to the ABRACADABRA web-based literacy intervention. *Journal of Research on Educational Effectiveness.*

Dede, C. (2007). Planning for neomillennial learning styles. *EDUCAUSE*. Retrieved, from http://net.educause.edu/ir/library/pdf/EQM0511.pdf.

Delpit, L. (1995). Other people's children: Cultural conflict in the classroom. New York: The New Press.

DeNike, L. (1976). An Exploratory Study of The Relationship of Educational Cognitive Style to Learning from Simulation Games. *Simulation & Games, 7*(1), 65–74. doi:10.1177/104687817600700105

Denis, G., & Jouvelot, P. (2005). Motivation-driven educational game design: Applying best practices to music education. In *Proceedings of the 2005 ACM SIGCHI international Conference on Advances in Computer Entertainment Technology* (Valencia, Spain, June 15 - 17, vol. 265, pp. 462-465). New York: ACM. DOI= http://doi.acm.org/10.1145/1178477.1178581

Denzin & Y.S. Lincoln (Ed.), *Handbook of Qualitative Research* (2nd ed.). Thousand Oaks, CA: Sage.

Denzin, N. K. (1989). *Interpretive Biography.* Thousand Oaks, CA: Sage Publications.

Denzin, N. K., & Lincoln, Y. S. (2000). *The discipline and practice of qualitative research.* In N.K.

Department of Health. (2001). *Valuing People: a new strategy for learning disability for the 21ˢᵗ century.* London: HMSO.

Dewey, J. (1899). The School and Society. Chicago, IL: University of Chicago Press.

Dewey, J. (1909). *Moral Principles in Education.* New York: Houghton Mifflin.

Dewey, J. (1916). *Democracy and Education.* New York: Macmillan.

Dewey, J. (1956). *The Child and the Curriculum.* Chicago: University of Chicago Press. (Original work published 1900)

Dibbel, J. (1993). *A rape in cyberspace.* Retrieved April 14, 2009, from Julian Dibbell's webpage http://www.juliandibbell.com/texts/bungle.html

Dibbell, J. (2007). The life of the Chinese gold farmer. *New York Times.* Retrieved from http://www.nytimes.com/2007/06/17/magazine/17lootfarmers-t.html?pagewanted=print

Dickey, M. D. (2005). Three-dimensional worlds and distance learning: Two case studies of Active Worlds as a medium for distance education. *British Journal of Educational Technology, 36*, 439–451. doi:10.1111/j.1467-8535.2005.00477.x

Dickson, K. L., Walker, H., & Fogel, A. (1997). The relationship between smile type and play type during parent–infant play. *Developmental Psychology, 33*, 925–933. doi:10.1037/0012-1649.33.6.925

Diehl, W. C., & Prins, E. (2008). Unintended outcomes in Second Life: Intercultural literacy and cultural identity in a virtual world. *Language and Intercultural Communication, 8*(2), 101–118. doi:10.1080/14708470802139619

Dietz W.H., Bandini L.G., Morelli J.A., Peers K.F., Ching P.L. Effect of sedentary activities on resting metabolic rate. *American Journal of Clinical Nutition, 59*, 556–559.

Dimberg, U. (1982). Facial reactions to facial expressions. *Psychophysiology, 19*, 643–647. doi:10.1111/j.1469-8986.1982.tb02516.x

Din, F. S., & Calao, J. (2001). The effects of playing educational video games on kindergarten achievement. *Child Study Journal, 31*(2), 95–102.

Disability Discrimination Act. (2005). *HMSO*. Retrieved March 23, 2006, from http://www.opsi.gov.uk/acts/acts2005/20050013.htm

Disability Rights Commission. (2004). *The Web: Access and Inclusion for Disabled People*. Retrieved May 8, 2009, from http://www.equalityhumanrights.com/en/publicationsandresources/Pages/webaccess.aspx?k=The%20Web:%20Access%20and%20Inclusion%20for%20Disabled%20People

DiSalvo, C. A., & Oswald, D. P. (2002). Peer-mediated interventions to increase the social interaction of children with autism: Consideration of peer expectancies. *Focus on Autism and Other Developmental Disabilities, 17*(4), 198–207. doi:10.1177/10883576020170040201

DiSessa, A. A. (2000). *Changing minds: Computers, learning, and literacy*. Cambridge, MA: MIT Press.

Distance education timeline. (n.d.). Retrieved April 14, 2009, from Baker's Guide http://www.bakersguide.com/Distance_Education_Timeline.

Donchin, E. (1989). The learning strategies project. *Acta Psychologica, 71*, 1–15. doi:10.1016/0001-6918(89)90002-4

Dreher, C., Reiners, T., Dreher, N., & Dreher, H. (2009). Virtual worlds as a context suited for information systems education: Discussion of pedagogical experience and curriculum design with reference to Second Life. *Journal of Information Systems Education, 20*(2), 211–224.

Driscoll, M. (2005). Psychology of Learning for Instruction, (3rd Ed.). Boston: Pearson Education.

Driscoll, M. P. GLE: Grade level evaluation: Ensuring academic success. Psychology of Learning for Instruction. Boston: Allyn & Bacon.

Driskell, J., & Dwyer, D. (1984). Microcomputer videogame based training. *Educational Technology, 24*(2), 11–15.

Duchenne, G. B. (1990). *The mechanism of human facial expression or an electro-physiological analysis of the expression of emotions* (Cutherbertson, R. A. (Trans. Ed.)). New York: Cambridge University Press. (Original work published 1862)

Duclos, S. E., & Laird, J. D. (2001). The deliberate control of emotional experience through control of expressions. *Cognition and Emotion, 15*, 27–56. doi:10.1080/0269993004200088

Duffy, T. M., & Cunningham, D. J. (1996). Constructivism: Implications for the Design and Delivery of Instruction. In D. H. Jonassen, (ed.), Handbook of Research for Educational Communications and Technology (pp. 170-198). New York: Macmillan Library Reference.

Duffy, T. M., & Jonassen, D. (Eds.). (1992). *Constructivism and the technology of instruction: A conversation*. Hillsdale, NJ: Lawrence Erlbaum Associates.

Duffy, T. M., & Jonassen, D. H. (1992b). Preface. In T. M. Duffy & D. H. Jonassen, (Eds.), Constructivism and the technology of instruction: A conversation. Hillsdale, NJ: Lawrence Erlbaum.

Duke, R. (1974). Toward a General Theory of Gaming. *Simulation & Games, 5*(2), 131–146. doi:10.1177/003755007452001

DuPaul, G. J., & Stoner, G. (2003). ADHD in the schools: Assessment and intervention strategies (2nd ed.). New York: Guilford.

DuPaul, G. J., Rutherford, L. E., & Hosterman, S. J. (2008). Attention-deficit/hyperactivity disorder. In Morris, R.J., & Mather, N. (Eds.), Evidence-based interventions for students with learning and behavioral challenges (pp. 42). New York: Routledge.

DuPaul, G., & Weyandt, L. (2006). School-based interventions for children and adolescents with attention-deficit/hyperactivity disorder: enhancing academic and behavioral outcomes. *Education & Treatment of Children, 29*, 341–358.

Dyck, J., Pinelle, D., Brown, B., & Gutwin, C. (2003). *Learning from Games: HCI Design Innovations in Entertainment Software*. Paper presented at the Graphics Interface Conference, Halifax, Canada.

Edelman, G. (2004). Wider Than the Sky: The Phenomenal Gift of Consciousness. New Haven, CT: Yale University Press.

Edelson, D. C., Gordin, D. N., & Pea, R. D. (1999). Addressing the challenges of inquiry-based learning through technology and curriculum design. Journal of the Learning Sciences, 8(3/4), 391–450. doi:10.1207/s15327809jls0803&4_3

Edirisingha, P., Nie, M., Pluciennik, M., & Young, R. (2009). Socialisation for learning at a distance in a 3-D multi-user virtual environment. *British Journal of Educational Technology, 40*, 458–479. doi:10.1111/j.1467-8535.2009.00962.x

Egli, E., & Meyers, L. (1984). The role of video game playing in adolescent life: Is there reason to be concerned? *Bulletin of the Psychonomic Society, 22*, 309–312.

Ehri, L., Nunes, R. S., Willows, D., Schuster, B. V., Yaghoub-Zadeh, Z., & Shanahan, T. (2001). Phonemic awareness instruction helps children learn to read: Evidence from the national reading panel's meta-analysis. *Reading Research Quarterly, 36*(3), 250–287. doi:10.1598/RRQ.36.3.2

Ekman, P., & Friesen, W. V. (1982). Felt, false, and miserable smiles. *Journal of Nonverbal Behavior, 6*, 238–252. doi:10.1007/BF00987191

Ekman, P., Levenson, R. W., & Friesen, W. V. (1983). Autonomivic nervous system activity distinguishes among emotions. *Science, 221*, 1208–1210. doi:10.1126/science.6612338

Ekpenyong, L. E. (1999). A Reformulation of the Theory of Experiential Learning Appropriate for Instruction in Formal Business Education. *Journal of Vocational Education and Training, 51*(3), 449–471. doi:10.1080/13636829900200092

Elder, J. (2006). *Different like me: My book of autism heroes*. London: Jessica Kingsley Publishers.

Engel, S. (1999). *Context is everything: The nature of memory*. London: Freeman.

Engeström, Y. (1987). *Learning by expanding: An activity-theoretical approach to developmental research*. Helsinki: Orienta-Konsultit.

Engeström, Y., & Escalante, V. (1996). Mundane tool or object of affection? The rise and fall of the Postal Buddy. In Nardi, B. A. (Ed.), *Conscious and consciousness: Activity theory and human-computer interaction* (pp. 325–373). London: MIT Press.

Engeström, Y., Engeström, R., & Karkkainene, M. (1995). Polycontextuality and boundary crossing in expert cognition. *Learning and Instruction, 5*(4), 319–336. doi:10.1016/0959-4752(95)00021-6

Entertainment and Leisure Software Publishers Association. (2006). *Unlimited Learning; Computer and Video Games in the Learning Landscape*. Retrieved from http://www.elspa.com/assets/files/u/unlimitedlearningtheroleofcomputerandvideogamesint_344.pdf

Entertainment Software Association. (2006). *Essential Facts about the Computer and Video Game Industry*. Retrieved January 11, 2007, from http://www.theesa.com/facts/index.php.

Epstein, J., Casey, B. J., Toney, S. T., Davidson, M. C., Reiss, A. L., & Garrett, A. (2007). ADHD and medication-related brain activation effects in concordantly affected parent-child dyads with ADHD. *Journal of Child Psychology and Psychiatry, and Allied Disciplines, 48*, 899–913. doi:10.1111/j.1469-7610.2007.01761.x

Esteves, M., Fonseca, B., Morgado, L., & Martins, P. (2009). Using Second Life for problem-based learning In computer science programming. *Journal of Virtual Worlds Research, 2* (1). Retrieved July 29, 2009 from https://journals.tdl.org/jvwr/article/view/419/462

Etuk, N. (2008). Educational gaming: From edutainment to bona fide 21st century teaching tool. *MultiMedia & Internet @Schools, 15*(6), 10-13.

Evans, E. M. (2008). Conceptual change and evolutionary biology: A developmental analysis. In Vosiandou, S. (Ed.), *International Handbook of Research on Conceptual Change*. New York: Routledge.

Evans, M.A. (in press). Mobility, games, and education. To appear in the Handbook of Research on Educational Games.

Evett, L., & Brown, D. (2005). Text formats and web design for visually impaired readers – Clear Text for All. *Interacting with Computers, 17*, 153 172. doi:10.1016/j.intcom.2005.04.001

Evett, L., Brown, D., Smith, P., & Hibberd, R. (2006). Cleaning up the environment – Accessible PowerPoint Presentations. In *Proceedings of NTU 6th Annual Learning and Teaching Conference* (pp. 26-44). March 2006. Nottingham, UK: Nottingham Trent University.

Eyal, K., Metzger, M. J., Lingsweiler, R. W., Mahood, C., & Yao, M. Z. (2006). Aggressive political opinions and exposure to violent media. *Mass Communication & Society, 9*(4), 399–428. doi:10.1207/s15327825mcs0904_2

Fabricatore, C. (2000). *Learning and videogames: An unexploited synergy.* Retrieved from www.learndev.org/dl/FabricatoreAECT2000.pdf

Facer, K., Ulicsak, M., & Sandford, R. (2007*).* Can computer games go to school? In *Emerging technologies 2007, BECTA.* Retrieved May 12, 2007 from www.becta.org.uk

Facione, P. (1990). Critical Thinking: A Statement of Expert Consensus for Purposes of Educational Assessement and Instruction. Millbrae, CA.

Factory, C. (2009). *Mobile Speak for Symbian OS.* Retrieved May 7, 2009, from http://www.codefactory.es/en/products.asp?id=24

Falmagne, J.-C., Cosyn, E., Doignon, J.-P., & Thiery, N. (2004). *The assessment of knowledge, in theory and in practice.* Retrieved February 20, 2006 from http://www.business.aleks.com/about/Science_Behind_ALEKS.pdf

Faraone, S. V., Biederman, J., Monuteaux, M. C., & Seidman, L. J. (2001). A psychometric measure of learning disability predicts educational failure four years later in boys with attention deficit hyperactivity disorder. *Journal of Attention Disorders, 4*, 220–230. doi:10.1177/108705470100400404

Farber, B. (1963). Interaction with Retarded Siblings and Life Goals of Children. *Marriage and Family Living, 25*(1), 96–98. doi:10.2307/349015

Faria, A. J. (1998). Business Simulation Games: Current Usage Levels - An Update. *Simulation & Gaming, 29*(3), 295 308. doi:10.1177/1046878198293002

Faria, A. J., & Wellington, W. J. (2004). A survey of simulation game users, former-users, and never-users. *Simulation & Gaming, 35*(2), 178–207. doi:10.1177/1046878104263543

Farrace-Di Zinno, A., Douglas, G., Houghton, S., Lawrence, V., West, J., & Whiting, K. (2001). Body movements of boys with attention deficit hyperactivity disorder (ADHD) during computer video game play. *British Journal of Educational Technology, 32*, 607–618. doi:10.1111/1467-8535.00229

Federation of American Scientists. (2006). *Findings and recommendations from the Summit on Educational Games: Harnessing the power of video games for learning. October 25, 2005.* Washington, DC: Author.

Federation of American Scientists. (2006). *Harnessing the power of video games for learning.* Report from the Summit on Educational Games. Retrieved March 12, 2009 from http://www.fas.org/gamesummit/Resources/Summit%20on%20Educational%20Games.pdf

Federation of American Scientists. (2006). *Summit on Educational Games* [White paper]. Retrieved from Federation of American Scientist, Washington, DC: http://www.fas.org/gamesummit/

Feldman, J. (1997). Embodiment is the Foundation, Not a Level. *The Behavioral and Brain Sciences, 20*(4), 746–747. doi:10.1017/S0140525X9727161X

Ferguson, C. J. (2007). The good, the bad, and the ugly: A meta-analytic review of positive and negative effects of violent video games. *The Psychiatric Quarterly, 78*, 309–316. doi:10.1007/s11126-007-9056-9

Ferguson, C. J. (2008). The school shooting/violent video game link: Causal relationship or moral panic? *Journal of Investigative Psychology and Offender Profiling, 5*, 25–37. doi:10.1002/jip.76

Ferguson, C. J., Rueda, S. M., Cruz, A. M., Ferguson, D. E., Fritz, S., & Smith, S. M. (2008). Violent video games and aggression: Causal relationship or byproduct of family violence and intrinsic violence motivation? *Criminal Justice and Behavior, 35,* 311–332. doi:10.1177/0093854807311719

Fernández-Dols, J. M., & Ruiz-Belda, M. A. (1995). Are smiles a sign of happiness? Gold medal winners at the Olympic Games. *Journal of Personality and Social Psychology, 69,* 1113–1119. doi:10.1037/0022-3514.69.6.1113

Fiertag & Berge. (2008). Training generation N: How educator should approach the Net Generation. *Education & Training, 50*(6), 457-464.

Fisch, S. M. (2005). *Making Educational Computer Games "Educational".* Paper presented at the 4th International Conference on Interaction Design and Children (IDC2005).

Fisher, B., Bruce, M., & Grieve, C. (2007). *The entry knowledge of Australian preservice teachers in the area of phonological awareness and phonics. Quality of School Education: Senate Standing Committee on Employment, Workplace Relations and Education (No. 172).* Canberra, Australia: Parliament of the Commonwealth of Australia.

Fisher, S. (1994). Identifying video game addiction in children and adolescents. *Addictive Behaviors, 19*(5), 545–553. doi:10.1016/0306-4603(94)90010-8

Fister, S. (1999). CBT fun and games. *Training Magazine, 36*(5), 68–70.

Fletcher, J. D. (2009, January). Education and training technology in the military. *Science, 323,* 72–75. doi:10.1126/science.1167778

Fletcher, J.D. & Chatelier. (2000). *An overview of military training* (Office of Under Secretary for Defense (P&R) (Readiness and Training. No. BE-2-1710). Washington, DC: Institute for Defense Analysis.

Foorman, B. R., Fletcher, J. M., Francis, D. J., Schatschneider, C., & Mehta, P. (1998). The Role of Instruction in Learning to Read: Preventing Reading Failure in At-Risk Children. *Journal of Educational Psychology, 90*(1), 37–55. doi:10.1037/0022-0663.90.1.37

Ford, Barlow & Lewis, (n.d.). *An initial analysis of the military potential of COTS games.* Retrieved from Australian Defence Force Academy Web Site: www.siaa.asn.au/get/2391114970.pdf

Foreman, J. (2004). Video game studies and the emerging instructional revolution. *Innovate: Journal of Online Education, 1.* Retrieved from http://www.innovationonline.info/index.php?view=article&id=2

Fortugno, N., & Zimmerman, E. (2005). *Learning to Play to Learn - Lessons in Educational Game Design.* Retrieved 8 July 2008, from http://www.gamasutra.com/features/20050405/zimmerman_01.shtml

Frazier, T., Youngstrom, E., Glutting, J., & Watkins, M. (2007). ADHD and achievement: Meta-analysis of the child, adolescent, and adult literatures and a concomitant study with college students. *Journal of Learning Disabilities, 40,* 49–65. doi:10.1177/00222194070400010401

Frea, W. D. (1995). Social-communicative skills in high-functioning children with autism. In Krogel, R. L., & Koegel, L. K. (Eds.), *Teaching children with autism: Strategies for initiating positive interactions and improving learning opportunities* (pp. 53–66). Baltimore: Brookes.

Freedman, D. H. (1994). The Schank Tank. *Wired magazine, 2.*08, August 1994.

Freeman, D. (2004). *Creating emotion in games.* San Francisco, CA: New Riders.

Friedl, M. (2003). Online game interactivity theory. London: Charles River Media.

Friedrich, S., Morgan, S. B., & Devine, C. (1996). Children's attitudes and behavioral intentions toward a peer with Tourette's syndrome. *Journal of Pediatric Psychology, 21,* 307–319. doi:10.1093/jpepsy/21.3.307

Fritz, J. (2005). Warum eigentlich spielt jemand Computerspiele? Macht, Herrschaft und Kontrolle faszinieren und motivieren. In *Bundeszentrale für politische Bildung, Thema Computerspiele*. Retrieved March 10, 2009 from http://www.bpb.de/themen/RSE41Q,0,Warum_eigentlich_spielt_jemand_Computerspiele.html.

Froehlich, T. E., Lanphear, B. P., Epstein, J. N., Barbaresi, W. J., Katusic, S. K., & Kahn, R. S. (2007). Prevalence, recognition, and treatment of attention-deficit/hyperactivity disorder in a national sample of U.S. children. *Archives of Pediatrics & Adolescent Medicine, 161*, 857–864. doi:10.1001/archpedi.161.9.857

Fromberg, D., & Bergen, D. (2006). *Play from Birth to 12*. New York: Routledge.

Fromme, J. (2003). Computer games as a part of children's culture. *The International Journal of Computer Game Research, 3*(1). Retrieved July 30, 2009 from http://gamestudies.org/0301/fromme/

Fromme, J. (2006). Socialisation in the Age of New Media. *MedienPädagogik. Zeitschrift für Theorie und Praxis der Medienbildung*. Retrieved January 17, 2009 from http://www.medienpaed.com/05-1/fromme05-1.pdf

Fu, D., Jensen, R., Ramachandran, S., Salas, E., Rosen, M., Upshaw, C., et al. (2007). *Authoring Effective Demonstrations*. Technical Report TR2007-01. San Mateo, CA: Stottler Henke.

Fu, F., Su, R., & Yu, S. (2009). EGameFlow: a scale to measure learners' enjoyment of e-learning games. *Computers & Education, 52*, 101–112. doi:10.1016/j.compedu.2008.07.004

Futurelab. (2009). *Futurelab – Innovation in Education*. Retrieved May 7, 2009, from http://www.futurelab.org.uk/

Gagne, R. (1987). *Instructional Technology Foundations*. Hillsdale, NJ: Lawrence Erlbaum Assoc.

Gagné, R. M. (1985). The conditions of learning and theory of instruction (4th ed.). New York: Holt, Rinehart and Winston.

Gagne, R. M., Walter, W. W., Golas, K., & Keller, J. (2005). Principles of instructional design: Fifth edition. Belmont, CA: Wadsworth.

Gailey, C. W. (1996). Mediated messages: Gender, class, and cosmos in home video games. In P.M.

Gaimster, J. (2008). Reflections on interactions in virtual worlds and their implication for learning art and design. *Art. Design & Communication in Higher Education, 6*(3), 187–199. doi:10.1386/adch.6.3.187_1

Games, I. A. (2008). Three Dialogs: a framework for the analysis and assessment of twenty-first century literacy practices, and its use in the context of game design within Gamestar Mechanic. *E-learning, 5*(4), 396–417. doi:10.2304/elea.2008.5.4.396

Gardner, H. (1983). Frames of mind: The theory of multiple intelligences. New York: Basic Books.

Gardner, H. (1999). Intelligence reframed: Multiple Intelligences for the 21st century. New York: Basic Books.

GaGarris, R., Ahlers, R., & Driskell, J. E. (2002). Games, motivation and learning. *Simulation & Gaming; An Interdisciplinary Journal of Theory. Practice and Research, 33*(4), 43–56.

Garris, R., Ahlers, R., & Driskell, J. E. (2002). Games, motivation, and learning: A research and practice model. *Simulation & Gaming, 33*(4), 441–467. doi:10.1177/1046878102238607

Garrison, D. R. (1991). Critical Thinking and Adult Education: A Conceptual Model for Developing Critical Thinking in Adult Learners. *International Journal of Lifelong Education, 10*(4), 287–303. doi:10.1080/0260137910100403

Garrison-Harrell, L., Kamps, D., & Kravits, T. (1997). The effects of peer networks On social-communicative behaviors for students with autism. *Focus on Autism and Other Developmental Disabilities, 12*(4), 241–256. doi:10.1177/108835769701200406

Gartner. (2000, May 9). Generation Y Web Shoppers Emerge as Mini-Boomers According to Gartner. *Gartner.*

Gbrown. (25 May 2009). Generation 'no effort.' why? *Chronicle.com*. Retrieved June 6, 2009 from http://chronicle.com/forums/index.php?topic=60658.0

Gee, J. (1989). Literacy, discourse, and linguistics: Introduction. *Journal of Education, 171*(1), 5–17.

Gee, J. (1996). Social linguistics and literacies: Ideology in Discourses (2nd ed.). London: Taylor & Francis.

Gee, J. (1999). An introduction to Discourse analysis. New York: Routledge.

Gee, J. (2000). Teenagers in new times: A new literacy studies perspective. *Journal of Adolescent & Adult Literacy, 43*(5), 412–420.

Gee, J. (2001). Reading as situated language: A sociocognitive perspective. *Journal of Adolescent & Adult Literacy, 44*(8), 714–725. doi:10.1598/JAAL.44.8.3

Gee, J. (2007). What Video Games Have to Teach Us about Learning and Literacy, (2nd Ed.). Basingstoke, UK: Palgrave Macmillan.

Gee, J. P. (1996). *Social linguistics and literacies: Ideology in discourses*. New York: Routledge.

Gee, J. P. (2003). *What computer games have to teach us about learning and literacy*. New York: Palgrave, Macmillan.

Gee, J. P. (2003, 2004). Good Video Games and Good Learning. Retrieved April 27, 2009 from http://www.academiccolab.org/resources/documents/Good_Learning.pdf

Gee, J. P. (2004). *Situated Language and Learning: A Critique of Traditional Schooling*. New York: Routledge.

Gee, J. P. (2005). *An introduction to discourse analysis*. Abingdon, UK: Routledge.

Gee, J. P. (2005). *Game-like learning: An example of situated learning and implications for the opportunity to learn* [Electronic Version]. Retrieved September 6, 2006 from http://www.academiccolab.org/resources/documents/Game-Like%20Learning.rev.pdf

Gee, J. P. (2005). Good video games and good learning. *Phi Kappa Phi Forum, 85*(2), 33–37.

Gee, J. P. (2008). Learning and games. In K. Salen (Ed) The Ecology of Games: Connecting Youth, Games, and Learning (pp 21-40). Cambridge, MA: The MIT Press.

Gee, J. P. (2008). Video Games and Embodiment. *Games and Culture, 3*(3-4), 253–263. doi:10.1177/1555412008317309

Gee, J. P. (2009). Discussant for the session Peering behind the digital curtain: Using situated data for assessment in collaborative virtual environments and games. AERA, San Diego, CA.

Gee, J. P., Hawisher, G., & Selfe, C. (2007). *Gaming lives in the twenty-first century: Literate connections*. New York: Palgrave/Macmillan.

Geertz, C. (1973). *The Interpretation of Cultures*. New York: Basic Books.

Gehlbach, H., Brown, S.W., Ioannou, A., Boyer, M.A., & Hudson, N., & Niv-Solomon, A.et al. (2008). Increasing interest in social studies: Social perspective taking and self-efficacy in stimulating simulations. *Contemporary Educational Psychology, 33*, 894–914. doi:10.1016/j.cedpsych.2007.11.002

Generation Fit. (2007). [Video File]. Video posted to http://www.generation-fit.com

Genocchio, B. (2008, March 12). Flying avatars admire the artwork. *The New York Times,* p. 36.

Gentile, D. A. (2005). *The psychology behind video games as excellent teachers: A dimensional approach*. Paper presented at the 91W EMS/Department of combat medical training education conference, San Antonio, TX.

Gentile, D. A., & Anderson, C. A. (2003). Violent video games: The newest media violence hazard. In D.A. Gentile (Ed.), Media violence and children. Westport, CT: Praeger Publishing.

Gentile, D. A., Lynch, P. J., Linder, J. R., & Walsh, D. A. (2004). The effects of violent video game habits on adolescent hostility, aggressive behaviors, and school performance. *Journal of Adolescence, 27*, 5–22. doi:10.1016/j.adolescence.2003.10.002

Gentry, J. W., Commuri, S. F., Burns, A. C., & Dickenson, J. R. (1998). The second component to experiential learning: A look back at how ABSEL has handled the conceptual and operational definitions of learning. *Developments in Business Simulation & Experiential Exercises*, *25*, 62–68.

Gibb, G., Bailey, J., Lambirth, T., & Wilson, W. (1983). Personality differences between high and low electronic video game users. *The Journal of Psychology*, *114*, 159–165.

Gibbons, L. J. (2009). Law and the Emotive Avatar. *Vanderbilt Journal of Entertainment and Technology Law*, *11*(4), 899–920.

Gibson, C., & Levine, P. (2003). *The Civic Mission of Schools*. New York: Carnegie Corporation.

Gibson, J. J. (1986). *The Ecological Approach to Visual Perception*. Hillsdale, NJ: Erlbaum.

Giere, R. (1991). *Understanding Scientific Reasoning* (3rd ed.). Fort Worth, TX: Holt, Rinehardt and Winston.

Giumetti, G., & Markey, P. M. (2007). Violent video games and anger as predictors of aggression. *Journal of Research in Personality*, *41*(6), 1234–1243. doi:10.1016/j.jrp.2007.02.005

Givens, S., & Monahan, J. (2005). Priming Mammies, Jezebels, and Other Controlling Images: An Examination of the Influence of Mediated Stereotypes on Perceptions of an African American Woman. *Media Psychology*, *7*(1), 87–106. doi:10.1207/S1532785XMEP0701_5

Glass, A. (2007). Understanding generational differences for competitive success. *Industrial and Commercial Training*, *39*(2), 98–103. doi:10.1108/00197850710732424

Glickman, C. (1984). Play in public school settings: A philosophical question. In Yawkey, T. D., & Pellegrini, A. D. (Eds.), *Child's play: Developmental and applied* (pp. 255–271). Hillsdale, NJ: Lawrence Erlbaum Associates.

Goffman, E. (1959). The presentation of self in everyday life. Garden City, NY: Doubleday.

Goldstein, H., Kaczmarek, L., & Pennington, R. (1992). Peer-mediated intervention: Attending to, commenting on, and acknowledging the behavior of preschoolers with autism. *Journal of Applied Behavior Analysis*, *25*(2), 289–305. doi:10.1901/jaba.1992.25-289

Gonzalez-Lopez, A., & Kamps, D. M. (1997). Social skills training to increase social interactions between children with autism and their typical peers. *Focus on Autism and Other Developmental Disabilities*, *12*, 2–14. doi:10.1177/108835769701200101

Goodson, F. T., & Norton-Meier, L. (2003). Motor oil, civil disobedience, and media literacy. *Journal of Adolescent & Adult Literacy*, *47*(3), 258–262.

Goodson, I. F., Knoebel, M., Lankshear, C., & Mangan, J. M. (2002). Cyber spaces/Social spaces: Culture clash in computerized classrooms. New York: Palgrave Macmillan.

Gosen, J., & Washbush, J. (1999). Perceptions of learning in TE simulations. *Developments in Business Simulation & Experiential Exercises*, *26*, 170–175.

Gosen, J., & Washbush, J. (2004). A review of scholarship on assessing experiential learning effectiveness. *Simulation & Gaming*, *35*(2), 270–293. doi:10.1177/1046878104263544

Gosenpud, J. (1990). Evaluation of Experiential Learning. In J. W. Gentry (ed.), Guide to Business Gaming and Experiential Learning, (pp. 301-329). London: Nichols/GP.

Gotthelf, C., & Peel, T. (1990). The Children's Television Workshop goes to school. *Educational Technology Research and Development*, *38*(4), 25–33. doi:10.1007/BF02314642

Gottlieb, J., & Gottlieb, B. W. (1977). Stereotypic attitudes and behavioral intentions toward handicapped children. *American Journal of Mental Deficiency*, *82*, 65–71.

Gould, L. J., & Corey, M. Social desirability in children: an extension and replication. *Journal of Consulting and Clinical Psychology*, 33-128.

Grabstats. (n.d.). Retrieved July 7, 2009, from http://www.grabstats.com/statcategorymain.asp?StatCatID=14

Grandin, T. (1995). *Thinking in Pictures: My Life with Autism*. New York: Doubleday.

Grandin, T., & Johnson, C. (2005). *Animals in translation*. New York: Scribner.

Gray, C. A., & Garand, J. D. (1993). Social stories: Improving responses of students with autism with accurate social information. *Focus on Autistic Behavior, 8*(1), 1–10.

Gray, D. E. (1993). Perceptions of stigma: The parents of autistic children. *Sociology of Health & Illness, 15*, 103–120. doi:10.1111/1467-9566.ep11343802

Gray, W. (1995). *Playing War: the Applicability of Commercial Conflict Simulations to Military Intelligence Training and Education. DIA Joint Military Intelligence College*. Washington, DC: Bolling Air Force Base.

Gray, W., & Fu, W. T. (2004). Soft constrains in interactive behavior: the case of ignoring perfect knowledge in-the-world for imperfect knowledge in-the-head. *Cognitive Science, 28*(3), 359–382.

Gray, W., Sims, C., Fu, W. T., & Schoelles, M. (2006). The Soft Constraints Hypothesis: A Rational Analysis Approach to Resource Allocation for Interactive Behavior. *Psychological Review, 113*(3), 461–482. doi:10.1037/0033-295X.113.3.461

Graybill, D., Kirsch, J., & Esselman, E. (1985). Effects of playing violent versus nonviolent video games on the aggressive ideation of aggressive and nonaggressive children. *Child Study Journal, 15*(3), 299–205.

Graybill, D., Strawniak, M., Hunter, T., & O'Leary, M. (1987). Effects of playing versus observing violent versus nonviolent video games on children's aggression. *Psychology: A Quarterly Journal of Human Behavior, 24*(3), 1-8.

Gredler, M. E. (1994). *Designing and evaluating games and simulations: A process approach*. Houston, TX: Gulf Publication Company.

Gredler, M. E. (1996). Educational games and simulations: A technology in search of a (research) paradigm. In Jonassen, D. H. (Ed.), *Handbook of research for educational communications and technology* (pp. 521–539). New York: Macmillan.

Gredler, M. E. (2004). Games and simulations and their relationships to learning. In Jonassen, D. H. (Ed.), *Handbook of research on educational communications and technology* (2nd ed., pp. 571–581). Mahwah, NJ: Lawrence Erlbaum Associates.

Green, C. S., & Bavelier, D. (2003). Action video game modifies visual selective attention. *Nature, 423*, 534–537. doi:10.1038/nature01647

Green, C. S., & Bavelier, D. (2007). Action-Video-Game Experience Alters the Spatial Resolution of Vision. *Psychological Science, 18*(1), 88–94. doi:10.1111/j.1467-9280.2007.01853.x

Green, M. C., & Brock, T. C. (2000). The role of transportation in the persuasiveness of public narratives. *Journal of Personality and Social Psychology, 79*, 701–721. doi:10.1037/0022-3514.79.5.701

Green, M. C., Strange, J. J., & Brock, T. C. (2002). Narrative impact: Social and cognitive foundations. Mahwah, NJ: Lawrence Erlbaum.

Green, M. E., & McNeese, M. N. (2008). Factors that predict digital game play. *The Howard Journal of Communications, 19*, 258–272. doi:10.1080/10646170802218321

Greenblat, C., & Duke, R. (1981). Principles and Practices of Gaming-Simulation. Beverly Hills, CA: Sage.

Greenfield & R.R. Cocking (Ed.). Interacting with Video (pp. 9-23). Norwood, NJ: Ablex Publishing. (Reprinted from Journal of Popular Culture, 27(1), 81-97, 1993)

Greenfield, P. A. (1984). Mind and media: The effects of television, video games and computers. Cambridge, MA: Harvard University Press.

Greenfield, P. M., Brannon, C., & Lohr, D. (1994). Two-dimensional representation of movement through three-dimensional space: The role of video game expertise. *Journal of Applied Developmental Psychology, 15*, 87–103. doi:10.1016/0193-3973(94)90007-8

Greenlaw, P. S., Herron, L. W., & Rawdon, R. H. (1962). Business Simulation in Industrial and University Education. Englewood Cliffs, NJ: Prentice-Hall, Inc.

Griffiths, M. (2004). Can videogames be good for your health? *Journal of Health Psychology, 9*(3), 340–343. doi:10.1177/1359105304042344

Griffiths, M. D., & Dancaster, I. (1995). The effect of type A personality on physiological arousal while playing computer games. *Addictive Behaviors, 20*(4), 543–548. doi:10.1016/0306-4603(95)00001-S

Gros, B. (2007). Digital games in education: The design of games-based learning environments. *Journal of Research on Technology in Education, 40*(1), 23–38.

Gross, R. (1995). *Psychology: The science of mind and behaviour* (4th ed.). Tonbridge, UK: Greengate Publishing.

Grossman, F. K. (1972). *Brothers and sisters of retarded children: An exploratory study.* Syracuse, NY: Syracuse University Press.

Grossman, R. J. (2008, May). Keep pace with older workers. *HRMagazine, 53*, 39–46.

Guest, T. (2008). Second Lives: a journey through virtual worlds. New York: Random House.

Guite, J., Lobato, D., Kao, B., & Plante, W. (2004). Discordance Between Sibling and Parent Reports of the Impact of Chronic Illness and Disability on Siblings. *Children's Health Care, 33*(1), 77–92. doi:10.1207/s15326888chc3301_5

Gunter, G., Kenny, R., & Vick, E. (2007). Taking educational games seriously: using the RETAIN model to design endogenous fantasy into standalone educational games. *Educational Technology Research and Development, 56*, 511–537. doi:10.1007/s11423-007-9073-2

Guralnick, D. (1996). An Authoring Tool for Procedural-Task Training. Evanston, IL: Northwestern University Press.

Guralnick, D. (2000). A Step Beyond Authoring: Process-Support Tools. WebNet 2000. San Antonio, TX: Association for the Advancement of Computing in Education.

Guralnick, D. (2005). Creating Online Simulations to Teach Social Skills. In *European Conference on E-Learning*, Amsterdam.

Guralnick, D. (2006). How to Design Effective, Motivating User Interfaces. In *American Society for Training & Development TechKnowledge Conference*, Denver, CO.

Guralnick, M. J., Connor, R. T., Hammond, M. A., Gottman, J. M., & Kinnish, K. (1996). The peer relations of preschool children with communications disorders. *Child Development, 67*(2), 471–489. doi:10.2307/1131827

Gutner, T. (2004). Special needs, crushing costs. *Business Week, Issue 3885.*Klein, E.B., Haddon, M. (2003). The Curious Incident of the Dog in the Night-time. United Kingdom: Jonathan Cape.

Hagiwara, T., & Myles, B. S. (1999). A multimedia social story intervention: Teaching skills to children with autism. *Focus on Autism and Other Developmental Disabilities, 14*(2), 82–95. doi:10.1177/108835769901400203

Hai-Jew, S. (2007). Gadgets, games, and gizmos for learning: Knowledge transfer from boomers to gamers?/ Gadgets, games and gizmos for learning. *Journal of Interactive Instruction Development, 20*(1), 42–45.

Hake, R. R. (2000). What *Can We Learn from the Physics Education Reform Effort?* Presented at the ASME Mechanical Engineering Education Conference, Fort Lauderdale, Florida.

Hakkarainen, P. (1999). Play and motivation. In Engeström, Y., Miettinen, R., & Punamäki, R. L. (Eds.), *Perspectives on activity theory* (pp. 232–249). Cambridge, UK: Cambridge University Press.

Hall, K., & Harding, A. (2003). A systematic review of effective literacy teaching in the 4 to 14 age range of mainstream school. In *Research Evidence in Education Library.* London: EPPI- Centre, Social Sciences Research Unit, Institute of Education.

Hall, S. (1980a). Encoding/Decoding. In S. Hall, et al. (Eds.), Culture, Media, Language, (pp. 128-138). London: Hutchinson.

Hall, S. (1980b). Cultural Studies: Two Paradigms. *Media Culture & Society*, 2(1), 57–72. doi:10.1177/016344378000200106

Hames, A. (2005). How younger siblings of children with learning disabilities understand the cognitive and social implications of learning disabilities. *European Journal of Special Needs Education*, 20(1), 3–19. doi:10.1080/0885625042000319052

Hanson, M. (2006). *Bodies in code: Interfaces with digital media*. London: Routledge.

Haring, T. G., & Breen, C. G. (1992). A peer-mediated social network intervention to enhance the social network intervention to enhance the social integration of persons with moderate and severe disabilities. *Journal of Applied Behavior Analysis*, 25, 319–333. doi:10.1901/jaba.1992.25-319

Harper, D. C. (1999). Social psychology of differences: Stigma, spread, and stereotypes in Childhood. *Rehabilitation Psychology*, 44, 131–144. doi:10.1037/0090-5550.44.2.131

Harper, E. (2006, September). World of Warcraft hits 7 million subscribers. *Joystiq*. Retrieved January 11, 2007 from http://www.joystiq.com/2006/09/07/world-of-warcraft-hits-7-million-subscribers/

Harris, M. J., Milich, R. C., Corbitt, E. M., Hoover, D. W., & Brady, M. (1992). Self-fulfilling effects of stigmatizing information on children's social interactions. *Journal of Personality and Social Psychology*, 63, 41–50. doi:10.1037/0022-3514.63.1.41

Harris, M., Lowendahl, J. M., & Zastrocky, M. (2007). *Second Life: Expanding higher education e-learning into 3-D*. Gartner Report No. G00149847.

Hattie, J. A. (2003). Teachers make a difference: What is the research evidence? *2003 Australian Council for Educational Research Conference*. Melbourne.

Hattie, J. A. (2005). *What is the nature of evidence that makes a difference to learning?* Paper presented at the Research Conference 2005 VIC: Australian Council for Educational Research.

Hawkridge, D., & Vincent, T. (1992). *Learning Difficulties and Computers*. London: Jessica Kingsley.

Haycock & Kemp. (2008). Immersive Learning Environments in Parallel Universes: Learning through Second Life. *School Libraries Worldwide*, 14(2), 89–97.

Hayden-Thomson, L., Rubin, K. H., & Hymel, S. (1987). Sex preferences in sociometric choices. *Developmental Psychology*, 23, 558–562. doi:10.1037/0012-1649.23.4.558

Hayes, E., & Games, I. A. (2008). Making computer games and design thinking: A review of current software and strategies. *Games and Culture*, 3(1), 309–332. doi:10.1177/1555412008317312

Hays, R. T. (2005). The effectiveness of instructional games: A literature review and discussion. Technical Report for the Naval Air Center Training Systems Division: Orlando, FL.

Haythornthwaite, C. (2007). Social networks and online community. In Joinson, A. M., McKenna, K. Y. A., Postmes, T., & Reips, U.-D. (Eds.), *The Oxford Handbook of Internet Psychology* (pp. 121–137). Oxford: Oxford University Press.

Hede, T., & Hede, A. (2002). *Multimedia effects on learning: Design implications of an integrated model*. Paper presented at the ASET.

Heidenreich, B. (1999). Vorwort. In B. Heidenreich (Ed.), Politische Theorien des 19. Jahrhunderts. I. Konservatismus (pp. 7-10). Wiesbaden.

Heider, F. (1958). *The Psychology of Interpersonal relations*. New York: Wiley. doi:10.1037/10628-000

Henning, P. (2003). Everyday Cognition and Situated Learning. In D. Jonassen (Ed.), Handbook of Research on Educational Communications and Technology. Mahwah, NJ: Lawrence Erlbaum Associates, Inc.

Henninger, A. (2009). On uncertainty. *The Modeling and Simulation Center Information Analysis Center Journal*, 4(1), 2.

Herold, D. K. (2009). Virtual education: Teaching media studies in Second Life. *Journal of Virtual Worlds Research, 2* (1). Retrieved July 27, 2009 from https://journals.tdl.org/jvwr/article/view/380/454

Herrmann, N. (1981). The creative brain. *Training and Development Journal, 35*(10), 10–16.

Herz, B., & Merz, W. (1998). Experiential Learning and the Effectiveness of Economic Simulation Games. *Simulation & Gaming, 29*(2), 238–250. doi:10.1177/1046878198292007

Herz, J. (1997). *Joystick nation. How videogames ate our quarters, won our hearts, and rewired our minds.* Princeton, NJ: Little Brown & Company.

Hess, U., Kappas, A., McHugo, G. J., Lanzetta, J. T., & Kleck, R. E. (1992). The facilitative effect of facial expression on the self-generation of emotion. *International Journal of Psychophysiology, 12,* 251–265. doi:10.1016/0167-8760(92)90064-I

Hick, J. (1977). *Evil and the God of Love.* San Francisco: Harper and Row.

Hickey, D. T. (2009). Designing assessments and assessing designs in educational videogames. Presentation at AERA 2009, San Diego, CA.

Hiemstra, R. (2006). More than three decades of self-directed learning: From whence have we come? *Adult Learning,* 5–8.

Hillestad, R. J., Bennett, B., & Moore, L. R. (1996). *AF Modeling for Campaign Analysis: Lessons for the Next Generation of Models: Executive Summary. Technical Report – MR-710.* RAND Corporation.

Hipps, G., Abrami, P. C., & Savage, R. (2005). ABRACADARA: The research, design development of web-based early literacy software. In Pierre, S. (Ed.), *Développement, intégration et évaluation des technologies de formation et d'apprentissage (DIVA). Innovations et tendances en technologies de formation et d'apprentissage* (pp. 89–112). Montreal, QC: Presses Internationales Polytechnique.

Hogle, J..G. (1996). *Considering games as cognitive tools: In search of effective "edutainment".*

Höglund, J. (2008). Electronic Empire: Orientalism Revisited in the Military Shooter. *GameStudies. The international journal of computer game research, 8*(1). Retrieved January 28, 2009 from http://gamestudies.org/0801/articles/hoeglund

Holbert, R. L. (2005). A typology for the study of entertainment television and politics. *The American Behavioral Scientist, 49,* 436–453. doi:10.1177/0002764205279419

Holbert, R. L., Shah, D. V., & Kwak, N. (2003). Political Implications of Prime Time Drama and Sitcom use: Genres of Representation and Opinions Concerning Women's Rights. *The Journal of Communication, 53*(1), 45–60. doi:10.1111/j.1460-2466.2003.tb03004.x

Holbert, R. L., Shah, D. V., & Kwak, N. (2004). Fear, authority, and justice: Crime-related TV viewing and endorsement of capital punishment and gun ownership. *Journalism & Mass Communication Quarterly, 81*(2), 343–363.

Hollander, E., DelGiudice-Asch, G., & Simon, J. (1999). B lymphocyte D8/17 and repetitive behaviors in autism. *The American Journal of Psychiatry, 156,* 317–320.

Holroyd, J., & MacArthur, D. (1976). Mental retardation and stress on the parents: a contrast between Down syndrome and childhood autism. *American Journal of Mental Deficiency, 4,* 431–436.

Holtz-Bacha, C. (1988). Unterhaltung ist nicht nur lustig. Zur politischen Sozialisation durch Medieninhalte. *Publizistik, 33*(2-3), 493–504.

Honey, P., & Mumford, A. (1982). Manual of Learning Styles. London: P. Honey.

Horkheimer, M., & Adorno, T. W. (2007). Dialektik der Aufklärung. Philosophische Fragmente. In A. Schmidt & G. Schmid Noerr (Eds.). Max Horkheimer. Gesammelte Schriften. Bd. 5, Frankfurt/Main, 11-290.

Horton, S. (2006). Access by Design: A Guide to Universal Usability for Web Designers. Berkeley, CA: New Riders. Retrieved January 3, 2009, from http://universalusability.com/index.html

Howard, J. (2008). *Quests: design, theory, and history in games and narratives*. Wellesley, MA: A.K. Peters Press.

Howes, A., & Payne, S. (1990). Display-Based Competence: Towards User Models for Menu-Driven Interfaces. *International Journal of Man-Machine Studies, 33*(6), 637–655. doi:10.1016/S0020-7373(05)80067-7

Huizinga, J. (1955). Homo Ludens: A Study of the Play Element in Culture. Boston: Beacon Press.

Hull, C. L. (1951). Essentials of behavior. New Haven, CT: Yale University Press.

Hull, G. A. (2003). Youth culture and digital media: New literacies for new times. *Research in the Teaching of English, 38*(2), 229–233.

Hunsberger, P. (2007). 'Where am I?' A call for 'connectedness' in literacy. *Reading Research Quarterly, 42*(3), 420–424. doi:10.1598/RRQ.42.3.7

Hutchins, E. (1995). How a Cockpit Remembers its Speeds. *Cognitive Science, 19*(3), 265–288.

Hutchins, E., & Klausen, T. (1996). Distributed Cognition in an Airline Cockpit. In L. Resneck, R. Saljo, C. Potecorvo & B. Burge (Eds.), Tools, and Reasoning: Essays in Situated Cognition. Vienna, Austria.

Hynd, G. W., Hern, K. L., Voeller, K. K., & Marshall, R. M. (1991). Neurobiological basis of Attention-Deficit Hyperactivity Disorder (ADHD). *School Psychology Review, 20*, 174–186.

Hynds, S. (1997). On the brink: Negotiating literature and life with adolescents. New York: Teachers College Press.

Iavaraone, A., Patruno, M., Galeone, F., Chieffi, S., & Carlomagno, S. (2007). Brief report: error pattern in an autistic savant calendar calculator. *Journal of Autism and Developmental Disorders, 37*, 775–779. doi:10.1007/s10803-006-0190-2

Irwin, M. J. (2009). Unlocking achievements: rewarding skill with player incentives. *Gamsutra.com*. Retrieved April 1, 2009 from http://www.gamasutra.com/view/feature/3976/unlocking_achievements_rewarding_.php

Irwin, R., & Gross, A. (1995). Cognitive tempo, violent video games, and aggressive behavior in young boys. *Journal of Family Violence, 10*, 337–350. doi:10.1007/BF02110997

Iuppa, N., & Borst, T. (2007). *Story and simulations for serious games: Tales from the trenches*. Boston: Focal Press.

Jäckel, M. (2005). Medienwirkungen. Ein Studienbuch zur Einführung. Wiesbaden, Germany: VS Verlag für Sozialwissenschaften.

Jacobson, M., & Spiro, R. (1993). Hypertext Learning Environments, Cognitive Flexibility, and the Transfer of Complex Knowledge. [Center for the Study of Reading.]. *Urbana (Caracas, Venezuela)*, IL.

Jarman, L., Traphagan, T., & Mayrath, M. (2008). Understanding project-based learning in Second Life with a pedagogy, training, and assessment trio. *Educational Media International, 45*, 157–176. doi:10.1080/09523980802283889

Jarmon, L., Traphagana, T., Mayratha, M., & Trivedia, A. (2009). Virtual world teaching, experiential learning, and assessment: An interdisciplinary communication course in Second Life. *Computers & Education, 53*(1), 169–182. doi:10.1016/j.compedu.2009.01.010

Jenkins, H. (2004). Game Design as Narrative Architecture. In N. Wardrip-Fruin & P. Harrigan (Eds.), First Person: New Media as Story, Performance, Game. Cambridge, MA: MIT Press.

Jenkins, H. (2005). Getting into the game. *Educational Leadership, 62*(7), 48–51.

Jenkins, H. (2006). *Confronting the challenges of participatory culture: Media education for the 21st Century*. Chicago, IL: John D. and Catherine A. MacArthur Foundation.

Jenkins, H. (2007). Keynote presented at the Games in Action Conference, Gothenburg, Sweden.

Jewitt, C. (2003). Computer-mediated learning: The multimodal construction of mathematical entities on screen. In C. Lankshear, M. Knobel, C. Bigum, & M. Peters (Series Eds.) & C. Jewitt & G. Kress (Vol. Eds.), New literacies and digital epistemologies: Vol. 4. Multimodal literacy (pp. 34-55). New York: Peter Lang.

Jiminez, C. (2007). The high cost of World of Warcraft. *BBC News.* Retrieved from http://news.bbc.co.uk/2/hi/technology/7007026.stm

Johnson, P. R., Brown, S. W., Lima, C. O., Boyer, M. A., & Hudson, N. (2006, April). *GlobalEd: A comparison of leadership in FTF and CMC environments.* Poster presented at the AERA conference, San Francisco, CA.

Johnston, R. S., & Watson, J. E. (2004). Accelerating the development of reading, spelling, and phonemic awareness skills in initial readers. *Reading and Writing: An Interdisciplinary Journal, 17,* 327–357. doi:10.1023/B:READ.0000032666.66359.62

Johnston, S., McDonnnell, A., & Hawken, L. (2008). Enhancing outcomes in early literacy for young children with disabilities: Strategies for success. *Intervention in School and Clinic, 43*(3), 210–217. doi:10.1177/1053451207310342

Joint Forces Quarterly. (2009). Gaming the 21st century: what to game? *Joint Forces Quarterly, 53*(2), 141–142.

Jonassen, D. H. (1992). Evaluating Constructivistic Learning. In T. M. Duffy & D. H. Jonassen, (eds.), Constructivism and the Technology of Instruction: A Conversation (pp. 137-148). Mahwah, NJ: Lawrence Erlbaum Associates, Publishers.

Jonassen, D. H., Peck, K. L., & Wilson, B. G. (1999). Learning with Technology; A Constructivist Perspective. New York: Prentice Hall.

Jonassen, D., Ambruso, D., & Olesen, J. (1992). Designing hypertext on transfusion medicine using cognitive flexibility theory. *Journal of Educational Multimedia and Hypermedia, 1*(3), 309–322.

Jonassen. (2006). *Modeling with Technology: Mindtools for Conceptual Change.* Columbus, OH: Pearson.

Jones, C. (Ed.). (2006). *Sensorium: Embodied experience, technology, and contemporary art.* Cambridge, Massachusetts: The MIT Press.

Jones, E. E. (1990). *Interpersonal Perception.* New York: W.H. Freeman.

Jones, S. (2003). *Let the Games Begin: Gaming Technology and Entertainment Among College Students.* Pew Internet and American Life Project. Retrieved July 17, 2009. Retrieved from http://www.pewinternet.org/Reports/2003/Let-the-games-begin-Gaming-technology-and-college-students.aspx

Jonsson, M., Tholander, J., & Fernaeus, Y. (2009). Setting the Stage - Embodied and Spatial Dimensions in Emerging Programming Practices. *Interacting with Computers, 21*(1-2), 117–124. doi:10.1016/j.intcom.2008.10.004

Jordan & Henderson. (1995). Interaction analysis: Foundations and practice. *Journal of the Learning Sciences, 4*(1), 39–104. doi:10.1207/s15327809jls0401_2

Jorgensen, A. (2004). *Marrying HCI/Usability and Computer Games: A Preliminary Look.* Paper presented at the Third Nordic conference on Human-Computer Interaction, Tampere, Finland.

Joy, E., & Garcia, F. (2000). Measuring learning effectiveness: A new look at no-significant-difference findings. *Journal of Asynchronous Learning Network, 4*(1). 15. Available online at http://www.aln.org/alnweb/journal/vol14_issue1/joygarcia.htm

Junemann, E., & Lloyd, B. (2003). Consulting for Virtual Excellence: Virtual teamwork as a task for consultants. *Team Performance Management: An International Journal, 9*(7/8), 182–189. doi:10.1108/13527590310507435

Juul, J. (2005). *Half-real: video games between real rules and fictional world.* Cambridge, MA: The MIT Press.

Juvonen, J. (1991). Deviance, perceived responsibility and negative peer reactions. *Developmental Psychology, 27,* 672–681. doi:10.1037/0012-1649.27.4.672

Juvonen, J. (1992). Negative peer reactions from the perspective of the reactor. *Journal of Educational Psychology, 84,* 314–321. doi:10.1037/0022-0663.84.3.314

Juvonen, J., & Weiner, B. (1993). An attributional analysis of students' interactions: the social consequences of perceived responsibility. *Educational Psychology Review*, 5(4), 325–345. doi:10.1007/BF01320222

Kafai, Y. B. (1995). *Minds in play: Computer game design as a context for children's learning.* Mahwah, NJ: Lawrence Erlbaum Associates, Inc.

Kafai, Y. B. (1996). Electronic play worlds: Gender differences in children's construction of video games. In Kafai, Y., & Resnick, M. (Eds.), *Constructivism in Practice: Designing, Thinking, and Learning in a Digital World* (pp. 97–123). Mahwah, NJ: Erlbaum.

Kafai, Y. B. (2006). Constructionism. In R. K. Sawyer (Ed.), The Cambridge Handbook of the Learning Sciences (pp. 35-46). Cambridge, UK: Cambridge University Press.

Kafai, Y. B. (2006). Playing and making games for learning: Instructionist and constructionist perspectives for game studies. *Games and Culture*, 1(1), 36–40. doi:10.1177/1555412005281767

Kafai, Y. B. (2008). Understanding Virtual Epidemics: Children's Folk Conceptions of a Computer Virus. *Journal of Science Education and Technology*, 17(6). doi:10.1007/s10956-008-9102-x

Kamps, D. M., Kravitz, T., Gonzalez-Lopez, A., Kemmerer, K., Potucek, J., & Harrell, L. G. (1988). What do peers think? Social validity of peer-mediated programs. *Education & Treatment of Children*, 21, 107–134.

Kane, S. K., Bigham, J. P., & Wobbrock, J. O. (2008). Slide Rule: Making mobile touch screens accessible to blind people using multi-touch interaction techniques. In *Proceedings of the ACM SIGACCESS Conference on Computers and Accessibility (ASSETS '08)*. New York: ACM Press. Retrieved May 5, 2009, from http://students.washington.edu/skane/sliderule/

Kapell, M. (2002). Civilization and its discontents: American monomythic structure as historical simulacrum. *Popular Culture Review*, 13(2), 129–136.

Kapp, K. M. (2007). *Gadgets, Games, and Gizmos for Learning.* San Francisco: John Wiley and Sons.

Kaptelinin, V. (1996). Computer-mediated activity: Functional organs. In Nardi, B. A. (Ed.), *Conscious and consciousness: Activity theory and human-computer interaction* (pp. 45–68). London: MIT Press.

Kaptelinin, V., & Nardi, B. A. (2006). *Acting with technology: Activity theory and interaction design.* London: MIT Press.

Karlsen, F. (September 2008). Quests in context: a comparative analysis of discworld and world of warcraft. *Game studies*, 8(1). Retrieved June 13, 2009 from http://gamestudies.org/ 0801/articles/karlsen

Kataria, S., Hall, C. W., Wong, M. M., & Keys, G. F. (1992). Learning styles of LD and NLD ADHD children. *Journal of Clinical Psychology*, 48, 371–378. doi:10.1002/1097-4679(199205)48:3<371::AID-JCLP2270480316>3.0.CO;2-F

Kayes, D. C. (2002). Experiential Learning and Its Critics: Preserving the Role of Experience in Management Learning and Education. *Academy of Management Learning & Education*, 1(2), 137–149.

Ke, F. (2008). Computer games application within alternative classroom goal structures: cognitive, metacognitive, and affective evaluation. *Educational Technology Research and Development*, 56, 539–556. doi:10.1007/s11423-008-9086-5

Ke, F. (2009). A Qualitative Meta-Analysis of Computer Games as Learning Tools. In R. E. Ferdig (Ed.), Handbook of Research on Effective Electronic Gaming in Education (Vol. 1-32). Hershey, PA: Information Science Reference.

Kearney, P. R. (2006). Immersive environments: What can we learn from commercial computer games. In Pivec, M. (Ed.), *Affective and emotional aspects of human-computer interaction: Emphasis on game-based and innovative learning approaches.* Amsterdam: IOS Press BV.

Kearney, P., & Pivec, M. (2007). *Immersed and how? That is the question.* Gothenburg, Sweden: Games in Action.

Kearney, P., & Pivec, M. (2007). Recursive loops of game based learning. *In Proceedings of World Conference on Educational Multimedia, Hypermedia and telecommunications* 2007 Vancouver BC, Canada, 2007, (pp. 2546 – 2553).

Keller, J. M. (1987). Development and use of the ARCS model of motivational design. *Journal of Instructional Development, 10*(3), 2–10. doi:10.1007/BF02905780

Kelley, H. H. (1967). Attribution Theory in Social Psychology. In D. Levine (Ed.), *Nebraska Symposium on Motivation, 1967.* Lincoln: University of Nebraska Press.

Kelly, H. (2005). Games, cookies, and the future of education. *Issues in Science and Technology, 21*(4), 33–40.

Kelly, H., Howell, K., Glinert, E., Holding, L., Swain, C., & Burrowbridge, A. (2007). How to build serious games. *Communications of the ACM, 50*(7), 44–49. doi:10.1145/1272516.1272538

Kelton, A. J. (2008). Virtual Worlds? «Outlook Good». *EDUCAUSE Review*, (September/October), 15-22. Retrieved July 30, 2009, from http://net.educause.edu/ir/library/pdf/ERM0850.pdf

Kennedy, C. H., & Souza, G. (1995). Functional analysis and treatment of eye poking. *Journal of Applied Behavior Analysis, 28*(1), 27–37. doi:10.1901/jaba.1995.28-27

Kenny, R. (2009). Evaluating cognitive tempo in the digital age. *Educational Technology Research and Development, 57*, 45–60. doi:10.1007/s11423-007-9035-8

Kesner, I. A. (2001). The Strategic Management Course: Tools and Techniques for Successful Teaching. In Hitt, M., Freeman, R. E., & Harrison, J. S. (Eds.), *Handbook of Strategic Management.*

Ketelhut, D. J., Nelson, B., & Schifter, C. (2009). Situated assessment using virtual environments of science content and inquiry. Presentation at AERA, San Diego, CA.

Kiely, R., Sandmann, L. R., & Truluck, J. (2004). Adult learning theory and the pursuit of adult degrees. *New Directions for Adult and Continuing Education, 103*, 17–30. doi:10.1002/ace.145

Kiili, K., & Lainema, T. (2008). Foundation for Measuring Engagement in Educational Games. *Journal of Interactive Learning Research, 19*(3), 169–188.

King, J. R., & O'Brien, D. G. (2002). Adolescents' multiliteracies and their teachers' needs to know: Toward a digital détente. In D. E. Alvermann (Ed.), Adolescents and Literacies in a Digital World (pp. 40-50). New York: Peter Lang.

Kirkley, S. E., & Kirkley, J. R. (2004). Creating next generation blended learning environments using mixed reality, video games and simulations. *TechTrends, 49*(3), 42–53. doi:10.1007/BF02763646

Kirschner, P., Sweller, J., & Clark, R. (2006). Why Minimal Guidance During Instruction Does Not Work: An Analysis of the Failure of Constructivist, Discovery, Problem-Based, Experiential, and Inquiry-Based Teaching. *Educational Psychologist, 41*(2), 75–86. doi:10.1207/s15326985ep4102_1

Kirsh, D. (2006). Distributed Cognition: A Methodological Note. *Pragmatics & Cognition, 14*(2), 249–262. doi:10.1075/pc.14.2.06kir

Kirsh, D., & Maglio, P. (1994). On Distinguishing Epistemic from Pragmatic Action. *Cognitive Science, 18*(4), 513–549.

Klabbers, J. H. G. (2003). Interactive learning of what? In Percival, F., Godfrey, H., Laybourn, P., & Murray, S. (Eds.), The international simulation & gaming yearbook, Vol. 11 (257-266). Edinburgh, UK: Napier University.

Klabbers, J. H. G. (2003). The gaming landscape: A taxonomy for classifying games and simulations. In M. Copier & J. Raessens, (Eds.), *Proceedings of Level Up: Digital Games Research Conference*, (pp. 54-68, 4-6). Utrecht, The Netherlands: University of Utrecht.

Klimmt, C. (2006a). Computerspielen als Handlung. Dimensionen und Determinanten des Erlebens interaktiver Unterhaltungsangebote. Köln, Germany: von Halem.

Klimmt, C. (2006b). *Computerspielkonsum und Politischer Konservatismus unter Jugendlichen.* Paper presented at the Workshop „Konstruktion von Politik und Gesellschaft in Computerspielen?" of the Arbeitskreis Visuelle Politik/Film und Politik der DVPW. München.

Klin, A., Warren, J., Schultz, R., & Volkmar, F. (2002). Visual fixation patterns during viewing of naturalistic social situations as predictors of social competence in individuals with autism. *Archives of General Psychiatry*, *59*(9), 809–816. doi:10.1001/archpsyc.59.9.809

Klingberg, T., Fernell, E., Olesen, P., Johnson, M., Gustafsson, P., & Dahlström, K. (2005). Computerized training of working memory in children with ADHD- A randomized, controlled trial. *Journal of the American Academy of Child and Adolescent Psychiatry*, *44*, 177–186. doi:10.1097/00004583-200502000-00010

Klopfer, E. (2008). *Augmented Learning; Research and Design of Mobile Educational Games*. Cambridge, MA: The MIT Press.

Klopfer, E., Osterweil, S., & Salen, K. (2009). Moving learning games forward: obstacles, opportunities, and openness. *The Education Arcade*. Cambridge, MA: Massachusetts Institute of Technology. Retrieved April 2, 2009 from: http://www.educationarcade.org/

Knowles, M. (1996). Androgogy: An emerging techology for adult learning. In R. Edwards, A. Hanson & P. Raggatt (Eds.), Boundaries of Adult Learning (pp. 82-96). London: Routledge.

Knowles, M. S. (1970). The Modern Practice of Adult Education: Andragogy vs. Pedagogy. New York: Association Press.

Knowles, M. S. (1980). The Modern Practice of Adult Education: from Pedagogy to Andragogy: Second edition. New York: Cambridge Books.

Knowles, M. S. (1980, August). My Farewell Address... Andragogy - No Panacea, No Ideology. *Training and Development Journal*, 48–50.

Knowles, M. S. (1984). The Adult Learner: A Neglected Species (3rd Ed.). Houston, TX: Gulf.

Knowles, M. S., & Associates. (1984). Andragogy in action: Applying modern principles of adult learning. San Francisco: Jossey-Bass.

Koedinger, K. R., Anderson, J. R., Hadley, W. H., & Mark, M. A. (1997). Intelligent tutoring goes to school in the big city. *International Journal of Artificial Intelligence in Education*, *8*, 30–43.

Kolb, A. Y., & Kolb, D. A. (2005). Learning styles and learning spaces: Enhancing experiential learning in higher education. *Academy of Management Learning & Education*, *4*(2), 193–212.

Kolb, A., & Kolb, D. (2008, October 10). The Learning Way. Meta-cognitive Aspects of Experiential Learning. *Simulation & Gaming*. doi:.doi:10.1177/1046878108325713

Kolb, A., & Kolb, D. A. (2008). *Experiential learning theory bibliography: Volume 2 2006-2008*. Cleveland, OH: Experience Based Learning Systems. Available from the Experience Based Learning Systems Web site, www.learningfromexperience.com

Kolb, D. (1984). Experiential Learning: Experience the Source of Learning and Development. Prentice-Hall, Inc, Englewood Cliffs.

Kolb, D. A., Boyatzis, R., & Mainemelis, C. (2001). Experiential learning theory: Previous research and new directions. In R. Sternberg, & L. Zhang, (Eds.), Perspectives on thinking, learning, and cognitive styles, (pp. 227-247). Mahwah, NJ: Lawrence Erlbaum.

Kolodner, J. L., Crismond, D., Gray, J., Holbrook, J., & Puntambekar, S. (1998). Learning by design from theory to practice. In *Proceedings of the International Conference of the Learning Sciences*, (pp. 16–22).

Konrad, K., Neufang, S., Hanisch, C., Fink, G. R., & Herpertz-Dahlmann, B. (2006). Dysfunctional attentional networks in children with attention deficit/hyperactivity disorder: Evidence from an event-related functional magnetic resonance imaging study. *Biological Psychiatry*, *59*, 643–651. doi:10.1016/j.biopsych.2005.08.013

Konstam, V., Drainoni, M., Mitchell, G., Houser, R., Reddington, D., & Eaton, D. (1993). Career choices and values of siblings of individuals with developmental disabilities. *The School Counselor*, *40*(4).

Koster, R. (2002). *Online world timeline*. Retrieved April 14, 2009, from Raph Koster's website: http://www.raphkoster.com/gaming/mudtimeline.shtml

Koster, R. (2004). Theory of Fun for Game Design. Phoenix, AZ: Paraglyph.

Kozma, R. B. (1994). Will media influence learning? Reframing the debate. *Educational Technology Research and Development*, *42*(2), 7–19. doi:10.1007/BF02299087

Kozol, J. (1975/1990). *The night is dark and I am far from home, new* (revised edition). New York: Simon & Schuster.

Krathwohl, D. R., Bloom, B. S., & Masia, B. B. (1964). Taxonomy of Educational Objectives: Classification of Educational Goals, Handbook II: Affective Domain New York: David McKay Co., Inc.

Kreijns, K., Kirschner, P. A., Jochems, W., & van Buuren, H. (2007). Measuring perceived sociability of computer-supported collaborative learning environments. *Computers & Education*, *49*, 176–192. doi:10.1016/j.compedu.2005.05.004

Kress, G. (2003). Genre and the multimodal production of 'scientificness.' In C. Lankshear, M. Knobel, C. Bigum, & M. Peters (Series Eds.) & C. Jewitt & G. Kress (Vol. Eds.), New literacies and digital epistemologies: Vol. 4. Multimodal literacy (pp. 173-186). New York: Peter Lang.

Kress, G., & Jewitt, C. (2003). Introduction. In C. Lankshear, M. Knobel, C. Bigum, & M. Peters (Series Eds.) & C. Jewitt & G. Kress (Vol. Eds.), New literacies and digital epistemologies: Vol. 4. Multimodal literacy (pp. 1-18). New York: Peter Lang.

Kress, G., & Van Leeuwen, T. (2001). Multimodal discourse: The modes and media of contemporary communication. London: Arnold.

Kriz, W. C. (2003). Creating effective learning environments and learning organizations through gaming simulation design. *Simulation & Gaming*, *34*, 495–511. doi:10.1177/1046878103258201

Kriz, W. C. (2008, June 20). A Systemic-Constructivist Approach to the Facilitation and Debriefing of Simulations and Games. *Simulation & Gaming*. doi:. doi:10.1177/1046878108319867

Kuhn, H.-P. (2000). Mediennutzung und politische Sozialisation. Eine empirische Studie zum Zusammenhang zwischen Mediennutzung und politischer Identitätsbildung im Jugendalter. Opladen.

Kuhn, T. E. (1962). *The structure of scientific revolutions*. Chicago: University of Chicago Press.

Kuhn, T. S. (1970). *The structure of scientific revolutions* (2nd ed.). Chicago: University of Chicago Press.

Labbo, L., Leu, D. Jr, Kinzer, C., Teale, W., Cammack, D., & Kara-Soteriou, J. (2003). Teacher wisdom stories: Cautions and recommendations for using computer-related technologies for literacy instruction. *The Reading Teacher*, *57*(3), 300–304.

Lacasa, P., Méndez, L., & Martínez, R. (2008). Bringing commercial games into the classroom. *Computers and Composition*, *25*, 341–358. doi:10.1016/j.compcom.2008.04.009

Lainema, T. (2007). Open System View Applied in Business Simulation Gaming. *International Journal of Advanced Technology for Learning on Game-based Learning*, *4*(4), 200–205.

Lainema, T. (2009). Perspective Making. Constructivism as a Meaning-Making Structure for Simulation Gaming. *Simulation & Gaming*, *40*(1), 48–67. doi:10.1177/1046878107308074

Lainema, T., & Lainema, K. (2007). Advancing Acquisition of Business Know-How: Critical Learning Elements. *Journal of Research on Technology in Education*, *40*(2), 183–198.

Lainema, T., & Nurmi, S. (2006). Applying an Authentic, Dynamic Learning Environment in Real World Business. *Computers & Education*, *47*(1), 94–115. doi:10.1016/j.compedu.2004.10.002

Landsberger, J. (2004). Gaming, teaching and learning: An interview with kurt squire. *TechTrends*, *48*(4), 4–7. doi:10.1007/BF02763436

Lanningham-Foster, L., Jensen, T., Foster, R. C., & Redmond, A. B. (2006, December). Energy expenditure of sedentary screen time compared with active screen time for children. *Pediatrics*, *118*(6). doi:10.1542/peds.2006-1087

Larkin, J. (1989). Display-Based Problem Solving. In D. Klahr & K. Kotovsky (Eds.), Complex Information Processing: The Impact of Herbert A. Simon. Hillsdale, NJ: Lawrence Erlbaum.

Lave, J., & Wenger, E. (1991). *Situated learning: Legitimate peripheral participation.* Cambridge, UK: Cambridge University Press.

Lawrence, V., Houghton, S., Tannock, R., Douglas, G., Durkin, K., & Whiting, K. (2002). ADHD outside the laboratory: boys'' executive function performance on tasks in videogame play and on a visit to the zoo. *Journal of Abnormal Child Psychology, 30,* 447–462. doi:10.1023/A:1019812829706

Learner-centered psychological principles revised. (1996). *Newsletter for Educational Psychologists, 19*(2), 10.

Lee, P. D. (2009). Using Second Life to teach operations management. *Journal of Virtual Worlds Research, 2* (1). Retrieved July 29, 2009 from https://journals.tdl.org/jvwr/article/view/431/464

Leemkuil, H., de Jong, T., & Ootes, S. (2000). *Review of educational use of games and simulations.* EC project KITS (Knowledge management Interactive Training System). EC project KITS (IST-1999-3078), KITS Deliverable D1, Enschede: KITS consortium. University of Twente, The Netherlands. Retrieved January 25, 2009, from http://kits.edte.utwente.nl/documents/D1.pdf

Leiner, A. C., Leiner, H., & Noback, C. R. (1997). *Cerebellar Communications with the Prefrontal Cortex: Their Effect on Human Cognitive Skills.* Palo Alto, CA: Channing House.

Lektorsky, V. A. (1999). Activity theory in a new era. In Engeström, Y., Miettinen, R., & Punamäki, R. L. (Eds.), *Perspectives on activity theory* (pp. 65–69). Cambridge, UK: Cambridge University Press.

Lenhart, A. (2008). *Pew Internet Project Data Memo.* Retrieved from http://www.pewinternet.org/pdfs/PIP_Adult_gaming_memo.pdf

Lenhart, A., Jones, S., & MacGill, A. (2008, December 7). *Adults and video games.* Retrieved July 17, 2009 from Pew Internet Website: http://www.pewinternet.org/Reports/2008/Adults-and-Video-Games.aspx?r=1

Lenhart, A., Kahne, J., Middaugh, E., Macgill, A. R., Evans, C., & Vitak, J. (2008). *Teens, Video Games and Civics: Teens' gaming experiences are diverse and include significant social interaction and civic engagement.* Washington, DC: Pew Internet and American Life Project.

Leont'ev, A. N. (1978). *Activity, consciousness, and personality.* Englewood Cliffs, NJ: Prentice Hall.

Leont'ev, A. N. (1981). *Problems of the development of the mind.* Moscow: Progress.

Leu, D. J. Jr, Castek, J., Henry, L. A., Coiro, J., & McMullan, M. (2004). The lessons that children teach us: Integrating children's literature and the new literacies of the Internet. *The Reading Teacher, 57*(5), 496–503.

Levy, F., & Murnane, R. (2004). *The New Division of Labor: How Computers are Creating the Next Job Market.* Princeton, NJ: Princeton University Press.

Liang, N., & Wang, J. (2004). Implicit mental models in teaching cases: An empirical study of popular MBA cases in the United States and China. *Academy of Management Learning & Education, 3*(4), 397–413.

Lieb, S. (1991) *Principles of adult learning* [White paper]. Retrieved from Honolulu Community College Web site: http://honolulu.hawaii.edu/intranet/committees/FacDevCom/guidebk/teachtip/adults-2.htm

Lim, C. P. (2008). Spirit of the game: Empowering students as designers in schools? *British Journal of Educational Technology, 39*(6), 996–1003. doi:10.1111/j.1467-8535.2008.00823_1.x

Lim, C., Nonis, D., & Hedberg, J. (2006). Gaming in a 3D multiuser virtual environment: Engaging students in science lessons. *British Journal of Educational Technology, 37*(2), 211–231. doi:10.1111/j.1467-8535.2006.00531.x

Limon, M. (2001). On the Cognitive Conflict as an Instructional Strategy for Conceptual Change: A Critical Appraisal. *Learning and Instruction, 11*(4-5), 357–380. doi:10.1016/S0959-4752(00)00037-2

Lincoln, Y. S., & Guba, E. G. (1985). *Naturalistic Inquiry.* Newbury Park, CA: Sage.

Linser, R. (2008) The Magic Circle – Game Design Principles and Online Role-Play Simulations. In *Proceedings of World Conference on Educational Multimedia, Hypermedia and telecommunications 2008* Vienna, Austria, 2008, (pp. 5290 - 5297).

Lipnack, J., & Stamps, J. (1999). Virtual teams: The new way to work. *Strategy and Leadership, 27*(1), 14–19. doi:10.1108/eb054625

Liu, E., & Lin, C. (2009). Developing evaluative indicators for educational computer games. *British Journal of Educational Technology, 40*(1), 174–178. doi:10.1111/j.1467-8535.2008.00852.x

Livingstone, D., & Kemp, J. (Eds.). (2006). *Proceedings of the Second Life Education Workshop at the Second Life Community Convention.* University of Paisley. Retrieved April 6, 2009 from http://www.simteach.com/SLCC06/slcc2006-proceedings.pdf.

Lloyd, J., Persaud, N., & Powell, T. E. (2009). Equivalence of Real-World and Virtual-Reality Route Learning: A Pilot Study. *Cyberpsychology & Behavior, 4*(12), 423–427. doi:10.1089/cpb.2008.0326

Lorimer, P. A., Simpson, R. L., Myles, B. S., & Ganz, J. B. (2003). The use of social stories as a preventative behavioral intervention in a home setting with a child with autism. *Journal of Positive Behavior Interventions, 4*(1), 53–60. doi:10.1177/109830070200400109

Lotherington, H. (2003). Emergent metaliteracies: What the Xbox has to offer the EQAO. *Linguistics and Education, 14*, 305–319. doi:10.1016/j.linged.2004.02.007

Lucas, K., & Sherry, J. L. (2004). Sex differences in video game play: A communication-based explanation. *Communication Research, 31*(5), 499–523. doi:10.1177/0093650204267930

Ludlow, P., & Wallace, M. (2007). The Second Life Herald: The virtual tabloid that witnessed the dawn of the metaverse. Cambridge, Massachusetts: The MIT Press.

Luke, A., & Elkins, J. (1998). Reinventing literacy in 'New Times.'. *Journal of Adolescent & Adult Literacy, 42*(1), 4–7.

Luppa, N., & Borst, T. (2007). *Story and simulations for serious games: Tales from the trenches.* Boston, MA: Focal Press.

Lyle, J. (2003). Stimulated recall: A report on its use in naturalistic research. *British Educational Research Journal, 29*(6), 861–878. doi:10.1080/0141192032000137349

Lyon, G. (1999). *The NICD research program in reading development, reading disorders, and reading instruction.* Washington, DC: National Center for Learning Disabilities.

Lyon, G. R., & Moats, L. C. (1997). Critical conceptual and methodological considerations in reading intervention research. *Journal of Learning Disabilities, 30*(6), 578–588. doi:10.1177/002221949703000601

Maccoby, E. E., & Jacklin, C. N. (1987). Gender segregation in childhood. In Reese, E. H. (Ed.), *Advances in child development and behavior* (*Vol. 20*, pp. 239–287). New York: Academic Press.

Macedonia, M. (2000). *Entertainment technology and virtual environments for military training and education.* Retrieved from the Educause Website net.educause.edu/ir/library/pdf/ffp0107s.pdf

Macedonia, M. (2002). Games, simulation, and the military education dilemma. In M. Devlin, R. Larson & J. Meyerson, (Eds), Internet and the University: 2001 Forum (pp. 157-167). Cambridge, MA: EDUCAUSE, MIT.

MacKeracher, D. (1996). Making Sense of Adult Learning. Toronto: Culture Concepts.

MacMahan, A. (2003). Immersion, engagement, and presence: A method for analysing 3-d video games. In Wolf, M. J. P., & Perron, B. (Eds.), *The video game theory reader* (pp. 67–86). New York: Routledge.

Maedgen, J., & Carlson, C. (2000). Social functioning and emotional regulation in attention deficit hyperactivity disorder subtypes.. *Journal of Clinical Child Psychology*, *29*, 30–42. doi:10.1207/S15374424jccp2901_4

Malliet, S. (2006). An exploration of adolescents' perceptions of video game realism. *Learning, Media and Technology*, *31*(4), 377–394. doi:10.1080/17439880601021983

Malone, T. (1981). Toward a theory of intrinsically motivating instruction. *Cognitive Science*, *4*, 333–369.

Malone, T. W. (1980). *What makes things fun to learn? Heuristics for designing instructional computer games*. Paper presented at the Joint Symposium: Association for Computing Machinery Special Interest Group on Small Computers and Special Interest Group on Personal Computers, Palo Alto, CA.

Malone, T. W. (1981). Toward a theory of intrinsically motivating instruction. *Cognitive Science*, *5*(4), 333–369.

Malone, T. W. (1981). What makes video games fun? *Byte*, *6*(12), 258–277.

Malone, T. W., & Lepper, M. R. (1987). *Aptitude, learning and instruction iii: Cognitive and affective process analysis*. Hillsdale, NJ: Lawrence Erlbaum Associates.

Malone, T. W., & Lepper, M. R. (1987). Making Learning Fun: A Taxonomy of Intrinsic Motivations for Learning. In R. E. Snow & M. J. Farr (Eds.), Aptitude, Learning and Instruction: Conative and affective process analyses (Vol. 3, pp. 223-254). Hillsdale, NJ: Lawrence Erlbaum Associates.

Maloney, A. (2007). *Generation-Fit, a Pilot Study of Youth in Maine Middle Schools Using an "Exerlearning" Dance Video Game to Promote Physical Activity During School*. Retrieved from http://clinicaltrials.gov/ct2/show/NCT00424918

Malouf, D. B. (1987). The effect of instructional computer games on continuing student motivation. *The Journal of Special Education*, *21*(4), 27–38. doi:10.1177/002246698802100406

Mane, A. M., Adams, J. A., & Donchin, E. (1989). Adaptive and part: Whole training in the acquisition of a complex perceptual-motor skill. *Acta Psychologica*, *71*, 179–196. doi:10.1016/0001-6918(89)90008-5

Mansfield, R. (2008). *How to do everything with Second Life*. New York: McGraw Hill.

Maras, P., & Brown, R. Effects of different forms of school contact on children's attitudes toward disabled and non-disabled peers. *The British Journal of Educational Psychology*, *70*(3), 337–351. doi:10.1348/000709900158164

Marcus, S., Wan, G., Kemner, J., & Olfson, M. (2005). Continuity of methylphenidate treatment for attention-deficit/hyperactivity disorder. *Archives of Pediatrics & Adolescent Medicine*, *159*, 572–578. doi:10.1001/archpedi.159.6.572

Marsh, J. (2004). The techno-literacy practices of young children. *Journal of Early Childhood Research*, *2*(1), 51–66. doi:10.1177/1476718X0421003

Marsick, V. J., & Watkins, K. E. (1990). Informal and Incidental Learning in the Workplace. London: Routledge.

Martínez Alemán, A. M. (2001). The ethics of democracy: Individuality and educational policy. *Educational Policy*, *15*(3), 379–403. doi:10.1177/0895904801015003003

Marx, K. (1956). Zur Kritik der Hegelschen Rechtsphilosophie. Einleitung. In Institut für Marxismus-Leninismus beim ZK der SED (Ed.), Marx/Engels Werke, Bd. 1 (pp. 378-391). Berlin: Dietz Verlag.

Marzano, R. J. (2009). *MRL Meta-Analysis Database Summary*. Retrieved 5th July 2009: http://files.solution-tree.com/MRL/documents/strategy_summary_6_10_09.pdf

Marzano, R. J., & Kendall, J. S. (2006). The New Taxonomy of Educational Objectives (2nd ed.). Thousand Oaks, CA: Corwin Press.

Maslow, A. H. (1946). A Theory of Human Motivation. In P. L. Harriman (Ed.), Twentieth Century Psychology: Recent Developments in Psychology (pp. 22-48). New York: The Philosophical Library.

Mateas, M. (2003). Expressive AI: Games and Artificial Intelligence. In *Proceedings of Level Up: Digital Games Research Conference*, Utrecht, Netherlands, Nov. 2003.

Mather, N., Bos, N., & Babur, N. (2008). Perceptions and knowledge of preservice and inservice teachers about early literacy instruction. *Journal of Learning Disabilities, 34*(5), 472–482. doi:10.1177/002221940103400508

Mautone, J. A., DuPaul, G. J., & Jitendra, A. K. (2005). The effects of computer-assisted instruction on the mathematics performance and classroom behavior of children with ADHD. *Journal of Attention Disorders, 9*, 301–312. doi:10.1177/1087054705278832

Mayall, H. J. (2002). *An Exploratory/Descriptive Look at Gender Differences in Technology Self-efficacy and Academic Self-efficacy in the GlobalEd Project.* Unpublished dissertation, University of Connecticut.

Mayer, R. (1987). Educational psychology: A cognitive approach. Boston: Little, Brown.

Mayes, J., Draper, S., McGregor, A., & Oatley, K. (1988). Information flow in a user interface: the effect of experience and context on the recall of MacWrite screens. In D. M. Jones & R. Winder (Eds.), People and Computers IV. Cambridge, UK: Cambridge University Press.

Maynard, T. (2002). Boys and literacy: Exploring the issues. New York: Routledge.

Mayo, M. J. (2009). Video games: A route to large-scale STEM education? *Science, 323*, 79–82. doi:10.1126/science.1166900

McCaskill, L. (2005). Internet based lessons learned project provides first hand assistance prior to deployments. *REDCOM Magazine,* Winter, 2005-2006.

McClure, R., & Mears, F. (1986). Videogame playing and psychopathology. *Psychological Reports, 59*, 59–62.

McCown, M. (2005). Strategic gaming for the national security community. *Joint Forces Quarterly, 39*(4), 34–39.

McDermott, L. (2001). Oersted Medal Lecture2001: Physics education research – The Key to Student Learning. *American Journal of Physics, 69*(11). doi:10.1119/1.1389280

McEvoy, M. A., & Odom, S. L. (1987). Social interaction training for preschool children with behavioral disorders. *Behavioral Disorders, 12*, 242–251.

McFarlane, A., Sparrowhawk, A., & Heald, Y. (2001). *Report on the Educational Use of Games.* Retrieved April 10, 2009, from http://www.teem.org.uk/publications/teem_gamesined_full.pdf

McGill, I., & Brockbank, A. (2004). *The action learning handbook: Powerful techniques for education, professional development & training.* London: Routledge-Falmer.

McGill, T., & Volet, S. (1997). A Conceptual Framework for Analyzing Students' Knowledge of Programming. *Journal of Research on Computing in Education, 29*(3), 276–297.

McGinnis, T. A. (2007). Khmer rap boys, X-Men, Asia's fruits, and Dragonball z: Creating multilingual and multimodal classroom contexts. *Journal of Adolescent & Adult Literacy, 50*(7), 570–579. doi:10.1598/JAAL.50.7.6

McGonigal, J. (2009, March/April). Museums as happiness pioneers. *Museum, 88*, 48–53.

McGrenere, J. (1996). *Design: Educational Electronic Multi-player Games – A Literature Review.* Technical Report 96-12, the University of British Columbia. Retrieved on 27 June 2003.http://www.cs.ubc.ca/nest/egems/papers/desmugs.pdf

McLuhan, M., & Fiore, Q. (1968). *War and peace in the global village.* New York: Bantam.

McMillan, S., & Wilhelm, J. (2007). Students' stories: Adolescents constructing multiple literacies through nature journaling. *Journal of Adolescent & Adult Literacy, 50*(5), 370–377. doi:10.1598/JAAL.50.5.4

McNeil, F. (2009). *Learning with the brain in mind.* London: Sage Publications.

McVey, M. H. (2008). Observations of expert communicators in immersive virtual worlds: Implications for synchronous discussion. *ALT-J. Research in Learning Technology, 16*, 173–180.

Meadows, M. (2008). I, Avatar: The culture and consequences of having a second life. Indianapolis: New Riders.

Menn, D. (1993) Multimedia in Education: Arming Our Kids For the Future. *PC World, 11*(October).

Merriam, S. B., & Caffarella, R. S. (1999). Learning in Adulthood: A comprehensive guide, (2nd Ed.). San Francisco: Jossey-Bass.

Messinger, P. R., Ge, X., Stroulia, E., Lyons, K., Smirnov, K., & Bone, M. (2008). On the relationship between my avatar and myself. *Journal of Virtual Worlds Research, 1*(2), 1–17.

Meyer, E., Abrami, P. C., Wade, A., Aslan, O., & Deault, L. (in press). Improving literacy and metacognition with electronic portfolios: Teaching and learning with ePEARL. *Computers & Education.* See http://dx.doi.org/10.1016/j.compedu.2009.12.005

Mezirow, J. (1978). Perspective Transformation. *Adult Education, 28*(2), 100–110. doi:10.1177/074171367802800202

Michael, D., & Chen, S. (2006). *Serious games: Games that educate, train, and inform.* Boston, MA: Thomson Course Technology.

Michaels, J. (1993). Patterns of video game play in parlors as a function of endogenous and exogenous factors. *Youth & Society, 25*(2), 272–289. doi:10.1177/0044118X93025002005

Michigan State University. (2004). *Children spend more time playing video games than watching TV.* Retrieved from http://www.newsroom.msu.edu/site/indexer/1943/content.htm

Mikos, L. (1994). Fernsehen im Erleben der Zuschauer: vom lustvollen Umgang mit einem popularen Medium. Berlin: Quintessenz-Verlagsgesellschaft.

Millar, A., & Navarick, D. J. (1984). Self-control and choice in humans: Effects of video game playing as a positive reinforcer. *Learning and Motivation, 15,* 203–218. doi:10.1016/0023-9690(84)90030-4

Millard, E. (2003). Towards a literacy of fusion: New times, new teaching and learning? *Reading, 37*(1), 3-8.

Miller, G. A. (2003). The Magical Number Seven, Plus or Minus Two: Some Limits on Our Capacity for Processing Information. In B. J. Baars, W. P. Banks & J. B. Newman (Eds.), Essential Sources in the Scientific Study of Consciousness (pp. 357-372). Cambridge, MA: MIT Press.

Mirvis, P. H. (1996). Historical foundations of organizational learning. *Journal of Organizational Change Management, 9*(1), 13–31. doi:10.1108/09534819610107295

Mislevy, R. J., Steinberg, L. S., & Almond, R. G. (2003). On the structure of educational assessment (with discussion). *Measurement: Interdisciplinary Research and Perspectives, 1*(1), 3–62. doi:10.1207/S15366359MEA0101_02

Moberly, K. (2008, September). Composition, computer games, and the absence of writing. Computers & Composition, 25(3), 284_299.

Moje, E. B. (2000). 'To be part of the story': The literacy practices of gangsta adolescents. *Teachers College Record, 102*(3), 651–690. doi:10.1111/0161-4681.00071

Morecroft, J. D. W. (1992). Executive Knowledge, Models and Learning. *European Journal of Operational Research, 59*(1), 9–27. doi:10.1016/0377-2217(92)90004-S

Moreno Ger, P., Blesius, C., Currier, P., Sierra, J. L., & Fernández-Manjón, B. (2008). Online Learning and Clinical Procedures: Rapid Development and Effective Deployment of Game-Like Interactive Simulations In Z. Pan, A. D. Cheok, W. Müller & A. E. Rhabili (Eds.), Transactions on Edutainment I (Vol. 5080/2008, pp. 288-304). Berlin Heidelberg: Springer Verlag.

Morgan, S. B., & Wisely, D. W. (1996). Children's attitudes and behavioral intentions toward a peer presented as physically handicapped: A more positive view. *Journal of Developmental and Physical Disabilities, 8,* 29–42. doi:10.1007/BF02578438

Morgan, S. B., Biebrich, A. A., Walker, M., & Schwerdt-feger, H. (1998). Children's willingness to share activities with a physically handicapped peer: Am I more willing than my classmates? *Journal of Pediatric Psychology, 23*(6), 1998. doi:10.1093/jpepsy/23.6.367

Morrison, G. R., Ross, S. M., & Kemp, J. E. (2006). Designing Effective Instruction (5 ed.). London: Wiley.

Mottron, L., Dawson, M., Soulieres, I., Hubert, B., & Burack, J. (2006). Enhanced perceptual functioning in autism: an update, and eight principles of autistic perception. *Journal of Autism and Developmental Disorders, 36*(1), 27–43. doi:10.1007/s10803-005-0040-7

Mukherjee, W. (2008). Nokia plans to design handsets for disabled. *The Economic Times*. Retrieved May 5, 2009, from http://economictimes.indiatimes.com/Nokia_plans_handsets_for_disabled/rssarticle-show/3830729.cms

Munro, A. (2009). Software support of instruction in game contexts. In O'Neil, H. F., & Perez, R. (Eds.), *Computer games and team and individual learning* (pp. 3–20). Amsterdam, The Netherlands: Elsevier Ltd.

Murray, J. (1997). *Hamlet on the holodeck: The future of narrative in cyberspace*. New York: The Free Press.

Myles, B. S., Simpson, R. L., Ormsbee, C. K., & Erikson, C. (1993). Integrating preschool children with autism with their normally developing peers: Research findings and best practice recommendations. *Focus on Autistic Behavior, 8*, 1–18.

Nabors, L. A., & Larson, E. R. (2002). The effects of brief interventions on children's playmate preferences for a child sitting in a wheelchair. *Journal of Developmental and Physical Disabilities, 14*, 403–413. doi:10.1023/A:1020339004125

National Academy of Science. (1998). *Teaching About Evolution and the Nature of Science*. Washington, DC: National Academy Press.

National Center for Educational Statistics. (2007, February 22). *The Nation's Report Card: Reading 2007*. Retrieved October 25, 2007, from http://nces.ed.gov/pubsearch/pubsinfo.asp? pubid=2007496

National Development Group for the Mentally Handicapped. (1977). *Day Services for Mentally Handicapped Adults*. London: Department of Health and Social Security.

National Library of Medicine. (2000). *Current bibliographies in medicine: Health literacy*. Bethesda, MD: National Institutes of Health, U.S. Department of Health and Human Services. Retrieved from http://www.nlm.nih.gov/pubs/cbm/hliteracy.html

National Reading Panel. (2000). *Teaching children to read: reports of the subgroups*. Mahwah, NJ: Lawrence Erlbaum Associates. Retrieved April 7, 2009 from http://www.nichd.nih.gov/publications/pubs_details.cfm?from=&pubs_id=88

Nelson, B., Ketelhut, D. J., Clarke, J., Bowman, C., & Dede, C. (2005). Design-based research strategies for developing a scientific inquiry curriculum in a multi-user virtual environment. *Educational Technology, 45*(1), 21–27.

Nessa, N. (2004). National Statistics: The health of children and young people, (pp. 1- 20).

Neulight, N., Kafai, Y. B., Kao, L., Foley, B., & Galas, C. (2007). Children's participation in a virtual epidemic in the science classroom: Making connections to natural infectious diseases. *Journal of Science Education and Technology, 16*, 47–58. doi:10.1007/s10956-006-9029-z

New London Group. (1996). A pedagogy of multiliteracies: Designing social futures. *Harvard Educational Review, 66*, 60–92.

New Media Consortium. (2008). *The 2008 horizon report*. Retrieved from New Media Consortium web site: http://wp.nmc.org/horizon2008/

Newacheck, P. W., Inkelas, M., & Kim, S. (2004). Health services use and health care Expenditures for children with disabilities. *Pediatrics, 114*, 79–85. doi:10.1542/peds.114.1.79

News, B. B. C. (2005). S Korean Dies After Games Session. Retrieved from http://news.bbc.co.uk/2/hi/technology/4137782.stm

Newschaffer, C. J., Falb, M. D., & Gurney, J. G. (2005). National autism prevalence trends from United States special education data. *Pediatrics*, *115*(3), 277–282. doi:10.1542/peds.2004-1958

Nieborg, D. B. (2004). *America's Army: More Than a Game*. Paper presented at the Transforming Knowledge into Action through Gaming and Simulation, Munchen: SAGSAGA.

Nielsen, J. (1993). Usability Engineering. San Diego, CA: Academic Press.

Nielsen, J., & Molich, R. (1990). Heuristic Evaluation of User Interfaces. In *Proceedings of the. ACM CHI'90 Conference* (Seattle, WA, 1-5 April), (pp. 249-256).

NLN. (2003). *Paving the Way – Developing standards for e-learning*. National Learning Network. Retrieved May 14, 2008, from http://www.nln.ac.uk/?p=Using

Nokia (2009b). Nokia maps application. Retrieved May 6, 2009, from http://www.nokia.co.uk/get-support-and-software/navigation

Nokia. (2009a). *Text-to-speech*. Retrieved May 6, 2009, from http://blind.wikia.com/wiki/Open_Letter_Initiative#Android_Accessibility

Norton-Meier, L. (2005). Joining the video-game literacy club: A reluctant mother tries to join the "flow.". *Journal of Adolescent & Adult Literacy*, *48*(5), 428–432. doi:10.1598/JAAL.48.5.6

Notbohm, E. (2005). *Ten Things Every Child with Autism Wishes You Knew*. Arlington, Texas: Future Horizons.

NRC. (1996). *National science education standards*. Washington, DC: National Academy Press.

NRC. (2006). *America's Lab Report: Investigations in High School Science*. Washington, DC: National Academy Press.

O'Brien, D. A., Lawless, K. A., & Schrader, P. G. (in press). A taxonomy of educational games: Genres and applications. In Baek, Y. K. (Ed.), *Gaming and Classroom-Based Learning: Digital Role Playing as a Motivator of Study*. Hershey, PA: Information Science Reference.

O'Brien, D., & Scharber, C. (2008). Digital literacies go to school: Potholes and possibilities. *Journal of Adolescent & Adult Literacy*, *52*(1), 66–68. doi:10.1598/JAAL.52.1.7

O'Neil, H., & Perez, R. (2009) *Computer games and team and individual learning*. Amsterdam, Netherlands: Elsevier Ltd. osmotic. (2008). *Merriam-Webster online dictionary*. Retrieved July 16, 2008, from http://www.merriam-webster.com/dictionary/osmotic

Oblinger, D. G. (2003). Boomers, gen-xers, and millennials: Understanding the new students. *Educase*, *38*(4), 37-47. Retrieved January 26, 2009, from http://www.educause.edu/ir/library/pdf/erm0342.pdf

Oblinger, D. G. (2004). The next generation of education engagement. *Journal of Interactive Media in Education*, *8*, 1–18.

Oblinger, D., & Oblinger, J. (2005). Is it age or IT: first steps toward understanding the net generation. In D. Oblinger & J. Oblinger (Eds.), *Educating the net generation* (p. 2.1-2.19). Educause. Retrieved from Educause Web site: www.educause.edu/educatingthenetgen/

Odom, S. L., McConnell, S. R., & Chandler, L. K. (1993). Acceptability and feasibility of classroom-based social interaction interventions for young children. *Exceptional Children*, *60*, 226–236.

Oerter, R. (1999). Psychologie des Spiels. Ein handlungstheoretischer Ansatz, Weinheim, Germany: Beltz.

Oerter, R. (2000). Spiel als Lebensbewältigung. In S. von Hoppe-Graff & R. Oerter (Eds.). Spielen und Fernsehen. Über die Zusammenhänge von Spiel und Medien in der Welt des Kindes, (pp. 439-454). Weinheim, Germany: Juventa.

Ogle, D. (1986, February). K-W-L: A teaching model that develops active reading of expository text. *The Reading Teacher*, *39*, 564–570. doi:10.1598/RT.39.6.11

Oizumi, J. J. (1997). Assessing maternal functioning in families of children with autism. *Dissertation Abstracts International Section B: The Sciences and Engineering*, *57* (7-B), 5720.

Okagaki, L., & Frensch, P. A. (1994). Effects of video game playing on measures of spatial performance: Gender effects in late adolescence. *Journal of Applied Developmental Psychology, 15,* 33–58. doi:10.1016/0193-3973(94)90005-1

Oliver, K. (1997). *A Case-Based Pharmacy Environment: Cognitive Flexibility + Social Constructivism.* Paper presented at the ED-MEDIA/ED-TELECOM, Calgary, Canada.

Omale, N., Hung, W.-C., Luetkehans, L., & Cooke-Plagwitz, J. (2009). Learning in 3-D multiuser virtual environments: Exploring the use of unique 3-D attributes for online problem-based learning. *British Journal of Educational Technology, 40,* 480–495. doi:10.1111/j.1467-8535.2009.00941.x

Ondrejka, C. (2008). Education unleashed: Participatory culture, education, and innovation in Second Life. In Salen, K. (Ed.), *The ecology of games: Connecting youth, games, and learning* (pp. 229–251). Cambridge, MA: The MIT Press.

Online Learning History. (2008). Retrieved April 14, 2009, from Moodle Website: http://docs.moodle.org/en/Online_Learning_History

Organisation for Economic Co-operation and Development. (2006). *Are students ready for a technology-rich world? What PISA studies tell us.* Paris: OECD Publications.

Organisation for Economic Co-operation and Development. (2007). Pisa 2006: science competencies for tomorrow's world. Volume 1 analysis. Paris: OECD Publications.

Organization for Economic Co-Operation and Developement. (2000). *Knowledge and skills for life: First results from PISA 2000 (Executive summary).*

Ota, K. R., & DuPaul, G. J. (2002). Task engagement and mathematics performance in children with attention-deficit hyperactivity disorder: Effects of supplemental computer instruction. *School Psychology Quarterly, 17,* 242–257. doi:10.1521/scpq.17.3.242.20881

Owen-Deschryver, J. S. (2004). Promoting social interactions between students with Autism and their peers in inclusive school settings. *Dissertation Abstracts International Section A: Humanities and Social Sciences, 64(9-A),* 3246.

Oxford english dictionary. (n.d.). New York: Oxford University Press.

Paley, V. (2004). *A child's work: The importance of fantasy play.* Chicago: University of Chicago Press.

Pantelidis, V. S. (1993). Virtual reality in the classroom. *Educational Technology,* 23–27.

Papert, S. (1980). *Mindstorms: Children, Computers, and Powerful Ideas.* New York: Basic Books.

Papert, S. (1993). *The Children's machine: rethinking school in the age of the computer.* New York: Basic Books.

Papert, S., & Harel, I. (1991). *Situating constructionism. Constructionism.* Norwood, NJ: Ablex.

Paras, B., & Bizzocchi, J. (2005). *Game, Motivation, and Effective Learning: An Integrated Model for Educational Game Design.* Paper presented at the DiGRA 2005 – the Digital Games Research Association's 2nd International Conference, Simon Fraser University, Burnaby, BC, Canada.

Partnership for 21st Century Skills. (2002). *Learning for the 21st Century.* Tucson, AZ: Partnership for 21st Century Skills. Retrieved March 1st, 2009 from http://www.21stcenturyskills.org/index.php?option=com_content&task=view&id=29&Itemid=185

Partnership for 21st Century Skills. (2009). *Skills framework.* Retrieved April 3, 2009, from http://www.21stcenturyskills.org/index.php?option=com_content&task=view&id=254&Itemid=120

Passionate about entertainment. (n.d.). Retrieved October 13, 2008, from http://corp.ign.com/

Payne, S. (1991). Display-Based Action at the User Interface. *International Journal of Man-Machine Studies, 35*(3), 275–289. doi:10.1016/S0020-7373(05)80129-4

Pearce, C. (2006). Productive Play: Game Culture From the Bottom Up. *Games and Culture, 1*(1), 17–24. doi:10.1177/1555412005281418

Pearce, C., & Ashmore, C. (2007). *Principles of emergent Design in Online Games: Mermaids Phase 1 Prototype*. Presented at the SIGGRAGH Sandbox, Sand Diego, California.

Pellegrino, J., & Scott, A. (2004). The Transition from Simulation to Game-Based Learning. Retrieved March 8, 2008 from http://www.learningarchitects.net/files/Transition_from_Sims_to_Games.pdf

Perkins, D. N. (1986). *Knowledge as Design*. Hillsdale, NJ: Erlbaum.

Peter, J. (2002). Medien-Priming - Grundlagen, Befunde und Forschungstendenzen. *Publizistik, 47*, 21–44. doi:10.1007/s11616-002-0002-4

Peterson, M. (2006). Learner interaction management in an avatar and chat-based virtual world. *Computer Assisted Language Learning, 19*, 79–103. doi:10.1080/09588220600804087

Petrovsky, A. V. (Ed.). (1986). *General psychology*. Moscow: Education Publishers.

Pew Internet and American Life Project. (2008). *Teens, Video Games, and Civics*. Pew Internet and American Life Project. Retrieved April 29, 2009 from http://www.pewinternet.org/~/media/Files/Reports/2008/PIP_Teens_Games_and_Civics_Report_FINAL.pdf.pdf

Pham, A. (2009, March 20). Video game revenue jumps 9% in February. *Los Angeles Times*. Retrieved from http://www.latimes.com/business/la-fi-cotown-games20-2009mar20,0,6765213.story

PhysOrg.com. (2008 October 29). Issue retrieved from http://www.physorg.com/news144510236.html

Piaget, J. (1932). *The moral judgement of the child*. London: Routledge & Keegan Paul.

Pierce, K., & Schreibman, L. (1995). Increasing complex social behaviors in children with autism: Effects of peer-implemented pivotal response training. *Journal of Applied Behavior Analysis, 28*, 285–295. doi:10.1901/jaba.1995.28-285

Piirainen-Marsh, A., & Tainio, L. (2009). Collaborative game-play as a site for participation and situated learning of a second language. *Scandinavian Journal of Educational Research, 53*(2), 167–183. doi:10.1080/00313830902757584

Pillay, H. (2003). An investigation of cognitive processes engaged in by recreational computer game players: Implications for skills of the future. *Journal of Research on Technology in Education, 34*(3), 336–350.

Pivec, M. (2007). Editorial: Play and learn: potentials of game-based learning. *British Journal of Educational Technology, 38*(3), 387–393. doi:10.1111/j.1467-8535.2007.00722.x

Pivec, M. (Ed.). (2006) Affective and emotional aspects of human-computer interaction; Game-Based and Innovative Learning Approaches. Vol.1: The Future of Learning (IOS Press, 2006), ISBN 1-58603-572-x

Pivec, M., & Moretti, M. (Eds.). (2008) Discover the Pleasure of Learning - Guidelines on Game- Based Learning. Pabst Vrlg. ISBN 978-3-89967-521-4

Pivec, M., & Pivec, P. (2008). Designing and implementing a game in an educational context. In Pivec, M., & Moretti, M. (Eds.), *Discover the Pleasure of Learning - Guidelines on Game-Based Learning*. Pabst.

Pivec, M., & Pivec, P. (2008a). Playing to Learn: Guidelines for Designing Educational Games. Proceedings of *World Conference on Educational Multimedia, Hypermedia and telecommunications 2008* Vienna, Austria, 2008, pp. 3247 - 3252

Pivec, M., & Pivec, P. (2009) Misconceptions about being Digital. Chapter in Zheng R. (Ed.): Adolescent Online Social Communication and Behavior: Relationship Formation on the Internet. (In press, 2009)

Pivec, M., Dziabenko, O., & Schinnerl, I. (2003). *Aspects of Game-Based Learning*. Paper presented at the Third International Conference on Knowledge Management (IKNOW 03), Graz, Austria.

Pivec, P. (2009). Presentation at the Game-Based Learning Conference, London.

Pivec, P., & Pivec, M. (2008b) Games in Schools. Commissioned report for Interactive Software Federation of Europe (ISFE) by the European Commission (EC). Retrieved November 30, 2008, from http://www.isfe.eu/

Ployhart, R. E., & Ehrhart, M. G. (2003). Be careful what you ask for: Effects of response instructions on the construct validity and reliability of situational judgment tests. *International Journal of Selection and Assessment, 11*, 1–16. doi:10.1111/1468-2389.00222

Poling, D., & Evans, E. (2002, March). Why do birds of a feather flock together? Developmental change in the use of multiple explanations: Intention, teleology and essentialism. *The British Journal of Developmental Psychology, 20*(1), 89. doi:10.1348/026151002166343

Popper, F. (2007). *From technology to virtual art.* Cambridge, Massachusetts: The MIT Press.

Popper, K. (1959). *The logic of scientific discovery.* London: Hutchinson.

Porter, G., & Starcevic, V. (2007). Are violent video games harmful? *Australasian Psychiatry, 15*, 422–426. doi:10.1080/10398560701463343

Porter, M. (1980). *Competitive Strategy.* New York: The Free Press.

Postman, N. (1986). *Amusing ourselves to death: Public discourse in the age of show business.* New York: Penguin USA.

Poulson, D. F., & Waddell, F. N. (2001). USERFIT: user centred design in assistive technology. In Nicholle, C. A., & Abascal, J. (Eds.), *Inclusive Guidelines for HCI.* San Francisco: Taylor and Francis.

Poulson, D. F., Ashby, M., & Richardson, S. (1996). USERFIT: A Practical Handbook on User-Centred Design for Assistive Technology. Brussels: TIDE European Commission, ECSC-EC-EAEC.

Preece, J., Rogers, Y., Sharp, H., Benyon, D., Holland, S., & Carey, T. (1994). *Human-computer interaction.* Harlow, UK: Addison-Wesley.

Prensky, M. (2001). Digital Game-Based Learning. New York: McGraw-Hill Companies.

Prensky, M. (2001a). "Simulations": Are they games? In Digital game-based learning (pp. 210-220). New York: McGraw-Hill.

Prensky, M. (2001b). Digital natives, digital immigrants. *Horizon, 9*(5), 1–6. doi:10.1108/10748120110424816

Prensky, M. (2002). The Motivation of Gameplay or the REAL 21st century learning revolution. *Horizon, 10*, 1–14.

Prensky, M. (2004). Digital Game-Based Learning. New York: McGraw-Hill.

Prensky, M. (2006). *Don't bother me mom – I'm learning: How computer and video games are preparing your kids for 21st century success – and how you can help.* St. Paul, MN: Paragon House.

Prensky, M. (2008). Students as designers and creators of educational computer games: Who else? *British Journal of Educational Technology, 39*(6), 1004–1019. doi:10.1111/j.1467-8535.2008.00823_2.x

Prensky, M. (Interviewee). (2007). *The rules of engagement.* [video file]. Interview with Sisomo on 20 January 2007. Retrieved from Sisomo web site: http://sisomo.com/interviews/Marc-Prensky.htm

Prensky, M., & Thiagrajan, S. (2007). *Digital game-based learning.* New York: McGraw Hill.

Prentice, S. (2008). *Using virtual worlds as a communications channel.* Gartner Report No. G00160043.

Pressley, M. (1998). *Reading instruction that works.* New York: Guilford Press.

Pressley, M. (2002). Effective beginning reading instruction. *Journal of Literacy Research, 34*(2), 165–188. doi:10.1207/s15548430jlr3402_3

Pressley, M., Wharton-McDonald, R., Allington, R., Block, C. C., Morrow, L., & Tracey, D. (2001). A study of effective first-grade literacy instruction. *Scientific Studies of Reading, 5*(1), 35–58. doi:10.1207/S1532799X-SSR0501_2

Price, R. V. (1990). Computer-aided instruction: A guide for authors. Pacific Grove, CA: Brooks/Cole Publishing Company.

Project Tomorrow. (2007). *Speak up 2007 for students, teachers, parents & school leaders - selected national findings.* Retrieved December 10, 2008 from http://www.tomorrow.org/docs/National%20Findings%20Speak%20Up%202007.pdf

Project Tomorrow. (2008). *Speak Up 2007 for Students, Teachers, Parents & School Leaders Selected National Findings - April 8, 2008.* Retrieved from http://www.tomorrow.org/docs/National Findings Speak U 202007.pdf

Provenzo, E. (1991). *Video kids: Making sense of Nintendo.* Cambridge, MA: Harvard.

Provenzo, E. (1992). What do video games teach? *Education Digest, 58*(4), 56–58.

Rademacher, R. J. (2009a). *An assessment of current pure online physics courses.* Presented at the American Association of Physics Teachers Winter meeting, Chicago.

Rademacher, R. J. (2009b). *A proposed framework for studying educational virtual worlds.* Presented at the Indipendent Massively multiplayer Game Developers conference, Las Vegas, Nevada.

Rademacher, R. J. (in press). Best practices in teaching and designing a pure online science classroom. In Y. Katz, (Ed.), Learning Management Systems Technologies and Software Solutions for Online Teaching: Tools and Applications. Hershey, PA: IGI Global.

Raines, C. (2002). *Managing Millennials.* Retrieved February 28, 2009, from, http://www.generationsatwork.com/articles/millenials.htm

Ramani, G., & Siegler, R. (2008). Promoting broad and stable improvements in low-income children's numerical knowledge through playing number board games. *Child Development, 79*(2), 375–394. doi:10.1111/j.1467-8624.2007.01131.x

Ramsberger, P. F., Hopwood, D., Hargan, C. S., & Underhill, W. G. (1983). *Evaluation of a spatial data management system for basic skills education. Final phase 1 report for period 7 october 1980 - 30 april 1983.* Alexandria, VA: Human Resources Research Organization.

Ratey, J. (2008). *Spark: The revolutionary new science of exercise and the brain.* New York: Little, Brown and Company.

Raybourn, E. (2007). Applying Simulation Experience Design Methods to Creating Serious Game-Based Adaptive Training Systems. *Interacting with Computers, 19*(2), 206–214. doi:10.1016/j.intcom.2006.08.001

Razzaq, L., Feng, M., Nuzzo-Jones, G., Heffernan, N. T., Koedinger, K. R., & Junker, B. (2005). The assistment project: Blending assessment and assisting. In *Proceedings of the 12th artificial conference on intelligence in education,* (pp. 555–562). Amsterdam: ISO Press.

Recreation. (n.d.). Retrieved April 9, 2009, from http://en.wikipedia.org/wiki/Fun

Redfern, S., & Naughton, N. (2002). Collaborative virtual environments to support communication and community in internet-based distance education. *Journal of Information Technology Education, 1*(3), 12.

Reeves, T. C., & Okey, J. R. (1996). Alternative assessments in constructivist learning environments. In B. G. Wilson (Ed.), Constructivist Learning Environments: Case Studies in Instructional Design, (pp. 191-202). Englewood Cliffs, NJ: Educational Technology Publications.

Reigeluth, C. M., Merrill, M. D., Wilson, B. G., & Spille, R. T. (1980). The elaboration theory of instruction: A model for sequencing and synthesizing instruction. *Instructional Science, 9*(3), 195–219. doi:10.1007/BF00177327

Report, H. (2007). *Trends in Online Learning.* The New Media Consortium.

Rettenburg, J. W. (2008). Quests in world of warcraft:

deferral and repetition. In Rettenburg, J. W., & Corneliussen, H. G. (Eds.), *Digital culture, play, and identity: a world of warcraft reader* (pp. 167–184). Cambridge, MA: The MIT Press.

Rettie, R. (2002). Net Generation Culture. *Journal of Electronic Commerce Research, 3*(4), 254–264.

Revans, R. (1980). *Action learning: New techniques for action learning.* London: Blond and Briggs.

RezEd.org. (2008, June). Re: What are virtual worlds? Message posted to http://www.rezed.org/forum/topic/show?id=2047896%3ATopic%3A7218

Ricci, K. E., Salas, E., & Cannon-Bowers, J. A. (1996). Do computer-based games facilitate knowledge acquisition and retention? *Military Psychology, 8*(4), 295–307. doi:10.1207/s15327876mp0804_3

Rice, M. L., Huston, A. C., Truglio, R., & Wright, J. (1990). Words from "Sesame Street": learning vocabulary while viewing. *Developmental Psychology, 26*(3), 421–428. doi:10.1037/0012-1649.26.3.421

Rideout, V. J., Vandewater, E. A., & Wartella, E. A. (2003). Zero to Six: Electronic Media in the Lives of Infants, Toddlers and Preschoolers. Menlo Park, CA: Kaiser Family Foundation.

Rideout, V., Roberts, D.F., & Foehr, U.G. (March, 2005). *Media in the lives of 8-18 year olds.* A Kaiser Family Foundation Study.

Rieber, L. (1996). Seriously considering play: Designing interactive learning environments based on the blending of microworlds, simulations, and games. *Educational Technology Research and Development, 44*(1), 43–58. doi:10.1007/BF02300540

Rieber, L. P. (1996). Seriously considering play: Designing interactive learning environments based on the blending of microworlds, simulations, and games. *Educational Technology Research and Development, 44*(2), 43–58. doi:10.1007/BF02300540

Rieber, L. P. (2004). Microworlds. In D. Jonassen (Ed.), Handbook of research for educational communications and technology: Second edition, (pp. 583-603). Mahwah, NJ: Lawrence Erlbaum Associates.

Rieber, L. P., & Noah, D. (2008). Games, simulations, and visual metaphors in education: Antagonism between enjoyment and learning. *Educational Media International, 45*(2), 77–92. doi:10.1080/09523980802107096

Roberts, N. (1976). Simulation gaming: A critical review. Cambridge, MA: Lesley College and Massachusetts Institute of Technology. (ERIC Document Reproduction Service No.ED 137165).

Rodriquez, F. G., & Nash, S. S. (2004). Technology and the adult degree program: The human element. *New Directions for Adult and Continuing Education, 103*, 73–79. doi:10.1002/ace.150

Roeyers, H. (1996). The influence of nonhandicapped peers on the social interactions of children with a pervasive developmental disorder. *Journal of Autism and Developmental Disorders, 26*, 303–320. doi:10.1007/BF02172476

Rogers, D., & Swan, K. (2004). Self regulated learning and Internet search. *Teachers College Record, 106*(9), 804–1824. doi:10.1111/j.1467-9620.2004.00406.x

Rogers, E. M. (2003). Diffusion of innovations (5th ed.). New York: Free Press.

Rogers, S. J. (2000). Interventions that facilitate socialization in children with autism. *Journal of Autism and Developmental Disorders, 30*, 399–409. doi:10.1023/A:1005543321840

Rogoff, B. (2003). *The cultural nature of human development.* Oxford, UK: Oxford University Press.

Rohbeck, J. (2004). Geschichtsphilosophie zur Einführung. Hamburg, Germany: Junius.

Rollings, A., & Adams, E. (2003). *Andrew Rollings and Ernest Adams on Game Design.* Retrieved from GameDev.net Web site: http://www.gamedev.net/reference/design/features/rollingsadams/

Rollings, A., & Morris, D. (2004). Game Architecture and Design: A New Edition. Berkeley, CA: New Riders Publishing.

Rorty, R. (1979). *Philosophy and the mirror of knowledge.*

Princeton, NJ: Princeton University Press.

Rosas, R., Nussbaum, M., Cumsille, P., Marianov, V., Correa, M., & Flores, P. (2003). Beyond Nintendo: Design and assessment of educational video games for first and second grade students. *Computers & Education, 40,* 71–94. doi:10.1016/S0360-1315(02)00099-4

Rosedale, P. (2007). Forward. In Rymaszewski, M. Wagner, J. A., Wallace, M., Winters, C. Ondrejka, C., Batstone-Cunninghan, B., & Second Life citizens. Second Life: The official guide. Hoboken, NJ: John Wiley & Sons, Inc.

Rosenbaum, P. L., Armstrong, R. W., & King, S. M. (1988). Determinants of children's attitudes toward disability: A review of the evidence. *Children's Health Care, 17,* 1–8. doi:10.1207/s15326888chc1701_5

Rosenthal, R. (1963). On the social psychology of the psychological experiment: The experimenter's hypotheses as unintended experimental results. *American Scientist, 51,* 268–283.

Rosenthal, R. (1989). Experimenter expectancy covert communication and meta-analytic methods. Address delivered to the 97th annual convention of the American Psychological Association, New Orleans.

Roskos-Ewoldsen, B., Davies, J., & Roskos-Ewoldsen, D. R. (2004). Implications of the mental models approach for cultivation theory. *Communications: The European Journal of Communication Research, 29*(3), 345–364.

Rosser, J. C., Lynch, P. J., Cuddihy, L., Gentile, D. A., Klonsky, J., & Merrell, R. (2007). The impact of video games on training surgeons in the 21st century. *Archives of Surgery, 142*(2), 181–186. doi:10.1001/archsurg.142.2.181

Rossi, P. H., Lipsey, M. W., & Freeman, H. E. (2004). *Evaluation: A Systematic Approach* (7th ed.). Thousand Oaks: Sage Publications.

Roth, W. M., & McGinn, M. K. (1998). Inscriptions: Toward a theory of representing as social practice. *Review of Educational Research, 68*(1), 35–59.

Rouse, R. (2001). *Game Design: Theory and Practice.*

Plano, TX: Wordware Publishing.

Rousseau, J. J. (2003). Émile. London: Orion Publishing Group. (Original work published in 1911)

Ruben, B. (1999). Simulations, Games and Experience-Based Learning: The Quest for a New Paradigm for Teaching and Learning. *Simulation & Gaming, 30*(4), 498–505. doi:10.1177/104687819903000409

Rubin, Z., & McNeil, E. B. (1983). *The psychology of being human* (3rd ed.). London: Harper and Row.

Ruble, L. A., Heflinger, C. A., Renfrew, J. W., & Saunders, R. C. (2005). Access and service use by children with autism spectrum disorders in medicaid managed care. *Journal of Autism and Developmental Disorders, 35,* 3–13. doi:10.1007/s10803-004-1026-6

Ryan, K. M. (1981). Developmental differences in reactions to the physically disabled. *Human Development, 24,* 240–256. doi:10.1159/000272685

Ryan, R. M., & Deci, E. L. (2000). Self-determination theory and the facilitation of intrinsic motivation, social development and well-being. *The American Psychologist, 55*(1), 68–78. doi:10.1037/0003-066X.55.1.68

Rymaszewski, M., Wagner, J. A., Wallace, M., & Winters, C. Ondrejka, C., Batstone-Cunninghan, B., & Second Life citizens (2007). Second Life: The official guide. Hoboken, NJ: John Wiley & Sons, Inc.

Sadler, T. D., Barab, S. A., & Scott, B. (2007). What do students gain by engaging in socioscientific inquiry? *Research in Science Education, 37,* 371–391. doi:10.1007/s11165-006-9030-9

Salem Darrow, M. (1995). Increasing research and development of virtual reality in education and special education: what about mental retardation? *VR in the Schools, 1*(3), 1–7.

Salen, K. (2007). Gaming literacies: A game design study in action. *Journal of Educational Multimedia and Hypermedia, 16*(3), 301–322.

Salen, K. (2008). Toward an Ecology of Gaming. In K.

Salen (Ed) The Ecology of Games: Connecting Youth, Games, and Learning (pp 1-17). Cambridge, MA: The MIT Press

Salen, K., & Zimmerman, E. (2003). *Rules of play: Game design fundamentals.* Cambridge, MA: MIT Press.

Salguero, R. A., & Moran, R. M. (2002). Measuring problem video game playing in adolescents. *Addiction (Abingdon, England), 97,* 1601–1606. doi:10.1046/j.1360-0443.2002.00218.x

Sallis, J. F., Hovell, M. F., Hofstetter, C. R., & Barrington, E. (1992). Explanation of vigorous physical activity during two years using social learning variables. *Social Science & Medicine, 34,* 25–32. doi:10.1016/0277-9536(92)90063-V

Salmon, G. (2002). E-tivities: the key to active on-line learning. *American Philosophy of Science, 24,* 148–156.

Salmon, G. (2009). The future for (second) life and learning. *British Journal of Educational Technology, 40,* 526–538. doi:10.1111/j.1467-8535.2009.00967.x

Saltzman, M. (Ed.). (1999). *Game design: Secrets of the sages.* Indianapolis: Brady.

Sample, M. L. (2008). Virtual Torture: Videogames and the War on Terror. *GameStudies. The international journal of computer game research, 8*(2). Retrieved January 28, 2009 from http://gamestudies.org/0802/articles/sample

Sasse, M. A. (1997). *Eliciting and Describing User's Models of Computer Systems.* Unpublished Doctoral Thesis, University of Birmingham, Birmingham.

Savage, R. S. (2006a). Effective early reading instruction and inclusion: Some reflections on mutual dependence. *International Journal of Inclusive Education: Special Issue, 10*(4-5), 347–361. doi:10.1080/13603110500221495

Savage, R. S. (2006b). Reading comprehension is not always the product of decoding and listening comprehension: Evidence from teenagers who are very poor readers. *Scientific Studies of Reading, 10*(2), 143–164. doi:10.1207/s1532799xssr1002_2

Savage, R. S., & Carless, S. (2008). The impact of reading interventions delivered by Teaching Assistants on Key Stage 1 performance. *British Educational Research Journal, 34*(3), 363–385. doi:10.1080/01411920701609315

Savage, R. S., & Pompey, Y. (2008). What does the evidence really say about effective literacy teaching? *Educational and Child Psychology, 25,* 21–30.

Savage, R., Abrami, P. C., Hipps, G., & Deault, L. C. (2009. (in press). A randomized control trial study of the ABRACADABRA reading intervention program in Grade 1. *Journal of Educational Psychology.*

Sawyer, B., & Smith, P. (2008). *Serious Games Taxonomy.* Retrieved 26 March, 2008, from http://www.dmill.com/presentations/serious-games-taxonomy-2008.pdf

Sawyer, R. K. (2006). *The Cambridge handbook of the learning sciences.* Cambridge, MA: Cambridge University Press.

Saxer, U. (2007). Politik als Unterhaltung. Zum Wandel politischer Öffentlichkeit in der Mediengesellschaft, Konstanz, Germany: UVK.

Scandura, J. M. (2003). Domain Specific Structural Analysis for Intelligent Tutoring Systems: Automatable Representation of Declarative, Procedural and Model-Based Knowledge with Relationships to Software Engineering. *Technology, Instruction. Cognition and Learning, 1,* 7–57.

Scandura, J. M. (2006). Abstract Syntax Tree (AST) infrastructure in problem solving research. *Technology, Instruction. Cognition and Learning, 3,* 1–13.

Scardamalia, M., & Bereiter, C. (1993-1994). Computer support for knowledge-building communities. Journal of the Learning Sciences, 3(3), 265–283. doi:10.1207/s15327809jls0303_3

Schaller, D. & Allison-Bunnell. (2008). *Wolfquest: How do we know if a learning game really works?* Presented at the Games+Learning+Society Conference, Madison, WI.

Schank, R. C. (1982). Dynamic Memory. Cambridge, UK: Cambridge University Press.

Schank, R. C. (1997). Virtual Learning: A Revolutionary Approach to Building a Highly Skilled Workforce. New York: McGraw-Hill Companies.

Schank, R., Fano, A., Bell, B., & Menachem, J. (1994). The Design of Goal-Based Scenarios. *Journal of the Learning Sciences, 3*(4), 305–345. doi:10.1207/s15327809jls0304_2

Schell, J. (2005). Understanding entertainment: story and gameplay are one. [CIE]. *Computers in Entertainment, 3*(1), 6. doi:10.1145/1057270.1057284

Schmelter, A., Jansen, P., & Heil, M. (2009). Empirical evaluation of virtual environment technology as an experimental tool in developmental spatial cognition research. *The European Journal of Cognitive Psychology, 21*(5), 724–739. doi:10.1080/09541440802426465

Schmidt, L., & Hawkins, P. (July 15, 2008). Children of the tech revolution. *Sydney Morning Herald*. Retrieved July 25, 2009 from http://www.smh.com.au/news/parenting/children-of-the-tech-revolution/2008/07/15/1215887601694.html

Schon, D. A. (1985). *The design studio: An exploration of its traditions and potentials*. London: RIBA Publications.

Schon, D. A. (1987). *Educating the reflective practitioner: Toward a new design for teaching and learning in the professions*. San Francisco: Jossey-Bass.

Schopler, E., & Mesibov, G. B. (Eds.). (1986). *Social behavior in autism*. New York: Plenum Press.

Schrader, P. G. (2008). Learning *in* technology: Reconceptualizing immersive environments. *AACE Journal, 16*(4), 457–475.

Schrader, P. G., & Lawless, K. A. (2008). Gamer Discretion Advised: How MMOG Players Determine the Quality and Usefulness of Online Resources. In K. McFerrin et al. (Eds.), Proceedings for the Society for Information Technology and Teacher Education (pp. 710-715). Chesapeake, VA: AACE.

Schrader, P. G., & McCreery, M. (2008). The acquisition of skill and expertise in massively multiplayer online games. *Educational Technology Research and Development, 56*(5-6), 557–574. doi:10.1007/s11423-007-9055-4

Schreibman, L., O'Neill, R. E., & Koegel, R. L. (1983). Behavioral training for siblings of autistic children. *Journal of Applied Behavior Analysis, 16*, 129–138. doi:10.1901/jaba.1983.16-129

Schroeder, R. (Ed.). (2002). *The social life of avatars: Presence and interacton in shared virtual environments*. London: Springer-Verlag.

Schroeder, R., & Axelsson, A.-S. (Eds.). (2006). *Avatars at work and play: Collaboration and interaction in shared virtual environments*. London: Springer-Verlag.

Schulz, W. (1989). Massenmedien und Realität. Die „ptomeläische" und die „kopernikanische" Auffassung. In M. Kaase & W. Schulz (Eds.), Massenkommunikation. Theorien, Methoden, Befunde (pp. 135-149). Opladen, Germany: Westdeutscher Verlag.

Schumann, P. L., Scott, T. W., & Anderson, P. H. (2006). Designing and introducing ethical dilemmas into computer based business simulations. *Journal of Management Education, 30*(1), 195–219. doi:10.1177/1052562905280844

Schutte, N., Malouff, J., Post-Gorden, J., & Rodasta, A. (1988). Effects of playing videogames on children's aggressive and other behaviors. *Journal of Applied Social Psychology, 18*(5), 454–460. doi:10.1111/j.1559-1816.1988.tb00028.x

Schwabe, W. (1994). *An Introduction to Analytic Gaming*. Technical Paper P-7864, RAND Corporation.

Schwabe, W., & Wilson, B. (1990). *Analytic War Plans: Adaptive Force-Employment Logic in the RAND Strategy Assessment System (RSAS)*. Technical Notes N-3051-NA. RAND Corporation.

Schwimmer, J. B., Burwinkle, T. M., & Varni, J. W. (2003, April 9). Health-related Quality of Life of Severely Obese Children and Adolescents. *Journal of the American Medical Association, 289*.

Scott, J., Clark, C., & Brady, M. (2000). *Students with autism: Characteristics and Instruction programming*. San Diego, CA: Singular.

Second Life hosts a dedicated education page at http://slife.com/education

Section 508. (2006). *Assistive technology resource.* section508.gov. Retrieved July 7, 2007, from http://www.section508.gov/

Seely-Brown, J., Denning, S., Groh, K., & Prusak, L. (2004). *Storytelling in Organizations: Why Storytelling is Transforming 21st Century Organizations and Management.* Burlington, MA: Elseiver.

Sehaba, K., Estraillier, P., & Lambert, D. (2005). Interactive Educational Games for Autistic Children with Agent-Based System. *Lecture Notes in Computer Science, 3711,* 422–432. doi:10.1007/11558651_41

Selfe, C. L., & Hawisher, G. E. (2004). *Literate Lives in the Information Age: Narratives On Literacy From the United States.* Mahwah, NJ: Erlbaum.

Serbin, L. A., & Sprafkin, C. (1986). The salience of gender and the process of sex-typing In three-to-seven year-old children. *Child Development, 57,* 1188–1199. doi:10.2307/1130442

Shaffer, D. W. (2004). Pedagogical praxis: The professional models for post-industrial education. *Teachers College Record, 106*(7). doi:10.1111/j.1467-9620.2004.00383.x

Shaffer, D. W. (2006). *How Videogames Can Help Children Learn.* New York: Palgrave McMillan. doi:10.1057/9780230601994

Shaffer, D. W., Squire, K. R., Halverson, R., & Gee, J. P. (2004). Video Games and the Future of Learning Retrieved March 10, 2008 from http://www.academiccolab.org/resources/gappspaper1.pdf

Shah, A., & Frith, U. (2006). An islet of ability in autistic children: a research note. *Journal of Child Psychology and Psychiatry, and Allied Disciplines, 24*(4), 613–620. doi:10.1111/j.1469-7610.1983.tb00137.x

Shaheen, J. G. (2001). Reel Bad Arabs. How Hollywood Vilifies a People. New York: Olive Branch Press.

Shalev, L., Tsal, Y., & Mevorach, C. (2007). Computerized progressive attentional training (CPAT) program: Effective direct intervention for children with ADHD. *Child Neuropsychology, 13,* 382–388. doi:10.1080/09297040600770787

Share, D. L. (1995). Phonological recoding and self-teaching: sine qua non of reading acquisition. *Cognition, 55*(2), 151–218. doi:10.1016/0010-0277(94)00645-2

Shasek, J. (2009). *Brainy Stuff* [PowerPoint slides]. Retrieved from http://www.slideshare.net/invenTEAM/brainy-stuff-1078097

Shaw, G. A. (1992). Hyperactivity and creativity: The tacit dimension. *Bulletin of the Psychonomic Society, 30,* 152–160.

Shaw, R., & Lewis, V. (2005). The impact of computer-mediated and traditional academic task presentation on the performance and behaviour of children with ADHD. *Journal of Research in Special Educational Needs, 5,* 47–54. doi:10.1111/J.1471-3802.2005.00041.x

Shaw, R., Grayson, A., & Lewis, V. (2005). Inhibition, ADHD, and computer games: The inhibitory performance of children with ADHD on computerized tasks and games. *Journal of Attention Disorders, 8,* 160–168. doi:10.1177/1087054705278771

Sheese, B. E., & Graziano, W. G. (2005). Deciding to defect: The effects of video-game violence on cooperative behavior. *Psychological Science, 16*(5), 354–357. doi:10.1111/j.0956-7976.2005.01539.x

Shepard, R. J. (1997). *Curricular Physical Activity and Academic Performance.* Pediatric Exercise Science.

Sherry, J. (2001). The effects of violent video games on aggression: A meta-analysis. *Human Communication Research, 27*(3), 409–431.

Shibuya, A., Ihori, A. S. N., & Yukawa, S. (2008). The effects of the presence and contexts of video game violence on children: A longitudinal study in Japan. *Simulation & Gaming, 39*(4), 528–539. doi:10.1177/1046878107306670

Shute, V. J. (2009). Simply assessment. *International Journal of Learning and Media*, *1*(2), 1–11. doi:10.1162/ijlm.2009.0014

Shute, V. J., Ventura, M., Bauer, M. I., & Zapata-Rivera, D. (2008). Melding the power of serious games and embedded assessment to monitor and foster learning: Flow and grow. In U. Ritterfeld, M.J. Cody, & P. Vorderer, (Eds.), The Social Science of Serious Games: Theories and Applications. Philadelphia, PA: Routledge/LEA.

Sicart, M. (2005, 16-20 June 2005). *The Ethics of Computer Game Design.* Paper presented at the DiGRA 2005 - the Digital Games Research Association's 2nd International Conference, Simon Fraser University, Burnaby, BC, Canada.

Sigelman, C. K. (1991). The effect of causal information on peer perceptions of children with a pervasive developmental disorder. *Journal of Applied Developmental Psychology*, *12*, 237–253. doi:10.1016/0193-3973(91)90014-U

Silton, N. (2009). *Fostering knowledge, positive intentions and attitudes of typical children towards children with autism.* Unpublished doctoral dissertation, Fordham University, USA.

Silvern, S., & Williamson, P. (1987). The effects of video game play on young children's aggression, fantasy and prosocial behavior. *Journal of Applied Developmental Psychology*, *8*, 453–462. doi:10.1016/0193-3973(87)90033-5

Simpson, E. J. (1972). The classification of educational objectives in the psychomotor domain: The psychomotor domain (Vol. 3). Washington, DC: Gryphin House.

Simpson, E., & Clem, F. (2008). Video games in the middle school classroom. *Middle School Journal*, *39*(4), 4–11.

Siperstein, G. N., & Bak, J. (1977). *Instruments to measure children's attitudes toward the handicapped: Adjective Checklist and Activity Preference List.* Unpublished Manuscript, University of Massachusetts, Boston.

Siperstein, G. N., & Bak, J. (1980). Improving children's attitudes toward blind peers. *Journal of Visual Impairment & Blindness*, 132–135.

Siperstein, G. N., & Chatillion, A. C. (1982). Importance of perceived similarity in Improving children's attitudes toward mentally retarded peers. *American Journal of Mental Deficiency*, *86*(5), 453–458.

Skinner, B. F. (1935). Two Types Of Conditioned Reflex And A Pseudo Type. *The Journal of General Psychology*, *12*, 66–77.

Skinner, B. F. (1974). *About behaviourism.* London: Penguin.

Skowronek, J. S., Leichtman, M. D., & Pillemer, D. B. (2008). Long-term episodic memory in children with Attention-Deficit/Hyperactivity Disorder. *Learning Disabilities Research & Practice*, *23*, 25–35. doi:10.1111/j.1540-5826.2007.00260.x

Slater, M. D., Rouner, D., & Long, M. (2006). Television dramas and support for controversial public policies: Effects and mechanisms. *The Journal of Communication*, *56*(2), 235–254. doi:10.1111/j.1460-2466.2006.00017.x

Slator, B. M., Hill, C., & Del Val, D. (2004). Teaching computer science with virtual worlds. *IEEE Transactions on Education*, *47*(2), 269–275. doi:10.1109/TE.2004.825513

Smith, B. H., Barkley, R. A., & Shapiro, C. J. (2007). Attention-deficit/hyperactivity disorder. In E.J. Mash, & R.A. Barkley, (Eds.), Assessment of childhood disorders, (4th ed.), (pp. 100-101). New York: Guilford Press.

Smith, M. W., & Wilhelm, J. D. (2002). Reading don't fix no chevys. Portsmouth, NH: Heinemann.

Smith, M. W., & Wilhelm, J. D. (2006). Going with the flow. Portsmouth, NH: Heinemann.

Smith, R. (n.d.). *The long history of gaming in military training.* Retrieved from the U.S. Army Program Executive Office of Simulation, Training, and Instrumentation, Orlando, FL, Website http://www.peostri.army.mil/CTO/FILES/RSmith_LongHistory_SG40.pdf

Snow, C. E., & Strucker, J. (1999). *Lessons from preventing reading difficulties in young children for adult learning and literacy (Vol. 1).* Washington, DC: National Center for the Study of Adult Learning and Literacy.

Snow, C. E., Burns, M. S., & Griffin, P. (Eds.). (1998). *Preventing reading difficulties in young children*. Washington, DC: National Academy Press.

Snow, R. E., & Mandinach, E. B. (1991). *Integrating assessment and instruction: A research and development agenda* (ETS Research Report No. 91-08). Princeton, NJ: ETS.

Soloway, E. (1998). No one is Making Money in Educational Software. *Communications of the ACM, 4*(12), 11–15. doi:10.1145/269012.269014

Spencer, T.J., Biederman, J., & Mick, E. (2007). Attention-deficit/hyperactivity disorder: diagnosis, lifespan, comorbidities, and neurobiology. *Journal of Pediatric Psychology, 6, Special issue: Attention-deficit/hyperactivity disorder*, 631-642.

Spiro, R., & Jehng, J. (1990). Cognitive Flexibility and Hypertext: Theory and Technology for the Nonlinear and Multidimensional Traversal of Complex Subject Matter. In D. Nix & R. Spiro (Eds.), Cognition, Education and Multimedia: Exploring Ideas in High Technology, (pp. 163-205). Hillsdale, NJ: Lawrence Erlbaum Associates.

Spiro, R., Feltovich, P., Jacobson, M., & Coulson, R. (1992). Cognitive Flexibility, Constructivism and Hypertext: Random Access Instruction for Advanced Knowledge Acquisition in Ill-Structured Domains. In T. M. Duffy & D. H. Jonassen (Eds.), Constructivism and the technology of instruction: A conversation. Hillsdale, NJ: Erlbaum.

Spiro, R., Vispoel, W., Schmitz, J., Samarapungavan, A., & Boerger, A. (1987). Knowledge Acquisition for Application: Cognitive Flexibility and Transfer in Complex Content Domains. In B. C. Britton, (Ed.), Executive Control Processes, (pp. 177-200). Hillsdale, NJ: Laurence Erlbaum Associates.

Squire, K. (2003). Video games in education. *International Journal of Intelligent Simulations and Gaming, 2*(1). Retrieved January 27, 2006 from http://cms.mit.edu/games/education/pubs/IJIS.doc

Squire, K. (2005). Changing the game: What happens when video games enter the classroom? *Innovate: Journal of Online Education, 1*(6). Retrieved from http://innovateonline.info.proxy.bc.edu/index.php?view=article&id=82

Squire, K. (2006). From content to context: Videogames as designed experience. *Educational Researcher, 35*(8), 19–29. doi:10.3102/0013189X035008019

Squire, K. (2008). Open-ended video games: A model for developing learning for the interactive age. In K. Salen (Ed.), The ecology of games: Connecting youth, games, and learning (pp. 167-198). Cambridge, MA: The MIT Press.

Squire, K. D., & Steinkuehler, C. A. (2006). Generating CyberCulture/s: The case of Star Wars Galaxies. In D. Gibbs & K. L. Krause (Eds.), Cyberlines: Languages and cultures of the Internet (2nd ed.). Albert Park, Australia: James Nicholas Publishers.

Squire, K. D., Giovanetto, L., DeVane, B., & Durga, S. (2005). From users to designers: Building a self-organizing game-based learning environment. *TechTrends, 49*(5), 34–42. doi:10.1007/BF02763688

Squire, K., & Durga, S. (2008). Productive gaming: The case for historiographic game play. In Ferdig, R. E. (Ed.), *Handbook of Research on Effective Electronic Gaming in Education (Vol. I)*. Hershey, PA: Information Science Reference.

Squire, K., & Jenkins, H. (2003). Harnessing the power of games in education. *Insight (American Society of Ophthalmic Registered Nurses), 3*, 6–33.

Squire, K., & Steinkuehler, C. (2005). MEET THE GAMERS. (cover story). *Library Journal, 130*(7), 38–41.

Squire, K., Barnett, M., Grant, J., & Higginbotham, T. (2004). *Electromagnetism supercharged!: learning physics with digital simulation games*. Paper presented at the Proceedings of the 6th international conference on Learning Sciences, Santa Monica, CA.

Standen, P. J., Brown, D. J., Anderton, N., & Battersby, S. (2006a). A systematic evaluation of current control devices used by people with intellectual disabilities in non-immersive virtual environments. *Cyberpsychology & Behavior, 9*(5), 608–613. doi:10.1089/cpb.2006.9.608

Standen, P. J., Karsandas, R., Anderton, N., Battersby, S., & Brown, D. J. (2006b). An evaluation of the use of a switch controlled computer game in improving the choice reaction time of adults with intellectual disabilities. In P. M. Sharkey (Ed.), *Proceedings of the sixth International conference on Disability, Virtual Research and Associated Technology,* (pp. 285-291).

Standen, P.J., Rees, F., & Brown, D.J. (2009. (in press). Effect of playing computer games on decision making in people with intellectual disabilities. *Journal of Assistive Technologies.*

Steinkhueler, C. (2005). Cognition and literacy in massively multiplayer online games. In D. Leu, J. Corio, C. Lankshear & C. Knobel (Eds.), *Handbook of research on new literacies.* Mahwah, New Jersey: Erlbaum. Retrieved October 18, 2006, from http://website.education.wisc.edu/steinkuehler/papers/ SteinkuehlerNEWLIT2005

Steinkuehler, C. (2006). Why Game (Culture) Studies Now? *Games and Culture, 1*(1), 97–102. doi:10.1177/1555412005281911

Steinkuehler, C. (2008). Pop cosmopolitanism, cognition, and learning on the virtual frontier. Keynote presentation at the International Society for the Learning Sciences (ICLS), Utrecht, Netherlands.

Steinkuehler, C. A. (2004). Learning in massively multiplayer online games. In Y. B. Kafai, W. A. Sandoval, N. Enyedy, A. S. Nixon, and F. Herrera, (ed.), *Proceedings of the Sixth International Conference of the Learning Sciences,* (pp. 521-8). Mahwah, NJ: Erlbaum.

Steinkuehler, C. A. (2005). The new third place: Massively multiplayer online gaming in American youth culture. *Tidskrift Journal of Research in Teacher Education, 3,* 17–32.

Steinkuehler, C., & Duncan, S. (2008). Scientific habits of mind in virtual worlds. *Journal of Science Education and Technology, 17*(6), 530–543. doi:10.1007/s10956-008-9120-8

Steinkuhler, C. A., & Williams, D. (2006). Where everybody knows your (screen) name: Online games as "third places.". *Journal of Computer-Mediated Communication, 11,* 885–909. doi:10.1111/j.1083-6101.2006.00300.x

Stephen, J., Parente, D. H., & Brown, R. C. (2002). Seeing the forest and the trees: Balancing functional and integrative knowledge using large scale simulation in capstone business classes. *Journal of Management Education, 26*(2), 164–193. doi:10.1177/105256290202600204

Stephens, C. E. (2005). Overcoming challenges and identifying a consensus about autism intervention programming. *International Journal of Special Education, 20*(1), 35–49.

Stephenson, W. (1999). The Microserfs are Revolting-Sid Meier's Civilization II. *Bad Subjects, 45.* Retrieved March 9, 2009 from http://bad.eserver.org/issues/1999/45/stephenson.html

Stone, J. C. (2007). Popular websites in adolescents' out-of-school lives: Critical lessons on literacy. In M. Knobel and C. Lankshear (Eds.), A New Literacies Sampler (pp. 49-66). New York: Peter Lang.

Strohmeier, G. (2005). Politik bei Benjamin Blümchen und Bibi Blocksberg. *Aus Politik und Zeitgeschichte, 41,* 7–15.

Sturmey, P. (2003). Video technology and persons with autism and other developmental disabilities. *Journal of Positive Behavior Interventions, 5*(1), 3–4. doi:10.1177/10983007030050010401

Subrahmanyam, K., & Greenfield, P. (1998). Computer games for girls: What makes them play? In Cassell, J., & Jenkins, H. (Eds.), *From Barbie to Mortal Combat: Gender and computer games.* Cambridge, MA: MIT Press.

Subrahmanyam, K., & Greenfield, P. M. (1994). Effect of video game practice on spatial skills in girls and boys. *Journal of Applied Developmental Psychology, 15,* 13–32. doi:10.1016/0193-3973(94)90004-3

Subrahmanyan, K., & Greenfield, P. (2001). The impact of computer use on children's and adolescent's development. *Journal of Applied Developmental Psychology, 22*(1), 7–30. doi:10.1016/S0193-3973(00)00063-0

Summit on Educational Games. (2006). Retrieved January 23, 2008 from http://www.fas.org/gamesummit/Resources/Summit%20on%20Educational%20Games.pdf

Susi, T., Johannesson, M., & Backlund, P. (2007). *Serious games: An overview. Technical Report HS- IKI -TR-07-001, University of Skövde.Tapscott, D. (1998). Growing Up Digital: The Rise of the Net Generation.* New York: McGraw-Hill.

Swaim, K. F., & Morgan, S. B. (2001). Children's attitudes and behavioral intentions toward a peer with autistic behaviors: Does a brief educational intervention have an effect? *Journal of Autism and Developmental Disorders, 31*(2), 195–207. doi:10.1023/A:1010703316365

Sweller, J. (1994). Cognitive load theory, learning difficulty, and instructional design. *Learning and Instruction, 4*(4), 295–312. doi:10.1016/0959-4752(94)90003-5

Tang, S. Martin Hanneghan, & El-Rhalibi, A. (2009). Introduction to Games-Based Learning. In T. M. Connolly, M. H. Stansfield & L. Boyle (Eds.), Games-Based Learning Advancements for Multi-Sensory Human Computer Interfaces: Techniques and Effective Practices (pp. 1-17). Hershey, PA: Idea-Group Publishing.

Tang, S., Hanneghan, M., & El-Rhalibi, A. (2007). *Pedagogy Elements, Components and Structures for Serious Games Authoring Environment.* Paper presented at the 5th International Game Design and Technology Workshop (GDTW 2007), Liverpool, UK.

Tanis, M. (2007). Online social support groups. In Joinson, A. M., McKenna, K. Y. A., Postmes, T., & Reips, U.-D. (Eds.), *The Oxford Handbook of Internet Psychology* (pp. 139–153). Oxford: Oxford University Press.

Tannock, R. (1997). Television, videogames, and ADHD: Challenging a popular belief. *The ADHD Report, 5*, 3–7.

Tapscott, D. (2009). *Grown up digital: How the net generation is changing your world.* New York: McGraw Hill.

Taylor, B. M., Pearson, P. D., Clark, K. F., & Walpole, S. (2000). Effective schools and accomplished teachers: Lessons about primary grade reading instruction in low-income schools. *The Elementary School Journal, 101*, 121–165. doi:10.1086/499662

Taylor, P., & Carpenter, S. (2002). Inventively Linking: Teaching and Learning with Computer Hypertext. *Art Education, 55*(4), 6–12. doi:10.2307/3193962

Taylor, T. L. (2006). *Play between worlds: exploring online game culture.* Cambridge, MA: The MIT Press.

Tech Special Report: "Virtual Life". *Business Week.* Retrieved April 13, 2009 from

TechDis. (2009). Accessibility Essentials Series. *JISC TechDis.* Retrieved January 16, 2009, from http://www.techdis.ac.uk/index.php?p=3_20

Technical Report HS- IKI -TR-07-001, University of Skövde.

Telfer, R. (1993). Aviation Instruction and Training. Aldershot, UK: Ashgate.

Tennyson, R., & Jorczak, R. (2009). A conceptual framework for empirical study of instructional games. In O'Neil, H. F., & Perez, R. (Eds.), *Computer games and team and individual learning* (pp. 3–20). Amsterdam, The Netherlands: Elsevier Ltd.

Tessmer, M., Jonassen, D. H., & Caverly, D. (1989). Non-programmer's guide to designing instruction for microcomputers. Littleton, CO: Libraries Unlimited.

Thatcher, D. C. (1990). Promoting learning through games and simulations. *Simulation & Gaming, 21*, 262–273. doi:10.1177/1046878190213005

The New Media Consortium & EDUCAUSE Learning Initiative. (2008). *The Horizon Report: 2008 Edition.* Stanford, California. Retrieved March 15, 2009, from http://www.nmc.org/pdf/2008-Horizon-Report.pdf

The Training Room. (2009). Retrieved February 29, 2009, from http://www.gamedesigncampus.com

The Harvard Brain. (Spring 2000) An interview with Temple Grandin. *Vol. 7.*http://www.hcs.harvard.edu/~husn/BRAIN/vol7-spring2000/grandin.html.

Theunert, H. (1999). Medienkompetenz. Eine pädagogische und alterspezifisch zu fassende Handlungsdimension. In F. Schell, E. Stolzenburg & H. Theunert, (Eds.), Medienkompetenz. Grundlagen und pädagogisches Handeln, (pp. 50-59). München, Germany: KoPäd-Verlag.

Theunert, H. (2005). Medien als Orte informellen Lernens im Prozess des Heranwachsens. In Sachverständigenkommission Zwölfter Kinder- und Jugendbericht (Ed.), Kompetenzerwerb von Kindern und Jugendlichen im Schulalter, Bb. 3, München (pp. 175-300).

Thomas, P., & Macredie, R. (1994). Games and the design of human-computer interfaces. *Educational Technology, 31*(2), 134–142.

Thompson, A. A., Stappenbeck, G. J., & Reidenbach, M. A. (2008). *GLO-BUS: Developing Winning Competitive Strategies*. New York: McGraw-Hill/Irwin, Inc.

Thorndike, E. L. (1933). A proof of the law of effect. *Science, 77*, 173–175. doi:10.1126/science.77.1989.173-a

Tiresias. (2008). *Checklists*. Retrieved January 3, 2009, from http://www.tiresias.org/research/guidelines/checklists/index.htm

Tomlinson, J. (1997). Inclusive learning: the report of the committee of enquiry into the post-school education of those with learning difficulties and/or disabilities, in England 1996. *European Journal of Special Needs Education, 12*, 184–196. doi:10.1080/0885625970120302

Tönnies, F. (2005). Gemeinschaft und Gesellschaft: Grundbegriffe der reinen Soziologie. Darmstadt, Germany: Wissenschaftliche Buchgesellschaft.

Torgesen, J. K. (2005). Recent discoveries from research on remedial interventions for children with dyslexia. In Snowling, M., & Hulme, C. (Eds.), *Presentations and Publications* (pp. 521–537). Oxford, UK: Blackwell Publishers.

Torgesen, J. K. (2005). Remedial interventions for students with dyslexia: National goals and current accomplishments. In Richardson, S., & Gilger, J. (Eds.), *Research-based education and intervention: What we need to know* (pp. 103–124). Boston: International Dyslexia Association.

Torrance, P. E. (1984). The role of creativity in identification of the gifted and talented. *Gifted Child Quarterly, 28*, 153–156. doi:10.1177/001698628402800403

Trend, D. (2007). The Myth of Media Violence: A Critical Introduction. Oxford, UK: Blackwell.

Tribune Business News, 1.

Tronstad, R. (2001, September). *Semiotic and non semiotic MUD performance*. Paper presented at the 2001 COSIGN conference. Retrieved June 11, 2009 from http://www.cosignconference.org/downloads/papers/tronstad_cosign_2001.pdf

Turkle, S. (1984). *The second self: Computers and the human spirit*. New York: Simon and Schuster.

Turkle, S. (1997). Life on the screen: Identity in the age of the internet. New York: Touchstone.

Turner Bell, D. (2009, March). *Exercise Gives The Brain A Workout, Too*. Retrieved from http://www.cbsnews.com/stories/2009/01/30/earlyshow/health/main4764523.shtml

Tuzun, H. (2006). Egitsel bilgisayar oyunlari ve bir örnek: *Quest Atlantis* (Educational computer games and a case: *Quest Atlantis*). *Hacettepe Universitesi Egitim Fakültesi Dergisi, 30*, 220–229.

U.S. Army. (2007). *Army Regulation 350-1: Army Training and Leadership Development*.

U.S. Department of Defense. (1995). *Joint Publication 3-07: Joint publication for operations other than war*.

Underwood, J. S. (2008). Effective feedback: Guidelines for improving performance. In *Proceedings of the International Conference of the Learning Sciences*, Utrecht, The Netherlands.

Underwood, J. S., Kruse, S., & Jakl, P. (2009). *Embedded assessment: Evaluating in-game data to adapt the learning environment*. Presentation at Games, Learning + Society Conference, Madison, WI.

Ustun, T. B. (2007). Using the international classification of functioning, disease and health in attention-deficit/hyperactivity disorder: Separating the disease from its epiphenomena. *Ambulatory Pediatrics, 7*(1S), 132–139. doi:10.1016/j.ambp.2006.05.004

Valve Developer Community. (2008). *GCFScape*. Retrieved March 2, 2008, from http://developer.valvesoftware.com/wiki/GCFScape

Van Cleave, J., & Leslie, L. K. (2008). Approaching *ADHD* as a chronic condition: Implications for long-term adherence. *Psychiatric Annals, 38*, 35–42. doi:10.3928/00485713-20080101-05

Van der Hulst, A. Muller, T.J., & Roos, C.I. (2008). *Handling serious gaming, Job Oriented Training*. Technical Report TNO-DV 2008 A340. Netherlands.

Van Eck, R. (2006). Digital game-based learning: It's not just the digital natives who are restless. *EDUCAUSE Review, 41*(2), 1–16.

Van Merrienboer, J., & Sweller, J. (2005). Cognitive Load Theory and Complex Learning: Recent Developments and Future Directions. *Educational Psychology Review, 17*(2), 147–177. doi:10.1007/s10648-005-3951-0

Van Merrienboer, J., Kirschner, P., & Kester, L. (2003). Taking the Load Off a Learner's Mind: Instructional Design for Complex Learning. *Educational Psychologist, 38*(1), 5–13. doi:10.1207/S15326985EP3801_2

Van Oers, B. (Ed.). (2008). *Learning and learning theory from a cultural-historical point of view*. Cambridge, UK: Cambridge University Press. doi:10.1017/CBO9780511499937

Vandewater, E. A., Shim, M., & Caplovitz, A. G. (2004). Linking obesity and activity level with children's television and video game use. *Journal of Adolescence, 27*(1), 71–85. doi:10.1016/j.adolescence.2003.10.003

Vasudevan, L. M. (2006). Looking for Angels: Knowing adolescents by engaging with their multimodal literacy practices. *Journal of Adolescent & Adult Literacy, 50*(4), 252–256. doi:10.1598/JAAL.50.4.1

Verte, S., Roeyers, A., & Buysse, A. (2003). Behavioral problems, social competence, and self-concept in siblings of children with autism. *Child: Care, Health and Development, 29*(3), 193–205. doi:10.1046/j.1365-2214.2003.00331.x

Virtual Heroes. (2008). *Serious Game Conceptualization as a Learning Objectives-Driven Process* [White paper]. Retrieved from Virtual Heroes of North Carolina Website http://www.virtualheroes.com

Virvou, M., Katsionis, G., & Manos, K. (2005). Combining software games with education: Evaluation of its educational effectiveness. *Educational Technology & Society, 8*(2), 54–65.

Voeltz, I. M. (1980). Children's attitudes toward handicapped peers. *American Journal of Mental Deficiency, 84*, 455–464.

Volkmar, F., & Pauls, D. (2003). Autism. *Lancet, 362*(9390), 1133–1141. doi:10.1016/S0140-6736(03)14471-6

Vorderer, P. (1996). Rezeptionsmotivation: Warum nutzen Rezipienten mediale Unterhaltungsangebote? *Publizistik, 41*, 310–326.

Vosniadou, S., & Brewer, W. (1987). Theories of Knowledge Restructuring in Development. *Review of Educational Research, 57*(1), 51–67.

Vygotsky, L. (1933). *Play and its role in the mental development of the child*. Retrieved from http://www.marxists.org/archive/vygotsky/works/1933/play.htm by *Psychology and Marxism Internet Archive (marxists.org)*.

Vygotsky, L. S. (1978). *Mind in society: The development of higher mental processes*. Cambridge, MA: Harvard University Press.

W3C. (1999). *Web Content Accessibility Guidelines 1.0, W3C Recommendation 5.5*. Retrieved July 7, 2007, from www.w3.org/TR/1999/WAI-WEBCONTENT-19990505, W3C

W3C. (2008a). *Web Content Accessibility Guidelines (WCAG) 2.0, W3C Recommendation 11 December 2008*. Retrieved May 4, 2007, from http://www.w3.org/TR/WCAG20/

W3C. (2008b). *How to Meet WCAG 2.0: A customizable quick reference to Web Content Accessibility Guidelines 2.0 requirements (success criteria) and techniques*. Retrieved May 4, 2007, from http://www.w3.org/WAI/WCAG20/quickref/

Wade, A., Abrami, P. & MacDonald, M. (2008, Feb.). *Inquiry Strategies for the Information Society in the Twenty-First Century (ISIS-21).* Final report prepared for Inukshuk Wireless. Montreal: Centre for the Study of Learning and Performance.

Wade, A., Abrami, P. C., & Sclater, J. (2005). An electronic portfolio for learning. *Canadian Journal of Learning and Technology, 31*(3), 33–50.

Wade, A., Abrami, P. C., White, B., Baron, M., Farmer, L., & Van Gelder, S. (2008). Information literacy: An essential competency in the twenty-first century. *IFLA School Libraries and Resource Centers Newsletter, 47,* 15–18.

Wagner, A. J. (2008, May 5). Special Report "Second Life Marketing: Still Strong"

Wagner, C. (2008). Learning experience with virtual worlds. *Journal of Information Systems Education, 19,* 263–266.

Wagner, U. (Ed.). (2008). Medienhandeln in Hauptschulmilieus. Mediale Interaktion und Produktion als Bildungsressource. München, Germany: KoPäd-Verlag.

Wainess, R. (2007). The potential of games & simulations for learning and assessment. In *2007 CRESST Conference: The Future of Test-based Educational Accountability,* Los Angeles, CA.

Walker, V. L. (2009). 3D virtual learning in counselor education: Using Second Life in counselor skill development. *Journal of Virtual Worlds Research, 2*(1). Retrieved July 27, 2009 from https://journals.tdl.org/jvwr/article/view/423/463

Wallerstein, I. (2004). Das moderne Weltsystem, 3 Bde. Wien, Germany: Promedia Verlagsgesellschaft.

Walsh, C. (2007, April 14). If One Life's Not Enough, Try A 2nd One. *Knight Ridder*

Waltz, M. (1993). Chapter 9 of Pervasive Developmental Disorders: Finding a Diagnosis and Getting Help. O'Reilly & Associates. Retrieved October 2, 2007, from, http://oreilly.com/medical/autism/news/social_skills.html

Warburton, S. (2009). Second Life in higher education: Assessing the potential for and barriers to deploying virtual worlds in learning and teaching. *British Journal of Educational Technology, 40,* 414–426. doi:10.1111/j.1467-8535.2009.00952.x

Ward, L., Hansbrough, E., & Walker, E. (2005). Contributions of Music Video Exposure to Black Adolescents' Gender and Sexual Schemas. *Journal of Adolescent Research, 20*(2), 143–166. doi:10.1177/0743558404271135

Waters, J. K. (2009). A 'Second Life' For Educators. *T.H.E. Journal, 36*(1), 29–34.

Watkins, S., & Sherk, J. (2008). Who serves in the U.S. military? *Center for Data Analysis.* Retrieved from National Defense Industry Association Web Site: http://www.ndia.org/Divisions/Divisions/SOLIC/Documents/Content/ContentGroups/Divisions1/Special_Operations_Low_Intensity_Conflict/CDA%20-%20Who%20Serves%20in%20the%20Military%209-17-08.pdf

Watters, C. B. (2009, March). Effective use of simulations in business training. *Talent Management, 5,* 32–35.

Webber, R., Ritterfeld, U., & Mathiak, K. (2006). Does playing violent video games induce aggression? Empirical evidence of a functional magnetic resonance imaging study. *Media Psychology, 8,* 39–60. doi:10.1207/S1532785XMEP0801_4

Weber, C., & Matthews, H. S. (2008). Quantifying the global and distributional aspects of American Household carbon footprints. *Ecological Economics, 66,* 379–391. doi:10.1016/j.ecolecon.2007.09.021

Weber, M. (1972). Wirtschaft und Gesellschaft, Tübingen, Germany.

Wechselberger, U. (2009). Einige theoretische Überlegungen über das pädagogische Potential digitaler Lernspiele. In T. Bevc & H. Zapf (Eds.), Wie wir spielen, was wir werden (pp. 95-111). Konstanz, Germany: UVK.

Wegerif, R. (1998). The social dimension of asynchronous learning networks. *Journal of Asynchronous Learning Networks, 2*(1), 34-49, Retrieved April 8, 2009 from http://www.sloan-c.org/publications/jaln/v2n1/pdf/v2n1_wegerif.pdf.

Weiner, B. (1979). A Theory of Motivation for Some Classroom Experiences. *Journal of Educational Psychology*, *71*(1), 3–25. doi:10.1037/0022-0663.71.1.3

Weiner, B. (1993). On sin versus sickness: A theory of perceived responsibility and social motivation. *The American Psychologist*, *48*, 957–965. doi:10.1037/0003-066X.48.9.957

Weinger, H. (1969). *Trends in Military Gaming*. Technical Paper P-4173, RAND Corporation.

Wenger, E. (1998). *Communities of practice: learning, meaning and identity*. Cambridge, UK: Cambridge University Press.

Wert, B. Y., & Neisworth, J. T. (2003). Effects of video self-modeling in spontaneous requesting in children with autism. *Journal of Positive Behavior Interventions*, *5*(1), 30–34. doi:10.1177/10983007030050010501

Westheimer, J., & Kahne, J. (2004). What kind of citizen? The politics of educating for democracy. *American Educational Research Journal*, *41*(2), 237–269. doi:10.3102/00028312041002237

Wexler, S., Schlenker, B., Bruce, B., Clothier, P., Miller, D. A., & Nguyen, F. (2008). Authoring & Development Tools. Santa Rosa, CA: The eLearning Guild.

Whitehead, M. J., & Quinlan, C. A. (2002). *Canada: An Information Literacy Case Study*. White Paper prepared for UNESCO, the U.S. National Commission on Libraries and Information Science, and the National Forum on Information Literacy, for use at the Information Literacy Meeting of Experts, Prague, The Czech Republic. Available at: http://www.nclis.gov/libinter/infolitconf&meet/papers/quinlan-fullpaper.pdf

Whitney, K. (2006). Simulations in Management Education. Chief Learning Officer, (pp. 48-51).

Wikipedia contributors. (2009). *Closed captioning*. Wikipedia, The Free Encyclopedia. Retrieved May 8, 2009, from http://en.wikipedia.org/w/index.php?title=Closed_captioning&oldid=288518912

Williams, D. (2006). Virtual Cultivation: Online Worlds, Offline Perceptions. *The Journal of Communication*, *56*, 69–87. doi:10.1111/j.1460-2466.2006.00004.x

Williamson, D., & Gee, J. P. (2006). *How computer games help children learn*. New York: Palgrave Macmillan. McGraw Hill.

Wilson, M. (2002). Six Views of Embodied Cognition. *Psychonomic Bulletin & Review*, *9*(4), 625–636.

Wilson, R. (1997). Pointers, Codes, and Embodiment. *The Behavioral and Brain Sciences*, *20*(4), 757–758. doi:10.1017/S0140525X97421611

Wing, J. M. (2006). Computational thinking. CACM Viewpoint, 49(3), 33–35.

Winter, D. (2008). *Welcome to PONG-Story: The Site of the First Video Game*. Retrieved from http://www.pong-story.com/intro.htm

Wisely, D. W., & Morgan, S. B. (1981). Children's ratings of peers presented as mentally Retarded and physically handicapped. *American Journal of Mental Deficiency*, *86*(3), 281–286.

Withrow, F. (2004). *Literacy in the digital age: Reading, writing, viewing, and computing*. Lanham, MD: Scarecrow Education.

Wittgenstein, L. (1953). *Philosophical Investigations*. Malden, MA: Blackwell Publishing.

Wolf, M. J. P., & Perron, B. (2003). Introduction. The Video Game Theory Reader. New York: Routledge.

Wood, D. J., Bruner, J. S., & Ross, G. (1976). The role of tutoring in problem-solving. *Journal of Child Psychology and Psychiatry, and Allied Disciplines*, *17*, 89–100. doi:10.1111/j.1469-7610.1976.tb00381.x

Wood, R. T. A. (2008). Problems with the concept of video game "addiction": Some case study examples. *International Journal of Mental Health and Addiction*, *6*, 169–178. doi:10.1007/s11469-007-9118-0

Wozney, L., Venkatesh, V., & Abrami, P. C. (2006). Implementing computer technologies: Teachers' perceptions and practices. *Journal of Technology and Teacher Education*, *14*(1), 173–207.

Wright, J., Stackhouse, J., & Wood, J. (2008). Promoting language and literacy skills in the early years: lessons from interdisciplinary teaching and learning. *Child Language Teaching and Therapy, 24*(2), 155–171. doi:10.1177/0265659007090292

Wright, P., Fields, R., & Harrison, M. (2000). Analyzing Human-Computer Interaction as Distributed Cognition: The Resources Model. *Human-Computer Interaction, 15*(1), 1–41. doi:10.1207/S15327051HCI1501_01

Yardley, R. J., Thie, H., Schank, J. F., Galegher, J. R., & Riposo, J. L. (2003) *Use of simulation for training in the U.S. Navy Surface Force*, Technical Report MR-1770-NAVY, RAND Corporation.

Yee, N. (2006). Motivations of Play in Online Games. *Journal of Cyber Psychology and Behavior, 9*, 772–775. doi:10.1089/cpb.2006.9.772

Yee, N. (n.d.). *Motivations of Play in MMORPGs. Results from a Factor Analytic Approach*. Retrieved February 26, 2009 from http://www.nickyee.com/daedalus/motivations.pdf

Yee, N., & Bailenson, J. (2007). The Proteus Effect: The effect of transformed self-representation on behavior. *Human Communication Research, 33*, 271–290. doi:10.1111/j.1468-2958.2007.00299.x

Young, K. S. (2004). Internet addiction: A new clinical phenomenon and its consequences. *The American Behavioral Scientist, 48*(4), 402–415. doi:10.1177/0002764204270278

Young, M. (2003). An Ecological Psychology of Instructional Design. In D. Jonassen (Ed.), Handbook of Research on Educational Communications and Technology. Mahwah, NJ: Lawrence Erlbaum Associates, Inc.

Young, M. (2004). *An ecological description of video games in education*. Retrieved July 14, 2009, from http://web2.uconn.edu/myoung/EISTA04Proceed.pdf

Young, M. F., Schrader, P. G., & Zheng, D. P. (2006). MMOGs as learning environments: An ecological journey into *Quest Atlantis* and the Sims Online. *Innovate, 2* (4). Retrieved March 20, 2006, from http://www.innovateonline.info/index.php?view=article&id=66

Young, M., Barab, S., & Garrett, S. (2000). Agent as detector: An ecological psychology perspective on learning by perceiving-acting systems. In D. H. J. S. M. Land (Ed.), Theoretical foundations of learning environments (pp. 147-172). Mahwah, NJ: Erlbaum.

Zantow, K., Knowlton, D. S., & Sharp, D. C. (2005). More than fun and games: Reconsidering the virtues of strategic management simulations. *Academy of Management Learning & Education, 4*(4), 451–458.

Zapata-Rivera, D. (2009). Assessment-based gaming environments. Presentation at AERA, San Diego, CA.

Zapata-Rivera, D., VanWinkle, W., Shute, V. J., Underwood, J. S., & Bauer, M. (2007). English ABLE. In R. Luckin, K. Koedinger, & J. Greer (Eds.), Artificial intelligence in education - Building technology rich learning contexts that work (pp. 323-330). Amsterdam, The Netherlands: IOS Press.

Zaphiris, P. & ang, C. S. (2007). HCI Issues in Computer Games. *Interacting with Computers, 19*(2), 135–139. doi:10.1016/j.intcom.2006.08.007

Zeichner, K., & Wray, S. (2001). The teaching portfolio in US teacher education programs: what we know and what we need to know. *Teaching and Teacher Education, 17*, 613–621. doi:10.1016/S0742-051X(01)00017-8

Zemke, R., Raines, C., & Filipczak, B. (2000). *Generations at Work: Managing the Clash of Veterans, Boomers, Xers, and Nexters in Your Workplace.* New York: Amacom.

Zentall, S. S., Cassady, J. C., & Javorsky, J. (2001). Social comprehension of children with hyperactivity. *Journal of Attention Disorders, 5*, 11–24. doi:10.1177/108705470100500102

Zhang, J. (1997). The Nature of External Representations in Problem Solving. *Cognitive Science, 21*(2), 179–217.

Zhang, J., & Norman, D. (1994). Representations in Distributed Cognitive Tasks. *Cognitive Science, 18*(1), 87–122.

Zihni, F., & Zihni, F. (1995). *The AZ method: The use of video techniques to develop language skills in autistic children.*

Zimmerman, B, J. (1989). A social cognitive view of self-regulated academic learning. *Journal of Educational Psychology, 81*, 329–339. doi:10.1037/0022-0663.81.3.329

Zimmerman, B. J. (2000). Attaining self-regulation: A social cognitive perspective. In Boekaerts, M., & Pintrich, P. R. (Eds.), *Handbook of self-regulation* (pp. 13–39). New York: Academic Press. doi:10.1016/B978-012109890-2/50031-7

Zuiker, S. (2009). Assessment for "Learning to Be" in educational videogames. Presentation at AERA, San Diego, CA.

Zyda, M. (2005). From Visual Simulation to Virtual Reality to Games. *Computer, 38*, 25–32. doi:10.1109/MC.2005.297

About the Contributors

Pavel Zemliansky is an Associate Professor in the School of Writing, Rhetoric, and Technical Communication at James Madison University, where he also coordinates the graduate program. Dr. Zemliansky teaches courses in writing, rhetoric, digital media, and technical communication. His latest book, which he co-edited with Kirk St. Amant, is *The Handbook of Research on Virtual Workplaces and the New Nature of Business Practices*, published by IGI-Global in 2008.

Diane Wilcox is an Assistant Professor in the College of Education at James Madison University where she teaches educational technology, materials design and development, visual communication, and research methods. Diane's interest in game design began in the late 1980s when she created computer graphics and animation for educational games published by Broderbund Software. After earning her Master's and Doctoral degrees in Educational Psychology at the University of North Carolina (UNC) in the 1990s, she co-designed and developed Mindforge Fractions, which used a visual approach, gaming elements, and rich media to motivate and engage students.

* * *

Philip C. Abrami is Professor, Research Chair, and Director of the Centre for the Study of Learning and Performance (CSLP), Concordia University, LB-581, 1455 de Maisonneuve Blvd. West, Montreal, Quebec, Canada H3G 1M8; e-mail: abrami@education.concordia.ca His research interests include educational technology, social psychology of education and research synthesis.

Sandra Schamroth Abrams recently completed her Ph.D. at Rutgers University, and her dissertation, *Real benefits from virtual experiences: How four avid video gamers used gaming as a resource in their literate activity*, addressed video game playing as a vehicle for learning and contributed to the burgeoning discussion of video games and meaning making. Dr. Abrams continues to be fascinated by the powerful dimensions of digital literacies, and her current research agenda includes additional investigations into the dynamics of the gaming world and the ways digital literacies can inform traditional and multimodal learning. Dr. Abrams will join the faculty at St. John's University in September, 2009.

Janice L. Anderson is an assistant professor of science education at the University of North Carolina at Chapel Hill. Prior to joining the faculty at UNC-Chapel Hill, she taught biology and anatomy in Ohio and worked in elementary classrooms in Massachusetts. Anderson received her Ph.D. in Curriculum and Instruction from Boston College with a focus on Science and Technology. Her dissertation research explored the use of a 3D virtual world (Quest Atlantis) to teach concepts related to water quality and ecosystems to urban fifth-grade students. Her research considers the impact of gender and learning outcomes on how students engaged with the game. The catalyst for her professional efforts has been the notion of improving students' engagement with science and technology particularly among populations that are underrepresented in science, based on both gender and race.

Suzanne C. Baker is professor of psychology at James Madison University in Harrisonburg, VA, where she also currently serves as assistant department head in psychology. She received her PhD in Biological Psychology from the University of Georgia in 1987. Baker is the author of articles and book chapters on topics related to teaching and curriculum. She frequently speaks at conferences on topics such as curriculum development in psychology, engaging undergraduate students in research, and the use of technology in teaching. She teaches a wide range of courses, including introductory psychology, animal behavior, and other topics.

Matt Barton is an Assistant Professor of English at St. Cloud State University in St. Cloud, Minnesota. His research and teaching interests include composition, rhetoric, professional writing, and new media. He is the author of *Dungeons and Desktops*, a history of computer role-playing games, and co-author of Vintage Games, a book about the most influential videogames of all time. He is also the co-editor of *Wiki Writing: Collaborative Learning in the Classroom*, and an advocate of wikis and social media.

Steven Battersby is a software design engineer for the Interactive Systems Research group and has worked on numerous projects concerned with Serious Games and assistive technology. Steven is currently completing a PhD on adaptive, assistive technology.

Tobias Bevc was awarded his PhD in 2004 in Augsburg, Germany in Political Theory. From 2004 - 2008, he has been a lecturer at the Lehrstuhl für Politische Wissenschaft at Technische Universität München. Since Spring 2008 he is lecturer at Goethe University of Frankfurt. One of his research foci since 2005 is the Construction of Society and Politics in Video Games. Further focus of research: Political Theory and History of Ideas, Visual Politics/Film and Politics. He was a consultant in the development of the 2007 published video game "Genius Politik" (Cornelsen Verlag). Recent Publications are: Tobias Bevc (ed.) (2007): Computerspiele und Politik. Zur Konstruktion von Politik und Gesellschaft in Computerspielen, Münster. (Videogames and Politics) and Tobias Bevc (2007), Politische Theorie, Konstanz. (Political Theory).

David Brown was promoted from Reader to Professor of Interactive Systems for Social Inclusion in 2007. His research focuses on the application of virtual environments for the education of people with an intellectual impairment and for rehabilitation. His research on virtual environments for people with learning disabilities has been funded by a range of government agencies, by EPSRC and the EU. He is consortium leader for *"Game on"*, to develop 3D role play games for the education and personal development of prisoners and those at risk of offending. He is the principle investigator for the GOAL and GOET European projects on serious educational games to develop prevocational skills in people with learning difficulties.

David E. Cavazos is an assistant professor of management at James Madison University. He holds a B.A in economics, a Master of public administration and a Ph.D. in business administration from Texas Tech University in Lubbock, TX. His research interests include industry political and self-regulation, interorganizational relationships and the social stratification of markets. David's most recent research has appeared in The Academy of Management Learning and Education, and Business and Society Review. Prior to his career in academia, David worked as a secondary Math teacher.

Gia Deleveaux is the Literacy Projects Coordinator at the Centre for the Study of Learning and Performance at Concordia University in Montreal, Quebec. Her areas of interest are many and varied ranging from literacy studies, testing and evaluation, to science education but her main focus of research is in critical edutainment. In her work, Gia looks at how the written and hidden curricula, structures, rules and regulations, the educator, and the learner influence what takes place in educational settings. As a critical pedagogue, she is keenly interested in exploring how constructivist theories and teaching praxis can help to motivate ALL learners become literate citizens.

Hasan Deniz is an Assistant Professor of Science Education, currently teaching masters level science methods courses. His background includes secondary teaching in Turkey and introductory college science and methods courses at Indiana University. Dr. Deniz is an active researcher in the areas of students' epistemological beliefs in science and teaching evolution.

Kim Dielmann, is an assistant professor in the Department of Psychology & Counseling at the University of Central Arkansas, USA. She teaches master's and doctoral level students in the School Psychology programs to consult with teachers and other school personnel to develop creative, innovative interventions for students with academic and behavioral needs. Her primary research interest is with individuals with Attention Deficit Hyperactivity Disorder. She has national and international publications on the topic. Dr. Dielmann has recently served as president of the Arkansas School Psychology Association. She is currently involved in the development of animated computer education games to help adolescents learn about their disabilities and methods of improving their decision-making as they mature.

Michelle Estes teaches in an Adult Education and Human Resource Development program at James Madison University. She also teaches Educational Technology courses and can draw on previous experience in business and higher education including the coordination of a Second Life project.

Michael A. Evans, assistant professor in the department of learning sciences and technologies at Virginia Tech, teaches courses and conducts research focusing on the application of human learning theory to the design and development of instructional materials and systems. Current projects include: 1) examining the effects of physical and virtual manipulatives on the mathematical reasoning of elementary students, 2) designing educational simulations and games for middle school students in STEM areas, and 3) developing instructional multimedia for mobile and wireless devices. He received his doctorate in instructional systems technology from Indiana University.

Lindsay Evett is a lecturer in the Computing & Technology Team. Her research is on accessibility and assistive technology, especially with respect to Serious Games, and web-based content. She is a lecturer in Artificial Intelligence, and a member of Nottingham Trent University's working group on accessibility. She is a co-investigator on the GOET European project on serious educational games to develop prevocational skills in people with learning difficulties.

Dr. George Font's work is exemplified by efforts to generate small-scale, mixed-method studies that contribute to the information base of literacy and technology related practices that affect classroom instruction. His pedagogy is defined by how he makes decisions about curriculum, teaching, and learning. It is a 21st Century learner-centered approach that involves interpretation, negotiation, and reconceptualization. His professional experience is embedded in a social constructivist agenda using strategies that integrate content, context, and community of practice. His research translates into two specific strands. One strand involves examining literacy and language instruction that draws on existing funds of knowledge to make connections with cultural tools in studying practices rooted in daily life circumstances of diverse learners. A second strand encourages teachers to reconsider reading programs to better meet the needs of readers in a post-typographic world by exploring connections between digital resources and literacy learning.

Scott Gallagher joined the faculty of James Madison University in 2000. He earned his PhD from Rutgers University (2000), holds a MPP degree from Harvard's John F. Kennedy School of Government (1991), and a BBA degree from the University of Texas at Austin (1989). His current research interests include management of innovation, standards, and strategic alliances.

Ivan Alejandro (Alex) Games is an assistant professor in Telecommunications, Information Studies and Media at Michigan State University. His research concentrates on the role that learning environments involving designing interactive technologies such as computer games and web-based online communities as their core learning experiences can have on children and young adults' development of thinking, language, and literacy skills necessary in the 21st century. His work as been featured in E-Learning, the International Journal of Web-based Communities, and the Proceedings of the International Conference of the Learning Sciences.

David Guralnick holds a Ph.D. in computer science from Northwestern University, where his work synthesized concepts from the fields of computer science, instructional design, and cognitive psychology. Dr. Guralnick designed and developed the first learn-by-doing simulation for corporate training use, as well as the first e-learning-specific authoring tool. Over the past 20 years, he has designed simulation-based training applications, electronic performance-support systems, and specialized authoring tools which allow non-technical people, such as writers and trainers, to build e-learning sites. The cornerstone of Dr. Guralnick's design philosophy is the concept of content-driven, goal-driven design using the information and the needs of the end-users, rather than the technology, to lead the design process. Dr. Guralnick is president of New York-based Kaleidoscope Learning; president of the International E-Learning Association; a regular keynote speaker at international conferences; chair of the International Conference on E-Learning in the Workplace; Senior Editor of the International Journal on Advanced Corporate Learning; and an Adjunct Professor at Columbia University. His work has been featured in Wired magazine, Training magazine (as an Editor's Choice), and the Wall Street Journal, and he is the recipient of numerous e-learning design awards.

Martin Hanneghan (BSc Hons, PhD) is Head of the Department of Information, Media and Computer Entertainment in the School of Computing and Mathematical Sciences at Liverpool John Moores University in the UK where he teaches on undergraduate and postgraduate courses in Computer Games Technology. He has served as a member of the programme and technical committees for a number of games conferences around the world including Cybergames, GAME-ON, GDTW and SBGames. His research interests include serious game applications and software engineering for games.

Steven R. Harper is an assistant professor of management and of engineering at James Madison University. He holds a B.S. in engineering physics from the University of California, Berkeley, an M.E. in electrical engineering from University of Virginia, an M.A. in national security and strategic studies from the Naval War College, an M.S. in business administration, and a Ph.D. in systems and entrepreneurial engineering from the University of Illinois, Urbana/Champaign. Prior to joining academia, Dr. Harper served 21 years as a Naval Submarine Officer and Acquisition Professional in the U.S. Navy. His research focuses on group decision-making, diversity, and decision analysis.

Jeremy Hawkins received his BA in English from James Madison University in 2005. He has been employed by the University Unions department since 2004, helping to create the community at JMU that encourages students to become educated and enlightened citizens who will lead productive and meaningful lives. He is an active member of both the Association of College Unions International and the Association of Collegiate Conference and Event Directors-International. Yemrej Harlow was born in SL on September 11, 2006, and continues to spend his time making the JMU virtual campus a more inviting and engaging place.

Ann Higgins D'Alessandro is the Director of the Applied Developmental Psychology (ADP) Graduate Program of Fordham University. Before coming to Fordham in 1989, Dr. Higgins-D'Alessandro was a Senior Researcher at the Center for Moral Development and Education, Harvard University, publishing with Dr. Lawrence Kohlberg. Dr. Higgins-D'Alessandro writes extensively on moral development, democratic and civic education, at-risk youth, and identity. For several years US Department of Education grants have supported her research evaluations of school reform and character education programs. She is also conducting research with ADP students on the social moral reasoning development of adolescents with Asperger's Syndrome, and on elementary school outcomes of children with early diagnosed autism. She is a founding member and past president of the international Association of Moral Education. Dr. Higgins-D'Alessandro's books, include *Lawrence Kohlberg's Approach to Moral Education* and *Science and Society: Informing Policy and Practice through Research in Developmental Psychology.*

Peter Jakl is President of Pragmatic Solutions, Inc. He has used his 28 professional years in technology to make effective use of data in a variety of business sectors. America's Army has afforded him the opportunity to adapt that knowledge and experience to enrich and promote learning in games.

Karen Kellison spent 18 years working in K-12 public education, as a classroom teacher, library media specialist, and administrator. She earned a doctorate in Educational Psychology with an emphasis in Instructional Technology from University of Virginia and is licensed as a Division Superintendent in the Commonwealth of Virginia. Her higher education experience includes teaching educational technology and leadership courses for Virginia Commonwealth University, University of Richmond, and is now full time with James Madison University. Dr. Kellison is program coordinator for the Educational Technology minor and master's programs at James Madison University. Her interests are in the application of technology to improve access and learning for all including: Universal Design for Learning; games, simulations, and virtual worlds; and visual literacy.

S. E. Kruck is an Associate Professor in the College of Business at James Madison University and teaches in the Computer Information Systems program. Dr. Kruck earned a PhD from the Department of Accounting and Information Systems at Virginia Polytechnic and State University and has published articles in *Journal of Computer Information System; Journal of End User Computing; Journal of Information Systems Education; Information Management and Computer Security; Journal of International Information Management; Journal of Accounting Education; and many others.* Dr. Kruck on the Editorial Board of *Journal of Computer Information System* and *Information Management and Computer Security*: and is also a CPA in the state of Virginia and has over twelve years of corporate accounting experience.

Stacy Kruse is Director of Education and Serious Games at Pragmatic Solutions, Inc. Over the last 17 years she has designed technology-driven educational and co-curricular programs for middle school and high school students, working closely with schools, youth service providers, and community stakeholders.

Timo Lainema Ph.D. is an Assistant Professor in Information Systems Science at the Turku School of Economics (TSE). He holds a Ph.D. and a master degree in economics and business administration from TSE with an emphasis on Information Management. His Ph.D. thesis focused on the use of business simulation games in business process education. His research interests are learning through simulation gaming, flow in games, knowledge sharing in virtual working contexts, and decision making under time pressure. He has participated in several projects related to innovative use of IT in management education. He has published articles in Computers and Education, Simulation & Gaming, the Journal of Information Technology Education, Journal of Research on Technology in Education, and the Journal of Interactive Learning Research, the International Journal of Advanced Technology for Learning on Games-Based Learning.

Kimberly Lawless is a professor and department chair of Educational Psychology at the University of Illinois at Chicago. Currently, she is the principal investigator on the Digital Literacy Assessment Project and the Global Ed II Project, which seek to understand middle schools students' use of content area literacy skills when engaged in online environments. In addition, Dr. Lawless has published more than 100 manuscripts in the areas of educational technology, instructional design and reading; and, serves on the editorial boards of the *American Educational Research Journal, Contemporary Educational Psychology* and *Instructional Science*.

Catherine LeBel is the Director of Design and Development at the CSLP, where she supervises the team of programmers and designers. Ms LeBel also teaches courses in the department of Design and Computation Arts at Concordia. She has worked for cultural organizations such as the National Gallery of Canada as well as for the private sector, developing her expertise in interactive design, graphic design and information architecture.

Christine Conroy Levy holds a B.S. in media from Northwestern University and an M.A. in Learning Sciences (an interdisciplinary program in education, cognitive science and computer science) from Northwestern's Institute for the Learning Sciences. She is experienced in the design and development of custom e-learning solutions for clients, the design of authoring tools for internal and client use to create and maintain these solutions, performing task analyses, usability, and client management. She has spent over fifteen years using technology to support learning, during which she has designed many training and educational software programs and Web sites for corporate clients and non-profit organizations.

Jennifer McCabe is the Assistant Director of East Campus Library Services at James Madison University. She works primarily with students and faculty in the Nursing department to develop their information seeking and health literacy skills. Jennifer is the principal investigator on the Institute for Museum and Library Services National Leadership Grant that funded the development of the health literacy game Face the Case as well as several simple games designed to develop information seeking skills. Jennifer taught an interdisciplinary course in healthcare informatics for several years at JMU and has published several articles and presented posters on health literacy and informatics. She received her Master's in Library and Information Sciences degree from the University of Wisconsin-Milwaukee.

Julie Meaux is an associate professor in the Department of Nursing at the University of Central Arkansas, USA. She is also a registered nurse with extensive research, publications, and grants in the areas of ADHD and stimulant medication use. Dr. Meaux has been a faculty excellence award finalist twice. She is a member of the Arkansas Children's Hospital Research Council and is a certified nurse educator. She is involved in the development of animated computer education games to help adolescents learn about their disabilities and methods of improving their decision-making as they mature.

Elizabeth J. Meyer is the ePortfolio Project Manager at Concordia University's Centre for the Study of Learning and Performance and a lecturer at McGill University. She is the author of *Gender, bullying, and harassment: Strategies to end sexism and homophobia in schools* and has had her work published in the *McGill Journal of Education, The Canadian Journal of Learning and Technology, Gender and Education,* and *LEARNing Landscapes.* For more on her current research projects please visit: http://lizjmeyer.googlepages.com.

Kevin Moberly is an Assistant Professor of English at Old DominionUniversity in Norfolk, VA. He received his Ph.D. in May 2005 from the University of Louisiana at Lafayette. His areas of expertise include new media, cultural and visual rhetoric and rhetorical theory. His research focuses on understanding how computer-enabled manifestations of popular culture reflect, contribute, and transform contemporary cultural and political discourses.

Paul Peachey is a senior lecturer in Enterprise and Entrepreneurship at the University of Glamorgan, Wales, UK. Although Paul's lecturing role is in the field of enterprise, Paul's primary area of research is in online pedagogies especially in the field of e-learning although he has a particular interest in games-based learning. Paul has been significantly involved in the development and delivery of two of Europe's biggest online courses and boasts a number of publications in the fields of enterprise, pedagogy and e-learning. Paul's overarching research objective is to determine ways with which GBL computer application programs may be incorporated into the pedagogy of e-learning courses.

Maja Pivec is Professor of Game-Based Learning and e-Learning at the University of Applied Sciences FH JOANNEUM in Graz, Austria. For her research achievements, Maja Pivec received in the year 2001 Herta Firnberg Award (Austria) in the field of computer science. In the 2003 she was awarded by European Science Foundation in form of a grant for an interdisciplinary workshop organisation in the field of affective and emotional aspects of human-computer interaction, with emphasis on Game-Based Learning and innovative learning approaches. Maja project lead the creation of the Engage Learning website (www.engagelearning.eu), a web portal facilitating the european community for best practices in Game-Based Learning. Maja's full academic resume can be viewed on http://www.majapivec.com.

Paul Pivec has worked in computing for over 30 years in all aspects of the industry. He has consulted to both game development and publishing companies, and teaches game development at tertiary level. He has a Masters degree in Computer Technology with specific emphasis on digital games. His thesis showed that multitasking skills are enhanced from player immersive computer games. He also has a graduate diploma in higher education and is currently working on his PhD in Game-Based Learning at Deakin University in Melbourne, Australia. Paul and Maja founded Pivec Labs (www.piveclabs.com) where structured methodology is utilised to predict the success of both educational and recreational video games. Paul's academic history can be seen at http://www.paupivec.com.

Dr. Ricardo Rademacher is a native Chilean who obtained his Physics PhD in 2002 and is the founder and CEO of Futur-E-Scape, LLC. Created in 2004, this company is dedicated to the creation and research of educational virtual worlds. In the last five years, Futur-E-Scape has received several grants and has been the subject of several published papers on the subject of educational virtual worlds. Related to his company's mission, Dr. Rademacher also teaches and creates courses for various pure-online universities. He also speaks at various educational and entertainment conferences and has written several publications on the subject. In his free time, he likes to watch grass grow.

Eeli Saarinen (M.Sc., Econ. & Bus. Adm.) currently holds a position as a researcher in Turku School of Economics (TSE) in the Department of Management and Organization. His current research interests in TSE include leadership and trust in virtual organizations, cross-cultural communication, knowledge management systems, networks and e-collaboration. He has also studied learning processes in different contexts and developed methods to enhance learning in computer-mediated environment. During his career as a researcher, he has participated in several international research projects focusing on topics like cross-cultural issues, leadership and dispersed work environment.

Juan Carlos Sanchez Lozano is a PhD Candidate in the Educational Technology program at Concordia University in Montreal, Canada. Applying his background in aerospace engineering research and simulation systems, his work underlines the importance of communication between instructional design and computer science. His research focuses on the development of games to teach software applications and programming, emphasizing the role of distributed and embodied forms of cognition. He is also interested in the design and development of digital media, particularly three-dimensional environments and their use in fields such as education, literature, and psychology.

Robert Savage is an Associate Professor and William Dawson Scholar at McGill University who has published over 50 research articles in international journals on children's early reading and spelling strategies in typical and atypical development. Research on basic cognitive processes in literacy continues (current projects explore analogy-use in reading acquisition, the 'Simple View of Reading', the nature and role of phonological awareness and rapid naming in acquisition, the basis of co-occurring attention and reading problems) alongside these other current projects: 1) Preventative early intervention projects for reading and spelling problems using the ABRACADABRA web-based reading intervention http://grover.concordia.ca/abra/php2006/ 2) The assessment of effective classroom teaching in Grade 1 3) The impact of inclusive education and the most effective support for children at-risk when transitioning to high school 4) The impact of French immersion on literacy and language development.

P.G. Schrader is an associate professor of Educational Technology at the University of Nevada, Las Vegas. Dr. Schrader's recent work involves understanding learning in complex nonlinear digital environments like Massively Multiplayer Online Games and Hypertext. In these contexts, he has examined aspects of expertise, literacy, and the dynamic exchange of information. His work has appeared in a number of journals, books, and national and international conferences.

Judy Shasek, M.S. ExerLearning is poised at the intersection of fitness, education and technology. The author contributes vital expertise and resources in each of these key areas. Judy Shasek has 17 years of experience as a fitness/education consultant and 12 years as a public school teacher, curriculum designer, teacher trainer and grant writer. By assimilating a massive amount of research and drawing on the invention and energy of many educators, researchers and fitness leaders around the country, ExerLearning was first delivered via Generation FIT. It is a program that developed organically over five years– in real schools with diverse students.

Nava Silton received her doctorate and Masters of Arts in Applied Developmental Psychology from Fordham University and her Bachelor of Science from Cornell University. Silton has worked in the Standards Department at Nickelodeon, the Education and Research Department at Sesame Street Workshop and has recently conducted research with Mediakidz. In conjunction with her freelancing and consulting work with children's educational programming, Dr. Silton's research focuses primarily on fostering sensitivity of typical children towards children with disabilities through educational media. In addition to her media interests, Silton has published articles on the experiences of rabbis' children, the biological substrates of personality and the temporality of Asperger's syndrome in the *Archive for the Psychology of Religion,* the *Journal of Clinical and Experimental Neuropsychology and the Journal of Phenomenological Psychology,* respectively. Silton has also served as a Senior Teaching Fellow and as an Adjunct Professor at Fordham University and Hunter College.

Nickolas Shopland is a software design engineer for the Interactive Systems Research group and has worked on numerous projects concerned with Serious Games and assistive technology. Nick is currently pursuing his research interests in accessible and open embedded technology.

Randell Snow is a former K12 educator for high-risk, drop out prevention. He has worked in pharmaceutical manufacturing and research as a Human Resource Analyst, and now incorporates Second Life in his undergraduate Human Resource Development courses. He is passionate about the potential of virtual world simulations to inspire and engage adult learners in their work and play.

Penny Standen's primary research interest is in evaluating ways of promoting the independence and quality of life of people with learning disabilities and her main area of research is developing and evaluating virtual environments and interactive software for people with learning disabilities.

Kathryn E. Stevens received her PhD in art history from the Virginia Commonwealth University in 2003. Currently she is the Director of the Madison Art Collection at James Madison University in Harrisonburg, Virginia. She teaches Art of the Ancient World, Art of Ancient Egypt, and Introduction to Museum Studies for the School of Art and Art History. Dr. Stevens has a strong interest in emerging technologies that allow arts and cultural collections to be transcribed virtually and used for public educational outreach. If you would wish to contact her in-world, send an instant message to Lykopis Darkstone.

Stephen Tang (BSc, MSc) is a Senior Lecturer in Computing at Department of Information, Media and Computer Entertainment in the School of Computing and Mathematical Sciences at Liverpool John Moores University (LJMU) in the UK where he teaches on undergraduate and postgraduate courses in Computer Games Technology and Computer Animation and Visualisation. Prior to joining LJMU he was a lecturer at Tunku Abdul Rahman College (TARC) in Malaysia where he taught on undergraduate courses in multimedia and computer games design and technologies. Stephen has also served as a member of programme and technical committee members for game conferences such as Asian Game Developers Summit, GDTW and CyberGames. He is a technical reviewer of the International Journal of Computer Games Technology. Stephen is currently a PhD candidate at LJMU. His research interests include game-based learning, serious games design and development, and model driven engineering.

Jane Thall developed in interest in gaming and simulation through her teaching in the Adult Education and Human Resource Development Graduate Program at James Madison University and her research in organizational middle management and the conversion of tacit to explicit knowledge. She holds a Master's degree from Johns Hopkins University and a doctoral degree in Education from George Washington University.

Jody S. Underwood, Ph.D., is Chief Scientist at Pragmatic Solutions, Inc. She has spent the last 20 years doing research and development of intelligent tutoring systems, e-learning environments, assessment design, and effective feedback. Before joining Pragmatic, Dr. Underwood worked as a Development Scientist in the Research Division of Educational Testing Service, and at the Math Forum, a renowned online mathematics education portal. Pragmatic Solutions is interested in forming partnerships with educational researchers and serious games designers to study data mining and create adaptive gaming environments.

Courtney Uram, M.S.Ed earned her Master's degree in Adult Education/ Human Resource Development with a concentration in instructional design from James Madison University in May 2009. While completing her degree, Courtney's work focused primarily on the integration of e-learning into workplace training and development. In June 2009, Windwalker Corporation brought Courtney on board as a Junior Instructional Designer for the Army Center for Substance Abuse Prevention (ACSAP) project. Here, she designs interactive training content for blended learning delivery using interactive technologies and media.

Anne Wade is Manager at the Centre for the Study of Learning and Performance at Concordia University, Montreal, Quebec. Her expertise is in information storage and retrieval, and in using technology to support learning. She has served as the Coordinator of the CSLP-LEARN e-portfolio project since its inception eight years ago and is currently leading a research and development project related to information literacy. Wade has also taught extensively in the field of information studies for twenty years.

Index

Symbols

21st century skills 126, 127, 128

A

ABalanced Reading Approach for Canadians Designed to Achieve Best Results for All (ABRACADABRA) 168, 170, 171, 172, 173, 174, 175, 176, 177, 178, 179, 180, 183, 184, 185

activities of daily living (ADLs) 325, 329, 332

activity theory (AT) 154, 155, 156, 157, 158, 159, 160, 161, 162, 163, 164, 165, 166, 167

Adequate Yearly Progress (AYP) 195

adolescent literacy 78

adult education 1, 5, 343, 347

adult learning 252, 253, 254, 255, 257, 258, 259, 261

Adult Literacy and Life Skills (ALLS) 169

adventure games 209

affordance 293, 294, 297, 298, 299, 300, 301, 302, 304, 307, 309

After Action Review (AAR) 350

andragogy 253, 260, 261

Annual Yearly Progress (AYP) 195

Applied Behavior Analysis (ABA) 322, 325, 335, 336, 338, 339

Assessment and Learning in Knowledge Spaces (ALEKS) 128, 139

assessment design 126, 130, 133, 137

assessment of learning through gaming 17

ATM 96

Attention Deficit Hyperactivity Disorder (ADHD) 235, 236, 237, 238, 239, 240, 241, 242, 243, 244, 245, 246, 247, 248, 249, 250, 251, , 319

attitudes 315, 322, 323, 324, 325, 333, 334, 335, 337, 338, 339, 340

attribute tracking system (ATS) 134

Attribution Theory 117

authentic context 32

autism spectrum 316, 317, 319, 320, 322, 324, 326, 329, 332, 333, 339

autism spectrum disorders (ASDs) 317, 318, 322, 332, 333, 339

avatar 378, 379, 380, 383, 384, 386, 387, 388, 389, 390, 391, 392

AYP 195

B

Balanced Literacy Toolkit (BLTK) 171

behavioral intentions 315, 322, 323, 324, 333, 335, 337, 338

blended learning 1, 11, 14, 119

blogging 351

board game 226, 227, 228, 229, 230

bridging literacies 78

Bulletin Board Systems (BBSs) 67

Business Policy 227

C

citizenship 189, 190, 192, 199, 200, 203

civic engagement 189, 190, 191, 192, 193, 196, 200, 201, 202, 203, 204

coaching 32, 33, 35, 36, 37, 40, 41, 45

cognitive attitudes 323, 324